PHILIPPIANS FOR PASTORS

JOHN A. KITCHEN

Philippians for Pastors
© 2018 by John A. Kitchen

ISBN: 978-1-934952-41-2

Published by Kress Biblical Resources
The Woodlands, TX 77393
www.kressbiblical.com

All rights reserved. No portion of this book may be reproduced in any form without the written permission of the publisher except for brief excerpts quoted in critical reviews.

Unless otherwise noted, Scripture quotations are taken from the NEW AMERICAN STANDARD BIBLE7, 1960, 1962, 1963, 1968, 1971, 1972, 1973, 1975, 1977, 1995 by The Lockman Foundation. Used by permission. www.Lockman.org

The Greek text used is *Novum Testamentum Graece, Nestle-Aland 27*th Edition. Copyright © 1993 Deutsche Bibelgesellschaft, Stuttgart, Germany.

Other versions used:

> Scripture quotations marked (ESV) are taken from The Holy Bible, English Standard Version™, copyright © 2001 by Crossway Bibles, a division of Good News Publishers. Used by permission. All rights reserved.
> Scripture quotations marked (HCSB) are from the Holman Christian Standard Bible®. HCSB®. Copyright ©1999, 2000, 2002, 2003 by Holman Bible Publishers. Used by permission. Holman Christian Standard Bible®, Holman CSB®, and HCSB® are federally registered trademarks of Holman Bible Publishers.
> Scripture quotations marked (KJV) are taken from the King James Version.
> Scripture quotations marked (NET) are from The NET Bible® Copyright © 2005 by Biblical Studies Press, L.L.C. www.bible.org All rights reserved.
> Scripture quotations marked (NIV) are taken from the New International Version®. Copyright © 1973, 1978, 1984 by International Bible Society. Used by permission of Zondervan Publishing House. All rights reserved.
> Scripture quotations marked (NKJV) are taken from *The New King James Version*. Copyright © 1979, 1980, 1982 by Thomas Nelson, Inc. Used by permission. All rights reserved.
> Scripture quotations marked (NLT) are taken from the *Holy Bible*, New Living Translation, copyright © 1996. Used by permission of Tyndale House Publishers, Inc., Wheaton, Illinois 60189. All rights reserved.
> Scripture quotations marked (NRSV) are taken from the New Revised Standard Version. Copyright © 1989 by the Division of Christian Education of the National Council of the Churches of Christ in the United States of America. All rights reserved.
> Scripture quotations marked (Phillips) are taken from The New Testament in Modern English, copyright © 1958, 1959, 1960 J.B. Phillips and 1947, 1952, 1955, 1957 The Macmillian Company, New York. Used by permission. All rights reserved.
> Scripture quotations marked (RSV) are taken from the Revised Standard Version of the Bible, Copyright © 1952, 1946, 1971 by the National Council of Churches of Christ in America.
> Scripture quotations marked (TEV) are taken from the Good News Translation in Today's English Version- Second Edition Copyright © 1992 by American Bible Society. Used by Permission.

Dedicated to

Dr. Vernon S. Olson
and
Dr. William J. Larkin, Jr.

Τοῦτο φρονεῖτε ἐν ὑμῖν ὃ καὶ ἐν Χριστῷ Ἰησοῦ
—Philippians 2:5

CONTENTS

Acknowledgements 9
Abbreviations 11
How to Use this Book 15
Philippians 17
    Introduction to Philippians 19
    Philippians 1 63
    Philippians 2 163
    Philippians 3 287
    Philippians 4 383
Appendix A: Preaching and Teaching Philippians 473
Appendix B: A Topical Index to the Ministry Maxims 497
Appendix C: Assorted Charts 501
Appendix D: Annotated Bibliography 505

ACKNOWLEDGEMENTS

No work of this nature is ever accomplished without the support of a number of people. I wish to express my thanks to those who reviewed the manuscript in part or in whole, offering insights and proofreading the text: Robin Angell, Rev. Dr. Rhett Dodson, Evelyn Mohr, and Lorrie Scheftic. Their service has contributed in valuable ways to the improvement of the manuscript. Any errors or deficiencies that remain are solely my responsibility.

I wish to also express my gratitude to the people of both the Plymouth Alliance Church and the Stow Alliance Fellowship. Over the years they both have eagerly joined me in the careful study of this letter. It was at Stow Alliance Fellowship that I circled back and gave myself to additional years of private, careful study of the text of this great letter, the result of which is the commentary you hold now in your hand.

I am grateful for Rick Kress of Kress Biblical Resources for believing in the value of this kind of study and for partnering to put tools in the hands of God's servants—tools which help them engage God's Word more deeply that they might know and love God more genuinely and serve Him more effectively.

As ever, I am grateful for my dear wife, Julie. Her support and encouragement enable me to keep moving forward; her joy and friendship make the journey immeasurably more enjoyable.

I am grateful for those who shepherd local churches across the globe, serving in many cases in obscurity and with little to no remuneration. I am thankful to stand among you as a brother in service to our Savior. My prayer is that this contribution will help us be more faithful to "the Great Shepherd of the sheep," who "through the blood of the eternal covenant" redeemed us and made us His own (Heb. 13:20).

ABBREVIATIONS

Old Testament

Gen.	Genesis	Eccl.	Ecclesiastes
Exod.	Exodus	Song of Sol.	Song of Solomon
Lev.	Leviticus	Isa.	Isaiah
Num.	Numbers	Jer.	Jeremiah
Deut.	Deuteronomy	Lam.	Lamentations
Josh.	Joshua	Ezek.	Ezekiel
Judg.	Judges	Dan.	Daniel
Ruth	Ruth	Hos.	Hosea
1 Sam.	1 Samuel	Joel	Joel
2 Sam.	2 Samuel	Amos	Amos
1 Kings	1 Kings	Obad.	Obadiah
2 Kings	2 Kings	Jonah	Jonah
1 Chron.	1 Chronicles	Mic.	Micah
2 Chron.	2 Chronicles	Nah.	Nahum
Ezra	Ezra	Hab.	Habakkuk
Neh.	Nehemiah	Zeph.	Zephaniah
Esth.	Esther	Hag.	Haggai
Job	Job	Zech.	Zechariah
Psa.	Psalm	Mal.	Malachi
Prov.	Proverbs		

New Testament

Matt.	Matthew	1 Tim.	1 Timothy
Mark	Mark	2 Tim.	2 Timothy
Luke	Luke	Titus	Titus
John	John	Philem.	Philemon
Acts	Acts	Heb.	Hebrews
Rom.	Romans	James	James
1 Cor.	1 Corinthians	1 Peter	1 Peter
2 Cor.	2 Corinthians	2 Peter	2 Peter
Gal.	Galatians	1 John	1 John
Eph.	Ephesians	2 John	2 John
Phil.	Philippians	3 John	3 John
Col.	Colossians	Jude	Jude
1 Thess.	1 Thessalonians	Rev.	Revelation
2 Thess.	2 Thessalonians		

Bible Translations

ESV	English Standard Version
HCSB	Holman Christian Standard Bible
KJV	King James Version
NASB	New American Standard Bible (1977)
NASU	New American Standard Bible: Updated Edition (1995)
NET	NET Bible
NIV	New International Version
NKJV	New King James Version
NLT	New Living Translation
NRSV	New Revised Standard Version
Phillips	The New Testament in Modern English
RSV	Revised Standard Version
TEV	Today's English Version

Miscellaneous

c.	*circa*, about
cf.	*confer*, compare
contra	contrary to
e.g.	*exempli gratia*, for example
etc.	*et cetera*, and the like
ff.	following (verses, pages, etc.)
ibid.	*ibidem*, in the same place
i.e.	*id est*, that is
LXX	Septuagint
n.	Footnote
n.d.	no date
NT	New Testament
OT	Old Testament
PE	Pastoral Epistles
rpt.	reprint

Footnotes

BDAG	*A Greek-English Lexicon of the New Testament and Other Early Christian Literature*, 3rd ed.
NIDNTT	*The New International Dictionary of New Testament Theology*
NIDNTT: Abridged	*The New International Dictionary of New Testament Theology: Abridged Edition*
TDNT	*Theological Dictionary of the New Testament*, 10 vols.
ZPEB	*The Zondervan Pictorial Encyclopedia of the Bible*, 5 vols.

HOW TO USE THIS BOOK

Allow me to share a word about how you may use this volume for your personal growth and for that of your congregation. Like the other commentaries in this series, the present work weaves three distinct features into the fabric of one volume. It will serve your needs in a number of different ways. Three of the most obvious ways it will serve you are as a commentary, a counselor, and a coach.

Commentary: You will find that *Philippians for Pastors* provides a wealth of exegetical information regarding the text of this NT epistle. I suggest you read the commentary with your Greek (or Interlinear Greek/English) New Testament open to the passage and follow the development of the passage. This, I trust, will aid you in personally understanding God's Word, in preaching and teaching these texts, and in explaining the meaning of these Scriptures to the people whom you shepherd.

Counselor: You will find generously dispersed throughout the text what I call Ministry Maxims. These are pithy, pointedly stated principles of ministry which arise from or are suggested by the verse where they are found. Each is stated in such a way as to distill the wisdom of the given Scripture into a pointed—and sometimes provocative—statement of principle which applies in ministry contexts of all cultures and at all times. Do you wonder if that is possible? Have a debate with one of the Ministry Maxims? Then they have served their purpose! They are stated in thought-provoking ways in order to stimulate your mind and rouse you to interaction with the truth. While the commentary speaks facts into your mind, the Ministry Maxims are designed to speak truth into your heart.

Coach: This companion never allows you to leave a section of Scripture without stopping to ponder how its truth applies to your life and ministry. It provides bridges of application from the truths found in the text of Scripture to the work of ministry in your local church. You will find Digging Deeper questions dispersed throughout the text. My hope is that these will stimulate reflection on how the truths of Philippians apply to life and local church ministry. If the commentary is designed to speak facts into your mind and the Ministry Maxims are designed to speak truth into your heart, then these Digging Deeper questions are intended to put skill into your hands as you serve the Lord by serving His people. Additionally, the appendices provide practical ideas on how you can use Philippians in personal ministry growth, counseling, and preaching/teaching.

Finally, may I suggest that *Philippians for Pastors*, just as with the other commentaries in this series, is suitable for diving, wading, and dipping. That is to say, you may want to dive in and immerse yourself in the fullness of its content. Or you may want to wade into a particular section of the epistle by studying the commentary at that point in the text. Or you may simply want to dip into its contents by perusing the Ministry Maxims, and only then stopping to examine the exegetical work behind those statements which pique your interest. In my mind, the deeper you dive the better, but there is benefit in all these approaches.

PHILIPPIANS

INTRODUCTION TO PHILIPPIANS

The story of the church in Philippi teaches us this simple principle: before there is *big* there is *small*. Big always follows small. Just about the only place small follows big is in the dictionary.

It is true in nature. An oak has its genesis in an acorn. Vast blankets of forest begin as one insignificant nut. Didn't Jesus Himself say something about the expansive, unexpected influence of a single mustard seed? Did He not teach us of a single grain of wheat bringing forth much life?

It is true also in history. A tiny, faithful band returned from decades of Exile, hoping for big things. When the foundation was laid for the temple they hoped to reconstruct, some rejoiced, but "the old men who had seen the first temple, wept with a loud voice when the foundation of this house was laid before their eyes" (Ezra 3:12). The prophet Haggai asked, "Who is left among you who saw this temple in its former glory? And how do you see it now? Does it not seem to you like nothing in comparison?" (Haggai 2:3). His compatriot queried: "Who has despised the day of small things?" (Zech. 4:10).

It is true in our personal experience as well. Nobody sets out on a noble quest for "the day of small things." Small isn't a dream people chase. Small is no one's passion, nobody's vision. Despising it is the particular danger of all who dream of big, but dwell in small. Yet in my own life a few words scrawled at the top of an otherwise insignificant ninth grade English assignment commanded much of the rest of my life. A few lines in a single book crystalized God's purpose for my life, and the years since have flowed out in obedience to Him. Big always begins with small.

Acts 16 tells of an incalculably big thing that began in a seemingly insignificant way. It's the story of the church in the city Philippi, but it is also the seed of a saga involving much, much more than just one church. Philippi became the site of an exceedingly strategic gospel beachhead. Let Ray Stedman spell it out for us:

> ... an obscure and apparently minor event ... in the reckoning of hindsight, has turned out to be one of the most significant and momentous occasions in human history. When the Apostle Paul and his small company crossed the Dardanelles, moving from Asia to Europe, they changed the whole course of Western civilization. Perhaps no single event since the cross of Jesus Christ has so affected the world as Paul's seemingly insignificant decision to cross a narrow neck of water. If the Emperor Claudius, who occupied the throne in Rome at that time, had been asked to name the most significant event of his reign, I'm sure he would never have dreamed of suggesting (had he even known about it) that it was the occasion when an obscure little bald-headed Jew decided to leave Asia for Europe. That is how little we understand the history we are living through! We don't know what the really great events are.[1]

It might surprise you to know the origin of the church in Philippi (and the expansive influence that grew from the advance of the gospel there) is reducible to the stories of three people. Those three people became not only an integral part of that church's story, but a part of the story of all of European history since that time. Indeed, not just European history but of all of Western civilization to this day.

What would you imagine these three to be like? A Roman Emperor? A great religious leader maybe? Or a foreign head of state? Your expectations would be underwhelmed upon meeting them. But your personal

---

1   Stedman, 83.

hope would swell, for few of us are well-positioned enough to arouse great expectations.

Big things start small. Acts 16 tells us of the first time the gospel moved into Europe.[2] When Paul and his missionary friends departed the coastline of Asia Minor at Troas and sailed overnight across a narrow neck of water, bypassing an island named Samothrace, they arrived at a place called Neapolis. Upon arrival they walked approximately eleven miles to the city of Philippi. There, for the first time on European soil, the name of Jesus was declared and believed upon.[3] Thus what happened in this city is really the story of a whole church, of a whole continent, and of the entirety of Western civilization.

Behold the power of a mustard seed! Watch and be amazed at a single grain of wheat!

The greatness of the story lies not simply in what happened *in* Philippi, but of what happened *from* that city. The Scriptures unfold their account and tell of a redeemed people who consistently and sacrificially supported Paul's continuing mission—a mission which spread the gospel of Jesus Christ throughout the Mediterranean world and in so doing launched it into a trajectory that would gather in all of Europe.

---

2 Acts 16 is the first *recorded* advance of the gospel into European soil. It may well be that the gospel had made its way to Rome by this time, though we have no record of just how it would have done so. It could have been carried there through those visitors from Rome who had been in Jerusalem for Pentecost when the Holy Spirit was poured out upon the followers of Jesus (Acts 2:10). This is a possible, though speculative, explanation of the origins of the Church in Rome. The renowned Church historian Philip Schaff calls the origin of the church in Rome an "impenetrable mystery" (*History of the Christian Church*, 1:366). Goodwin, quoting Meyer, similarly adds, "The *origin* of the Roman church cannot … be determined with any certainty" (220, emphasis original).

3 Vincent says: "With the arrival of Paul at Neapolis the gospel first entered Europe" (ICC, xix). Martin calls the founding of the church in Philippi "the entrance of the gospel of the Lord Jesus Christ into Europe" (15). Müller says Philippi was, "… the first city on European soil where a Christian Church was founded by Paul" (13). Comfort says Philippi was "where the Good News of Christ was proclaimed for the first time in Europe" (145). Boice says that the arrival of Paul and his small missionary band constituted "the official opening of Europe to Christianity and with it the gospel began the long westward march that eventually brought it to us" (275). Baxter calls the church in Philippi: "the first Christian church ever planted in Europe" (181). Of these events Munck says simply, "Thus Christianity entered Europe" (158).

But then, we shouldn't be surprised, for big things start small. What happened in that first European town, Philippi, has set the pace for all that has happened since. It is reducible to the story of a wealthy business woman (Acts 16:11-15), of a demon-possessed slave girl (vv.16-24), and a hardhearted, retired military man now working at the local jail (vv.25-34). God influenced all subsequent history through them. Big things always start small.

I hope that sounds like hope to you. It does to me. Few of us are toiling in big right now. Life is made up of many mundane, but essential and unavoidable responsibilities. There is little flash, not much pizzazz, precious few moments when we feel like we've hit the big time. Few are the relationships that seem as strategic as we'd like. But every person's story—yours included, and those of the people God has placed in your life—is strategic in God's hand and for His plan. The story of the church in Philippi is a story divinely intended for you. I pray that as you undertake the study of this New Testament epistle, God will make it intensely personal and that your story—like that of the Philippians themselves—will not be simply a tale of what God does *in* your life, but *from* your life.

As we prepare to immerse ourselves in the text of Philippians, let's turn our attention first to a few matters we need to understand before we can most fruitfully engage this magnificent letter.

Authorship: Who Wrote This Epistle?

The Author of the Letter

At one level the answer to this question is obvious. The letter itself claims Paul as its author (Phil. 1:1). That the Apostle may have employed an amanuensis to aid him in writing some of his letters is not largely in doubt (e.g., Rom. 16:22). At such times Paul would often affix his signature to the letter to assure that the scribe had faithfully conveyed his words (e.g. 1 Cor. 16:21; 2 Thess. 3:17). This may have been the case with the present letter as the Apostle's opening greeting includes Timothy (1:1), though there is nothing else within the letter to commend this idea. In fact, the evidence points in the opposite direction, to Paul as the single author of the letter. Details like the repeated use of first-person singular pronouns and the detail and manner of reporting his personal circumstances (1:12-26; 4:10-23) point to Paul as the author.[4] In fact, the commendation of Timothy (2:19-24) would point away from Timothy serving in the role of amanuensis. Furthermore, the mention of Timothy alongside Paul in the opening salutation (1:1) may have prepared the readers for the news that Timothy would soon be coming their way (2:19-24).[5]

That Paul was responsible for the writing of the letter to the Philippians was universally accepted within the early church. Irenaeus, Tertullian and Clement of Alexandria are all early and authoritative voices attributing the letter to the Apostle Paul. The words and expressions of the letter appear often in quotations and allusions of the early church.[6] The earliest canons of Scripture (including those of Marcion and the Muratorian fragment) include the letter to the Philippians and attribute it to the Apostle Paul.

This early consensus stood as the unquestioned view throughout subsequent church history, until scholars in the nineteenth century presented alternative theories. While their skepticism over Pauline authorship has found more traction in the debate over others of his New Testament letters (e.g. Colossians, 1 and 2 Timothy, Titus), Paul's authorship of Philippians has remained widely unquestioned even in our day. Again, the letter itself claims to have been written by Paul (1:1). The references to Paul's associates ring of authenticity and attest to its genuineness. The circumstances to which the author refers within the letter are known from the larger corpus of Scripture and conform to what we know of the Apostle's life and ministry. The expressions, theology, and ideas of the letter are consistent with what we have become accustomed to from the pen of the Apostle Paul.[7]

---

4   Harmon, 21-22.

5   Ibid., 23.

6   Lightfoot says, "The quotations from this letter in early Christian writers are not so numerous as they would probably have been if it had contained more matter which was directly doctrinal or ecclesiastical" (85). Yet he goes on to cite the following as quoting from or using allusions to the wording of Philippians: Clement of Rome, the *Testaments of the Twelve Patriarchs*, the *Letter to Diognetus*, Justin Matyr, and the *Acts of Thomas* (86-87).

7   Kent, 11:96.

The Unity of the Letter

While the matter of Pauline authorship has not been largely questioned across the landscape of Church history, a more widespread and sometimes contentious debate revolves around the unity of the letter. Conceding that Paul wrote the various parts of the letter as we have it now, some debate whether they were originally composed in the present document or represent various portions drawn together by Paul or another editor into their present form.

The use of "Finally" (Τὸ λοιπόν) in 3:1 and the rather jarring transition between 3:1 and 2 have been central features in the discussion. The embers of debate have been fanned, also, by the fact that the early church father Polycarp (A.D. 69-155) spoke in the plural when referring to the Apostle Paul's written correspondence with the church in Philippi.[8] Some believe that the structure of Philippians is not consistent with the typical form of Pauline epistles. Still others are bothered by the fact that Paul does not get around to expressing thanks for the financial contribution of the Philippian believers until the end of the letter (4:10ff).

These have led to much conjecture as to the number of original documents involved and just where the breaks for each portion are to be found. Ironically, in attacking the unity of the letter there has been little unity among dissenting scholars as to the original form of these assumed portions. Among those who believe in multiple fragments knit together into the present form, many see three originals, but others discern two.[9]

A good deal of scholarship has been dedicated to the question of the epistle's unity. The debate grows complex and intricate. But in the final analysis all the objections to the unity and integrity of the letter as presented to us can be answered reasonably.

---

8   "For neither am I, nor is any other like me, able to follow the wisdom of the blessed and glorious Paul, who when he was among you in the presence of the men of that time taught accurately and stedfastly the word of truth, and also when he was absent wrote letters to you, from the study of which you will be able to build yourselves up into the faith given you." (*Polycarp to the Philippians*, 3.2; http://www.earlychristianwritings.com/text/polycarp-lake.html).

9   David E. Garland, "the Composition and Unity of Philippians: Some Neglected Literary Features," *NovT* 27 (1985), 141. Garland identifies twenty-four scholars in favor of three portions and six who see two fragments. Cited in Hansen, 15.

1. No manuscript evidence exists supporting the notion that this was once multiple, separate pieces of written communication. Hansen can rightly assert, "All the theories of multiple letters rest on conjectural speculation, not on textual evidence."[10]

2. Polycarp's comment may mean nothing more than the fact that not all the Apostle's written communication to the church in Philippi has been preserved for us by God. That which we do have was given under inspiration of the Holy Spirit (2 Tim. 3:16; 2 Peter 1:21) and preserved for us as Holy Scripture (2 Peter 3:15-16). Alternatively, Polycarp may have used the plural ("letters") because he was referring to all of Paul's epistles to the churches of Macedonia (1 and 2 Thessalonians included). Or perhaps Polycarp read Philippians 3:1b ("To write the same things *again* is no trouble to me and it is a safeguard for you," emphasis added) and concluded that the Apostle had written previously to the congregation.[11] Besides this, Polycarp speaks later in the same letter using the singular form, speaking of Paul's "Epistle" to the Philippians.[12]

3. The expression "Finally" (Τὸ λοιπόν, 3:1), as explained in the commentary, is often used when the author wishes to transition to a new matter (1 Cor. 7:29; Phil. 3:1; 4:8; 2 Thess. 3:1). This is especially true "when it comes near the end of a literary work."[13] The expression is used adverbially, indicating the manner in which the verbal action (χαίρετε, "rejoice") is to be taken.[14] In 3:1 it might also mean something like "as far as the rest is concerned," "beyond that," or "in addition."[15] It is not used because

---

10   Hansen, 17.

11   Ibid.

12   "But I have neither perceived nor heard any such thing among you, among whom the blessed Paul laboured, who are praised in the beginning of his Epistle." (11:3a, http://www.earlychristianwritings.com/text/polycarp-lake.html). Brockmuehl, cites this, acknowledging that it "is textually uncertain," (22).

13   BDAG, 4612.3.b.

14   Wallace, 200-201, 293.

15   Ibid.

Paul is moving to bring the letter to a close.[16] Rather he is turning from the immediate discussion of the sending of Timothy and Epaphroditus (2:19-30), but what he says now does not depart from the major theme of "joy" and "rejoicing" that he has been weaving throughout the letter. In time the expression came to be used as almost equivalent to οὖν.[17] This seems to be the case here (and in 4:8) as it simply signals a transition in what follows.[18] Silva's comment is also germane: "What would lead an editor to incorporate a separate document at such an awkward point? … Editorial revisions are normally undertaken with a view to attenuating, not aggravating, literary problems and inconsistencies."[19] It may be said fairly that "partition theories have turned out to raise more questions than they answer."[20]

4. *Too much has probably been made regarding a standard form for Pauline letters and using it as a rubric to exclude letters otherwise accepted as from his hand.* While there is some general concurrence among some of his letters (e.g. Ephesians and Colossians), is that form inviolable? Was the Apostle incapable of adapting his form to the audience he addressed and the needs at hand (compare, for instance, Galatians and 1 Thessalonians)?

5. *There is little unanimity among the proponents of the fragment theory.* They cannot agree if the editor used three existing documents or two. Even when scholars agree as to the total number, they do not achieve consensus regarding the limits of those fragments within the present text of Philippians.[21] The proponents of the fragment theory are themselves fragmented when it comes to their own hypothesis. Without unity among themselves their arguments do not ring with authority.

6. *There may be any number of reasons Paul withheld the expression of his thanks for their monetary gift until the end of the letter,* none of which

---

16 Ibid., 493, n.114.
17 Robertson, *Grammar*, 1146; cf. Kennedy, 448; Lenski, 826; Vincent, ICC, 90.
18 Harmon, 304; O'Brien, 348; Sumney, 69.
19 Silva, 13.
20 Bockmuehl, 25.
21 Hansen, 18.

had anything to do with multiple letters and an editor's work to join their fragments together. Perhaps he wanted his gratitude to be what remained upon their minds most prominently at the end of the letter's public reading. Perhaps he wanted to lead with the news he believed they were most concerned about, his imprisonment. As a whole the argument seems to be built upon social mores of the twenty-first century rather than those of the first century.[22] And why would an otherwise competent editor bypass the supposed social etiquette of the day and leave the expression of gratitude to the end? If we cannot accept Paul's doing so, why should we accept the notion of an editor doing the same?

Thus there appears to be no compelling reason to approach Philippians as anything other than what it presents itself to be—a genuine letter penned by the Apostle Paul under the inspiration of the Holy Spirit and preserved under divine providence in its present state for the welfare of the people of God. J.B. Lightfoot says that the evidence, when fairly examined by an unbiased reader, puts "the genuineness of the letter to the Philippians beyond the reach of doubt."[23]

Origin: From Where Was Philippians Written?

If, then, Paul did indeed pen the letter, where was he when he did so? Clearly the letter was penned from an imprisonment (Phil. 1:7, 13, 14, 17), but which one of Paul's imprisonments and in what location? Students of the Bible have championed three basic answers to this question as it relates not only to the writing of Philippians, but the other prison epistles as well: Ephesians, Colossians, and Philemon. Though they may not all have been written at precisely the same moment in Paul's incarceration, generally they are understood to have all arisen from the

---

22 Fee exposes the silliness of the argument, noting, "… since we would not produce a letter like this, then in all likelihood neither did Paul" (21; unless otherwise noted all footnotes marked "Fee" refer to his volume in the NIC series).

23 Lightfoot, 84.

same imprisonment. Scholars view the letter as having originated either in Ephesus, Caesarea or Rome.[24] Let's explore the evidence for these options.

1. Ephesus. Some assign the letter's origin to an imprisonment in Ephesus. They conjecture that the Apostle was imprisoned in Ephesus sometime during his three to three-and-one-half years in that city (Acts 19:10, 22; 20:31). Let us first consider the evidence that may support such a notion.

- Paul testified to the Corinthian believers, saying, "I fought with wild beasts at Ephesus" (1 Cor. 15:32). Some take this as descriptive not merely of the upheaval described more generally in Acts 19:23-20:1, but as inclusive of an imprisonment they wish to find during Paul's time in Ephesus.
- When Paul wrote to the believers in Corinth (in the mid-fifties), he could say that he had been "in far more imprisonments" than his opponents in Corinth (2 Cor. 11:23). The plural ("imprisonments") would seem to require multiple incarcerations, some of which would not have been recorded for us in the book of Acts. Thus they conjecture Ephesus as a legitimate possibility for one of those imprisonments and as the place of origin for the letter to the Philippians.
- Similarly, Paul told the Corinthian believers that while in Ephesus matters became so desperate that he "despaired even of life" (2 Cor. 1:8) and that he and his companions "had the sentence of death within" themselves (v.9). Again, this is viewed as suggestive of an imprisonment.
- The strength of these suggestive notations may be buttressed, it is contended, by noting that both Acts (16:12; 20:1, 3, 6) and 2 Corinthians (1:16; 2:13; 7:5; 13:1) hint that Paul had visited Philippi at least three times. But Philippians suggests

---

24 In 1731 G. L. Oeder argued for Corinth as the location from which the letter was written. Dockx revived the hypothesis in 1973. Support for this view has never been strong. We have no mention of Paul ever being imprisoned in Corinth. The view is without evidence and, therefore, speculative at best. Cf. Hawthorne/Martin (xl) or Melick (38) for more on this view.

he had not seen them since "the first preaching of the gospel" (4:15). Thus it is argued that Philippians must have been written prior to 2 Corinthians (A.D. 55), placing the multiple imprisonments prior to that time and making Philippians refer to an earlier imprisonment.[25]

- The single strongest argument for an Ephesian imprisonment as the place of origin for the letter is its relative proximity to Philippi. The book of Philippians may suggest as many as six to eight trips between Philippi and the place of Paul's imprisonment.[26] A trip between Philippi and Ephesus would have taken approximately one week. Conversely, travel between Philippi and Rome (the traditional place of Paul's imprisonment and authorship of the letter) would have taken upwards of a month. Proponents of an Ephesian imprisonment contend that the limits of time would make it highly unlikely that such travel might fit within the timeframe of Paul's two year imprisonment in Rome (Acts 28:30) and would be more likely to be undertaken if his imprisonment were closer at hand as would be the case in Ephesus.
- Additionally, we know that Timothy was with Paul in Ephesus (Acts 19:22; cf. Phil. 1:1) and that he traveled from Ephesus to Macedonia (1 Cor. 16:10; cf. Phil. 2:19-24), as did the Apostle Paul upon his departure (Acts 20:1; 2 Cor. 1:8; 2:13; cf. Phil. 2:24).[27] This, it is conjectured, would almost certainly have included a stop in Philippi.[28]

---

25 Bockmuehl, 26.

26 Kent (11:98) suggests that these trips may have included: 1) Arrival in Philippi of the news of Paul's imprisonment (Phil. 1:12ff), 2) Epaphroditus' travel to Paul with a gift (1:25, 30; 4:18), 3) Arrival in Philippi of the news that Epaphroditus had fallen ill (2:26), 4) Arrival to Epaphroditus and Paul of the news that the believers in Philippi were deeply concerned for his welfare (2:26), 5) a journey by Timothy to Philippi (2:19-24), 6) a return trip by Timothy to once again join the Apostle Paul (2:19). Hansen projects the possibility of eight trips (21).

27 Bockmuehl, 27.

28 Harmon, 36.

- The telling expression "Caesar's household" (Phil. 4:22), we are told, could refer, not to personal family members of Caesar (unlikely to be living in Ephesus), but to slaves or freedmen who were in the employ of the Emperor. Such could legitimately be imagined to have been located in Ephesus. Archeology has, in fact, uncovered first century Latin inscriptions from Ephesus that mention both "Praetorium" (1:13) and "Caesar's household" (4:22).[29]

Other scholars, however, have responded to these evidences by pointing out the unlikely nature of an Ephesian imprisonment. Among them are these important considerations.

- All the suggested possibilities notwithstanding, we have no actual record of Paul ever being imprisoned in Ephesus, whether from Acts or elsewhere.
- Even if one conjectures an Ephesian imprisonment, there are serious questions as to whether the conditions there would have fit with the evidence from Philippians concerning the Apostle's imprisonment at the time of writing the letter. Philippians says he was incarcerated on a capital charge and he is uncertain about life and death (Phil. 1:13-14, 20; 2:17). Yet Acts not only doesn't mention an Ephesian imprisonment, the impression is that while there he enjoyed freedom of travel and ministry, to the extent that he changed his plans and stayed on in the city (Acts 19:8-10, 20-22; 1 Cor. 16:6-9). Clearly Paul experienced some kind of harrowing experience in Ephesus so that he "despaired even of life" (2 Cor. 1:8), but this could easily be from the events described in Acts 19:23-20:1.[30] From the available evidence, an Ephesian imprisonment seems unlikely to have

---

29 Ibid., 37.

30 Bockmuehl, 27.

led Paul to a concern for his execution, for he could have always appealed to Caesar—which in fact he did do when imprisoned in Caesarea (Acts 25:11).[31]
- The fact that Paul does not mention, in the text of the letter, later visits to Philippi is not insignificant, but in the final analysis it is an argument from silence. It is also true that he doesn't mention the collection for the saints in Judea (though while in Ephesus he was busy organizing it (1 Cor. 16:1-4; 2 Cor. 8-9). This actually makes better sense if he wrote from Rome, well after the collection had been completed. True, Paul makes no mention in Philippians of visits subsequent to his first, but the following passages from Philippians are compatible with a "growing acquaintance and repeated personal contact" by the apostle over a number of years: 1:5, 27; 2:12; 3:17-18; cf. 2:22; 4:9.[32]
- The depiction in the Book of Acts of Paul's time in Ephesus seems to leave little room for an imprisonment, particularly of the length necessary for the various trips made between Philippi and Ephesus. Furthermore, the likelihood of Paul as a Roman citizen facing a prolonged imprisonment in Ephesus seems less likely than one in Rome after his appeal to Caesar.[33]
- Some scholars point to the existence of inscriptions discovered in Ephesus to a *praetorianus* (a member of the Praetorian Guard; cf. Phil. 1:13) being present in the city.[34] It has been shown, however, that these refer to a former member of the Guard who later served in the province of Asia.[35]
- In Philippians 1:13 and 4:22 Paul appears to delight in telling the Philippian believers of the penetration of the gospel

---

31 Harmon, 38.
32 Bockmuehl, 28.
33 Ibid.
34 Bockmuehl, 28; Harmon, 37-38.
35 Bruce, *Philippians*, 11.

into the power center of the Empire. These statements and the encouragement they seem intended to convey would be far more likely to have achieved their goal if they arose from an imprisonment in the capital of Rome, rather than from Ephesus. Citizens of Philippi, a Roman colony, would be far more impressed by the former than the latter.[36]

- It is argued that as the capital of a Roman province, Ephesus would very possibly have had a Praetorium. But, as the commentary will show, the phrase "praetorian guard" (1:13) probably refers to a people, not a place. The addition of the adjective "whole" (ὅλῳ, 1:13) makes it more likely that the noun refers to a group of soldiers than a physical location or place.[37] This argues against an Ephesian origin and in favor of a Roman origin.
- At any rate, the fact that Ephesus was part of a senatorial rather than an imperial province means that the governor's palace would not have been called a Praetorium.[38]
- It is not a certainty that it was the trouble in Ephesus/Asia that led Paul to despair of life itself (2 Cor. 1:8-9). Nor is it clear that the affliction had anything to do with prison.[39]
- Philippians 1:14-18 seems to say the local believers were divided over Paul and his ministry, but Luke's account of Paul's extended ministry in Asia (Acts 19) reveals great favor among the saints and no such division. Again, this argues against an Ephesian imprisonment.[40]
- It is said that when Paul speaks to the Romans of a projected visit beyond them to Spain (Rom. 15:24) this contradicts his plans to visit Philippi again (Phil. 2:24). Rather, it is said,

---

36 Bockmuehl, 28.
37 Harmon, 37.
38 Fee, 35, n.87.
39 Harmon, 37.
40 Ibid., 38.

Paul's comments about visiting Philippi fit better with an Ephesian imprisonment. But five years of imprisonment could change anyone's plans. Thus if Paul had to rethink the timing of his anticipated journey into the uncharted territory of Spain and plan instead to revisit some of his earlier scenes of ministry, it should not come as a surprise.[41]

Thus, while a somewhat brief imprisonment in Ephesus cannot be ruled out, the available evidence weighs against an Ephesian imprisonment and against the letter to the Philippians being penned from that city. Such a view faces, as Bockmuehl states it, "overwhelming difficulties" and it "remains an improbable hypothesis."[42]

2. Caesarea. Other scholars believe the letter to the Philippians came from the Apostle Paul while he was incarcerated in Caesarea. In favor of this view are several lines of evidence put forward by those who champion its merits.

- We have historical record of Paul spending two years under arrest in Caesarea prior to his appeal to Rome (Acts 23:31-24:27; A.D. 57-59).
- The "whole praetorian guard" (Phil. 1:13) could be a reference to Herod's facilities in Caesarea (Acts 23:35), though there is debate as to whether that would be the most natural understanding of the term (as per arguments above and also in the commentary at 1:13).
- The scathing rebuke of Judaizers in Philippians 3:2-3 would perhaps be more fitting if the letter arose from Caesarea, given its closer proximity to Judea and Jerusalem and the known animosity of the Jews there toward Paul (Acts 21:27-24:9).

---

41 Kent, 11:98.
42 Bockmuehl, 27.

There are, however, as with the Ephesian hypothesis, some telling lines of evidence that speak against Caesarea as the place of origin for Philippians.

- Paul seemed to expect release in the near future (Phil. 2:24) and the narrative of Acts describing his Caesarean imprisonment gives no reason to believe he enjoyed such optimism during that incarceration. Such hope would have evaporated entirely after he appealed to Caesar (Acts 25:10-12).
- There seems to be little evidence from the accounting in Acts that Paul's life was ever in any imminent danger of ending while imprisoned in Caesarea, while in Philippians Paul seems genuinely uncertain, though confident, regarding the outcome of his trial (Phil. 1:21-23; 2:17).[43]
- Additionally, Colossians seems to depict dynamic missionary activity taking place around the Apostle (Col. 4:3-4, 10-14) despite his imprisonment. If the two letters are from the same imprisonment, there is no evidence that Paul could have organized any such ministry by his co-laborers during his imprisonment in Caesarea.

As with Ephesus, it seems unlikely that Caesarea would have served as the place from which the Apostle Paul penned the letter to the Philippians.

3. Rome. After his two years of imprisonment in Caesarea and seeing that his case might proceed poorly, Paul appealed to Rome (Acts 25:11; 26:32; 28:19). Thus constrained, Festus sent Paul on to Rome (25:12). After a frightful voyage at sea in which God miraculously preserved the life not only of Paul, but the lives of all who journeyed with him, Paul and his captors arrived in Rome (Acts 27:1-28:14). "And he stayed two full years in his own rented quarters and was welcoming all who came to him, preaching the kingdom of God and teaching concerning the Lord Jesus Christ with all openness, unhindered" (Acts 28:30-31). The traditional and most widely

---

43 Ibid., 30.

held view is that Paul wrote the letter of Philippians (along with Ephesians, Colossians and Philemon) from this first Roman imprisonment.

The great objection put forth is the matter of distance and the number of trips made between the place of the letter's origin and the city of Philippi. With a journey between Philippi and Rome taking a month under reasonable conditions, it is conjectured that the necessary number of trips would not have been possible. It is, however, possible that some of the trips would not have involved the full distance between the two locations. For example, Epaphroditus may have fallen ill en route to Rome. One of the traveling party or another traveling in the opposite direction may have carried word of his illness back to the church. Other possibilities also exist which may reduce the number or length of the trips involved. Even if there were up to six trips involved, the time frame of Paul's two years of incarceration in Rome (Acts 28:30) allows for those trips to be undertaken with the time necessary on either end of the individual journeys to complete the matters at hand. If one protests that the travail of such extensive travels appear too much to expect of the parties involved, let it be remembered that these are men who had proven again and again that they were fully devoted to Christ and to the advance of the gospel. They would echo with Paul, "I do not consider my life of any account as dear to myself, so that I may finish my course and the ministry which I received from the Lord Jesus, to testify solemnly of the gospel of the grace of God" (Acts 20:24).

With the matter of distance removed, the remaining objections to a Roman origin of the letter are enfeebled and the evidence in favor of it overwhelms protests to the contrary.

Philippians may have been written during a different portion of this imprisonment than the other Prison Epistles. Colossians, Ephesians and Philemon—because of their similarities—were probably written in close proximity to one another. All three of these letters (along with a letter to the Laodiceans, Col. 4:16) were probably sent about the same time and carried by Tychicus (Eph. 6:21; Col. 4:7). Philippians was likely carried by the hand of Epaphroditus upon his return to Philippi from the Apostle's side (Phil. 2:25-30).

It is the view of this commentary that the most likely place of origin was Rome, during Paul's first imprisonment there (Acts 28:16-30). This means that Philippians and the other Prison Epistles were probably written sometime between A.D. 60-62. Though it is impossible to be dogmatic, the available evidence seems to point to Philippians being written toward the latter portion of Paul's Roman imprisonment. Thus a date closer to A.D. 62 seems most likely.[44]

Recipients: To Whom Was This Epistle Written?

The city of Philippi was located in the eastern portion of the Roman province of Macedonia, approximately eleven miles from Neapolis, a port city located on the Aegean Sea (cf. Acts 16:11). The two cities were connected by the major east-west thoroughfare, the Via Egnatia. It's being placed so strategically for both foot and sea travel gave Philippi a certain cosmopolitan feel and brought influences from beyond its immediate sphere. It also meant that over the years Philippi was subject to the whims of many who sought power and riches. It was located between the Strymon and Nestos Rivers, near a stream known as the Gangites. The latter may be the location of the prayer meeting Paul first visited upon arrival in Philippi (Acts 16:13). Through the ages the region had benefited agriculturally from the fertile plain upon which the city set, the gold mines located in the surrounding mountains, and its considered placement on the Via Egnatia.

The ancient name of the city was Krenides, which means something like "springs"[45] or "The Little Fountains."[46] In either case the name was due to the prevalence of springs in the surrounding area. Philip II of Macedon, father of Alexander the Great, seized control of the region in 356 B.C. to protect it from the Thracians and to mine the gold discovered in the surrounding mountains. At that time he renamed the city Philippi in his own

---

44 Fee, 37; O'Brien, 26.

45 A. Ruprecht, "Philippi," *The Zondervan Pictorial Encyclopedia of the Bible*, (1975, 1976), 4:759.

46 Vincent, ICC, xiii.

honor. The gold enabled him both to upgrade the local economy and to strengthen the grip of his own military.

Control of the region passed to the Romans in 168 B.C. after their victory at the battle of Pydna. The Romans originally divided the region into four districts, but in 146 B.C. the entire territory was consolidated into a singular Roman province. When in 42 B.C. the Republican armies of Brutus and Cassius were defeated by the Imperial forces of Octavian and Mark Anthony at Philippi, the city gained the status of a Roman colony and was given the name *Colonia Iulia Philippensis*. Just over a decade later (31 B.C.) Octavian (whom the Roman Senate later titled Augustus) was victorious over Mark Anthony and the city was made the dwelling of military veterans loyal to the latter as they were dispossessed of their holdings in Rome. At that time the name was changed again, now to *Colonia Agustua Iulie (Victrix) Philippensium*.[47]

The city's standing as a "Roman colony" (Acts 16:12) brought many residual benefits. Philippi was on equal footing with any of the Roman colonies in Italy. Citizens of Philippi were considered also to be citizens of Rome. The governance of Philippi, as a Roman colony, was independent of the provincial rulers.[48] The constitution of the city reflected that of Rome itself. The layout of Philippi was designed after the pattern of the city of Rome. Its people adorned themselves in Roman dress.[49] Citizens of Philippi enjoyed exception from poll and property taxes, and possessed the right to full ownership of their lands. As a colony, Philippi was made in every way possible to be "a miniature reproduction of the city of Rome."[50] The official language of the city was Latin, though Greek continued as a necessity for daily interactions. Roman architecture began to dominate the city. "Roman arches, bathhouses, forums, and temples dominated" the city's landscape.[51] Religiously, temples to gods of Greek,

---

47 M.N. Tod, 'Philippi,' *The International Standard Bible Encyclopaedia*, (1939), 4:2369.
48 Ruprecht, 4:760.
49 O'Brien, 4.
50 Hiebert, 285.
51 Hansen, 2.

Phrygian, and Egyptian origin were known, but "the imperial cult was the most prominent in the city. With impressive altars and temples dedicated to the emperor and members of his family, the city's religious life centered on the worship of the emperor."[52] Any departure from the imperial cult was viewed as seditious and unpatriotic.

Little wonder that Paul's persecutors in Philippi charged him and Silas with "proclaiming customs which it is not lawful for us to accept or to observe, being Romans" (Acts 16:21). Strategically, Paul used his Roman citizenship as leverage when the city officials tried to scurry him out of town (v.37). The depth of local loyalty to Caesar and his empire is evident in the change of behavior among the city's officials when the news of Paul and Silas's Roman citizen reached them (v.38).

This background information becomes significant as we interpret various portions of the letter, including Paul's references to "citizenship" (Phil. 3:20; cf. 1:27), "the whole praetorian guard" (1:13) and "those of Caesar's household" (4:22). Paul employed as titles for Jesus Christ those which in normal parlance were reserved for Caesar: "Lord" (2:11, 19; 3:8; 4:23) and "Savior" (3:20). He promised "the peace of God" (4:7) from "the God of peace" (v.9) rather than the *Pax Romana* offered by Caesar.[53] All this factors decidedly as one sifts the data and makes a decision regarding the location of Paul's imprisonment and thus the place from which Paul wrote this letter to the Philippians.

The ethnicity of Philippi's citizens included the Roman colonists who had been transplanted there, the original Macedonian peoples, as well as an assortment of peoples who had come into the area from the east. The largest percentage were the original Macedonian peoples, the more influential and powerful the Romans.[54] The fledgling church itself seems to have been primarily—if not exclusively—Gentile in makeup. Of the four personal names recorded in relationship to the church in Philippi, three are Greek (Lydia, Acts 16:40; Euodia and Syntyche, Acts 4:2-3) and the

---

52 Ibid., 3.

53 Ibid.

54 Hiebert, 285.

fourth is Roman (Clement, 4:3).[55] History seems to imply that women enjoyed an unusual prominence in the public life of Macedonia[56] and it is of note that the early history of the church in Philippi was marked also by the prominent place of women.[57] One such woman was Lydia, who was among the women to whom Paul and his companions first spoke of Christ upon entering the city (Acts 16:13-15) and in whose home the church originally met (Acts 16:40). Other women of the church, whose names are recorded for us, though for perhaps less noble reasons, include Euodia and Syntyche (Phil. 4:2-3).

Philippi had, by the time of the Apostle Paul's arrival on the scene, apparently attracted only a few Jews. This may have been due to the city's strengths lying in the area of agriculture and the military, rather than commercial interests.[58] There was no synagogue in the city, something that required a minimum of ten Jewish men to establish. Rather any Jews that existed in the city and the God-fearers who joined them gathered for prayer along the river outside of town (Acts 16:13). The church, then, would have been "composed primarily, if not exclusively, of Gentiles."[59]

There has been considerable debate over Luke's statement that Philippi was "a leading city of the district of Macedonia" (Acts 16:12). A variety of answers have been offered, but no consensus has been reached. Ramsay believed that Luke, "the beloved physician" (Col. 4:14), may have been a native of Philippi.[60] The city was the site of a well-known medical school

---

55   Fee, 26.

56   Martin (16) quotes Tarn and Griffith as saying, "If Macedonia produced perhaps the most competent group of men the world had yet seen, the women were in all respects the men's counterparts; they played a large part in affairs, received envoys and obtained concessions for them from their husbands, built temples, founded cities, engaged mercenaries, commanded armies, held fortresses, and acts on occasion as regents or even co-rulers."

57   "In fact it is not too much to say that the author's portrayal of the church at Philippi 'from the first day' (Phil 1:5) presents those women as absolutely essential partners in the foundational development of that congregation that Paul loved 'with the affection of Christ Jesus' (1:8, NIV)." (Luter, 419)

58   Hiebert, 286.

59   Cousar, 6.

60   Ramsay, 201-205.

from which physicians were dispatched into the wider Mediterranean world. If Philippi was not Luke's hometown, it may have been the location of his alma mater. This is uncertain speculation, of course, but it is strengthened perhaps by the famous interruption in Luke's second biblical work, the book of Acts. After Acts 16:12-40 (cf. specifically vv.16, 17) Luke drops the pronoun "we" from the narrative until resuming its use in Acts 20:5, suggesting that Luke may have remained in Philippi with the other believers after Paul's forced departure. If it was home or at least home to his years of study and preparation as a physician it would make sense that he would desire to remain there to nurture the faith of those who made up the fledgling church. The notion that Luke is the man from Macedonia that appeared to Paul in the dream through which he was called to enter Europe (Acts 16:8-10) is interesting, but cannot rise above the level of conjecture.

Occasion: What Circumstances Gave Rise to the Writing of this Epistle?

The text of Philippians points to several matters that prompted the Apostle Paul to write the letter. We do well to consider this both from the angle of the recipients as well as those of the author of the letter.

<u>The Circumstances of the Recipients</u>
The believers in Philippi were being challenged on two fronts at the time of Paul's writing. As is often the case for God's people, one test came from without and the other from within.

The pressure coming upon them from outside the community of faith took the form of opposition. This conflict presented itself in a multifaceted front. There was the more generalized pressure of the pagan Roman culture in which they were immersed. As we have already seen, this pressure would have been particularly prevalent in Philippi since it enjoyed the status of a Roman Colony. Loyalty to Rome and to its Caesar was a conspicuous thread in the fabric of Philippian society and culture. Loyalty to all things Rome was not only part of how things worked in first century

Philippi, it was a matter of identity, self-perception and pride. In Rome (and its colonies, like Philippi) god and country were entwined in one and the same person. Elevation of anything approaching Caesar's level would be considered treasonous. They, no less than we, lived "in the midst of a crooked and perverse generation" (2:15). Paul urged them to "in no way [be] alarmed by your opponents" (1:28).

In that light it is interesting to note Paul's conspicuous use of titles normally reserved in Roman culture for Caesar alone, now applied uniquely to Christ. In this regard Paul's use of σωτήρ ("Savior") as a designation for Jesus (3:20) is notable. Those of us accustomed to the Christian subculture of the twenty-first century read that as commonplace, but in first century Roman society it would have been scandalous, for to the public mind Caesar was savior and any good citizen was ready at any time to confess him so verbally. Similarly, Paul's application of κύριος ("Lord") to Jesus was remarkable—not to mention dangerous. It rolls off the tongue perhaps too casually in our day. But Paul employed it fifteen times in the letter (1:2, 14; 2:11, 19, 24, 29; 3:1, 8, 20; 4:1, 2, 4, 5, 10, 23), perhaps most notably in the triumphant and climactic confession of all intelligent creation: "every tongue will confess that Jesus Christ is Lord, to the glory of God the Father" (2:11).

Thus Paul writes to a people thoroughly immersed in the conflict of loyalties that confronts believers in any age, but which, in the early part of the seventh decade A.D. had unique and painful edges to it in Philippi. The Apostle's call is not to a nuanced expression of faith that panders to and plays word-games with civil religion. Rather he demands absolute and unequivocal loyalty to Jesus Christ above all others. Paul does so by using the very terminology of their earthly privilege as citizens of Rome and applying it to their heavenly calling. In his demand to "conduct [πολιτεύομαι] yourselves in a manner worthy of the gospel of Christ" Paul uses a verb that pointed to one's conduct as a citizen. He used a cognate noun later in a similar expression: "For our citizenship [πολίτευμα] is in heaven, from which also we eagerly wait for a Savior, the Lord Jesus Christ" (3:20). The effect is to set the one loyalty over against the other and give the heavenly the greater value.

Another front of outward pressure facing the Philippian believers was perhaps more potential than actual, but the Apostle was concerned enough that he included this word in the letter: "Beware of the dogs, beware of the evil workers, beware of the false circumcision; for we are the true circumcision, who worship in the Spirit of God and glory in Christ Jesus and put no confidence in the flesh" (3:2-3). The warning concerned the presence and influence of Judaizers who had wreaked such havoc upon other congregations (e.g. Galatians). It is not clear whether the threat qualified as a clear and present danger or only a likelihood or possibility, but it provided the believers one more thing to factor into their faith. The entire description of Paul's personal pursuit of Christ that follows (3:4-14) flows out of this warning and the passion with which he expresses himself underscores the seriousness of the issues involved and the threats they imposed upon the believers in their path.

Yet another front from which the believers in Philippi faced opposition was from the debauched moral standards of the multitudes around them. Immorality was often a central feature of the pagan religions in which they had grown up and out of which they had come to faith in Christ. If the Judaizers (3:2-3) threatened by way of legalism, these warred against their souls by means of licentiousness. Many "walk," then as now, as "enemies of the cross of Christ" (3:18). Their "end is destruction," their "god is their appetite," and their "glory is in their shame," for they "set their minds on earthly things" (3:19) not on the things of Christ.[61] Both over-reliance upon the law and a resolute lawlessness can derail believers.

The second front upon which the believers must vigilantly stand guard was against an enemy from within their own ranks: division. Most notably (and uncharacteristically) Paul named two women who had become embroiled in some unnamed conflict: "I urge Euodia and I urge Syntyche to live in harmony in the Lord" (4:2). So serious was their rift that others in the congregation were vulnerable to being drawn into the fray, and soon the church would be divided in its loyalties. Paul directly calls a

---

61 See the commentary for evidence that some bearing the name of Christ had already fallen prey to such thinking.

prominent individual in the church to take the lead in seeing these two reconciled: "Indeed, true companion, I ask you also to help these women who have shared my struggle in the cause of the gospel ..." (v.2a). But behind this most obvious point of fracture, there lies the recurrent theme of unity found running throughout the letter (see below under "Theology: What Does Philippians Teach Us?"). The pervasive and multi-faceted presentation of this call to oneness underscores the dangers of division that confront them. In addition to specifically addressing the two women and speaking more pervasively, but indirectly to emphasize unity, Paul also spoke pointedly at times, calling the believers of Philippi to the kind of lives that adorn the gospel with love and unity (1:27-28; 2:1-4).

This is a congregation that had repeatedly and sacrificially invested in the advance of the gospel through the Apostle Paul (1:5, 7; 4:16). The knowledge of Paul's imprisonment had sent shockwaves through their fellowship. They wondered what had become of the Apostle (1:12) and, in his incarceration, what would become of the gospel (1:13-18). Paul wrote to put their minds at ease regarding his welfare personally (1:19-26) and with regard to the ongoing triumph of the gospel (1:12), even at the nerve center of Rome's power (1:13) and within Caesar's own household (4:22). The Apostle offers sage counsel as to how one can enter into "the peace of God" by drawing near "the God of peace" (4:6-9).

Paul knew what it was to be "afflicted on every side," facing "conflicts without, fears within" (2 Cor. 7:5). He wrote to strengthen the believers to face all these pressures and to find joy under the circumstances in which God had appointed them to live out their discipleship to Jesus Christ.

The Circumstances of the Author
Consider also the circumstances of the Apostle Paul himself as he wrote this letter. As already noted, Paul was in prison (Phil. 1:7, 13, 14, 17). Though the Apostle was full of faith and enjoyed a measure of confidence (1:19-20a, 24-26), the consequences hanging in the balance were matters of life and death (1:20b-23). We understand this to be his house arrest in Rome (see above: "Origin: From where was Philippians written?") as he awaited trial before the Emperor (Acts 28:30-31). Though we have no

word as to the specific point in that imprisonment when Paul took up pen to write to the believers in Philippi, the available evidence seems to point to the latter portion of his two years of imprisonment in Rome.[62] During this time the Apostle received a visit from Epaphroditus (Phil. 2:25), who had fallen ill en route or shortly after arrival at Paul's side (vv.26-27). It is likely that Epaphroditus, despite his illness, was able to inform the Apostle of conditions in the church in Philippi and of the threats that confronted the believers. Paul, then, wrote in response to their generous gift of support (4:10-20) and in view of the challenges they faced (see above: "The Circumstances of the Recipients") as they sought to continue faithfully in the way of Christ.

The Chronology of Relationship

It will aid us to gather up the details and provide a chronological development of the relationship between the Apostle Paul and the believers in Philippi.

It all began when the Apostle, under divine guidance (Acts 16:6-10), left Asia Minor (along with Silas, Timothy and Luke) and sailed to Macedonia (v.11). This took place in approximately A.D. 51. Upon landing, their first stop was Philippi, about 11 miles inland (v.12). Finding no synagogue in the city, Paul and his party went to a place of prayer for God-fearers near a river (v.13). There Lydia (and apparently at least the others in her "household") believed the gospel (vv.14-15). We are uncertain just how long the party stayed in Philippi, though the narrative seems to suggest a series of events that would have required at least a few weeks ("we were staying in this city for some days," v.12b). After unrest broke out over the deliverance of a demon-possessed girl (vv.16-21), Paul and Silas were jailed (vv.22-24; cf. 1 Thess. 2:2; Phil. 1:30). God miraculously delivered them (vv.25-26) and used the events to bring the jailer and his family to faith in Christ (vv.27-34). Upon release, Paul was asked by the authorities to leave Philippi (vv.35-40).

Paul left Luke with the believers in Philippi and journeyed on with Silas and Timothy, coming first to Thessalonica (17:1-9; note the

---

62 Fee, 37; O'Brien, 26.

dropping of the pronoun "we" at 17:1 when the narrative transitions away from Philippi, and note how it is only picked up again in 20:5-6 when the narrative returns again to Philippi, after an interval of some six or seven years[63]). The three stayed in Thessalonica about three weeks (v.2). It was a difficult time, fraught with opposition (vv.5-9). Multiple times during those three weeks Paul received financial gifts from the believers in Philippi (Phil. 4:16; cf. 1 Thess. 2:9; 2 Thess. 3:6-10).

Under persecution, Paul and the others traveled onward (Acts 17:10a). They ministered in Berea (vv.10-15), Athens (vv.16-34), and Corinth (Acts 18:1-18a). Paul stayed in Corinth for eighteen months (v.11), again supporting himself (vv.2-4). There may have been additional gifts from Philippi at this time, though we cannot be certain (Phil. 4:15).[64] Silas and Timothy, who had been left behind for ministry in Berea (Acts 17:14), at some point again joined Paul in Corinth (Acts 18:5; 2 Cor. 1:19). Then Paul devoted himself fulltime to the proclamation of the gospel (Acts 18:5).

Paul determined it was time to return to his supporting church in Antioch. The route included visits to Cenchrea (Acts 18:18), Ephesus (v.19), and Caesarea (v.22a). We are not certain how long Paul remained in Antioch ("having spent some time there ..." v.23a).

It was probably in A.D. 54 that the Apostle set out on his third missionary journey (Acts 18:23-21:14). A main emphasis of the trip was to collect money from the Gentile believers in support of the famine-struck Jewish believers of Jerusalem and Judea (1 Cor. 16:1-4; 2 Cor. 8-9; Rom. 15:25). This journey included travels through Macedonia (Acts 20:1-2). This would no doubt have involved a stop in Philippi, given its strategic location along the Via Egnatia. In fact, it seems likely that Paul would have visited the church in Philippi twice as part of this journey, once on his travel from Ephesus to Corinth (v.2) and again on his return trip (v.6). Given the larger context of the Apostle's ministry and the growing resistance of the Judaizers, Paul surely would have warned the Philippians about the teachings, influence and threat of these Judaizers. When the Philippian believers

---

63   Goodwin, 67.

64   Ibid., 77.

heard of the offering to be taken to their Jewish brethren, they begged for the opportunity to contribute to the fund (2 Cor. 8:1-5).

Paul, with a delegation from the Gentile churches (Acts 20:4), took the offering to Jerusalem (A.D. 58; Acts 21:1-16). After initial acceptance and a warning concerning of the growing tensions over his gospel (vv.17-26), Paul was then arrested and examined (21:18-23:22). He was subsequently imprisoned for two years in Caesarea (A.D. 58-59; Acts 21:23-24:27). The Philippian believers probably heard of the Apostle's imprisonment, but would have found it difficult to help in any tangible way. Was this because of their own poverty (2 Cor. 8:1-4)? Or was it because of a lack of means to deliver their aid to him?

When on trial before Festus, the Apostle Paul appealed his case to Caesar (A.D. 59; Acts 25:1-26:32). Paul set sail for Rome under Roman guard (27:1-28:10; A.D. 59 or 60). After miraculous deliverance from a storm at sea (27:13-28:10), Paul arrived in Rome and began to serve his two years under arrest and to progress through the various legal levels of his case (Acts 28:11-31).

The Philippians surely heard of Paul's appeal and journey to Rome. Given their heart for the Apostle and the consistency with which they had supported the mission of the gospel through him (Phil. 4:15-16), they would have wished to offer him aid during his incarceration. At some point they determined to send Epaphroditus to Paul in Rome (2:25) with a gift to aid him. But either on the way or upon his arrival in Rome, Epaphroditus fell ill (vv.26-27). The report of Epaphroditus' illness reached Philippi and they were deeply concerned (v.26). News of the Philippians' concern for Epaphroditus' welfare reached Paul and Epaphroditus in Rome (v.26). Paul penned the letter to the Philippians (A.D. 61-63). Paul dispatched the now healthy Epaphroditus to carry the letter back to the church in Philippi (vv.28-30). Paul told the believers in Philippi to expect a visit from Timothy at a time in the not too distant future (vv.19-24). At an undesignated time beyond that, the Apostle himself planned to visit them (v.24).

Thus the Apostle Paul probably would have visited Philippi three times prior to the writing of the NT letter of Philippians: his original, evangelizing visit (Acts 16), again when he traveled from Ephesus to Corinth (20:1-2), and again on the return journey from Corinth (v.6).

The first visit would have happened in approximately A.D. 51. The second and third visits probably took place somewhere between A.D. 54 and 58. The letter was written sometime during Paul's first Roman imprisonment (A.D. 61-63) and probably in the latter portion of those two years. Thus from first encounter to the time of the letter there was a span of approximately one decade.

Purpose: Why Did Paul Write Philippians?

We are able, then, from the text itself, to identify several purposes that lie behind the Apostle's letter.

1. Paul would soon be sending Epaphroditus back to the congregation which had dispatched him to bear their gift to the Apostle and to presumably remain on in ministry at his side (2:25). Epaphroditus, however, fell ill while en route or perhaps after his arrival. Word had leaked back to the believers and they were rightly concerned for their envoy's wellbeing (2:26). Paul realized he would need to explain the presence of Epaphroditus back in Philippi (2:27-30).

2. Paul wished to acknowledge the financial gift from the believers in Philippi and to express his thanks for their support (4:10-19). Their longstanding investment in funding the mission of the gospel through the Apostle (Phil. 4:15; cf. 2 Cor. 8:1-7) had been renewed (v.10) and he wished to enhance that partnership through written communication.

3. Paul believed it prudent to address the seed of division that was beginning to germinate within the church. We know that two women in the congregation were at odds with one another (Phil. 4:2-3) and it may have been that others were feeling the strain. The Apostle wished to mend this rift before it gashed the congregation in two.

4. Paul wished to prepare the congregation for a visit from Timothy (Phil. 2:19-24). Perhaps because of the threat of division within the church, the Apostle thought it prudent that an apostolic designate be on site to help the congregation with the challenges at hand.

5. *Paul wished to update these loyal supporters on his circumstances in prison and to explain how God's purposes in the gospel had not been spoiled by his incarceration* (Phil. 1:12-26). The bond between the Apostle and the believers in Philippi was warm, and he wanted to ease their concerns for his welfare. He wanted also to underscore the triumph of the gospel over all opposition, particularly the powers of Rome (1:13; 4:22).

Theology: What Does Philippians Teach Us?

For a letter as brief as Philippians, there are a surprising number of well-developed themes running through its lines. I will not treat them exhaustively here, but provide enough evidence to move you to the text of the letter (and the commentary), assisting you to further mine these rich veins of truth through your own study. Let's consider seven veins of gold (Psa. 19:10; 119:72, 127; Prov. 2:4; 8:10) running through the strata of Philippians.

1. *Joy.* Perhaps the best and most beloved of these themes is that of joy. In one form or another, the vocabulary of joy is found in every stratum of the letter, sixteen times in all: χαίρω: 1:18 [2x]; 2:17, 18, 28; 3:1; 4:4 [2x], 10; συγχαίρω: 2:17, 18; χαρά: 1:4, 25; 2:2, 29; 4:1.

2. *Unity.* Just as pervasive is the theme of unity among God's people. The Apostle employs a breadth of expression and vocabulary to both explicitly and with great pastoral nuance call the people of the church in Philippi toward the unity that is theirs in Christ. Paul directly, overtly and repeatedly calls the congregation in Philippi to unity (e.g., 1:27; 2:1-4; 4:2, 3, 5, 7, 9). He uses more understated means to pursue unity as well. The pervasive use of the adjective πᾶς ("all") is a subtle nuance by the Apostle as he at every turn speaks inclusively and universally to the believers in Philippi (e.g. 1:1,4, 7, 8, 25). Lightfoot comments, "It is impossible not to connect this recurrence of the word with the strong and repeated exhortations to unity which the letter contains."[65]

Paul employs the power of example in making his plea for unity. The explicit call to unity in 1:27-2:4 is followed by the example of Christ's

---

65   Lightfoot, 94.

attitude, the kind of thinking that makes for peace among God's people (2:5-11). The call for unity in 2:12-18 is followed by the example of humble service in Timothy (2:19-24) and Epaphroditus (2:25-30) serving gladly side-by-side under the Apostle's leadership. Paul pictures the ultimate end of all history as a unified creation all giving glory to God through Christ (2:11).

The use of the plural reflexive pronoun ἑαυτῶν ("your") in 2:12 is a call for the collective body of believers to so live with one another that the salvation of Christ they have each experienced is given fullest expression and finds its logical outworking in the midst of their relationships with one another. In 2:14 Paul calls the believers away from the "grumbling or disputing" which would breed ill-will and dissention in their midst. Three times Paul uses the expression ("you all") in addressing the believers (1:7, 8; 2:26). He reminded them, "you all are partakers of grace with me" (1:7). He reminds them they are together the object of his own affection, which is actually the expression of Christ's own affection for them (1:8). It is this shared grace which then bound the Philippian believers together in joint concern for Epaphroditus after they learned he had fallen ill (2:26). Seven times Paul addressed the whole of them as "brethren" (ἀδελφοί, 1:12; 3:1, 13, 17; 4:1, 8, 21).

In 3:15 the plural form of the personal pronoun ὑμῖν ("you") may indicate that the problem threatening the unity of the church in Philippi was more than a single person within the congregation, but at least potentially was made up of a movement of folks who had begun to trend in contrary directions, dividing the congregation. Thus Paul's repeated calls for unity may have been intended in this direction, though there may have been other areas of conflict and division within the church as well.

In 3:16 Paul uses the verb στοιχέω ("let us keep living") to call the believers to right living. If a hint of the military background of the word remains here, this may serve as another subtle call to move forward together in unity, marching as one toward the goal.[66]

---

66 O'Brien, 442.

In 3:21 the Apostle looks to that day in which Christ will "subject all things [τὰ πάντα] to himself." Paul was willing to lose his whole world (τὰ πάντα, "all things," v.8) so that "all things" might come under the rule of Christ (v.21). Here again this simple adjective (used over thirty times in the letter) is used as a subtle reminder of the unity which the Apostle was seeking throughout the letter. The unity of the local church under Christ is a reflection and foretaste of the universal submission of "all things" at the return of Christ. If we, like Paul, direct all our desire and energy toward that day (vv.8, 14), we will dwell together in unity as God's people here and now.

Throughout the letter Paul employs fifteen different terms prefixed by the preposition σύν ("with")[67], "indicating a pattern of usage implying partnership and unity."[68] At the height of his most direct address of the matter of division, in 4:3, Paul chose four words with a σύν ("with") prefix in order to make his point (σύζυγε, "companion"; συλλαμβάνου, "help"; συνήθλησάν, "shared my struggle"; συνεργῶν, "fellow workers").[69] He thus continues consistently driving home the theme of unity in both subtle and overt ways. Paul concludes the letter by binding every believer in Philippi to "Greet every saint" (4:21), thus insisting that they must acknowledge one another as God's redeemed, justified children. There has been a good bit of discussion over the lack of any formal greetings at the close of the letter. But even this may have been a part of Paul's mission of unity: "Paul may have omitted all personal salutations so as not to give any suggestion of partiality."[70]

We should not lose sight of the fact that Paul was living under the ill effects of disunity among the believers where he was imprisoned (1:14-17).

---

67 See the chart "Does Paul's use of σύν in Philippians Contribute to the Theme of Joy?" in Appendix C.

68 Luter, 415.

69 Luter suggests we add to these the proper name Συντύχην ("Syntyche," 4:2), seeing an intended irony between her name and the division she was party to: "That there is also an implication for Syntyche to live up to her name here is made more likely by the clustering of this *syn*-terminology in 4:3" (Ibid.).

70 O'Brien, 553.

Yet even here the gospel-lenses through which he processes these tensions are a lesson in what it takes to live in peace-seeking, unity-maintaining relationships (v.18).

3. *Relationships*. Having tasted of Paul's panoply of methods in holding forth and calling the believers of Philippi to unity, it comes as no great surprise that there is a great deal to learn in this letter about relationships. We discern in this brief letter something of Paul's pastoral savvy (as noted above in his call to unity) and the power of grace to influence thinking (2:5), words (2:14) and actions (2:12-13) in relationships (2:14-16). Some have expressed great consternation over the fact that Paul waited until the end of his letter to express his gratitude for their financial gift (4:10-20). But instead of sitting in judgment of the text of Scripture, should we not come under its authority and seek to discover just why he may have done this? And how it may reveal the ways of grace and the wisdom of the Spirit?

There is also much in this letter that is instructive concerning dealing with opposition (1:7, 15-18, 27-29; 2:5-11, 15-16; 3:2, 18-21).

4. *Ministry Partnership*. We learn a good deal about material partnership in ministry not only from the text of Philippians itself but from the entire history of the Apostle's relationship to this church. Paul reminded them that they were "partakers with me of grace" (1:7) and how out of this grew their "partnership in the gospel" (1:5). Time and again they supported Paul in his ministry (4:15-16). And they went beyond all expectation in their support of those suffering in Judea, even though they themselves dwelt in meager circumstances (2 Cor. 8:1-5). Their financial giving was an extension of their commitment to Christ and His gospel (1:5) and its advance (1:12; 2:22), as well as an expression of their personal love for the Apostle himself ("your concern for me," 4:10). Their concern over the effect the Apostle's imprisonment would have upon the advance of the gospel (1:12-18) reveals that they did not merely "write a check," but truly bought-in to Christ's Great Commission (Matt. 28:19-20; Acts 1:8). In all this their material gifts were "a fragrant aroma, an acceptable sacrifice, well-pleasing to God" (4:18).

5. *Example.* We learn here about the divine gift of example, and thus of mentoring. Paul held forth the powerful examples of Jesus (2:5-11), Timothy (2:19-24), Epaphroditus (2:25-30), and himself (3:2-14). He explicitly called them to imitate him: "The things you have learned and received and heard and seen in me, practice these things, and the God of peace will be with you" (4:9). It should be noted, in this light, that the Apostle used these very Macedonian believers as examples for the Corinthians to consider in regard to the matter of generosity, sacrifice and faith (2 Cor. 8:1-7).

6. *Suffering.* Philippians has much to teach us about how to face suffering for Christ's sake. We know by now that Paul writes from a Roman imprisonment (Phil. 1:7, 13, 14, 17). But incarceration is not the only suffering in view. The Philippians were surely counted among the impoverished of Macedonia of whom Paul made mention in his correspondence with the church in Corinth (2 Cor. 8:1-5). Then too Epaphroditus suffered in carrying out the will of God and ministering to Paul on behalf of the other Philippian believers (2:25), for he was not only "sick," but deeply "distressed" over the effect this news would have upon the church in Philippi (v.26). His sickness had been "to the point of death" (v.27) and "he came close to death for the work of Christ" (v.30).

Suffering is in fact a multi-dimensional reality. Suffering may be both external (Phil. 1:7a) and internal (1:22-23, 30). It may be both physical (1:7, 13, 14, 17) and emotional (2:27; 4:6-7). It may be inward and highly personal (1:22) and yet also interpersonal (4:2). Even when the suffering is personal in nature, it almost always involves highly relational elements (1:15, 17). Suffering may be religious (3:2), moral (1:18), political/social (2:15; 1:27; 3:20-21), or financial (4:12a) and material (4:12b). It may be caused by "envy and strife" (1:15) or by deep love and care (4:3). It may divide people (1:15-17) or it can, when submitted to God, draw His people together (4:3) through prayer (1:19) and giving (4:12, 14).

Whatever its cause and whatever forms it may take, suffering cannot derail God's purpose for my life (1:6) nor stop the advance of His gospel. In fact it may be used, in the providence of God, to actually advance the gospel (1:12-13). My suffering may move others to more serious discipleship and embolden them in more intentional evangelization (1:14). Epaphroditus' suffering marked him out relationally ("brother"), occupationally ("worker"), militarily ("fellow soldier") and missionally ("your messenger and minister to my need," 2:25).

Suffering often helps us sift, sort, and value, identifying that which is precious and ushering it to the head of our priorities (1:15-18). Suffering is an opportunity to draw nearer to Christ (1:21). Indeed, suffering is often one of God's key tools in sanctification. Suffering serves to refine our purpose to exalt Christ in all things, whatever the outcome may be (1:20). Suffering reminds us that living well is the best kind of vengeance (1:28). Suffering is an unavoidable part of living as the "children of God in the midst of a crooked and perverse generation" (2:15). Our calling is to "appear as lights in the world" (2:15) and to be "holding fast the word of life" (2:16).

There is a kind of suffering which is self-imposed for the purposes of discipleship and longing after Christ (3:12-14). Paul could say "I have counted as loss" (3:7), "I count all things to be loss" (v.8a), and "I have suffered the loss of all things" (v.8b). All this was in pursuit of the "fellowship of His sufferings, being conformed to His death" (v.10). And it was by this pursuit of Christ above all things that Paul could come to say, "I have learned to be content in whatever circumstances I am" (4:11), "I know how to get along in humble means" (v.12a), "in any and every circumstance I have learned the secret of being filled and going hungry, both of having abundance and suffering need" (v.12b).

7. *The Mind*. We learn also about the central place the mind plays in discipleship to Christ. The verb φρονέω ("to think") is used twenty-six times in the NT, twenty-three of those by Paul. Of those, ten appear in this brief letter (1:7; 2:2 [2x], 5; 3:15 [2x], 19; 4:2, 10 [2x]), more than any other single book. This signals the emphasis which the Apostle intends to place upon the realm of one's thoughts. Paul is concerned not merely with the individual thoughts of the believer, but also with developing "the mind of Christ" (1 Cor. 2:16) in His people. The fact that nine of the ten usages of the verb in Philippians appear in the present tense underscore the abiding way of thinking that Paul desires for Christ's disciples.

There is, then, toward the conclusion of the letter that great call: "Finally, brethren, whatever is true, whatever is honorable, whatever is right, whatever is pure, whatever is lovely, whatever is of good repute, if there is any excellence and if anything worthy of praise, dwell on these things" (4:8). The Christian mind involves intentionally forgetting as much as it does purposefully thinking (3:13). So pervasive is the theme of the mind in Philippians that the entire letter may be outlined after this rubric:

- A United Mind (Philippians 1)
- An Unselfish Mind (Philippians 2)
- An Undistracted Mind (Philippians 3)
- An Undivided Mind (Philippians 4)[71]

The hungry heart and active mind will mine these rich themes, as well as discover many other treasures in the text of this God-breathed masterpiece, the NT letter to the Philippians.

Bibliography

Alford, Henry. *Alford's Greek Testament: An Exegetical and Critical Commentary.* 5 vols. Grand Rapids, Michigan: Baker Book House, reprint 1980 from the 1871 version.

Barclay, William. *The Letters to the Philippians, Colossians, and Thessalonians.* The Daily Study Bible. Philadelphia: The Westminster Press, 1959.

Bateman, Herbert W., IV. "Were the Opponents at Philippi Necessarily Jewish?" *Bibliotheca Sacra* 155 (January-March 1998): 39-61.

Batten, Jim. "Touchstones of God's Economy: The Divine Economy in Philippians." *JETS* 7/1 (April 2002): 61-67.

---

71 For the full outline see Appendix A: Expositional Outlines: Single Message; cf. Wiersbe's outline of Philippians after the theme of the mind (63)

Bauer, Walter. *A Greek-English Lexicon of the New Testament and Other Early Christian Literature*. Edited by Frederick W. Danker. 3rd ed. Chicago: University of Chicago Press, 2000. BibleWorks. v.9.

Baxter, J. Sidlow. *Explore the Book*. Grand Rapids: Zondervan Publishing House, 1960.

Black, David Alan. "Paul and Christian Unity: A Formal Analysis of Philippians 2:1-4." *JETS* 28/3 (September 1985): 299-308.

Bockmuehl, Markus. *The Epistle to the Philippians*. Black's New Testament Commentary. Grand Rapids: Baker Publishing Group, 1998.

Boice, James Montgomery. *An Expositional Commentary – Philippians*. Paperback ed. GrandRapids, MI: Baker Books, 2006. WORDsearch CROSS e-book.

Brown, Colin, ed. *The New International Dictionary of New Testament Theology*. 3 vols. Grand Rapids, Michigan: Zondervan Publishing House, 1975.

Bruce, F.F. *Paul, Apostle of the Heart Set Free*. Grand Rapids: William B. Eerdmans Publishing Company, 1977.

_____. *Philippians*. New Interational Biblical Commentary of the New Testament. Peabody: Hendrickson Publishers, 1989.

Buchanan, Mark. *Spiritual Rhythm*. Grand Rapids: Zondervan, 2010.

Bullinger, E.W. *Figures of Speech Used in the Bible: Explained and Illustrated*. Grand Rapids: Baker Book House, 1898, reprinted in 1988.

Burk, Denny. "On the Articular Infinitive in Philippians 2:6: A Grammatical Note with Christological Implications." *Tyndale Bulletin* 55.2 (2004): 253-274.

Carson, D.A. *Basics for Believers: An Exposition of Philippians*. Grand Rapids: Baker Academic, 1996.

Comfort, Philip W., "Philippians." *Cornerstone Biblical Commentary – Volume 16: Ephesians-2 Thessalonians, Philemon*. Carol Stream, IL: Tyndale House, 2008. WORD*search* CROSS e-book.

Cousar, Charles B. *Philippians and Philemon: A Commentary*. The New Testament Library. Louisville: Westminster John Knox Press, 2009.

Dana, H.E. and Julius R. Mantey. *A Manual Grammar of the Greek New Testament*. Toronto: The Macmillan Company, 1927, 1955.

Fee, Gordon D. *God's Empowering Presence: The Holy Spirit in the Letters of Paul*. Peabody, Massachusetts: Hendrickson Publishers, 1994.

_____. *Paul's Letter to the Philippians*. New International Commentary on the New Testament. Grand Rapids: William B. Eerdmans Publishing Company, 1995.

_____. "To What End Exegesis? Reflections on Exegesis and Spirituality in Philippians 4:10-20." *Bulletin for Biblical Research* 8 (1988): 75-88.

Foulks, Francis "Philippians." *The New Bible Commentary: Revised*. Donald Guthrie and J.A. Motyer, editors. Grand Rapids: William B. Eerdmans Publishing Company, 1970.

Friberg, Timothy, Barbara Friberg and Neva F. Miller. *Analytical Lexicon of the Greek New Testament*. Victoria, British Columbia: Trafford Publishing, 2005.

Garland, David E. "Philippians," *The Expositor's Bible Commentary: Revised Edition*, vol. 12. Grand Rapids: Zondervan, 2006.

Greenlee, J. Harold. *An Exegetical Summary of Philippians*. 2nd ed. Dallas: Summer Institute of Linguistics, 1992, 2008.

Gilbrant, Thoralf, ed. *The Complete Biblical Library – Galatians-Philemon*. Springfield, IL: World Library Press, Inc., 1995. WORD*search* CROSS e-book.

Goodwin, Frank J. *A Harmony of the Life of St. Paul: According to the Acts of the Apostles and the Pauline Epistles*. Grand Rapids: Baker Book House, 1951.

Harmon, Matthew. *Philippians: A Mentor Commentary*. Fern: Christian Focus Publications, 2015.

Hansen, G. Walter. *The Letter to the Philippians*. The Pillar New Testament Commentary. Grand Rapids: William B. Eerdmans Publishing Company, 2009.

Harris, Murray J. *Colossians and Philemon*. Exegetical Guide to the Greek New Testament. Grand Rapids: Eerdmans Publishing Company, 1991.

Hawthorne, Gerald F. and Ralph P. Martin. *Philippians*. Word Biblical Commentaries 43. Nashville: Thomas Nelson, 2004. WORD*search* CROSS e-book.

_____. *Word Biblical Themes: Philippians*. Waco: Word Books, 1987.

Hellerman, Joseph H. *Philippians*. Exegetical Guide to the Greek New Testament. Nashville: Broadman and Holman Publishing Group, 2015.

_____. "Brothers and Friends in Philippi: Family Honor in the Roman World and in Paul's Letter to the Philippians." Biblical Theology Bulletin 39.1 (February 2009): 15-25.

_____. "The Humiliation of Christ in the Social World of Roman Philippi, Part 1." Bibliotheca Sacra 160 (July-September 2003): 321-336.

_____. "The Humiliation of Christ in the Social World of Roman Philippi, Part 2." *Bibliotheca Sacra* 160 (October-December 2003): 421-433.

Hendriksen, William. *Philippians, Colossians and Philemon*. New Testament Commentary. Grand Rapids: Baker Book House, 1962.

_____, *Thessalonians, Timothy and Titus*. New Testament Commentary. Grand Rapids: Baker Book House, 1979.

Henry, Matthew. *Matthew Henry's Commentary on the Whole Bible: Complete and Unabridged in One Volume*. Peabody, Massachusetts: Hendrickson Publishers, Inc., 1991.

Hiebert, D. Edmond. *An Introduction to the Pauline Epistles*. Chicago: Moody Press, 1954.

Keener, Craig S. *The IVP Bible Background Commentary – New Testament*. Downers Grove, IL: InterVarsity Press, 1993. WORD*search* CROSS e-book.

Kennedy, H.A.A., "The Epistle to the Philippians." In *Expositor's Greek Testament*. Ed. W. Robertson Nicoll. London: Hodder and Stoughton, 1903.

Kent, Homer A., Jr. *Philippians*. The Expositor's Bible Commentary, vol.11. Grand Rapids: Zondervan Publishing House, 1978.

Kitchen, John A. *Colossians and Philemon for Pastors*. The Woodlands, Texas: Kress Biblical Resources, 2012.

_____. *Embracing Authority*. Ross-shire, Scotland: Christian Focus Publications, 2002.

_____. *The Pastoral Epistles for Pastors*. The Woodlands, Texas: Kress Biblical Resources, 2009.

Kittel, Gerhard and Gerhard Friedrich. *Theological Dictionary of the New Testament*. 10 vols. Translated by Geoffrey W. Bromiley. Grand Rapids: William B. Eerdmans Publishing Company, 1964-1976.

Lenski, R.C.H. *The Interpretation of St. Paul's Epistles to the Galatians, Ephesians and Philippians*. Minneapolis: Augsburg Publishing House. Copyright 1937, Lutheran Book Concern, 1946, The Wartburg Press. Copyright assigned to Augsburg Publishing House, 1961.

Liddell, Henry George, and Robert Scott. *A Greek-English Lexicon: With a Revised Supplement*. Edited by Sir Henry Stuart Jones and Roderick McKenzie. 9th ed. Oxford: Clarendon, 1996. BibleWorks, v.9.

Lighfoot, J.B. *Philippians*. The Crossway Classic Commentaries, Alistar McGrath and J.I. Packer, editors. Wheaton: Crossway Books, 1994.

Lightner, Robert P. "Philippians." *The Bible Knowledge Commentary: New Testament*, John F. Walvrood and Roy B. Zuck, Editors. Victor Books, 1983.

Llewelyn, Stephen Robert. "Sending Letters in the Ancient World: Paul and the Philippians." *Tyndale Bulletin* 46.2 (1995): 337-356.

Louw, Johannes E., and Eugene A. Nida. *Greek-English Lexicon of the New Testament: Based on Semantic Domains*. 2 vols. 2nd ed. New York: United Bible Societies, 1989. BibleWorks, v.9.

Luter, Boyd A. "Partnership in the Gospel: The Role of Women in the Church at Philippi." JETS 39/3 (September 1996): 411-420.

MacArthur, John. *MacArthur New Testament Commentary – Philippians*. Chicago: Moody Press, 2001. WORDsearch CROSS e-book.

MacLeod, David J. "Imitating the Incarnation of Christ: An Exposition of Philippians 2:5-8." *Bibliotheca Sacra* 158 (July-September 2001): 308-330.

_____. "The Exaltation of Christ: An Exposition of Philippians 2:9-11." *Bibliotheca Sacra* 158 (October-Decembber 2001): 437-450.

Marshall, I. Howard. "The Christ-Hymn in Philippians 2:5-11." *Tyndale Bulletin* 19 (1968): 104-127.

Martin, Ralph P. *The Epistle of Paul to the Philippians: An Introduction and Commentary*. Tyndale New Testament Commentaries, R.V.G. Tasker, General Editor. Grand Rapids: William B. Eerdmans Publishing Company, 1959, reprint 1980.

McClain, Alva J. "Doctrine of the Kenosis in Philippians 2:5-8." *Grace Journal* 8.2 (Spring 1967): 3-13.

Melick, Richard R. *New American Commentary – Volume 32: Philippians, Colossians, Philemon.* Nashville, TN: Broadman Press, 1991. WORD*search* CROSS e-book.

Moulton, J. H., and G. Milligan. *Vocabulary of the Greek Testament.* London: Hodder and Stoughton, 1930. BibleWorks, v.9.

Mounce, William D. Gen. Ed. *Mounce's Complete Expository Dictionary of Old and New Testament Words.* Grand Rapids: Zondervan, 2006.

Müller, Jac. J. *The Epistle of Paul to the Philippians.* New International Commentary on the New Testament. Grand Rapids: William B. Eerdmans, 1984.

Munck, Johannes. *The Acts of the Apostles.* The Anchor Bible. New York: Doubleday and Company, Inc. 1967.

Murry, George W. "Paul's Corporate Witness in Philippians." *Bibliotheca Sacra* 155 (July–September 1998): 316-326.

Murray, John. *Redemption—Accomplished and Applied.* Grand Rapids: William B. Eerdmans Publishing Company, 1955.

Newman, Jr., Barclay M. *A Concise Greek-English Dictionary of the New Testament.* Stuttgart: Deutsche Bibelgesellschaft, 1993. BibleWorks, v.9.

O'Brien, Peter T. *The Epistle to the Philippians.* The New International Greek Testament Commetnary. Grand Rapids: William B. Eerdmans Publishing Company, 1991.

Orr, James, Gen. Ed., *The International Standard Bible Encyclopaedia.* Grand Rapids: William B. Eerdmans Publishing Company, 1939, 1956.

Peterlin, Davorin. "Paul's Letter to the Philippians in the light of Disunity in the Church." *Tyndale Bulletin* 45.1 (1994): 207-210.

Ramsay, William M. *St. Paul the Traveller and the Roman Citizen.* 1905. 8th ed. London: Hodder & Stoughton.

Reumann, John. *Philippians.* The Anchor Yale Bible Commentaries. Yale University Press, 2008.

Rienecker, Fritz. *A Linguistic Key to the Greek New Testament.* Translated by Cleon L. Rogers, Jr. Grand Rapids, Michigan: Zondervan Publishing House, 1976, 1980.

Robertson, Archibald Thomas. *Grammar of the Greek New Testament in the Light of Historical Research.* London: Hodder & Stoughton. Third edition, 1919.

_____. *Paul's Joy in Christ: Studies in Philippians.* Grand Rapids: Baker Book House, 1917 by Fleming H. Revell Company, Baker reprint, 1979.

_____. *Word Pictures in the New Testament.* 6 vols. Grand Rapids, Michigan: Baker Book House, reprint n.d. from 1930 Sunday School Board of the Southern Baptist Convention.

Russell, Ronald. "Pauline Letter Structure in Philippians." *JETS* 25/3 (September 1982): 295-306.

Silva, Moisés. *Phlippians.* Baker Exegetical Commentary on the New Testament. Grand Rapids: Backer Academic. Second edition, 2005.

Snyman, A.H. "Philippians 4:10-23 from a Rhetorical Perspective." *Acta Theologica* 2007:2: 168-185.

Stedman, Ray C. *When the Church Was Young: An Exposition of Acts.* Palo Alto: Discovery Foundation. 1989.

Strimple, Robert B. "Philippians 2:5-11 in Recent Studies: Some Exegetical Conclusions." *WTJ* 41.2 (Spring 1979): 247-268.

Sumney, Jerry L. *Philippians: A Greek Student's Intermediate Reader.* Peabody, Massachusetts: Hendrickson Publishers, Inc., 2007.

Swift, Robert C. "The Theme and Structure of Philippians." *Bibliotheca Sacra* 141 (July–September 1984): 234-254.

Tenney, Merrill C. *The Zondervan Pictorial Encyclopedia of the Bible.* Grand Rapids: Zondervan Publishing House. 1975, 1976.

Thayer, Joseph H. *Thayer's Greek-English Lexicon of the New Testament.* Peabody, Massachusetts: Hendriksen Publishers, Inc., reprinted 2003 from the 4th edition originally published by T&T Clark, Edinburgh, 1896.

Thielman, Frank S. *Philippians.* NIV Application Commentary. Grand Rapids: Zondervan, 1995.

Thompson, Alan J. "Blameless Before God? Philippians 3:6 in Context." *Themelios* 28/1: 5-12.

Tozer, A.W. *The Pursuit of God.* Harrisburg: Christian Publications, 1982.

Verbrugge, Verlyn D., ed. *New International Dictionary of New Testament Theology: Abridged Edition.* Grand Rapids: Zondervan, 2000.

Vincent, Marvin R. *A Critical and Exegetical Commentary on the Epistles to the Philippians and to Philemon.* The International Critical Commentary. Edinburgh: T. & T. Clark, 1897.

_____. *Vincent's Word Studies in the New Testament.* McLean, Virginia: MacDonald Publishing Company, n.d.

Vine, W.E. *Vine's Expository Dictionary of New Testament Words.* McLean, Virginia: MacDonald Publishing Company, n.d.

Wallace, Daniel B. *Greek Grammar: Beyond the Basics.* Grand Rapids: Zondervan, 1996.

Walvrood, John F. *Philippians: Triumph in Christ.* Everyman's Bible Commentary. Chicago: Moody Press, 1971.

Wiersbe, Warren W. *The Bible Exposition Commentary: New Testament*, vol. 2. Colorado Springs: Victor Books, 2001.

Wright, N.T. "ἁρπαγμός and the Meaning of Philippians 2:5-11," *Journal of Theological Studies*, NS 37 [1986].

Wuest, Kenneth S. *Philippians in the Greek New Testament for the English Reader.* Grand Rapids: William B. Eerdmans Publishing Company, 1942.

PHILIPPIANS 1

Verse 1 – Paul and Timothy, bond-servants of Christ Jesus, To all the saints in Christ Jesus who are in Philippi, including the overseers and deacons:

If big begins with small, we should not be surprised that a letter of such incalculable influence written to a church of enduring, global effect would begin with a simple greeting. Simple though this greeting may be, it is anything but perfunctory. The Holy Spirit does not inspire perfunctory; all He has spoken is profound and calculated for the good of the faith-filled listener. This is true even in the seemingly mundane greetings in the NT letters.

The first word we encounter is the author's name (Παῦλος, "Paul"), as is his custom in all his NT letters. "Paul" was born the son of a Roman citizen (Acts 22:28) and was given both a Roman name (Παῦλος, "Paul") and a Hebrew name (Σαῦλος, "Saul"). It is his Hebrew name that dominates the early Biblical record (e.g., Acts 7:58; 8:1, 3; 13:1, 2, 7, 9). This is probably because he was still primarily associated with the Jewish people. After his call as an apostle to the Gentiles his Roman name became the regular way of referring to him. Missing here is the normal practice of referring to himself as an apostle, something that he does in every one of his letters save 1 and 2 Thessalonians and here. This is probably because, as O'Brien says, Paul's apostolic authority "was not under challenge either in Philippi or in the other Macedonian church, Thessalonica (cf. 1 Thes. 1:1; 2 Thes. 1:1), with whom Paul had special bonds of affection."[1]

The Apostle is joined (καί, "and") by his frequent associate "Timothy" (Τιμόθεος). Timothy is similarly designated in the salutations of 2 Corinthians, Colossians, 1 and 2 Thessalonians, and Philemon. Paul met Timothy and discovered him to be a disciple when he made his return to Lystra (Acts 16:1). While on his first visit to the city, the Apostle had been taken initially for a god after healing a lame man. But soon the populace turned on him, stoning him nearly to death at the provocation of the local Jewish citizenry (Acts 14:8-20). The Apostle spent only a short time there before moving on. There is no word of Timothy's conversion at that time. Had he been one listening at the fringes of the crowd as Paul preached? It is possible his heart had been moved and, when he witnessed the Apostle's resolute faith in the face of death (2 Tim. 3:11), he put his faith in Christ. At whatever point the genesis of Timothy's faith might be placed and whatever the final impetus to trust in Christ, he was a well-known disciple of Christ at the time of Paul's return to Lystra. He was known in his hometown (the same locale in which the Apostle had been stoned to the point of death!) and throughout the region as an effective disciple of Christ (Acts 16:2). Paul desired that Timothy travel at his side in the cause of the gospel, so that he might further nurture his faith and equip him for ministry (Acts 16:3). Paul and Timothy had logged many miles together and had experienced much of life and ministry side-by-side.

Now, with Paul in a Roman prison, Timothy is found faithfully at his side. It is not expressly clear whether Timothy was likewise imprisoned or simply available as his servant and associate. It seems likely it was the latter. In any case Timothy was present to care for the Apostle's needs and to carry out his instruction, facilitating ministry under his direction. In relationship to the church at Philippi, Timothy had been intimately

---

1   O'Brien, 45.

involved since its birth. He was there when the church began (Acts 16:1, 3; 17:14). He may have visited the church at least three times since[2] and was now on the verge of yet another visit to Philippi (Phil. 2:19) since, insists the Apostle, "I have no one else of kindred spirit who will genuinely be concerned for your welfare" (v.20).

Clearly Timothy was present with Paul at the time of writing. We are left, however, with the question as to whether the expression "and Timothy" (καὶ Τιμόθεος) is to be understood as including Timothy in the composition or recording of this letter. The words as they stand could point to Timothy's role as an amanuensis, recording the words as Paul dictated them. But it appears Paul was the sole author of this epistle, for in verse 3 he will say, "I thank *my* God" (Εὐχαριστῶ τῷ θεῷ μου; emphasis added). This is in contrast to Colossians 1:3 where he says, "*We* thank God" (Εὐχαριστοῦμεν τῷ θεῷ; emphasis added).[3] O'Brien also points out that Paul uses the personal pronouns "I," "me," or "my" more than fifty times in this epistle.[4] The Apostle owns these words as his own and, as with all Scripture, they came under the inspiration of the Holy Spirit (2 Tim. 3:16).

Paul designated both himself and Timothy as "bond-servants of Christ Jesus" (δοῦλοι Χριστοῦ Ἰησοῦ). This is unique, for though he also uses it in the salutations of Romans (1:1) and Titus (1:1), each of those times it is in the singular, referring to himself alone. The noun "slaves" (δοῦλοι) was assigned to those who had sold themselves into slavery, generally for economic reasons. They had voluntarily given themselves up to the will of another, albeit under negative conditions. The word "bond-slave" captures the meaning better than "servants" (NIV, NRSV, etc.), though the word is somewhat archaic and lost on contemporary audiences. It is only in Biblical translation and in early American history that the word "servant" has been substituted for "slave."[5] Paul uses the noun literally to speak of those who are enslaved to earthly masters (e.g., Eph. 6:5-8; Col. 3:11, 22-25; Titus

---

2 Lightfoot, 91.

3 O'Brien, 44.

4 Ibid.

5 BDAG, 2089.1.

2:9). He used it as a negative image for slavery to sin (Rom. 6:16, 19-20) and to men (1 Cor. 7:23). He could use it to speak of one who is "Christ's slave" (1 Cor. 7:22; Eph. 6:6) and of a slave to righteousness (Rom. 6:19). It thus became a title which he gladly applied to himself (Rom. 1:1; Gal. 1:10; Titus 1:1) and others (Phil. 1:1; Col. 4:12). All who serve Christ should be glad to take this title (2 Tim. 2:24). Paul, for Christ's sake, could even say he was a bond-slave of others (2 Cor. 4:5). Ultimately, as he will soon make clear in this letter, the image is dignified and elevated by the fact that Christ willingly took "… the form of a bond-servant" (Phil. 2:7).

The order "Christ Jesus" (Χριστοῦ Ἰησοῦ) is Paul's preferred order in this letter (Phil. 1:1 [2x], 6, 8; 2:5; 3:3, 8, 12, 14; 4:7, 19, 21), though he proves he can freely reverse the order to "Jesus Christ" (1:11, 19; 2:11, 21). Note "the Lord Jesus Christ" (1:2; 2:11; 3:20; 4:23) and "Christ Jesus my Lord" (3:8).

Paul addresses his letter to "all the saints" (πᾶσιν τοῖς ἁγίοις). The plural form of the noun (τοῖς ἁγίοις, "saints") is a familiar NT expression that refers to believers in Jesus Christ generally, not to a special order or class of believers. The adjective (πᾶσιν, "all") makes his concern inclusive of everyone who has been given the standing of "saints." The inclusive adjective is "the first of many references that should be connected with the repeated exhortations to unity throughout the letter."[6] To a church struggling with division (cf. 4:2-3) Paul now gathered up the whole of the church and dealt with them as one.[7] Lightfoot observes:

> "There is a studied repetition of the word 'all' in this letter, when the Philippian church is mentioned: see 1:4, 7 ('about all of you'), 8, 25; 2:17; 4:21. It is impossible not to connect this recurrence of the word with the strong and repeated exhortations to unity which the letter contains (1:27; 2:1-4; 4:2, 3, 5, 7, 9). The apostle seems to say, "I make no difference between man and man, or between party and party: my heart is open to all; my prayers, my thanksgivings, my hopes, my obligations, extend to all."[8]

---

6 O'Brien, 44.

7 Wuest, 27.

8 Lightfoot, 94.

But to narrow the frame of reference he says they are "in Christ Jesus who are in Philippi" (ἐν Χριστῷ Ἰησοῦ τοῖς οὖσιν ἐν Φιλίπποις). It is only by being "in Christ Jesus" that one can be deemed a saint. It is union with the perfectly righteous Christ that makes it possible for anyone to be counted a saint. Spiritually their identity is "in Christ Jesus" (ἐν Χριστῷ Ἰησοῦ), but physically as those "who are in Philippi" (τοῖς οὖσιν ἐν Φιλίπποις). The former tells me *who* I am, the latter *where* I am. They are "saints in Christ Jesus," specifically (and literally) "the ones being in Philippi" (τοῖς οὖσιν ἐν Φιλίπποις). The articular participle (τοῖς οὖσιν, "who are") is used substantivally. The present tense underscores their abiding nature as such.

Their union with Christ defines their life, their physical location the arena in which they live this out. Our identity as those in union with Jesus Christ must always be lived out in a specific place in a specific time immersed in a specific set of circumstances. For these people that arena was "in Philippi" (ἐν Φιλίπποις). Philippi was a city in the ancient Roman province of Macedonia. The story of the Apostle Paul's first encounter there and how the gospel came to the city is found in Acts 16:11-40. During his second missionary journey Paul came to the city and on the Sabbath found a gathering of women at the river. There he spoke of Christ, and Lydia came to faith. When Paul later delivered a demon-possessed girl, those who had benefitted from her were outraged and started a riot. Paul and Silas were beaten and imprisoned. But as they sang hymns at midnight, God miraculously shook the jail so as to open the doors. As the jailer was about to commit suicide at the thought of having lost all his prisoners, the Apostle Paul called out to him. He was led to faith in Christ and was baptized with his family that very night. In the morning, the leaders of the community attempted to hustle Paul and Silas out of town, but Paul pressed their Roman citizenship, frightening their

> **Ministry Maxim**
>
> Every believer has both a spiritual and physical address—the former provides an identity, the latter the arena of its expression.

captors. Before leaving they visited those who had declared faith in Christ, encouraging them in their newfound faith. All told, they had been in the city "for many days" (v.18), an ambiguous designation, but one which assures that they left behind a small, young, but strong church.

Indeed, the Apostle writes not only to the general populace of the church in Philippi, but to the officers of the church: "including the overseers and deacons" (σὺν ἐπισκόποις καὶ διακόνοις). O'Brien observes that "the preposition σὺν ('with') is to be taken inclusively, 'to all the saints, *including* the overseers and deacons', not exclusively, that is, 'to all the saints *together* with the overseers and deacons', for the latter implies that they are not to be numbered among 'all the saints in Christ Jesus'."[9]

The first, "overseers" (ἐπισκόποις), are elsewhere in the NT also designated "elders" (πρεσβύτεροι). The two terms are interchangeable in Acts 20:27, 28 and Titus 1:5 and 7 (cf. 1 Tim. 3:1-7). While both terms describe the same office, each does so from a unique angle. The term "elder" points to the dignity of the office, while "overseer" points to the function of the role. The term used here is a compound word made up of "over" (ἐπί) and "a watchman or observer" (σκοπός). The root word appears in the NT only in Philippians 3:14 where Paul says, "I press on toward the *goal* [i.e., that which one set his eye upon] for the prize of the upward call of God in Christ Jesus" (emphasis added). Thus as "overseers" the elders are charged with watching over the congregation as a whole, to protect the congregation in its entirety as well as its individual members and also to guard the purpose and mission of the church.

To this Paul adds (καὶ, "and") a second office, "deacons" (διακόνοις). The noun is used twenty-nine times in the NT, twenty-one of which are found in Paul's writings. It is often used more generally in the sense of a servant, helper or minister (e.g., Matt. 20:26; Rom. 15:8; 1 Tim. 4:6). But it also came to designate a second office within the growing church, and is therefore translated here "deacons." The overseers/elders focused upon leadership and teaching while the deacons majored on serving the physical needs of the congregation, particularly the needy (such as widows, cf.

---

9   O'Brien, 48.

Acts 6:1-7). The Acts 6 passage does not employ the title "deacons" with reference to the seven men chosen to serve the needs of widows, but the related noun διακονία is used twice (vv.1, 4) and the verb διακονέω is used once (v.2). It appears that these men may have filled a role which the church came to see as essential in all the congregations, paving the way for a second office within the local church. The role of deacon is not as clearly defined as is the overseer/elder. There appears to be no prototype within the Jewish synagogue which may have given rise to this office in the early church. Probably in the outworking of the life and ministry of the church such ministry became clearly necessary and the office grew and was defined by the needs that existed within the local churches. Many of the qualifications laid upon the overseers/elders (1 Tim. 3:1-7) are repeated in the list of qualifications for deacons (1 Tim. 3:8-10), but some are unique to each office. For example, deacons are not required to be "able to teach" (1 Tim. 3:2). The emphasis upon service signals that the deacons' service probably freed the overseers/elders to focus on their God-given ministries of leadership and teaching (cf. Acts 6:4).

The Apostle's salutation sets a tone of ministry and mutuality from the beginning. We each have a spiritual *identity* ("saints in Christ Jesus")—it is foundational for all believers and defines who we are. We each have a physical *locality* ("who are in Philippi")—it is situational and makes up the earthly arena in which we live out our identity as believers in Christ together. We each have a ministry *capacity* (in this case, "including the overseers and deacons")—it is vocational, and though not all will serve as overseers or deacons, all are gifted by the Spirit (1 Cor. 12:7-11) in a way that defines how the reality of Christ's life is expressed through them.

Verse 2 – Grace to you and peace from God our Father and the Lord Jesus Christ.

Paul now wishes or prays for the wellbeing of his readers. The phrasing of this entire verse is repeated exactly in the openings of Romans, 1 and 2 Corinthians, Galatians, Ephesians, 2 Thessalonians and Philemon. The phrase "Grace to you and peace" (χάρις ὑμῖν καὶ εἰρήνη), in addition to these eight letters, is repeated verbatim also at the beginning of Colossians and 1 Thessalonians. His three remaining letters, the Pastoral Epistles (1 and 2 Timothy and Titus), also include these words in their opening, though not with the precise same phrasing. That this is to come "from God our Father" (ἀπὸ θεοῦ πατρὸς) is also found in every one of his letters, except 1 Thessalonians (though cf. 1 Thess. 1:2b where he acknowledges calling upon God for them).

"Grace" (χάρις) may serve as a one word summary of all Pauline theology. It both declares and reminds that all which comes to us from God in salvation is a free, unmerited gift. Paul uses it also to close this letter (4:23), thus wrapping its contents in an inclusio of grace. The word "peace" (εἰρήνη) reverberates with echoes of the Hebrew *shalom* (שָׁלוֹם), the emphasis being not so much on an inward serenity of heart, but on the full-orbed wholeness of a life at rest with God. This the Apostle extends "to you" (ὑμῖν), using the plural form to address all those just classified in verse 1.

These are not graces that arise from within the Apostle himself or that can be drawn from some reserve of personal virtue. Rather they must come "from God our Father and the Lord Jesus Christ" (ἀπὸ θεοῦ πατρὸς ἡμῶν καὶ κυρίου Ἰησοῦ Χριστοῦ). The single preposition (ἀπὸ) governs both "God our Father" and "the Lord Jesus Christ." This indicates that both the Father and the Son together are the only source of grace and peace known to man. As Harris says with regard to this wording in Philemon, "Of no mere human being could it be said that, together with God, he was a fount of spiritual blessing; the deity of Christ is thus implicitly affirmed."[10] Paul grounds this grace and peace in the initiative of the Father and in the accomplishment of the Son. The Spirit will also figure prominently in the Apostle's words here (Phil. 1:19; 2:2; 3:3).

The full title "Lord Jesus Christ" (κυρίου Ἰησοῦ Χριστοῦ) is instructive. The personal name "Jesus" (Ἰησοῦ) speaks of his historical personage and true human nature. Yet it also reminds us of His divine mission in the world: "you shall call His name Jesus, for He will save His people from

---

10 Harris, 246.

their sins." (Matt. 1:21). The title "Christ" (Χριστοῦ), like its OT counterpart (מָשִׁיחַ, i.e., "Messiah"; cf. Dan. 9:25-26; John 1:41; 4:25), means "Anointed One." As kings and priests were set apart to their service by anointing with sacred oil, so Jesus was set apart by God the Father for His earthly ministry by the anointing of the Holy Spirit (Luke 4:18; Acts 4:27; 10:38; Heb. 1:9). "Lord" (κυρίου) is the term used over 9,000 times in the LXX, some 6,000 of which are used to translate the Hebrew יְהוָה (*Yahweh*), the covenant name of God.[11] Its frequent and free application to Jesus in the NT is, therefore, an explicit statement regarding His deity. The confession of Jesus as "Lord" became the hallmark of the early church (1 Cor. 12:3) and put them at odds with the larger Roman culture and its enforcers who demanded that the allegiance of its citizens be expressed through the expression "Caesar is Lord." Robertson comments that, "Thus by 'Lord Jesus Christ' Paul really presents the statement that Jesus is a real man, is the Jewish Messiah of promise, and is divine, Son of God and Son of man (cf. Luke 2:11 'the Saviour, who is Christ the Lord')."[12]

> **Ministry Maxim**
>
> Beginning with blessing is more than the way of wisdom; it is the way of the gospel.

Digging Deeper:

1. In what way do your earthly circumstances give opportunity to better know and experience your spiritual identity? (v.1)
2. How do they give opportunity to live out and show forth your true identity in Christ in relationship to others?
3. Upon whom do you need to speak the blessing of God's grace today? What form must that expression take? (v.2)

---

11 Mounce, 422.
12 Robertson, *Paul's Joy in Christ*, 53.

Verse 3 – I thank my God in all my remembrance of you,

Paul now begins a sentence that will run all the way through verse 7. At times it is difficult to know just how to understand the interconnection of the various clauses throughout this prayer, which is so imbued with emotion. As Lightfoot says, Paul "repeats words and accumulates clauses in the intensity of his feeling."[13] What is clear is that he immediately gets to the heart of the sentence: "I thank my God" (Εὐχαριστῶ τῷ θεῷ μου). The present tense of the verb indicates this is a standing or abiding activity for Paul—

> **Ministry Maxim**
>
> Gratitude spans the gulf created by miles and years, keeping the pathways of relationship flowing freely.

he is continuously grateful. It is from this word that we derive our word *Eucharist*—the time of remembering and giving thanks to God for His love expressed to us through Jesus Christ. That thanks, says Paul, goes to "my God" (τῷ θεῷ μου). The noun with the article makes specific the object of the Apostle's gratitude—God; not just any god, but, literally, "*the* God." And He is "my" (μου) God—the One who has made me, redeemed me, and now rules and owns my life. Paul uses "my God" as an inclusion to open the letter here and to close it in 4:19 (ὁ ... θεός μου; cf. also Rom. 1:8; 1 Cor. 1:4; 2 Cor. 12:21; Philem. 4).

This ongoing flow of gratitude occurs, says Paul to the Philippian believers, "in all my remembrance of you" (ἐπὶ πάσῃ τῇ μνείᾳ ὑμῶν). There is debate about just how to translate this phrase. All the major English translations follow something like the NASU's rendering. O'Brien, however, believes the entire clause must be understood as causal (one of three reasons for his thanksgiving) rather than temporal (indicating the frequency of his thanksgiving) and that this might be rendered: "for your every remembrance of me."[14] The former would be the more natural way of reading the text, while the latter remains a possibility and would anticipate verse 5

---

13 Lightfoot, 93.
14 O'Brien, 58-61; cf. Martin, 59-60.

(not to mention 4:10-20). The preposition "in" (ἐπί) might more literally be rendered "on" or "upon." It is used metaphorically "of that upon which any action, effect, condition, rests as a basis or support; properly, *upon the ground of.*"[15] The noun τῇ μνείᾳ ("remembrance") points to the mental act of consciously calling something to mind. It is used seven times in the NT, all by Paul. Six of those describe Paul's prayers, usually with regard to his expressions of thanksgiving (Rom. 1:9; Eph. 1:16; Phil. 1:3; 1 Thess. 1:2; 2 Tim. 1:3; Philem. 4). In four of those six, excluding this one, it appears in tandem with ποιέω ("making"). The adjective (πάσῃ, "all"), when used with articular nouns means "all the" or "the whole."[16] Thus the idea is that the entirety of all Paul's thoughts of them is filled with joyful thanksgiving. As already pointed out Paul could be using the genitive pronoun (ὑμῶν, "of you") either objectively (the remembrance you have, in this case meaning the Philippian believers remember Paul; i.e., with a financial gift of support) or subjectively (referring to Paul's remembrance of them). I understand the text to be pointing to the latter.

Paul is ten years removed from his first evangelistic efforts in Philippi and now is 800 miles away in a Roman prison[17], but his heart is still full of joy and gratitude over them. Through the years and over the miles the believers in Philippi have continued their interest in, prayer for and support of the Apostle in his ministry. This is a beautiful picture of the fellowship that can be ours in the gospel.

Verse 4 – always offering prayer with joy in my every prayer for you all,

The main clause (v.3) is now qualified by two extended participial phrases, the first in verses 4 and 5, the second in verses 6 and 7.

Maintaining the original word order the clause might be woodenly rendered as "always in every prayer of mine on behalf of all you, with

---

15 Thayer, 233.

16 Ibid., 492.

17 Lightner, 2:649.

joy the prayer making." The participle (ποιούμενος, "offering") comes at the end of the clause. It means simply "to do" or "to make." The present tense underscores the regular, repeated nature of Paul's praying. The middle voice may emphasize Paul acting upon himself to undertake the praying. Prayer is a discipline as well as an urge; an activity which one chooses to undertake. That which is thus undertaken is "prayer" (τὴν δέησιν). Rienecker reports, "The verb from which the noun is derived had the meaning 'to chance upon,' then 'to have an audience w[ith] a king,' to have the good fortune to be admitted to an audience, so to present a petition. The word was a regular term for a petition to a superior and in the papyri it was constantly used of any writing addressed to the king."[18] Note the definite article; it is "*the* prayer" to which Paul refers. Vincent says, "The article refers to *every supplication*."[19] This prayer is offered "with joy" (μετὰ χαρᾶς). Joy (χαρᾶς) is a theme running through this letter, what Robertson calls "the undertone of the whole Epistle"[20] (χαίρω: 1:18 [2x]; 2:17, 18, 28; 3:1; 4:4 [2x], 10; συγχαίρω: 2:17, 18; χαρά: 1:4, 25; 2:2, 29; 4:1). The preposition (μετὰ, "with") indicates that this joy is woven into the very fabric of Paul's praying.

> **Ministry Maxim**
>
> Joy as an experience usually follows thanksgiving as a discipline.

This Paul does "always" (πάντοτε). The adverb of time indicates that this is the repeated and all-pervasive way of the Apostle's prayers. Indeed, Paul does this, he affirms, "in my every prayer for you all" (ἐν πάσῃ δεήσει μου ὑπὲρ πάντων ὑμῶν). Note the frequency with which Paul uses the adjective πᾶς ("all"; cf. vv. 1, 3, and twice here in v. 4) in this letter, a total of thirty-three times. With every attempt to gather the believers in Philippi into a unified whole, he speaks in all-pervasive terms, seeking to cast his words as widely as possible.

---

18 Rienecker, 618-619.
19 Vincent, *Word Studies*, 3:416.
20 Robertson, *Paul's Joy in Christ*, 60.

Verse 5 – in view of your participation in the gospel from the first day until now.

Paul's joyful prayer on behalf of the Philippians (v.4) is "in view of" (ἐπὶ) something in particular. The preposition is used here "of the reason or motive underlying words and deeds, so that ἐπὶ is equivalent to *for, on account of.*"[21] That foundation, says Paul, is "your participation in the gospel" (τῇ κοινωνίᾳ ὑμῶν εἰς τὸ εὐαγγέλιον). The word rendered "participation" (τῇ κοινωνίᾳ) is perhaps more familiar to us by the translation "fellowship" (KJV, NKJV). The noun form which we meet here is found nineteen times in the NT, twice more here in Philippians (2:1; 3:10). The verb form is found eight times (cf. Phil. 4:15) and the related noun (κοινωνός) is found another ten times in the NT, five of those in Paul's letters (1 Cor. 10:18, 20; 2 Cor. 1:7; 8:23; Philem. 17).

Broadly speaking, the noun is used in three ways in the NT: *participation* (association by shared experience; 1 Cor. 10:16; Phil. 1:5; 2:1; 3:10), *fellowship* (association by shared life; 1 Cor. 1:9; 2 Cor. 6:14; 13:14 [13]; Gal. 2:9), and *giving* (association by shared goods, i.e. a gift/contribution; Rom. 15:26; 2 Cor. 8:14; 9:13), though the line of demarcation between the first two is not always easily drawn.[22]

It may well be in the first sense that the Apostle uses the word here. Note the presence of the definite article. Perhaps it points to "*the* participation" which could point to salvation itself, that which marks one as a child of God and a part of the fellowship of Christ's church. It could also be that Paul used it in the third sense; in view of the fact that Paul is writing to express his thanks for their recent monetary gift (4:10-19). In this sense their "participation" was a financial and material investment in the

> **Ministry Maxim**
> Fellowship gives tangible, relational, enduring expression to the union we have in Christ.

---

21 Thayer, 233.
22 TDNT, 3:798-809.

spread of the gospel by which they had been saved. Lightfoot may strike the right note when he says, "it denotes cooperation in the widest sense, their participation with the apostle whether in sympathy with suffering or in active labor or in any other way. At the same time their almsgiving was a signal instance of this cooperation and seems to have been foremost in the apostle's mind."[23] And this participation is not simply "in the gospel" (εἰς τὸ εὐαγγέλιον), but as the preposition's force might be rendered: "*into* the gospel" (cf. the same phrasing in 2:22). It is full, earnest abandon to the good news of Jesus Christ. In view of this "participation in the gospel" the Philippian believers have come to the "fellowship of the Spirit" (Phil. 2:1) and may even come into "the fellowship of His [Christ's] sufferings" (3:10).

This, the Apostle says, has gone on without interruption "from the first day until now" (ἀπὸ τῆς πρώτης ἡμέρας ἄχρι τοῦ νῦν). A period of some ten years has passed. The Apostle has logged many miles since his visit to Philippi. They themselves have faced many challenges since that time. But they never forgot the one who brought them the life-giving, soul-saving hope of Jesus Christ. And they have not failed in that entire time to continue investing themselves personally, prayerfully and materially in that gospel and in the Apostle who brought it to them, enabling him to spread that salvation to as many as possible. Indeed, what a reason for joyful thanksgiving! When he was with them, they shared their homes (Lydia, Acts 16:14-15, 40; the Philippian jailer, 16:33-34) and the substance of their lives (16:34). Upon his departure from their midst they repeatedly sent monetary gifts of support to him in Thessalonica (Phil. 4:15-16) and Corinth (2 Cor. 11:9) and even now, ten years removed from those events, while he was in Rome they sent their financial support via Epaphroditus (Phil. 4:10).

---

23   Lightfoot, 94-95; cf. O'Brien, 62-63.

> **Digging Deeper:**
> 1. Is there someone to whom you could write a long-overdue note expressing your gratitude for them and their ministry? (v.3)
> 2. Where in your life and ministry has joy been most absent of late? (v.4)
> 3. How can intentional and sustained expressions of disciplined gratitude to God pave the way for a fresh inflow of joy? (vv.3-5)

Verse 6 – *For I am* confident of this very thing, that He who began a good work in you will perfect it until the day of Christ Jesus.

Paul now adds another extended participial clause (vv.6-7) to the one already found in verses 4 and 5. Both modify Paul's statement "I thank my God" (Εὐχαριστῶ τῷ θεῷ μου) in verse 3.

In Paul's gratitude he is "confident" (πεποιθὼς). Paul uses this verb in Philippians more times than in any other one book (1:6, 14, 25; 2:24; 3:3, 4). The participle is perfect tense in form, though present tense in meaning.[24] The word itself points toward trust, reliance, conviction, confidence, and assurance. It can mean "to convince someone to believe something and to act on the basis of what is recommended."[25] The participle is used in a causal sense, setting forth a reason for Paul's thanksgiving (v.3). That of which Paul is so confident is "this" (τοῦτο). To this demonstrative pronoun Paul adds a personal pronoun (αὐτὸ) which is employed "as equivalent to a demonstrative pronoun" and is used "to direct attention exclusively to a person or thing, placed in the predicate position."[26] Thus together the pronouns emphasize "this very thing." Paul uses the formula frequently (Rom. 9:17; 13:6; 2 Cor. 5:5; 7:11; Gal. 2:10; Eph. 6:22; Phil.

---

24 BAGD, 639; O'Brien, 63.
25 Louw and Nida, 33.301.
26 Friberg, 82.

1:6; Col. 4:8). It is used outside of Paul only one other time in the NT (2 Pet. 1:5). The pronouns do not point back to what has already been spoken of in verse 5 (the participation/partnership/giving of the Philippians), but forward to God's work of salvation.[27]

What is "this very thing" of which Paul is so "confident"? The remainder of the verse tells us: "that He who began a good work in you will perfect it until the day of Christ Jesus" (ὅτι ὁ ἐναρξάμενος ἐν ὑμῖν ἔργον ἀγαθὸν ἐπιτελέσει ἄχρι ἡμέρας Χριστοῦ Ἰησοῦ). The conjunction ὅτι ("that") introduces a clause which will identify "this very thing." The participle is used substantivally (ὁ ἐναρξάμενος, "*He* who began"; emphasis added). God the Father is surely the subject here, for "God" was the last one mentioned at the head of the sentence (v.3) and Paul will soon mention "Christ Jesus" at the end of the verse and for this to refer to the Son here would be a redundancy.[28] The verb is used only two times in the NT. Here it speaks of the beginning God made in the believers. In Galatians 3:3 it describes the beginning they made by the Spirit. It is a compound word made up of ἐν ("in") and ἄρχομαι ("to begin"). The aorist tense notes the definite beginning God has made to this work. The middle voice indicates that it was God's volitional choice and personal initiative which set the work in motion. This is something which He chose to set in motion "in you" (ἐν ὑμῖν). The pronoun (ὑμῖν, "you") is plural, so Paul is speaking not just of each individual believer in the Philippian church, but also to the church as a whole. He has in view not merely the events of his original visit to Philippi, but the inward, eternal, saving, spiritual work which on that occasion God set in motion within them (cf. Acts 16:11-40).

> **Ministry Maxim**
>
> God both initiates and consummates my salvation, thus I can be assured He will not misstep in between.

---

27 O'Brien, 63.

28 NET Bible.

What God began in those days was "a good work" (ἔργον ἀγαθὸν). The two-word combination is used extensively throughout the NT (e.g. Rom. 2:7; 2 Cor. 9:8; Eph. 2:10), and especially in the Pastoral Epistles (e.g., 2 Tim. 2:21; 3:17; Tit. 1:16; 3:1). In every other passage it refers to good works that believers do or should carry out. Only here does it refer to God as the one performing the "good work."[29] God's "good work" of salvation produces "good works" through the believer, works which He has "prepared before hand so that we would walk in them" (Eph. 2:10b). The Apostle will soon enough hold divine sovereignty in balance with human responsibility by commanding the believers, "work out your salvation with fear and trembling; for it is God who is at work in you, both to will and to work for His good pleasure" (Phil. 2:12b-13).

Paul's joy comes from his confidence that God will "perfect" (ἐπιτελέσει) this work of His. It is a compound verb comprised of ἐπί ("on"/"upon") and τελέω ("to bring to an end," "to complete," "to finish"). The preposition in compound intensifies the root verb and thus points to "will *fully* finish" the work He began.[30] It means "*to bring to an end, accomplish, perfect, execute, complete.*"[31] God both initiates and consummates our salvation.[32] Thus Paul's great confidence! With God as the Alpha and the Omega of our salvation, He can be trusted with all that stands between that beginning and its culmination. Christ possesses "the power ... to subject all things to Himself" (Phil. 3:21b) and is more than a match for anything that would threaten to derail the good work God has begun in us. Paul is utterly confident that God shall continue to "perfect" His work in us "until the day of Christ Jesus" (ἄχρι ἡμέρας Χριστοῦ Ἰησοῦ; cf. v.10). This is Paul's way of referring to the Second Coming of Jesus Christ. In verse 10 and 2:16 he will call it "the day of Christ" (cf. 1 Cor. 1:8). Paul believed in the imminent coming of Christ. Yet he was realistic about the possibility of his own death arriving first (Phil. 1:19-24).

---

29 In agreement with Kent, 11:105, 107, Martin, 61. O'Brien, 64; contra Lightfoot, 95-96.
30 Robertson, *Word Pictures*, 4:436.
31 Thayer, 244.
32 Robertson, *Word Pictures*, 4:436.

There are two sides to the good news found in this verse. The first is that Jesus has a plan by which He will perfect us, to make of us what He always designed for us to be. Indeed, says the Apostle John, in that day "we will be like Him, because we will see Him just as He is" (1 John 3:2). This work lies in His hands. He will do it; meaning we cannot do it. We must participate through our willing, yielded obedience to Him. He will not do it apart from us, but we must be clear that only He can do this. This is not a self-reformation project. God began the good work; He alone will perfect it.

The second edge of this good news might feel a bit like both bad news and good news. It is the fact that our perfection awaits the coming of Christ. It is only in a new world with a fully-redeemed body, soul and spirit that we shall be all that we were designed to be. This means waiting, which sounds like bad news. And it is, but the good news is that we can adjust our expectations for our experience in the present. We are not perfect now. We will not be perfect in this world. God knows this. He has told us this. He is working to perfect us, but He does not expect perfection out of us yet, not till Jesus comes back. Therefore, do not slack up even in the slightest in your pursuit of holiness and Christlikeness, but in pressing forward with all Christ's strength within you (Phil. 3:7-14), cut yourself some slack. God deals in grace for a reason. You need it. There will never be a time you don't need His grace. Rest in it. Live in it. Delight in it.

> **Digging Deeper:**
>
> 1. In what way does the knowledge of God as both the initiator and finisher of your salvation give you confidence in his providential dealings with you in the moments and details of life?
> 2. To whom might you express confidence about what you see God doing in their life? What form should that expression take? What effect might it have on that person's life?

Verse 7 – For it is only right for me to feel this way about you all, because I have you in my heart, since both in my imprisonment and in the defense and confirmation of the gospel, you all are partakers of grace with me.

Paul now elaborates on the confidence he expressed in verse 6. The subordinating conjunction "For" (Καθώς) has a causal sense, perhaps "since" would serve as a good alternate translation.[33] The subject of the clause is expressed by an infinitive phrase: "to feel this way about you all" (τοῦτο φρονεῖν ὑπὲρ πάντων ὑμῶν). The present tense of the infinitive reveals that this is Paul's ongoing view with regard to the Philippian believers. Of the twenty-six times the word appears in the NT, all but three are in Paul's writings. Ten of these occurrences are here in Philippians (1:7; 2:2 [2x], 5; 3:15 [2x], 19; 4:2, 10 [2x]). It means to think, to form or hold an opinion, or to judge; here with the specific meaning to "*think* or *feel in a certain way about someone.*"[34] The demonstrative pronoun (τοῦτο, "this") refers back either to the confidence expressed in verse 6[35] or to the whole of his sentiments expressed in verses 3-6.[36] The apostle's confidence is not in one or two of the Philippian believers, perhaps the leadership (v.1b) rather than the general church membership or vice versa, but with regard to (ὑπὲρ, "about") "you all" (πάντων ὑμῶν). The phrase (ὑπὲρ πάντων ὑμῶν, "about you all") is an exact repetition of what we have in verse 4.[37] The joyful prayer of verse 4 has become the glad confidence of verse 7. This was a healthy congregation and it brought joy and anticipation to the Apostle's heart. Such a view, said Paul, "is only right" (ἐστιν δίκαιον). The adjective (δίκαιον, "right") is used in a broad sense of "*upright, righteous,*

---

33   Thayer, 315.
34   BDAG, 7819.1.
35   Vincent, ICC, 9.
36   Lenski, 711; O'Brien, 66.
37   Lenski, 711.

virtuous."[38] This was a perspective of the church that was personal to Paul (ἐμοὶ, "for me").

The reason Paul had this unique perspective on and experience with the church in Philippi goes beyond simply his initial ministry among them (Acts 16:12-40). This additional foundation is explained in the remainder of the verse which also forms the end of the sentence that began in verse 3. He introduces it with "because" (διὰ); he will lay down the basis of that which forms his evaluation of the Christians in Philippi.

The Apostle says to them in deeply endearing terms, "I have you in my heart" (τὸ ἔχειν με ἐν τῇ καρδίᾳ ὑμᾶς). Grammatically it is possible to translate this in the opposite direction: "you hold me in your heart" (NRSV).[39] Yet "I have you in my heart" seems the more likely because of the original word order and the fact that in verse 8 Paul seems to reinforce this notion with an oath.[40] Robertson says, "There is no way to decide which is the idea meant except to say that love begets love. The pastor who, like Paul, holds his people in his heart will find them holding him in their hearts."[41] The infinitive (ἔχειν, "I have") serves with the preposition (διὰ) to indicate a causal relationship of this to what precedes.[42] The present tense indicates the ongoing way in which Paul holds the Philippian believers in the dearest regards. In the NT "heart" (καρδίᾳ) describes the seat of the mind (2 Cor. 4:6), emotions (Eph. 6:22), and will (2 Cor. 9:7). The "heart" is the core and center of the individual.

This affection of the Apostle arose from a deep and abiding fellowship in the grace of God: "you all are partakers of grace with me" (συγκοινωνούς μου τῆς χάριτος πάντας ὑμᾶς ὄντας). The noun rendered "partakers" (συγκοινωνός) is used only four times in the NT, three of them by Paul (Rom. 11:17; 1 Cor. 9:23; Phil. 1:7; Rev. 1:9). It is a compound word comprised of σύν ("with") and κοινωνός ("partner," "companion"),

---

38 Thayer, 148.
39 NET Bible; Robertson, *Word Pictures*, 4:436.
40 Alford, 3:155; O'Brien, 68.
41 Robertson, *Word Pictures*, 4:436.
42 BDAG, 1823.B.2.c; O'Brien, 68.

the latter being from the familiar κοινωνία word group (cf. Phil. 1:5; 2:1; 3:10; 4:15). The prefix (συν-) may emphasize "share to the full with."[43] It is followed by "the addition of the genitive of the person with whom one is partaker of a thing" (μου, "with me").[44] Thus the personal pronoun (μου, "me") is rightly connected with "partakers" (συγκοινωνούς) and not with "grace" (τῆς χάριτος).[45] This sharing was "of grace" (τῆς χάριτος). Note the definite article. It is a particular "grace" in which they became partakers along with the apostle. The genitive is objective ("the grace Paul receives") rather than subjective ("the grace Paul gives").[46] Such "partakers," Paul can truthfully say, "you all are" (πάντας ὑμᾶς ὄντας). It might more literally be rendered, "all of you being." Here again he gathers up "all" (πάντας) the Philippian believers as just that: "believers," regardless of other distinguishing marks among them. The present tense of the participle (ὄντας, "are") underscores the ongoing nature of their participation.

That particular grace which they came to share along with the Apostle is that which came by their sharing "both in my imprisonment and in the defense and confirmation of the gospel" (ἔν τε τοῖς δεσμοῖς μου καὶ ἐν τῇ ἀπολογίᾳ καὶ βεβαιώσει τοῦ εὐαγγελίου). This extended and complex prepositional phrase has two prongs—roughly to be thought of as *suffering* ("my imprisonment") and *speaking* ("the defense and confirmation of the gospel"). That he does so is signaled by the use of the conjunction τε ("both") and the repeated preposition ἐν ("in"): "both [τε] in [ἐν] my imprisonment and in [ἐν] the defense and confirmation of the gospel." These, then, are hinged together by the first instance of the coordinating conjunction καὶ ("and"). Both uses of ἐν ("in") are locative in meaning, describing the sphere in which the Philippians and Paul together shared their experiences and thus the grace that God poured out on them.

The first prong, then, is "my imprisonment" (τοῖς δεσμοῖς μου). The noun (τοῖς δεσμοῖς, "imprisonment") is used eighteen times in the

---

43 Robertson, *Paul's Joy in Christ*, 65.
44 Thayer, 593.
45 Martin, 63; O'Brien, 70; Vincent, ICC, 10; Wuest, 33.
46 Robertson, *Word Pictures*, 4:437.

NT, eight of them by Paul and four of those here in the first chapter of Philippians (1:7, 13, 14, 17). He adds the definite article, marking the present circumstances in which he finds himself as a prisoner of Rome (Acts 28:16, 30-31). The word refers literally to bonds, chains or fetters (e.g., Luke 8:29; Acts 16:26) and by metonymy it can then be used to speak of imprisonment generally (e.g., Col. 4:18) as it does here.[47] Paul adds the personal pronoun (μου, "my") to make emphatic that this is his very own experience, though in some measure he believes the Philippian believers to have shared in it with him.

The second prong is doubled up, the two lines coordinated by the second instance of καὶ ("and"): "the defense and confirmation of the gospel" (τῇ ἀπολογίᾳ καὶ βεβαιώσει τοῦ εὐαγγελίου). On the front end of the clause both nouns are governed by the one preposition (ἐν, "in") and by one definite article (τῇ, "the"), in the middle they are coordinated by the conjunction καὶ ("and"), and at the end they both are described by the genitive "of the gospel" (τοῦ εὐαγγελίου). All this to indicate that they are to be considered closely tied to one another, though they do not seem to form a hendiadys ("defense for confirmation").[48]

The first noun (ἀπολογίᾳ, "defense") is the word from which we get our English word *apologetics*. The word was a technical term from the legal world which described a verbal defense of oneself or one's position. Paul would use it of the legal process in his final Roman imprisonment (2 Tim. 4:16).

The second noun (βεβαιώσει, "confirmation") is used only here and in Hebrews 6:16: "For men swear by one greater than themselves, and with them an oath given as confirmation [βεβαίωσιν] is an end of every dispute." It too was a technical term from the legal world which was used for "guaranteeing" or "furnishing security."[49] It described "a legally valid confirmation" or an action which thus served as *"confirmation,"*

---

47 Friberg, 106.

48 Vincent, ICC, 10.

49 BDAG, 1448.

"*verification*" or a "*making sure*" of something.⁵⁰ If a third party caused a buyer to be in doubt about the authenticity of that which he purchased, the original seller would offer such a "confirmation."⁵¹ Thus it described an act which was "to cause something to be known as certain."⁵² It was the kind of thing Paul was doing in Acts 28:23: "When they had set a day for Paul, they came to him at his lodging in large numbers; and he was explaining to them by solemnly testifying about the kingdom of God and trying to persuade them concerning Jesus, from both the Law of Moses and from the Prophets, from morning until evening."⁵³

> **Ministry Maxim**
>
> There is no shortcut to love—it takes shared life and shared grace in the midst of it to bind hearts together as one.

These two terms were surely tied to Paul's impending trial, but probably also were a reference more generally to the whole tenor and substance of his gospel ministry. The former (ἀπολογίᾳ, "defense") and the latter (βεβαιώσει, "confirmation") may be thought of respectively in broad terms as the negative ("removing obstacles and prejudices") and positive ("the direct advancement and establishment of the gospel") aspects of speaking for the gospel.⁵⁴

The Apostle's words remind us that through prayer, financial support, and other means of contact the missionary and his/her supporters have a true and actual bond. It is more than a psychological bond, for they actually together share in the "grace" (τῆς χάριτος) God pours out commonly upon both, though they are separated by many miles and perhaps by a different language, culture and other vastly different sets of immediate circumstances. This bond is spiritual and is as true, or truer, than if they had merely been present physically in his trials.

---

50 Friberg, 90.
51 Kent, 11:107.
52 Louw-Nida, 28.44.
53 O'Brien, 69.
54 Lightfoot, 97.

Here too verses 6 and 7 reveal a discernable pattern with importance in ministry relationships. In service to Christ along with others we want to have a deep confidence (v.6) in those alongside of whom we serve. But how does this come about? Such confidence is an outgrowth of personal intimacy and relationship ("it is only right for me to feel this way about you all, because I have you in my heart," v.7a). In turn, such intimacy of relationship comes from a mutual experience of a common grace from God ("you all are partakers of grace with me," v.7c). And such experiences of God's grace grow out of shared experiences in which you trust God together ("both in my imprisonment and in the defense and confirmation of the gospel," v.7b). Thus there is a progression from shared experience (v.7c) to mutual grace (v.7b) to personal intimacy (v.7a) to assured confidence (v.6). This pattern has implications for how we seek to reproduce disciples of Jesus Christ and how we train workers and leaders for kingdom work. It also offers some explanation for why we may feel a certain way about certain fellow servants and why they may feel as they do about us.

> **Digging Deeper:**
> 1. How does this progression (shared experience → mutual grace → personal intimacy → assured confidence) encourage you to take a step toward someone else in relationship today?
> 2. If you desire deep relationships with other believers, what investments must you make in those relationships today?

Verse 8 – For God is my witness, how I long for you all with the affection of Christ Jesus.

The conjunction "For" (γάρ) signals that Paul is further explaining why it is right for him to feel (v.7) as he does about them (i.e., confident, v.6). The Apostle calls in the highest evidence: "God is my witness" (μάρτυς ... μου ὁ θεός). Paul similarly calls God as witness in Romans 1:9, 2 Corinthians 1:23, 1 Thessalonians 2:5, 10 (cf. Rev. 1:5; 3:14). That to which God is able to bear witness is "how I long for you all" (ὡς ἐπιποθῶ πάντας ὑμᾶς). The conjunction ὡς, when used after verbs of knowing or saying, is equivalent to ὅτι ("that").[55] Yet Thayer adds, "there is this difference between the two, that ὅτι expresses the thing itself, ὡς the mode or quality of the thing (hence, usually rendered how)."[56] The verb "I long for" (ἐπιποθῶ) is a compound, with a prefixed preposition (ἐπί) that gives direction to the yearning.[57] The word is a strong one, describing an intense longing after something (2 Cor. 5:2) or someone (Rom. 1:11; 2 Cor. 9:14; Phil. 1:8; 2:26; 1 Thess. 3:6; 2 Tim. 1:4). It is a word of which the Apostle Paul is especially fond, as seven of its nine NT usages are found in his letters. The Apostle's intense yearning was indiscriminate toward all the believers in Philippi (πάντας ὑμᾶς, "you all")—another subtle contribution to the Apostle's theme of unity.

> **Ministry Maxim**
>
> The height of ministry is when Jesus loves people through you.

But it was no mere human emotion that possessed the Apostle. No, he yearned after them "with the affection of Christ Jesus" (ἐν σπλάγχνοις Χριστοῦ Ἰησοῦ). The noun rendered "the affection" (σπλάγχνοις) refers more literally to the "*bowels, intestines* (the heart, lungs, liver, etc.)."[58] In the ancient world these were considered the seat of the emotions. To the Greek poets they were the center of "the more violent passions, such as anger and love, but by the Hebrews as the seat of the tenderer affections, especially kindness, benevolence, compassion."[59]

Just how should we understand the preposition (ἐν, "with")? Is it to be understood as locative and thus describe the sphere "in" which these emotions are found or experienced? And how should we understand the genitive (Χριστοῦ Ἰησοῦ, "of Christ Jesus")? Does Paul intend it as a subjective genitive (the affection which Christ brings) or as an objective genitive (the

---

55 BDAG, 8075.5.

56 Thayer, 681; cf. Robertson, *Grammar*, 1032; Vincent, ICC, 10; contra, O'Brien, 71.

57 Rienecker, 545.

58 Thayer, 584.

59 Ibid.

affection which Christ Himself feels)? The latter might be similar to Luke 1:78: "Because of the tender mercy of our God." The noun appears again in Philippians 2:1 where the Apostle wonders if they have experienced any "encouragement in Christ" (παράκλησις ἐν Χριστῷ) and continues the query with regard to "compassion" (σπλάγχνα). Here the locative sense of the pronoun is clear, making the expression closer to the idea of the objective genitive. The noun is used three times in Philemon (Philem. 7, 12, 20), in the last of which the Apostle asks Philemon, "refresh my heart in Christ" (ἀνάπαυσόν μου τὰ σπλάγχνα ἐν Χριστῷ). Here too the preposition appears to be used in a locative sense of the sphere in which the reality pointed to by the noun is experienced.

For these reasons it seems wisest to take Paul's words here in Philippians in the sense of his coming to share in the very affection, compassion, heart or emotions of Christ Jesus by virtue of his faith union with Him. Paul is asserting that he has come to share the Lord's own compassion for the Philippians.

O'Brien can thus say this is "nothing less than Christ's love expressing itself through Paul" and that "Christ loves the Philippians in and through Paul."[60] Bengel says, "It is not Paul who lives within Paul, but Jesus Christ, which is why Paul is not moved by the bowels of Paul but by the bowels of Jesus Christ."[61] Vincent says "Christ loves them in him [i.e., the Apostle Paul]."[62] Lightfoot calls it "A powerful metaphor describing perfect union."[63] Wuest says that Paul's "heart ... beat as one with the heart of Jesus."[64] Robertson contends that "Paul longs for the Philippians ... in mystic union with Christ with the very heart-throb of Jesus Himself."[65] God Himself, says the Apostle, could bear witness to this fact. And this

---

60 O'Brien, 71, 72.
61 Quoted by O'Brien, 72.
62 Vincent, ICC, 11.
63 Lightfoot, 98.
64 Wuest, 34.
65 Robertson, *Paul's Joy in Christ*, 66.

explains his feelings expressed in verse 7 and ultimately his confidence as expressed in verse 6.

> **Digging Deeper:**
> 1. Who in your life right now is most difficult to love?
> 2. What does this verse teach you about what is possible in that relationship? What would it look like for Jesus to love that person through you?
> 3. What does this verse teach you about what more is possible in the relationships with the people you already love most?

Verse 9 – And this I pray, that your love may abound still more and more in real knowledge and all discernment,

Having expressed his gratitude for the Philippians (1:3-8), Paul now gives them a glimpse into his petitions (hinted at in v.4) on their behalf (vv.9-11). The conjunction Καὶ ("And") serves to move the Apostle's thought along from his gratitude for them (vv.3-8) to his intercession on their behalf (vv.9-11). The verb προσεύχομαι ("I pray") is in the present tense, underscoring the ongoing nature of the way he prays for them. It is the most general word for prayer in the NT. The demonstrative pronoun τοῦτο ("this") points forward, "introducing the *substance* of the prayer" while the conjunction ἵνα points to the *aim* of Paul's prayer for them.[66] The ἵνα takes "the place of the explanatory inf[initive] after a demonstrative" pronoun (τοῦτο, "this").[67]

Paul's prayer, then, for the Philippian believers is that "your love may abound still more and more" (ἡ ἀγάπη ὑμῶν ἔτι μᾶλλον καὶ μᾶλλον περισσεύῃ). The heart of Paul's intercession is that they might know and experience "love" (ἡ ἀγάπη). Note the definite article, for this is not just love as a concept nor is it love defined according to the Philippian's present

---

66   Alford, 3:156.

67   BDAG, 3715.2.e.

feelings or circumstances. No, this is "*the* love" of all loves—the love of God for them through Jesus Christ poured in and through them until it can legitimately be called "*your* love" (ἡ ἀγάπη ὑμῶν, emphasis added). The genitive plural form of the personal pronoun (ὑμῶν, "your") points to the love which will unify any divisions (4:2-3), overcome any false teachings (3:1ff) and heal any wounds (2:1-5).

Paul prays that this love will "abound" (περισσεύῃ). The verb depicts having more than enough of something, to have leftovers of something, for something to be extremely rich or abundant. Paul will use it four more times in this letter (1:26; 4:12 [2x], 18). Here it may have the meaning "grow" until it is in such a state of abundance.[68] The present tense pictures this as an ongoing, unending process. The subjunctive mood hints that its reality depends upon God answering Paul's prayer.

As if this abounding were not enough, it is to happen "still more and more" (ἔτι μᾶλλον καὶ μᾶλλον). The adverb ἔτι ("still") is used "of that which is added to what is already at hand"[69] The adverb μᾶλλον means "to a greater degree." And then this is doubled up (μᾶλλον καὶ μᾶλλον, "more and more"). Thus Paul makes his point that whatever love they may already have experienced as recipients of God's grace in Christ (2:1), his prayer is that this will be multiplied until it abounds, overflows, exists in excess of all measure of need and that it may do this over and over again. Lightfoot justly calls it "An accumulation of words to denote superabundance."[70] "The expression builds layer upon layer to make the point. 'More' would have sufficed, 'more and more' was better, but 'still more and more' accentuated the point being made."[71]

> **Ministry Maxim**
>
> Love that rests upon something less than deepening knowledge and penetrating insight is not true love.

---

68 Ibid., 5868.1.a.δ.

69 Ibid., 3188.2.b.

70 Lightfoot, 98.

71 Melick, 62.

This abounding, overflowing love will express itself in a two-pronged fashion: "in real knowledge and all discernment" (ἐν ἐπιγνώσει καὶ πάσῃ αἰσθήσει). The preposition ἐν ('in') governs both nouns and is to be understood as locative, expressing the spheres in which love properly operates.[72] The first way in which such super-abounding love will express itself is "real knowledge" (ἐπιγνώσει). It is a compound word comprised of ἐπί ("upon") and γνῶσις ("knowledge"). The prefix intensifies the root word and points to a fullness, depth and completeness of knowledge. In each of the four epistles written from Paul's first Roman imprisonment this becomes part of his prayer for the recipients (Eph. 1:17; Phil. 1:9; Col. 1:9; Philemon 6).[73] Lightfoot says, "Its more frequent occurrence thus corresponds to the more contemplative aspect of the gospel presented in these letters."[74]

This is joined (καὶ, "and") with "discernment" (αἰσθήσει). The noun is used only here in the NT, but the verb appears in Luke 9:45 and a related noun in Hebrews 5:14. The latter of these tells us that though this faculty is ultimately a gift from God it is also something that can be trained and developed: "But solid food is for the mature, who because of practice have their senses [τὰ αἰσθητήρια] trained to discern good and evil." It does appear more frequently in the LXX, especially in Proverbs where it often renders the Hebrew word *da'at* (דַּעַת), which points to a knowledge that is not merely intellectual, but deeply personal and experiential (e.g., Prov. 1:4, 7; 2:5). Martin says "it is the employment of the faculty which makes a person able to make a moral decision."[75] It is "a moral action of recognizing distinctions and making a decision about behavior."[76] It means "to have the capacity to perceive clearly and hence to understand the real nature of something."[77] Robertson says, "This word denotes the fineness

---

72 O'Brien, 75.
73 Vincent, ICC, 12.
74 Lightfoot, 98.
75 Martin, 65.
76 Friberg, 38.
77 Louw-Nida, 32.28.

of spiritual perception that comes from alertness and practice."[78] Similarly Vincent contends, "It is the faculty of spiritual discernment of the bearings of each particular circumstance or case which may emerge in experience. It is more specific than ἐπίγνωσις with the practical applications of which it deals."[79] To this is affixed the adjective "all" (πάσῃ). Here it includes "everything belonging, in kind, to the class designated by the noun."[80] O'Brien says it "points to insight for all kinds of situations as they arise."[81]

The two nouns when held up against one another provide a composite picture of Paul's prayer for these dear saints. The former points to "intellectual perception" while the latter to "moral understanding."[82] Vincent says that the former "is the general regulator and guide" while the latter applies the former "to the finer details of the individual life, and fulfils itself in the various phases of Christian tact."[83] Lightfoot adds, "While **knowledge** deals with general principles, **insight** is concerned with practical applications."[84] Robertson contends that the latter "calls for the practical application of" the former.[85]

Paul told the Corinthian believers, "Knowledge makes arrogant, but love edifies" (1 Cor. 8:1). But his prayer for the Philippians proves that this need not be the case. Indeed, love and knowledge are not mutually exclusive; rather love operates in the sphere of true, deep, personal, experiential knowledge of God as it is applied in the real-world issues of our daily relationships and responsibilities. Paul went on to tell the believers in Corinth that "If I … know all mysteries and all knowledge … but do not have love, I am nothing" (1 Cor. 13:2).

---

78 Robertson, *Paul's Joy in Christ*, 68.
79 Vincent, ICC, 12.
80 BDAG, 5722.5.
81 O'Brien, 77.
82 Ibid.
83 Vincent, ICC, 12.
84 Lightfoot, 99, emphases original.
85 Robertson, *Paul's Joy in Christ*, 68.

Love without deep knowledge and penetrating insight is sentimental. Deep knowledge and penetrating insight without love may become tyrannous. Wed together they are a force to be reckoned with in a world comprised of equal parts ignorance, blindness, and selfishness.

Verse 10 – so that you may approve the things that are excellent, in order to be sincere and blameless until the day of Christ;

The purpose or intended result (εἰς τὸ plus the infinitive, "so that") of Paul's praying that they may thus abound in this knowing, discerning love (v.9) is now set forth. The infinitive "may approve" (δοκιμάζειν) has both the sense of testing (2 Cor. 13:5) and, as here, approving something, or approving something after testing. The word was used in the world of metallurgy to describe the scrutiny employed to test the genuineness of metal. As such, then, it was used to describe both the scrutiny itself and the resulting approval of the genuine article.[86] The present tense describes the action as simply happening—they may possess such discernment at whatever time they need it. The Apostle uses the plural form of the pronoun to show he prays this will become true for all the believers in Philippi (ὑμᾶς, "you"). The articular participle (τὰ διαφέροντα, "the things that are excellent") is used as a substantive. When used intransitively it has the basic meaning of "differ" or "be different." But here it has the idea of "differ to one's advantage fr[om] someone or someth[ing]" which is equivalent to saying "be worth more than, be superior to."[87] Used absolutely it can be translated "the things that really matter."[88] It points to

> **Ministry Maxim**
>
> Passing the discernment-tests of today is the only way to pass the final exam on "the day of Christ."

---

86 Thayer, 154.

87 BDAG, 1937.4.

88 Ibid.

what is "worthwhile, excellent, vital."[89] Paul's goal, then, in praying that they might be discerning (v.9) is that they would be able at any given moment in their walk of discipleship to identify what is God's appointed way and will for their lives and embrace it with obedience.

This too is done for a specific purpose (ἵνα, "in order to"). The verb (ἦτε, "to be") is in the subjunctive mood, pointing to what is possible, though its reality depends upon the fulfillment of certain conditions—in this case that they are indeed able to "approve the things that are excellent." The present tense points to what Paul prays may be continually true of them. That which they are "to be" is two-fold. First, is "sincere" (εἰλικρινεῖς). It has been conjectured that the compound word is composed of εἴλη or ἔλη ("sunlight") and κρινῶ ("to judge"), meaning, then, to be "found pure when unfolded and examined by the sun's light."[90] Others have supposed that it is a compound using ἒιλος, ἐίλειν which comes then to mean "sifted and cleansed by rapid movement or rolling to and fro."[91] Most seem to side with the former etymology. Boice describes what may have been behind the imagery:

> In ancient times the biggest industry in the world was the pottery industry. And pottery varied in quality just as cars, office supplies, or household goods vary today. The cheapest pottery was thick and solid and did not require much skill to make. It is found everywhere at archaeological sites. The finest pottery was thin. It had a clear color, and it brought a high price. Fine pottery was very fragile both before and after firing, and it would often crack in the oven. Cracked pottery should have been thrown away. But dishonest dealers were in the habit of filling in the cracks with a hard pearly wax that would blend in with the color of the pottery. This made the cracks practically undetectable in the shops, especially when painted or glazed; but the wax was immediately

---

89   Rienecker, 545.

90   Thayer, 175.

91   Ibid.

detectable when the pottery was held up to light, especially the sun. It was said that the artificial element was detected by "sun-testing." Honest dealers marked their finer product by the caption *sine cera*—"without wax."[92]

Whatever the etymological background, the resulting meaning is that which is found to be unalloyed, unmixed, genuine or "sincere" after examination. Wiersbe reminds us that our English word "sincere" comes from a Latin root which means "unadulterated, pure, unmixed."[93]

Second, Paul adds (καὶ, "and") that they might be "blameless" (ἀπρόσκοποι). The word is the alpha-prefix (α-) affixed as a negation to προσκόπτω ("to strike/stumble"). The resulting word then means, transitively, "*having nothing for one to strike against; not causing to stumble;*" or intransitively "*not striking against or stumbling; metaphorically, not led into sin; blameless.*"[94] If we understand the word as a transitive then the two words together describe "respectively the relation to God (**pure**) and the relation to men (**blameless**)."[95] If, however, we understand "blameless" in its intransitive sense then the two words express the positive (remaining pure) and the negative (shunning sin).[96]

Paul prays that the Philippian believers would be both of these "until the day of Christ" (εἰς ἡμέραν Χριστοῦ). The preposition (εἰς, "until") is used in a temporal way to speak of the time "up to which someth[ing] continues."[97] But it seems to be more than simply temporal. Kennedy is probably right when he says it "has the meanings 'with a view to' and 'until,' which here shade off into each other."[98] He has already referred to

---

92 Boice, 47.
93 Wiersbe, 66.
94 Thayer, 70.
95 Lightfoot, 99, emphasis original.
96 Ibid.
97 BDAG, 2291.2.a.α.
98 Kennedy, 422; cf. Alford, 3:156; Lightfoot, 99; O'Brien, 79; Vincent, ICC, 14; Vincent, *Word Studies*, 3:418.

"the day of Christ Jesus" (1:6) and in 2:16 will again speak of "the day of Christ." The expressions look to the day of Christ's second advent and the revelation and judgment that will take place at that time.

Verse 11 – having been filled with the fruit of righteousness which *comes* through Jesus Christ, to the glory and praise of God.

Verse 11 brings to a close both the sentence begun in verse 9 and the opening section of the epistle describing Paul's prayers for the Philippian believers (vv.3-11). The whole of the verse comprises a participial clause which describes the background of that set forth in verse 10 (i.e., that which prepares one to be "sincere and blameless until the day of Christ").

The participle (πεπληρωμένοι, "having been filled") leads the clause. The verb is used four times in Philippians (1:11; 2:2; 4:18, 19), while it is found nearly ninety times in the whole of the NT. It can be used both of filling physically or spatially and in a more figurative sense. It is in the latter sense that he employs it here.[99] When used figuratively it can mean to fill persons with some kind of powers or qualities.[100] Paul speaks of believers being filled with the Holy Spirit (Eph. 5:18), indeed, with God Himself (Eph. 1:23; 3:19). That with which Paul speaks of people being filled includes joy and peace (Rom. 15:13), knowledge (Rom. 15:14), comfort (2 Cor. 7:4), and, as here, the fruit of righteousness (Phil. 1:11). It is used here in the perfect tense indicating that they had been filled at some point in the past and continue in that settled state. The passive voice indicates that another (in this case, God) must do this filling, not the Philippian believers themselves. It is not their effort which will produce this, but God's grace (2:12-13).

> **Ministry Maxim**
>
> Living righteousness is the proof of one's legal righteousness before God.

---

99 Mounce, 251.

100 BDAG, 5981.1.b.

That with which they are being filled is "fruit" (καρπὸν). The singular is a collective noun. Fruit, of course, is the product of a process. It is the outworking of something else (cf. "the fruit *of the Spirit*," Gal. 5:22, emphasis added). Fruit is the product, not the process itself. It is, in this case, the fruit "of righteousness" (δικαιοσύνης). How shall we understand the genitive? It could be a subjective genitive, "the fruit which consists of righteousness." Or it could be an objective genitive, meaning "the fruit which righteousness produces." Surely it must be the latter.[101]

The fruit is not the same as the righteousness. It is the result of righteousness that is in view. Righteousness brings forth a life which is the proper outworking of that righteousness. But just what does this mean? Does it mean "your efforts at living a righteous life"? Or does it mean "the gift of righteousness imputed by God to you through Christ"? The phrase "the fruit of righteousness" has its roots in the LXX (e.g., Prov. 3:9; 11:30; 13:2; Amos 6:12). In the NT compare Hebrews 12:11 and James 3:18.

The noun ("righteousness," δικαιοσύνης) is used three more times in Philippians. It can describe a righteousness pursued by human effort—the kind of righteousness which Paul had attained as a scrupulous Jew (Phil. 3:6). This is clearly not the righteousness Paul champions here (as the context of 3:6 makes clear). The other two occurrences follow quickly upon the heels of this reference and hold forth a very different kind of righteousness. Paul says his longing is to "be found in Him, not having a righteousness of my own derived from the Law, but that which is through faith in Christ, the righteousness which comes from God on the basis of faith" (v.9). This is the righteousness whose fruit Paul speaks of believers being filled with here. Indeed, it is a righteousness "which comes through Jesus Christ" (τὸν διὰ Ἰησοῦ Χριστοῦ). The additional definite article (τὸν) indicates that it is the fruit that "comes through Jesus Christ." "None of it can they produce by their own powers, hence this second and attributive (τὸν) qualification."[102] "The emphasis is thus on the character of the fruit

---

101 Vincent, ICC, 14.

102 Lenski, 720.

with which we are ever to be filled."¹⁰³ That the verb is passive in voice (πεπληρωμένοι, "having been filled") is confirmed in that this is "not ... a righteousness of my own ... but that which ... comes from God" (v.9). It is the imputed righteousness of Christ Himself. It is the very righteous life of Jesus put to our account as a gift of God's grace.

This fact having been settled for us by God's gracious declaration, Paul pictures the believer as coming to a state in which they are filled with the supernatural outworking ("fruit") "of [such] righteousness." Justification (in which the believer is declared righteous before God by virtue of the alien, perfect, imputed righteousness of Christ) is a declaration arising from outside of ourselves, made by God, from heaven, over us. Yet that declaration, that imputation spoken over us and concerning us, is more than merely judicial (though it is certainly that). It then begins to fill the recipient of that declarative gift of righteousness "with *the fruit of* righteousness" (emphasis added). That is to say it produces not just a verdict outwardly set upon us, but it releases also the logical and life-giving "fruit" of that declaration in a moral explosion within the believer. The objective righteousness of Christ put to our ledger in heaven sets off an expansive experience of life within us and through us on earth.

Herein, then, Paul weds two essential doctrines of our salvation: justification and regeneration. For this "righteousness" is legally imputed to us by God through Christ as a gracious gift received through faith alone. Yet it produces "fruit," which is not merely a legal declaration but bespeaks a living process. This tells us that salvation is not merely (but not less than!) a legal declaration made over us in heaven by another (God Himself), but that it is also the impartation of a new Life, which must of necessity show itself in the product of this new life—"fruit"!

In this Paul also reminds us that justification precedes and makes way for sanctification. Salvation is a free gift imparted to us by God, a new standing declared over us on the basis of Christ's righteousness and sacrifice on our behalf. This new standing and relationship having been established, God then works by His grace to produce in us the righteousness He

---

103 Ibid.

has procured for us and pronounced over us. The order is always imputed righteousness and then imparted righteousness.

And all this is "to the glory and praise of God" (εἰς δόξαν καὶ ἔπαινον θεοῦ). The "glory" (δόξαν) of God is of special concern to the Apostle in this letter. He looks for the day when "every tongue will confess that Jesus Christ is Lord, to the glory of God the Father" (2:11). Indeed, in that day He "will transform the body of our humble state into conformity with the body of His glory ..." (3:21a). In the meantime all that is required to carry out His will He provides "according to His riches in glory in Christ Jesus" (4:19). He closes this letter with the benediction: "Now to our God and Father be the glory forever and ever. Amen" (4:20). But he knows also there are many "whose end is destruction, whose god is their appetite, and whose glory is in their shame" (3:19). The "glory" of God is the outshining of His own nature, the sum total of His divine perfections. He couples this (καὶ, "and") with the "praise of God" (ἔπαινον θεοῦ). Later he will tell the Philippian believers to set their minds on "anything worthy of praise [ἔπαινος]" (4:8). Here it is "The homage rendered to God as a God of 'glory.'"[104] The genitive (θεοῦ, "of God") does not point to the praise that comes from God, but the praise that goes "to" (εἰς) God. Glory is the manifestation of His true nature; praise the recognition of this by humans.[105] Compare with Ephesians 1:6, 12, 14.

Paul's prayer for the Philippians, then, keeps telescoping outward. He prays that their discerning love may abound (v.9) so that they might approve the things that are most excellent (v.10a), so that they might be sincere and blameless until Christ's coming (v.10b), at which time they might be found full of the fruit that comes from being made right with God by His grace through Jesus Christ (v.11).

---

104 Vincent, ICC, 15.

105 Lightfoot, 100; Vincent, *Word Studies*, 3:418.

> **Digging Deeper:**
> 1. Initiate a conversation with someone about the interrelationship of discernment and love (cf. vv.9-10). Afterward ask yourself: What did I learn? What was I able to share?
> 2. What does this prayer teach us about the one who claims justification by faith but shows little "fruit of righteousness" in his life (v.11)?
> 3. Take time now to turn Paul's prayer (vv.9-11) into your prayer for your family and the people who make up the local fellowship of believers where you worship and serve.

Verse 12 – Now I want you to know, brethren, that my circumstances have turned out for the greater progress of the gospel,

The postpositive conjunction δὲ ("Now") signals that the Apostle is shifting his focus to a new topic. Having communicated his heart of prayer (vv.3-11), Paul now says, "I want you to know" (Γινώσκειν ... ὑμᾶς βούλομαι) something. The main verb "I want" (βούλομαι) readies us to hear what is upon the Apostle's heart in this new turn of the letter. This verb is different from the one he will use in 2:13 (θέλω, "to will"). As Thayer points out, the distinction between the two is that "the former seems to designate the will which follows deliberation, the latter the will which proceeds from inclination."[106] That is to say βούλομαι expresses more strongly than θέλω the "deliberate exercise of the will."[107] It describes "choice, purpose, or intention and desire or longing."[108] Given that θέλω is used five times more frequently in the NT than βούλομαι, it would seem Paul had good

---

106 Thayer, 286.

107 Vine, 301, 1240-1241.

108 Mounce, 773.

reason for selecting the verb he did in this case.[109] The Apostle had carefully considered that which he is about to express.

This desire of his is directed toward all the believers in Philippi (ὑμᾶς, "you," plural). And that desire is for them "to know" (Γινώσκειν) something. The verb tends to stress the personal and experiential nature of the knowledge (cf. the verb οἶδα in vv.16, 19, 25, which may at times emphasize the informational nature of knowledge; in those cases referring to his own knowledge or that of others near to him). The present tense stresses the ongoing nature of the knowledge he wishes for them. The infinitive comes first in the sentence, giving it special emphasis. Paul is urgent in his desire that they might understand his present circumstances.

In this he addresses them as ἀδελφοί ("brethren"). He will address them this way often in this letter (3:1, 13, 17; 4:1, 8, 21; cf. also 1:14; 2:25). Paul used the expression far less frequently of the Colossian or Ephesian believers (two of the other letters written from his first Roman imprisonment; cf. Eph. 6:23; Col. 1:2; 4:15). Paul obviously felt a deep bond of spiritual kinship and affection with the Philippian believers. He did not want his dear brothers and sisters in Christ to be confused about what had befallen him in prison. The entirety of the opening clause may signal that the Philippians had become concerned about Paul's wellbeing and had inquired (perhaps through Epaphroditus, 2:25) as to what his situation meant for him and for the gospel cause. They surely knew of his house arrest in general terms (Acts 28:30-31), but perhaps some more recent turn of events (his being transitioned to the Praetorian Guard for further processing of his legal case?) had increased their concern and anxiety.

The conjunction ὅτι serves to distinguish "that" which the Apostle wants them "to know." His goal is to communicate to them that "my circumstances have turned out for the greater progress of the gospel (τὰ κατ' ἐμὲ μᾶλλον εἰς προκοπὴν τοῦ εὐαγγελίου ἐλήλυθεν). When Paul speaks of "my circumstances" (τὰ κατ' ἐμὲ, more lit., "the things with respect to me"), he is referring to his arrest and ultimate imprisonment under house arrest in Rome (Acts 21:27-28:31). Paul uses the exact expression also in

---

109 Thayer, 286.

Ephesians 6:21 and Colossians 4:7, another signal that these three letters may have been written from the same circumstances and within the same general timeframe. The main verb of the clause is held off to the end (ἐλήλυθεν, "have turned out"). The perfect tense indicates that an abiding state of things has come about because of his arrest and imprisonment. The resulting state is "for the greater progress of the gospel" (μᾶλλον εἰς προκοπὴν τοῦ εὐαγγελίου). The adverb μᾶλλον ("greater") may mean something simple like "more" (quantitative), but here seems to mean "rather" (or "instead").[110] The KJV rendered it: "the things which happened unto me have fallen out *rather* unto the furtherance of the gospel" (emphasis added). The Philippians had drawn conclusions about what the Apostle's circumstances meant, but Paul was anxious for them to know that it had the opposite effect.

> **Ministry Maxim**
>
> Under the care of a sovereign God, what appears negative may prove to be precisely the opposite.

That which is thus magnified is "the ... progress" (προκοπὴν). The noun is used in the NT only here, 1:25, and 1 Timothy 4:15. The cognate verb demonstrates that the word can be used both positively (Luke 2:52; Rom. 13:12; Gal. 1:14) and negatively (2 Tim. 2:16; 3:9, 13), for "not every 'advance' is also 'growth'."[111] It is a compound comprised of πρό ("before") and κόπτω ("to cut" or "to strike"). It has the notion of "to cut forward." Some see military imagery behind the word. Vincent, for instance, contends that the imagery "is supposed to be that of pioneers *cutting* a way *before* an army, and so *furthering* its march."[112] Robertson similarly suggests "cutting a way ahead, blazing a trail before an army to come afterwards."[113] Wuest adds "it is thought to have been used of an army of pioneer wood cutters which precedes the regular army, cutting

---

110 O'Brien, 90; contra BDAG, 4696.1, which contends for "to a greater or higher degree."
111 DNTT, 2:130.
112 Vincent, ICC, 16.
113 Robertson, *Paul's Joy in Christ*, 74.

a road through an impenetrable forest, thus making possible the pioneer advance of the latter into regions where otherwise it could not have gone."[114] Others see nautical imagery in the term, in which a ship is seen "to make headway in spite of blows" against which it prevails.[115] Still others see the imprint of the blacksmith's hammer, as the word was used to describe the lengthening out of iron under his blows.[116] Whatever the correct etymological background of the word, it did become a technical term in the world of Stoic philosophy, describing an advance toward wisdom. Whether this philosophical background has influenced Paul is a matter of debate among scholars.[117]

Obviously the noun is used here in a positive sense. Given the rarity of the noun in the NT, it seems clear that Paul uses it as an inclusio to open the new paragraph (v.12) and to move toward its close (v.25).[118] He begins with concern for the "progress" of the gospel and closes by expressing his concern for the "progress" of the Philippian believers in the gospel. The Philippians may have been worried about Paul, but his great concern, and word of comfort to them, was about "the gospel" (τοῦ εὐαγγελίου). Paul saw himself as expendable (Phil. 1:21-23), but "the gospel" as all-important (1:15-18). The genitive seems to be objective (the advance of the gospel itself) rather than subjective (the advance which the gospel brings).[119]

For a visual rendering of the logical flow of thought in verses 12-18 see the chart "Gospel Work and Gospel Motives" in Appendix C.

---

114 Wuest, 39-40.

115 TDNT, 6:704.

116 Ibid.

117 Hawthorne, WBC, 43.

118 O'Brien, 88.

119 NET Bible; contra Hellerman, 42 (unless otherwise noted, all footnotes marked "Hellerman" refer to his voume in the EGGNT).

Verse 13 – so that my imprisonment in *the cause of* Christ has become well known throughout the whole praetorian guard and to everyone else,

The sentence began in verse 12 and extends on through verse 14, the remainder being composed of two parallel infinitive clauses, one here in verse 13 and the other in verse 14. This extended and double emphasis begins with the subordinating conjunction ὥστε ("so that"). It points to the result of Paul's new set of circumstances (v.12). Thus the two infinitive clauses (coordinated by καὶ, "and," v.14a) present two results of Paul's new circumstances: unbelievers are aware that the gospel is the reason for his imprisonment (v.13) and believers are emboldened to speak the gospel (v.14).[120]

The word order of the first infinitive clause (v.13) is somewhat unusual and presents us with challenges in how to understand Paul's thought. A very literal rendering which preserves the word order would be: "the bonds of me manifest in Christ to become in all the praetorium." Paul clearly speaks again of "my imprisonment" (τοὺς δεσμούς μου). He uses the noun with its definite article and a personal pronoun in the genitive as in verse 7 (see the comments there) and again in verses 14 and 17 (cf. Col. 4:18). Paul uses the same noun elsewhere without the pronoun while still referring to his own personal imprisonment (2 Tim. 1:9; Philem. 10, 13). Next comes the word translated "well known" (φανερούς). It means visible, clear or manifest. But just what had become manifest is not so clear. The familiar Pauline expression "in Christ" (ἐν Χριστῷ) comes next. Does this mean that Paul's imprisonment is "in Christ" (i.e., that he is most fundamentally and spiritually a captive of Christ and only secondarily a captive of Rome; cf. KJV, NKJV) or that he is imprisoned "because of Christ" (i.e., that his imprisonment is primarily physical and Roman and is because of his spiritual relationship to Christ; NASU, cf. ESV, NIV, NLT)? The word order speaks against the former, but the meaning

---

120 Ibid.

is probably wider than the latter.¹²¹ Ultimately the correct answer probably includes both ideas. Paul has ended up in a Roman prison because his heart and life had already been taken captive by Jesus Christ. In a cataclysmic encounter with the heavenly Lord, Paul became a glad captive of Christ and everything else about his life and ministry from that point on took place "in Christ." He experienced imprisonment "in [union with] Christ" (cf. Acts 23:11; 27:23-24) and because of Christ. Paul's present imprisonment is a part of what it is to know "the fellowship of His sufferings" (Phil. 3:10).

Only now do we meet the infinitive, "has become" (γενέσθαι). The object is "my imprisonment." The aorist tense points to what had come about already. The middle voice presents the manifestation of Paul's imprisonment as coming about as you would expect, by its own natural course. This manifestation took place toward two groups. First, it was "throughout the whole praetorian guard" (ἐν ὅλῳ τῷ πραιτωρίῳ). The preposition ἐν is rendered "throughout" because it is followed by the adjective "whole" (ὅλῳ), which means "whole, intact, entire, all" and when used with a noun, as here ("the ... praetorian guard"), it indicates the totality of that noun.¹²²

Just what does Paul intend his readers to understand by "the ... praetorian guard" (τῷ πραιτωρίῳ)? The noun originally referred to "the praetor's tent in camp, w[ith] its surroundings." Over time the word also came to designate the official residence of the governor.¹²³ This is the meaning it appears to have in the Gospels (e.g., Matt. 27:27; Mk. 15:16; John 18:28 [2x], 33; 19:9). In Acts it refers to the Palace of Herod in Caesarea (Acts 23:35). But what does it refer to here in Philippians, its only other appearance in the NT? The answer to that largely depends

> **Ministry Maxim**
>
> My manifest suffering with Christ may be my best witness for Christ.

---

121 O'Brien, 91-92.

122 Friberg, 280.

123 BDAG, 6123.

upon what one concludes regarding the place of Paul's imprisonment. If one concludes, as some have, that Paul writes from a Caesarean imprisonment, then it refers to those in the Palace of Herod (cf. Acts 23:35). If, however, one concludes (as I have) that Paul most likely wrote from a Roman imprisonment, then it probably refers to the elite troops of "the … praetorian guard."

The term has been understood in four primary ways.[124] Some understand it as referencing the emperor's own palace. But we have no record of the word being used in this way. Others believe it refers to the barracks at the imperial palace where the praetorian guard assigned to the emperor stayed. But, as O'Brien says, "there is no authority for the use of the term to denote these barracks and, furthermore, the space was too limited to warrant using the phrase 'in the whole praetorium'."[125] Still others believe it refers to the larger, established camp where all the praetorian guard stayed just outside the walls of Rome. "But," O'Brien again demonstrates, "this camp, too, was not known as the 'praetorium'."[126] Finally, it is understood not as reference to a place, but to a people—the men who formed "the praetorian guard." This is the conclusion Lightfoot reached and most scholars seem to have followed him since.[127] This usage is supported by much evidence from various ancient inscriptions and in view of the fact that the two nouns (τῷ πραιτωρίῳ and τοῖς λοιποῖς) of the phrase are governed by a single preposition (ἐν) and since the second part of the phrase ("and to everyone else") refers to people, it would naturally follow that this first part of the phrase would likewise refer, not to a place, but to a people.[128]

The elite corps of soldiers known as the praetorian guard were responsible for the immediate safety of the Emperor himself. In this sense,

---

124 Lightfoot, 113-116.

125 O'Brien, 93.

126 Ibid.

127 Fee, writing almost thirteen decades after Lightfoot, could say Lightfoot's "arguments on this matter have never been overturned" (113).

128 Bockmuehl, 75; Hellerman, 44; Müller, 49; O'Brien, 92-93, Sumney, 20.

originally "The term stood for the emperor's bodyguard of nine cohorts."[129] A cohort was the tenth part of a legion and normally was comprised of 600 men. The Emperor had such a concentration of these special soldiers in Rome as special protection for himself, the capital city, its people, and the powers essential to the Empire's safety, health, and continuance. The praetorian guard was originally formed by Augustus in 27 B.C., but in A.D. 23 Tiberius' minister Seianus accelerated their number (up to 10,000[130]) and their role. From that time the praetorian guard played "a sinister role that they assumed in the setting up and pulling down of emperors."[131] To have cracked the external shell of such an elite corps of soldiers with the gospel would have been a truly remarkable advance of the good news. Lightfoot explains how this happened: "According to Roman custom he was bound by the hand to the soldier who guarded him and was never left alone day or night. As the soldiers would relieve guard in constant succession, they were brought one by one into communication with the 'prisoner of Jesus Christ,' and thus he was able to affirm that his chains had born witness to the gospel 'throughout the whole palace guard.'"[132] Wuest describes it this way: "He lived for two years with a Roman soldier chained to his wrist. As the different soldiers would take their turn guarding Paul, they would hear the conversations he had with his visitors, conversations full of the gospel and of the Saviour of sinners. They would hear the apostle pray, and would listen as he dictated the epistles he wrote. The noble prisoner would talk to them about their souls, talking in the international Greek so common in those days. Thus, the gospel went through the barracks of the Roman soldiers, a place where it would not have gone, if Paul had not been a prisoner there."[133]

Secondly (καὶ, "and"), the manifestation of the cause of Paul's imprisonment took place "to everyone else" (τοῖς λοιποῖς πάσιν). The adjective

---

129 Melick, 70.

130 Robertson, *Paul's Joy in Christ*, 76.

131 ZPEB, 4:832.

132 Lightfoot, 26-27.

133 Wuest, 40-41.

with the definite article is used as a substantive (τοῖς λοιποῖς) and means something like "the remaining ones" or, in better English, "the others."[134] To this is added the indefinite adjective (πᾶσιν), which might be translated "all." So with this brief, but sweeping expression the Apostle gathers up all others which the Philippians might understand to be included within the populace of Rome. During his imprisonment Paul was afforded the privilege of "welcoming all who came to him" (Acts 28:30) and he could speak of Christ and His Kingdom "with all openness, unhindered" (v.31b). This does not mean, of course, that every last citizen of Rome heard the gospel from Paul personally.[135] It is, rather, the Apostle's way of expressing the remarkable and unpredictable way his imprisonment had permitted the advance of the gospel into places and lives probably unreachable in any other way. The impression left upon the Philippian believers must have been profound.

Verse 14 – and that most of the brethren, trusting in the Lord because of my imprisonment, have far more courage to speak the word of God without fear.

Here Paul adds (καὶ, "and") the second of two infinitive clauses, the first making up verse 13. There he described how his imprisonment for the gospel had effect among the unbelieving. This second clause describes its effect upon his fellow believers. The infinitive itself (τολμᾶν, "have ... courage") means to "have the courage" or "be brave enough" for something.[136] The previous infinitive (γενέσθαι, "has become," v.13) is aorist in tense; this one is in the present tense. Lenski notes that, "The fact result (aorist) is followed by the continuous effect result (present). The fact was published far and wide that Paul's imprisonment was connected with no crime or criminal charge but with 'Christ,' and the effect of this was the

---

134 BDAD, 4612.2.b.a.

135 Lightfoot, 48.

136 BDAG, 7191.a.α.

greater daring with which so many brethren told the Word of God."[137] Using an adverb as a comparative, Paul says this courage was "far more" (περισσοτέρως) than would have been the case without his imprisonment. It is "used as a comparative to denote that a state or action is beyond what is ordinary or expected."[138]

This unexpected, surprising, disproportional courage took place in "most of the brethren" (τοὺς πλείονας τῶν ἀδελφῶν). By referring to "the brothers" (τῶν ἀδελφῶν) Paul probably isn't attempting a gender designation. Whether or not believing women were involved is not his point here. The lines are not drawn along the line of gender, but of belief. Some translations use this as an opportunity to express gender neutrality: "the believers" (NLT), "the brothers and sisters" (NET, NIV, NRSV).

Having drawn the line between believers and unbelievers, Paul further divides the believing by referring to "most" (τοὺς πλείονας) of the believing. The adjective is also a comparative and may mean either "the majority" or "the others, the rest" in contrast to a minority.[139] There were more believers who took exceeding courage from Paul's stalwart faith under the bondage of imprisonment than those believers who did not. The difference seems to be that the majority were "trusting in the Lord" (ἐν κυρίῳ πεποιθότας). The prepositional phrase "in the Lord" (ἐν κυρίῳ) could be understood as qualifying the previous noun (τῶν ἀδελφῶν, "the brothers") so that Paul was referring to them as "brothers in the Lord" (NIV, HCSB; cf. KJV, NKJV). Most other English translations take the prepositional phrase with the participle "trusting" (πεποιθότας) (i.e., "trusting in the Lord," NASB, NASU, ESV, RSV, NRSV, etc.). Paul uses this particular verb more times in Philippians than in any other one letter (1:6, 14, 25; 2:24; 3:3, 4). It is perfect tense in form, though present tense in meaning.[140] The word itself points toward trust, reliance, conviction, confidence, and assurance. As noted above (under

---

137 Lenski, 723-724.

138 Friberg, 310.

139 BDAG, 6061.1.b.β.ℵ. and 1.1.b.β.ג.

140 Ibid., 5754.2.

v.6) it describes that which is translated into action, for it means "to convince someone to believe something and to act on the basis of what is recommended."[141] If such confidence in believers (τῶν ἀδελφῶν, "the brethren") is not "in the Lord" (ἐν κυρίῳ), then where would it be placed? We understand, then, that ἐν κυρίῳ ("in the Lord") is to be taken with πεποιθότας ("trusting"). The fact that the prepositional phrase is placed before the verb makes the prepositional phrase emphatic by position. Thus "ἐν κυρίῳ is the ground of the confidence (πεποιθότας) and τοῖς δεσμοῖς is an instrumental dative ('by [my] bonds')."[142] Vincent wraps up the idea nicely, saying, "By Paul's bonds the brethren have had their confidence in the Lord strengthened."[143]

We can see, then, that the instrument by which they were provoked to trust in the Lord was, as Paul says, "my imprisonment" (τοῖς δεσμοῖς μου). Paul has already used this precise phrase in verse 6 (see the comments there) and will do so again in verse 17. Taken at face value the phrase seems not to provide an adequate stimulus to provoke "having confidence" (NET) in the Lord. How would the fact of the great Apostle himself, the champion of the gospel, the great driving force—humanly speaking— behind the advance of the gospel now being confined in prison engender confident trust in the Lord? Paul had been imprisoned in Caesarea for at least two years prior to his appeal to Caesar and subsequent voyage to Rome (Acts 24:27), where he spent two more years in confinement before his release (28:30). How would four years of Paul's confinement provoke confidence in other believers? It seems reasonable, therefore, to conclude that it was not simply "because of my imprisonment," but because of how he conducted himself in that imprisonment and the way the Lord used him in that imprisonment that provoked the

> **Ministry Maxim**
>
> My manifest suffering with Christ may be the best mobilizer of Christians.

---

141 Louw and Nida, 33.301.

142 O'Brien, 95; cf. Vincent, ICC, 17.

143 Vincent, ICC, 17.

majority of the believers to act with greater confidence and courage in their own realm of influence. The words "because of" are the translator's attempt to express the intent of the dative case of the noun and its definite article (τοῖς δεσμοῖς, "the imprisonment"). Many other English translations understand it similarly (NET, NIV, NLT, RSV), while some opt for "by" (ESV, KJV, NKJV, NRSV) or "from" (HCSB).

That which this newfound courage provoked in them was "to speak the word of God without fear" (ἀφόβως τὸν λόγον λαλεῖν). The infinitive (λαλεῖν, "to speak") is in the present tense, underscoring the continuous or ongoing nature of the action. They were speaking not just once, but repeatedly. That which they spoke was "the word" (τὸν λόγον). By this Paul means the gospel. This is made clear in Ephesians 1:13 where he refers to "the word [τὸν λόγον] of truth, the gospel of your salvation." Some manuscripts have τοῦ θεοῦ ("of God") added following τὸν λόγον ("the word"). Several versions, including the NASU, follow this reading (NASB, NIV, NLT, RSV). But others are not convinced of its genuineness and thus do not include it (ESV, HCSB, NET, NRSV, KJV, NKJV). The facts are hard to read, but perhaps the weight rests in favor of the shorter reading.[144] This speaking of the gospel they now did "without fear" (ἀφόβως). The adverb is comprised of the α–privative (for negation) and the common noun φόβος ("fear"). It appears only three other times in the NT (Lk. 1:74; 1 Cor. 16:10; Jude 12).

Thus Paul's imprisonment has resulted in the unbelieving hearing the gospel (v.13) and the believing speaking the gospel more courageously (v.14). In this, he contends, the Philippian believers should see the hand of God and rejoice.

---

144 See the NET Bible for a good recap of the issues.

> **Digging Deeper:**
> 1. If Paul was interpreting the events of his life through the lenses of gospel-advance(vv.12-14), what lenses does the average person in your church interpret their life-events through? How does one change such a perception and interpretation of life—in oneself and in others?
> 2. If the story of a suffering and triumphant Christ is best promulgated through suffering, triumphant Christ-followers, what might this require of you?
> 3. How have the faithful sufferings of other believers encouraged you toward increased faithfulness to the Lord and the spread of His gospel?

Verse 15 – Some, to be sure, are preaching Christ even from envy and strife, but some also from good will;

Paul twice uses the plural pronoun τινὲς ("some … some") to designate the subjects of this sentence. Though a new sentence begins here, these pronouns find their antecedent in the expression "most of the brethren" in verse 14. Paul is now breaking down that larger group into two subgroups. Further he delineates the comparison of the two groups by use of the formula μὲν … δὲ, which is sometimes rendered "on the one hand … on the other hand." Both elements of this comparative construction are paired with the conjunction καὶ.

That which is common to both groups is expressed through the main verb and object: "are preaching Christ" (τὸν Χριστὸν κηρύσσουσιν). The verb is in the present tense, underscoring the ongoing nature of the activity. They "are [and keep on] preaching Christ." This verb enlarges upon what Paul meant by "to speak" (λαλεῖν) in the previous verse. That general word for vocalizing is made more specific now by "preaching" (κηρύσσουσιν), which speaks more specifically of proclamation of or "preaching" the gospel. The word describes the activity of one sent as an authorized and commissioned representative of a higher authority. Such a one delivers an authoritative message as if the ruling power were present personally to speak the word. In this case the message is simply described as "Christ" (τὸν Χριστὸν). Note the definite article, literally "the Christ"—the prophesied, long awaited One! This is the One who came, lived, died and rose again "according to the Scriptures" (1 Cor. 15:3-4). Thus it was out of those Holy Scriptures that the one "preaching" would detail the person and message of the Christ.

The burden of this sentence is really not what is similar in these two groups, but what holds them in distinction from one another. Those he has referred to as "most of the brethren" (v.14) are in some way divided. Vincent suggests that here καὶ "introduces another and a different class, and not the same class with the addition of a subordinate and baser motive."[145] That is to say, the people he first introduces here are a different bunch than those who are referred to in the previous verse as τοὺς πλείονας ("most"). But it seems best to understand Paul as not introducing a new group to the discussion, but dividing the one he has already spoken of in verse 14. As O'Brien quotes Michael as saying, "Unless he means that these two classes are two sections of the preachers of ver. 14, his language is decidedly misleading."[146]

On the one hand (μὲν καὶ, "to be sure") there are among "most of the brethren" (v.14) those who make their proclamation "from envy and strife" (διὰ φθόνον καὶ ἔριν). The first occurrence of καὶ is used emphatically ("indeed," ESV, KJV, NKJV, RSV). The combination (μὲν καὶ) almost serves as a concession on the part of the Apostle ("It is true ...", NIV; "It's true ...", NLT). It's as if someone, having heard his reasoning in verse 14, raised their hand to object. That which he concedes is that not all who are now boldly speaking of Christ (v.14) are doing so from the purest of motives.

Some, says the Apostle, preach Christ "from envy" (διὰ φθόνον). The preposition (διὰ, "from") governs both nouns and is used to designate the

---

[145] Vincent, ICC, 18; cf. Alford, 3:158; Kennedy, 424.
[146] O'Brien, 98.

reasons for their action.[147] It describes the motives by which their "preaching" takes place and might here be rendered "out of."[148] By "envy" (φθόνον) he means a negative response prompted by the success of another. Paul frequently uses the term in his lists of vices (Rom. 1:29; Gal. 5:21; 1 Tim. 6:4; Tit. 3:3). It is used to describe unregenerate humanity (Rom. 1:29; Titus 3:3) and is one of the deeds of the sinful nature (Gal. 5:21). It is what motivated those who delivered over Jesus to be killed by the Jewish religious leaders (Matt. 27:18; Mark 15:10). Added (καὶ, "and") to this is "strife" (ἔριν). It describes "conflict resulting from rivalry and discord."[149] Indeed, Kennedy believes the word should on this occasion be translated "rivalry" rather than "strife."[150] Their preaching was "as much against Paul as in favour of Christ."[151] One can easily picture how "rivalry" breaks out as "strife."

It is difficult, however, to picture just what this means. How does one preach the gospel out of this kind of "envy and strife"? Against whom was this "envy and strife" directed? Clearly it was against the Apostle Paul himself (v.17). But in what sense are they envious toward him who has been imprisoned for years because of his faithfulness to God and His word? How are they striving against Paul? Some believe it was Judaizers such as he battled in Galatia and elsewhere.[152] Yet it is difficult to see just how Paul could in anyway affirm the preaching of those whom he so vigorously opposed in his other letters. Sticking with the Jewish angle, it may have been Jewish believers "who disliked the note of universality in Paul's message and feared that he did

> **Ministry Maxim**
> Ministry is fertile soil for a bumper crop of envy.

---

147 BDAG, 1823.2.a.

148 Ibid.

149 Louw-Nida, 39.22.

150 Kennedy, 424.

151 Robertson, *Paul's Joy in Christ*, 82.

152 Robertson, *Word Pictures*, 4:438-439; Lightfoot, 102-103.

not sufficiently guard the interests of Judaism."[153] Vincent believes they were "Pauline Christians who were personally jealous of the apostle, and who sought to undermine his influence. It may be … that as the Roman church before Paul's arrival had no definite leadership, it was easy for ambitious and smaller men to obtain a certain prominence which they found menaced by the presence and influence of the apostle."[154] This seems the most plausible view.

Yet on the other hand there are "also" (δὲ καὶ) others who make Christ known "from good will" (δι᾽ εὐδοκίαν). The preposition (δι᾽, "from") is used as it was earlier in the sentence (see above). The noun "refers to the good motives and well wishes from which an action comes."[155] These motives too are directed toward the Apostle Paul personally (v.16). In support of the Apostle and with thankful and longing hearts toward him, there were those who stepped out to proclaim Christ when he was chained and unable to travel, preach, and establish churches. O'Brien believes the word's orientation is God-ward, not man-ward. In which case it would point to divine acceptance of Paul's ministry, thus removing any offense some might take over Paul's imprisonment.[156] Yet this would seem to disrupt the comparison of motives that Paul intends within this verse and upon which he enlarges in the next two verses. One might look to the lengthy list of names Paul includes in Romans 16 as examples of those who may have made up this group.[157]

Verse 16 – the latter *do it* out of love, knowing that I am appointed for the defense of the gospel;

In verses 13 and 14 the Apostle divided between the unbelieving and the believing in distinguishing the effect of his imprisonment on each group.

---

153 Robertson, *Paul's Joy in Christ*, 82.
154 Vincent, ICC, 19; cf. Robertson, *Paul's Joy in Christ*, 82.
155 Rienecker, 546.
156 O'Brien, 99-100.
157 Hellerman, 49.

Then in verse 15 he divided the believing into two subgroups. He now, in verses 16 and 17, expands upon the two groupings of believers from verse 15. The former group ("Some ... are preaching Christ even from envy and strife," v.15a) are taken up in verse 17, while the latter group ("some also from good will," v.15b) are expanded upon here in verse 16. The KJV and NKJV follow the Textus Receptus and its inferior manuscript testimony in reversing the order of verses 16 and 17 to make them conform to the order of verse 15. The best manuscript evidence retains the order we find here and in all other major English translations. The effect of this creates a chiastic arrangement:

A "Some ... are preaching Christ even from envy and strife" (v.15a)

B "some also from good will" (v.15b)

B' "the latter do it out of love" (v.16)

A' "the former ... out of selfish ambition" (v.17)

In this the formula μὲν ... δὲ appears again (vv.16a, 17a), as it did in the previous verse. In verse 15 these two elements were paired with τινὲς ... τινὲς ("Some," "some"). Here they are paired with the nominative plural definite articles οἱ ... οἱ ("the latter," v.16; "the former," v.17). The present construction serves to mark a contrast between the first (those who preach Christ out of love, v.16) and the second (those who preach Christ from ill motives, v.17).[158]

In verse 15 the main verb and object were "are preaching Christ" (τὸν Χριστὸν κηρύσσουσιν). So too this present clause has as its main verb and object "proclaim Christ" (τὸν Χριστὸν καταγγέλλουσιν, v.17). Note the change of verbs over the course of these verses: λαλεῖν ("to speak," v.14), κηρύσσουσιν ("are proclaiming," v.15), and καταγγέλλουσιν ("proclaim," v.17). The first emphasizes the vocalization, the second the authority and accountability, the third the element of announcement.

---

158 Wallace, 212-213.

Those who speak of Christ "from good will" (v.15b) are said to do so "out of love" (ἐξ ἀγάπης). Their proclamation arises out of (ἐξ) a motive of "love" (ἀγάπης). The Apostle has already told the Philippian believers that his prayer is "that your love [ἡ ἀγάπη ὑμῶν] may abound still more and more in real knowledge and all discernment" (v.9). In some Roman believers (v.9) he was already seeing the kind of answer to his prayers he desired also for the Philippians (vv.15b, 16).

These of good motive speak the gospel "knowing that I am appointed for the defense of the gospel" (εἰδότες ὅτι εἰς ἀπολογίαν τοῦ εὐαγγελίου κεῖμαι). The participle (εἰδότες, "knowing") employs a verb (οἶδα) also used in verses 19 and 25 (also in 4:12, 15). It can stress the informational nature of knowledge; as opposed to γινώσκω (cf. 1:12; 2:19, 22; 3:10; 4:5), which can stress the personal and experiential nature of the knowledge. The perfect tense has a present tense meaning. Their new courage in speaking out boldly for Christ arises from a particular mindset, from something of which they are convinced. Thinking leads to speaking; knowledge begets proclamation. What is known is the real reason for Paul's imprisonment.

> **Ministry Maxim**
>
> Rarely do we know the epic nature and far-ranging effect of the struggle we are currently facing.

He is imprisoned "for the defense of the gospel" (εἰς ἀπολογίαν τοῦ εὐαγγελίου). The preposition (εἰς, "for") designates that unto which Paul, in his imprisonment, was set apart: "the defense" (ἀπολογίαν) of the gospel. The noun has already been used in verse 7 (see the comments there). Though the noun is anarthrous the translators of the NASU have added the definite article ("*the* defense," emphasis added). They see Paul as describing his imprisonment and legal case as something epic and defining for the larger purposes of the gospel. Paul had been set in prison that he might serve uniquely as a legal confirmation of the validity and truthfulness and power of "the gospel" (τοῦ εὐαγγελίου). Paul has been preoccupied with the gospel thus far in the letter (vv.5, 7, 12) and will continue to be (1:27 [2x]; 2:22; 4:3, 15). And to this end Paul says, "I am appointed" (κεῖμαι). This main verb of the clause is held to the end for emphasis. The verb is a simple one, meaning "lie" or "recline." But when used figuratively, as here, it can have the meaning "*be appointed, set, destined ... for someth*[ing]"[159] (cf. Luke 2:34; 1 Thess. 3:3). The passive voice pictures another taking the action upon Paul, in this case, God. The present tense of this verb has the sense of a perfect tense and became a virtual stand-in for the passive of τίθημι ("to put," "to place").[160] Thus there is a note of abiding state here—Paul has been and continues to be divinely "appointed" for such a "defense of the gospel."[161] This imprisonment and its effect for the purposes of the gospel is God's doing. Paul is, as Martin puts it, "as much 'on duty' as the guards who are posted to watch over him are on duty in the service of Rome."[162] The Philippians are to see, as Paul has, that heaven is working out larger purposes than the natural eye can discern.

Verse 17 – the former proclaim Christ out of selfish ambition rather than from pure motives, thinking to cause me distress in my imprisonment.

Paul completes here the chiastic arrangement he began in verse 15 (see comments at the beginning of v.16) and offers the contrast to those in verse 16. The οἱ μὲν ... οἱ δὲ combination ("the latter," v.16; "the former," v.17) plays out and completes the contrast of this and the previous verse. By "the former" (οἱ μὲν), he refers to "Some ... [who] are preaching Christ even from envy and strife" (v.15a).

The main verb and object of the two clauses that make up verses 16 and 17 are "proclaim Christ" (τὸν Χριστὸν καταγγέλλουσιν). This matches "preaching Christ" (τὸν Χριστὸν κηρύσσουσιν) from verse 15, which in turn links with "to speak the word" (τὸν λόγον λαλεῖν) of verse 14. The present verb (used again in v.18) was reserved for "solemn religious

---

159 BDAG, 4179.3.a.

160 Hellerman, 50.

161 Kennedy, 425; Lenski, 731; O'Brien, 101; Robertson, *Paul's Joy in Christ*, 86.

162 Martin, 73.

messages"¹⁶³ and means "to announce, declare, promulgate, make known; to proclaim publicly, publish."¹⁶⁴ The preposition prefix (κατά) may, in compound, intensify the root verb, resulting in a meaning of "making fully known."¹⁶⁵ The first verb emphasized the verbalization of the message, the second the divine authority of the proclamation, and if there is to be any distinction in this latter verb it may be in that it describes the solemn, thorough nature of the announcement of the gospel.

> **Ministry Maxim**
>
> Honorable actions do not guarantee honorable motives, for even the goodwill of the gospel can be harnessed to the ill-will of the human heart.

Those under consideration here in verse 17 make their proclamation of Christ "out of selfish ambition" (ἐξ ἐριθείας). This is in contrast to those who do so "out of love" (ἐξ ἀγάπης, v.16). Again, as in verse 16, the preposition (ἐξ, "out of") indicates the origin out from which the proclamation arises. In the present case that origin is "selfish ambition" (ἐριθείας). The noun comes "from ἐριθεύω (*serve for hire*), which is from ἔριθος (*day-laborer*)" and thus denotes "an attitude of self-seeking *selfish ambition, self-interest, rivalry.*"¹⁶⁶ Rienecker explains that "A hired worker was looked down upon because his laboring was wholly for his own interest."¹⁶⁷ The noun appears only seven times in the NT, five of those in Paul's writings (Rom. 2:8; 2 Cor. 12:20; Gal. 5:20; Phil. 1:17; 2:3; James 3:14, 16). There is an implicit contrast between the theme of their preaching (τὸν Χριστὸν, "Christ") and the driving force behind their preaching (ἐριθείας, "selfish ambition"). Paul draws this out in even more stark and bold ways in 2:3 and 5-8 where he contrasts Christ's mindset with that of selfish

---

163 Friberg, 217.

164 Thayer, 330.

165 Rienecker, 546.

166 Friberg, 172 (emphasis original).

167 Rienecker, 546.

ambition. The effect is to draw out the moral incongruity between Christ and selfish ambition.[168]

This stimulus is "rather than from pure motives" (οὐχ ἁγνῶς) or, more literally and simply, "not purely." The adverb ἁγνῶς ("pure") is found only here in the NT. The negative adverb (οὐχ) is used in litotes, a figure of speech in which the affirmative is stated by means of the negative of the contrary.[169] It denies the reality to which it is applied.[170] Thus the point is that the motives are impure.

Such people, says Paul, do what they do "thinking to cause me distress in my imprisonment" (οἰόμενοι θλῖψιν ἐγείρειν τοῖς δεσμοῖς μου). The participial phrase adds specificity to the prepositional and adverbial phrases already affixed to "proclaim Christ" (τὸν Χριστὸν καταγγέλλουσιν). The verb itself (οἰόμενοι, "thinking") is used only two other times in the NT (John 21:25; James 1:7). It describes "making a mental evaluation but without certainty."[171] Vincent says it denotes "a belief or judgment based principally upon one's own feelings, or the peculiar relations of outward circumstances to himself."[172] Paul appears to deliberately contrast "knowing" (εἰδότες, v.16) with "thinking" (οἰόμενοι, v.17). The former being certain and accurate; the latter uncertain and misguided.

That which they are thus thinking is "to cause me distress" (θλῖψιν ἐγείρειν). It more literally might be rendered "affliction to raise up." The noun (θλῖψιν, "distress") means pressure or a pressing and thus points to distress brought on by outward circumstances and the pressure they bring. These people purposely act in order to create circumstances and situations that press upon Paul's soul. That is to say they seek "to cause" (ἐγείρειν) this effect upon Paul. The word means to "raise up" or to "bring into being."[173] They speak the gospel, not for its saving effects, but for the

---

168 Lightfoot, 103.

169 BAGD, 590.

170 Ibid.

171 Friberg, 279.

172 Vincent, ICC, 21.

173 BDAG, 2172.5.

purpose of giving rise to circumstances that will create negative pressure upon the heart and soul of the Apostle Paul. And they do so, says Paul, "in my imprisonment" (τοῖς δεσμοῖς μου). See the same phrase in verses 7, 13, and 14 as well as our comments on each (cf. 4:18).

Before God we each must answer pointed and uncomfortable questions about our motives in gospel ministry. Have I found my identity in the gospel or in the ministry of the gospel? The two are not the same and their proximity to one another makes the differentiation all the more difficult. Have I used the ministry of the gospel to create downward pressure (θλῖψιν, "distress") on a brother? Have I used the ministry of the gospel to raise myself up (ἐριθείας, "selfish ambition")? Am I climbing upward in "the ministry" by climbing over or stepping on someone else? Because the ministry of the gospel is forever linked to the beauty of the gospel itself, it is easy to believe every motive for and every action taken in such ministry is also beautiful. This is not always the case and is precisely why we must first and always preach the gospel to ourselves.

> **Digging Deeper:**
> 1. When it comes to your fellow servants in ministry, at what point are you weakest against the assault of envy? What is your first best step toward overcoming ministerial envy? (v.15)
> 2. How might your current struggle in life and ministry serve as confirming evidence of the truth and beauty of the gospel? (v.16)
> 3. How might you be tempted to use the work of the gospel for non-gospel purposes? (v.17)

Verse 18 – What then? Only that in every way, whether in pretense or in truth, Christ is proclaimed; and in this I rejoice. Yes, and I will rejoice,

"What then?" (Τί γάρ) serves as an exclamatory question meaning something like "What does it matter?"[174] It is Paul's rhetorical means of initiating the transition from explanations about his circumstances and how they affect the gospel (vv.12-17) to the implications they have for him personally (vv.18-26). There are several textual variants related to πλὴν ὅτι ("Only that"). The Textus Receptus does not contain ὅτι, while a couple of manuscripts have ὅτι, but are missing πλὴν.[175] The great majority of the best manuscripts support the fuller reading, as we have it here.[176]

The main clause expresses the key to Paul's understanding of his circumstances: "Christ is proclaimed" (Χριστὸς καταγγέλλεται). The same combination appears in verse 17 (see the comments there). It is important to string together again the key phrases of Paul's argument so we can see the priority of "the gospel" (v.12b) in his heart: "speak the word of God" (v.14b), "preaching Christ" (v.15a), "proclaim Christ" (v.17a), "Christ is proclaimed" (v.18). The present tense here underscores the present and ongoing nature of the proclamation of the gospel of Jesus Christ. The passive voice pictures that gospel as being taken up by the preachers and given voice through their words.

Leading up to this are several qualifying clauses. The first is "Only that in every way" (πλὴν ὅτι παντὶ τρόπῳ) Christ is proclaimed. By "only that" (πλὴν ὅτι) Paul is narrowing the field of what brings him joy. It could mean either "*In any case ...*"[177] or "*except that ...?*"[178] By "in every way" (παντὶ τρόπῳ) he then broadens that field to include every possible way

---

174 BDAG, 7377.1.β.ה; Hellerman, 52.

175 Vincent, 22.

176 O'Brien, 97.

177 BDAG, 5977.1.c.

178 Ibid, 5977.1.d.

of preaching Christ. He now expands upon and defines "in every way" by saying "whether in pretense or in truth" (εἴτε προφάσει εἴτε ἀληθείᾳ).[179]

The formula εἴτε ... εἴτε means "whether ... or" (e.g., 1 Cor. 3:22; 8:5; 10:31; 12:13; Phil. 1:20, 27) and serves to introduce two or more competing possibilities. In this case the first is "in pretense" (προφάσει). Of the noun's six NT usages, Paul uses it only twice (here and 1 Thess. 2:5). It is a "pretext" or "ostensible reason" for something.[180] It is used "of what is made to appear to others to hide the true state of things."[181] This characterized the Jewish scribes (Mk. 12:40; Luke 20:47) and the world more generally (John 15:22; cf. Acts 20:30). But it is something Paul had avoided using in his ministry (1 Thess. 2:5). It is clear that there were some who "proclaimed Christ" in Rome at the time of Paul's first imprisonment who did so from alloyed motives. They presented the outward front of genuine, earnest preachers of the Christ, but inwardly they undertook their activity with some admixture of spite for the incarcerated Apostle.

The alternate possibility is proclaiming Christ "in truth" (ἀληθείᾳ). As it is used here the word stresses "reality ... as opposed to mere appearance."[182] In such preachers their *apparent* motives are their *true* motives. Transparency, honesty, sincerity and genuineness are their calling card. The dative forms for both nouns express the manner in which the preaching takes place.[183]

Paul now adds (καί, "and") his evaluation of these events. By "in this" (ἐν τούτῳ) he points back to the fact that "Christ is proclaimed" (Χριστὸς καταγγέλλεται). Whatever the motives, wherever Christ is preached, Paul can say "I rejoice" (χαίρω). The present tense points to the ongoing, repeated nature of Paul's rejoicing—it abounds and remains and abides and grows. With this verb Paul conspicuously carries forward one of the rich themes of the letter, that of joy and rejoicing:

---

179 Vincent, ICC, 22.

180 BDAG, 6369.2.

181 Friberg, 336.

182 BDAG, 324.3.

183 Rienecker, 546.

χαίρω (1:18 [2x], 2:17, 18, 28; 3:1; 4:4 [2x], 10); συγχαίρω (2:17, 18); χαρά (1:4, 25; 2:2, 29; 4:1).

There are questions about punctuation and the relationship of the following clause to that which surrounds it. Does "Yes, and I will rejoice" (Ἀλλὰ καὶ χαρήσομαι) attach to with what follows (as the NASU renders it, cf. HCSB, NET, ESV, NIV, NRSV) or does it go with what precedes (NASB, cf. KJV, NKJV, RSV)? Or does it stand alone (NLT)? The trend appears to be toward reading it with what follows. Note the transition from the NASB to the NASU and from the RSV to the NRSV. Most newer translations tend in this direction as well. This seems the better of the two options.[184] The future tense transitions from his present joy (χαίρω, "I rejoice") to that which he anticipates as a continuing experience (χαρήσομαι, "I will rejoice") as the circumstances he anticipates come to reality (v.19). Future tense verbs will dominate the sentence running through verse 20.[185] Here the passive voice pictures Paul as being moved by the preaching of Christ—as Christ is proclaimed the Apostle will, as always, be moved with joy.

> **Ministry Maxim**
>
> Motives matter, but the gospel's proclamation matters even more.

Verse 19 – for I know that this will turn out for my deliverance through your prayers and the provision of the Spirit of Jesus Christ,

Having informed the Philippians of the surprising, supernatural advance of his gospel (vv.12-18b), Paul now unfolds for them the adversity of his imprisonment (vv.18c-26). He explains (γὰρ, "for") the ground of the joy he presently experiences ("I rejoice," v.18b) and anticipates as a continuing experience ("I will rejoice," v.18c) despite his circumstances. For Paul continuing joy rests upon something "I know" (οἶδα). The perfect

---

184 Hawthorne, WBC, 48; Hellerman, 57; Kennedy, 426; O'Brien, 108; Vincent, ICC, 23.
185 O'Brien, 107.

tense has a present tense meaning. The verb is also used in verses 16, 25 (also in 4:12, 15; cf. γινώσκω used in 2:19, 22; 3:10; 4:5). It serves as an inclusion for the present passage, bracketing the entire section (vv.19-26). Similarly the theme of joy also forms another inclusion ("I will rejoice," v.18c; "joy," v.25). Thus we discover here the knowledge that enables one to experience joy at the intersection of "life" (vv.20, 21, 22, 25) and "death" (vv.20, 21, 23).

And "that" (ὅτι) which is known is "this will turn out for my deliverance" (τοῦτό μοι ἀποβήσεται εἰς σωτηρίαν). The phrase ὅτι τοῦτό μοι ἀποβήσεται εἰς σωτηρίαν ("that this will turn out for my salvation") corresponds precisely to Job 13:16 in the LXX.[186] Hawthorne says, "Paul understood and interpreted his situation in terms of Job's experience."[187] See especially O'Brien's discussion regarding the context of the statement in Job and how it informs our present passage.

But we must ask, as it regards our present passage, to what does "this" (τοῦτό) refer? What precisely is it which will "turn out for [Paul's] deliverance"? In the previous verse the same demonstrative pronoun referred to the preaching of Christ. In this verse, however, it seems best to understand "this" (τοῦτό) as a broader reference to all of his current affairs—his imprisonment (v.7), the new vistas for personal proclamation of Christ that imprisonment has afforded him (vv.12-13), the new impetus others have received for preaching Christ (vv.14-18), his impending trial (v.7), and its outcome (v.20).

What he has come to know concerns him personally (μοι, "my"). The verb ἀποβήσεται ("will turn out") is used only four times in the NT. Twice it is used to describe disembarking or stepping down out of a boat (Luke 5:2; John 21:9). It is also used idiomatically to refer to a resulting state of things (i.e., "will turn out"; Luke 21:13).[188] This seems to be the idea in this passage. The future tense points to what Paul believes will be the result of his trial. The middle voice pictures the anticipated outcome as

---

186 Lenski, 735-736; Martin, 74-75; O'Brien, 108-109.
187 Hawthorne, WBC, 48; cf. Fee, 130-131.
188 Friberg, 65.

the outworking of the events surrounding his life and imprisonment. The evidence, the process, the people involved, all of them will culminate in the anticipated decision. That resulting decision will be "for ... deliverance" (εἰς σωτηρίαν). More literally it could be rendered "unto salvation." But just what does Paul intend by "salvation" (σωτηρίαν)? Some view it as Paul's anticipated release from prison.[189] Others have understood it in its more usual sense of ultimate salvation into the presence of God forever.[190] O'Brien calls it "his vindication in the heavenly court."[191] The context (vv.20b-21) seems to confirm that Paul uses it here in this latter, more normal sense. While at times used of physical deliverance from danger (e.g., Acts 27:34), Paul never uses it of anything other than spiritual salvation. He likewise never uses the cognate verb (σῴζω) in any other sense than that of spiritual salvation.[192] Writing from his second Roman imprisonment—which did end in his martyrdom—Paul tellingly used this same verb: "The Lord will rescue [ῥύσεταί] me from every evil deed, and will bring me safely [σώσει] to His heavenly kingdom; to Him be the glory forever and ever. Amen" (2 Tim. 4:18). It is of note that Paul used a different verb to describe his physical "rescue" (ῥύσεταί), while reserving σῴζω to describe his spiritual salvation ("will bring me safely [σώσει] to His heavenly kingdom").[193] Thus we conclude that in the present passage Paul anticipates his vindication before God in and through all he faces before the Roman tribunal.

The Apostle knows and confesses that this will come about only "through" (διά) certain means which God will employ. This preposition governs both noun clauses that follow. Those means are "your prayers and the provision of the Spirit of Jesus Christ" (τῆς ὑμῶν δεήσεως καὶ ἐπιχορηγίας τοῦ πνεύματος Ἰησοῦ Χριστοῦ). By including in these means "your prayers" (τῆς ὑμῶν δεήσεως) the Apostle is reminding the Philippian believers of the

---

189 E.g. Hawthorne, WBC, 49; Kennedy, 426.

190 E.g., Alford, 3:159; Bockmuehl, 83; Harmon, 132-133; Vincent, ICC, 23.

191 O'Brien, 110.

192 Harmon, 132-133.

193 Bockmuehl, 83; Harmon, 133.

privilege they as believers have in calling upon God and in seeing Him respond. Paul has already used the noun (δεήσεως, "prayers") twice in verse 4 (see our comments there) to refer to his prayers on behalf of the believers in Philippi. The personal pronoun is in the attributive position, tucked between the noun and its definite article, thus emphasizing the qualitative nature of the prayers— they are the prayers of these specific believers. They are not prayers someone else will pray, but those they themselves will utter. Paul, in this way, winsomely calls them to the throne of God on his behalf. It is instructive to note that while the pronoun is plural (ὑμῶν, "your") the noun is singular (δεήσεως, lit., "prayer"). O'Brien says, "δέησις appears in the singular and directs attention to the single, specific nature of the request, while ὑμῶν, placed first for emphasis, is plural and points to the united offering of prayer by the Philippians for this particular object."[194]

> **Ministry Maxim**
>
> The prayers of God's people are intricately tied up in the fullness of God's Spirit in His gospel-servants.

Added (καί, "and") to this is "the provision of the Spirit of Jesus Christ" (ἐπιχορηγίας τοῦ πνεύματος Ἰησοῦ Χριστοῦ). The fact that this and the preceding noun clause are both governed by a single preposition (διά, "through") and definite article (τῆς) indicates that "The supply of the Spirit is the answer to his friends' prayer."[195] When he speaks of "the provision" (ἐπιχορηγίας) he uses a rare word which is found only here and Ephesians 4:16 in the NT. Rienecker says, "The simple noun originally indicated a payment for the cost of bringing out a chorus at a public festival. Then it signified provisions for an army or expedition. The word w[ith] the prep[osition] in compound was a technical term for describing the provision of food, clothing, etc., which a husband is obligated to make for his wife."[196] The verbal form of the word is found five times in the NT (2 Cor. 9:10; Gal. 3:5; Col. 2:19; 2 Pet. 1:5, 11). The noun is

---

194 O'Brien, 111.

195 Ibid., 110.

196 Rienecker, 532.

followed by a phrase with double genitives "of the Spirit of Jesus Christ" (τοῦ πνεύματος Ἰησοῦ Χριστοῦ). How are we to understand the first genitive (τοῦ πνεύματος, "of the Spirit") and its relationship to the noun? Is the Spirit Himself "the provision" (objective genitive)? Or "the provision" something the Spirit gives (subjective genitive)? Perhaps in some sense it is both.[197] Luke is not shy in calling the Holy Spirit the promise (Luke 24:49; Acts 1:4) and gift of the Father (Acts 2:38; 10:45). Yet the Spirit is the down payment upon and foretaste of all we will receive from the Father (Rom. 8:23; 2 Cor. 1:22; 5:5; Eph. 1:14). So the Spirit is both the gift and the provider of all God's grace to us. Having answered that, how should we understand the second genitive (Ἰησοῦ Χριστοῦ, "of Jesus Christ")? Does Paul mean Jesus Christ's own Spirit (objective genitive)? Or does he mean the Spirit which Jesus Christ gives (subjective genitive)? Luke can refer to the Holy Spirit as "the Spirit of Jesus" (Acts 16:7), both Paul and Peter call Him "the Spirit of Christ" (Rom. 8:9; 1 Pet. 1:11) and Paul designates Him "the Spirit of His Son" (Gal. 4:6). Yet Jesus is also the one who gives the Spirit (John 15:26; Acts 2:32-33). While this is true, Paul more regularly refers to the Father as the one giving the Spirit (1 Cor. 6:19; Eph. 1:17; Gal. 3:5; 1 Thess. 4:8). Perhaps it is best to understand Jesus as giving us of His very own Spirit.[198]

Verse 20 – according to my earnest expectation and hope, that I will not be put to shame in anything, but *that* with all boldness, Christ will even now, as always, be exalted in my body, whether by life or by death.

Just what is the phrase "according to my earnest expectation and hope" (κατὰ τὴν ἀποκαραδοκίαν καὶ ἐλπίδα μου) intended to qualify? It could qualify either what precedes—the verb "will result" (ἀποβήσεται, v.19; KJV, NKJV, NASB, NASU)[199]—or what follows—the coordinate verbs

---

[197] Lightfoot, 105; Robertson, *Paul's Joy in Christ*, 90.

[198] O'Brien, 112.

[199] Ibid.; Vincent, ICC, 25.

"I will not be put to shame" (ἐν οὐδενὶ αἰσχυνθήσομαι) and "Christ will … be exalted" (μεγαλυνθήσεται Χριστός, v.20b; HCSB, NET, NIV, NLT, RSV, NRSV).[200] The former seems the more likely. Paul has confidently asserted how he believes his present circumstances "will turn out" (ἀποβήσεται, v.19).

In wrapping up the sentence he tells us this outcome will be "according to" (κατὰ) two internal anchors: "my earnest expectation and hope" (τὴν ἀποκαραδοκίαν καὶ ἐλπίδα μου). Both nouns are governed by a single definite article (τὴν), making both specific and tying them integrally together. Both are Paul's personally (μου, "my"). The first noun, "earnest expectation" (ἀποκαραδοκίαν), is used only here and Romans 8:19 in the NT. The noun came from the verb ἀποκαραδοκεῖν, which is a double compound comprised of ἀπό ("from"), κάρα ("the head") and δοκεῖν ("to watch").[201] It means, then, "to watch with head erect or outstretched, to direct attention to anything, to wait for in suspense."[202] The prefix (ἀπό) may serve to intensify the meaning.[203] Kennedy says it conveys "The concentrated intense hope which ignores other interests (ἀπό) and strains forward as with outstretched head (κάρα, δοκεῖν)."[204] This, not surprisingly, is held in parallel (καὶ, "and") with "hope" (ἐλπίδα). The rarity of the first noun is balanced by the familiarity and frequency of this second noun, which is found over fifty times in the NT.

The ὅτι points to the object of Paul's "earnest expectation and hope"[205] and introduces Paul's more precise identification of that which fills his heart in this regard. This object is stated in a two-fold fashion, first negatively and then positively. Negatively, Paul declares, "I will not be put to shame in anything" (ἐν οὐδενὶ αἰσχυνθήσομαι). The verb (αἰσχυνθήσομαι, "I will not be put to shame") is used five times in the NT (Luke 16:3; 2

---

200 Martin, 75.

201 Thayer, 62.

202 Ibid.

203 O'Brien, 113.

204 Kennedy, 427.

205 Vincent, ICC, 25; cf. O'Brien, 113.

Cor. 10:8; Phil. 1:20; 1 Pet. 4:16; 1 John 2:28). The passive voice here pictures circumstances having the effect of disappointing one's hope.[206] The future tense anticipates a possible scenario which is as yet unrealized. This, however, Paul assures, will happen "in nothing" (ἐν οὐδενὶ). The pronoun denies the matter absolutely. The Apostle foresees no possibility of a failure of hope.

In stark contrast (ἀλλ᾽, "but") to the possibility of his hope being disappointed, Paul states the matter positively, "Christ shall ... be exalted" (μεγαλυνθήσεται Χριστὸς). At root the verb means to make large, to make long or to magnify. Then, figuratively, it could designate to exalt, glorify, magnify or to speak highly of.[207] By Paul's carefully chosen words, "Christ becomes the subject ... and Paul is simply the instrument by which the greatness of Christ shines out."[208] The future tense points to what Paul anticipates of his circumstances and the result of them. The passive voice pictures God acting "with Paul being the instrument in the divine hands."[209] The Name, renown and honor of Christ is the great passion of the Apostle. He is confident that his present circumstances and their eventual outcome will enable him to accomplish, by God's grace, what he has labored toward and longed after since he met Christ—glorifying his Savior.

> **Ministry Maxim**
>
> The only assurance I have that I would die for Christ someday is that I die to self today.

Paul can see himself accomplishing this "with all boldness" (ἐν πάσῃ παρρησίᾳ). The noun described "*outspokenness, frankness, plainness*" of speech "that conceals nothing and passes over nothing."[210] Thus it is sometimes rendered "openness," "boldness" or "confidence."[211] It is "the

---

206 BDAG, 217.2.

207 Ibid., 4760.2.

208 O'Brien, 115; cf. Lenski, 737.

209 Ibid.

210 BDAG, 5720.1.

211 Rienecker, 575.

courage appropriate to the free man, which acts openly even in a hostile atmosphere."[212] No circumstance, however dark, will move Paul to curtail his preaching of Christ. This "boldness" (παρρησίᾳ) is in contrast to any possible "shame" (αἰσχυνθήσομαι).[213] Paul will act in this bold confidence without restriction and in full concentration (ἐν πάσῃ, "in all"). Paul's "all" (πάσῃ) stands as the direct opposite of "nothing" (οὐδενί).[214] Assured that the future holds this course for him, the Apostle says that "as [he has] always" (ὡς πάντοτε) exalted Christ in the past so "even now" (καὶ νῦν) he is doing so in the present. The order is essential: ὡς πάντοτε ("as always") must come before καὶ νῦν ("even now"). The best indicator of future performance is past performance. And Paul's future course was sure because his past record and present experience set a trajectory of Christ-exalting faithfulness in which he could anticipate God's continued supply of grace and picture the continuing determined set of his will. The only assurance one can have that he would be willing to die for Christ someday is the fact that he dies to self today.

And this exaltation, says Paul, will take place "in my body" (ἐν τῷ σώματί μου). The precise phrase is used one other time in the NT, when Paul says "(I bear on my body [ἐν τῷ σώματί μου] the brand-marks of Jesus" (Gal. 6:17). The preposition (ἐν, "in") depicts Paul's body as "the scene or sphere" of the action.[215] The Apostle is stressing that this is a corporeal experience, not simply spiritual. It is not merely a state of mind, but an experience in which the whole of his being will be involved. Indeed, Paul intends to exalt Christ "whether by life or by death" (εἴτε διὰ ζωῆς εἴτε διὰ θανάτου). The familiar formula εἴτε ... εἴτε ("whether ... or," cf. vv. 18, 27) holds the two possibilities in parallel relationship. The doubling up of the preposition διά ("by," signifying the means by

---

212 Ibid, 547.
213 Alford, 3:160.
214 Vincent, ICC, 26.
215 O'Brien, 115.

which Christ will be exalted[216]) heightens the simple, plainly stated contrast. Paul uses ζωή ("life") rather than βίος, for the former stresses existence and is more naturally the antithesis of "death" (θάνατος) while the latter tends to be used of the period, means, or manner of existence.[217] The former is more readily used of men; the latter of animals. He will use ζωή again in the next verse, signaling that already in his mind, the Apostle is thinking about more than mere human, biological existence. He is thinking of "life" in all its original, God-intended, Christ-purchased fullness. If God chooses to exalt Christ through Paul by "life," it will mean more than brainwaves and heartbeats. It will mean life lived in union with Christ Himself! Paul was "always carrying about in the body the dying of Jesus, so that the life of Jesus also may be manifested in [his] body." (2 Cor. 4:10).

> **Digging Deeper:**
> 1. Is the power of the gospel hindered by the motives of the gospel-bearer? (v.18)
> 2. What anointing of the Spirit and what deliverance from trouble awaits your commitment to rally the people of God to pray for you? (v.19)
> 3. What gives you confidence that whatever your life may hold you will glorify Jesus Christ? (v.20)

Verse 21 – For to me, to live is Christ and to die is gain.

The conjunction (γάρ, "For") introduces an explanation of Paul's previous confidence regarding the two possible outcomes of his current trial. The first word in the sentence is Ἐμοὶ ("to me"). And with this in the emphatic position the Apostle introduces his personal evaluation of the contrasting

---

[216] "Note that διὰ is to express means, and that the agent in the passive (the Spirit of Jesus Christ) is the one who employs the means." Lenski, 738.

[217] Thayer, 102.

possibilities of life and death which he introduced in verse 20. Robertson calls the pronoun a "Fine example of the ethical dative."[218]

The brevity of language and terseness of expression make the statement all the more powerful as it holds the two dramatic possibilities side by side. On the one hand is "to live" (τὸ ζῆν). The presence of the definite article (τὸ) indicates that we should understand the infinitive as the subject of the clause.[219] There is no finite verb ("is") in the original, though it is rightly understood here by the translators. The present tense of the infinitive underscores the continuous nature of the living. For Paul "to live" = "Christ" (Χριστός). The expression bespeaks the mystery of the believer's union with Christ (cf. 2 Cor. 4:11; Gal. 2:20; Col. 1:27). If Paul's physical life continues it will be an opportunity for "Christ, who is our life" (Col. 3:4) to manifest Himself through the Apostle's words and works. "Christ will even now ... be exalted in my body ... by life" (v.20).

Is Paul merely using artful expression or is he describing an existential reality? Is his brevity mistaken for more than he intends? Or has he taken off his sandals because he is walking on holy ground and measuring his words lest he misspeak (Eccl. 5:2)? The life of the indwelling Christ was a daily, moment-by-moment reality for Paul. He seems to have especially sensed this reality in times of extremity: "we are afflicted in every way, but not crushed; perplexed, but not despairing; persecuted, but not forsaken; struck down, but not destroyed; always carrying about in the body the dying of Jesus, so that *the life of Jesus also may be manifested in our body*. For we who live are constantly being delivered over to death for Jesus' sake, so that *the life of Jesus also may be manifested in our mortal flesh*" (2 Cor. 4:8-11, emphasis added). The actual, fleshly, earthly engagement of life and all its realities is the arena wherein Jesus personally shows up with the manifestation of His life in and through His child. Thus Paul can say, "to live is

> **Ministry Maxim**
>
> The living Christ living His life in and through me—this is life indeed.

---

218 Robertson, *Word Pictures*, 4:440.

219 Wallace, 235.

Christ." He can confess in another place "it is no longer I who live, but Christ lives in me" (Gal. 2:20). He reminds the Colossian believers that it is "Christ, who is our life" (Col. 3:4). Jesus commanded His followers, "Abide in me, and I in you" (John 14:4a). This is mystery deep, but it is also life indeed.

Held in parallel relationship (καὶ, "and") to this is "to die" (τὸ ἀποθανεῖν). Again, as with the previous infinitive, the presence of the definite article (τὸ) indicates that we should understand this infinitive as the subject of its clause. The word is a compound comprised of ἀπό ("from") and θνήσκω ("to die"). Commentators are divided over how to understand the aorist tense of the infinitive. Some demand it is not to be understood as punctiliar action, denoting rather the consequence of dying or the state of death.[220] Others demand that the aorist tense points to the act of dying, not the process.[221] This seems the more usual way of understanding the aorist tense.

In physical death the immaterial part of us (soul/spirit) is separated from our physical body. To be thus released from this body and this physical world "is gain" (κέρδος). Again, "is" has been added by the translators to render the bare text of the original into readable English. The noun describes whatever might be to one's profit, advantage, or gain. It is used only two other places in the NT, both by Paul (Phil. 3:7; Tit. 1:11). See the cognate verb in Philippians 3:8 (κερδήσω, "I may gain"). For Paul "to die" = "gain." To die is "to depart and be with Christ" (v.23). The word was used at times in the first century to describe gains realized through interest. Thus Robertson can say that to die "is to cash in both principal and interest and so to have more of Christ than when living."[222] Death is gain "because it will introduce him to complete union with Christ, unhampered by limitations of the flesh."[223] "Christ will even now ... be exalted in my body ... by death" (v.20b).

---

[220] Lightfoot, 106; Wuest, 45.

[221] Lenski, 740; Martin, 76; O'Brien, 122; Robertson, *Paul's Joy in Christ*, 95.

[222] Robertson, *Word Pictures*, 440.

[223] Vincent, ICC, 27.

Verse 22 – But if *I am* to live *on* in the flesh, this *will mean* fruitful labor for me; and I do not know which to choose.

Paul's grammar is becoming increasingly more difficult to unravel. Martin well says, "The agitation of Paul's mind is clearly to be seen in the broken syntax of his writing."[224]

The post positive conjunction δέ is used as an adversative ("But") to show Paul standing at a crossroads, uncertain which of two paths ("to live ... to die," v.21) to take. The condition (εἰ, "if") is assumed true for the sake of the argument. The infinitive with its definite article is repeated from verse 21 (τὸ ζῆν, "to live"). The definite article functions "both as a substantiver of the infinitive and anaphorically."[225] Wallace renders it literally "Now if **the** living [on] in the flesh ...", but says it is more smoothly translated as "now if I am to live on in the flesh."[226] The present tense points to the ongoing process of living, thus the translators have added "on" to give that impression. It is life "in the flesh" (ἐν σαρκί) that Paul has in mind.

> **Ministry Maxim**
>
> Life is given us not first that we might enjoy it, but that we bear fruit in it—joy comes in fruitfulness.

The protasis (εἰ, "if") is now followed by what amounts to the apodosis.[227] By "this" (τοῦτό) Paul means his continuing "to live on in the flesh." There is no verb, so the translators have added "will mean." The rendering "fruitful labor" (καρπὸς ἔργου) is correct for this is an example of the attributed genitive, a form in which the first noun functions as an attributive adjective.[228] Taken as an attributive genitive it would mean "laboring fruit," which is nonsensical.[229] And all this is gauged from Paul's

---

224 Martin, 77.

225 Wallace, 235.

226 Ibid., emphasis original.

227 O'Brien, 124.

228 Wallace, 89-90.

229 Ibid., 90.

own perspective (μοι, "for me"). The dative form might be rendered "*to me*," but this could sound like the "fruitful labor" is something performed by another on Paul or for his benefit. Rather Paul is explaining what the effect of continued bodily life here on earth would mean from his perspective—he would go on living and serving and bearing fruit by God's grace and for God's glory.

Contemplating the two paths before him, Paul adds (καί, "and")[230] a further confession: "I do not know which to choose" (τί αἱρήσομαι οὐ γνωρίζω). The interrogative pronoun (τί, "which") opens the clause, and the word order might literally be rendered "which to choose? I do not know." The verb translated "to choose" (αἱρήσομαι) is used in the NT only here and 2 Thessalonians 2:13 and Hebrews 11:25. The former speaks of God's electing choice, while the latter a personal choice of Moses in the face of temptation. Here the tense is future and expresses Paul's bewilderment as he looks at the possibilities before him. All three NT usages are in the middle voice, which speaks "of taking for oneself" and thus "*choose, select*" or, here "as choosing between alternatives" with the idea "*prefer*."[231]

Thus surveying the two options, Paul says "I do not know" (οὐ γνωρίζω) which to choose. The negation "denies simply, absolutely, categorically, directly, objectively" the action of the verb.[232] The verb (γνωρίζω, "I ... know") in the NT has either the sense of "make known"/"reveal" or "know." Strong authorities point us toward the latter sense.[233] Yet the prevailing NT sense of the word is toward the former.[234] The idea would then be that Paul has "nothing to make known" or "nothing to say" regarding the two options. Perhaps, as Lohmeyer suggests, it is simply that the Apostle is confessing that God has not revealed His mind to him and he,

---

230 BDAG (3845.1.b.θ) suggests καί is used "to introduce an abrupt question, which may often express wonder, ill-will, incredulity, etc." and they offer a rendering of "then which shall I choose?"

231 Friberg, 37.

232 Thayer, 408.

233 E.g., BDAG, 1661.2; Friberg, 100; cf. Bultmann who says, "When we turn to the NT we find this meaning only at Phil. 1:22" (TDNT, 1:718).

234 Lightfoot, 107; O'Brien, 127-128; cf. Vincent, 28.

therefore, "has nothing to declare 'from the Lord' regarding the options of living or dying."[235]

> **Digging Deeper:**
> 1. To what degree are you operating in the power and grace of the indwelling life of Christ right now? (v.21)
> 2. Using Paul's words here how would you counsel a person who comes to you because they are afraid of death?
> 3. What is happening right now in your life that gives you confidence that continued physical life will mean fruitfulness for Christ? (v.22)

Verse 23 – But I am hard-pressed from both *directions*, having the desire to depart and be with Christ, for *that* is very much better;

Again (as in verse 22) we meet the postpositive conjunction δὲ. It has here the role of both continuing, by way of explanation, what has been said before and yet also setting this present statement apart from what precedes.[236] The verb συνέχομαι ("I am hard-pressed") is a compound word comprised of σύν ("with") and ἔχω ("to hold") with the resulting idea of "to hold together." The verb is used frequently in the Gospels and Acts to describe being in the grip of diseases (Matt. 4:24; Luke 4:38; Acts 28:8), fear (Luke 8:37), pressing crowds (Luke 8:45), feelings (Luke 12:50), and enemy armies (Luke 19:43) or soldiers (Luke 22:63). Paul's only other usage is in 2 Corinthians 5:14 where it is the love of Christ which "constraineth" (KJV) us. The image is that of two pressures exerting their force upon one from different sides. The present tense depicts the unending pressure Paul feels. The passive voice pictures him being squeezed to the point of immobility between the opposing forces that press upon his heart.

---

235 Cited in O'Brien, 128; cf. Lenski, 745.

236 Vincent, ICC, 28.

In Paul's case the pressure comes "from both directions" (ἐκ τῶν δύο). The preposition (ἐκ, "from") may here have the rare meaning of "between,"[237] but it seems rather to indicate the source out of which the two opposing pressures come upon Paul.[238] He is pressed from two sides, by two opposing desires, which impinge upon him from different directions, making it impossible for him to incline toward one or the other. The definite article (τῶν) is employed because the two opposite pressures have already been identified: "to live" in ongoing fellowship with and "fruitful labor" for Christ and "to die" which is to "gain" the fullness of His presence (vv.21-22).[239]

The issues of living fellowship with Christ and dying entrance into Christ's full presence press upon the Apostle. Yet he confesses to "having the desire to depart and be with Christ" (τὴν ἐπιθυμίαν ἔχων εἰς τὸ ἀναλῦσαι καὶ σὺν Χριστῷ εἶναι). The participle (ἔχων, "having") is in the present tense, stressing the abiding nature of the desire Paul feels. The participial form is used to describe attendant circumstances. That is to say, while Paul is being "hard-pressed" between the options, his personal preference is "to depart" this physical life and to "be [more fully and finally] with Christ." That which is thus had is "the desire" (τὴν ἐπιθυμίαν). In itself it is a morally neutral term, designating any strong and overwhelming desire. Paul uses the noun nineteen times in his letters, always in a negative sense, except here and in 1 Thessalonians 2:17. This powerful desire is personal, for the definite article may be used to designate possession (i.e., "*my* desire").[240]

> **Ministry Maxim**
>
> Our hope is set upon a person, not simply a concept or even a place.

---

237 Wallace, 135.

238 Kennedy, 428; Lenski, 745.

239 Lenski, 745.

240 Lightfoot, 107; O'Brien, 129; Vincent, ICC, 28.

That desire which Paul has in mind is now spelled out with a purpose clause (εἰς τὸ + two infinitives).[241] Or the formula may indicate "grammatically the direction of the apostle's strong desire."[242] The first infinitive stresses the anticipated exit from this life: "to depart" (τὸ ἀναλῦσαι). Appropriately the infinitive is an aorist, stressing the punctiliar nature of the action. Death occurs at a singular moment in time—"it is appointed for men to die once" (Heb. 9:27). The word Paul chooses here is used elsewhere in the NT only in Luke 12:36. It is a compound comprised of ἀνά ("up") and λύω ("to loose," "to untie"). It means "to break up," "to unloose," or "to undo" and was used of loosing a ship from its moorings, of a party breaking camp, and then, as here, as a metaphor for death.[243] Paul uses the cognate noun to describe his own death in 2 Timothy 4:6.

Added (καὶ, "and") to this is a second infinitive which stresses the resulting state of the first: "be with Christ" (σὺν Χριστῷ εἶναι). Both infinitives are governed by the one definite article (τὸ), indicating just how closely related and ultimately inseparable are the two: "to depart" is to "be with Christ."[244] From a verb used only two times in the NT, Paul now turns to one used over 2,400 times. The present tense is fitting for describing the believer's abiding state of fellowship with Christ which will be enjoyed after death. This stands in contrast to the singular (aorist tense) event of the departure from this life. The momentary event of death opens to an eternal, ongoing experience with Christ. The preposition and noun (σὺν Χριστῷ, "with Christ") are placed before the infinitive for emphasis. To "be absent from the body" is "to be at home with the Lord" (2 Cor. 5:8). Paul here pictures death as immediately ushering the believer consciously into the presence of the Lord, in open fellowship with Him. O'Brien says, "the preposition σὺν ('with') was suited to express intimate personal union with Christ."[245]

---

241 Robertson, *Word Pictures*, 4:441.

242 O'Brien, 129.

243 Rienecker, 547.

244 O'Brien, 130.

245 Ibid., 132.

Paul adds an explanatory (γὰρ, "for")[246] evaluation of the Christ-option: "that is very much better" (πολλῷ ... μᾶλλον κρεῖσσον). The Apostle piles up the descriptors in an attempt to approach the qualitative superiority of being in God's presence. It was probably this piling up of comparatives that created angst for some scribes, and thus explains the variety among the manuscripts at this point.[247] This, being the more difficult reading, is to be preferred.[248] Literally, it might be rendered "much more better."[249] Commentators vary in calling it either a "double comparative"[250] or a "triple comparative,"[251] but by either accounting the Apostle piles up the expressions to establish the relative value of being with Christ following death. The dative adjective πολλῷ ("very") is used to express "the degree to which the comparison is true or the degree of difference that exists in the comparison."[252] The adverb μᾶλλον ("much") means "to a greater degree."[253] The adjective κρεῖσσον ("better") functions as the comparative of ἀγαθός ("good") and here has the idea of "more useful," "more advantageous," and thus "better."[254]

Paul has, for the moment, allowed his heart to soar with the possibility of leaving this life to enter immediately into Christ's direct presence. There is something deeply personal, intimate, and precious in hearing the Apostle's wistful longing expressed so tenderly. His willingness to reveal his heart through his pen on this occasion has drawn out the same longing in struggling, home-sick believers for two-millennia.

---

246 There is some debate about the authenticity of γὰρ, but the evidence seems to rest in favor of considering it a genuine part of the text.

247 O'Brien, 131.

248 Ibid, 116.

249 Vincent, *Word Studies*, 3:425.

250 Müller, 63.

251 Martin, 79.

252 Wallace, 166-167.

253 BDAG, 4696.1.

254 Ibid., 4394.2.a.

Verse 24 – yet to remain on in the flesh is more necessary for your sake.

Having allowed his heart to soar with the thought of actually being "with Christ" (v.23), the Apostle now contrasts (δὲ, "yet") that "desire" with what he knows to be the more likely and needed scenario for the present time. That is "to remain on in the flesh" (τὸ ... ἐπιμένειν [ἐν] τῇ σαρκὶ). The verb is a compound, composed of ἐπί ("upon") and μένω ("remain"; cf. this uncompounded root verb in the next verse).

> **Ministry Maxim**
>
> In ministry, the necessity of others overrides personal desire.

The preposition in compound "implies rest in a place and hence at a more protracted stay."[255] The word conveys the active sense of persisting in something, rather than the passive notion of simple continuance.[256] As in verse 22 the presence of the definite article (τὸ) marks the infinitive as a substantive.[257] The preposition ἐν ("in") is found in some important manuscripts, but it is not common for this preposition to be found with the verb (1 Cor. 16:8 is the only other example).[258] The preposition is not necessary[259], but it "may have been due to early scribes seeking to make the expression correct grammatically."[260] Paul can sometimes use "the flesh" (τῇ σαρκὶ) to refer to man's fallen propensity toward sin (Rom. 8:3, 12; Gal. 5:13), but here he uses it in its more natural sense of the human body (Gal. 4:14; Col. 2:5).

This, he says, "is more necessary" (ἀναγκαιότερον). The text does not contain the verb ("is"), but expects us to mentally supply it, as the translators have done. The adjective is used only eight times in the NT, five of

---

255 Rienecker, 547-548.
256 Harris, *Colossians & Philemon*, 60.
257 Wallace, 235.
258 O'Brien, 116.
259 Robertson, *Word Pictures*, 4:441.
260 O'Brien, 116.

which are from Paul's pen (Acts 10:24; 13:46; 1 Cor. 12:22; 2 Cor. 9:5; Phil. 1:24; 2:25; Titus 3:14; Heb. 8:3). It is used as a comparative here, thus it is "*more* necessary."[261] But "more necessary" than what? Than that which is "very much better" (v.23)! And what makes Paul's remaining on in this life and in active ministry so "very much better" is that it is done "for your sake" (δι' ὑμᾶς). The plural pronoun shows that Paul has the whole body of believers in Philippi in mind. Yet it is unlikely that Paul is thinking only of the Philippian believers, but all those who need his care, leadership and witness for the gospel.[262] "Later he will urge his readers to consider the good of others (2:4). Here he sets the example himself."[263]

Digging Deeper:
1. Which is the stronger desire right now in your life: living and bearing fruit for Christ or departing to live immediately in His presence forever? Is there any desire higher than these in your life? (v.23)
2. What personal sacrifice is required of you right now to meet some necessity in the lives of others around you? (v.24)

Verse 25 – Convinced of this, I know that I will remain and continue with you all for your progress and joy in the faith,

The NASU leaves the opening καὶ untranslated (but cf. NASB, "And"). Having expressed uncertainty about which desire to choose (vv.21-24) Paul is now certain of something, for he says "I know" (οἶδα). The perfect tense has a present tense meaning. This same verb is also used in verses 16, 25 (also in 4:12, 15; cf. γινώσκω in 2:19, 22; 3:10; 4:5). Paul's certainty rests upon a foundation: "Convinced of this" (τοῦτο πεποιθὼς).

---

261 Friberg, 48; emphasis added.
262 O'Brien, 131.
263 Ibid.

Paul uses this verb in Philippians more times than in any other one book (1:6, 14, 25; 2:24; 3:3, 4). Here again the perfect tense has a present tense meaning.[264] The word itself points toward trust, reliance, conviction, confidence, and assurance. It means "to convince someone to believe something and to act on the basis of what is recommended."[265] That of which the Apostle is "Convinced" is "this" (τοῦτο)—referring to the necessity of him continuing on in the flesh for the sake of the believers in Christ (v.24).

But what does Paul "know"? This he expresses by way of a ὅτι clause ("that"). That which Paul knows is "I shall remain and continue with you all" (μενῶ καὶ παραμενῶ πᾶσιν ὑμῖν). The two verbs are held in parallel relationship by the coordinating conjunction καὶ ("and"). The two are also obviously related—the first is the more basic μενῶ ("I shall remain") and the second is a compound built off of this same root (παραμενῶ, "continue"; cf. the same root verb compounded with a different prefix in the preceding verse). The second is comprised of παρά ("beside") and μένω ("I continue"). The former means simply "I remain," while the second means "I remain *with*" someone.[266] It, of course, in this context has the sense of remaining alive. The second verb is often followed by a dative form used to express those with whom the person is remaining, in this case "you all" (πᾶσιν ὑμῖν). Paul similarly combines a root verb and a compound verb built off of it in 2:17 (χαίρω καὶ συγχαίρω, "I rejoice and share my joy").[267]

> **Ministry Maxim**
>
> A gospel-servant's desires must often be secondary to others' joy and progress in the faith.

Paul's continuance in this life has a goal (εἰς, "for"). That goal is "your progress and joy in the faith" (τὴν ὑμῶν προκοπὴν καὶ χαρὰν τῆς πίστεως). The two nouns (προκοπὴν καὶ χαρὰν, "progress and joy") are

---

264 BDAG, 5205; O'Brien, 63.

265 Louw and Nida, 33.301.

266 BDAG, 4816.1, 5608.1.b.

267 Robertson, *Word Pictures*, 4:441.

both governed by one definite article (τὴν). The personal pronoun (ὑμῶν, "your") is in the plural form, indicating that all of the Philippian believers are in view. It is in the attributive position, tucked between the definite article and the first noun, thus doubly emphasizing (along with its genitive case) the personal nature of both the "progress" and the "joy." The noun "progress" (προκοπὴν) is used only three times in the NT, all by Paul and two of them here in Philippians (Phil. 1:12, 25; 1 Tim. 4:15). The cognate verb is a compound comprised of πρό ("before") and κόπτω ("to cut" or "to strike"). Given the rarity of the noun in the NT it is apparent that the Apostle uses it as an inclusio, using it to open this extended section (v.12) and now employing it as he moves to close the discussion.[268] See our comments on verse 12 for more on the word's meaning. Coordinate (καὶ, "and") to this "progress" is a personal and collective "joy" (χαρὰν). Once again the Apostle dips into the flow of one of this letter's special themes (χαίρω: 1:18 [2x], 2:17, 18, 28; 3:1; 4:4 [2x], 10; συγχαίρω: 2:17, 18; χαρά: 1:4, 25; 2:2, 29; 4:1).

Both the progress and joy are specifically "in the faith" (τῆς πίστεως). The genitive form might more literally be rendered "*of* the faith" (cf. KJV; NKJV). The genitive should be read with both nouns, as was the genitive personal pronoun (ὑμῶν, "your").[269] The definitive article may be intended to express personal possession ("of *your* faith," NLT, emphasis added) or to point not so much to "faith" as personal trust, but to the body of truth which makes up the Christian faith ("*the* faith," HCSB, ESV, RSV, NASB, NASU, NET, NIV, emphasis added). The latter seems the more likely, but of course the two cannot and must not be separated if one is to truly experience the "joy" that comes from resting oneself upon "the truth" of the gospel. And we must note also that personally embracing "the truth" of the gospel launches one into a process of growth and maturity which can only demand and result in "progress"—the gospel changes you both instantly and continuously.

---

268 O'Brien, 139-140.

269 Lightfoot, 109; Vincent, ICC, 30.

Verse 26 – so that your proud confidence in me may abound in Christ Jesus through my coming to you again.

Paul's continuance in life—rather than martyrdom—(v.25) will have its effect. But is ἵνα ("so that") to be understood as indicating purpose[270] or result?[271] Though most English versions translate with "so that" rather than "in order that," it seems best to read this as indicating the purpose, goal or objective of God choosing to have Paul continue in life and in ministry (v.25). This purpose is that "your proud confidence ... may abound" (τὸ καύχημα ὑμῶν περισσεύῃ). The articular noun (τὸ καύχημα, "proud confidence") is used again in 2:16 and denotes "that which constitutes a source of pride."[272] It designates, not the act of boasting, but "the ground or reason for boasting."[273] In this case it is "the faith" (v.25), the gospel which is the "proud confidence" of the Philippian believers (ὑμῶν, "your," subjective genitive).[274] This confidence "may abound" (περισσεύῃ). Paul has already used the verb (1:9, see our comments there) and will use it three more times in this letter (4:12 [2x], 18). Here it may have the meaning "be present in abundance."[275] The present tense has the sense of ongoing, ever-abounding.

> **Ministry Maxim**
>
> The goal of ministry is to so live that others are proud of following Christ.

Three prepositional phrases follow. Each progressively narrows the field in which the Philippian believer's "proud confidence" in the gospel "may abound." We will consider them in the order they confront us in the Greek text.

---

270 BDAG, 3715.1.a.δ; O'Brien, 140; Sumney, 32.

271 Harmon, 151.

272 BDAG, 4172.1.

273 Rienecker, 548.

274 Alford, 4:162; Kennedy, 429, O'Brien, 141.

275 BDAG, 5868.1.a.β.

This "proud confidence" takes place "in Christ Jesus" (ἐν Χριστῷ Ἰησοῦ). This phrase is properly connected to "may abound" (περισσεύῃ), not "proud confidence" (τὸ καύχημα).[276] Christ is the sphere (ἐν) "in" which Paul and the Philippian believers hear, believe and "abound in" the gospel.[277]

The "proud confidence" of the Philippian believers is focused upon Paul (ἐν ἐμοί, "in me"). While the whole of their abounding in their boast (the gospel) takes place "in Christ," the immediate "ground" or "special cause" of it is "in" (ἐν) Paul.[278] He is the immediate causative sphere ("in me") within the larger, all-encompassing sphere of being "in Christ." It is Paul's continued physical life and fruitful ministry that is in view (vv.24-25).

Obviously, then, the effective trigger of their abounding in their "proud confidence" in the gospel is "through my coming to you again" (διὰ τῆς ἐμῆς παρουσίας πάλιν πρὸς ὑμᾶς). The preposition (διὰ, "through") designates the immediate agent through which their abounding will take place. The possessive adjective (ἐμῆς, "my") is emphatic.[279] Vincent explains nicely the awkward grammar: "The ground of glorying is first, and comprehensively, in Christ; then in Paul as representing Christ; then in Paul's personal presence again with them."[280]

The "proud confidence" of the Philippian believers will be realized in the *arena* of their relationship to Jesus ("in Christ"), upon the *ground* of Paul's life lived faithfully for Christ ("in me"), and through the immediate *agency* of Paul's coming to them once again ("through my coming to you again"). So too we desire that as other believers stand "in Christ," our lives lived in faithfulness to Jesus may become the ground of their confidence in the gospel as we actively fellowship with and minister to them.

---

276 Vincent, ICC, 31.

277 Kennedy, 429.

278 Vincent, ICC, 31.

279 Lenski, 750.

280 Vincent, ICC, 31.

Eventually, Paul was released from his first Roman imprisonment (as described in Acts 28:16-31), traveled, ministered in various locations, and perhaps during that time revisited Philippi.[281] Subsequently, he was rearrested and imprisoned again in Rome, from which he penned Second Timothy shortly before he was martyred (2 Tim. 4:6-8).[282]

> **Digging Deeper:**
> 1. How have you had to lay aside your legitimate longings and desires in order to faithfully serve the good of God's people? (v.25)
> 2. In what way must your life become the arena in which others glory in Christ? (v.26) For this to become reality, what is demanded of you?

Verse 27 – Only conduct yourselves in a manner worthy of the gospel of Christ, so that whether I come and see you or remain absent, I will hear of you that you are standing firm in one spirit, with one mind striving together for the faith of the gospel;

Paul now, in a sentence that extends through verse 30, begins his exhortations to the Philippian believers.[283] The main verb is the imperative "Conduct yourselves" (πολιτεύεσθε). The verb is used only here and in Acts 23:1 where it is again in Paul's mouth as he testifies to the Jewish ruling Council, "Brethren, I have lived my life [πεπολίτευμαι] with a

---

[281] We have no independent verification that Paul did indeed revisit Philippi after release from his first Roman imprisonment. Paul also expressed desire to visit Colossae upon release (Philem. 22). Perhaps he also wished to visit the churches in the nearby cities of Laodicea and Hierapolis (Col. 2:1; 4:12-13). Goodwin calls these *"conjectural* travels" (176, emphasis original) in his harmony of the life of the Apostle Paul. But he adds regarding Paul's wish to revisit Philippi: "This seems to me the most probable of the conjectural travels of Paul" (177).

[282] Cf. the author's *The Pastoral Epistles for Pastors*, 18-19.

[283] See the alternating pattern of exhortation and example in 1:27-4:9 as evidenced in the exegetical outline of Appendix A.

perfectly good conscience before God up to this day." The word literally means to "live as a citizen."[284] In Hellenistic writings it means "*to conduct oneself as pledged to some law of life*"[285] or to "discharge your obligations as citizens."[286] Philippi had been granted the status of "colonia," which raised it to the status of a "mini-Rome,"[287] and thus the citizenry took their privileges and obligations as a matter of pride. As Paul wrote from Rome to Philippi, it was a natural word for him to employ. Indeed, during his first visit to Philippi, he had called upon his Roman citizenship personally and the city's standing as a Roman "colonia" when they arrested him (Acts 16:12, 37-38).[288] Perhaps the Apostle played upon all this in his choice of the word here. He certainly called upon it later in the letter, employing the cognate noun: "For our citizenship [τὸ πολίτευμα] is in heaven, from which also we eagerly wait for a Savior, the Lord Jesus Christ" (3:20). Paul seems to be intentionally selecting his vocabulary to call the believers away from their innate pride of Roman citizenship as first allegiance and to absolute allegiance to Christ and to citizenship in His Kingdom. There is a sense of obligation and accountability inherent in the word, and it fits the Apostle's need perfectly as he seeks to exhort them in the pathway of Christian discipleship. The present tense imperative calls for behavior that becomes an abiding pattern, a way of life.

Indeed, this way which lies before them is constricted and obligatory (Μόνον, "Only"), eliminating other options and narrowing the field of one's choices. When employed as an adverb, as it is here, it is "used to limit or separate an action or state to the one designated in the verb."[289] Paul is reducing the whole of the Christians' responsibility to one thing "Only." This one thing will serve as the rubric under which all else in 1:27-2:18

---

284 Friberg, 321.

285 Thayer, 528.

286 BDAG, 6035.3.

287 Rienecker, 548.

288 Lightfoot, 120.

289 Friberg, 266.

will fall.²⁹⁰ With this adverb, says Kennedy, Paul "gives the aim for which he wishes to remain alive."²⁹¹ And we should read this not simply with ἀξίως ("a manner worthy"), but with "the whole of the imperatival sentence as well."²⁹² Compare also the singularity with which Paul pursues Christ (Phil. 3:7-14) and to which also he calls the Philippian believers (3:15ff.).

Indeed, it is "in a manner worthy of the gospel of Christ" (ἀξίως τοῦ εὐαγγελίου τοῦ Χριστοῦ) that they must conduct themselves. The adverb (ἀξίως, "in a manner worthy"), when followed by the genitive, means "worthily" or "suitably."²⁹³ It depicts that which is "equivalent," as in that which would balance the scales.²⁹⁴ In the other five NT occurrences of the adverb it is followed by "of the saints" (Rom. 16:2), "of the calling with which you have been called" (Eph. 4:1), "of the Lord" (Col. 1:10), "of the God who calls you" (1 Thess. 2:12), and "of God" (3 John 1:6). How should we understand the genitive (τοῦ εὐαγγελίου τοῦ Χριστοῦ)? Müller suggests that it might be understood as both objective and subjective at the same time: "The gospel emanating from Christ is also the gospel concerning Christ. Christ is both author and content of the gospel."²⁹⁵ In any case the genitive clause ("of the gospel of Christ") is pictured as placed on one side of the scales and the lives of the Philippian believers placed on the other. Their obligation, then, is to so live that the scales balance. That is not to say that the believer's life can repay God's grace, but that it should be lived in light of and commensurate with the magnitude of the grace received from God.

This should happen "whether I come and see you or remain absent" (εἴτε ἐλθὼν καὶ ἰδὼν ὑμᾶς εἴτε ἀπὼν). For the third and last time in this letter Paul uses the combination formula εἴτε … εἴτε ("whether … or,"

---

290 O'Brien, 145-146.

291 Kennedy, 430.

292 O'Brien, 145.

293 BDAG, 780.

294 Rienecker, 530.

295 Müller, 68.

cf. vv.18, 20). It serves to introduce two competing possibilities. The first possibility is "I come and see you" (ἐλθὼν καὶ ἰδὼν ὑμᾶς). The two aorist participles contemplate the event of Paul arriving in person to visit the Philippian believers. The second possibility is "remain absent" (ἀπὼν). Paul now changes from the aorist to a present participle. The change in tense pictures the present reality (Paul being "absent" from the Philippians) continuing on without interruption.

Their living this way has a specific purpose ("so that"), as signaled by the use of ἵνα with the subjunctive verb (ἀκούω). The purpose of their living in light of the gospel is that the Apostle might receive (ἀκούω, "I will hear") a good report "of them" (τὰ περὶ ὑμῶν; lit., "the things concerning of you").

Paul wants to hear "that" (ὅτι)[296] they are living in unity: "you are standing firm in one spirit, with one mind striving together for the faith of the gospel" (στήκετε ἐν ἑνὶ πνεύματι, μιᾷ ψυχῇ συναθλοῦντες τῇ πίστει τοῦ εὐαγγελίου). The verb (στήκετε, "standing firm") can simply describe the act of physical standing (Mark 3:31; 11:25), but Paul, as he does here, is more likely to use it in the sense of standing firm or steadfast (1 Cor. 16:13; Gal. 5:1; Phil. 4:1; 1 Thess. 3:8; 2 Thess. 2:15).[297] Lohmeyer says, "The word indicates the determination of a soldier who does not budge one inch from his post."[298]

If this is to be accomplished together it must be "in one spirit" (ἐν ἑνὶ πνεύματι). Many want to see "spirit" (πνεύματι) as a reference to the Holy Spirit. Paul's reference in 2:1 to the "fellowship of the Spirit," might point this direction. Yet it probably is used here "in a general sense as unity of spirit and insight."[299] That they might find such unity among themselves could only be an achievement of the Holy Spirit, but—in the words of O'Brien—"in our judgment ἐν ἑνὶ πνεύματι is not an *explicit* reference to

---

296 The ὅτι clause is in apposition to τὰ περὶ ὑμῶν ("the things concerning you"), so that it might be rendered "the things concerning you, namely that ..." (NET Bible).

297 BDAG, 6823.2.

298 Quoted in Rienecker, 548.

299 Müller, 68.

the Holy Spirit."³⁰⁰ That this is how we should understand "spirit" is clear because it is matched with "soul" (ψυχῇ) in the next clause.³⁰¹ And again there, in this inward part of themselves, they must be "one" (μιᾷ). In just a moment, using this root in compound, Paul will appeal to them to be "united in spirit" (σύμψυχοι, 2:2; lit., "one soul").

Though this must become an inward reality, it will be seen outwardly as they are "striving together" (συναθλοῦντες). The word is used only here and in 4:3, where it is applied to two specific women in the church in Philippi. It is a compound made up of σύν ("with") and ἀθλέω ("to strive/compete" as in an athletic context, used only in the NT two times in 2 Tim. 2:5). The meaning, of course, is not that they should strive *against* one another, but *with* or alongside one another ("fighting together," NLT). And that for which they fight together is "the faith of the gospel" (τῇ πίστει τοῦ εὐαγγελίου). How should we understand the genitive (τοῦ εὐαγγελίου, "of the gospel")? It could be a genitive of apposition ("the faith that is the gospel"), or a genitive of source ("the faith that originates from the gospel") or an objective genitive ("faith in the gospel").³⁰² O'Brien calls it a genitive of origin ("the faith which is based on the gospel").³⁰³ The genitive of apposition seems the most probable—"the faith" which has been once for all delivered to the saints.

> **Ministry Maxim**
>
> There is no apologetic for the gospel more effective than unity among those who claim to believe it.

Whatever comes, with or without Paul, the Philippians must continue to let the gospel govern their lives and do so together as one in Christ.

---

300 O'Brien, 150; cf. Müller, 68.

301 Müller says, "The contrast between ψυχή and πνεῦμα (where they do not appear as synonyms, as is often the case) lies in the fact that ψυχή denotes more especially the inward feeling and will, the soul as the seat of desires and emotions, whereas with πνεῦμα the emphasis falls on the mind or spirit with its activities of thought and reflection," 68.

302 NET Bible.

303 O'Brien, 152.

Verse 28 – in no way alarmed by *your* opponents— which is a sign of destruction for them, but of salvation for you, and that *too*, from God.

Strangely, the coordinating conjunction (καὶ) is not translated by either the NASU or NASB (but cf. "and," ESV, KJV, NKJV, NET, RSV, NRSV). It serves to hold the previous participle (συναθλοῦντες, "striving together," v.27) and the one here in parallel relationship, both subordinate to the finite verb "standing firm" (στήκετε).

The participial phrase here is "in no way alarmed" (μὴ πτυρόμενοι ἐν μηδενὶ). The verb is used only here in the NT. It means simply to frighten or to scare, but in the passive as we have it here it means to "be frightened" or to "let oneself be intimidated."[304] Secular Greek usages from the time indicate that it may have been used especially of frightened horses.[305] Rienecker suggests that it may have been "an allusion to Cassius who at the battle of Philippi committed suicide at the fear of defeat."[306] The Philippian believers are not to allow this to happen to them. The Greek text contains two negations, the combination of which makes for a strengthened negative statement. It might literally be rendered "not [μὴ] being frightened in nothing [μηδενὶ]." The first, a particle, "denies the thought of the thing, or the thing according to the judgment, opinion, will, purpose, preference, of someone (hence, as we say technically, indirectly, hypothetically, subjectively)."[307] The second, an indefinite pronoun, broadens the frame of reference and makes the expression emphatic.[308] It thus means something like "in no way" or "in no respect."[309] The New English Bible renders it in powerful, picturesque language: "without so

---

304 BDAG, 6414.

305 Alford, 3:163; Rienecker, 548; Vincent, *Word Studies*, 3:428.

306 Rienecker, 548.

307 Thayer, 408.

308 Hellerman, 81.

309 BDAG, 4889.2.b.δ.

much as a tremor." The preposition (ἐν, "in") accompanying this indefinite pronoun specifies the sphere of their existence and non-intimidation.

Then Paul specifies those who might seek to intimidate: "by your opponents" (ὑπὸ τῶν ἀντικειμένων). We meet another participle, this one appearing with a definite article and used as a substantive. The verb is a compound made up of "against" (ἀντί) and "lay" (τίθημι). It means to be opposed or to be opposed to someone (Gal. 5:17; 1 Tim. 1:10).[310] It can also be used absolutely, as it is here, of an opponent or enemy (1 Cor. 16:9). It is used both of the antichrist (2 Thess. 2:14) and the devil (1 Tim. 5:14). The present tense pictures their continual opposition. The verb is deponent so the middle/passive form has an active meaning.[311] The preposition (ὑπὸ, "by") designates the "opponents" as the agents of such attempts at terror.

The question is, then, just who were these "opponents"? Were they Jewish[312] or pagan[313] or were they perhaps assailed from both sides?[314] Ultimately we may be unable to decide with absolute assurance.[315] Yet the stern opponents Paul faced while in Philippi were Gentiles (Acts 16:16-40) and he calls upon that experience here in verse 30. Historical evidence points to a very small Jewish population in Philippi, for it lacked even a synagogue. Though Paul warns of Judaizers (Phil. 3:2-4) it seems he speaks of a problem that might come to pass, rather than one which already exists. Thus we are justified in concluding that the "opponents" were probably pagan Gentiles, though opposition to the gospel from any front would qualify.

Paul now adds a powerful statement: "which is a sign of destruction for them" (ἥτις ἐστὶν αὐτοῖς ἔνδειξις ἀπωλείας). But the question is, to what does the relative pronoun (ἥτις, "which") refer? Just what is the "sign": the

---

310 Spicq, 1:128-130.
311 Greenlee, 75; Sumney, 37.
312 Hawthorne, WBC, 72; Martin, 87.
313 Comfort, 166; Kennedy, 431; Lenski, 755; O'Brien, 153; Wuest, 53.
314 Alford, 3:163-164; Kent, 11:119; Müller, 69; Vincent, ICC, 34.
315 Melick, 89; Müller, 69.

enemy's opposition or the believers' fearlessness in the face of that opposition? The relative pronoun's singular form does not match either the first participle (πτυρόμενοι, "alarmed") or the second (τῶν ἀντικειμένων, "opponents"), both of which are plural in form. The prepositional phrase (ἐν μηδενί, "in no way") is singular and it seems likely that the relative pronoun (ἥτις, "which") points to the fact that the believers are able to remain steady, unintimidated and fearless before those who oppose them.[316]

This fearlessness, says the Apostle, "is a sign of destruction for them" (ἐστὶν αὐτοῖς ἔνδειξις ἀπωλείας). The verb is present tense, emphasizing the enduring nature of the action. The plural personal pronoun (αὐτοῖς, "for them") clearly points to the "opponents." The dative form directs the action at those who oppose. Wallace classifies it as a dative of both reference and disadvantage, but with the emphasis on the latter.[317]

The noun ἔνδειξις ("a sign") is used four times in the NT, all by Paul (Rom. 3:25, 26; 2 Cor. 8:24; Phil. 1:28).[318] The word literally means "a pointing out" and was used in the legal world of "a writ of indictment."[319] It can, therefore, refer to evidence, a demonstration or proof of something. The other three NT usages tend toward that meaning, but here it has the sense of a "sign" or "omen."[320] Kennedy suggests that "It denotes proof obtained by an appeal to facts."[321]

This "sign" is one "of destruction" (ἀπωλείας) for those who oppose the believers. It is a strong word. The antichrist is called "the son of destruction" (ὁ υἱὸς τῆς ἀπωλείας, 2 Thess. 2:3). The same phrase is used to call Judas "the son of perdition" (ὁ υἱὸς τῆς ἀπωλείας, John 17:12). The word is used to speak of the destruction waiting down the broad path (Matt.

---

316 Vincent, ICC, 35; Robertson, *Paul's Joy in Christ*, 106.

317 Wallace, 143-144.

318 Though the cognate verb ἐνδείκνυμι ("show," "demonstrate") is used eleven times (Rom. 2:15; 9:17, 22; 2 Cor. 8:24; Eph. 2:7; 1 Tim. 1:16; 2 Tim. 4:14; Tit. 2:10; 3:2; Heb. 6:10, 11) and the related noun ἔνδειγμα is used once ("a plain indication," 2 Thess. 1:5).

319 Vincent, *Word Studies*, 3:427.

320 BDAG, 2601.1.

321 Kennedy, 431.

7:13). It pictures the lot of those who go to hell (Rev. 17:8, 11). Peter used the word five times in rapid succession in his description of false prophets, speaking of both the current destructiveness of their ways and teaching (2 Peter 2:1) and of the eschatological judgment awaiting them (2 Peter 2:1, 3; 3:7, 16). Thayer says the word describes "the destruction which consists in the loss of eternal life."[322] The genitive form is probably a subjective genitive, the fearlessness of the Philippian believers will be the sign which points toward the destruction of their opponents.

> **Ministry Maxim**
>
> A believer's faithfulness in persecution is a sign that points in two directions: one for the persecutor and one for the persecuted.

This opposition, which serves as a sign pointing to the opponents' destruction, is at the same time another kind of sign for the believers: "but of salvation for you" (ὑμῶν δὲ σωτηρίας). The conjunction (δὲ) is clearly used as an adversative ("but") to contrast the role the sign plays in the case of the believers. The plural personal pronoun (ὑμῶν, "for you") points to all the believers who make up the Philippian church. The noun "salvation" (σωτηρίας) was already used in verse 19 (cf. also 2:12) where it was translated "deliverance." It is the opposite of the "destruction" (ἔνδειξις) of which he has just spoken. O'Brien says, "The point is not that the adversaries themselves see this ... but that it seals their doom as the enemies of the gospel and confirms the eternal salvation of the faithful who endure to the end."[323]

We should note the shift and contrast between the dative (αὐτοῖς, "for them") and the genitive (ὑμῶν, "for you"). We might render it that this destruction is *to them* and the salvation is *of you*. "The dative accents what will happen *to the enemies* ... while the genitive accents what the believers will *possess* (and, in fact, *do already* possess, as v. 29 makes

---

322 Thayer, 71.

323 O'Brien, 155.

clear)."³²⁴ Wallace says, "… the enemies of the gospel do not possess their destruction, but are the unfortunate recipients of it; but believers do possess their salvation."³²⁵

Paul adds (καὶ, "and") one additional thought: "that from God" (τοῦτο ἀπὸ θεοῦ). The demonstrative pronoun "that" (τοῦτο) could refer to one of four referents: the "sign,"³²⁶ the "destruction," the "salvation" or the entire preceding statement.³²⁷ It seems the latter is the more likely. But whichever way, be it "sign," "destruction," "salvation" or all of the above, we know that they arise entirely "from God" (ἀπὸ θεοῦ).³²⁸ Lightfoot sees here an allusion to the sign from the crowds in the amphitheater during the gladiatorial contests. The thumbs up meant life; the thumbs down meant death. But "The Christian gladiator does not anxiously await the signal of life or death from the fickle crowd. The great Gladiator himself has given him a sure token of deliverance."³²⁹

Digging Deeper:

1. Go through this day and every circumstance, encounter, event, and decision it contains asking one question: "What does/can/should the gospel look like here?" (v.27a)
2. If unity is one of the greatest apologetics for the gospel, what then is the effect of disunity? (v.27b)
3. How does understanding the sign-nature of persecution help overcome the fear it seeks to impose? (v.28)

---

324 NET Bible; cf. Lenski, 756.

325 Wallace, 143-144.

326 Lightfoot, 120; Robertson, *Paul's Joy in Christ*, 106; Wuest, 53.

327 Lenski, 757; Vincent, ICC, 35.

328 "ἀπὸ θεοῦ is always used by Paul with reference to God's gracious working" (O'Brien, 157).

329 Lightfoot, 120-121.

Verse 29 – For to you it has been granted for Christ's sake, not only to believe in Him, but also to suffer for His sake,

Paul now continues this lengthy sentence (begun in v.27 and not ending until v.30) by expanding upon what he meant by "from God" (ἀπὸ θεοῦ) in verse 28, particularly in regards to "salvation."[330] He makes the connection by way of the subordinating conjunction ὅτι ("For"). It introduces a fuller explanation of what "from God" means.

It is "from God" that something "has been granted" (ἐχαρίσθη). The word emphasizes that the action is undertaken "freely as a favor" or is "graciously" given.[331] It is used in 2:9 of the Father bestowing upon Christ "the name which is above every name." Paul uses the same verb to describe the act of forgiveness (2 Cor. 2:7, 10; 12:13; Eph. 4:32; Col. 2:13; 3:13). He uses it to describe the gracious act of God's giving in response to prayer (Philem. 22) and in all we shall inherit in Christ (1 Cor. 2:12; Rom. 8:32). It describes God's giving of the covenant to Abraham (Gal. 3:18). The aorist tense looks back upon a definite event: "The aorist points to the original bestowment of the gift."[332] The passive voice means that another (in this case, God) has acted upon the Philippian believers in this giving.[333] God has thus, graciously and freely given us, as we shall discover momentarily, the grace to believe and the gift of suffering for His sake! And it is "to you" (ὑμῖν) this gift has been directed, the plural form pointing to all the believers in Philippi. The personal pronoun is thrust forward for emphasis,[334] underscoring the remarkable and unmerited nature of the divine bestowal (perhaps with the sense: "to you, *you* yourself, you of all people!").

While believers are the object of this divine bestowal, the believer is not the goal of giving. That which has been given to them is "for Christ's sake" (τὸ ὑπὲρ Χριστοῦ). The preposition is used to denote "the moving

---

330 O'Brien, 158.

331 BDAG, 7893.1.

332 Vincent, ICC, 36.

333 Sumney, 37-38.

334 Hellerman, 84; Vincent, ICC, 35.

cause or reason" for God's giving.[335] The preposition is notably tucked between the noun and its definite article. The definite article turns this entire prepositional phrase into a substantive, indicating the subject of the verb "has been granted" (ἐχαρίσθη).[336] The result is difficult to render in English. Lenski likens it to a "precious jewel" which is "God's dearest gift to them, which is engraved: IN BEHALF OF CHRIST."[337]

Two articular infinitives follow and are in apposition to this phrase, explaining just what it is that has been granted "for Christ's sake."[338] In each case another prepositional phrase is tucked between the article and the infinitive, bringing further clarity to Paul's intentions. Wallace provides this literal translation: "**the** on-behalf-of-Christ thing has been given to you, namely, not only **the** believing in his name, but also **the** suffering for him."[339]

That which has been "granted for Christ's sake" is now identified more specifically through the two infinitive clauses. As Robertson says, "the two infinitives following, each with τὸ, explain the first τὸ."[340] These two infinitive clauses are framed by the formula "not only … but also" (οὐ μόνον … ἀλλὰ καὶ). The contrast is stark and bold. Perish the thought that one would think that what was given was only "to believe"! No, it is also "to suffer"!

That which is "granted for Christ's sake" is first of all "to believe in Him" (τὸ εἰς αὐτὸν πιστεύειν). The infinitive is accompanied by the definitive article (τὸ … πιστεύειν). The present tense underscores the ongoing nature of the trusting faith. As already noted, the prepositional phrase is placed between the infinitive and its definite article: "in Him" (εἰς αὐτὸν). The preposition conveys not only believing "in" Christ, but perhaps more pointedly "into" Christ. Paul rarely combines this verb and the preposition

---

335 BDAG, 7538.2.

336 Sumney, 38.

337 Lenski, 758.

338 Wallace, 236, 607.

339 Ibid., 236, emphasis original.

340 Robertson, *Grammar*, 777.

(cf. Rom. 10:14; Gal. 2:16), but John finds joy in doing so (John 2:11; 3:16, 18; 4:39; 6:40; 7:5, 31, 39, 48; 8:30; 9:36; 10:42; 11:45, 48; 12:37, 42). Kennedy calls it "The deepest aspect of faith, the intimate union into which the soul is brought."[341] The opportunity, inclination, ability, and act of believing in Christ are a gift from God (cf. Eph. 2:8-9).

The second thing which is granted for Christ's sake" is "to suffer for His sake" (τὸ ὑπὲρ αὐτοῦ πάσχειν). Once again the infinitive is accompanied by the definite article (τὸ ... πάσχειν). And once again the present tense underscores the ongoing nature of the action—for the believer suffering is not an occasional experience, but an abiding way of life in this world. Until we reach heaven faith and suffering will always lie side by side and extend together into the far horizon of our earthly experience. As with faith, so with suffering—the opportunity, inclination, ability, and act of suffering with and for Christ are a gift from God's hand.

Such suffering is not only from His hand, but is "for His sake" (ὑπὲρ αὐτοῦ). While both infinitives are held in coordinate relationship by καὶ ("and") Paul's emphasis is upon the latter: "to suffer." This is clear in that he repeats "for His sake" (ὑπὲρ αὐτοῦ) here. See our comments just above concerning the meaning of the preposition. This is the preposition that is also used to speak of Christ's substitutionary, vicarious sufferings and death in our place (Rom. 5:6-7; Gal. 2:20; 1 Pet. 3:18). In this sense Paul may intend to say that Christ suffered and died in our place to secure our salvation, and now we as His body are given the gift of suffering in His place (not in an atoning sense, which He alone can accomplish on our behalf and in our place) as we take the message of His salvation to the world.[342] This seems to be what Paul had in mind in Colossians 1:24: "Now I rejoice in my sufferings for your sake,

> **Ministry Maxim**
>
> Believing in and suffering for Christ are both gifts straight from God's hand— we can take credit for neither.

---

341 Kennedy, 432.

342 Wuest, 54.

and in my flesh I do my share on behalf of His body, which is the church, in filling up what is lacking in Christ's afflictions" (cf. 1 Pet. 2:21). Certainly Christ's sufferings lacked nothing in regards to saving power, but He did not personally preach the gospel to all creation. He has charged us with that task and it is a task which must of necessity require suffering. "That you suffer with Christ proves your union with him, and your union with Christ insures your salvation."[343] Soon enough Paul will say that he wants to "know Him and the power of His resurrection and the fellowship of His sufferings, being conformed to His death" (Phil. 3:10; cf. Rom. 8:17; 2 Thess. 1:5; 2 Tim. 2:12).

Verse 30 – experiencing the same conflict which you saw in me, and now hear *to be* in me.

Paul moves now to close the sentence that has extended from verse 27. The participle (ἔχοντες, "experiencing") means more simply, "having." The present tense indicates that the Philippian believers were in current, immediate possession of this gift of suffering. The participle may be used instrumentally[344] or, more likely, adverbially to point to the manner in which they "suffer."[345]

That which they thus possess is "the same conflict" (τὸν αὐτὸν ἀγῶνα). The noun is used only six times in the NT, five of those by Paul (Phil. 1:30; Col. 2:1; 1 Thess. 2:2; 1 Tim. 6:12; 2 Tim. 4:7; Heb. 12:1). Our word *agony* arose from this root. The noun can speak of an athletic contest such as a race (Heb. 12:1), but more often, as it does here, it speaks of a conflict, struggle, or fight for the gospel (Phil. 1:30; Col. 2:1; 1 Thess. 2:2).[346] O'Brien says, "It involves untiring toil and labour, an intense wres-

---

343 Vincent, ICC, 35.
344 NET Bible.
345 Hellerman, 87.
346 BDAG, 101.2.

tling and struggle for the spread, growth, and strengthening of the faith as the goal of his mission."[347]

This which the Philippian believers now experience is not unprecedented, for it is the "same" (αὐτὸν) as that which they observed in the Apostle himself. The adjective in the attributive position stresses the qualitative nature of the "conflict," it is a shared kind of experience. Paul has modeled this for them. They saw in his experience a prototype of their own. The singular form of the noun (ἀγῶνα, "conflict") indicates that whatever the differences in their individual circumstances and sufferings, it is just one, singular, common "conflict" in which they share. The details may change, the locations differ, the times be separate, but as one in Christ and serving together in the advance of the same gospel they share in a common "conflict" and agony. "These two sets of circumstances, separated in time and by distance, are part of the one apostolic ἀγών for the gospel."[348]

> **Ministry Maxim**
>
> Persecution is both something you are in and something that is in you.

The relative pronoun οἷον ("which") means "of what sort" or "such as." It is used of that which is "similar to something else in some respect."[349] It stresses the qualitative nature of the comparison. The precise details of their suffering may not be just like Paul's but it is qualitatively the same in that they are both suffering for Christ.

Two verbal clauses are now held in coordinate relationship by καὶ ("and"). The first is "you saw in me" (εἴδετε ἐν ἐμοὶ). The Philippian believers were eyewitnesses to Paul's sufferings when he was among them (Acts 16:16-40; cf. 1 Thess. 2:2 where he also uses ἀγών). He and Silas had been physically "seized" and "dragged" into the public marketplace (v.19). They were falsely accused before the magistrates (vv.20-21). They were the victims of mob violence (v.22), being stripped and beaten.

---

347 O'Brien, 161.

348 Ibid., 162.

349 Louw-Nida, 64.1.

They were "severely flogged" and were thrown in prison (v.23). In the deepest belly of the prison they were secured in the stocks. After a miraculous earthquake opened the prison, they led the jailer and his family to faith in Christ (vv.25-34). They were deprived of due process when the leaders simply wanted to release them (vv.35-37). In all this the Philippian believers watched on and took note.

Not only in the past had they seen the circumstances in which Paul suffered and the conflict that raged within him, but in the present they hear of the same (through Epaphroditus, cf. 2:25). The second verbal clause is "now hear to be in me" (νῦν ἀκούετε ἐν ἐμοί). The former was historical ("you saw," aorist tense); this is present (νῦν, "now"). The former was visual (εἴδετε, "saw"); this is auditory (ἀκούετε, "hear"). While the timing and the external conditions of each experience may have changed, the internal "conflict" was the same. In both clauses the preposition ἐν ("in") is used to describe the sphere of the "conflict." The twice repeated prepositional phrase ἐν ἐμοί ("in me") reminds me that it is not the struggle I am "in" which defines me as much as the struggle that is "in me." One believer may face the unjust recriminations of a violent government crackdown on Christians. Another may be afflicted by the more subtle pressures of a pagan culture which wars on his soul. The "conflict" they are "in" is different, but the "conflict" that is "in" them is the same.

Digging Deeper:

1. If both faith *in* and suffering *for* Christ are gifts from God, how are they similar and how are they different? (v.29)
2. What are the interrelationships of Christ dying in my place (for gospel-atonement) and me suffering in His place (for gospel-advancement)? (v.29)
3. In what way is suffering both something you are "in" and something that is "in" you? (v.30)

PHILIPPIANS 2

Verse 1 – Therefore if there is any encouragement in Christ, if there is any consolation of love, if there is any fellowship of the Spirit, if any affection and compassion,

What flows now from the pen of the Apostle Paul and runs through verse 11 makes up one of the most sublime pieces of literature the world has ever known. The elegance and flow, the pacing and phraseology combine with the exalted and rich nature of the subject to not only capture the heart with its beauty, but to move the will in worship of the One whose name is above every name (v.9).

The sentence begun here runs through verse 4. The present verse is comprised of four conditional clauses, all assumed to be true.[1] They move along, one after another, setting up the imperative of verse 2 ("make my joy complete"). Each contains the indefinite adjective τις ("any," or in one case the neuter τι) which serve to broaden the scope of that which is under consideration. In each case the verb is absent from the Greek text, but to be understood by the readers ("is"). Paul leads the way with the inferential conjunction (οὖν, "Therefore"), indicating he is preparing logical ground by which to move the Philippians to the action indicated in

---

1   They might in that regard be rendered "Since ..." or "If, as is obviously the case, ..."

the imperative to come in verse 2.[2] The inference is back to 1:27 and the banner-like heading for this entire section: "Only conduct yourselves in a manner worthy of the gospel of Christ." The Apostle followed that immediately with a summons to unity ("standing firm in one spirit, with one mind striving together for the faith of the gospel") and now he returns to that call here (vv.2-4). What follows here are descriptions of four "supernatural, objective realities."[3] These are not hoped-for qualities, but "objective realities" which the Philippian believers would recognize as authentic in their Christian experience. Life in Christ is more than an idea, a philosophy, a worldview or a rationale—we do not misspeak when we talk of our Christian *experience*. Christ, by His indwelling life, brings us into actual life-change. It is these demonstrable realities that Paul uses now as leverage to call the believers in Philippi to unity.

The first conditional statement is "if there is any encouragement in Christ" (Εἴ τις ... παράκλησις ἐν Χριστῷ). The noun παράκλησις ("encouragement") is cognate to the more frequently used verb παρακαλέω (used twice in 4:2). It is a compound word meaning "to call" (καλέω) "alongside" (παρά). The noun has a range of meaning that spans from comfort (2 Cor. 1:3; Philem. 7) to admonition (Rom. 12:8; 1 Tim. 4:13). The majority of commentators appear to lean toward understanding it as "exhortation" in this case. Yet there seems to be good reason to see it as tending here toward the softer side of "comfort" or "consolation," which is the most frequent way Paul uses the word.[4] O'Brien well says "παράκλησις ἐν Χριστῷ [encouragement in Christ] is the first ground of Paul's exhortation, not the exhortation itself."[5] This "comfort" is found "in Christ" (ἐν Χριστῷ), that is to say, in union with Him.

---

2 The conjunction οὖν is oddly placed, being the third word in the sentence rather than the second. This is because of the formulaic Εἴ τις, which, as O'Brien says, "was considered to be one word" (174).

3 O'Brien, 167.

4 Ibid., 170.

5 Ibid.

The second conditional statement is "if there is any consolation of love" (εἴ τι παραμύθιον ἀγάπης). The noun "consolation" (παραμύθιον) is found only here in the NT. It is a compound word in which the preposition (παρά) may have the force of "aside," as in "the converse which draws the mind aside from care."[6] The cognate verb is found four times in the NT (John 11:19, 31; 1 Thess. 2:12; 5:14) and a cognate feminine noun is found in 1 Corinthians 14:3. Our noun designates "that which causes or constitutes the basis for consolation and encouragement."[7] In this case that which does the persuading is "love" (ἀγάπης). The genitive is subjective, pointing to the love of Christ which brings consolation to their hearts.[8] Love is the reasoned argument that brings the soul "consolation" in its discouragements and fears.

The third conditional statement is "if there is any fellowship of the Spirit" (εἴ τις κοινωνία πνεύματος). Broadly speaking, the noun "fellowship" (κοινωνία) is used in three ways in the NT: *participation* (association by shared *experience*; 1 Cor. 10:16; Phil. 1:5; 2:1; 3:10), *fellowship* (association by shared *life*; 1 Cor. 1:9; 2 Cor. 6:14; 13:14 [13]; Gal. 2:9), and *giving* (association by shared *goods*, i.e. a gift/contribution; Rom. 15:26; 2 Cor. 8:14; 9:13), though the line of demarcation between the first two is not always easily drawn.[9] In this case it is further defined as "of the Spirit" (πνεύματος). Should we understand this as a reference to the person of the Holy Spirit (as most English translations do) or to a more general, communal reality (as in 1:27)? And just how should we understand the genitive? It could be understood as a subjective genitive—the fellowship which the Spirit brings ("Any

> **Ministry Maxim**
>
> Christ is true apart from our experience, but if we experience no life-change we might question the truth of our relationship to Him.

---

6   Rienecker, 549.
7   Louw-Nida, 25.154.
8   O'Brien, 172.
9   TDNT, 3:798, 804-809.

fellowship together in the Spirit," NLT or "any fellowship in the Spirit," NET). Or it could be an objective genitive—the fellowship we have with the Spirit Himself ("if any fellowship with the Spirit," HCSB, NIV). Or it could be understood as an attributive genitive—"spiritual fellowship." Most English translations treat it as referring to the Holy Spirit, and this seems best given the parallel to "Christ" in this verse and the similarities with 2 Corinthians 13:13. The call between the objective and subjective genitive is a difficult one. Again the parallel with "in Christ" seems to tip the scales in favor of the objective genitive: "fellowship with the Spirit" (HCSB, NIV). The Apostle took it as a commonplace that there was some demonstrable, experiential reality to their "fellowship with the Spirit" to which his words connected in their consciousness.

The fourth conditional statement is "if any affection and compassion" (εἴ τις σπλάγχνα καὶ οἰκτιρμοί).[10] The noun σπλάγχνα ("affection") was already used in 1:8. It refers literally to the "*bowels, intestines* (the heart, lungs, liver, etc.)."[11] In the ancient world these were considered the seat of the emotions. To the Greek poets they were the center of "the more violent passions, such as anger and love, but by the Hebrews as the seat of the tenderer affections, especially kindness, benevolence, compassion."[12] Paired with (καὶ, "and") this is οἰκτιρμοί ("compassion"). It is described as "a motivating emotion" such as pity, compassion, mercy, etc.[13] Paul uses the word only four times. God is the "Father of mercies" (2 Cor. 1:3) and in view of "the mercies of God" we are to offer ourselves as living sacrifices (Rom. 12:1).[14] As those chosen by God we are to "put on" that which characterizes our Father (Col. 3:12). There the two nouns

---

[10] There is some debate as to the text. Is it τις σπλάγχνα (as we have it here)? Or is it τίνα σπλάγχνα? The former has the weightier manuscript evidence behind it, but the "form is irregular and difficult to explain" (Müller, 73).

[11] Thayer, 584.

[12] Ibid.

[13] Friberg, 279.

[14] In the LXX this word is used 23 of 26 times to designate God's mercies. Thus it seems likely that it is so used here, without losing the assumption that what is true of God is to become true of those who know Him (O'Brien, 175).

are paired together and rendered as "a heart of compassion." In the present case Vincent says the former "is the organ or seat of compassionate emotion" while the latter "are the emotions themselves."[15]

Verse 2—make my joy complete by being of the same mind, maintaining the same love, united in spirit, intent on one purpose.

Having set before us the four conditional clauses of verse 1, Paul comes now to the single imperative to which they lead: "make my joy complete" (πληρώσατέ μου τὴν χαρὰν). The verb is a common one, being used some eighty-six times in the NT. It generally conveys the notion of making full or filling up completely.[16] Here the aorist imperative conveys urgency and demands the action be taken immediately. The fact that it is to be made "complete" implies that the Apostle already found joy in these believers (1:4; 4:1). This is his way of urging them forward to completion in the area of unity (1:27). That which is to thus be filled up or completed is the Apostle's (μου, "my") "joy" (τὴν χαρὰν). We have already met this noun in 1:4 and 25 (χαρά: 1:4, 25; 2:2, 29; 4:1; cf. also χαίρω: 1:18 [2x], 2:17, 18, 28; 3:1; 4:4 [2x], 10; συγχαίρω: 2:17, 18). Paul is convinced he will remain alive "for your ... joy in the faith" (1:25). Here he asks the Philippian believers to fill up the measure of his own joy. Clearly Paul envisions Christian relationships which produce a reciprocating mutuality in joy.

The first clause is "being of the same mind" (τὸ αὐτὸ φρονῆτε). The verb appears twenty-six times in the NT, of which twenty-three are by Paul. Of those twenty-three usages ten of them appear here in Philippians, more than any other NT book (1:7; 2:2 [2x], 5; 3:15 [2x], 19; 4:2, 10 [2x]). This demonstrates a significant emphasis upon the mind throughout the book. The verb means "to have an opinion with regard to someth[ing]"; to

---

15 Vincent, ICC, 54; cf. Lightfoot, 122; Robertson, *Paul's Joy in Christ*, 114.

16 Friberg, 317.

"think, form/hold an opinion" or to "judge."[17] Thus is seems to speak not merely of individual thoughts, but of "a certain way of looking at things, thus 'mindset.'"[18] Might we say, worldview? The desired mindset/worldview will be more fully unfolded (vv.6-11) after Paul uses the verb again in verse 5.[19] Paul's frequent use of the word underscores the significance he places upon the Christian mind. The present tense looks for action that is abiding, continual, or habitual. The subjunctive mood with the ἵνα normally forms a final clause, but in this case is not used to indicate purpose.[20] Rather it is used epexegetically in relationship to the "joy" which Paul calls upon them to complete.[21] That is to say it specifies just what fulfilling Paul's joy would consist of (i.e., "being of the same mind"). This is supported by the translation "by" (NASB; cf. ESV, NET, NIV, NLT). This would mean that the clauses that follow (through verse 4) show how the Philippian believers are to accomplish this (including utilizing four participles of means).[22] These clauses describe more fully what making Paul's joy complete looks like.

The articular personal pronoun (τὸ αὐτὸ) is rendered "the same." Being singular it emphasizes the singularity and commonality of that which they are thus to think together. Since the verb will be repeated in verse 5 in ordering, "Have this attitude [φρονῆτε] in yourselves which was also in Christ Jesus," the "mind" or "attitude" they each have is to be set to that which Christ had. Christ is the tuning fork and as each mind is set to His thinking, they will together have "the same mind."

The second clause is "maintaining the same love" (τὴν αὐτὴν ἀγάπην ἔχοντες). Paul has just directed their minds and hearts to the love Christ has for them (v.1). His great love becomes the fount from which they love one another. "We love, because He first loved us" (1 John 4:19). The

---

17 BDAG, 7819.1.

18 Fee, 185.

19 Ibid.

20 Robertson, *Grammar*, 992.

21 NET Bible; O'Brien, 177; Sumney, 41; Wallace, 476.

22 Wallace, 628-630.

pronoun is repeated from the previous clause, but it now serves as an intensifying adjective (αὐτὴν, "same").[23] Being in the attributive position it emphasizes the qualitative nature of the love demanded. And as in the previous clause, we ask again: Does the comparative inference of "same" (αὐτὴν) correspond to Christ or to one another within the Body of Christ? That is to say, by "same" does Paul intend Christ's love for the believers (v.1) or does he mean that the "same" love as is found in one believer ought to be found in the others around him? Since unity is the theme, Paul probably has in mind loving one another without distinction; loving one another the "same," without variance according to external standards or inward bias. This, however, will only happen as they take up the love Christ demonstrates toward them (v.1); "the love of God [which] has been poured out within our hearts through the Holy Spirit" (Rom. 5:5). This love we are to be "maintaining" (ἔχοντες), or, more literally, "having." The present tense underscores the continual maintenance Paul has in mind here. The participle describes the means by which the Philippian believers are to have "the same mind."

> **Ministry Maxim**
>
> True unity comes from looking at Christ, not at one another.

This "maintaining the same love" is the first of four participles (running through verse 4) which indicate the means by which the desired unity is achieved. To these four can also be added the next clause, which, though it is missing the participle, takes the tally up to five means by which unity is achieved in the local church.

The second mark of true unity that produces joy is communicated through a single word σύμψυχοι ("united in spirit"). Some want to connect this to the final clause (e.g., "working together with one mind and purpose," NLT).[24] However, this seems best taken as an independent thought.[25] This masculine plural adjective is used only here in the NT. It is

---

23 Wallace, 349-350.

24 Fee, 183; Müller, 74.

25 O'Brien, 178.

a compound made up of σύν ("with") and ψυχή ("soul") and might literally be rendered "fellow souled."[26] It describes "total agreement in attitude."[27] It is variously translated as "united in spirit" (NASU, NASB, NET), "one in spirit" (NIV), "in full accord" (ESV, NRSV, RSV), "of one accord" (KJV, NKJV), and "sharing the same feelings" (HCSB). With their thoughts and affections (first two clauses) calibrated to the mind and heart of Christ, they will enjoy a true likeness of soul with one another. Though the word is used only here in the NT, note that Paul does use two other compounds formed from the root ψυχή elsewhere in this chapter (εὐψυχέω, 2:19 and ἰσόψυχος, 2:20) as well as the noun itself (1:27; 2:30).[28] Sumney observes, "By using these various compounds of ψυχή, formed with prefixes that relate to togetherness, good will, and equality, Paul is seeking to emphasize the unity to which he is calling the Philippians."[29]

The third means of unity is to be "intent on one purpose" (τὸ ἓν φρονοῦντες). Paul again uses the verb just employed earlier in this verse (see comments there) and will use it again in verse 5. It is in the present tense underscoring again the continual nature of the mindset being enjoined. Again, the participle is used to describe means. Whereas the opening clause called for being of the "same" (τὸ αὐτὸ) mind, here they are called upon to think "one" (τὸ ἓν) thing. The former clause is the more general expression; this is the stronger and more specific.

O'Brien suggests that the four clauses found in verse 2 may in fact form a chiasmus of sorts:

A   "being of the same mind" (τὸ αὐτὸ φρονῆτε)
    B   "maintaining the same love" (τὴν αὐτὴν ἀγάπην ἔχοντες)
    B¹ "united in spirit" (σύμψυχοι)
A¹ "intent on one purpose" (τὸ ἓν φρονοῦντες).[30]

---

26 Ibid.
27 Friberg, 363.
28 O'Brien, 178-179.
29 Sumney, 41.
30 O'Brien, 165, 177, 179.

In this the first and fourth emphasize the world of the mind, while the second and third draw in the world of feeling.[31]

> **Digging Deeper:**
> 1. What demonstrable, experiential evidence is there that you enjoy the "fellowship of the Spirit"? (v.1)
> 2. In what sense is the completeness of your joy dependent upon the behavior of others? Who are they? What must they do? (v.2a)
> 3. Using the text of verses 1 and 2 explain to someone precisely how unity is evidenced within the body of Christ.

Verse 3 – Do nothing from selfishness or empty conceit, but with humility of mind regard one another as more important than yourselves;

There is a way a Christian should think (φρονῆτε, being "of … mind," v.2) and a way he should not think. Paul first presents a negative way of thinking which is to be shunned: "Do nothing from selfishness or empty conceit" (μηδὲν κατ' ἐριθείαν μηδὲ κατὰ κενοδοξίαν). The repeated preposition (κατ' … κατὰ, "from") is used as a "marker of norm of similarity or homogeneity" of something and in this case "to indicate the nature, kind, peculiarity or characteristics of a thing."[32] Or, as Lenski well states it, "nothing … that smells of" selfishness is acceptable among God's people.[33] The repeated negation (μηδὲν … μηδὲ, "nothing … or") makes absolute the nullification and indicates that the first half of the lesson comes by way of a strong prohibition. The imperative "Do" is added by the translators. Yet the whole of the verse (as with verse 2b and 4 as well) is subordinate to the finite verb φρονῆτε ("being of the same mind") in

---

31 Fee, 185.
32 BDAG, 3938.5.b.β..
33 Lenski, 766.

verse 2, with this third verse forming the fourth means of unity. Thus the idea is stronger than "Do nothing." It is "Don't even *think* any thoughts motivated by selfish ambition."[34]

That which is to be thus shunned is, first, "selfishness" (ἐριθείαν). The word was already used in 1:17 to describe the ill motives of some preachers of the gospel who "proclaim Christ out of selfish ambition [ἐριθείας]." Surely there is no accident that the Apostle takes up the noun again here. The noun comes "from ἐριθεύω (*serve for hire*), which is from ἔριθος (*day-laborer*)" and thus denotes "an attitude of self-seeking *selfish ambition, self-interest, rivalry*."[35] Rienecker explains that "A hired worker was looked down upon because his laboring was wholly for his own interest."[36] He further said that it stood for "the ambition which has no conception of service and whose only aims are profit and power."[37] The noun appears only seven times in the NT, five of those in Paul (Rom. 2:8; 2 Cor. 12:20; Gal. 5:20; Phil. 1:17; 2:3; James 3:14, 16).

This is paired with "empty conceit" (κενοδοξίαν). The word appears only here in the NT. It is a compound word comprised of κενός ("empty") and δόξα ("glory"). The latter is used extensively in Philippians (1:11; 2:11; 3:19, 21; 4:19, 20). Tracing these out and comparing what they tell us of true glory will set this "empty glory" in its proper place. The lexicons variously describe it as "*vain-glory, groundless self-esteem, empty pride,*"[38] "empty conceit, vain pride, (groundless) boasting,"[39] "vanity, conceit,

---

34 "There is no main verb in this verse; the subjunctive φρονῆτε (*phronēte*, 'be of the same mind') is implied here as well. Thus, although most translations supply the verb 'do' at the beginning of v. 3 (e.g., 'do nothing from selfish ambition'), the idea is even stronger than that: 'Don't even *think* any thoughts motivated by selfish ambition.'" (NET Bible; cf. also Alford, 3:165; Lenski, 766; Müller, 75; Robertson, *Paul's Joy in Christ*, 118; Vincent, 55; O'Brien says, "Although this is possible, it is unnecessary," 179)

35 Friberg, 172.

36 Rienecker, 546.

37 Ibid., 549.

38 Thayer, 343.

39 Friberg, 228.

excessive ambition,"[40] and "a state of pride which is without basis or justification – 'empty pride, cheap pride, vain pride.'"[41] The emphasis seems to be not only pride, but *baseless* pride. Robertson says, "The Jewish element had the pride of privilege, the Gentile element the pride of culture."[42] Both were in error and missed the way of Christ.

The first word describes one obsessed with what he may gain, the second a person who is impressed with what he (wrongly) thinks he already possesses. Moody says, "Strife is knocking another down—vainglory is setting oneself up."[43] The first may describe "partisan pride," the second personal egotism.[44]

There is, in contrast to this, a different, Christ-like kind of thinking (cf. vv.5-8). This we must pursue at all costs. Paul sets it over against what he has just described by means of the strong adversative ἀλλὰ ("but").

The verb (ἡγούμενοι, "regard") means to think, consider or regard.[45] It denotes "a belief resting not on one's inner feeling or sentiment, but on the due consideration of external grounds, the weighing and comparing, of facts."[46] It is thus "the deliberate estimate and preference of others, not a momentary impulse of politeness."[47] The present tense presents the action as continual or habitual. The verb is deponent, thus the middle voice form has an active meaning. The participle, with the two that came before in verse 2 and the one that follows in verse 4, designates the means by which they are to be "of the same mind." Paul uses the verb

> **Ministry Maxim**
>
> Interpersonal unity begins with an intrapersonal peace accord.

---

40 BDAG, 4189.1.
41 Louw-Nida, 88.221.
42 Robertson, *Paul's Joy in Christ*, 118.
43 Quoted in Robertson, *Paul's Joy in Christ*, 119.
44 Robertson, *Paul's Joy in Christ*, 118.
45 BDAG, 3410.2.
46 Thayer, 276.
47 Robertson, *Paul's Joy in Christ*, 120.

eleven times in his writings, six of those here in Philippians (2:3, 6, 25; 3:7, 8 [2x]). Significantly, Paul uses it to refer to Christ's inward reckoning when he "did not regard [ἡγήσατο] equality with God a thing to be grasped" (2:6). Also significantly, he uses it three times to describe his own inward reckoning regarding his own self-righteousness (3:7-8).

This must be done "with humility of mind" (τῇ ταπεινοφροσύνῃ). The noun is made emphatic by its position.[48] Though the word does not occur in the OT, as O'Brien has shown, ταπεινός does, and in abundance.[49] The non-Christian world used the present word negatively, but with the coming of Christ the word was transformed.[50] Jesus called out, "Take My yoke upon you and learn from Me, for I am gentle and humble [ταπεινός] in heart" (Matt. 11:29a). Robertson can thus say, "It is the crowning social grace and is Christian in origin and spirit."[51] Paul uses the word five times (Eph. 4:2; Phil. 2:3; Col. 2:18, 23; 3:12). It is generally used in a positive sense, as it is here, to describe "a quality of voluntary submission and unselfishness *humility, self-effacement.*"[52] But it can also be used in a pejorative sense, meaning "a misdirected submission in cultic behavior *self-abasement, (false) humility, self-mortification.*"[53] In those cases it described the misguided practices taught by the false teacher(s) at work in Colossae (Col. 2:18, 23). But clearly in this case Paul has in view the possibility of a right, godly, Spirit-produced practice of humility. Vincent says, "The virtue itself is founded in a correct estimate of actual littleness conjoined with a sense of sinfulness. It regards man not only with reference to God, but also with reference to his fellow men, as here."[54] Bockmuehl adds, "The biblical view of humility is precisely *not* feigned or groveling, nor a

---

48 Lenski, 766.

49 See Bockmuehl (110-111) and O'Brien (180-181) for helpful discussion of the OT background of this word.

50 Note the cognate verb used of Christ in Phil. 2:8: "He humbled [ἐταπείνωσεν] Himself"

51 Robertson, *Paul's Joy in Christ*, 120.

52 Friberg, 375.

53 Ibid.

54 Vincent, ICC, 56.

sanctimonious or pathetic lack of self-esteem, but rather a mark of moral strength and integrity. It involves an unadorned acknowledgement of one's own creaturely inadequacies, and entrusting one's fortunes to God rather than to one's own abilities or resources."[55] The dative form may be causal—giving the ground from which such thinking is undertaken[56] or it may indicate manner (i.e., "in humility")[57] or means.[58] The definite article "probably denotes the virtue considered abstractly or generically," though it could be considered possessive ("*your* lowliness") or as "the *due* lowliness" each one should show.[59]

The last verb (ὑπερέχοντας, "as more important than") is found only five times in the NT, four of those by Paul and three of those here in Philippians (Rom. 13:1; Phil. 2:3; 3:8; 4:7). The verb is a compound comprised of ὑπέρ ("over/above") and ἔχω ("to have/hold"). He uses the verb in this letter to describe "knowing Christ" as of "surpassing value" (3:8) and the peace of God as that which "surpasses all comprehension" (4:7). Here the present tense describes continual, habitual action. Such regard for others is to be the standing order of the day for a Christian's thinking toward others.

But how can this be? Perhaps you are certain that in some area you surpass another in knowledge or skill. Are you simply to pretend that the other is better than you at this particular thing? Lenski helpfully explains that what God demands is not that we pretend the facts are other than they are, but that we determine that all others in all situations are "deserving first attention from us."[60] We purposefully think of them before we think of ourselves.

---

55 Bockmuehl, 110.

56 Alford, 3:165; O'Brien, 181.

57 O'Brien, 181.

58 Lenski, 766-767.

59 Vincent, ICC, 56; cf. Lenski, 766 and O'Brien, 181.

60 Lenski, 767.

Note also how Paul combines the reciprocal and reflexive pronouns.[61] The reciprocating pronoun (ἀλλήλους, "one another") indicates "an interchange between two or more groups."[62] There is a correct way of thinking ("regard") not only about "one another," but in active relationship with one another. Such thinking is like the information flowing up and down a fiber optics line—moving actively in both directions, back and forth from one end to the other in constant motion. As such it is never simply one sided, but "live," in motion, and moving back and forth between the parties under consideration. This is interpersonal action. The reflexive pronoun (ἑαυτῶν, "yourselves"), on the other hand, indicates that the subject participates in the verbal action.[63] This is inward, self-directed action. It is not interpersonal action (as with the reciprocating pronoun), but intrapersonal—action taken upon oneself. The emphasis then is something like this: consider the back-and-forth relationships with others as more significant than simply what you think and reason and feel about and within yourself. The plural forms indicate that this needs not only to be applied individually by each Christian, but collectively in the groups within which they gather themselves. There may have been within the church in Philippi a jostling to take sides in the conflict between the two women called out by name in 4:2. Each believer must practice this thinking and encourage their fellow believers to do the same.

James reminds us that interpersonal conflict begins with an intrapersonal conflict: "What is the source of quarrels and conflicts among you? Is not the source your pleasures that wage war in your members?" (James 4:1). Just so the decision for interpersonal unity and harmony begins with an intrapersonal peace accord—I have signed on the dotted line in a contract with myself that I will regard you as better than myself. Another way of saying this is that relationships ("one another") matter more than ego, pride, and self-esteem ("yourselves").

---

61 Robertson says that the reflexive can be used in a reciprocal sense, though he contends that here in Philippians 2:3 "each word retains its own idea." (Robertson, *Grammar*, 690). O'Brien adds that ἀλλήλους "is used precisely and distinctly from ἑαυτῶν." (O'Brien, 182).

62 Wallace, 351.

63 Ibid., 350.

Verse 4 – do not *merely* look out for your own personal interests, but also for the interests of others.

As Paul now moves to close the sentence he began in verse 1, he does so by way of a vivid and emphatic contrast: "do not [μὴ] … but [ἀλλὰ]." On one side of the contrast is "look out for your own personal interests" (τὰ ἑαυτῶν ἕκαστος σκοποῦντες). The verb (σκοποῦντες, "look out for") is used only six times in the New Testament, five of those by Paul (Luke 11:35; Rom. 16:17; 2 Cor. 4:18; Gal. 6:1; Phil. 2:4; 3:17). It means "to pay careful attention to" or "look out" for or "take notice" of,[64] with the sense of "care for, have regard to" something.[65] The present tense calls for a constant vigilance. The participle is the fourth and serves to introduce the last of

> **Ministry Maxim**
>
> Personal responsibility for other-centeredness is a basic essential of corporate Christian experience.

the five means by which the Philippians are to be "of the same mind" (vv.2-4).[66] At the same time it seems to carry some imperatival force.[67] That which is to be carefully discerned can be positive (Phil. 3:17) or negative (Rom. 16:17). The action can be directed at others (Rom. 16:17; Phil. 3:17) or at one's self (Luke 11:35; Gal. 6:1). Here is it "your own personal interests" (τὰ ἑαυτῶν ἕκαστος) that are in view. The plural definite article stands alone and is used as a substantive, rendered "interests." The reflexive pronoun (ἑαυτῶν, "personal") indicates the subject is also the object of the action. The action prohibited is one taken upon oneself and thus basically selfish in orientation. The plural reflexive pronoun (ἑαυτῶν) is paired with the singular adjective (ἕκαστος, "your own"). For unselfishness to characterize the collective relationships of Christ's people the prohibition must be personally and individually embraced by each

---

64 BDAG, 6715.
65 Thayer, 579.
66 Wallace, 628-630.
67 Sumney, 43; Robertson, *Paul's Joy in Christ*, 121.

one. Such thinking would stand in contrast to "they all seek their own interests, not those of Jesus Christ" (Phil. 2:21). "Let no one seek his own good, but that of his neighbor" (1 Cor. 10:24; cf. v.33). Love "does not seek its own" (1 Cor. 13:5).

On the other side of the stark contrast ("but," ἀλλὰ) is care "for the interests of others" (τὰ ἑτέρων ἕκαστοι). No verb exists in this half of the phrase but the influence of the participle from the first half of the contrast (σκοποῦντες, "look out for") continues to direct the action. Many western texts have dropped the καὶ ("also"), but there seems to be strong external support for its inclusion and the overall majority of manuscripts include it.[68] Alford says, "The καὶ shews that the first is to be taken with some allowance, for by our very nature, each man must" give some heed to his own concerns.[69] This likely motivated the translators of the NASU to add "merely" in the first line.

In contrast to ones "own personal interests" it is now "the interests of others" that are in view. As in the first half of the verse the plural definite article stands alone and is used as a substantive, rendered as before "the interests." Continuing the contrast the singular (ἕκαστος, "your own") has now become plural (ἕκαστοι, untranslated in NASU and most modern English translations, but contrast "every man" in KJV). This is the only example of this adjective in the plural in the New Testament.[70] Instead of a singular focus upon yourself (ἕκαστος, "your own"), your eyes should be set upon the multitude "of others" (ἑτέρων) whom God has set around you. Paul could easily have used ἄλλων ("one another"), but he chose ἕτερος because it includes people of another class, those who are distinctively different than you are.[71]

Momentarily Paul will explain why he is sending Timothy to them, it is because others "seek after their own interests, not those of Christ Jesus" (v.21). So we see that Paul is laying foundational principles (what

---

68   NET Bible.
69   Alford, 3:166; cf. O'Brien, 185, Vincent, ICC, 56.
70   Robertson, *Grammar*, 292
71   Robertson, *Paul's Joy in Christ*, 121.

Fee calls a "miniature expression of the heart of Pauline ethics"[72]) which he will next illustrate, supremely through Jesus Christ (vv.5-11) and then through Timothy (vv.19-24) and Epaphroditus (vv.25-30).

Paul has now identified by use of four participles of means just how God's people are to be "of the same mind" (v.2a). This happens by "having the same love" (v.2b), being "intent on one purpose" (v.2d), "with humility of mind regard[ing] one another as more important than yourselves (v.3), and looking out "for the interests of others" (v.4). To this the orphaned "united in spirit" (v.2c) can be added.

> **Digging Deeper:**
> 1. Do you think it is possible to actually live so as to "Do nothing from selfishness"? (v.3a)
> 2. In the immediacy of your personal relationships as they currently are configured, what does it mean for you to "regard one another as more important than" yourself? (v.3b)
> 3. If total self-forgetfulness is not the point ("not *merely* ... but also"), where is the line dividing appropriate self-concern and sinful selfishness? (v.4)

Verse 5 – Have this attitude in yourselves which was also in Christ Jesus,

Having laid the foundation of their personal and collective experience in Christ (2:1) and then called the believers to unified (v.2), unselfish living (vv.3-4), the Apostle now illustrates what he has called for from the believers. He begins with the supreme illustration of selfless, humble love, Jesus Christ Himself. (vv.5-11). He will then follow later with the examples of two of Christ's disciples, Timothy (vv. 19-24) and Epaphroditus (vv.25-30), before turning to his own pattern of life (3:4-17).

---

72 Fee, 191.

The sentence Paul begins here runs through verse 8. It describes the self-embraced humiliation of Christ and the sentence that follows (vv.9-11) describe the exaltation that was His reward for his self-demotion through incarnation, earthly life, and death on our behalf. The mysteries explored, the pattern of selflessness exposed, the beauty of expression employed all make the exploration of these verses holy ground. Let us take off our shoes and tread reverently, earnestly, lightly. Yet the sheer volume of literature produced over these verses can be almost numbing in its effect. If one begins to digest even a bit of the vast volume of literature on this passage it quickly becomes overwhelming. One feels simply overcome and soon realizes the rose's beauty can easily be lost in the dissection of its petals. God help us to search deeply, but to do so with ever-worshipful hearts.

Much discussion centers on the nature of the material: Is it poetry? A preexisting hymn? Pauline? Adapted from another by Paul? If so, to what degree has he adapted the material? What was the purpose of the original? What was Paul's purpose in taking it up here? These are not unimportant questions, but given the sheer volume of words already spent on these matters, I believe it suffices to say that whatever else it may or may not have been, whether Paul was using existing material or writing it himself at the time of this letter's composition, Paul was under the inspiration of the Holy Spirit as he wrote. If he was using something already in existence, he was, by using it, endorsing it as fully his own and in accord with the truth as it is in Christ Jesus. It is beautiful purely for its literary qualities, which bear the marks of a poetic hand. But its real beauty is in the truth that it portrays, which shines beyond even the beauty of how that is stated.

Paul opens by commanding, "Have this attitude" (Τοῦτο φρονεῖτε).[73] The present active imperative demands that action be taken repeatedly or habitually.[74] It might literally be rendered "This think!" The verb is used twenty-six times in the NT, twenty-three of those by Paul. Of those twenty-three usages, ten of them are found here in the short letter to the

---

73 Some manuscripts include γὰρ, but the oldest manuscripts do not support its inclusion.

74 Some manuscripts have the passive singular (φρονείσθω) at this point, but the evidence is in support of the plural active as we have it here (φρονεῖτε).

Philippians (1:7; 2:2 [2x], 5; 3:15 [2x], 19; 4:2, 10 [2x]). Paul places a disproportionate emphasis upon the mind of the believer in this letter.

> **Ministry Maxim**
>
> That which goes on in the individual mind is the foundation of society, so no thought is a purely private matter.

The word describes the realm of the mind: to think, to have an attitude, to form an opinion. It means, "to develop an attitude based on careful thought"[75] and thus "signifies the general mental attitude or disposition."[76] This conveys not just the individual thoughts a believer is to entertain, but *how* they think and reason through life, relationships, temptations, and opportunities. We must aim for more than control of our individual *thoughts*, but the development of a Christian *mind*. We pursue "the mind of Christ" (1 Cor. 2:16), "the mind of the Lord" (Rom. 11:34).

That to which "this" (Τοῦτο) points has been a matter of some debate. It could point backward to the exhortations just issued (vv.2-4) or it could point forward to the example of Christ about to be recounted (vv.6ff).[77] In the other two occasions in this letter when Paul uses this demonstrative pronoun and verb (1:7; 3:15), the demonstrative pronoun refers to what has gone before.[78] It would seem, therefore, that he uses it in the same way here. This is underscored by the fact that the verb in this verse ("Have ... attitude," φρονεῖτε) has already appeared twice ("the same mind [τὸ αὐτὸ φρονῆτε]" and "one purpose [τὸ ἓν φρονοῦντες]," v.2).[79] The reference, then, is to the exhortations to unselfishness and humility which have been issued (vv.3-4). But this will immediately be reinforced and vividly portrayed for the readers through the depictions of Christ's example as the foundation for the exhortations. This verse, in fact, serves as

---

75 BDAG, 7819.3

76 Vincent, ICC, 57.

77 Sumney, 44.

78 O'Brien, 204.

79 Ibid.

a transitional mechanism—looking back to the exhortations that have come before (vv.2-4) and preparing the reader for what is about to be recounted regarding Christ (vv.6-11).

This attitude is to be "in yourselves" (ἐν ὑμῖν). The preposition can describe the sphere in which something exists or transpires, but here, because of the plural form of the personal pronoun (ὑμῖν, "yourselves"), it seems likely to communicate the idea of "among" (NASU margin, ESV, RSV).[80] Paul is speaking not just to the individual believers in Philippi, but to all of them collectively as the people of God. He is demanding a collective way of thinking (and thus of valuing and relating), not merely an individual's personal thoughts. Of course each believer must adopt this mindset if the whole of the believing body is to embrace it as their functional mindset or attitude. It might be rendered "in your community (of faith and love)" or "in your common life."[81]

It is an attitude "which was also in Christ Jesus" (ὃ καὶ ἐν Χριστῷ Ἰησοῦ). The relative pronoun (ὃ, "which") agrees in gender (neuter) and number (singular) with the preceding demonstrative pronoun (Τοῦτο, "this"). There is no verb in this clause. The question becomes which verb, if any, is to be understood here. Many conclude (as have the translators of the NASU) it is most natural to include something like "was" (or "is," ESV, RSV).[82] Others believe it most natural to read the verb from the parallel and previous line: "think."[83] Still others deem there is no need to read a verb into the text because the point is that the thinking we are to take up is that which was first (καὶ, "also") found in our Lord.[84] Perhaps Lenski is right in saying that the verb we supply "makes little difference, for we can in no way stress what is absent in Greek."[85]

---

80 Ibid., 205.

81 Rienecker, 550.

82 E.g., Fee, 200; Sumeny, 45; Wuest, 61.

83 E.g., Kennedy, 434; Robertson, *Paul's Joy in Christ*, 122-123; Silva, 96.

84 O'Brien, 205.

85 Lenski, 771.

The prepositional phrase (ἐν Χριστῷ Ἰησοῦ, "in Christ Jesus") would be most naturally understood as describing sphere—the One in whom this mindset is first and perfectly displayed. But in view of the way the same preposition has just been used (ἐν ὑμῖν, "in [among] yourselves") it is possible that it conveys something like: "have the same thoughts among yourselves as you have in your communion with Christ Jesus."[86] This would be "… rather than simply seeing Jesus' own attitude as a model for us to follow."[87] It seems more clearly, however, to refer to the thinking that was found "in Christ Jesus,"[88] which, of course, then is to be replicated in the community life and thinking of His people. Jesus' own pattern of thought and way of reasoning is the pattern to which we seek to conform our thinking. Some object to this on the grounds that the two ἐν clauses must be read in the same way in the same context.[89] While in general terms this is sound hermeneutically, one should not make a principle into a master that rules every text inviolably.[90]

Verse 6 – who, although He existed in the form of God, did not regard equality with God a thing to be grasped,

The sentence continues as the relative pronoun ὅς ("who") picks up upon Χριστῷ Ἰησοῦ ("Christ Jesus") from verse 5, agreeing in gender and number with its antecedent. So Paul now sets out to unfold the mysteries of the thinking that was "in Christ Jesus" (v.5) and which then must become the pattern of our individual thinking and community relations. Christ's thinking is set forth in the negative here in verse 6 (that is to say, a way of thinking He shunned) and positively in verses 7 and 8 (the way of thinking He embraced).

---

86 BDAG, 7819.3.
87 NIDNTT: Abridged, 593.
88 Sumney, 45; O'Brien, 205.
89 Vincent, 57; cf. Lenski, 770.
90 Fee, 200; cf. Sumney, 45.

There was a way of thinking that Christ "did not regard" (οὐχ ... ἡγήσατο). The verb is the same one just used in verse 3 to describe how believers are to think of "one another." The cast of such social-spiritual relations finds its die in the thinking of Jesus. Paul will use the verb four more times in this letter, all to describe his own way of reckoning relationally (2:25) and personally (3:7, 8 [2x]). It means "to engage in an intellectual process" and thus to *think, consider, regard*."[91] It denotes "a belief resting not on one's inner feeling or sentiment, but on the due consideration of external grounds, the weighing and comparing, of facts."[92] The negation (οὐχ) denies the matter "absolutely, categorically, directly, objectively."[93] Paul speaks in definitive terms regarding Christ's repudiation of the kind of thinking under consideration here.

That which was thus repudiated in Christ's thoughts had to do with His "equality with God" (τὸ εἶναι ἴσα θεῷ). Most literally it might be rendered "the to be equal with God." The adjective (ἴσα, "equality") is used only here in the NT epistles. It is used five times in the Gospels (Matt. 20:12; Mark 14:56, 59; Luke 6:34; John 5:18) and once each in Acts (11:17) and Revelation (21:16). It is found thirty-three times in the LXX. Generally speaking it pertains to "being equivalent in number, size, quality."[94] The Jewish leaders, hearing Jesus call God His Father, concluded that He was "making himself equal [ἴσον] with God" (John 5:18). When in the neuter plural, as it is here, it is often used as an adverb. So the entire infinitive phrase can be rendered "equality."[95]

Functioning, then, as an adverb it modifies the action of the verb (εἶναι, "to be"). In simplistic form, the statement "he ran" may be modified by the addition of the adverb "quickly." "He ran quickly" adds the manner in which the running took place. "He ran slowly" leaves the action unchanged (he still "ran"), but the manner has changed. It might be said

---

91 BDAG, 3410.2, emphasis original.
92 Thayer, 276.
93 Thayer, 408.
94 BDAG, 3744.
95 Robertson, *Word Pictures*, 4:444; Sumney, 46.

that adverbs describe the manner in which the action is manifested. Thus the fact is that, prior to His incarnation, Christ was eternally preexisting "in the form of God" (ἐν μορφῇ θεοῦ). Prior to His incarnation He did so before the eyes of all the beings of heaven manifestly in "equality with God" (τὸ εἶναι ἴσα θεῷ). He might at the incarnation change the manner in which He manifested Himself (v.7). He eternally, preexistently and rightly manifested Himself in "equality with God" (v.6), but at the incarnation, having taken on also "the form of a bond-servant" (μορφὴν δούλου), He manifested Himself to the world in humility (v.7). He was no longer openly and manifestly utilizing and demonstrating all the fullness of His deity in the same manner as He had previously, but the fact of His full divinity remained unchanged.

We need also to determine the function of the definite article (τὸ) and the infinitive (εἶναι). Wright has argued attractively[96] for viewing the definite article as anaphoric (the use of an expression the understanding of which depends upon another expression in the context), pointing back to the substantive which has already been mentioned, in this case, "existed in the form of God" (ἐν μορφῇ θεοῦ ὑπάρχων). Wallace, on the other hand, believes that the definite article simply and most naturally serves to mark the infinitive as the object of the verb.[97] It seems simply and most obviously to be roughly synonymous[98] with what Paul meant by "existing in the form of God" (for which see our comments below). The infinitive (εἶναι) is in the present tense, speaking of an ongoing reality. Alford said that His "equality with God" is "no mere new thing" which Christ refused to grasp after, "but His state already existing."[99] The Son's equality with God the Father is eternal and this current expression points to His preexistent standing with and relationship to the Father.

---

96 N.T. Wright, "ἁρπαγμός and the Meaning of Philippians 2:5-11," *JTS*, NS 37 [1986] 344.

97 Wallace, 220, 635; cf. Robertson, *Grammar*, 1059.

98 "... not in the sense that the two phrases are identical, but that both point to the same reality. Together, therefore, they are among the strongest expressions of Christ's deity in the NT." (Fee, 207-208).

99 Alford, 3:167.

There has been much discussion around and ink spilled over just what Paul had in mind when he used the noun ἁρπαγμὸν. It is tucked between the negation (οὐχ, "not") and verb (ἡγήσατο, "regard"). Being anarthrous the noun is generalized, emphasizing not a specific thing, but the quality of that which is described. Being masculine in gender and singular in number it agrees with ὅς ("who") which in turn agrees with Χριστῷ Ἰησοῦ ("Christ Jesus," v.5). In the accusative case, it is part of a double accusative along with the definite article (τὸ, already considered above).

Just what does Paul mean by ἁρπαγμὸν ("a thing to be grasped")? Arriving at an answer is complicated by the fact that the word is rare, found only here in the NT, being non-existent in the LXX, and found only rarely in Greek literature generally. The noun arose from the verb ἁρπάζω, which described "snatching" or "seizing," often with a sense of violence or suddenness.[100] This understanding, however, "is next to impossible"[101] in the present verse which is due to a lack of object.[102]

The noun may have either an active sense (emphasizing the verbal idea from which it arose; i.e., "robbing") or a passive sense (in which case it serves more purely as a noun by pointing to something concrete and thus referring to a thing gained).[103]

The various possibilities of meaning have classically been broken down into three options.[104] The first emphasizes "holding fast to someth[ing] already obtained."[105] The second, "the appropriation to oneself of someth[ing] that is sought after."[106] These first two would emphasize the verbal idea inherent in the noun. The third possibility sees it as "something

---

100 Fee, 205.

101 BDAG, 1122.1.

102 TDNT, 1:474.

103 Rienecker, 550.

104 Fee, 206; cf. Comfort, 169; Vincent, 3:432; TDNT, 1:473-474.

105 BDAG, 1122.2a.

106 Ibid.

to be clung onto."¹⁰⁷ This would view the noun in a more static fashion, as referring to a thing to be grasped rather than the action of grasping.

How do we evaluate these possibilities? Clearly the second is impossible since Christ already possessed a divine nature and equality with God. The first likewise appears out of the question since Jesus never "obtained" equality with God, but had eternally existed in that state. That leaves number three as our remaining possibility. This could then also be understood in two ways: "He did not regard equality with God as a gain, either in the sense of something not to be let slip, or in the sense of something not to be left unutilised."¹⁰⁸ Of these two options the former would seem to locate the matter in time and space¹⁰⁹ (i.e., something accomplished during Jesus' earthly life), but the entire context seems to speak of a state existing before time. This seems to be confirmed by the fact that "nouns ending in *–mos* do not ordinarily refer to a concrete expression of the verbal idea in the noun but to the verbal idea itself."¹¹⁰ The sense here then is seen "as not forcefully retaining something for one's own advantage."¹¹¹ It is not something to be held on to or seen as a bit of good fortune to be exploited.¹¹² The point is that "Christ did not use His equality w[ith] God in order to snatch or gain power and dominion."¹¹³

As Moule put it, equality with God did not mean "grasping," but "giving away."¹¹⁴ MacLeod says, "He did not regard His divine prerogatives as something to use for His own advantage" and "Christ saw Godlikeness essentially as giving Himself. Being equal with God did not mean taking

---

107 Fee, 206.
108 TDNT, 1:474.
109 Ibid.
110 Fee, 206.
111 Friberg, 75.
112 Ibid.
113 Rienecker, 550.
114 Moule, 272, quoted by Fee, 206.

everything to Himself, but just the opposite—giving everything away."[115] Similarly, Wright says, "The preexistent Son regarded equality with God not as excusing Him from the task of (redemptive) suffering and death, but actually as uniquely qualifying Him for that vocation."[116]

The noun (μορφῇ, "form") is used again in the next verse (μορφὴν δούλου, "the form of a bond-servant") and then only one other time in the NT (in the disputed passage of Mark 16:12). Given such a limited usage, its occurrence in verse 7 must influence our understanding of it here. Of note also is the use of σχῆμα in the next verse as well[117] ("Being found in appearance [σχήματι] as a man"). In this last regard it should be noted that σχῆμα ("appearance") denotes "that which appeals to the senses and which is changeable" while μορφή ("form") "is identified with *the essence* of a person or thing."[118] The σχῆμα ("appearance") "may change without affecting the" μορφή ("form").[119]

O'Brien nicely summarizes the various interpretations of μορφή under five categories.[120] First, there is the view that it derived its meaning from Greek philosophy, with special emphasis upon Aristotle's usage. Lightfoot, for example, saw this as conveying Christ's "essential nature and character of God." Little evidence has surfaced, however, to demonstrate that Paul used the word in this philosophical sense.[121] Second, μορφή was equated with God's glory

> **Ministry Maxim**
>
> I cannot cling to all that is rightly mine and still be fully His.

---

115 David J. MacLeod, "Imitating the Incarnation of Christ: An Exposition of Philippians 2:5-8," *Bibliotheca Sacra* 158 (July-September 2001), 316.

116 N.T. Wright, "ἁρπαγμός and the Meaning of Philippians 2:5-11," *Journal of Theological Studies* 37 (1986), 345.

117 There is a differentiation in verse divisions in the Greek text and that of the English text; the phrase appears at the end of verse 7 in the Greek text and at the beginning of verse 8 in the NASU.

118 Vincent, *Word Studies*, 3:430-431.

119 Ibid.

120 O'Brien, 207-210.

121 TDNT, 4:752.; O'Brien, 207.

(δόξα).¹²² However, finding clear examples of the two words being used as synonyms has been difficult.¹²³ Third, μορφή has been equated with εἰκών ("image"). This views Paul's entire statement (vv.6-11) under the rubric of a contrast between Adam and Christ.¹²⁴ There is, however, nothing in the context to suggest that Paul has any such contrast in mind. Fourth, is the view that μορφή must be viewed through its usages in other existing Greek literature which includes the worldview of Hellenistic religious dualism. Paul is seen, then, as speaking against "the Gnostic myth of the 'heavenly Man', whose position was equal with God."¹²⁵ Again, there is insufficient internal evidence that Paul is addressing such a problem in the church of Philippi. Fifth, is the view that μορφή refers to a "condition" or "status" and is thus "referring to Christ's original position vis-à-vis God."¹²⁶ This view suffers, however, from a lack of evidence for such an understanding in Greek literature.¹²⁷

What then is our conclusion as to the meaning of μορφή here in verse 6? Clearly it does not point to physical form, for "God is spirit" (John 4:24) and has no essential physical form. Then too we must admit the English word "form" is inadequate to convey the concept in Paul's mind, though we have no other word that would serve better.¹²⁸ The Greek noun (μορφή) "always signifies a form which truly and fully expresses the being which underlies it."¹²⁹ It refers to the "outward display of the inner reality or substance" of a thing.¹³⁰ Fee says regarding its appearance here and in the next verse, "*Morphē* was precisely the right word for this dual usage, to

---

122 TDNT, 4:751.

123 O'Brien, 208-209.

124 Ibid., 209.

125 Ibid.

126 Ibid., 210.

127 Ibid.

128 Fee, 204; Vincent, ICC, 57.

129 Moulton and Milligan, *Vocabulary of the Greek New Testament*, 417.

130 Rienecker, 550.

characterize both the reality (his being God) and the metaphor (his taking on the role of a slave), since it denotes 'form' or 'shape' not in terms of the external features by which something is recognized, but of those characteristics and qualities that are essential to it. Hence it means *that which truly characterizes a given reality.*"[131]

Does this not draw us near to option two above in our effort to describe the indescribable? While μορφή and δόξα may not be synonyms, is not the outshining of God's inner reality always perceived as "glory"?[132] Does this approach what Jesus had in mind when He prayed, "Now, Father, glorify Me together with Yourself, with the glory which I had with You before the world was" (John 17:5)? Is this what is meant by Jesus being "the radiance of His glory and the exact representation of His nature" (Heb. 1:3)? It would seem that we are nearing the borders beyond which human intelligence cannot pass and from which we can only peer in worshipful wonder at the glorious Triune God.

It was thus "in the form of God" (ἐν μορφῇ θεοῦ) that Christ "existed" (ὑπάρχων). The present tense participle points to Christ's preexistent state, to the abiding nature of the preexistent Christ. It stands, in this regard, in contrast (along with εἶναι) to the aorist tenses that surround it.[133] From verse 6 through 8 there are nine verbal forms; seven of them are aorist and only these two are in the present tense. Clearly when Paul speaks of Christ's being, he pictures it as an ongoing, pre-temporal matter. The Son was eternally, continually, without interruption and in an ongoing state of being fully divine.

Just how should we understand the participle to function? Many translate it as introducing a concession: "although He existed in the form of God" (NASU, NASB; cf. ESV, NET, NLT, RSV, NRSV).[134] This would view Christ's action as being taken in contradistinction to His divine nature. Others argue for translating the participle as indicating cause:

---

131 Fee, 204, emphasis original.

132 O'Brien, 210-211; Rienecker, 550.

133 Hendriksen, 103.

134 Melick, 100; Wallace, 634-635.

"because He was God."¹³⁵ This marks Christ's action as arising out of His divine nature. Perhaps the best view is to read the participle as simply the "fact as a link in the logical chain, 'subsisting as He did;' without fixing the character of that link as a causal or concessive."¹³⁶ Thus the NIV: "*being* in very nature God"; and also the KJV: "*being* in the form of God" (emphases added).

The meaning of the verb itself has also been a matter of debate. It is a compound word, being made up of ὑπό ("under") and ἀρχή ("beginning"). The etymology of the word woodenly can be rendered "under the beginning" and it stressed "the original state of affairs."¹³⁷ This notion "of continuity with a previous state" did fade in the later Greek writings¹³⁸ and in Hellenistic Greek literature it became roughly synonymous with εἶναι, but here may retain the notion of "'be inherently (so)' or 'be really'."¹³⁹ Moulton and Milligan concede that "the meaning 'being originally' ... cannot be pressed" here, but then they quickly add, "though the thought is probably present."¹⁴⁰ It at least "suggests Christ's preexistence prior to his incarnation."¹⁴¹ So, whether or not it can be proven by the time element in this one word, the point Paul is making is that Christ eternally preexisted in a fully divine nature and shared alike with the Father and Spirit in the full embrace of divinity. As Alford says, "Less cannot be implied in this word than eternal pre-existence."¹⁴²

The ancient sage declared, "... humility goes before honor" (Prov. 18:12b). He "in whom are hidden all the treasures of wisdom and knowledge" (Col. 2:3) demonstrated this by stepping out of eternity and into time, taking to Himself a human nature and a human body in order to

---

135 Comfort, 168; Hawthorne, WBC, 85; O'Brien, 214.

136 Alford, 3:166.

137 Melick, 100.

138 Moulton and Milligan, 650.

139 BDAG, 7525.2.

140 Moulton and Milligan, 650.

141 NIDNTT: Abridged, 377.

142 Alford, 3:166.

redeem us. "For you know the grace of our Lord Jesus Christ, that though He was rich, yet for your sake He became poor, so that you through His poverty might become rich" (2 Cor. 8:9).

Verse 7 – but emptied Himself, taking the form of a bond-servant, *and* being made in the likeness of men.

In stark and dramatic contrast (ἀλλὰ, "but") to the thought of Christ using His eternal, preexistent deity for selfish ends (v.6), He took action that is described by two finite verbs, one here (ἑαυτὸν ἐκένωσεν, "emptied himself") and the other in verse 8 (ἐταπείνωσεν ἑαυτὸν, "humbled Himself"). These two verbs and the clauses they represent are held in a parallel relationship with one another by καὶ. Then together they are held in a parallel, but contrasting relationship (via the οὐχ ... ἀλλὰ formula, "not ... but") with "regard" (v.6). The thinking Christ turned away from (v.6) is set in contrast to the actual action He took (vv.7-8). All three verbs are aorist active indicatives. In fact the two finite verbs and four participles of verses 7 and 8 are all in the aorist tense and stand in contrast to the present tense ὑπάρχων ("He existed," v.6). The actions Christ took to humble Himself that He might come and save us (vv.7-8) stand in contrast to what one might expect from One who was eternally preexisting deity in "the form of God" (v.6).

The meaning of the verb "emptied" (ἐκένωσεν) has been a matter of great debate. It is used only twice in the LXX (Jer. 14:2; 15:9) and in the NT only five times, all by Paul (Rom. 4:14; 1 Cor. 1:17; 9:15; 2 Cor. 9:3; Phil. 2:7). The literal sense of the word is clear enough, to "remove the content of something."[143] However, it is not used literally in the Scriptures, but figuratively. In the other NT usages it means "to cause to be without result or effect."[144] But here it describes "taking away the prerogatives of status or position,"[145] "eliminating all privileges or prerogatives associated

---

143 Friberg, 228.

144 BDAG, 4194.2.

145 Friberg, 228.

with" a certain status.¹⁴⁶ Clearly Christ did not empty Himself of His essential deity, but "gave up *the appearance* of his divinity and took the form of a slave."¹⁴⁷ "He emptied Himself of *the display* of His deity for personal gain."¹⁴⁸ Christ did not insist on the continuing manifestation of His "equality with God" (τὸ εἶναι ἴσα θεῷ). The context tells us that this was action taken by the preexistent Christ, rather than descriptive of His incarnate state. Some have argued for the latter, viewing the action as the process of "the outpouring of himself in life and also on the cross" rather than the act of the preexistent Christ.¹⁴⁹ This, however, would appear to go against what the context clearly indicates—that we are speaking of the very act of becoming incarnate, which of course then assumes the life of humility and even death that followed.

Paul used the reflexive pronoun "Himself" (ἑαυτὸν). This stresses that the subject is also the object of the verb's action.¹⁵⁰ Christ took this action knowing He would be the one who would experience the consequences in Himself. By His own gracious choice the consequences came upon Himself, the benefits upon us. The emphatic position of the pronoun "points to the humiliation of our Lord as *voluntary, self-imposed*."¹⁵¹

He did not give up "equality with God," but chose not to make it the way He made Himself known to the world. How He showed Himself to the world is explained by the clauses that follow.¹⁵² Let us confine our thoughts to these actual words of Scripture rather than chasing down speculative philosophical and theological possibilities.

This main verb (ἐκένωσεν, "emptied") is modified by two aorist participles: "taking" (λαβών) and "being made" (γενόμενος). The first participle, "taking the form of a bond-servant" (μορφὴν δούλου λαβών), is

---

146 Louw-Nida, 87.70.

147 BDAG, 4194.1.b. (emphasis added).

148 Riencecker, 550 (emphasis added).

149 NIDNTT, 1:548-49.

150 Wallace, 350-351.

151 Lightfoot, 125.

152 Vincent, ICC, 59.

explanatory of the main verb ("emptied")[153] and the time is simultaneous with that of the main verb.[154] This provides us "the *method in which*"[155] or the means by which He emptied Himself.[156] Though perhaps a bit counterintuitive, we discover that the emptying consisted of "taking," not divesting. It was an emptying by addition, not subtraction. The aorist tense describes an act rather than a process. That which was thus taken was "the form of a bond-servant" (μορφὴν δούλου). And this in direct contrast to "the form of God" (μορφῇ θεοῦ, v.6) in which He had eternally preexisted. It is of note that it is nowhere said that Christ put off "the form of God" in order to take "the form of a bond-servant." Rather the emptying consisted precisely in taking to Himself this "form of a bond-servant."[157] The eternally divine, preexistent Son of God who forever had "existed in the form of God" took to Himself a fully human nature and body. He thus was fully divine and fully human, the true God-man. For the word "form" (μορφὴν) see the discussion on verse 6. It refers to the "outward display of the inner reality or substance" of a thing.[158] As the beings of heaven had discerned the eternal Son of God "in the form of God," so in His incarnation all creation looked upon Christ and saw "the form of a bond-servant."

---

153 Ibid.

154 Alford, 3:168; Lightfoot, 125; Robertson, *Grammar*, 1114; "The aorist participle denotes simultaneous action. Therefore the meaning is: 'He emptied Himself *by taking* the form of a servant." (Müller, 82).

155 Alford, 3:168 (emphasis original); Sumney, 46.

156 Wallace, 630.

157 "… Paul seems to have hinted at this meaning in his instructions to the saints in v.3: '[Think] nothing from selfishness or conceit (κενοδοξίαν).' The Philippians were told not to puff themselves up with 'empty glory' (κενοδοξίαν), because Christ was an example of one who emptied his glory. If this connection is intentional, then the *Carmen Christi* has the following force: Do not elevate yourselves on empty glory, but follow the example of Christ, who, though already elevated (on God's level), emptied his glory by veiling it in humanity." (Wallace, 630)

158 Rienecker, 550.

It is not that Christ "*exchanged* the form of God for the form of a slave, but that he *manifested* the form of God in the form of a slave."[159] In this way he "reveals not only what Jesus is truly like but also what it means to be God."[160] As Fee says, "God is not an acquisitive being, grasping and seizing, but self-giving for the sake of others."[161]

More broadly the noun "bond-servant" (δούλου) described one who had sold himself into slavery, generally for economic reasons. Such a one had voluntarily given himself up to the will of another. The word "bond-slave" captures the meaning better than "servant" (ESV, NIV, RSV). The application of such a word to the eternally divine Son of God is breathtaking. The distance covered in this self-embraced humility is beyond comprehension. As the Apostle calls the Philippian believers (and through him the Holy Spirit calls us as well) to unity through self-chosen humility, who can protest before a Savior like this? In fact the title "bond-slave" became something of a badge of honor for the followers of Christ. Paul opened this letter by using the noun in the plural to describe himself and Timothy (1:1). He could use the noun literally to speak of those who are enslaved to earthly masters (e.g., Eph. 6:5-8; Col. 3:11, 22-25; Titus 2:9). He used it as a negative image for slavery to sin (Rom. 6:16, 19-20) and to men (1 Cor. 7:23). But he delighted to use it to speak of one who is "Christ's slave" (1 Cor. 7:22; Eph. 6:6) and a slave to righteousness (Rom. 6:19). It thus became a title which he readily applied to himself (Rom. 1:1; Gal. 1:10; Titus 1:1) and others (Phil. 1:1; Col. 4:12). All who serve Christ should be glad to take this title (2 Tim. 2:24). Paul, for Christ's sake, could even say he was a bond-slave of others (2 Cor. 4:5).

> **Ministry Maxim**
>
> Embracing the role of servant never diminishes one's true essence, it merely reveals it.

---

159 Bruce, *Philippians*, 46.

160 O'Brien, 216.

161 Fee, 211.

But of whom was Christ a "bond-servant"?[162] Perhaps it can be most simply said that Christ served the Father by serving us and He served us by serving the Father. He met our need by putting Himself under the Father's plan, direction and will. He took his cue from our need, but He took His commands from the Father.

Is there something deeper behind Paul's use of the imagery of slavery? The notion of Christ making Himself subject to demonic powers in order to free us from their power by His death seems wholly out of touch with the present context.[163] It has been suggested that Isaiah's servant of the Lord theme (Isa. 42-53) stands behind the Apostle's words here. Some counter, saying this cannot be, because in Isaiah the title "servant of the Lord" is a badge of honor, while here Christ's service is seen clearly as wholly negative.[164] But doesn't the "servant of the Lord" theme in Isaiah culminate and climax in chapter fifty-three, with the sufferings and atoning death of the "Servant"? Is that not the very echo of Paul's current trajectory in speaking of Christ's self-embraced humility here (v.8)? Additionally, it is noted that the linguistic parallels break down at the vital point of the key term itself. For "servant" in Isaiah the LXX uses παῖς, while Paul uses δοῦλος. This may hint that there is not a *direct* reliance, but, as Fee notes, "It is hard to imagine that early Christians, therefore, would not rather automatically have heard this passage with that background in view."[165] Even if the connection may not be direct, it does not therefore follow that it is nonexistent.[166] Paul need not quote in order to purposefully connect to Isaiah's words. One does not have to embrace all that some proponents of this connection have suggested in order to see some level of dependence. Indeed, Christ

---

162 Kennedy demands that "It is needless to ask whose δοῦλος He became. The question is not before the Apostle." (437). Nevertheless the question continues to be asked, and we ought not avoid it.

163 Fee, 212; O'Brien, 219.

164 Cousar, 53.

165 Fee, 212.

166 See the excellent discussion of the linguistic connections between Isaiah and Paul in Harmon, 201-204, 211-212.

is the ultimate "servant of the Lord" to which all previous revelation looked and for which all creation longed.[167]

Then too there is the question of a conscious dependence upon the account of Jesus serving the disciples by washing their feet (John 13:3-17). A number of commentators have postulated an intentional dependence of Paul upon John.[168] As with Isaiah's "servant of the Lord" theme, it appears difficult to prove direct dependence. There does, however, seem the appropriate and valuable use of John's account of Christ's service to the disciples as an illustrative example of the kind of thing of which he speaks here.

The second participial clause which modifies the main verb (ἐκένωσεν, "emptied") is "being made in the likeness of men" (ἐν ὁμοιώματι ἀνθρώπων γενόμενος). Here too, as with the previous participle, the action is simultaneous with the main verb ("emptied").[169] And again, the participle describes the means or manner by which Christ "emptied Himself."[170] Wuest identifies this as an example of the ingressive aorist "which signifies entrance into a new state."[171] Lenski, however, contends that all the aorists in verses 6 and 7 are punctiliar and historical in nature.[172] The verb itself stresses not the idea of being born, but of becoming. It is "to experience a change in nature and so indicate entry into a new condition" and thus to become something.[173] The dative form of ὁμοιώματι ("likeness") is a dative of reference—with reference to "the likeness of men" Christ was made.[174] It is used "to qualify a statement that would otherwise typically

---

167 Hendriksen, 109.

168 Bruce, 46; O'Brien, 224;

169 Alford, 3:168; Müller, 82.

170 Hellerman, 114; Sumney, 46.

171 Wuest, 68.

172 Lenski, 779.

173 BDAG, 1646.5.

174 Wallace, 146.

not be true."[175] With the preposition (ἐν) it describes a state of being.[176] We should note the contrast between ὑπάρχων ("existed") and γενόμενος ("being made"). The former stresses "being by nature," while the later "becoming."[177] Paul stands Christ's eternal pre-existence (v.6) over against His incarnation in time and space (v.7).[178] In "passages where it is specified who or what a person or thing is or has been rendered," γίνομαι especially denotes "quality, condition, place, rank, character."[179]

The noun translated "likeness" (ὁμοιώματι) stresses not exactness, but similarity. It described that which had been made after the likeness of something else, thus a figure, image, likeness or representation.[180] Resemblance not exactness is the idea.[181] Paul used it in Romans 8:3 to describe God the Father "sending His own Son in the likeness [ὁμοιώματι] of sinful flesh." Jesus came in "the likeness of sinful flesh," and thus permitted Himself to be "tempted in all things as we are, yet without sin." (Heb. 4:15) He fully took sinless humanity in body and nature to Himself ("the form of a bond-servant"), but when it came to our frailty to sin, it was only a "likeness." It can in this regard be rightly said that Paul "… uses our word to bring out both that Jesus in his earthly career was similar to sinful humans and yet not totally like them."[182] The likeness was genuine and real. His was no "phantom humanity" as the Docetists held.[183] He was fully human, though His fullness was greater than His humanity. Note also the plural form here

---

175 Ibid., 144-145.

176 BDAG, 1646.5.c.

177 Kennedy, 437.

178 Hellerman, 115-116.

179 Thayer, 116.

180 Ibid., 445.

181 Ibid.

182 BDAG, 5296.3.

183 Robertson, *Word Pictures*, 4:445.

(ἀνθρώπων, "of men") and the singular form in the next line (ἄνθρωπος, "a man"). The plural here is near to saying "humanity."[184]

As in the previous verse there is a variation in versification at this point in the text. Prominent versions of the Greek text include the next line in verse 7.[185] Correspondingly some English versions follow the former (e.g., NET, NLT, NRSV) and some the latter (e.g., NASU, NIV, RSV). The text remains the same; it is simply a matter of where the verse notation falls, thus we will follow the text as the NASU sets it before us.

Verse 8 – Being found in appearance as a man, He humbled Himself by becoming obedient to the point of death, even death on a cross.

We meet now the second of the two finite verbs that together make up the contrast to what Christ "did not regard" (οὐχ ... ἡγήσατο, v.6). The καὶ serves to hold "emptied Himself" (ἑαυτὸν ἐκένωσεν, v.7) and "He humbled Himself" (ἐταπείνωσεν ἑαυτὸν) in parallel relationship.[186] As with the first verb this is an aorist active indicative form. Again, all the aorist tenses of verses 7-8 stand in contrast to the present tense ὑπάρχων ("He existed," v.6). His eternal, preexisting deity in "the form of God" stands in contrast to the actions Christ took to humble Himself to come and save us. Thus the aorist tense here points to a definite act. The active voice, coupled with the reflexive pronoun (ἑαυτὸν, "Himself") may be designated a "reflexive active," emphasizing that the subject (Christ) acted upon himself,[187] "that the humiliation was freely self-imposed."[188]

The verb could be used literally to speak of lower elevation or of being made lower, as in Luke 3:5: "Every ravine shall be filled up, And every mountain and hill shall be brought low [ταπεινωθήσεται] ...". It also was

---

184 Kennedy, 438.
185 NA[27] and UBS[4].
186 O'Brien, 226.
187 Wallace, 413-414.
188 Hellerman, 116.

used metaphorically as it is here. That which brings one low may be God (2 Cor. 12:21; implied in Luke 14:11; 18:14) or one's circumstances. In the latter case Paul could say later in this very letter, "I know how to get along with humble means [ταπεινοῦσθαι], and I also know how to live in prosperity; in any and every circumstance I have learned the secret of being filled and going hungry, both of having abundance and suffering need" (4:12). He learned this, of course, from consideration of the life of His Lord.

In the NT, however, it is most often used to describe action one takes upon oneself (Luke 14:11; 18:14; 2 Cor. 11:7; James 4:10; 1 Pet. 5:6). Indeed, the reflexive pronoun (ἑαυτὸν, "Himself") appears here again as it did with the previous finite verb in verse 7. As before it again points to action Christ took upon Himself. It may thus point to "the voluntary nature" of Christ's actions.[189] Its position, however, in relationship to the finite verb has changed. In verse 7 it preceded the verb, laying special stress upon the pronoun. Here it follows the verb, emphasizing the act.[190]

The finite verb (ἐταπείνωσεν, "humbled") is modified by two participial phrases, as was ἐκένωσεν ("emptied"). The first of these is, "Being found in appearance as a man" (σχήματι εὑρεθεὶς ὡς ἄνθρωπος). There is some debate as to whether this should be read as a third participle qualifying "emptied"[191] or as modifying "humbled."[192] The balance of opinion seems to fall with seeing it as qualifying "humbled."[193] In this case the participle precedes the verb and may be considered to summarize what the previous two participles have told us about Christ's incarnation and to

---

189 Sumney, 47-48.

190 "This time, ἑαυτὸν does not precede, because ... in ver. 7 the pragmatic weight rested on the *reflexive reference* of the act, but here on the *reflexive act* itself," Alford, 3:168; cf. Robertson, *Paul's Joy in Christ*, 132; Vincent, ICC, 60.

191 Sumney, 46-47.

192 O'Brien, 226; Silva, 105-106.

193 Alford, 3:168; Kennedy, 438; Vincent, *Word Studies*, 3:434.

thus lay the ground for the verb that follows immediately upon its heels ("humbled").[194]

The meaning of the noun "appearance" (σχήματι) has garnered a lot of attention, particularly as it relates to the previous terms "form" (μορφή, vv.6-7) and "likeness" (ὁμοίωμα, v.7). The first (μορφή, "form") emphasizes the essence of a thing, the second ("likeness," ὁμοίωμα) the resemblance of it to the original, and this third ("appearance," σχήματι) denotes the outward presentation of the thing. It is "the form or nature of something, with special reference to its outer form or structure."[195] It refers to "the generally recognized shape or form in which someth[ing] appears."[196] The σχῆμα is what is observable to the senses.[197] Thus the σχῆμα "may change without affecting the" μορφή.[198]

> **Ministry Maxim**
>
> Obedience that falls short of all that is required is not obedience at all, but rebellion.

Note again the transition from the plural (ἀνθρώπων, "men") to the singular (ἄνθρωπος, "man"). In the previous participial phrase Christ embraced the likeness of all "men" (i.e., humanity). Here He became a particular one of that race, "*a* man" (emphasis added). This is how Christ was "found" (εὑρεθείς). The passive voice depicts the action of others beholding, seeing, encountering Christ and what they thus perceived of Him. The aorist pictures those encounters as definite and singular acts. The participial form again designates the means by which Christ "humbled Himself." What they thus beheld of Christ was that He was "as" (ὡς) "a man" (ἄνθρωπος), a singular example of all that humanity is. The comparative ὡς ("as") is used as a "marker introducing the perspective from which a pers[son], thing, or activity is viewed or understood as to

---

194 Silva, 106.

195 Louw-Nida, 58.7.

196 BDAG, 7204.1.

197 TDNT, 7:954; cf. Robertson, *Paul's Joy in Christ*, 131-132; Vincent, ICC, 60.

198 Vincent, *Word Studies*, 3:430-431.

character, function, or role" with a particular "focus on quality, circumstance, or role."[199] Christ was completely man, though He was more than merely a man. He was everything we are, except for sin, and yet He was not entirely defined by that nature. He was entirely divine, not surrendering anything of His divinity in order to accomplish His incarnation.

The main verb ἐταπείνωσεν ("humbled") is also qualified by a second participial phrase: "by becoming obedient to the point of death" (γενόμενος ὑπήκοος μέχρι θανάτου). The participle (γενόμενος, "becoming") is the same verb just used in verse 7 ("being made"). What Christ became was "obedient" (ὑπήκοος; cf. Rom. 5:19; Heb. 5:8). Here too the participle designates the means by which the main verb ("humbled") was accomplished. And again the aorist points to a definite event. By citing Christ's obedience Paul lays the exemplary foundation for the obedience of the Philippian believers which he has sought (vv.2-4) and to which he will immediately return after this poetic ode to Christ (vv.12-13).[200] It was a thorough obedience for it was "to the point of death" (μέχρι θανάτου). The preposition μέχρι ("to the point of") serves here as a "marker of degree or measure."[201] It is not that Christ was obedient "to death," but "*unto the point of* death."[202] Christ was obedient to the Father (Gal. 1:4; Heb. 10:7), not to death. He was obedient *to* the Father "*unto the point of* death." At the end of the chapter Paul will use the word to speak of Epaphroditus who "came close to [μέχρι] death for the work of Christ" (v.30a). He came up to the point of death, but came short of it. Christ, however, took obedience to the farthest horizon; He wrote the last and definitive chapter on what obedience means. There is no greater step beyond obedience unto death.

---

199 BDAG, 8075.3.a.γ.

200 Fee, 216.

201 BDAG, 4883.3.

202 Wuest, 70.

As if this were not enough, Paul adds "even death on a cross" (θανάτου δὲ σταυροῦ). The δὲ is used emphatically or intensively ("even").[203] It "introduces another and more striking detail of the humiliation, and leads on to a climax."[204] We should note that "*on* a cross" is more literally "*of* a cross" (genitive). It emphasizes not so much the location of the death ("*on* a cross") as the quality and nature of the death ("*of* a cross").[205] The absence of the definite article (it is rightly "*a* cross" not "*the* cross") emphasizes the character and nature of His death.[206] Not only was crucifixion the most torturous of deaths, to the Jewish mind it denoted the utter dregs of shame (Heb. 12:2) and marked one as under the curse of God. "Christ redeemed us from the curse of the Law, having become a curse for us-- for it is written, 'CURSED IS EVERYONE WHO HANGS ON A TREE'" (Gal. 3:13, quoting Deut. 21:22-23; cf. Acts 5:30; 10:39). Joshua hung the king of Ai (Josh. 8:29) and the five kings of key Canaanite cities (10:26) upon a tree to broadcast the cursed nature of their existence and death. So entirely did Christ trust His Father's wisdom that He submitted to the worst of physical deaths and in so doing bore the mark of His curse for people who had revolted against Him and whose sins He did not commit. The cross was the "bottom rung in the ladder from the Throne of God."[207] These opening lines of Paul's depiction of Christ's example "take us down, down, down to the deepest, darkest hellhole in human history to see the horrific torture, unspeakable abuse, and bloody execution of a *slave* on a *cross*."[208] This is the loving obedience of utter faith; all else falls silent before this supreme example.

---

203 Dana and Mantey, 244; cf. O'Brien, 230.

204 Vincent, ICC, 60.

205 Sumney mentions this as a possibility, 48; Lenski calls it "the characterizing genitive 'of a cross,'" 785; "*on* a cross" would view it as a genitive of place; Wallace prefers to see it as a genitive of production, "death produced by, brought about by a cross," 105.

206 Wuest, 70.

207 Robertson, *Word Pictures*, 4:445.

208 Hansen, 159, emphasis original.

> **Digging Deeper:**
> 1. Outline practical steps you and other Christ-followers where you worship might take in order to pursue the mind of Christ. (v.5)
> 2. What good thing that is rightfully yours might you have to surrender in order to be like Christ for the good of others? (v.6)
> 3. What humbling step of obedience is Christ asking you to embrace for His glory and the good of others? (v.7)
> 4. Discuss with someone you respect: Is there a limit to how much God may ask a person to surrender in order to fully obey Him? (v.8)

Verse 9 – For this reason also, God highly exalted Him, and bestowed on Him the name which is above every name,

In verse 5 Paul set out to unfold the thinking that was "in Christ Jesus." Christ's thinking has been set forth in the negative (v.6; a way of thinking He shunned) and positively (vv.7-8; the way of thinking He embraced). Now we come to the crescendo of God's affirmation upon such thinking and acting. This serves as the prototype of how God rewards those who likewise "Have this attitude in [themselves] which was also in Christ Jesus" (v.5).

The conjunction (διό) is inferential ("For this reason") and introduces a logical conclusion from the kind of thinking Christ embraced (vv.6-8). When in combination with καί ("also"), as it is here, it denotes that the inference is self-evident.[209]

That which is self-evident is that it was precisely because Christ thought and acted in this way (vv.6-8) that "God highly exalted Him" (ὁ θεὸς αὐτὸν ὑπερύψωσεν). Exaltation is what God gives to one who has embraced humility. What the Father has done for His Son, Christ's own may expect to receive as well: "… he who humbles [ταπεινῶν] himself will be exalted" (Luke 14:11b; cf. 18:14). "Humble yourselves [ταπεινώθητε]

---

209 BDAG, 2013; Friberg, 117; cf. Louw-Nida, 89.47.

in the presence of the Lord, and He will exalt you" (James 4:10). "Therefore humble yourselves [Ταπεινώθητε] under the mighty hand of God, that He may exalt you at the proper time" (1 Pet. 5:6).

The verb (ὑπερύψωσεν, "highly exalted") is used only here in the NT. It is a compound word comprised of ὑπέρ ("above") and ὑψόω ("lift up"). The preposition in compound strengthens the idea of the root verb[210] so that it is "'perfective' or intensive" of the verbal idea.[211] It points to Christ's "exaltation being a super-eminent one."[212] It means "to raise to a high point of honor."[213] Christ was thus not simply "exalted" (ὑψόω), but preeminently, supremely exalted. "The force of the prep[osition] in compound is not to describe a different stage in Christ's existence in a comp[arative] sense, but to contrast His exaltation w[ith] the claim of other high powers, and thereby to proclaim His uniqueness and absoluteness."[214] The aorist tense points to an historical act.[215] It includes the entire sweep of Jesus' resurrection, ascension, glorification, and session. Exaltation is the note with which the great song of the Suffering Servant began, "Behold, My servant will prosper, He will be high and lifted up and greatly exalted" (Isa. 52:13). Before the suffering was recounted, the outcome was known. It was "for the joy set before Him" that Jesus "endured the cross, despising the shame, and has sat down at the right hand of the throne of God" (Heb. 12:2). That for which Jesus prayed the very night of His betrayal, is now His: "Now, Father, glorify Me together with Yourself, with the glory which I had with You before the world was" (John 17:5).

This exaltation was coupled with (καὶ, "and") the appropriate designation. It was "bestowed on Him" (ἐχαρίσατο αὐτῷ). The verb emphasizes that the action is undertaken "freely as a favor."[216] It is used in 1:29 of the

---

210 TDNT, 8:609.

211 Dana and Mantey, 111.

212 Alford, 3:169.

213 BDAG, 7582.

214 Rienecker, 551.

215 Alford, 3:169.

216 BDAG, 7893.1.

Father giving the Philippian believers not only the grace "to believe in Him, but also to suffer for His sake." Paul uses the same verb to describe the act of forgiveness (2 Cor. 2:7, 10; 12:13; Eph. 4:32; Col. 2:13; 3:13). He uses it to describe the gracious act of God's giving in response to prayer (Philem. 22) and in all we shall inherit in Christ (1 Cor. 2:12; Rom. 8:32). It describes God's giving of the covenant to Abraham (Gal. 3:18). The aorist tense again looks back upon a definite event and is coincident with the previous verb (ὑπερύψωσεν, "highly exalted").[217] Marvelously, "Christ obtained as a gift what he renounced as a prize."[218]

That which was so freely given to Christ is "the name which is above every name" (τὸ ὄνομα τὸ ὑπὲρ πᾶν ὄνομα). Note that it is not just "*a* name," but "*the* name" (τὸ ὄνομα). Note also the repetition of ὑπὲρ ("above") which was just used in compound (ὑπερύψωσεν, "highly exalted"). Verses 6 through 8 depicted a definite downward movement of humility; verses 9-11 have reversed the direction now in exaltation. The clause (τὸ ὑπὲρ πᾶν ὄνομα, "which is above every name") follows and is in apposition to "the name" (τὸ ὄνομα), thus more fully identifying it.[219]

The preposition (ὑπὲρ, "above") and the adjective (πᾶν, "every") are in the attributive position, tucked between the definite article (τὸ, "the") and its noun (ὄνομα, "name"). This serves to highlight the qualitative nature of "the name" that is under consideration. There is no verb ("is" has been added by the NASU translators to make for smooth English). The nuance of the phrase, therefore, might be rendered "*the* name—the above-every-name."[220]

To what does "the name" (τὸ ὄνομα) point? There has been no little discussion in the search for an answer to this question. Lightfoot insists that it does not point to any definite appellation, but to a generalized sense of dignity, title, office, or rank.[221] Others insist it means "Jesus," which is

---

217 Lenski, 787; O'Brien, 237.

218 Vincent, ICC, 62.

219 Lenski, 789.

220 cf. Ibid., 787.

221 Lightfoot, 126-127.

mentioned in the next verse.[222] This would point to His earthly, human nature. What had changed for the glorified Christ (over against what had been His in his pre-incarnate state) is the addition of His *glorified* humanity.[223] Yet He bore the name "Jesus" prior to His ascension and glorification. Indeed, it was given to Him before birth (Matt. 1:21; Luke 1:31). Others insist that "the name" points to the combination, "Jesus Christ," which is mentioned in verse 11. Vincent insists that this underscores both His glorified humanity ("Jesus") and His office as the Anointed of God ("Christ").[224] Others demand that "the name" is "Lord," which also is designated His in verse 11. The LXX often used κύριος ("Lord") where the OT authors used Yahweh.[225] The NT writers followed this pattern. The Jew's reverence for the Tetragrammaton ("the unpronounceable name"[226]) is well established. In lieu of speaking the unutterable name they would often simply say "the name" (cf. 3 John 7).[227] Is this what Paul intended by τὸ ὄνομα? The nuanced meaning of "*the* name—the above-every-name" would lend dignity to this possibility. If so, then when Paul asserted that every tongue will acknowledge that Jesus Christ is "Lord" (κύριος) he was simply putting a single word to that unutterable name, "the name" (τὸ ὄνομα) that has now become utterable in worship of the exalted Lord Jesus Christ.

So what is "the name"? It is that name which uniquely belongs to God, what had been the unspeakable name for long ages has become the one name by which every tongue will confess that "Jesus [the fully human one] Christ [the anointed Messiah of God]" is indeed "Lord" (κύριος), the one who has come from heaven to earth,

> **Ministry Maxim**
>
> Exaltation arises from humility—always, by God's own hand, avowed by His Word.

---

222 E.g., Alford, 3:169; Silva, 110-111.

223 Robertson, *Paul's Joy in Christ*, 136.

224 Vincent, ICC, 62.

225 Martin, 104.

226 Robertson, *Paul's Joy in Christ*, 138.

227 Fee, 221.

from the heights to the grave, from glory to death and back to glory for the redemption of His people.

This is indeed breathtaking. He has gone on record, saying, "I am the LORD [Hebrew: יְהוָה; Greek: κύριος], that is My name; I will not give My glory to another" (Isa 42:8).[228] Yet here is the incarnate, crucified, now raised, glorified, enthroned Jesus, the Christ, rightful possessor of the unutterable "name"!

God the Father "raised [Jesus] from the dead and seated Him at His right hand in the heavenly places, far above all rule and authority and power and dominion, and every name that is named, not only in this age but also in the one to come. And He put all things in subjection under His feet, and gave Him as head over all things to the church" (Eph. 1:20-22). Hallelujah, glorious Lord!

Verse 10 – so that at the name of Jesus EVERY KNEE WILL BOW, of those who are in heaven and on earth and under the earth,

The crescendo having been reached (v.9), the closing note is sustained by means of an extended purpose clause (ἵνα, "so that") that is two-pronged and extends through verse 11. Wallace classifies this as indicating both purpose and result, saying "it indicates both the intention and its sure accomplishment."[229] If this is the case then Paul is underscoring the certainty with which these things can be counted upon.

The Father has thus highly exalted the Lord Jesus Christ to the utmost place and bestowed on Him the most exalted of names with an express outcome in mind. The first prong of that surely-to-be-realized purpose is that "EVERY KNEE WILL BOW" (πᾶν γόνυ κάμψῃ). To bend the knee is a key demonstration of obeisance, submission, deference, and homage. This was Pharaoh's command for every Egyptian citizen with regard to Joseph: "He had him ride in his second chariot; and they proclaimed

---

228 O'Brien, 238.

229 Wallace, 473; cf. Fee, 223; O'Brien, 239.

before him, 'Bow the knee!'" This was precisely how Pharaoh demonstrated and the people acknowledged that he had "set him over all the land of Egypt" (Gen. 41:43). Having taken his stand before wicked king Ahab, this is the position Elijah took before God in prayer: "And he bowed himself down on the earth and put his face between his knees" (1 Kings 18:42, ESV). When Elijah later commiserated before the Lord that he was the only one faithful to Him, He told the prophet, "Yet I will leave 7,000 in Israel, all the knees that have not bowed to Baal and every mouth that has not kissed him" (1 Kings 19:18; cf. Rom. 11:4). Little wonder that this is the position to which we are called in worship: "Come, let us worship and bow down, Let us kneel before the LORD our Maker" (Psalm 95:6). Paul himself had already taken up his position: "For this reason I bow my knees before the Father" (Eph. 3:14).

Though the biblical background for the act is rich, it appears that the Apostle directly quotes from one particular passage: "I have sworn by Myself, The word has gone forth from My mouth in righteousness And will not turn back, That to Me every knee will bow, every tongue will swear allegiance" (Isa. 45:23). What was a future indicative in the LXX of Isaiah ("will bow") is an aorist subjunctive here in Philippians. The subjunctive mood is necessary for the sake of ἵνα and the purpose clause. The aorist casts what the prophet originally spoke of in future, predictive terms as taking place in an actual event in history.

In the context of Isaiah's original prophecy, the one speaking is the "Lord" (Yahweh) Himself (v.21). Indeed, he says, "Is it not I, the Lord? And there is no other God besides Me, A righteous God and a Savior; There is none except Me." (v.21b). And He adds this demand for exclusive worship, "Turn to Me and be saved, all the ends of the earth; For I am God, and there is no other" (v.22).

This in turn, then, is applied by the Apostle under the inspiration of the Holy Spirit to Jesus. This which Yahweh ("the Lord") rightly demands, will take place "at the name of Jesus" (ἐν τῷ ὀνόματι Ἰησοῦ). It is difficult to imagine a more direct, powerful statement to the divine nature and prerogatives of Christ.

The more explicit dependence upon Isaiah 45 here in verse 10 firms up the support for our contention that "the Lord" (Yahweh) should be seen as "the name" of verse 9 and that an intentional connection exists between the "bond-servant" in verse 7 and the suffering servant of Isaiah 52:13-53:12.

Similarly, in Romans 14, where Paul is making the point that "we will all stand before the judgment seat of God" (v.10b), he immediately backs up his argument with a fuller quotation from Isaiah 45:23: "For it is written, 'AS I LIVE, SAYS THE LORD, EVERY KNEE SHALL BOW TO ME, AND EVERY TONGUE SHALL GIVE PRAISE TO GOD'" (v.11).

Just how should we understand the preposition ἐν?[230] English versions almost universally translate it with the word "at." A more wooden rendering might be "in." This, however, makes for an unusually stated English sentence. The preposition should not be made to indicate means (Jesus is the means or medium "by" or "through" which the Father is worshiped), for it is clear in the next verse that it is Jesus who receives the worship and that this takes place "to the glory of God the Father." While it is not easy to render it in English, the preposition probably has some such notion as "in honor of the name of Jesus" (GNB).[231]

Also, how should we understand the genitive "of Jesus" (Ἰησοῦ)? Does this mean the mention of the name "Jesus"? Or does it refer to the name given to Jesus (i.e., "Lord")? The latter better fits the overall context.[232] The Apostle is not looking for a habitual genuflecting every time the name Jesus is intoned, but the submission of heart and life to Him as Lord of all.

This is the first direct reference to the name "Jesus" in the hymn and this is not inconsequential.[233] It is the name by which His humanness

---

230 It has been variously designated the "accompanying circumstance," "efficient cause" (the first of which O'Brien rejects and the latter of which he embraces, 240), "object," "medium" (the first of which Fee rejects and the latter of which he embraces, 223), or "ground" (Kennedy, 439) of the knee-bowing.

231 Fee, 223; Hellerman, 121; O'Brien, 239-240.

232 Fee, 223.

233 O'Brien, 240.

is most graphically emphasized. The very one who humbled Himself to become man and then to die the ignominious death of the cross is the one who is now glorified and worshiped.

The universality of this homage to Christ is expressed through a string of three adjectives. The knees that will bow to Christ include all "of those who are in heaven and on earth and under the earth" (ἐπουρανίων καὶ ἐπιγείων καὶ καταχθονίων). Each is in the genitive case, which could be understood as a genitives of place ("every knee should bow, in the heavenly and earthly and subterranean places")[234], but probably should be understood as possessive genitives," referring to those whose knees are bent ('the knees of those who are in heaven, etc.')."[235]

Each is masculine and plural.[236] After designating the genitives as genitives of place, Sumney then says the plural forms may be used to substantivize the adjectives "so [they] stand for all those who live in these realms."[237] The net is the same. The plural forms serve also to indicate an all-inclusive sweep of all found in each of these regions.

Just how are the three divisions to be understood? They have, according to Lightfoot, been understood variously as "Christians, Jews, and heathens; or angels, men, and devils; or the angels, the living, and the dead; or the souls of the blessed, people on earth, and souls in purgatory."[238] In other words, a great deal of guesswork has been applied to this question over the years.

---

234 Sumney, 50.

235 Wallace, 124-125.

236 The forms may be identified as either masculine or neuter. Some have opted for the latter and believe the Apostle is not pointing to "intelligent/rational beings" in each realm, but simply sweeping all of creation as participating in the grand submission to Christ. While the Scriptures do emphasize the full submission of all creation to Christ (e.g., Rom. 8:22; Eph. 1:22), the present passage would seem to have something more along the line of intelligent/rational beings in view. The express description of knees bowing and tongues confessing, while not without intelligent counter argument (e.g., Lightfoot, 115; H.C.G. Moule, 69-70; Silva, 116), seems to point us in this direction. The one does not rule out the other; we simply have to decide which one Paul has in view in the present passage.

237 Sumney, 50.

238 Lightfoot, 128.

The first (ἐπουρανίων, "in heaven") is used by Paul elsewhere to speak of the location of Christ's present session at God's right hand (Eph. 1:20; 2:6), the repository of our spiritual blessings in Christ (Eph. 1:3), a place where "rulers and authorities" reside and from which they observe the wisdom of God displayed in we who make up His church (Eph. 3:10), and where "spiritual forces of evil" dwell and work (Eph. 6:10). It marks the nature and locus of God's kingdom (2 Tim. 4:18).

The second (ἐπιγείων, "on earth") describes that which is terrestrial. It is at times set over against the first (John 3:12; 1 Cor. 15:40). It is the place of our present dwelling with a body made appropriate for it (2 Cor. 5:1), a place that is characterized by a kind of thinking (Phil. 3:19) and a "wisdom" (James 3:15) which is not yet redeemed and sanctified. In the latter case it is paired with what is "natural" and "demonic" (James 3:15) and is the opposite of God's wisdom. Such "wisdom" is characterized by the very kind of "bitter jealousy and selfish ambition" (James 3:14) Paul is seeking to counteract here in Philippi (cf. Phil. 2:3-4).

> **Ministry Maxim**
>
> Unity is the automatic and undisputed outcome of truly seeing Jesus.

The third (καταχθονίων, "under the earth") is used only here in the LXX and the NT. It is a compound word comprised of "against/under" (κατά) and "the earth" (χθών).[239] It refers to that which is subterranean.[240] It may well be "a reference to the dead, generally regarded as inhabiting a dark region under the ground."[241]

In all this Paul may not be attempting to speak as specifically as we might wish him to or to categorize with as much distinction as we might desire. His emphasis may be on the all-inclusive nature of the homage paid to Jesus rather than to the specificity of enumerating precisely who in each region is intended. The emphasis is upon "EVERY" (πᾶν) without

---

239 Thayer, 338.

240 BDAG, 4096.

241 Louw-Nida, 1.17; cf. Friberg, 223.

enumerating the subcategories of all beings along the way. Not one (living or dead, angel or demon, principality or power,[242] etc.) in any realm above, below or around will avoid rendering to Jesus the honor that is due to Him. "And every created thing which is in heaven and on the earth and under the earth and on the sea, and all things in them, I heard saying, 'To Him who sits on the throne, and to the Lamb, be blessing and honor and glory and dominion forever and ever'" (Rev. 5:13).

Many wonder, is this universal bowing of the knee performed willingly or unwillingly? Or, to put it another way: Does this imply the salvation of all? To which we may reply: Of course not! This statement does not erase the rest of God's revelation. As I have written elsewhere:

> There is a time coming when the sound of countless millions of knees will be heard as they hit the dust in humble submission to Christ (Philippians 2:10-11). Some will bow willingly, having practiced for that day in untold times of personal worship during their sojourn upon earth. They will bend low in joy as they pass into a life of bliss forever in the presence of their Savior and Lord. Others will have their unyielding knees bent low under the awesome weight of the unveiled glory of God in Christ. Having never acknowledged Christ in this life, they will be compelled to bend low in worship before Him then. Theirs will be a parting admission of His rightful place even as they pass out of His presence forever into eternal torment. Either way, all will bow.

> Likewise we are told every tongue will utter the confession "He is Lord!" To some it will be the sweet, final echoes of their heart's song, having been sung through difficult days as they trod this life. Their song will become an eternal song of worship. Others will find the words forced over lips that have cursed and slandered His name all their lives. Even as their teeth begin to gnash and

---

242 While Paul surely includes the demonic here, he does not as specifically single it out as he does in Colossians (e.g., 1:16; 2:14-15), where the matter is more specifically a concern of the false teacher(s) at work in that community.

their eyes begin to weep, without any hope of comfort throughout eternity, they will finally utter those words: "He is Lord!" All alike, however, will verbally acknowledge what will have become the most obvious conclusion of all creation—Jesus is Lord![243]

Fee helpfully points out the eternity-to-eternity sweep of the Apostle's hymn.[244] Beginning in eternity past ("existed in the form of God," v.6), he moves to the incarnation ("being made in the likeness of men," v.7), the cross ("he humbled Himself by becoming obedient to death, even death on a cross," v.8), on to glorification ("God highly exalted Him," v.9; which assumes the resurrection and ascension), and finally brings us to God's appointed eschatological conclusion ("at the name of Jesus EVERY KNEE WILL BOW … every tongue will confess that Jesus Christ is Lord, to the glory of God the Father," vv.10-11).

Verse 11 – and that every tongue will confess that Jesus Christ is Lord, to the glory of God the Father.

The second (καὶ, "and") prong of the Father's assured purpose (ἵνα, "so that", v.10) in supremely exalting Jesus is "that every tongue will confess" (πᾶσα γλῶσσα ἐξομολογήσηται).

The verb (ἐξομολογήσηται, "will confess"), like its partner in the other half of the purpose statement (κάμψῃ, "WILL BOW"), is an aorist subjunctive.[245] Here, as with the previous verb, the subjunctive is coupled with ἵνα ("so that," v.10) to form the purpose statement, and the aorist points to a definite event. Here the middle voice is deponent, having an active meaning. The preposition in compound (ἐκ) may emphasize either that the confession comes *"forth from the heart"* or that it is given *"freely,*

---

243 Kitchen, *Embracing Authority*, 208.

244 Fee, 223.

245 Some manuscripts have the future indicative, but given the parallel to the verb in the previous clause and the strength of the manuscripts in which the aorist subjunctive is found it is more likely to be the original (Sumney, 50).

or publicly, openly."²⁴⁶ In this case it is probably the latter, since not all will give this praise out of the joyful experience of true salvation and thus "from the heart." It seems, then, to have the idea of "to declare openly in acknowledgment" or, in other words, to "*profess*" or "*acknowledge*."²⁴⁷ It is used "of open expression of allegiance to someone."²⁴⁸

This will be true of "every tongue" (πᾶσα γλῶσσα). There is no good reason to limit "every" to the truly redeemed. Its intent is all encompassing; "every" single voice will finally be united in the same confession. The world—above, below and around—will finally be unified. Only the sight of Jesus returning in His glory will achieve such unity. What Paul exhorted for the Philippians to make true in time and space within the circle of the redeemed ("being of the same mind," v.2) will then be true of all created beings. That "mind" will find a voice (γλῶσσα, "tongue"). The noun is used as a synecdoche, the lesser representing the greater. The "tongue" indicates not simply the physical organ within the mouth, but the entire ability to vocalize and intone what the mind has recognized, to give expression to what is true of the whole person.

The translators of the NASU cast the previous half of this purpose statement in all capitals²⁴⁹ ("EVERY KNEE WILL BOW"), indicating that it is a direct quotation from the text of Isaiah 45:23. Here, however, they display it in lowercase characters (as with the rest of the sentence), indicating the direct quotation has ceased. Yet that text says: "I have sworn by Myself, The word has gone forth from My mouth in righteousness And will not turn back, That to Me every knee will bow, *every tongue will swear allegiance*" (Isa. 45:23, emphasis added). Paul appears to continue the application of that text to Jesus at His return. The text here is identical to that of the LXX except that, as in the previous clause (v.10), the LXX has the verb as a future indicative, while Paul casts it in the aorist subjunctive.

---

246 Thayer, 224.

247 BDAG, 2807.3.

248 Friberg, 156.

249 A general change of practice from the original NASB when it comes to NT quotations of the OT.

It is unclear, therefore, to me just why the translators have not also set this visually as a direct quotation from Isaiah.

That which is universally confessed is "that Jesus Christ is Lord" (ὅτι κύριος Ἰησοῦς Χριστός). The conjunction (ὅτι, "that") introduces and identifies the content of that which is thus confessed.[250] Here now "the name which is above every name" (v.9) is identified (see comments above under verse 9). "Lord" (κύριος) is cast forward in the clause to place emphasis upon it. In cases where the predicate nominative (κύριος, "Lord") is anarthrous (lacks the definite article) and is thrown forward before the subject (Ἰησοῦς Χριστός, "Jesus Christ") and lacks the verb (the NASU translators have added "is"), the predicate nominative is considered definite (i.e., "*the* Lord").[251] "For Paul, to confess that Jesus is Lord is to confess that he is Yahweh."[252]

The fullness of the confession is significant. "Jesus" is His human name—the name under which He embraced humble downward movement into humanity and in which He walked that road all the way "to the point of death, even death on a cross" (v.8). "Christ" points to His rightful office as the anointed of God, the One who fulfills all God promised and prophesied prior to His arrival. And "Lord" unveils His all-encompassing supremacy and marks Him as truly divine (again, see comments above under verse 9). The humble One ("Jesus") is now the exalted One ("Lord"). The anointed One ("Christ") is now openly acknowledged as such. God has come—personally, physically—to redeem His people and has utterly and all-inclusively triumphed in doing so.

It is not without significance that this is precisely the place the psalter ends: "Let everything that has breath praise the LORD. Praise the LORD!" (Psa. 150:6). John saw this day and rejoiced: "And every created thing which is in heaven and on the earth and under the earth and on the sea, and all things in them, I heard saying, 'To Him who sits on the

---

250 Fee suggests therefore that "these are the actual words of the confession" (225).

251 Wallace, 269-270.

252 Ibid., 188.

throne, and to the Lamb, be blessing and honor and glory and dominion forever and ever'" (Rev. 5:13).

All Jesus has done and all the Father will do in rightly honoring Him before the watching creation is done "to the glory of God the Father" (εἰς δόξαν θεοῦ πατρός).[253] The prepositional phrase modifies both clauses of the purpose statement (vv.10-11). That is to say, both the knee-bowing and tongue-confessing will be "to the glory of God the Father." Isaiah had simply "to God" (τῷ θεῷ), using the dative and the definite article to make the point. Paul strengthens that intent by employing the preposition (εἰς, "to") which might be used to point to the intended goal[254] and be rendered "unto." The Son has joined the Father in His quest and done all for the express purpose of gaining glory for Him.

> **Ministry Maxim**
>
> Time is on the side of the believer, for the vindication of confessing Christ as Lord is inevitable.

Coming thus to the end of the Apostle's magnificent hymn (vv.6-10) let us stand back and examine where he has brought us. Note that even in His glorified, exalted, fully-revealed and acknowledged state, Jesus willingly serves "to the glory of God the Father." This too serves the Apostle in making his point to the Philippians when he called them to "Do nothing from selfishness or empty conceit, but with humility of mind regard one another as more important than yourselves" and when he warned "do not merely look out for your own personal interests, but also for the interests of others" (vv.3-4). Indeed, this is precisely what it means to "Have this attitude in yourselves which was also in Christ Jesus" (v.5). Even in His exaltation, Jesus is thinking of, serving the purpose of, and exalting "God the Father." This, then, is what it means when the Apostle confesses, "for me to live is Christ" (Phil. 1:21).

---

253 Fee says that this closing phrase "goes with the whole narrative (from v.6), not just the final clause (226).

254 Sumney, 51; BDAG, 2291.4.

This signals that what the Apostle depicts here is not truly the end of the end. The universal confession of Christ as Lord works to an even greater end ("the glory of God the Father"). Is there a forward glimpse of what he describes in 1 Corinthians 15:24-28?

> Then the end will come, when he hands over the kingdom to God the Father after he has destroyed all dominion, authority and power. For he must reign until he has put all his enemies under his feet. The last enemy to be destroyed is death. For he "has put everything under his feet." Now when it says that "everything" has been put under him, it is clear that this does not include God himself, who put everything under Christ. When he has done this, then the Son himself will be made subject to him who put everything under him, so that God may be all in all.

Again, if I may, allow me to quote from my work elsewhere.

> History is linear, not cyclical. We are not caught in an unending experience of living through the past's reruns. We are headed somewhere. There is coming a time, in "the end", when the authority invested in Christ by the Father will have been brought to its end goal. The kingdom of God will win. Justice will be served. All opposition will be put down. All "dominion, authority and power" will have been destroyed. Christ will be Victor! Finally, and forever all that displeases and dishonors God will be under His feet! Having won the battle He was sent for, Jesus will hand the kingdom over to the Father once again. He then "will be made subject to him who put everything under him." Think of it! Mystery of mysteries! How can the co-eternal, co-equal Son eternally subject Himself to the Father with Whom He shares all the prerogatives and essence of Deity? ... Though our minds cannot fully comprehend it, this implies no inferiority of the Son to the Father either in His person, nature, or dignity. It simply means that even the Son, without surrendering His deity

or dignity, is willing to subject Himself eternally to the Father so that the authority of the triune God might be forever a wonder the new creation can't take its eyes off of.

When these unsearchable events have played themselves out, then "God will be all in all." The end goal of all the universe—from creation to consummation—will have been achieved! God will have been seen to be the source from which all things flow and the goal toward which all things progress. His glory will be manifested in its fulness! This has been the target from time immemorial. "As I live, all the earth will be filled with the glory of the Lord" (Numbers 14:21). This was God's repeated promise and prophecy throughout the Old Testament. This was the affirmed pledge of God Himself as His people stood upon the threshold of the promised land and refused to be part of His grand progress toward this display of His own Glory (Numbers 14:21). Such was the desire of Solomon at the height of the Old Testament kingdom's glory. "Praise be to his glorious name forever; may the whole earth be filled with his glory" (Psalm 72:19). This was the heart cry of the prophets of the Lord as they beheld the corruption of God's people and the crumbling of the Old Testament kingdom during its final centuries. "For the earth will be filled with the knowledge of the glory of the Lord, as the waters cover the sea" (Habakkuk 2:14). "… the earth will be full of the knowledge of the Lord as the waters cover the sea" (Isaiah 11:9). "The Lord will be king over the whole earth. On that day there will be one Lord, and his name the only name" (Zechariah 14:9). Now, through Christ, this is the blessed hope of every child of God. "But our citizenship is in heaven. And we eagerly await a Savior from there, the Lord Jesus Christ, who, by the power that enables him to bring everything under his control, will transform our lowly bodies so that they will be like his glorious body" (Colossians 2:20-21). One day a rider on a white horse will split the skies and bring in a glorious flood of God's glory throughout all creation

(Revelation 19:11-21). Finally and forever all opposition to God will be put down (Revelation 20).[255]

To this we can only agree with John, adding our voice to say, "Amen. Come, Lord Jesus" (Rev. 22:20b).

> **Digging Deeper:**
> 1. Explain how verse 9 puts hope into following the hard path exemplified by Christ in verses 6 through 8.
> 2. Why is submission to Christ in the present the wisest and safest step anyone can take? (vv.10-11)
> 3. If all things end at "the glory of God" (v.11) then what can you do to make each thing in your life serve that same end?

Verse 12 – So then, my beloved, just as you have always obeyed, not as in my presence only, but now much more in my absence, work out your salvation with fear and trembling;

The hymn of verses 6-11 is so stunning in its phraseology and exalted in its subject that a close consideration of it leaves one in breathless wonder and worship. Yet, having completed the hymn, the Apostle indulges in no pause, but immediately launches back into the kind of exhortation which led him into the hymn to begin with (1:27-2:5). The inferential conjunction Ὥστε ("So then") links what Paul is about to say with what has gone before and reveals that the following exhortations grow logically out of the truths of Christ just presented (vv.5-11). As Christ fully submitted to His Father and obeyed (v.8), so must we (v.12). Christ adopted a certain mindset (v.5) and so too must we; its outworking is addressed here (vv. 12-18) before being further exemplified by Timothy (vv.19-24) and Epaphroditus (vv.25-30).

---

255 Kitchen, *Embracing Authority*, 206-208.

Paul's appeal is direct (vocative) and especially passionate, for he addresses the readers as "my beloved" (ἀγαπητοί μου). Paul used this same form ("beloved," ἀγαπητοί) to address the believers in Rome (12:19), Corinth (1 Cor. 10:14; 2 Cor. 7:1), Thessalonica (1 Thess. 2:6), and believing slave owners more generally (1 Tim. 6:2). It is used also by the author of the letter to the Hebrews (6:9), by James (1:16, 19; 2:5), Peter (1 Pet. 2:11; 4:12; 2 Pet. 3:1, 8, 14, 17), John (1 John 2:7; 3:2, 21; 4:1, 7, 11), and Jude (3, 17, 20). Paul will use it again twice to address the Philippians in 4:1. The addition of the personal pronoun in the genitive (μου, "my") underscores the personal nature and depth of his feelings for these believers (cf. 1 Cor. 10:14; 15:58; Phil 4:1).

The sentence begun here runs through verse 13. The main verb is the command in the phrase "work out your salvation" (τὴν ἑαυτῶν σωτηρίαν κατεργάζεσθε), though it is preceded by several clauses. Twenty of the twenty-two times the verb appears in the NT it is from Paul's pen. It is a compound word comprised of κατά ("down") and ἐργάζομαι ("to work"). The preposition in compound either intensifies the root verb or emphasizes the downward motion of the effort[256], perhaps then being "perfective" in that it "views the linear progress down to the goal" and thus means "work on to the finish."[257] It means, then, "to do something with success and/or thoroughness."[258] Harmon notes that the word "commonly refers to the cultivation of land contracted to farmers, with an emphasis on the result of the work."[259] The present imperative calls for sustained, repeated, or habitual effort. Sanctification cannot be reduced merely to an event, but must be lived as an ongoing process. Paul casts a vote in favor of the believer's active—though thoroughly dependent—role in sanctification

> **Ministry Maxim**
>
> God makes your obedience your responsibility.

---

256 Thayer, 339.
257 Rienecker, 552.
258 Louw-Nida, 42.17.
259 Harmon, 241.

(as does Peter, 2 Pet. 1:10). Yielding and trusting are major elements in NT sanctification, but so is active, responsible initiative. While salvation is entirely of God and extended to us as a gift, it demands of us our utmost effort in embracing it and experiencing it to the fullest. The latter does not deny the former, but dignifies it for the genuine grace it is. For those who feel threatened by such an exhortation, the next verse will balance this emphasis on human responsibility with a strong word about divine sovereignty.

That which they are thus to work out successfully to its farthest extremities is "your salvation" (τὴν ἑαυτῶν σωτηρίαν). The relationship of salvation and works is one to which Paul has devoted a great deal of attention and in which he has come out squarely on the availability of salvation as a free gift of grace apart from works of the Law (cf. Rom. 3:20-28; Gal. 2:16). The Apostle emphatically says that salvation comes "to the one who does not work" (τῷ ... μὴ ἐργαζομένῳ, Rom. 4:5).[260] Clearly Paul is against any form of works-righteousness. "For by grace you have been saved through faith; and that not of yourselves, it is the gift of God; not as a result of works, so that no one may boast" (Eph. 2:8-9). But he is also against any so-called salvation that does not produce good works: "For we are His workmanship, created in Christ Jesus for good works, which God prepared beforehand so that we would walk in them" (v.10). The command issued here will be balanced and explained by the end of the sentence (v.13).

We should note that the command is issued to the whole of the believing body of people in Philippi, for both the verb and the reflexive pronoun (ἑαυτῶν, "your") are plural. The reflexive pronoun is in the attributive position, tucked between the noun and its definite article, thus emphasizing the qualitative nature of the salvation being considered. The emphasis of the reflexive pronoun is the subject taking action upon itself. The plural form then calls all the believers in Philippi to undertake this action. Paul is calling the collective body of believers to so live with one another that the salvation of Christ they each have experienced as a free gift of God's

---

260 Silva, 118.

grace is given fullest expression and finds its logical outworking to the nth degree in their relationships with one another. Thus Paul cues us that he is still on the theme of unity which he has been sounding for some time now (cf. 1:27-2:5). We need not divide into the either/or discussion of whether the Apostle is here discussing individual salvation vs. the collective health of the group. Personal salvation always impacts the believing community and the believing community is the context in which all personal faith finds expression. We each must believe, but we never believe in isolation or without larger relational impact.

As mentioned earlier, this command is preceded by several modifying clauses. The first of which is that this is to be fulfilled "just as you have always obeyed" (καθὼς πάντοτε ὑπηκούσατε). The verb (ὑπηκούσατε, "obeyed") meant "to answer the door" and thus "to obey as a result of listening."[261] The prepositional prefix (ὑπό) underscores the notion of submission that is present in the word.[262] Paul has just set before them in most graphic and beautiful terms the perfect and complete obedience of Christ (vvv.6-11) and now calls them to emulate that obedience and see it worked out in and through Christ's body. Such obedience—reflective of their Savior's own (ὑπήκοος, v.8)—has been their pattern in the past (πάντοτε ὑπηκούσατε, "you have always obeyed"). They have walked in selfless, loving relationships and experienced the resulting unity.

Paul does not make explicit to whom the obedience has been rendered and to whom he expects it will continue to be offered. Debate has raged needlessly. Clearly Paul intends obedience to the Father; as with Christ (v.8) so with His disciples (v.12). This would not, however, preclude obedience to Paul as the divinely called and commissioned Apostle, for such is Paul's certainty of His mission and message that to disobey his inspired word is to disobey God's Word.

---

261 Rienecker, 552.
262 Ibid.

Such obedience, says the Apostle, is to be worked out further "not as in my presence only" (μὴ ὡς ἐν τῇ παρουσίᾳ μου μόνον).²⁶³ The negation (μὴ, "not") is coupled with the adversative ἀλλὰ ("but") to form a strong contrast between what had been their record in the past and what Paul was calling for going forward. The comparative forms καθὼς ("just as") and ὡς ("as") serve to bring before their minds scenes of their past interactions with the Apostle.

At the time of his writing it likely had been over ten years since Paul's initial visit to the city of Philippi and the founding of the church there. He probably had visited the city and its believers three times, once at the church's founding (Acts 16:11-40) and later when Paul came and went through Macedonia again (Acts 20:1-6; 2 Cor. 1:16). During those times Paul had found the disciples teachable, responsive, and quick to obey the word of the Lord. They clearly held a high opinion of the Apostle Paul, for they saw themselves as intricately part of his wider ministry and lent him their support in advancing the gospel (1:5; 2:25-30; 4:10-20). Their sacrifice and generosity were exemplary (2 Cor. 8:1-5). A number from the believing community in Philippi were counted by the Apostle as partners in ministry, including Euodia, Syntyche (4:2-3a), Clement (4:3b), and Epaphroditus (2:25-30). Clearly the believers in Philippi had proven their readiness to obey God and the word He sent them through His Apostle. But Paul is now looking for more from the disciples (μὴ ... μόνον, "not ... only").

Just what additionally he has in mind is signaled by the words "but now much more" (ἀλλὰ νῦν πολλῷ μᾶλλον). Qualitatively he wants "more" (μᾶλλον) of the same kind of obedience he had come to expect from them. Quantitatively the current crisis will require "much" (πολλῷ) more in the way of obedience. Temporally the obedience must be worked out in the

---

263 Some point out that this clause is connected to the command "work out" rather than to the verb "obeyed" (e.g. Alford, 3:170; Vincent, ICC, 64; O'Brien, 280-282). The point is they should continue to "work out" their salvation even if he never physically visits them again. Robertson says, "Technically here the structure of the sentence shows that the clause about presence and absence belongs to 'work out.' Still, the idea covers obedience also" (*Paul's Joy in Christ*, 142) and Lenski adds, "'As' modifies both phrases" (796-797).

midst of (νῦν, "now") days of real of persecution (1:27-30), false teaching (3:2-3), and division (4:2-3).

Relationally this must happen, says Paul, "in my absence," (ἐν τῇ ἀπουσίᾳ μου). The noun "absence" (τῇ ἀπουσίᾳ) is found only here in the NT. We hear in this an echo of Paul's earlier words: "Only conduct yourselves in a manner worthy of the gospel of Christ, so that whether I come and see you or remain absent, I will hear of you that you are standing firm in one spirit, with one mind striving together for the faith of the gospel" (Phil. 1:27). Note also his return to this matter of his absence after this round of exhortations (2:19-24). As Paul called the bond-servants of Ephesus to relate to their masters, so he calls all the believers in Philippi to obey his directives, "not by way of eyeservice, as men-pleasers, but as slaves of Christ, doing the will of God from the heart" (Eph. 6:6).

Viscerally, this is to take place "with fear and trembling;" (μετὰ φόβου καὶ τρόμου). Of these two nouns the former (φόβου, "fear") is far more common in the NT. In fact τρόμος ("trembling") only occurs five times in the NT, but four of those are in combination with φόβος ("fear"). Paul, reflecting on his previous visit to the Corinthians, said, "I was with you in weakness and in fear [φόβῳ] and in much trembling [τρόμῳ]" (1 Cor. 2:3). Later he spoke to them of Titus's love for them, saying, "His affection abounds all the more toward you, as he remembers the obedience of you all, how you received him with fear [φόβου] and trembling [τρόμου]" (2 Cor. 7:15). He called the slaves of Ephesus to "be obedient to those who are your masters according to the flesh, with fear [φόβου] and trembling [τρόμου], in the sincerity of your heart, as to Christ" (Eph. 6:5). The latter emphasizes the sensation ("trembling" or "quivering"[264]), the former the "fear" from which it arises. The latter serves to strengthen the concept of the former.[265] Together they, in the present context, emphasize that the obedience to which the Philippians are called is to arise from a deep, reverent fear of the Lord.

---

264 BDAG, 7443.

265 Robertson, *Paul's Joy in Christ*, 145.

Paul will soon enough hold forth how the imperative to work out one's salvation is exemplified in his own life (3:4-14).

Verse 13 – for it is God who is at work in you, both to will and to work for *His* good pleasure.

Paul now provides the undergirding reason (γάρ, "for") why he can issue the command that the Philippian believers "work out" their salvation (v.12). What Paul says in verse 13 "supplies at once the stimulus to and the corrective of" the command of verse 12.[266] They can be expected to "work out" (κατεργάζεσθε) their salvation only because "it is God who is at work in you" (θεὸς ... ἐστιν ὁ ἐνεργῶν ἐν ὑμῖν). There is debate about the grammar at this point, particularly in identifying the subject of the sentence. The NASU translators have treated "God" as a personal name and view it as the subject of the sentence. The articular participle (ὁ ἐνεργῶν, "is at work"), however, is more likely to be the subject, with "God" (θεὸς) as the predicate nominative. If so, the position of θεὸς ("God") at the head of the sentence places stress upon the priority of His role, which serves to balance the responsibility laid upon the believer in verse 12. If this is the case it might be rendered "for the one working in you is God."[267]

Note the explicit contrast between "work *out*" (κατεργάζεσθε) and "at work *in*" (ὁ ἐνεργῶν ἐν, emphasis added). The common root (ἔργον) and the contrast between the prefixed κατά ("out") and ἐν emphasizes that while the believers are responsible for their obedience, in that obedience they are utterly dependent upon the work of God in them. The participle and its definite article (ὁ ἐνεργῶν, "who ... at work") is used substantively to emphatically describe God (θεὸς) and His activity. The present tenses of both the participle and the finite verb (ἐστιν, "is") emphasize the continual presence and activity of God in the midst of His people (ὑμῖν, "you" is plural).

---

266 Rienecker, 552.

267 Wallace, 46, 264-265; cf. Harmon, 245.

Given the plural form of the pronoun (ὑμῖν, "you"), the preposition ἐν could be translated "among" rather than "in," emphasizing the collective life of the body rather than the individual experience of each believer.[268] This would not deny the necessary, indwelling work of God within the individual believer, but would see Paul's emphasis here as being that saving reality worked out within the context of the believing community of God's people.

God is present and active in and among His people "both to will and to work" (καὶ τὸ θέλειν καὶ τὸ ἐνεργεῖν). God's active presence in His people is two pronged (καὶ ... καὶ, "both ... and"). There is a question about how to view the two infinitives. Wallace suggests that they should be viewed as substantives ("the willing" and "the working") and thus as the direct objects of ὁ ἐνεργῶν. This requires reading the verb as transitive (meaning "who is producing") rather than intransitive (meaning "who is at work"). This, Wallace argues, would "explicitly ... affirm the divine initiative in the process of sanctification."[269]

Wherever one lands on the specifics of these grammatical matters it seems the Apostle is bent on setting forth God as both the initiator (τὸ θέλειν, "to will") and the fulfiller (τὸ ἐνεργεῖν, "to work") of what has been commanded of believers. The first (τὸ θέλειν, "to will") describes the initial, inward impulse to obey. The second (τὸ ἐνεργεῖν, "to work") points to the ongoing fulfillment of what was inwardly initiated as the will was set. The very ability to decide for God and His will is a work done by God within us. Any and every actual step of concord with God's Word is possible only because of the immediate and personal inflow of God's life and power in us.

When we choose the will of God, it is evidence of God's presence and work within us (τὸ θέλειν, "to will"). When we actively move to fulfill the will of God through obedience, it is evidence of God's power flowing through us (τὸ ἐνεργεῖν, "to work"). The responsibility is ours, the ability God's alone. The responsibility was laid upon us by God and He also

---

268 Sumney, 53.

269 Wallace, 602-603; cf. Sumney, 53.

provides the ability to meet the responsibility. He who lays down the responsibility unfailingly makes available the ability to fulfill it. Divine imperatives always rest upon divine indicatives. We thus step forward to obey God's Word knowing that the very inclination to do so arises because of God's initiative within us. We take that step to obey knowing that as we cooperate with God's initiative within us He will empower and enable the fulfillment of what He has begun within us. Augustine well said, "We will, but God works the will in us. We work, therefore, but God works the working in us."[270]

> **Ministry Maxim**
>
> Every divine command is not only an obligation but an invitation.

Is this not an echo of the Apostle's opening words: "He who began a good work in you will perfect it until the day of Christ Jesus" (1:6)? Indeed, "our adequacy is from God" (2 Cor. 3:5). "Faithful is He who calls you, and He also will bring it to pass" (1 Thess. 5:24).

God's "will" and "work" are extended within us "for His good pleasure" (ὑπὲρ τῆς εὐδοκίας). The preposition (ὑπὲρ, "for") serves as a "marker of the moving cause or reason" and thus means "because of" or "for the sake of."[271] That which moves God to "both will and to work" within us is not something that arises within us, but something that arises within Himself: "His good pleasure" (τῆς εὐδοκίας). The translators rightly have taken the definite article as indicating possession ("His," i.e. God's).[272] The word was already used in 1:15 to describe the motive of some in preaching the good news. Here it is viewed as that within God[273] which moves Him to activity in and among His creatures. God wills and works to save because it brings Him pleasure to do so. God's saving impulse and activity arises not because of either the pitifulness or attractiveness of the creature, but because of the beauty and benevolence of His own nature. It

---

270 Quoted by Vincent, *Word Studies*, 3:438.

271 BDAG, 7538.2.

272 "In hundreds of instances the article has the force of 'his' ..." (Lenski, 800).

273 "that which pleases someone" (in this case, God), Louw-Nida, 25.88.

brings joy to God to work in and through His people. When we respond by joining our wills to His and take up His indwelling power to obey Him, God is pleased and we as His people enter into His joy. The Apostle John's exclamation is a reflection of the heart of God over His children: "I have no greater joy than this, to hear of my children walking in the truth" (3 John 4).

Does this make God then the opposite of what He has called His people to be (vv.3-4)? Is God, then, ultimately selfish by working in us what brings Him pleasure? Certainly not! Fee states the matter well: "… all that God does he does for his pleasure; but since God is wholly good, his doing what pleases him is not capricious, but what is wholly good for those he loves. God's pleasure is pure love, so what he does 'for the sake of his good pleasure' is by that very fact also on behalf of those he loves. After all, it delights God to delight his people."[274]

At the end of time, the universal confession of Jesus Christ as Lord will be "to the glory of God the Father" (εἰς δόξαν θεοῦ πατρός, v.11). So now joining our will to His and exercising His powerful working within us in obedience is "for His good pleasure" (ὑπὲρ τῆς εὐδοκίας, v.13).[275] The Father is glorified most when He is most pleased in His people. Just as He will make us intimate sharers of His glory (Phil. 3:20-21), so God calls us to share in His pleasure now through our obedience.[276] It will be universal then ("glory"); so make it particular now ("pleasure"). There shall be a creation-wide glory at His coming (vv.10-11), so let His pleasure be realized in the individual and collective obedience of His people in the present (νῦν, "now" v.12).

---

[274] Fee, 240.

[275] "Conceptually, the phrase is roughly equivalent to εἰς δόξαν θεοῦ (to the glory of God), though its distinctive thrust is different" (Silva, 131).

[276] For the interrelationship of God's glory and pleasure see my *Long Story Short*, 29-31.

> **Digging Deeper:**
> 1. How can we justly be held accountable ("work out") for that which only God can produce within ("work in") us?
> 2. In what specific point of your ongoing sanctification do you need to rely more deeply upon God being at "work in" you? (v.13)
> 3. In what specific point of your ongoing sanctification do you need to take personal responsibility and act in reliance upon God's grace? (v.12)
> 4. What is the proper balance between Christ-dependence (v.13) and personal responsibility (v.12)?

Verse 14 – Do all things without grumbling or disputing;

Having initially sounded the call to take up the obedience of Christ (v.8) and make it their own (vv.12-13), Paul now, in a sentence that extends through verse 16, continues to press the application of the thinking-that-makes-for-unity which He has been calling for since 1:27. Though there is no conjunction to indicate the immediate relationship, more specifically and immediately Paul gives practical expression to just what it means to "work out your salvation with fear and trembling" (vv.12-13).

Such application is all-encompassing, including "all things" (Πάντα). The neuter plural form gathers up the whole of life as the readers may know it in the present or at any future point. Every thought, feeling, choice, relationship, word, task, duty, obligation, necessity, pleasure, decision—everything and "all things" are in view.

These they are commanded to "do" (ποιεῖτε). The present imperative calls for continual or habitual action. The plural form scans the entire Christian fellowship in Philippi and leaves none excluded from the obligation.

While the scope of that which they must "do" (ποιεῖτε) is all-inclusive (Πάντα, "all things") there are, in this process, two things which they are to do "without" (χωρὶς). The word is used as a preposition and calls for the absence or lack of something. In this case it calls for undertaking their obedience "without making use of someth[ing]" or "without expressing or practicing someth[ing]."[277]

That which is rejected is "grumbling or disputing" (γογγυσμῶν καὶ διαλογισμῶν). The first, "grumbling" (γογγυσμῶν), is used only four times in the NT. The people of Israel did this concerning Jesus (John 7:12). The Hellenistic Jews of Jerusalem grumbled when there were inequities in the distribution of food among the believers (Acts 6:1). Peter exhorts his readers to "practice hospitality without grumbling" (1 Pet. 4:9). The word was used in the LXX to describe the murmurings of Israel (e.g., Ex. 16:7, 8 [2x], 9, 12; Numb. 17:20, 25). And that may stand as a backdrop in the Apostle's mind here.[278] The kindred verb was so used in 1 Corinthians 10:10: "Nor grumble [γογγύζετε], as some of them did."[279] Thus the idea here seems to be "murmuring against the dictates of God's will."[280] It may thus describe "secret talk" or "whispering,"[281] the kind of half-voiced, under-the-breath sort of muttering that sows seeds of discontent in a field wider than one's own heart.

> **Ministry Maxim**
>
> Personal discontent all too quickly becomes a corporate rallying cry.

To this is added (καὶ, "and") "disputing" (διαλογισμῶν). The word is a compound comprised of διά ("through") and λογισμός ("thought"). It came to describe "a thinking back and forth, deliberation."[282] While it could depict "evil thoughts," it could also be used of doubting (cf. 1 Tim 2:8, KJV).[283] Lightfoot, for this reason, calls it "intellectual rebellion

---

277 BDAG, 8013.1.b.β.

278 TDNT, 1:735-736.

279 The link to Israel's wilderness murmurings is strengthened by the fact that the next clause (v.15) draws directly upon Deuteronomy 32:5.

280 Silva, 124; Vincent, ICC, 67.

281 BDAG, 1667.

282 Rienecker, 620.

283 TDNT, 2:96-98.

against God."²⁸⁴ Paired with "grumbling" (γογγυσμῶν) it probably means something more like "disputing" or "arguing." But it may combine the two thoughts and point to "skeptical questionings or criticisms."²⁸⁵ When vocalized it becomes the "verbal exchange that takes place when conflicting ideas are expressed."²⁸⁶

"The murmuring" says Vincent, "is the moral, the doubting the intellectual rebellion against God."²⁸⁷ But some see these words as descriptive of murmurings and disputes between men, rather than with God.²⁸⁸ But the two need not be separated, for displeasure with God's doings and demands quickly becomes verbalized and once verbalized a matter of public debate, dispute, disagreement, and ultimately of division. Is this not precisely what the Israelites' grumblings against God show us? For their disputes with God found open form in their complaints against and opposition to Moses, which then divided the community.²⁸⁹ The plural forms for both nouns depict the variety of ways in which these things might find expression both inwardly/personally (e.g., Luke 5:22; 6:8; 24:38) and outwardly/relationally.²⁹⁰

Verse 15 – so that you will prove yourselves to be blameless and innocent, children of God above reproach in the midst of a crooked and perverse generation, among whom you appear as lights in the world,

---

284 Lightfoot, 131.

285 Vincent, ICC, 67.

286 BDAG, 1874.3.

287 Vincent, *Word Studies*, 3:438-439; cf. Robertson, *Paul's Joy in Christ*, 149).

288 E.g., Alford, 3:171-172; Fee, 243-244; Kennedy, 441; Martin, 113; O'Brien, 290-292.

289 Silva speculates that the problem in Philippi may have been disrespect for leadership and that the unusual mention of "the overseers and deacons" in 1:1 could be evidence of this. He also suggests that 2:29 may be a sign that leaders were not being treated with full respect (124).

290 O'Brien reasons in the opposite direction, beginning with people's disputes with one another and seeing Paul as hinting that their real complaint is with God, 291-292.

Continuing upon what he has said in verse 14 the Apostle now explains the purpose (ἵνα, "so that") behind the prohibition (vv.15-16a). He will then promptly complete the sentence with a clause expressing the desired result of their obedience (v.16b).

The goal is that "you will prove yourselves to be" (γένησθε). The subjunctive mood is combined with the ἵνα to express purpose. The aorist tense points to what "may definitely and permanently be."[291] The verb most simply means "to be," but is highly flexible and has a broad range of meanings. Perhaps here it means "to come into a certain state or possess certain characteristics" and thus "*to be, prove to be,* turn *out to be.*"[292] This may imply their culpability with regard to the "grumbling and disputing" confronted in verse 14.[293]

That which they are to be proven as is described in several ways. First, they are to be "blameless and innocent" (ἄμεμπτοι καὶ ἀκέραιοι). The first of the pair, "blameless" (ἄμεμπτοι), is used only five times in the NT, two of which are here in Philippians (2:15; 3:6). It meant to be "free from fault or defect" and thus "deserving no censure."[294] It obviously, then, described "pers[ons] of exceptional merit."[295] Luke, under the inspiration of the Holy Spirit, deemed Zechariah and Elizabeth to be "walking blamelessly" (Luke 1:6). Paul saw himself in his pre-conversion state as blameless "as to the righteousness which is in the Law" (Phil. 3:6). He prayed that the Thessalonian believers might love one another "so that He may establish your hearts without blame [ἀμέμπτους] in holiness before our God and Father at the coming of our Lord Jesus with all His saints" (1 Thess. 3:13). It points not to sinless perfection, but to living in such a way that there is no legitimate

> **Ministry Maxim**
>
> Refusal to complain is a powerful witness in itself.

---

291 Lenski, 802.

292 BDAG, 1646.7.

293 Martin, 113-114; Wuest, 76.

294 Thayer, 31.

295 BDAG, 394.

basis for blame by others. To this is added (καὶ, "and") "innocent" (ἀκέραιοι). The adjective is used only two other times in the NT, once as Jesus called His disciples to be "innocent as doves" (Matt. 10:16) and again when Paul told the Roman believers to be "innocent as to what is evil" (Rom. 16:19). It literally means to be "unmixed" (as with metals or wine) and thus is used figuratively in the NT of that which is pure and innocent.[296] Lightfoot observes that the first (ἄμεμπτοι, "blameless") "relates to the judgment of others," while the second (ἀκέραιοι, "innocent") describes the intrinsic character."[297]

By refusing to grumble and complain (v.14) they are to be seen as "children of God" (τέκνα θεοῦ). Paul seemed to appreciate the designation (Rom. 8:16, 17, 21; 9:8; Eph. 5:1) as did the Apostle John (John 1:12; 11:52; 1 John 3:1, 2, 10; 5:2). Elsewhere Paul will also speak of "sons" of God (Rom. 8:14; 9:26; Gal. 3:26). The noun "children" (τέκνα) is neuter and thus refers to both male and female as "children of God." Adam was designated the son of God (Luke 3:38). Israel was designated God's firstborn son (Exod. 4:22; Isa. 1:2-3; 43:6-7; 44;2; 49:14-15; 54:1-3; Jer. 3:19-20; Hosea 1:10). David was called God's son (2 Sam. 7:14). The prophets promised a son of David who would reign over God's people (e.g., Isa. 7:13-14; 9:1-7; Jer. 23:5-6; Ezek. 34:23-24; 37:24-28; Zech. 12:7-10). This came to full bloom in the NT where Jesus is both the Son of David (Matt. 1:1-17; 15:22; 20:30-31; 21:9) and the Son of God (Matt. 3:17; Mark. 15:39; Luke 4:41; John 1:34; Rom. 1:4; Heb. 4:14). Those who belong by grace through faith to Jesus are, as Paul says in our present passage, likewise called "sons of God." Jesus called His disciples to live uprightly before the unbelieving world "in order that you may be sons of your Father who is in heaven" (Matt. 5:45). Harmon puts it succinctly when he says, "What Adam and Israel could never be because of their disobedience, believers are because they are identified with Jesus Christ" and

---

296 Ibid., 260.

297 Lightfoot, 131.

"When the largely Gentile Christians in Philippi do all things without grumbling they show themselves to be the true children of God."[298]

To be "children of God" is to bear the likeness of the Father and to share His mind, mission, values, and perspective. Thus they must be proven to be "above reproach" (ἄμωμα). Note the assonance of the predicate adjectives as Paul piles them up: ἄμεμπτοι ("blameless"), ἀκέραιοι ("innocent"), ἄμωμα ("above reproach"). It is possible that this third predicate adjective, like the previous two, may go back to γένησθε ("will prove … to be"), but because its gender and number (neuter plural) matches τέκνα ("children") and because of its proximity to the noun it seems more likely to modify "children of God."[299] The word ἄμωμα ("above reproach") was used literally to speak of the absence of defect in an animal bound for sacrifice. Christ was, as the Lamb of God, blameless (Heb. 9:14; 1 Peter 1:19). It came then to be used in a religious and moral sense to speak of that which is without fault or blameless.[300] Believers are chosen from eternity past for this purpose (Eph. 1:4). We are thus to prove ourselves blameless, yet it is ultimately Christ who keeps us so that He may present us to Himself in this state (Jude 24), a glorious, beautiful bride (Eph. 5:27).

This all must become reality as we dwell "in the midst of a crooked and perverse generation" (μέσον γενεᾶς σκολιᾶς καὶ διεστραμμένης). The adjective μέσον ("in the midst") in the neuter form serves as an adverb and when, as here, it appears with the genitive it serves as a preposition[301], picturing the total immersion of the believers in a particular context. That context is designated by the collective noun γενεᾶς ("of a … generation"). It describes "the sum total of those born at the same time, expanded to include all those living at a given time and freq[uently] defined in terms of specific characteristics."[302] The term is used of Jesus looking "upon the

---

298 Harmon, 254 and 257; I am indebted to Harmon for this fuller understanding of the phrase "sons of God."

299 Hellerman, 136; Sumney, 54.

300 Friberg, 47.

301 BDAG, 4830.1.c.

302 Ibid., 1613.2.

whole contemp[orary] generation of Israel as a uniform mass confronting him" (Matt. 11:16; 12:41f; 23:36; 24:34; Mk 13:30; Luke 7:31; 11:29-32, 50f; 17:25; 21:32).[303]

That which characterizes this generation is two-fold. First it is "crooked" (σκολιᾶς). The word was used literally to describe that which had deviated from what is straight (Luke 3:5). It is from this word that we derive our word *scoliosis*. It is here used in a figurative sense, describing what is morally bent, twisted or crooked (cf. Acts 2:40). We are immersed in a generation which has as a collective whole deviated from God's way—and who call crooked, straight. Then also (καί, "and") this generation is "perverse" (διεστραμμένης). It was used literally "of an object on the potter's wheel" which had "*become misshapen*" and then figuratively it meant to "*pervert, corrupt, distort.*"[304] Jesus used the word to describe the generation in which He lived (Matt. 17:17; Luke 9:41). Jesus was accused of "misleading" (διαστρέφοντα) the Jewish nation (Luke 23:2). It was used of the demonically inspired magician Elymas in his attempts to turn the heart of the proconsul of Cyprus away from the truth of the gospel (Acts 13:8, 10). Paul used it to warn the elders of Ephesus that "from among your own selves men will arise, speaking perverse [διεστραμμένα] things, to draw away the disciples after them" (Acts 20:30). Our environment is such that it lays its hands upon one's perception of reality and seeks to reshape it after its own perverse design. The perfect tense describes the state in which this "generation" exists. The passive voice indicates that a malevolent hand has brought this state upon this "generation."

Paul strongly relies upon Deuteronomy 32:5 here. There Moses describes Israel as "a perverse and crooked generation" (γενεὰ σκολιὰ καὶ διεστραμμένη). Paul uses nearly identical terms to describe the unredeemed of his day, "a crooked and perverse generation" (γενεᾶς σκολιᾶς καὶ διεστραμμένης).[305] Harmon notes, "By refusing to grumble like the

---

303 Ibid.

304 Friberg, 112.

305 See Harmon (256-257) for an extensive enlargement on the connection between Deuteronomy 32:5 and Philippians 2:15.

Israelites did (cf. Phil. 2:14), believers show themselves to be what Israel never could be: without blemish in the midst of a crooked and twisted generation."³⁰⁶ The clear allusion to Moses' words here makes it more likely that Paul did have the wilderness generation in mind in verse 14 when he warned of "grumbling or disputing." Note also that here Paul calls the Philippian believers "children of God" (τέκνα θεοῦ) and in Deuteronomy 32:5 Moses calls the Israelites "not His children" (οὐκ αὐτῷ τέκνα).³⁰⁷

Note that "crooked and perverse" (σκολιᾶς καὶ διεστραμμένης) stand as the opposite of "blameless and innocent" (ἄμεμπτοι καὶ ἀκέραιοι).³⁰⁸ The contrast between the two is what makes believers to "appear as lights in the world" (φαίνεσθε ὡς φωστῆρες ἐν κόσμῳ). Note again Paul's emphasis on being engulfed by or immersed in the current culture or generation (ἐν οἷς, "among whom"). This is precisely where they are to "appear" (φαίνεσθε). The word means to "shine" or "to produce light" (cf. ESV, KJV, NET, NIV, NKJV, NRSV, RSV).³⁰⁹ The present tense indicates the continual or abiding nature of the action. The form may be either middle or passive. If the former, it pictures the inward-outward nature of the radiance. If passive then it pictures another—presumably, God—producing this light through them. It is not uncommon for older commentators to demand that the middle/passive cannot be translated "shine," but it has been demonstrated that this form can carry that meaning.³¹⁰ English translations clearly prefer the rendering "shine" (e.g., ESV, KJV, NET, NIV, NKJV, NRSV, NLT, RSV). The form may also be read either as indicative or imperative. Most English translations render it as an indicative. They are to do so "as lights in the world" (ὡς φωστῆρες ἐν κόσμῳ). The noun φωστῆρες ("lights") could be used of "any light-producing object in the sky, such as the sun, moon, and other planets and

---

306 Ibid., 257.

307 Lightfoot, 131.

308 Sumney, 55.

309 BDAG, 7678.1.b.

310 Ibid.; O'Brien, 295.

stars."[311] Given the morally dark nature of the "generation" under discussion perhaps "stars" is a good translation (cf. NIV, NRSV).

Paul alludes here to Daniel 12:3. The connection is confirmed by the fact that we have thus "the only two places in the Bible where the phrase 'shine as stars' occurs."[312] What Daniel saw as only possible at the time of the end when all are raised from the dead (v.2), Paul assigns as a possible, present experience of Christ's followers. The risen Christ inhabits His people even now by His Spirit and thus enables them to live out a foretaste in the present of what will be the fuller reality at His coming.

The preposition ἐν ("in") is the third emphasis in the latter part of the verse upon the immersion they exist in (μέσον, "in the midst"; ἐν οἷς, "among whom"; ἐν, "in"). While most English translations render κόσμῳ as "the world" (e.g., ESV, NASU, NET, NRSV), others render it as "a dark world" (NEB; Phillips) or "the sky" (NIV, TEV). The noun has a broad range of meaning, and can be used in an all-inclusive sense—"the sum total of everything here and now," of "the creation in its entirety."[313] It certainly includes the earth and all its inhabitants (as "generation" would indicate), but probably also includes the spiritual world as well. After all, Paul could tell the Ephesian believers that God called him as an apostle "to bring to light what is the administration of the mystery which for ages has been hidden in God who created all things" and that this was for the purpose that "the manifold wisdom of God might now be made known through the church to the rulers and the authorities in the heavenly places" (Eph. 3:9-10). Jesus told His disciples, "You are the light of the world. A city set on a hill cannot be hidden" (Matt. 5:14). Perhaps it is best to read "the world" (κόσμῳ) as synonymous with "a crooked and perverse generation" (γένησθε ἄμεμπτοι καὶ ἀκέραιοι).[314]

---

311 Louw-Nida, 1.27.

312 Harmon, 258.

313 BDAG, 4371.3.

314 O'Brien, 295.

Verse 16 – holding fast the word of life, so that in the day of Christ I will have reason to glory because I did not run in vain nor toil in vain.

Paul moves now to bring the sentence he began in verse 14 to a close by adding "holding fast the word of life" (λόγον ζωῆς ἐπέχοντες). The verb (ἐπέχοντες, "holding fast") is in the present tense, depicting the action as ongoing and abiding.[315] There is some debate about the meaning of the verb. Does it mean "holding *forth*" (KJV) or "holding *fast*" (NKJV; emphases added to both)? One means to provide and the other to protect; one intends to give and the other to guard. Most modern English versions go with the latter. The lexicons appear to be split between the former[316] and the latter.[317] The word is a compound comprised of the prefix ἐπί ("upon") and the basic verb ἔχω ("to hold"). In question is just how the preposition in compound is to be understood.[318] But the precise meaning of the word may well depend upon how one understands the role of the participle in the sentence. Sumney says its role may be understood in three different ways.[319] First, it could be understood as modifying "appear" (φαίνεσθε) in verse 15, being either explanatory of, and thus equivalent to, that verb (epexegetical), or indicating the way in which believers are to "appear" (instrumental),[320] or serving as a participle of means.[321] Second, it could be understood as beginning a new sentence and then be viewed as having imperatival force. Or thirdly, it could be dependent upon ἵνα

---

315 Reumann, 394; contra. Hellerman, 137.

316 Thayer says it means "to hold towards, hold forth, *present*: λόγον ζωῆςn as a light, by which illumined ye are the lights of the world," 231. Mounce says it is transitive and means "*to hold out, present, exhibit, display*," 1150. Vine adds, "of holding forth the word of life," 564.

317 BDAG, 2911.1; Friberg, 161; interestingly neither TDNT (relegated to a passing comment in n.1 in 2:816) or NIDNTT reference the word.

318 Müller insists the prefixed ἐπί means "to hold before, to hold out to others, to hold forth, like a torch which is held out before the bearer" (94).

319 Sumney, 55.

320 Silva, 126.

321 Harmon, 261; Rienecker, 553.

γένησθε ἄμεμπτοι καὶ ἀκέραιοι ("so that you will prove yourselves to be blameless and innocent") in verse 15.

The third, while possible grammatically, is too far removed to be probable. The second seems an unnatural way to read the line. It seems more likely to see the participle qualifying the preceding verb (φαίνεσθε, "appear") and thus being used in one way or another to describe just what form that appearance takes. Thus does the verb mean "holding fast" or "holding forth"? The Apostle's concern thus far in the letter seems to have leaned more in the direction of the propagation of the gospel (1:12-15, 17-18), though the protection of the gospel is not absent in his concern (1:7, 16).[322] Perhaps it is possible to say that we only "hold fast" the gospel by "holding forth" the gospel. Is this not what the Apostle was testifying of in his imprisonment? Paul's "defense and confirmation of the gospel" (1:7, 16) was achieving "the greater progress of the gospel" (1:12). By its very nature the gospel is lost by failing to share it; it is kept only by giving it away. It is in its propagation that the gospel is best protected.[323]

That which is thus to be guarded by giving is "the word of life" (λόγον ζωῆς). The reference is the gospel itself (cf. John 1:1; 1 Pet. 1:23; Heb. 4:12). Just how should we understand the genitive "of life" (ζωῆς)? It is probably best to view it such that "the word" is viewed as producing the "life."[324] Or perhaps as being the origin from which "life" arises.[325] As

---

[322] Interestingly both sides of the debate call upon context in support of their view. "Hold fast": "the context focuses on the blameless behavior of the Philippians, not their evangelistic outreach" (Harmon, 261; cf. Hellerman, 138); "Hold forth": "the rendering 'holding forth' or 'holding out' … would seem to be best suited to the context. As for the missionary idea, this is already present in the words, 'among whom you are shining as stars in the universe.'" (Hendriksen, 125). O'Brien argues both ways, saying on the one hand "… the rendering 'holding forth' … would appear to be well suited to the context," and on the other he supports the translation "holding fast" by saying "the general context of 1:27-2:18 has to do with standing firm in the faith against the attacks of external opponents" (297).

[323] Martin says, "The two meanings of the verb happily dovetail. Only as we firmly 'hold fast' to the gospel truth can we effectively 'hold it forth'" (118).

[324] Harmon, 262; Reinecker, 553; Sumney, 56.

[325] O'Brien, 298.

the gospel is distributed life is disseminated. Even if that proclamation culminates in martyrdom—"whether by life or by death" (1:20)— it produces life, both for the one who bears that witness (v.21) and for him who observes it and in it hears the gospel testimony (v.22). Note the transition from "lights" (v.15) to "life" (v.16) and compare with John's "In Him was life, and the life was the Light of men" (John 1:4).[326]

Paul calls upon the Philippian believers to live thus with a specific purpose in mind (εἰς, "so that"). This purpose is connected not merely to "holding fast the word of life" (v.16a) but to the whole of verses 15-16a.[327]

> **Ministry Maxim**
>
> The gospel is best protected not by hiding it away, but by holding it out.

What Paul has in view is that "I will have reason to glory" (καύχημα ἐμοί). The pronoun is emphatic (ἐμοί, "I"). The verb is missing, "will have" being added by the translators. The noun καύχημα ("reason to glory") appears eleven times in the NT, ten of which are used by Paul. It often expresses his "taking pride in someth[ing]" or designates "that which constitutes a source of pride" for the Apostle.[328] More often in Paul it is used in the latter sense and so here the translators render it "I will have reason to glory."[329] Paul's ultimate concern is for the glory of God (Phil. 1:11; 2:11; 4:19), but he foresees a day when God "will transform the body of our humble state into conformity with the body of His glory" (3:21), thus giving us a share in His glory. So Paul was concerned that his conduct in the present be such that the Philippians might "glory" in him (1:26). Now he wants them to so live that he might "have reason to glory" in them. They are, he says later, "my joy and crown" (Phil. 4:1). Paul spoke also of this mutual pride in relationship with the Corinthians: "we are your reason to be proud [καύχημα] as you also are ours, in the day of our Lord Jesus" (2 Cor. 1:14). He felt similarly regarding the Thessalonian

---

326 Kennedy, 442.

327 O'Brien, 298.

328 BDAG, 4172.1.

329 Sumeny, 56.

believers: "For who is our hope or joy or crown of exultation? Is it not even you, in the presence of our Lord Jesus at His coming? For you are our glory and joy" (1 Thess. 2:19-20).

As with the Corinthians, so Paul's concern here, even in the present, is what will be true "in the day of Christ" (εἰς ἡμέραν Χριστοῦ). He has already exhorted them to "be sincere and blameless until the day of Christ" (1:10)[330] and now demonstrates just how that motive works out in his own heart. Paul longs to be found without fault on that day and to receive his praise from God. He has already affirmed his confidence that God would finish the good work He began in the Philippian believers "until the day of Christ Jesus" (1:6). Paul ever had that last day in view (2:9-11).

What he has stated positively ("I will have reason to glory") Paul now states negatively. Paul longs not simply for divine praise on the final day, but that it might come to him "because" (ὅτι) two things will not have proven true of his life and ministry. In two parallel and roughly synonymous clauses Paul expresses this hope. The first reason will be that "I did not run in vain" (οὐκ εἰς κενὸν ἔδραμον). Paul uses the imagery of running to describe either the Christian life generally (1 Cor. 9:24, 26; Gal. 5:7) or ministry in Christ's name more specifically (Gal. 2:2; 2 Thess. 3:1). The verb conveys the intensity of the effort being made.[331] The same reality is viewed in the second clause as "toil" (ἐκοπίασα). Here too the term is often used by Paul, either to describe the Christian life (1 Tim. 4:10) or ministry in Christ's name (Rom. 16:6, 12; 1 Cor. 4:12; 15:10; 16:16; Gal. 4:11; Col. 1:29; 1 Thess. 5:12; 1 Tim. 5:17; 2 Tim. 2:6). The verb emphasizes the wearisome nature of the toil. In both cases the verbs are in the aorist tense, viewing the whole of his ministry as one event from the perspective of "the day of Christ" when it shall all be brought into review at the throne. Through both metaphors Paul expresses his hope that at the throne, under the gaze of divine omniscience, his ministry will not

---

330 This phrase is used only in Philippians. The more usual expression is "the day of the Lord" (e.g., 1 Cor. 1:8; 5:5; 2 Cor. 1:14; 1 Thess. 5:2; 2 Thess. 2:2).

331 Rienecker, 553.

have proven to have been "in vain" (εἰς κενὸν). The word generally means "empty" and here has the idea of without effect or result.[332] Paul does not want to appear at God's throne, after a lifetime of ministry, empty-handed (1 Cor. 15:10; Gal. 2:2; 1 Thess. 2:1; 3:5). Kennedy observed, "As the Apostle advanced in years the final result of his labours would have increasing prominence in his thoughts."[333]

Harmon identifies here an echo of Isaiah 49:4a: "But I said, 'I have toiled in vain, I have spent My strength for nothing and vanity.'" If this be the case then Paul is intentionally taking up the words of God's "Servant" to express that he "understood his life and ministry as the fulfillment of the Servant's mission to be a light to the nations because Jesus Christ, the Suffering Servant, lived in and through him (Gal. 1:15-16; 2:20)."[334] Significantly, Isaiah 49:6 continues the thought: "He says, 'It is too small a thing that You should be My Servant To raise up the tribes of Jacob and to restore the preserved ones of Israel; I will also make You a light of the nations So that My salvation may reach to the end of the earth.'" Is this also echoed here ("you appear as lights in the world," 2:15)? Certainly one can imagine the draw of this passage upon Paul, Apostle to the Gentiles.

In this one verse Paul has worked hard the preposition εἰς, employing it four times. Once it clearly is a temporal designation ("in [εἰς] the day of Christ"). The other three times it has its more typical directional sense ("indicating motion into a thing or into its immediate vicinity or relation to something"[335]).

---

332 BDAG, 4191.3.

333 Kennedy, 442.

334 Harmon, 264.

335 BDAG, 2291.

> **Digging Deeper:**
> 1. Prayerfully identify the precise area in which you are currently struggling with a grumbling spirit. (v.14)
> 2. Discuss with a friend: Why is grumbling so much easier for us and natural to us than gratitude?
> 3. In what way is grumbling directly connected to the success of our mission in the world? (vv.15-16)

Verse 17 – But even if I am being poured out as a drink offering upon the sacrifice and service of your faith, I rejoice and share my joy with you all.

As Paul followed his exhortations to unity (1:27-2:4) with the example of Christ (2:5-11), so now he will follow the present exhortations to unity (2:12-18) by recounting the examples of Timothy (2:19-24) and Epaphroditus (2:25-30). But first he must here draw to a close his present exhortations (2:12-18). As Paul moves to do so he makes a dramatic turn by use of the strong adversative Ἀλλὰ ("But"). Just what his present words are meant to contrast has been a matter of some discussion. It is possible that the contrast is not so much between something in the immediate context and what he now says, but the Apostle reaches far back to his confidence of deliverance from present imprisonment and its dangers (1:25-26) and contrasts this with the hypothetical possibility that it may end in his death. It may be more likely that he is contrasting the ongoing running/toiling of verse 16 with the final, climatic "being poured out as a drink offering" (v.17).[336]

The hypothetical nature of what he proposes is set before us through a concessive conditional clause (εἰ καὶ, "even if"). The condition (εἰ plus the present indicative) is viewed as fulfilled, in this case as a hypothetical statement for the sake of making a point. Although Paul elsewhere expressed

---
336 Lightfoot, 143; Sumney, 56.

his expectation of release from his present imprisonment (1:24-26; cf. 2:24), he here leaves open the possibility that it could end in his death. The emphatic use of καί ("even") amounts to a concessive statement. That which is conjectured is "I am being poured out as a drink offering" (σπένδομαι). The word is used only two times in the NT, both by Paul. He will use it again when in his second imprisonment and facing a more certain martyrdom (2 Tim. 4:6). Drink offerings were common among the pagans (Deut. 32:38) and among the Hebrews before Sinai (Gen. 28:18; 35:14). But when the Law was given to Moses, God prescribed that drink offerings should accompany many of the sacrifices (Exod. 29:40, 41). Usually consisting of wine, the offering was poured out as the final act of the sacrifice (Num. 15:4, 5, 7, 10, 24) or continual burnt offering (28:7-8). It was a regular part of worship on all Sabbaths (28:9-10) and feasts (28:14-31; 29:6-39). The wine may have been used by the Israelites as a substitute for the blood of pagan libations (Psa. 16:4).[337] Speaking of Paul's use of the word in 2 Timothy 4:6 Hendriksen well says, "Since this wine *was gradually poured out*, was *an offering*, and was *the final act* of the entire sacrificial ceremony, it pictured most adequately *the gradual ebbing away* of Paul's life, the fact that he was presenting this life to God as *an offering*, and the idea that while he viewed his entire career of faith as 'a living sacrifice' (Rom. 12:1; cf. 15:16), he looked upon *the present* stage of this career as being *the final act of sacrifice*."[338]

The present tense of the verb may vividly picture the sacrifice as already underway or it could look forward to what may become a present reality. The passive voice pictures not Paul himself pouring out his own life, but his being acted upon by another. That may reference the Roman Empire generally or Caesar more specifically. It seems, however, more likely that Paul would have in mind God as the active agent. Thus any such death would be ultimately in the hands of his sovereign King, who would pour out His servant's lifeblood—which had long before been offered as a living sacrifice (Rom. 12:1)—in one final act of service and worship. What

---

337 Fee, 288-289.

338 Hendriksen, *Thessalonians, Timothy and Titus*, 313.

Paul now contemplates as only a possibility would one day become a reality (2 Tim. 4:6).

The picture is of Paul's life being poured out in death "upon the sacrifice and service of your faith" (ἐπὶ τῇ θυσίᾳ καὶ λειτουργίᾳ τῆς πίστεως ὑμῶν). Paul's life and death are pictured as poured out to God over (ἐπὶ, "upon") the worshipful life of faith lived by the Philippian believers. Whether Paul has in mind Jewish or pagan religious ritual has been a matter of much discussion. On the one hand he is writing to a church primarily made up of former pagans, but on the other hand it is difficult to imagine Paul calling upon pagan ritual rather than his Jewish background. The point is made without the necessity of exact identification of the background from which he draws his illustration.[339] This then leads to the discussion of the precise intent of ἐπὶ ("upon"). Does it mean *around, on, over, at, upon* or *in addition to*?[340] Probably the point is not so much the exact location of the libation's landing, but its crowning nature.

> **Ministry Maxim**
>
> A pastor's death and his people's lives of faith are all of one piece as sacrifices of worship to God.

Paul reminds them that their active expression of faith is, first, a "sacrifice" (τῇ θυσίᾳ).[341] The word is used often in the LXX in a cultic context and, thus not surprisingly, often in Hebrews in the NT. It is used more sparingly in Paul's writings; only five times. Once he uses it of sacrifices under the Mosaic Law (1 Cor. 10:18), but otherwise he employs it metaphorically. One's entire body is to become "a living sacrifice" (Rom. 12:1) offered to God. Believers' active love for one another is, like Christ's own sacrifice, to be "an offering and a sacrifice to God as a fragrant aroma" (Eph. 5:2). And closer to home, Paul uses the word later in this letter to describe the gift of money the Philippians sent to him in his imprisonment

---

339 Hendriksen, 127; Kent, 11:130; Robertson, *Word Pictures*, 4:448.

340 In pagan practice the libation was poured over the sacrifice; in Jewish ritual it was poured out around the altar upon which the sacrifice was offered (Müller, 95-96).

341 The two nouns are joined together (καὶ, "and") and governed by one definite article (τῇ, "the").

("a fragrant aroma, an acceptable sacrifice [θυσίαν], well-pleasing to God," Phil. 4:18). Their faith is also "service" (λειτουργίᾳ) rendered to God and others in His name. As with its mate this word is used more frequently in the LXX than in the NT, and especially of cultic service of priests under the Mosaic Law (cf. Luke 1:23; Heb. 9:21). That system has been surpassed by the offering of Christ (Heb. 8:6). Now it can be used of monetary gifts of God's people (2 Cor. 9:12) and more generally of the life of "service" believers live to God as they serve others (Phil. 2:17, 30). Paul pictured the faith of the Philippians as both the sacrificial gift (τῇ θυσίᾳ, "the sacrifice") and the process by which that gift is offered (λειτουργίᾳ, "service").[342]

Thus, clearly, Paul pictures "your faith" (τῆς πίστεως ὑμῶν) through the lenses of OT worship. What had been offered repeatedly on a Jewish altar through physical sacrifices has been forever accomplished through the "once for all" sacrifice of Christ on our behalf (Heb. 7:27; 9:12, 26; 10:10). And in view of this supreme sacrifice the believers' unfolding and active lives of faith become thank offerings to God in view of the finished work of Christ.

Should "your faith" (τῆς πίστεως ὑμῶν) be read with the Philippians viewed as the priests offering up their faith to God[343] or with Paul as the priest offering their faith to God as evidence of His ministry?[344] The latter often references 1 Corinthians 15:16 as an example of Paul serving as priest offering to God the faith of the gentile believers. The former emphasizes the priesthood of all believers (1 Pet. 2:5). Martin points out that the passive voice of the verb (σπένδομαι, "I am being poured out as a drink offering") makes the latter view impossible.[345] In balance it seems more likely that Paul is depicting the Philippian believers as offering themselves up to God as "living sacrifices" (Rom. 12:1) as an expression of

---

342 Kennedy, 443.

343 Fee, 251-253; Hendriksen, 127; Kent, 11:130; Lightfoot 144; Martin, 119-120; O'Brien, 309; Robertson, *Paul's Joy in Christ*, 155-156; Silva, 129; Sumney, 57; Vincent, ICC, 71.

344 Alford, 3:178; Wallace, 116.

345 Martin, 120.

their faith in Christ. His possible martyrdom is then viewed as the crowning addition made to the offering of their lives.³⁴⁶

Even in this Paul keeps his call to unity in view. For what more intimate picture of oneness could he give than to depict himself as potentially dying far away from the Philippian believers whom he loved and by whom he was loved, and in that distant and ultimate physical act of faith being joined as one with them in worship to God? What they did and how they lived in Philippi was one act of worship with what Paul did and how he lived out faith in Christ in Rome. Two locations, multiple believers, one God, one act of worship! Thus, it may be indirectly implied, if the Philippians continue down a path of disintegration and disunity, what becomes of the Apostle's ultimate sacrifice to God?

And so "even if" (εἰ καὶ) all of that comes true in the present moment, if they and he remain as one in worship to God, Paul can say, "I rejoice" (χαίρω).³⁴⁷ Paul frequently used this precise expression to tell his people of his joy over their obedience (Rom. 16:19), fellowship with him (1 Cor. 16:17), repentance (2 Cor. 7:9, 16), and of his sufferings on their behalf in the cause of Christ (Col. 1:24). He rejoiced over the proclamation of the gospel (Phil. 1:18). And so presently he rejoiced over the thought of them all unified in a life of sacrificial faith lived in worship to God. The joy was not Paul's alone for in addition ("and," καὶ) Paul can say "I … share my joy with you all" (συγχαίρω πᾶσιν ὑμῖν). The verb is a compound form of the word just used, σύν ("with") and χαίρω ("rejoice").³⁴⁸ It thus points to shared joy, to rejoicing together with another. Thus Paul does not identify himself with a faction within the Philippian church or with a fraction of

---

346 Harmon, 268-269.

347 Here again Paul sounds the rich theme of joy which runs like a vein of gold through this letter (χαίρω: 1:18 [2x]; 2:17, 18, 28; 3:1; 4:4 [2x], 10; συγχαίρω: 2:17, 18; χαρά: 1:4, 25; 2:2, 29; 4:1).

348 Lightfoot insisted (144) that the compound word means "congratulate," since it would be awkward to speak of them already rejoicing (v.17) just before he commands them to "rejoice" (v.18, ESV). This seems an unnecessary attempt to resolve a perceived problem that has other answers.

their number, but "with you all" (πᾶσιν ὑμῖν). The Apostle never wastes an opportunity to underscore his theme of unity.

Verse 18 – You too, *I urge you*, rejoice in the same way and share your joy with me.

The joy that Paul lives in (v.17) he desires the Philippian believers to enter into. He calls them to join him: "You too" (καὶ ὑμεῖς). The pronoun is plural, calling them out of any divisions that may have fractured their relationships and into a shared response to God's grace. The καὶ ("too") is employed as if to underscore that if Paul, in prison, can "rejoice" (v.17) can't they in the bonds of their relational struggles manage to do the same (v.18)?

"I urge you" has been added by the translators and is not found in the Greek text. The NASB translators translated the δὲ ("And," cf. NET, NRSV) though the NASU has dropped it, presumably in search of a smoother English rendering.

Now the Apostle issues a command that they join him (v.17) and "rejoice" (χαίρετε). The present imperative calls for repeated or habitual action. The plural form calls each and every believer in Philippi to the same response. They are to fulfill this "in the same way" (τὸ ... αὐτὸ) Paul has (v.17). The pronoun and definite article function adverbially[349] and might be rendered "similarly" or "in the same way" (HCSB, NET, NRSV).

As Paul personally rejoiced ("I rejoice," v.17), so he commanded them to "rejoice" (v.18). And as Paul rejoiced with them ("share my joy with you all," v.17), now he calls them also (καὶ, "and") to "share your joy with me" (καὶ συγχαίρετέ μοι). The verb is the same one he used in the previous verse to speak of his shared joy with them. Now the sharing is to be reciprocated and flow in the reverse direction. Paul in this way seeks to bring the fractured and divided believers of Philippi into a unified response that

> **Ministry Maxim**
>
> Unity finds its crescendo in the shared joy of mutual sacrifice.

---

349 Robertson, *Grammar*, 487.

centers in their common relationship to their founding Apostle. The joy is in Christ, but the earthly locus is their collective bond with Paul. While they may be struggling to look at one another and agree, he calls them to look away to Christ and His Apostle and then, as they respond to them, to come to the realization that they are unified once again around something (or more accurately, someone) and sharing alike in the same reality—joy!

> **Digging Deeper:**
> 1. How can joint-worship take place among people separated by miles and circumstances? (v.17)
> 2. Discuss with someone how one person's joy can be a rebuke to another person's grumbling. (vv.17b-18)

Verse 19 – But I hope in the Lord Jesus to send Timothy to you shortly, so that I also may be encouraged when I learn of your condition.

As he followed the exhortations of 1:27-2:5 with the supreme example of Christ (2:6-11), so now he follows the exhortations of 2:12-18 with the examples of Timothy (2:19-24) and Epaphroditus (2:25-30). He again will offer a brief exhortation (3:1-3) before offering himself as an example (3:4-14).

By means of the mild adversative δὲ ("But") Paul transitions from the future possibilities of his ultimate sacrifice of martyrdom as added to their sacrificial life of faith (vv.17-18) to the present realities of their needs and his plans. In his absence he intends "to send Timothy" (Τιμόθεον ... πέμψαι) to them. At the moment of writing it is not absolutely certain he will be able to do so, thus he says "I hope" (Ἐλπίζω). He has an ongoing, abiding "hope" (present tense) to

> **Ministry Maxim**
> Shared news of joint obedience to a common Lord makes up the sinews by which the body of Christ is held together.

"send" Timothy to them at a given moment (aorist tense) in the future. While he cannot be definite in his statement, his is a hope that rests "in the Lord Jesus" (ἐν κυρίῳ Ἰησοῦ). Christ Himself is the sphere in which lie Paul's entire life and hope. The phrase ἐν κυρίῳ ("in the Lord") occurs nine times in Philippians (and over forty-five times in all his letters), setting forth the sphere of their trust (1:14; 2:24), hope (2:19), relationships (2:29), joy (3:1; 4:4, 10), stability (4:1), and unity (4:2).[350] "This favorite Pauline idiom is not a mere pious phrase, but represents the very core of Paul's philosophy of life. Jesus is the circumference of all his thoughts and activities. Christ is both the center and the circumference of the circle of life for Paul."[351] The Lord of the Church is the bedrock of Paul's hope with regard to the local expression of His Church in Philippi. He can be trusted to "fulfill every desire for goodness and the work of faith with power" (2 Thess. 1:11) as it relates to His people. It is by living out of his union with Christ and within the sphere (ἐν) of His sovereign will that Paul has confidence concerning his release from prison (1:25-26), of the extension of his life to receive the news Timothy will bring to him of their response to his letter (2:19), and of his future personal visit to them (v.24).

Upon his return to Derbe and Lystra, Paul found Timothy an active disciple of Christ (Acts 16:1-2). "Paul wanted this man to go with him" (v.3) and so it appears that Timothy would have been with him when he soon after arrived in Philippi for the first time (vv.12-40). So his sending Timothy to them now was to send one whom they respected, who had been a part of the founding of their fellowship. He would be not only known by them, but recognized as a ministry partner of the Apostle who would carry his authority when among them on his behalf.

That he will send his emissary "to you" (ὑμῖν) not only signals his ongoing care for them, but the approaching accountability they will face upon Timothy's arrival. The grumbling and divisive behavior had best be dealt with before his arrival. In fact he may arrive "shortly" (ταχέως) so they must deal with these matters not only thoroughly, but swiftly. Timothy

---

350 cf. similar expressions in 1:13, 26; 2:1; 3:3, 14; 4:7, 19, 21; cf. Fee, 264.

351 Robertson, *Paul's Joy in Christ*, 159.

will be dispatched "as soon as I see how things go with me" (v.23), so they best be prepared to give evidence they are heeding his exhortations.

That this tone of loving accountability stands behind the Apostle's plans is signaled by the purpose clause that he adds ("so that," ἵνα plus the subjunctive verb). His aim is that "I also may be encouraged" (κἀγὼ εὐψυχῶ). The verb appears only here in Biblical literature, though it was commonly used in grave inscriptions, wishing the departed a blessing in the afterlife. Did Paul use this in light of the possibility of his martyrdom (1:20; 2:17)? He clearly had expectation of release from prison rather than death (1:19, 25-26; 2:24), but it is possible he used this verb specifically to underscore the seriousness of the events in which he found himself entangled. The word has the sense of being heartened, gladdened or having courage, with a special emphasis on a release from anxiety.[352] It might be considered a variant on the theme of joy that runs through the letter. The present tense pictures an ongoing positive outlook toward the Philippian believers that replaces whatever anxiety has arisen in his heart after hearing from Epaphroditus of their current condition (2:25-30; 4:18).

By use of κἀγὼ ("I also," a combination of καὶ and ἐγώ) Paul makes the pronoun ("I") emphatic. But in just what way will he "also" be encouraged? The "also" probably signals that he expects the Philippians to be encouraged by his letter and by Timothy's visit and that he "also" wants to get in on the encouragement when he hears Timothy's report.[353] That is to say, the encouragement becomes reciprocal and shared among them. Less likely is the supposition that in addition to what he has received from them (their financial support, 4:10-20) he "also" wants to receive from them encouragement over their response to his present exhortations.

Such encouragement, says Paul, will only take place "when I learn of your condition" (γνοὺς τὰ περὶ ὑμῶν). The participle (γνοὺς) is translated as indicating a temporal relationship ("*when* I learn") between his

---

352 BDAG, 3326.

353 "as well as you, by your reception of news concerning me," Alford, 3:174; "by the tidings which I shall hear from you, as you by the accounts of me," Vincent, ICC, 73.

encouragement and the knowledge that releases it in his heart.³⁵⁴ It might also be regarded as instrumental or as indicating the means by which he will be encouraged ("by knowing") or as causal ("because I know").³⁵⁵ The aorist is probably ingressive ("come to know").³⁵⁶ The phrase "of your condition" (τὰ περὶ ὑμῶν, lit. "the things concerning you") was used in 1:27 ("of you") and will be used again in the next verse ("for your welfare").³⁵⁷ He has obviously received a report of their condition from Epaphroditus; that report has stirred enough concern for him to write this letter. That his peace over them rests upon again learning of their condition implies his expectation that they will change things among themselves based upon what he is writing in this letter. It is tantamount to saying, "I will be encouraged when I see how you respond to and apply what I am now writing to you."

Verse 20 – For I have no one *else* of kindred spirit who will genuinely be concerned for your welfare.

Paul now explains (γὰρ, "For") his choice of sending Timothy to them. Their experience with Timothy will underscore the Apostle's confession: "I have no one else" (οὐδένα ... ἔχω) like Timothy to send. The present tense of the verb may be understood to indicate there is no one else presently at his disposal, as if "he's the best I can offer right now, given my circumstances."³⁵⁸ But in view of how Paul universally praises Timothy both in personal terms (1 Cor. 4:17; 1 Tim. 1:2, 18; 2 Tim. 1:2) and

---

354 Rienecker, 553.

355 Harmon, 278.

356 Kennedy, 444; O'Brien, 318; Robertson, *Paul's Joy in Christ*, 160.

357 cf. also τὰ κατ' ἐμὲ ("my circumstances") in 1:12 and τὰ περὶ ἐμὲ ("how things go with me") in 2:23; and also τὰ ἑαυτῶν ἕκαστος ("your own personal interests") and τὰ ἑτέρων ἕκαστοι ("the interests of others") in 2:4 along with τὰ ἑαυτῶν ("their own interests") in contrast to τὰ Ἰησοῦ Χριστοῦ ("those of Jesus Christ," v.21); In light of all these subtle connections throughout the text Fee observes, "one seeks 'the interests of Jesus Christ' when one 'looks out for the interests of others,' instead of 'one's own,'" 260; cf. also Harmon, 278.

358 "to have at hand, have at one's disposal," BDAG, 3353.1.c.

in terms of his gospel service (Rom. 16:21; 1 Cor. 16:10; Phil. 1:1; 1 Thess. 3:2, 6) or both (Phil. 2:22), his point is probably more sweeping than that. Had he all his fellow gospel servants at hand, there would be none like Timothy. Timothy's uniqueness is partly due to the distinctive relationship Timothy shares with the Philippians, having been with Paul through the trying experiences of seeing the church birthed there (Acts 16:1-40). Others would not have these formative shared experiences with them. But apart from shared experience there was also a unique quality of character within Timothy.

These facts make Timothy exceptional in two ways. First is the fact that he is "of kindred spirit" (ἰσόψυχον). In Biblical literature the word is found only here and in the LXX of Psalm 54:14 where it is translated "my equal," describing someone close to David who betrays him. It is a compound word comprised of ἴσος ("equal") and ψυχή ("soul"). It has the basic meaning of being "equal in soul."[359] It may be a play on words with εὐψυχῶ ("I ... may be encouraged") in verse 19.[360] That to which Timothy's soul corresponds or is equal is Paul's own, in the matter of care for the Philippian believers.[361] They were both present at their birth and through their early testing. There is a bond that Paul, Timothy and they share, forged in the fires of spiritual birth and common persecution.

> **Ministry Maxim**
>
> Rare is the one you can trust not only to do a job, but to represent your heart.

---

359 Thayer, 307.

360 Moulton and Milligan, 2029; Harmon (279) identifies additional possible connections with 1:27 (μιᾷ ψυχῇ, "one mind"), 2:2 (σύμψυχοι, "united in spirit"), and 2:30 (ψυχῇ, "life").

361 Technically the wording would allow an understanding of this as a comparison to Timothy, and many able scholars have understood it this way (e.g., Hendriksen, 134; Kennedy, 444; Kent, 11:132; Lenski, 813; Lightfoot, 146; Martin, 123-124; Müller, 98; Robertson, *Word Pictures*, 4:448; Wuest, 79-80). It has even been suggested as a comparison to the Philippians themselves (Martin, 124, n.1; see also BDAG, 3748). But it seems most natural to read it as a reference to Paul, especially in light of the father/son relationship described in verse 22 (Alford, 3:174; Comfort, 185; Fee, 266; Harmon, 279; MacArthur, 196; Melick, 116; O'Brien, 318; Silva, 140; Vincent, ICC, 73).

Then also there is no one like Timothy, "who will genuinely be concerned for your welfare" (ὅστις γνησίως τὰ περὶ ὑμῶν μεριμνήσει). This relative clause may explain the ground or reason for Timothy's like-mindedness.[362] The indefinite pronoun "who" (ὅστις) designates an "undetermined person belonging to a class or having a status" and is used "to emphasize a characteristic quality, by which a preceding statement is to be confirmed."[363] The verb "will be concerned for" (μεριμνήσει) comes last in the sentence and thereby receives emphasis. The future tense extrapolates expected outcome based on the present character of Timothy. The word can be used negatively of anxiety or positively of appropriate care for someone or something. Paul will use the word in 4:6 to forbid being "anxious about anything." He uses it four times in 1 Corinthians 7 to contrast being anxious about the things of the Lord and being anxious about the things of the world (vv.32-34). He uses it in 1 Corinthians 12:25 in the context of spiritual gifts to say that each member ought to have "the same care" for all the other members of the body. Here it describes a commendatory quality in Timothy. This he will do "genuinely" (γνησίως). The adverb appears only here in Biblical literature. Its original sense was "born in wedlock" (and thus "legitimate"), but this was obscured by the later development of the word.[364] But then Timothy was present with Paul when they and their church were birthed spiritually. The cognate adjective is used to describe Timothy as Paul's "true [γνησίῳ] child in the faith" (1 Tim. 1:2) and he will describe how Timothy served alongside him "like a child serving his father" (Phil. 2:22). The word came in time to identify that which is "genuine," "faithful," and "sincere."[365] Timothy's concern does not arise from a mercenary spirit or from mere duty. He truly loves the believers in Philippi.

The phrase τὰ περὶ ὑμῶν ("your welfare") is repeated verbatim from the previous verse (see our comments there). In this Timothy provides a

---

362 Robertson, *Grammar*, 960, 961, 996.

363 BDAG, 5406.2.b.

364 Moulton and Milligan, 862.

365 Thayer, 119.

Philippians for Pastors

good example of being "of the same mind" (2:2) and of "not merely looking out for your own personal interests, but also for the interests of others" (2:4). He is one who has "this attitude" in himself "which was also in Christ Jesus" (2:5). He embodies the kind of love Jesus showed for all of us (2:6-8). Timothy shows what it is like to "conduct yourselves in a manner worthy of the gospel of Christ" and to stand "firm in one spirit, with one mind striving together for the faith of the gospel" (1:27).

Verse 21 – For they all seek after their own interests, not those of Christ Jesus.

Paul now explains (γὰρ, "For") why it is he has "no one of kindred spirit" (v.20) to send to them other than Timothy. All others (οἱ πάντες, "they all") are of a different sort. The expression is a strong one and allows exception to no one. They "seek after" (ζητοῦσιν) something different. The verb means "to devote serious effort to realize one's desire or objective."[366] The present tense pictures the regularity and habitual bent of their search. The others are committed to themselves first for, instead of being "genuinely ... concerned for [the Philippian believers'] welfare" they run after "their own interests" (τὰ ἑαυτῶν). These self-oriented

> **Ministry Maxim**
>
> Mercenary Christian service is neither true service nor genuinely Christian.

commitments and pursuits stand in marked contrast (οὐ, "not"), not to those of the Philippians or even of Paul himself, but to "those of Jesus Christ" (τὰ Ἰησοῦ Χριστοῦ). Previously he has charged them to "regard one another as more important than yourselves" (v.3) and to "not merely look out for your own personal interests, but also for the interests of others" (v.4). When Paul said he was confident he would live on, it would be "for your progress and joy in the faith" (1:25). The selflessness was directed horizontally toward one another. But now the primary concern has become vertical, with putting Christ and His concerns first. Given the

---

366 BDAG, 3381.3.b.

way Paul repeatedly uses the substantivized definite article along the way to express the various life circumstances of the parties involved[367] Fee's observation again stands out in even bolder relief: "one seeks 'the interests of Jesus Christ' when one 'looks out for the interests of others,' instead of 'one's own.'"[368] When we look out for Christ's interests first, we will look out for one another's interests before our own. And when we look out for one another's interests before our own we will be taking up Christ's own interests. The story of my relationship to Jesus Christ is told in the quality of my earthly relationships with others.

The question arises as to how Paul could use such strong and definitive language of all his fellow gospel workers. His concern certainly included, but could not be limited to those described in 1:15-17. Was not Luke present with him in Rome, as well as Aristarchus, Mark and other "fellow workers" in the gospel of Christ (Philemon 23-24; Col. 4:10, 14)? He will later send greetings from "the brethren who are with me" (Phil. 4:21). Many explanations have been offered, all of which are speculative and none of which are entirely satisfying. It is telling that Paul does not at the conclusion of this letter include greetings from some of these well-known servants of Christ, as he does in other letters written from this imprisonment (cf. Colossians and Philemon), though he does offer the more general greeting: "The brothers who are with me greet you. All the saints greet you, especially those of Caesar's household" (4:21b-22). It is possible that at the time of writing this letter they had been dispatched to other fields and endeavors. Perhaps the best that can be said is that none of the others present with Paul at the time of writing would also have been present at the conversion of the core of the Philippians who make up the church. In this sense they could not have been as "genuinely" (see original root of the word above, v.20) interested in their affairs, as him who served as midwife when they came to faith in Christ.

---

367 See n.357 above.

368 Fee, 260.

Verse 22 – But you know of his proven worth, that he served with me in the furtherance of the gospel like a child *serving* his father.

Timothy stands in contrast (δὲ, "But") to those committed to self-interest (v.21). This is no new news to the Philippian believers, for Paul says "you know of his proven worth" (τὴν ... δοκιμὴν αὐτοῦ γινώσκετε). The noun "proven worth" (τὴν ... δοκιμὴν) is used only seven time in the Bible, all by Paul (Rom. 5:4 [2x]; 2 Cor. 2:9; 8:2; 9:13; 13:3; Phil. 2:22). The word describes both the process of testing and that which emerges from the test. The product is proven by the process that produces it. That which emerges is genuine and trustworthy; it can be counted on. The Philippian believers know something of the process through which Timothy (αὐτοῦ, "of his") had passed (side-by-side with Paul, and many of them) and had observed first hand his emergence from the test as true gospel-gold (cf. Acts 16:1-40).

This they "know" (γινώσκετε; cf. its use in 1:12; 2:19; 3:10; 4:5; and cf. the verb οἶδα in 1:16, 19, 25; 4:12 [2x], 15). They had probably had Timothy in their midst at least three times to this point (Acts 16:13; 19:22; 20:3f.).[369] The present tense simply underscores that there was no further research or experience needed; the Philippian believers were already in possession of these facts of Timothy's character and conduct.

What they had observed is framed by the end of the sentence. The ὅτι introduces what the Philippians know. The metaphor could literally be rendered "as to a father a child" (ὡς πατρὶ τέκνον). It is a picturesque metaphor from which many rays of application may rightly emanate. It represents filial love, humility, intimacy, tenderness, commitment, trust, faithfulness and much more. Paul was not shy in expressing this relationship with Timothy, calling him not only "my fellow worker" (Rom. 16:21) and a "brother" (2 Cor. 1:1; Col. 1:1; Philem. 1), but "my beloved and faithful child in the Lord" (1 Cor. 4:17), my "true child in the faith" (1 Tim. 1:2), "my son" (1 Tim. 1:18), and "my beloved son" (2 Tim. 1:2).

---

369 Lenski, 815; Robertson, *Word Pictures*, 4:448.

The particular point of the imagery here, however, is made clear: "he served with me" (σὺν ἐμοὶ ἐδούλευσεν). The preposition and personal pronoun are simple (σὺν ἐμοὶ, "with me") but convey so much relationally, personally, emotionally and mentally.[370] Paul was not the one served, nor was Timothy. Rather, Timothy was at Paul's side (σὺν, "with"), apprenticing as it were, with his own father in the family business. Side-by-side with the Apostle "he served" (ἐδούλευσεν). The verb depicts the service of a slave to his master.[371] One may serve sin (Rom. 6:6), the Law (Rom. 7:25), one's own appetites (Rom. 16:18), idols (Gal. 4:8; 1 Thess. 1:9), "weak and worthless elemental things" (Gal. 4:9), "various lusts and pleasures" (Tit. 3:3), and literal, earthly masters (Eph. 6:7; 1 Tim. 6:2). Or, by the mercies of God, one can serve the Lord (Rom. 12:11; Eph. 6:7), Christ (Rom. 14:18), the "Lord Christ" (Rom. 16:18; Col. 3:24), "the living and true God" (1 Thess. 1:9). Such service is enabled by the Spirit (Rom. 7:6) and finds expression in service to one another (Gal. 5:13). Furthermore, the verb is related to the noun (δοῦλος) used to designate a slave, which Paul uses to identify both himself and Timothy (1:1) and, more significantly, the Lord Jesus (2:7) Himself, whose "attitude" (2:5) Timothy exemplifies in his service.

> **Ministry Maxim**
>
> Christian service is always family business.

In this case the "family business" in which Timothy apprenticed with his spiritual father and the goal to which they labored together was "in the furtherance of the gospel" (εἰς τὸ εὐαγγέλιον). It might be more literally rendered, "into the gospel." The precise phrase has already been used in Philippians 1:5 to describe the Philippian believers' "participation in the gospel" (εἰς τὸ εὐαγγέλιον). By taking up the phrase again here he is including himself, Timothy and the Philippian believers in a tight circle of fellowship into which they have all immersed themselves. Indeed, the preposition is full of meaning here and some, like the NASU ('in the

---

370 Paul wrote "of his intimate and affectionate relations with Timothy. Accordingly he wrote '*with* me' instead of 'me.'" (Vincent, ICC, 74); "Paul's delicacy of feeling made him use *sun* rather than *emoi* alone," (Robertson, *Word Pictures*, 4:448).

371 Hendriksen suggests the translation, "he slaved with me" (136).

furtherance of"), have taken it as expressive of the forward movement of the gospel: "advancing" (NET), "in the work of" (NIV, NRSV), "in preaching" (NLT).[372] The master which Timothy serves is not the Apostle. Paul depicts himself and Timothy as co-slaves (together "servants of Christ Jesus," Phil. 1:1), both serving the Lord whose business is the dissemination of the gospel to all the peoples of the earth. In this both Paul and the believers in Philippi recognize that Timothy has proven his worth and can be trusted. Kennedy calls it "A mixed construction, the result of refined feeling," explaining that "Paul first thinks of Timothy as his son in the Gospel, serving him with a son's devotion. But before the sentence is finished, his lowliness reminds him that they are both alike servants of a common Lord, equal in His sight."[373]

This is not the only time Timothy has pulled this kind of duty and it is not the only time Paul has applied this kind of imagery to their relationship: "For this reason I have sent to you Timothy, who is my beloved and faithful child in the Lord, and he will remind you of my ways which are in Christ, just as I teach everywhere in every church" (1 Cor. 4:17). He could testify further to the Corinthian believers, "he is doing the Lord's work, as I also am" (1 Cor. 16:10). And in this Timothy was "our brother and God's fellow worker in the gospel of Christ" (1 Thess. 3:2).

Verse 23 – Therefore I hope to send him immediately, as soon as I see how things *go* with me;

Paul now explains to the Philippian believers the actions he anticipates taking in the future, on the one hand (μὲν) regarding Timothy in the near term (v.23) and on the other (δὲ, "but") with regard to himself in the still not too distant future (v.24). This is only logical to Paul (οὖν, "Therefore"), given Timothy's "proven character" (v.22) and personal interest in the Philippians (v.20). The use of οὖν ("Therefore") signals that, having set forth Timothy's qualifications (vv.20-23), Paul is returning to the matter

---

[372] "εἰς here means: with a view to, in the interest of, for the expansion of" (Müller, 99).

[373] Kennedy, 444.

of sending him to Philippi (v.19).[374] Having set forth so graphically the trustworthiness of Timothy, Paul now keeps the emphasis upon him by positioning the pronoun τοῦτον ("him") at the head of the sentence. A wooden rendering of the word order might be "This one [τοῦτον] on the one hand therefore I hope to send."

Paul returns to his intent when he first mentioned Timothy for he repeats the two verbs and their exact forms from verse 19: "I hope to send" (ἐλπίζω πέμψαι). Again the present tense (ἐλπίζω) depicts an abiding "hope" that at a specific moment (aorist tense) he might "send" (πέμψαι) Timothy to them.

Circumstantially that time is not yet, but he anticipates this taking place "immediately" (ἐξαυτῆς). The word is placed at the end of the clause for emphasis. While the verbs are the same as verse 19, this adverb is different. There he anticipated sending Timothy "shortly" (ταχέως), using an adverb he will employ in verse 24 to describe his anticipated visit. The word here (ἐξαυτῆς, "immediately") is a compound comprised of ἐκ ("out of/from") and αὐτῆς ("of her") which strictly means "at the very time."[375] It is used only six times in the NT and this is Paul's sole usage. The other usages point to action

> **Ministry Maxim**
>
> Earthly circumstances do not rule the believer's life, but they must be accounted for.

that is undertaken without the slightest delay (Mark 6:25; Acts 10:22; 11:11; 21:32; 23:30). The adverb Paul used of sending Timothy in verse 19 (and which he will use again of his own coming in verse 24) also speaks of the swiftness of the action, though clearly Paul's arrival (v.24) will follow Timothy's (v.23). In this context we are probably unwise to seek fine distinctions of meaning or time between the two adverbs. Most English translations combine ὡς ἄν (see below) and ἐξαυτῆς, despite the distance between them in the sentence. The result is a translation something like

---

374 Thus οὖν has both inferential and resumptive qualities. In that it picks up again the notion of verse 19 it is resumptive; in relation to verses 20-22 it presents the logical outworking of Timothy's unique qualifications as Paul's ambassador to Philippi.

375 Friberg, 154.

the NIV: "as soon as I see how things go with me" (cf. ESV, NET, NRSV). The NASU recognizes the distinction and translates as separate expressions (cf. KJV, NKJV).

The only thing that stands between the writing of the letter and the sending of Timothy is "as soon as I see how things go with me" (ὡς ἂν ἀφίδω τὰ περὶ ἐμὲ). The combination ὡς ἂν ("as soon as") is used in a temporal sense with the subjunctive verb (ἀφίδω, "I see") "of the time of an event in the future."[376] "The construction ... indicates the uncertainty which surrounds the whole prospect."[377] Paul seems to have used the expression to speak of events which he anticipates, but which require that other matters first fall into place. Paul used the same formula in telling the Roman believers of his longstanding desire to visit them "whenever [ὡς ἂν] I go to Spain" (Rom. 15:24). He used it similarly when describing his future plans to the believers in Corinth: "The remaining matters I will arrange when [ὡς ἂν] I come" (1 Cor. 11:34).

That which is as yet unresolved is τὰ περὶ ἐμὲ (lit., "the things concerning me"). Paul first referenced "my circumstances" (τὰ κατ' ἐμὲ) in 1:12, knowing the believers in Philippi were concerned for his welfare. But he was equally concerned for the circumstances among them (τὰ περὶ ὑμῶν, 1:27). This is only appropriate for we are each not to be concerned for our own circumstance (τὰ ἑαυτῶν ἕκαστος), but those of others (τὰ ἑτέρων ἕκαστοι, 2:4). Thus Paul tells the believers in Philippi that he will be cheered when he knows "of your condition" (τὰ περὶ ὑμῶν, v.19). The very reason he contemplates sending Timothy is because he has no one like him who is similarly concerned for "your condition" (τὰ περὶ ὑμῶν, v.20). This is rare for most are only concerned for "their own concerns" (τὰ ἑαυτῶν) and not "those of Jesus Christ" (τὰ Ἰησοῦ Χριστοῦ, v.21).

Just what Paul in this instance intended by τὰ περὶ ἐμὲ is difficult to say with precision. He may have had in mind matters related to his trial and anticipated release, some other pastoral assignment for which

---

376 BDAG, 8075.8.c.α.

377 Rienecker, 554.

he required Timothy, or other circumstances which it is impossible for us to reconstruct.

Paul clearly exemplified Christ in being more concerned for others than himself (2:5-8). This birthed his plan to send Timothy to them (vv.19, 23) and then come to them himself (v.24). Yet for the moment he must "see" (ἀφίδω) how the events of this imprisonment and trial will turn out. The word is a compound, comprised of ἀπό ("from/away from") and ὁράω ("to look"). The preposition in compound emphasizes the looking away "from" (ἀπό) all other distractions to concentrate on his present circumstances in order to discern how they shall play out. The verb is rare, used only here and in Hebrews 12:2 ("fixing our eyes [ἀφορῶντες] on Jesus") in the NT. It is used once in the LXX, of Jonah going outside the city "until he could see [ἀπίδῃ] what would happen in the city" (Jonah 4:5). It describes "giving attention to one thing to the exclusion of all else"[378] and thus means "to develop a more precise knowledge" of something.[379] The aorist tense in the present passage looks to a moment when it shall come clear to the Apostle just how things will fall out for him. Until that time sending Timothy will have to do for the concerns of everyone—Paul, Timothy, and the Philippian believers themselves.

Verse 24 – and I trust in the Lord that I myself also will be coming shortly.

Paul does not want the sending of Timothy (v.23) to be understood as a solitary act, expected to fully satisfy either himself or the Philippians. The uncertainty regarding his circumstances (v.23) is now tempered with a confidence concerning coming to them. The δέ ("and") pairs with μέν of verse 23, giving a sense of "on the one hand" (μέν) and "on the other hand" (δέ).

The plans are not inevitable, though he hopes they become reality and expects that they will, for he says, "I trust in the Lord" (πέποιθα … ἐν

---

378 Friberg, 84.

379 BDAG, 1339.2.

κυρίῳ). The prepositional phrase "in the Lord" (ἐν κυρίῳ) both depicts the realm in which Paul's trust exists and echoes the sentiments with which he began this paragraph (ἐν κυρίῳ Ἰησοῦ, "in the Lord Jesus," v.19). All the Apostle's life, plans, and hopes were founded upon the sovereign will of his Savior.

In verse 19 it was the "hope" (ἐλπίζω) of sending Timothy (v.19) which rested "in the Lord Jesus," here he says "I trust" (πέποιθα) in Him for my own coming to you. The word means "to be so convinced that one puts confidence in" it.[380] The shift from ἐλπίζω ("I hope," vv.19, 23) to πέποιθα ("I trust") "may be Paul's way of subtly assuring the Philippians that his own coming to them again, in spite of immense obstacles, is more certain than the expected arrival of Timothy."[381] Paul has used the word already to speak of his confidence that God will complete the work He has begun in the Philippian believers (1:6) and that he will himself live on and serve the Lord and His people (1:25). Compare the similar verbiage in 1:14 where most of the believers are "trusting in the Lord" (ἐν κυρίῳ πεποιθότας) in a fresh way because of Paul's imprisonment. See also his use of the verb in 3:3 and 4. Here the perfect tense of the verb pictures trust that had been definitively established in Christ in the past and which has now become a settled state of confidence.

> **Ministry Maxim**
>
> When our confidence rests "in the Lord" the likelihood of it being rewarded increases exponentially.

The specific nature of Paul's trust is set forth (ὅτι, "that"). Paul is confident that "I myself also will be coming shortly" (καὶ αὐτὸς ταχέως ἐλεύσομαι). The emphatic emphasis upon Paul ("I myself") is made by adding the singular form of the pronoun (αὐτός) to the first person singular form of the verb (ἐλεύσομαι, "I will be coming"). The future tense of the verb looks forward to events Paul trusts will become reality. His coming will be in addition to (καί, "also") that of Timothy (v.23).

---

380 BDAG, 5754.2.a.

381 Hawthorne, WBC, 153.

All this Paul is relying upon the Lord to bring about without delay (ταχέως, "shortly"). Here again is the adverb used in verse 19 with reference to Paul's hope of sending Timothy. See our comments on verses 19 and 23 for this word.

Compare the plan and sentiments of verses 23-24 with Paul's words to the Corinthians on another occasion: "For this reason I have sent to you Timothy, who is my beloved and faithful child in the Lord, and he will remind you of my ways which are in Christ, just as I teach everywhere in every church. Now some have become arrogant, as though I were not coming to you. But I will come to you soon, if the Lord wills, and I shall find out, not the words of those who are arrogant but their power" (1 Cor. 4:17-19).

> **Digging Deeper:**
> 1. Which do you value more in your ministry partners—a gospel-heart or great giftedness? Why?
> 2. Who in your ministry partnerships has demonstrated "proven worth" (v.22)? How have they done so?
> 3. How does one determine when written (or electronic) communication will suffice, and when only face-to-face communication will do? (vv.23-24)

Verse 25 – But I thought it necessary to send to you Epaphroditus, my brother and fellow worker and fellow soldier, who is also your messenger and minister to my need;

Having set forth and justified his plans for sending Timothy (vv.19-23) and his own plans for visiting (v.24), Paul now takes up the matter of Epaphroditus' unexpected appearance back in Philippi (vv.25-30). He makes the transition by use of δὲ, which has mild adversative force. By thrusting the adjective Ἀναγκαῖον ("necessary") to the head of the sentence Paul casts the entire matter as essential, given certain circumstances which he will shortly explain. The adjective appears only eight times in the

NT. Paul uses it five of those times, two of which are here in Philippians (Acts 10:24; 13:46; 1 Cor. 12:22; 2 Cor. 9:5; Phil. 1:24; 2:25; Titus 3:14; Heb. 8:3). Paul clearly is working with circumstances that require decisions be made and actions taken.

The decision is indicated by "I thought it" (ἡγησάμην). Half of Paul's ten uses of this verb are here in Philippians (2:3, 6, 25; 3:7, 8 [2x]). It speaks of entering into an intellectual process[382] and denotes "a belief resting not on one's inner feeling or sentiment, but on the due consideration of external grounds, the weighing and comparing, of facts."[383] It is significant that this is the very verb used to charge them to "regard [ἡγούμενοι] one another as more important than yourselves" (2:3) and to describe Christ when He "did not count [ἡγήσατο] equality with God a thing to be grasped" (v.6). "In doing so Paul invites the Philippians to view his decision as thinking of their needs above his own."[384] Here in verse 25 the aorist tense may present the process as having culminated in a point of deduction and the drawing of a conclusion. Most scholars, however, treat it as an epistolary aorist, with the action viewed from the vantage point of the readers, and render it "I think" (NIV, NRSV).[385] If this is the case then it probably means that Epaphroditus personally delivered the letter upon his return to Philippi, a conclusion that seems likely given verses 29 and 30.

After careful consideration, the Apostle determined that the required action in this case was "to send to you Epaphroditus" (Ἐπαφρόδιτον ... πέμψαι πρὸς ὑμᾶς). All we know of Epaphroditus we learn in this letter.[386] Apparently he was dispatched from the Philippi by the believers to take a gift to Paul to sustain him in his imprisonment (Phil. 4:18). He was thus

---

382 BDAG, 3410.2.

383 Thayer, 276.

384 Harmnon, 287.

385 Fee, 274; Lenski, 818; Lightfoot, 146; Martin, 128; O'Brien, 330; Robertson, *Paul's Joy in Christ*, 166; Silva, 140; Sumney, 63; Vincent, ICC, 75.

386 Epaphras (Col. 1:7; 4:12; Philem. 23) is a contracted form of the name, though it does not refer to the same person under consideration here.

considered a trustworthy servant by his fellow-believers. He was a man of action, being willing to put feet to the wishes of the congregation. He was brave for he undertook this mission knowing there was some danger involved in such travel in the first century (2:29). He became ill (v.26) in the process of executing his assignment and nearly died (v.27). He was a man of feeling for "he was longing" for his brothers and sisters in Philippi and "was distressed" because of their worry over his welfare (v.26).

Epaphroditus was a remarkable man indeed! This is signaled not only by what the larger context of Philippians tells us, but by the fact that in this sentence Paul separates the subject (Ἐπαφρόδιτον, "Epaphroditus") from the verb and object (πέμψαι πρὸς ὑμᾶς, "send to you") by a great distance, filling that distance with five qualifiers descriptive of his stature and role. Paul begins by describing Epaphroditus in a three-fold relationship to himself. The three nouns are governed by one definite article (τὸν) that heads the list (which signals the definitive nature of Epaphroditus in these roles) and by the common genitive personal pronoun that brings up the rear (μου, "my"). The three are strung together in parallel relationship by the twice-repeated καὶ ("and ... and").

Primary is the fact that he is Paul's "brother" (ἀδελφὸν). This, of course, means that Epaphroditus is a fellow believer, having found, like Paul, new life in Jesus Christ which has bound them together as spiritual family members. It is the same designation Paul has used to describe his relationship with the Philippian believers as a whole (1:12; 3:1, 13, 17; 4:1, 8) and with others who speak of Christ (1:14) and those that surround Paul presently (4:21).

Epaphroditus is also, then, Paul's "fellow worker" (συνεργὸν). The word is a compound, comprised of σύν ("with") and ἔργον ("worker"). It designates a co-laborer, someone who works with another. The word is a favorite of Paul, twelve of its thirteen usages coming from his pen. He uses it of figures well known (Rom. 16:21) and obscure (16:9), of males (Philem. 24) and

> **Ministry Maxim**
>
> Putting your reputation on the line for one whose reputation is unjustly in question is Christ-likeness in action.

females (Rom. 16:3; Phil. 4:3), of individuals (Philem. 24) and married couples (Acts 16:3), of Jews (Col. 4:11) and of Gentiles (2 Cor. 8:23). He uses it of those who work in concert with himself (2 Cor. 8:23) and other believers (Philem. 1). He uses it of himself as working in concert with other believers (1 Cor. 1:24). And he uses it of himself and all believers as those who so work with God (1 Cor. 3:9; 1 Thess. 3:2). Those who thus labor together do so "in Christ Jesus" (Rom. 16:3, 9), for the gospel (Phil. 4:3; 1 Thess. 3:2), the kingdom of God (Col. 4:11), and for the joy of believers (1 Cor. 1:24). God's saving power in the lives of His people is "a good work [ἔργον]" which He has begun and will complete (Phil. 1:6). The ministry of the gospel is generally called "the work [ἔργον] of Christ" (2:30; cf. 1:22), work in which Epaphroditus was engaged on behalf of the Philippian believers when he nearly died (2:30).

Epaphroditus is also designated as Paul's "fellow soldier" (συστρατιώτην). Again the word is a compound, comprised of σύν ("with") and στρατιώτης ("soldier"). The word appears only here and in Philemon 2 where Paul uses it also of Archippus, probably the leader of the house church in Colossae. Clearly Paul considers Epaphroditus to be an especially trusted ministry associate, enlisted in the same force, warring side-by-side with all true soldiers of the Lord (cf. 2 Tim. 2:3).

The three designations mark Epaphroditus out as family ("brother"), a laborer ("fellow worker"), and a warrior ("fellow soldier"). Lightfoot observes that there is an ascending scale in the three terms: "common sympathy, common work, common danger and toil and suffering."[387] The fact that Paul designates Epaphroditus in all three roles in relationship to himself (μου, "my") rather than in relationship to all of them as believers (himself and the Philippian Christians collectively) in effect elevates Epaphroditus to a place that the rest of the Philippian believers do not occupy. It dignifies Epaphroditus in their midst and serves as a subtle protector against any criticism he might face by what some could consider a premature return to Philippi.

---

387 Lightfoot, 148; cf. Lenski, 819; O'Brien, 330.

Philippians 2

This having been accomplished Paul then adds (δὲ, "also") two descriptors to remind the Philippian believers of Epaphroditus' relationship to them (ὑμῶν, "your").[388] Yet even in these two roles he places Epaphroditus in a unique position among them. The pronoun (ὑμῶν, "your") is made emphatic by its forward position.

Epaphroditus functioned as the Philippian believers' "messenger" (ἀπόστολον). The word is the one which marks out the original disciples of Jesus as a special class (e.g., Matt. 10:2; Acts 1:2, 26; 2:37). To this Paul also was added as an "apostle" (e.g., Acts 14:14; Rom. 1:1) sent specifically to the Gentiles (Rom. 11:13), though he considers himself "one untimely born" and "the least of the apostles, and not fit to be called an apostle, because [he] persecuted the church of God" (1 Cor. 15:8, 9). The word could also be used more generally of others who labored in advancing the message of Christ from location to location (2 Cor. 8:23). Here it is used more simply in the sense of "messenger," Epaphroditus being commissioned and sent by the Philippian church to go from their midst to Paul in his imprisonment in Rome. In their commissioning and sending of Epaphroditus it is only logical that he now return and report to them of his ministry on their behalf. Having been originally sent to Paul by his fellow believers (ἀπόστολον, "messenger"), Epaphroditus is now sent (πέμψαι πρὸς ὑμᾶς, "to send to you") by the Apostle back to the believers in Philippi. The Apostle's appointment trumps that of the Philippians.

And also (καὶ, "and") Epaphroditus served as a "minister" (λειτουργὸν) of the Philippian believers. The word was used in secular circles of those who performed public and political service. Paul so used it to designate political entities (Rom. 13:6). It also developed religious overtones and was used in cultic contexts. It was used in the LXX of the priests and Levites (e.g., Ezra 7:24; Neh. 10:40; Isa. 61:6).[389] It was natural therefore for Paul to use the word to designate servants of Christ (Rom. 15:16) as he does here. This may give the connotation that the gift of the Philippians, sent through

---

388 Note how by placing μου ("my") and ὑμῶν ("your") side by side Paul heightens the contrast (Robertson, *Word Pictures*, 4:449).

389 TDNT, 4:215-231.

Epaphroditus to Paul in Rome, was viewed by the Apostle as a spiritual sacrifice unto God.[390] The word appears only five times in the NT; in addition to Paul's three usages the author of Hebrews uses it to designate angels as those who do God's bidding (Heb. 1:7) and of Jesus Himself as our High Priest (8:2). It is kindred to the word "service" (λειτουργίᾳ) that describes the faith of the Philippians in verse 17 and their service to Paul in verse 30. Epaphroditus thus served physically on behalf of the larger body of believers in Philippi, carrying out what they would have done if they had been able to be present with Paul in his Roman imprisonment. He was sent by them to give attention "to my [Paul's] need" (τῆς χρείας μου). The church in Philippi had repeatedly proven their commitment to meeting such needs for the Apostle (which he calls a θυσίαν, "sacrifice," 4:16)[391] and dispatching Epaphroditus to Rome was simply the latest expression of such practical ministrations of love.

Verse 26 – because he was longing for you all and was distressed because you had heard that he was sick.

Paul now gives the ground or cause (ἐπειδὴ, "because") of the necessity in sending Epaphroditus back to the Philippian church (v.25). That reason arose not because of something inside of Paul, but because of something going on inside Epaphroditus himself. He could not shake an ongoing pair of inward realities. The imperfect tense of the verb ἦν ("he was") underscores the ongoing, unshakable nature of these realities.[392]

Two participles serve as predicate adjectives[393], telling us just what it was that so plagued Epaphroditus. Both are in the present tense and were ongoing issues from which Epaphroditus had found himself incapable of escape. The emphasis is upon the first, for it actually precedes the verb. He

---

390 Kennedy, 446.

391 Robertson, *Paul's Joy in Christ*, 167.

392 O'Brien, 334; NIDNTT, 3:1193; Robertson, *Grammar*, 888, 1120; Robertson elsewhere suggests it is a periphrastic construction, *Paul's Joy in Christ*, 167; cf. Fee, 277; Hellerman, 158.

393 Sumney, 64.

was "longing for you all" (ἐπιποθῶν ... πάντας ὑμᾶς). The verb was already used to describe Paul's yearning after the Philippians: "I long [ἐπιποθῶ] for you all with the affection of Christ Jesus" (1:8). It is a compound, with a prefixed preposition (ἐπί) that gives direction to the yearning.[394] The word is a strong one, describing an intense longing after something (2 Cor. 5:2) or someone (Rom. 1:11; 2 Cor. 9:14; Phil. 1:8; 2:26; 1 Thess. 3:6). It is a word of which the Apostle Paul is especially fond, as seven of its nine NT usages are found in his letters. Just as it was with Paul, so it was with Epaphroditus, the object of his yearning was "you all" (πάντας ὑμᾶς). Paul uses this expression a third time here in Philippians and perhaps it explains why their hearts were so bound together with one another: "you all [πάντας ὑμᾶς] are partakers of grace with me" (Phil. 1:7). It was not something superior within the Philippian believers, Epaphroditus or even Paul which bound them together in such care that they longed for one another when apart. It was something that arose from within God and which He granted to each of them that bound them together. The secret of unity is shared grace.

> **Ministry Maxim**
>
> Being more worried over my worry for you than over your own illness is love in action.

In addition (καί, "and") to this longing, Epaphroditus was "distressed" (ἀδημονῶν). The word depicts a powerful inward reality, for the only two other usages of the word in Biblical literature describe Jesus as He prayed in the Garden of Gethsemane (Matt. 26:37; Mark 14:33). The derivation of the word is a matter of debate. Some see the word arising from ἀδήμων, which in turn came from the compound of the negating alpha privative (α-, "not") and δῆμος (a people, the populace of a city).[395] This gives the word the sense of "uncomfortable" as in "not at home."[396] Others, however, route its background through a different course.[397] Perhaps Kennedy's

---

394 Rienecker, 545.

395 Thayer, 11.

396 Ibid.

397 Moulton and Milligan, 58; cf. O'Brien, 334.

agnosticism on the matter is correct: "The derivations usually given are doubtful."[398] Lightfoot says, "The word describes the confused, restless, half-distracted state which is produced by physical derangement, or by mental distress such as grief, shame, disappointment, etc."[399] Something had overcome Epaphroditus from which he could not escape. It had rendered him nearly incapable of any other thought.

The cause of this (διότι, "because") was quite easily identified.[400] The conjunction is a contracted form of διὰ τοῦτο ὅτι and means "for the reason that" or "in view of the fact that."[401] That reason was "you had heard that he was sick" (ἠκούσατε ὅτι ἠσθένησεν). The transition from the present tense nature of his struggles to the aorist tense of their hearing of his illness paints the picture. His ongoing inward struggles (present tense) arose from an event ("you heard") which arose from another event ("he was sick").[402] The verb "he was sick" (ἠσθένησεν) generally described weakness and could be used of a spectrum of matters from physical illness (including that which might lead to death, v.27) to moral weakness (Rom. 4:19) to the social weakness of economic poverty (Acts 20:35).[403] Epaphroditus' struggle was physical in nature.

Just how they heard this news we do not know. Nor do we know precisely the nature of the illness and when it befell Epaphroditus. Nor do we know just how Epaphroditus knew they had become aware of his illness.[404] But we do know it created grievous, unbearable inward struggle

---

398 Kennedy, 446; cf. Rienecker, 554.

399 Lightfoot, 148.

400 "In Ph. 2:26 διότι is causal and ὅτι is declarative," (Robertson, *Grammar*, 964).

401 BDAG, 2028.1.

402 "ἠσθένησεν has sometimes been taken as an ingressive aorist ... though in the light of v.27, where the verb is repeated, it is perhaps better to regard the aorist as summing up Epaphroditus's whole experience as a single fact," (O'Brien, 335). If it is an example of the ingressive aorist it could be translated "had fallen sick," cf. Kennedy, 446; cf. Müller, 101; Robertson, *Paul's Joy in Christ*, 168.

403 Friberg, 78.

404 Kennedy suggests the Philippians sent a letter to Rome inquiring after Epaphroditus' condition, making the present letter of Paul an answer to their previous letter, (446).

for Epaphroditus. The illness was of the utmost seriousness, as the next verse will make clear. But it was the awareness that his fellow believers in Philippi knew of this sickness and may have been worried over him that consumed him. By being driven to distraction, not by his own nearly fatal illness, but by the unremitting concern of his fellow believers for his welfare, Epaphroditus clearly embodied what it means to "regard one another as more important than yourselves" (v.3).

It is clear that Paul's words here were not what informed the Philippian church of Epaphroditus' illness; of this they were already aware. Rather Paul's words here were to inform them of the inward struggle that accompanied Epaphroditus' illness—one which arose because of his love and longing for them and their welfare. This they could not have known except through the personal testimony of Epaphroditus who now expectantly stood before them. So now Paul gives an authoritative, eyewitness, confirming testimony of the commendable reason for his return to Philippi.

Verse 27 – For indeed he was sick to the point of death, but God had mercy on him, and not on him only but also on me, so that I would not have sorrow upon sorrow.

Having raised the issue of Epaphroditus' sickness (v.26) Paul now more fully explains it (γὰρ, "For"), doing so with an exclamation point (καὶ, "indeed"). That "he was sick" (ἠσθένησεν) was not a revelation to the Philippian church, but that it was "to the point of death" (παραπλήσιον θανάτῳ) may have been fresh and dramatic news. The neuter form of the adjective παραπλήσιος, παραπλήσιον ("to the point of") is used only here in Biblical literature and seems to function as an improper preposition in an adverb phrase.[405] It is a compound comprised of παρά ("beside") and πλησίον ("near/close").[406] It pertains "to coming alongside or near" something.[407] O'Brien renders the phrase literally as "a near neighbour to

---

405 O'Brien, 336; Robertson, *Grammar*, 646; Thayer, 485.

406 Robertson, *Grammar*, 646.

407 BDAG, 5622.

death."⁴⁰⁸ Epaphroditus had "a brush with death."⁴⁰⁹ The matter of "death" (θανάτῳ) has already been considered a possibility for Paul (Phil. 1:20) and was held forth as the ultimate expression of selflessness on the part of Christ (2:8). Being "conformed to His death" (3:10) is Paul's great goal. Here, then, is Epaphroditus, pictured with death sidling up next to him while in dispatch from the Philippian church to take their offering to Paul in his imprisonment in Rome and to become there the personal embodiment of their longing to minister to the Apostle's needs. We do not know how or when or where the illness came to Epaphroditus, nor precisely its nature, but we do know where its trajectory threatened to take him.

It is a grave picture indeed. Yet God intervened in a most powerful and personal way. The contrast between the close shave with death and the resulting action of God is stark (ἀλλά, "but"). The darkest night has often been penetrated with the grand testimony that always begins with: ἀλλὰ ὁ θεὸς ("but God")! Indeed, this is the very story of the gospel itself: "And you were dead in your trespasses and sins ... But God ... even when we were dead in our transgressions, made us alive together with Christ" (Eph. 2:1, 4, 5). The story of Epaphroditus is a physical illustration of all our testimonies on the spiritual plane.

As death drew near to Epaphroditus God "had mercy on him" (ἠλέησεν αὐτόν). The aorist tense pictures a specific moment when the tables turned for Epaphroditus. It was God's own hand that turned the events for good. The word stresses the pity and compassion that moves one to take action to relieve the suffering of another. It is used in the Gospels of people crying out to God for physical healing (e.g., Matt. 9:27; 17:15; 20:30, 31) and of God's action in delivering from demonic powers (Mark 5:19). God Himself thus looked upon Epaphroditus and acted on his behalf.

But there was more to God's act (δέ, "and") than just the obvious benefit to Epaphroditus. The mercy was "not on him only" (οὐκ αὐτὸν ... μόνον). With the strongest of contrasts (ἀλλά, "but") Paul could say God had mercy "also on me" (καὶ ἐμέ). Here is another of Paul's subtle messages

---

408 O'Brien, 336.

409 Spicq, 3:36.

urging the unity of the body of Christ. He told the Corinthian believers "And if one member suffers, all the members suffer with it" and "if one member is honored, all the members rejoice with it" (1 Cor. 12:26). Paul's heart was bound up with that of Epaphroditus. Here was a man he did not request, bringing a gift he did not solicit, who either was ill upon arrival or shortly thereafter became so, and instead of rendering service to the Apostle required his energies and those of what other fellow servants Paul had at his disposal. He was, after all, a man imprisoned. Yet Paul counted himself one with Epaphroditus. Paul kept his own counsel to "Rejoice with those who rejoice, and weep with those who weep" (Rom. 12:15). Could the Philippians not so live with one another despite their differences?

Paul believed that God extended mercy to Epaphroditus for a purpose that extended beyond the life of Epaphroditus himself. The mercy was personal to Epaphroditus and because God loved him, but it had effect upon more than simply his life. Such is life in the body of Christ. Using a negative purpose clause (ἵνα μὴ, "so that … not"; or "lest") Paul points to that end in his own life: "I would … have sorrow upon sorrow" (λύπην ἐπὶ λύπην σχῶ). Vincent says ἐπὶ has "a sense of motion," meaning "'sorrow upon sorrow,' or 'after' sorrow, as we say 'wave upon wave.'"[410] For similar constructions in the LXX see Psalm 69:27; Isaiah 28:10, 13; and Ezekiel 7:26[411] and in the NT see Matthew 24:2.[412] Here the aorist tense pictures the contemplated moment of death

> **Ministry Maxim**
> God often sends the current of mercy down the conductor of human relationships.

and the grief that would have swept over the Apostle. The subjunctive mood serves the negative purpose clause. Identifying the first "sorrow" as Epaphroditus' death and second as Paul's imprisonment[413] or the first as

---

410 Vincent, ICC, 76; cf. Alford, 3:176; Kennedy, 446.

411 O'Brien, 338.

412 Robertson, *Paul's Joy in Christ*, 169.

413 E.g., Martin, 131; O'Brien, 338; Robertson, *Paul's Joy in Christ*, 169.

Epaphroditus' illness and the second as his death[414] may get at the truth, but it may also be wringing more from the metaphor than Paul intended. The expression may simply point to the intensity of the sorrow.[415] Within the letter's theme of rejoicing (χαίρω: 1:18 [2x]; 2:17, 18, 28; 3:1; 4:4 [2x], 10; συγχαίρω: 2:17, 18; χαρά: 1:4, 25; 2:2, 29; 4:1) Paul here reminds us that joy is found not in perfect circumstances, but in the midst of the hard and painful realities of life. Pain and joy are not mutually exclusive, but the latter triumphs in the midst of the former.

God never wastes motion, but with each act touches as many lives as possible for good. His work in one life is never just for the benefit of that one life, but for all the lives connected relationally to that single life. Mercy to one is mercy to all.

Verse 28 – Therefore I have sent him all the more eagerly so that when you see him again you may rejoice and I may be less concerned *about you*.

The conjunction οὖν ("Therefore") is employed as it was in in verse 23 (where it was resumptive with regard to verse 19, but inferential with regard to verses 20-22).[416] Similarly here it is resumptive with regard to verses 25, but inferential with regard to verses 26-27. The aorist tense verb (ἔπεμψα, "I have sent") is to be understood as epistolary (cf. ἡγησάμην, "I thought," v.25).[417] Paul is speaking from the standpoint of the recipients reading the letter upon its arrival, having been delivered by Epaphroditus (αὐτόν, "him"). It may be translated as a present tense, as most English versions do (e.g., ESV, NIV). The adverb σπουδαιοτέρως ("more eagerly") is used by Paul only here and 2 Timothy 1:17 and Titus 3:3 (and only one other time in the NT, Luke 7:4). It describes action undertaken earnestly, diligently, or urgently. Here it is a comparative which is superlative in

---

414 E.g., Lenski, 822; Müller, 102.

415 Sumney, 66.

416 O'Brien, 325.

417 Dana and Mantey, 198; Wallace, 563.

meaning: "as quickly as possible."⁴¹⁸ There is an emphasis upon haste due to the importance of the task at hand.⁴¹⁹

The purpose (ἵνα, "in order that") in sending Epaphroditus with such urgency and haste had both the Philippians and Paul in view. He wanted to heighten their joy and lessen his concerns. The Apostle is convinced that joy (χαρῆτε, "you may rejoice") will be the result "when you see him again" (ἰδόντες αὐτὸν πάλιν). The aorist tense (χαρῆτε, "you may rejoice") depicts an immediate reaction on their part, precipitated by the sight of Epaphroditus. The subjunctive mood serves with ἵνα to form the purpose clause. The passive voice pictures this rejoicing being brought about by another. The precipitating event that would spark this response is set forth by the participle (ἰδόντες) and is temporal in nature: "*when* you see him." Paul thus artfully binds their response to Epaphroditus to the letter's theme of joy (χαίρω: 1:18 [2x]; 2:17, 18, 28; 3:1; 4:4 [2x], 10; συγχαίρω: 2:17, 18; χαρά: 1:4, 25; 2:2, 29; 4:1).

> **Ministry Maxim**
>
> Intent supersedes attempt—if the goal is met the means are secondary.

Should πάλιν ("again") be read with the main verb (χαρῆτε, "you may rejoice")⁴²⁰ or with the participle (ἰδόντες, "when you see")?⁴²¹ If it is the former, Paul is building off the Philippian believer's distress over Epaphroditus' wellbeing. They had heard he was sick (v.26). Now they will be able to return to joy because of his wellbeing and return home. If it is connected to the latter Paul is building off of the fact that seeing Epaphroditus "again" (πάλιν) was not their expectation, at least not so soon. In this case we might ask, was Paul voicing his honest expectation of the Philippian believers' response? Or was he subtly coaching them on how they ought to view the return of Epaphroditus?

---

418 Friberg, 354; cf. Thayer, 585.

419 BDAG, 6781.1.

420 Alford, 3:176; O'Brien, 339; Rienecker, 554; Vincent, ICC, 77.

421 Lenski, 823; Martin, 132; Robertson, *Paul's Joy in Christ*, 170; Silva, 141; Wuest, 85.

Paul too anticipates a personal benefit from sending Epaphroditus home: "and I may be less concerned" (κἀγὼ ἀλυπότερος ὦ). Paul's κἀγὼ ("and I") brings together the conjunction καί ("and") and the personal pronoun ἐγώ ("I"). So it serves to both coordinate (καί) from one motive to another and to make emphatic the effect upon Paul himself (ἐγώ, "I"). The present tense of the verb (ὦ, "I may be") looks to an abiding state into which Paul wishes to transition. The subjunctive mood again matches the ἵνα to form the purpose clause.

Paul puts subtle pressure upon the Philippian believers to respond to Epaphroditus in such a way that his desire might be achieved. They had originally sent Epaphroditus to care for Paul's needs (v.25), so now if their motives were still true to this original sentiment they will minister to Paul's needs by receiving Epaphroditus back into their midst with joy. That which Paul hopes to become is "less concerned" (ἀλυπότερος). The comparative adjective is used only here in biblical literature, though it was common in wider Greek literature. It arose from combining λύπη ("sorrow"/"grief"/"anxiety") with the alpha-privative as a negation.[422] Alford calls it "one of the Apostle's delicate touches of affection."[423] The root word was used twice in the previous verse: λύπην ἐπὶ λύπην ("sorrow upon sorrow").[424] Paul was able, in sending a well Epaphroditus back to the Philippian church, to swing from multiplied sorrows (v.27) to the elimination of sorrow over this incident ("free from anxiety," NET; "free from all anxiety,"[425] v.28). They sent Epaphroditus originally to lessen Paul's concerns, so now they can fulfill their original intent by receiving Epaphroditus back into their immediate fellowship. Though that which achieved their original intent is the opposite of what they undertook (receiving instead of sending Epaphroditus) there should be joy and relief all around.

---

422 Robertson, *Word Pictures*, 4:449.

423 Alford, 3:176.

424 Harmon, 295.

425 BDAG, 358.

Verse 29 – Receive him then in the Lord with all joy, and hold men like him in high regard;

Paul culminates (οὖν, "then") the matter of Epaphroditus' return (vv.25-28) by issuing two commands (v.29) regarding the Philippian church's reception and ongoing relationship to Epaphroditus and then giving the reason for those commands (v.30). Paul commands two actions of the believers in Philippi with regard to Epaphroditus: "receive" (προσδέχεσθε) and "hold" (ἔχετε). The first imperative is placed at the head of the sentence, while the second closes out its clause by taking up the final positon. Both are therefore emphatic by position. Between the two are qualifiers which explain the commands more fully. Both imperatives are in the present tense. The first pictures their "enduring welcome"[426] of him whom they originally sent out and who has now returned unexpectedly and early. The second depicts their ongoing estimation of him. The antecedent of αὐτὸν ("him") is clearly Epaphroditus who has been under consideration since verse 25.

The first command (προσδέχεσθε ... αὐτὸν, "receive him") is qualified by two prepositional phrases. The first is ἐν κυρίῳ ("in the Lord"). The preposition (ἐν, "in") depicts the arena or sphere in which their welcome of Epaphroditus is to take place. Paul shows how much hinges on being ἐν ("in") Him. Because they are in union with Christ, they are "saints in [ἐν] Christ Jesus" (1:1). Paul longs for them all "with [ἐν] the affection of Christ Jesus" (1:8). It is "in [ἐν] the Lord" that other servants of Christ have become more confident through Paul's imprisonment (1:14). It is "in [ἐν] Christ Jesus" that the Philippian believers are to rejoice when Paul comes to them again (1:26). It is "in [ἐν] one spirit" that they are to stand firm (1:27). It is "in [ἐν] Christ" that they have come to have encouragement, along with consolation of love, fellowship of the Spirit, affection and compassion (2:1). It is "in [ἐν] Christ

> **Ministry Maxim**
>
> When we honor those who sacrifice for Christ we honor the Christ of the sacrifice.

---

426 O'Brien, 340.

Jesus" that they find the mindset which they are to live by (2:5). It is "at [ἐν] the name of Jesus" that every knee will bow and tongue confess His Lordship (2:10). It is "in [ἐν] the Lord Jesus" that Paul's hope of sending Timothy to them resides (2:19). It is "in [ἐν] the Lord" that Paul's hope of coming to them himself rests (2:24). It is "in the Lord" (ἐν κυρίῳ) that they are all to rejoice together (3:1; 4:4) and stand firm (4:1). It is "in the Lord" (ἐν κυρίῳ) that Paul will entreat Euodia and Syntyche to resolve their differences (4:2) and that Paul rejoices in the revived concern of the Philippian church's for his welfare and ministry (4:10).

Thus here in verse 29 Paul wraps their welcome of Epaphroditus into the very fabric of their own relationship to Jesus Christ and their enjoyment of all the graces they enjoy because of their union with Him. In effect Paul is drawing a circle around the Philippian Christians, a circle in which He includes Jesus Christ, himself and Epaphroditus. All that they enjoy within that circle with Christ, they must likewise extend to Epaphroditus as well. How they relate to Epaphroditus will affect the quality of relationship they enjoy with both Paul and the Lord Jesus.

The second way He qualifies the command to "receive" Epaphroditus is μετὰ πάσης χαρᾶς ("with all joy"). As we have seen, "joy" is one of the most dominate themes in this letter (χαίρω: 1:18 [2x]; 2:17, 18, 28; 3:1; 4:4 [2x], 10; συγχαίρω: 2:17, 18; χαρά: 1:4, 25; 2:2, 29; 4:1). By weaving joy into the matter of their reception of Epaphroditus, Paul is reminding them that all he desires for them is wrapped up in their response to this man. By adding the adjective (πάσης, "all") he removes all boundaries and restrictions in lavishing Epaphroditus with a joyous welcome.[427] Their reception of Epaphroditus should be a glad event, not muted by any disappointment, suspicion or reserve.

The second command (ἔχετε, "hold") is joined (καὶ, "and") to the first. It signals what should follow the jubilant reception of Epaphroditus and form their abiding estimation of the man. Two qualifiers are added to this second imperative. The first regards those to whom it applies (τοὺς τοιούτους, "men like him"). Epaphroditus is still under consideration, but

---

427 It serves here as a "marker of the highest degree of" joy (BDAG, 5722.3.a).

Paul further esteems him by classing him together as part of a heroic body of Christ's servants. The definite article marks Epaphroditus as one among a special class of individuals, an elite corps of gospel servants. The expression might more literally be rendered "such ones." The specifics of what marks out such a group harken back to verse 25 ("brother ... fellow worker ... fellow solider ... messenger ... minister"). Indeed, the next verse will raise the bar even higher by indicating that in the fulfillment of these roles Epaphroditus "came close to death for the work of Christ" (v.30). This is the spiritual equivalent of honoring our veterans of foreign wars.

The second qualifier speaks to just how they are to "hold" Epaphroditus in their mind's eye (ἐντίμους, "in high regard"). The adjective is used only here by Paul. Peter applies it to the Father's estimate of Jesus Christ ("precious," 1 Pet. 2:4, 6). "That Epaphroditus is to be publicly esteemed for risking his life in the service of a crucified Messiah (v.30) ... represents an utter inversion of the social values of the dominant culture."[428] Yet in doing so they follow the pattern God Himself will evoke at the end of time as He brings forth universal acclaim for His own dear Son (2:6-11).

By virtue of these two commands, then, the Apostle has set the tone for how the Philippian believers are to initially "receive" Epaphroditus and the abiding esteem in which they are to "hold" him.

Verse 30 – because he came close to death for the work of Christ, risking his life to complete what was deficient in your service to me.

The Apostle now gives the ground (ὅτι, "because") for the two imperatives he has just issued (v.29). The reason that stands as a motivating factor behind the imperatives is that "he came close to death for the work of Christ" (διὰ τὸ ἔργον Χριστοῦ μέχρι θανάτου ἤγγισεν). Epaphroditus is still the assumed subject as he has been since verse 25.

The stunning news is that "he came close to death" (μέχρι θανάτου ἤγγισεν). Lest the Philippian believers, in their shock of seeing Epaphroditus

---

428 Hellerman, 163.

so quickly back home, assume that he somehow fell short of his commissioned service, Paul clarifies that his obedient service took him "close to death" (μέχρι θανάτου). The expression is used by Paul only here and in verse 8 where he employed it in reference to Christ and his obedience "to the point of death."[429] This highlights the fact that Paul is purposefully offering Epaphroditus as a human illustration of the kind of "attitude ... which was also in Christ Jesus" (v.5). It also serves to heighten in vivid fashion the stature of Epaphroditus in the estimation of his fellow believers. The aorist tense of the verb (ἤγγισεν, "he came") depicts the dramatic moment of the event itself.

The διὰ ("for") with the accusative (τὸ ἔργον, "the work") introduces the reason for Epaphroditus coming near to death. The genitive (Χριστοῦ, "of Christ") should be understood as objective.[430] It was work done for Christ and His Kingdom, under the commission of Christ. This was of a piece with the "good work" (ἔργον ἀγαθὸν) going on still in the Philippian believers themselves (1:6), with the "fruitful labor" (καρπὸς ἔργου) which also stood before the Apostle as he contemplated whether his imprisonment would end in his death or his freedom (1:22), and with the Philippians' repeated prayers and financial gifts that "the work of Christ" might go on (4:10). The entire phrase is pushed to the fore of the clause so as to emphasize that it was for Christ and His cause that Epaphroditus suffered nigh unto death.

Epaphroditus did so "risking his life" (παραβολευσάμενος τῇ ψυχῇ). The verb is used only here in biblical literature.[431] It is "from παράβολος, 'venturesome,' the verbal part expressing the energy of βάλλω, instead

---

429 Fee, 274.

430 There are several textual variants at this point. One manuscript (C) contains no genitive at all, leaving simply "the work." Several others (e.g, ℵ, A, P) substitute (κυρίου, "the Lord"). Χριστοῦ has good external support (𝔓⁴⁶, B, F, D) and appears to be the more difficult and therefore the more likely to have been "corrected" by a copyist. As it stands it is a descriptor not used elsewhere by Paul. Compare Acts 15:38 where "the work" (τὸ ἔργον) is used objectively (cf. Sumney, 67).

431 It, according to Fee, "occurs here for the first time in known literature." But "Paul did not invent the word" (Fee, 282).

of being static as in παραβολή."⁴³² It is a graphic word that was used in other Greek writings to describe gambling, often in high stakes games that were determined by a roll of the dice. It came then also to describe risky endeavors which put one's life in danger. In that sense it could be used of a friend endangering himself in the interest of a friend mired in legal difficulties. It could also be used of merchants who risked their lives for financial gain or of a fighter in the arena whose life was endangered to the point of death. "In the post-apostolic church a group called the 'paraboloni' risked their lives by nursing the sick and burying the dead."⁴³³ Here the participle is used circumstantially, noting the precipitating decision that meant Epaphroditus "came close to death." The aorist tense again pictures the event itself as a dramatic moment in time. The middle voice is deponent, having an active meaning.⁴³⁴ The definite article is correctly understood as possessive ("his"). Whether this depicts the seriousness of the illness that befell Epaphroditus (vv.26-27) or an additional danger in addition to that, we cannot be completely positive. Some see here a hint that Epaphroditus fell ill en route to Rome with the gift from the Philippians, but forged ahead despite the danger of exacerbating the illness with potentially dire consequences.⁴³⁵ This may have been the case, but what we have here would constitute little more than a hint in that direction. The specific details of the illness and brush with death remain beyond us.

This risk was taken with a specific purpose (ἵνα, "to") in mind. That was to "complete what was deficient in your service to me" (ἀναπληρώσῃ τὸ ὑμῶν ὑστέρημα τῆς πρός με λειτουργίας). Epaphroditus put himself within a hair's breadth of death because something was "deficient" (τὸ ... ὑστέρημα) apart from his action. The noun describes an insufficiency in or absence of something. Here it "refers to a present religious and ethical

---

432 Moulton and Milligan, 3158.

433 Rienecker, 555; cf. Vincent, ICC, 77.

434 Sumney, 68.

435 E.g., Fee, 283.

obligation."[436] Paul used the word eight of the nine times it is found in the NT (Luke 21:4; 1 Cor. 16:17; 2 Cor. 8:14 [2x]; 9:12; 11:9; Phil. 2:30; Col. 1:24; 1 Thess. 3:10). Five of those times it is found, as here, with compounded forms of the verb πληρόω ("to fill"): with ἀναπληρόω (1 Cor. 16:17; Phil. 2:30), προσαναπληρόω (2 Cor. 9:12; 11:9), and ἀνταναπληρόω (Col. 1:29). In this case there "is no rebuke in the word for the only 'deficiency' is that they could not be w[ith] him themselves, to do him service."[437] In fact Vincent says of the entire clause, "The expression is complimentary and affectionate, to the effect that all that was missing in the matter of their service was their ministration in person, which was supplied by Epaphroditus."[438] Paul's use of the word in Colossians 1:24 ("what is lacking [τὰ ὑστερήματα] in Christ's afflictions") makes clear that it need not imply anything negative in the lack.[439]

> **Ministry Maxim**
>
> Personal sacrifice may be necessary for accomplishment of the group's objective.

The singular action of Epaphroditus stood in the place of what the whole church (ὑμῶν, "your") should have supplied. The plural pronoun is in the attributive position, tucked between the definite article and the noun. It thus emphasizes the qualitative nature of the deficit. The genitive may simply indicate that the lack was the Philippian's.[440] Lenski makes the genitive objective, indicating that what was lacking was the Philippians themselves.[441] The deficit is not that they themselves were absent, but that something they might have supplied could not be supplied because of their absence.

---

436 TDNT, 5:933.

437 Rienecker, 555; similarly, Alford, 3:177; Kennedy, 447, Vincent, ICC, 78.

438 Vincent, *Word Studies*, 3:442.

439 Silva, 142.

440 Vincent, ICC, 78.

441 Lenski, 824.

A second articular noun in the genitive case follows: "service" (τῆς ... λειτουργίας). The genitive is objective, indicating that which is lacking.[442] Paul just used the same word to describe his own life pictured as being poured out as a drink offering "upon the sacrifice and service [λειτουργίᾳ] of your faith" (v.17). And he has just used the kindred word to describe Epaphroditus as the Philippian believers' own "minister [λειτουργὸν] to my need" (v.25). See there for more information on the background of the word. In the present case Paul clearly esteemed this as a spiritual ministry, a sacred, priestly "service." We might conclude, as some do[443], that this applies to the monetary gift which Epaphroditus bore to Paul from the Philippian congregation. But given the Apostle's delight over their gift and his insistence upon dependence upon God for the meeting of all his needs (4:10-19) it seems unlikely that he would now describe it as lacking in any way. The gift lacked only in its delivery to the Apostle in Rome. This Epaphroditus cared for at the risk of his own life. It probably also applies to the intended fuller ministry of support and encouragement that Epaphroditus was commissioned to fulfill on the Apostle's behalf.

The prepositional phrase "to me" (πρός με) is in the attributive position, positioned between the definite article (τῆς) and the noun (λειτουργίας, "service"). This serves to emphasize the qualitative nature of the service as that directed to Paul himself. The service in mind was to be directed to Paul (πρός με, "to me") while the deficit in fulfilling this was theirs (ὑμῶν, "your"), and that simply because they could not be physically present to render the service.

To resolve this Epaphroditus sought to "complete" (ἀναπληρώσῃ) what the other believers from Philippi could not do because of physical distance. The word is a compound, comprised of ἀνά ("up") and πληρόω ("to fill"). When used, as here, with the genitive of persons it can mean to "make up for someone's absence or lack" or to "represent one who is absent."[444] Paul used the verb in a similar circumstance with the believers

---

442 O'Brien, 344; Sumney, 68.

443 TDNT, 4:227.

444 BDAG, 547.3.

in Corinth: "I rejoice over the coming of Stephanas and Fortunatus and Achaicus, because they have supplied what was lacking [ἀνεπλήρωσαν] on your part" (1 Cor. 16:17). The aorist tense again pictures the entire ministry journey of Epaphroditus to Rome as a singular event. The subjunctive form serves with the ἵνα to identify this as a purpose clause.

> **Digging Deeper:**
> 1. Is there someone to whom you could loan your honor in order to rescue theirs? (v.25)
> 2. How can you honor Christ by honoring one of His servants?
> 3. Is there someone your local church should "hold … in high regard" (v.29) but does not? What can you do about that?

PHILIPPIANS 3

Verse 1 – "Finally, my brethren, rejoice in the Lord. To write the same things *again* is no trouble to me, and it is a safeguard for you."

Having exhorted the believers in Philippi to unity (1:27-2:4, 12-18) and having set forth the "attitude" (2:5) that will be necessary to achieve such unity, and having illustrated that "attitude" through Jesus (2:6-11) and both Timothy (2:19-24) and Epaphroditus (2:25-30), Paul now transitions in his thought and approach.

The expression Τὸ λοιπόν ("Finally") is often used when the author wishes to transition to a new matter (1 Cor. 7:29; Phil. 3:1; 4:8; 2 Thess. 3:1). This is especially true "when it comes near the end of a literary work."[1] The expression can be used adverbially, indicating the manner in which the verbal action (χαίρετε, "rejoice") is to be taken.[2] Here, however, it might mean something like "as far as the rest is concerned," "beyond that," or "in addition."[3] Paul is not moving to bring the letter to a close.[4]

---

1   BDAG, 4612.3.b. Contra Vincent who considers that Paul began to close the letter when he suddenly remembered the matter of the Judaizing teachers (v.2) and their influence upon the church and then decided to carry the letter onward (Vincent, *Word Studies*, 3:442); cf. also Alford, 3:177.

2   Wallace, 200-201; 293.

3   BDAG, 4612.3.b.

4   Wallace, 493, n.114.

Rather he is turning from the immediate discussion of the sending of Timothy and Epaphroditus (2:19-30), but what he says now does not depart from the major themes of "joy"/"rejoicing" and unity that he has been weaving throughout the letter. In time the expression came to be used as almost equivalent to οὖν.[5] This seems to be the case here (and in 4:8) as it simply signals a transition in what follows.[6]

We might thus see Paul as adding to the examples of Timothy (2:19-24) and Epaphroditus (2:25-30) that of himself (3:7-14) in contrast to the negative example of the Judaizers (3:2-6).[7] In himself, then, Paul offers an additional example of the mind of Christ (2:5) worked out in a human life, though perhaps now in the face of different challenges to their unity and joy. Indeed, he calls them to "join in following my example, and observe those who walk according to the pattern you have in us" (3:17). And this in contrast to the "enemies of the cross of Christ" (3:18-19).

Paul addresses the Philippian believers as "my brethren" (ἀδελφοί μου). The expression is not gender specific and includes both male and female believers ("my brothers and sisters, NRSV). Paul called Epaphroditus "my brother" (τὸν ἀδελφὸν ... μου, 2:25), so now he addresses all of the believers in Philippi as "my brethren" (ἀδελφοί μου). This is a familial circle of fellowship that included Paul and the church in Philippi (1:12; 3:1, 13, 17; 4:1, 8), including their messenger and minister, Epaphroditus (2:25), but it also included others beyond them (1:14), including those in Rome from which Paul wrote this letter (4:21). The Apostle's efforts at building unity continue even in these seemingly ordinary expressions.

He commands the believers in Philippi to "rejoice" (χαίρετε).[8] The present imperative demands the action be undertaken repeatedly or habitually. The ongoing pattern of their lives is to be one of rejoicing. The plural form demands that they do this together, rather than becoming mired

---

5   Robertson, *Grammar*, 1146; cf. Kennedy, 448; Lenski, 826; Vincent, ICC, 90.

6   Harmon, 304; O'Brien, 348; Sumney, 69.

7   Harmon, 303-304.

8   The thematic nature of rejoicing in the letter seems to mitigate against the suggestion that χαίρετε here is equivalent to Paul's "goodbye."

in controversy and division. The command enables Paul to transition (Τὸ λοιπόν, "Finally") but to show that he is not departing from this theme of joy (χαίρω: 1:18 [2x]; 2:17, 18, 28; 3:1; 4:4 [2x], 10; συγχαίρω: 2:17, 18; χαρά: 1:4, 25; 2:2, 29; 4:1).

Their rejoicing is to be "in the Lord" (ἐν κυρίῳ). Paul uses the phrase nine times in the letter (1:14; 2:19, 24, 29; 3:1; 4:1, 2, 4, 10). As he uses ἀδελφοί μου ("my brothers") as a connective to one another he now uses ἐν κυρίῳ ("in the Lord") to remind them of the union they all have together with the risen Christ, sharing together in His very life. Given the exceedingly strong warning against Judaizers that will immediately follow in verse 2, this command to "rejoice in the Lord" may be pregnant with meaning. Perhaps we could insert into this brief phrase the kind of teaching we find in the letter to the Galatians, with its stress on freedom from the Law and the fullness found in Christ. Thus the present command to rejoice "in the Lord" (ἐν κυρίῳ) may find an echo in the contrast between "in Christ Jesus" (ἐν Χριστῷ Ἰησοῦ) and "in the flesh" (ἐν σαρκὶ) in verse 3. It may further be a subtle preparation for the emphasis upon union with Christ in verses 9 and 10.

Paul begins a new sentence by pointing to his present letter and that which goes into its composition. "To write" (γράφειν) is a present infinitive. The present tense simply views his action from his personal vantage point as he pens the letter. The infinitive is used substantively to designate the subject of the verb.[9] That which he is writing are "the same things" (τὰ αὐτὰ). There is significant question regarding to what this refers. Scholars have formulated a variety of possibilities. 1) Some view it as a reference backward to ground already covered in this letter (chapters 1-2). 2) Others see it as a reference to the command to "Rejoice" (v.1a), since he has

> **Ministry Maxim**
>
> No believer ever matures to a state in which the ministry of reminder is unnecessary.

---

9 Wallace, 600-601.

already issued that command (2:18) and will do so again (4:4 [2x]).[10] It seems improbable, however, that the repetition of this command is given as a "safeguard" for them. In what meaningful sense can the command to rejoice serve as a "safeguard" for the Philippians?[11] 3) Yet others believe it reflects upon things previously communicated to them, perhaps in letters now lost to us (cf. Phil. 3:18).[12] Such warnings may have been specifically about the Judaizers he is about to mention in verse 2.[13] 4) There are those who believe it is a reference to the things that Epaphroditus and Timothy would verbally communicate to the Philippian believers upon their arrival.[14] 5) And there are those who despair of our ever knowing to what this refers.[15] But I believe the best course is to see it as a reference forward, to the things he is about to expound upon. Sumney observes[16] that Τὸ λοιπόν simply introduces a new section of the letter and thus directs our thoughts forward and that ἀσφαλές ("a safeguard") seems to point forward to the warnings that follow (vv.2ff).[17] This may include a review of Paul's theology [18] and the warnings that follow.[19] It seems most appropriate to view these as things Paul has orally taught them in the past, rather than what had been written in previous communication, for Paul specifically speaks of those "of whom I often told you" in verse 18.[20] In any case it clearly refers to things spoken to the Philippians themselves (ὑμῖν, "to you"; not translated by the NASU) and not just generally to other believers.

---

10   Alford, 3:177; Harmon, 306.
11   Müller, 105; O'Brien, 351.
12   Vincent, ICC, 91-92.
13   Kennedy, 448; Wuest, 87.
14   Rienecker, 555.
15   Robertson, *Paul's Joy in Christ*, 175-176; Vincent, *Word Studies*, 3:442.
16   Sumney, 70.
17   Cf. also Fee 288, n.11, 293; Hellerman, 169.
18   Silva, 152.
19   Lenski, 827; Martin, 135-136.
20   Fee, 292-293; O'Brien, 352.

Whatever the referent may be, Paul contrasts the effect of his present writing upon himself and upon the Philippians. He does so by the familiar formula μὲν … δὲ ("on the one hand … on the other"). Neither clause has a verb, but ἐστιν ("is") should be read in both as the NASU models. As it regards Paul himself, to write the same things to them again, he says "is no trouble to me" (ἐμοὶ μὲν οὐκ ὀκνηρόν). The word "trouble" (ὀκνηρόν) is used only two other times in the NT. It is used once to characterize as "lazy" the slave who misinterpreted his master's character (Matt. 25:26) and again by Paul in Romans 12:11 to exhort those believers to "not be lagging behind [ὀκνηροί] in diligence." In the LXX it appears exclusively in Proverbs, and there twelve times, most often depicting the "sluggard" (Prov. 6:6, 9; 11:16; 18:8; 20:4; 21:25; 22:13; 26:13, 14, 15, 16; 31:27). The adjective has the sense of hesitation, reluctance or a holding back from something.[21] Here Paul has "no" (οὐκ) such hesitation with regard to writing to them along the same lines of his previous exhortations.

As regards Paul's writing again to the Philippian believers, he says, "it is a safeguard to you" (ὑμῖν δὲ ἀσφαλές). There is a contrast between what the letter does "to me" (ἐμοί) and what it does "to you" (ὑμῖν). It is the contrast of singular to plural, of Apostle to disciples, of church planter to church members. However unified they may be in Christ, the present letter stands in unique relationship to them both. This is Paul's only use of the adjective (ἀσφαλές, "a safeguard"). It is a compound comprised of the alpha-privative for negation (α-) and σφάλλω ("to make fall" or "to cause to stumble"). It is thus "used to describe anything which has stability and firmness enough *not* to be overthrown."[22] Luke employs it when speaking of "certain, precise or exact knowledge" (Acts 21:34; 22:30; 25:26).[23] The author of Hebrews uses it to describe the "sure" nature of the hope which is the anchor of our souls (Heb. 6:19). Interestingly, as with the previous adjective, this one also appears in the LXX only in Proverbs (Prov. 3:18; 8:28; 15:7). It can be used to describe that which is stable or firm, or

---

21 BDAG, 5248.

22 Rienecker, 555.

23 Spicq, 1:217-218.

figuratively of that which is certain. In this case it describes what is, by being firm and certain, in the best interests of the Philippian believers.[24] It serves as a sure, certain word of counsel. And by their listening to it they find a firm foundation for their lives. It is thus "a safeguard" for them that Paul writes as he does. They need this because, as the next verse will show, there are other messages of a different nature being circulated about.

> **Digging Deeper:**
> 1. How does a dependence upon self-attained righteousness work against true joy? Explain.
> 2. What is it about us that makes the ministry of reminder so essential?

Verse 2 – "Beware of the dogs, beware of the evil workers, beware of the false circumcision;"

Paul's tone now suddenly seems to change.[25] His words become terse and sharp-edged. The staccato repetition of the thrice repeated imperative βλέπετε ("Beware") rings with the cry of danger, commanding alertness to a heretofore unmentioned foe. The present imperative form places responsibility squarely upon the Philippian believers. It demands a continuous watchfulness. They are to "see!" something which they may be prone to miss and which they are to observe because of its inherent danger. Paul uses this command not infrequently in his letters (1 Cor. 1:26; 8:9; 10:18; 16:10; 2 Cor. 10:7; Gal. 5:15; Eph. 5:15; Col. 2:8). The intent of the command might be brought out by any of several expressions in English such as "watch out," "beware," "look out," "see to it," all capturing the urgency of Paul's concern. In an example of the literary device known as asyndeton

---

24 BDAG, 1230.

25 Though his tone here is not entirely new, for he has already spoken of "your opponents" (1:28) and of the believers' role in a dark world (2:14-16). He will soon enough warn them about the "enemies of the cross" (3:18-19). Cf. O'Brien, 347.

Paul drops all conjunctions and allows the spare words of the rapidly fired commands to have their powerful rhetorical effect.²⁶

That for which they are to watch so carefully is in each case identified by an articular noun in the accusative case (and in the second instance the addition of an adjective in the attributive position). The definite articles mark each out as a specific class or group. The first two are masculine plurals; the last is a feminine singular, used as a collective noun. In each case the translators of the NASU have given us "of," but the Greek text is more abrupt: "Beware the dogs! Beware the evil workers! Beware the false circumcision!"

In all three cases Paul is referring to false teachers; specifically, Judaizers who attempted to make Torah observance a required component of salvation. Paul does not nuance his thoughts here. The strength of his language in assigning these descriptors leaves no doubt as to how Paul views these dirty, devilish, dangerous individuals. He employs alliteration to heighten the rhetorical effect of his warning, all three expressions beginning with the Greek letter kappa (κ-).

He first calls them "the dogs" (τοὺς κύνας). This is Paul's only use of the term and it appears but four other times in the NT. It clearly is a term of derision. In ancient times "dogs" were not domesticated pets, but dirty, dangerous scavengers to be avoided. Dogs in the ancient world were "without a home and without an owner, feeding on the refuse and filth of the streets, quarrelling among themselves and attacking the passer-by."²⁷ The term could be used to describe a male prostitute (Deut. 23:19). They are paired with "evildoers" in a prophetic foreshadowing of those who crucified our Lord (Psa. 21:17). The Jews employed it as a reference to Gentiles (Matt. 15:26; Mark 7:27). The disciples are ordered by the Lord, "Do not give what is holy to dogs, and do not throw your pearls before

> **Ministry Maxim**
>
> Caustic irony should not have first place in our apologetics, but that does not mean it has no place.

---

26   Robertson, *Grammar*, 949.

27   Lightfoot, 158.

swine" (Matt. 7:6a). In an echo of Proverbs 26:11 Peter also paired dogs and ritually unclean swine (2 Pet. 2:22). The pathetic estate of Lazarus was found in the fact that "the dogs were coming and licking his sores" (Luke 16:21). In the end "dogs" will be found outside the New Jerusalem, along with "the sorcerers and the immoral persons and the murderers and the idolaters, and everyone who loves and practices lying" (Rev. 22:15). Paul uses what was surely the Judaizers' own epithet and turns it back upon them—they who glory in Judaism and in its distinguishing mark of circumcision are the unclean, Gentile dogs they so roundly condemn!

Then the Apostle calls the Judaizers, "the evil workers" (τοὺς κακοὺς ἐργάτας). Surprisingly, Paul only uses the noun four times.[28] It can be used in a positive sense of a "workman who does not need to be ashamed" because of his "accurately handling the word of truth" (2 Tim. 2:15). It is similarly used of Elders who labor well, especially in preaching and teaching (1 Tim. 5:18). But he also uses it in a negative sense, as he does here, of "deceitful workers" (2 Cor. 11:13) who seek to undermine the ministry of the gospel. The adjective is in the attributive position, giving special emphasis to the "evil" (κακοὺς) nature and character of these "workers." In this case "the adjective receives greater emphasis than the substantive."[29] Thus the emphasis lies not so much upon their work, but upon its *evil* nature. There may be, however, by the use of ἐργάτας ("workers') a secondary, subtle and ironic emphasis upon the Judaizers' emphasis upon works (or *the* "work" of circumcision) as the means of true inclusion in God's favor.[30] Silva says, "In this context, the phrase is surely meant to refute the Judaizers' claim that they were doing the works of the law."[31]

Finally, in a powerful and ironic twist, Paul calls the Judaizers "the false circumcision" (τὴν κατατομήν). The word is used only here in biblical literature. The cognate verb (κατατέμνω) is used in the LXX of cuttings that

---

28 By way of contrast, in his NT letters Paul uses the kindred noun ἔργον over 60 times and cognate verb ἐργάζομαι 18 times.

29 Robertson, *Grammar*, 776.

30 Harmon, 310; Martin, 137.

31 Silva, 147.

are characteristic of pagan rites and thus forbidden by the Mosaic Law (Lev. 21:5; cf. 1 Kings 18:28; Hos. 7:14; Isa. 15:2). The word has proven a challenge for translators as the various renderings demonstrate: "those who mutilate the flesh" (ESV, NET, NRSV), "those mutilators of the flesh" (NIV), "the mutilation" (NKJV), "the concision" (KJV). We have here a play on words with ἡ περιτομη ("the true circumcision") in verse 3. The prepositions in compound seem to tell the story of the contrast intended. In the first case, it is a cutting *off* (κατά) which is pictured, and thus a "mutilation" (NKJV; cf. ESV, NET, NIV, NLT, NRSV). In the second case it is a cutting *around* (περί) which is envisioned. "In an ironic play on words Paul brings against his adversaries the objection that their vaunted circumcision (περιτομή) is in reality dissection (κατατομή)."[32] In this way Paul "apostrophises and presses to absurdity a claim of his adversaries."[33]

Paul's "bitter and aggressive irony"[34] is not unlike his words to the Galatians: "I wish that those who are troubling you would even mutilate [ἀποκόψονται] themselves" (Gal. 5:12). There instead of cut *around* (περιτέμνω) he has cut *off* (ἀποκόπτω).

For Paul circumcision is a matter of the heart, not the body and is found in repentance and faith, not the sharp edge of a knife (Rom. 2:28-29; Col. 2:11; Eph. 2:11). Lenski says, "What Christ had abrogated they demanded as essential; what now counted as nothing (Gal. 6:15) they counted as everything."[35]

Verse 3 – "for we are the *true* circumcision, who worship in the Spirit of God and glory in Christ Jesus and put no confidence in the flesh,"

Paul now gives the reason (γάρ, "for") for the last of the invectives in verse 2. Those powerful, cutting words make sense because "we are the true

---

32 TDNT, 8:110-111.

33 Ibid., 8:110.

34 Ibid., 8:111.

35 Lenski, 829.

circumcision" (ἡμεῖς γάρ ἐσμεν ἡ περιτομή). Having used the rare and derogatory word in verse 2 (κατατομή), Paul now employs the standard word for "circumcision" (περιτομή). The NASU translators have added "false" and "true" respectively in an attempt to highlight Paul's intention.

Circumcision was widely practiced throughout the ancient world, but it had been owned particularly by the Jewish people since God gave it to Abraham as a sign of His covenant with him and his descendants (Gen. 17:1-14). But even in the OT God had begun to consistently set forth the primacy not of the physical act of circumcision in the flesh, but of the "circumcision of the heart" (Deut. 10:16; 30:6; Jer. 4:4; 6:10 ["their ear is uncircumcised," KJV]; 9:26; Ezek. 44:7, 9). It seems clear that the Apostle is calling upon such imagery at the present time. What had been demanded in the Old Covenant has now been accomplished through Christ for everyone in union with Him by grace through faith (Rom. 2:28-29; Col. 2:11). Being physically circumcised or uncircumcised is now irrelevant in the Lord (Col. 3:11). Physical circumcision counts for nothing (1 Cor. 7:19; Gal. 5:6; 6:15) all that matters is "a new creation" (Gal. 6:15) that results in "faith working through love" (Gal. 5: 6) to produce obedience (1 Cor. 7:19). Clearly, "circumcision is that which is of the heart" (Rom. 2:29). Faith and justification always preceded circumcision (Rom. 4:9-12). Christ has ushered in a new day in God's dealings with humanity and the present tense verb (ἐσμεν, "we are") presents the things as they presently stand.

Some see here an indication that Paul makes the church the new Israel. Yet he does no such thing. Circumcision was given to Abraham only after his faith and justification (Rom. 4:11). Circumcision was given to Abraham long before Jacob and his sons existed. Circumcision was a distinguishing mark set upon Abraham and his descendants well before the Law was given. There is no replacement of Israel by the church to be found here. Rather he is saying that the state of heart that was to be witnessed by circumcision is now realized through becoming "a new creation" (Gal. 6:15) through repentance and faith in Jesus Christ and is witnessed to by "faith working through love" (Gal. 5:6) in an obedient life (1 Cor. 7:19), whatever may be your physical state of circumcision or uncircumcision (Rom. 3:30; Col. 3:11).

Paul explains more fully just who he intends by the plural pronoun "we" (ἡμεῖς). And note that the plural pronoun stands emphatically at the head of the sentence and thus in contrast to the "dogs," "the evil workers," "the false circumcision" of verse 2.[36] He uses three participial clauses to identify true believers, just as he employed three descriptors for the Judaizers (v.2). In fact Harmon sees here a positive, corresponding answer to each of those negatives expressed by way of a chiastic construction.

> A – dogs
>> B – evildoers
>>> C – those who mutilate the flesh
>>> C^1 – circumcision
>> B^1 – worship in the Spirit
> A^1 – glory in Christ Jesus and put no confidence in the flesh[37]

The first descriptor is that "we" are those "who worship in the Spirit of God" (οἱ πνεύματι θεοῦ λατρεύοντες). The articular participle (οἱ ... λατρεύοντες) is used as a substantive to designate the subject of the clause. The word is used sparingly by Paul, only four times in all. He uses it of his own service to the Lord (Rom. 1:9; 2 Tim. 1:3). He also uses it to describe the degraded worship of "the creature rather than the Creator" (Rom. 1:25). In secular Greek it could be used of work for pay, but it is used extensively throughout the LXX and in its NT occurrences to describe "the carrying out of religious duties, esp[ecially] of a cultic nature."[38] Vincent observes, "A Jew would be scandalized by the application of this term to

---

36 Lenski, 830; Sumney, 71; To further emphasize the contrast, O'Brien says, "The attributive use of the definite article after the verb 'to be' signifies that 'we, and we only, are *the circumcision*'" (358).

37 Harmon, 312.

38 BDAG, 4524.

Christian service. It is purposely chosen with reference to ἡ περιτομή."³⁹ The Jew believed that a life of service/worship to God was to be found only among the ranks of Israel. The Gentile could not live such a life unto God without becoming a part of Israel. Paul's application of the term to the followers of Jesus (both Jewish and Gentile) would have been scandalous to the Jews.

The real question here in how to understand the rest of the clause. There are difficulties in determining the text. Most read the genitive θεοῦ (i.e., "worship by the Spirit of God"). Other important manuscripts have the dative θεῷ and thus render it "worship God by the Spirit." The highly regarded manuscript 𝔓⁴⁶ omits the divine name altogether. Which then is to be considered the correct text? It is likely that the dative (θεῷ) would have been a scribal "correction" since they may have regarded the intent of πνεύματι as a matter of question and wanted to follow the general practice of ascribing worship to "God" rather risking the idea of worship being rendered to the "Spirit." It would be most likely that the omission of the divine name altogether was a scribal oversight, for there seems to be little room for a scribe to have intentionally removed it. Thus the reading of our text, the genitive "of God" (θεοῦ), seems the more likely text.⁴⁰ Thus the dative πνεύματι ("in the Spirit") is used instrumentally. ⁴¹Some translate it by "in" (NASU, NKJV, NRSV) while other opt for "by" (ESV, NET, NIV, NLT). It describes a person worshiping "prompted by" or "filled with" the Spirit of God.⁴² The genitive θεοῦ ("of God") specifies which "Spirit" is under discussion. The pair (πνεύματι θεοῦ) is in the attributive position, tucked between the definite article and its participle—emphasizing the nature of this religious service/worship. In this way Paul puts true service/worship—"in spirit and in truth" (John 4:23-24)—squarely in the camp of the followers of Jesus Christ and denies it

---

39 Vincent, ICC, 93.

40 Cf. NET Bible; Silva, 153; Sumney, 72.

41 Fee, 300 n.62; Hansen, 221 n.46; Hellerman, 173; Robertson, *Grammar*, 540; TDNT, 7.131-132

42 Thayer, 373.

is found among those Jews who seek it in the externals of rites and trappings of their ancestral religion.

Then also (καὶ, "and") "we" are those "who glory in Christ Jesus" (καυχώμενοι ἐν Χριστῷ Ἰησοῦ). All three participles are governed by one definite article (οἱ) so this present participle is also used as a substantive to designate the subject ("*who* glory"). The middle voice is deponent and therefore active in meaning. The verb is a favorite of Paul. Thirty-five of its thirty-seven appearances in the NT come from his pen. "It is used chiefly to define two extremes of religious attitude; either proud self-confidence (e.g. Gal. vi. 13), or humble submission to God's grace as revealed in the cross of Jesus (e.g., Gal. vi. 14)."[43] One may "glory" (or "boast," as it is often translated) in all manner of things, including self (1 Cor. 1:29), men (1 Cor. 3:21), and the Law (Rom. 2:23). Currently Paul is concerned with those who "glory" in their flesh, in their keeping of the Law, in the fact of their physical circumcision. But God has purposely made salvation by grace through faith in Jesus Christ, "not as a result of works, so that no one may boast" (Eph. 2:9). Paul told the Galatians that "those who are circumcised do not even keep the Law themselves, but they desire to have you circumcised so that they may boast in your flesh. But may it never be that I would boast, except in the cross of our Lord Jesus Christ, through which the world has been crucified to me, and I to the world" (Gal. 6:13-14). He told the Colossians, "there is no … Greek and Jew, circumcised and uncircumcised … but Christ is all, and in all" (Col. 3:11). This is why he could say, "may it never be that I would boast, except in the cross of our Lord Jesus Christ, through which the world has been crucified to me, and I to the world" (Gal. 6:14). To the Corinthians Paul said, "we preach Christ crucified, to Jews a stumbling block and to Gentiles foolishness" (1 Cor. 1:23) and "I determined to know nothing among you except Jesus

> **Ministry Maxim**
>
> True life is lived out in worshipful service to God through faith in Jesus Christ by the enabling of the Holy Spirit.

---

43 Martin, 139.

Christ, and Him crucified" (1 Cor. 2:2). In all this there seems to be an echo of Jeremiah's words: "'... let him who boasts boast of this, that he understands and knows Me, that I am the LORD who exercises loving-kindness, justice and righteousness on earth; for I delight in these things,' declares the LORD. 'Behold, the days are coming,' declares the LORD, 'that I will punish all who are circumcised and yet uncircumcised'" (Jer. 9:23-24).

Note that Paul speaks of the Trinity as it relates here to our salvation: the Father (θεοῦ, "God"), "the Spirit" (πνεύματι), and "Christ Jesus" (Χριστῷ Ἰησοῦ).

Finally, Paul adds (καὶ, "and") that "we" are those who "put no confidence in the flesh" (οὐκ ἐν σαρκὶ πεποιθότες). Again the participle is governed by the same definite article (οἱ) and is like the previous two a substantive participle designating the subject. The first two participles along with the main verb they qualify are in the present tense, picturing the ongoing, abiding nature of the action. This participle, however, is in the perfect tense, though it carries on the idea of the present.[44] The verb describes being so convinced of something that you put your trust in it.[45] It is used six times in this letter, describing how certain Paul is of God finishing the good work He'd begun in the Philippian believers (1:6), the increased confidence most brothers in Christ received from hearing of Paul's imprisonment (1:14), Paul's confidence that his imprisonment will result not in his death, but life and continuing service to the Philippians (1:25), and his confidence that he will be soon released and come to visit Philippi (2:24). Then he uses it here and similarly in the next verse.

The negation (οὐκ, "no") denies the matter absolutely and categorically.[46] Note the contrast which the double use of the preposition ἐν ("in") creates between "in Christ Jesus" (ἐν Χριστῷ Ἰησοῦ) and "in the flesh" (ἐν σαρκὶ). As the following lines will show those who "put

---

44 BDAG, 5754.2; Rienecker, 554, 556.

45 BDAG, 5754.2.a.

46 Thayer, 408.

confidence in the flesh" are the Jews. We, in emphatic contrast, honor the Father as we worship by the Spirit, resting our confidence in Christ.

Paul can use "flesh" (σαρκὶ) in a variety of nuanced ways. Sometimes it is a clear reference to the physical body (e.g., Phil. 1:22, 24) and at other times it points to that part of the believer that tends away from God (e.g. Rom. 8:4-13; Gal. 5:13-24). But here, given the centrality of the matter of circumcision, he clearly is using it of the physical body and the physical act which is performed upon it by insistence of the Judaizers. But here it is not a reference *merely* to physical circumcision, but (as Paul's own example will illustrate, vv.4-6) to circumcision as representative of all the external privileges (vv.4-5a) and personal efforts at righteousness (vv.5b-6) upon which the Jews rested their confidence, rather than upon Christ.

The Apostle's words to the Galatians are apropos here: "Those who desire to make a good showing in the flesh [ἐν σαρκί] try to compel you to be circumcised, simply that they may not be persecuted for the cross of Christ. For those who are circumcised do not even keep the Law themselves, but they desire to have you circumcised so that they may boast in your flesh [ἐν τῇ ὑμετέρᾳ σαρκι]. But may it never be that I would boast, except in the cross of our Lord Jesus Christ, through which the world has been crucified to me, and I to the world. For neither is circumcision anything, nor uncircumcision, but a new creation" (Gal. 6:12-15).

Digging Deeper:
1. When, if ever, would the kind of name-calling Paul employs in verse 2 be appropriate in a contemporary context?
2. In what way does circumcision reach its fulfillment in the salvation found only in Jesus Christ?
3. What essential spiritual reality did circumcision represent which must be realized still, even if the religious use of circumcision does not remain valid? How is that personally realized through faith in Jesus?

Verse 4 – "although I myself might have confidence even in the flesh. If anyone else has a mind to put confidence in the flesh, I far more:"

Paul had strong words for those who insist on circumcision as necessary for salvation (v.2) and declared that the true people of God "put no confidence in the flesh" (v.3). Now he completes the sentence begun in verse 3 by making a concession ("although"). The Apostle makes the point unambiguously by utilizing both καίπερ[47] and the participle ἔχων ("have") with concessive intent.[48] In fact the combination is used to make an emphatic opposing point.[49] The concession does not introduce a point which might weaken his arguments against reliance upon the flesh, but which powerfully reinforces them. He is making a unique avowal, an emphatic, autobiographical statement (ἐγώ, "I myself"). The switch from the first person plural (ἡμεῖς, "we") in verse 3 to the first person singular (which will predominate until verse 15 when the plural is reintroduced) is stark and vigorous.[50]

He who made such scathing remarks against any such dependence upon the "flesh" (circumcision and all the other external privileges or personal performances to which Jews might be tempted to look as in any way essential to their acceptance with God) now admits that he, above all others, "might have confidence even in the flesh" (ἔχων πεποίθησιν καὶ ἐν σαρκί). The verb (ἔχων, "might have") is in the present tense, pointing to realities which Paul still possessed at the time of writing and might therefore be relied upon, as did other Jews. The NASU renders it as "*might* have," but it is more definite than that. There is no question as to Paul actually possessing the qualities in question. In this way, for the sake of the argument, he speaks of actually possessing this ground of "confidence." The simple "have" (ESV, NIV, NRSV) is to be preferred. The noun (πεποίθησιν, "confidence")

---

47   This is Paul's sole use of the conjunction καίπερ (cf. Heb. 5:8; 7:5; 12:17; 2 Pet. 1:12).
48   Robertson, *Grammar*, 1129.
49   Ibid., 1154; cf. Lenski, 832; Rienecker, 556.
50   O'Brien, 366.

arose from the verb πείθω ("confidence"), used in the previous verse and about to be used at the end of this verse. Paul "put no confidence in the flesh" (v.3) even though he "might have confidence even in the flesh" (v.4). His utter dependence upon Jesus Christ and Him alone arose not because he could not measure up on the Jewish scale of pedigree and performance, but because he had come to see the utter bankruptcy of such dependence. It is not that Paul was not rich in the currency of Jewish religious ideals (as he shall shortly demonstrate in verses 5-6); it is that he realized God worked on a different economy altogether.

What, we may ask, is the role of καί? It could be emphatic: "*even* in the flesh." Or it might signal an addition: "in the flesh *also*" (ESV, RSV; cf. NKJV).[51] The latter seems the more likely. In that case, is it signaling confidence found not only in Christ, but "also" in Torah observance? Or does it signal Paul placing himself alongside of the opponents and saying "I also could place my confidence in my record in the flesh"? The second of these seems unlikely given the conjunction's distance from the emphatic pronoun (ἐγώ, "I myself"). So it seems Paul is saying that as far as human, earthly, merely religious credentials go, apart from His rightly placed confidence in Christ's righteousness, he might do as his opponents have done.

Indeed, Paul says "If anyone else has a mind to put confidence in the flesh, I far more" (Εἴ τις δοκεῖ ἄλλος πεποιθέναι ἐν σαρκί, ἐγὼ μᾶλλον). Paul momentarily, for the sake of argument, allows his hypothetical Jewish opponents their ground of argument. He steps onto their plane, offering to play by their rules, that he might make his point the more powerfully. The conditional statement (Εἴ plus the present indicative verb) is assumed true for the sake of the argument. This is no contest between David and Goliath. Paul (note the emphatic ἐγώ, "I") stands toe to toe with the best "anyone" (τις, he casts his net as

> **Ministry Maxim**
>
> It is a powerful thing when one has what everyone is chasing, but renounces it for what can be found in Christ alone.

---

51 Ibid., 367; Vincent, ICC, 95.

widely as possible, willing to take on any and all comers) among the Jews might offer and demonstrates that he is "far more" (μᾶλλον[52]) than their equal. Whoever imagines (δοκεῖ, "has a mind"[53]) they can compete with Paul on the plane of Jewish religious pedigree and performance is invited to step forward. As he will demonstrate in verses 5 and 6 no one will have more reason "to put confidence in the flesh" (πεποιθέναι ἐν σαρκί) than he does. The verb is the same one used in the previous verse and cognate to the noun just used in this verse. As noted in the previous verse, the perfect tense has a present meaning.

Paul's sentence runs through verse six and will consist of seven points at which he might find reason for "confidence in the flesh." The number seven in the Hebrew Scriptures is often symbolic of completeness and may have been employed here by the Apostle as an additional, subtle device to meet and overcome his opponents on their own ground. What follows describes as fully as possible the kind of resume a strict Jew might wish to present before God's throne.

Paul had been forced to take this line of argumentation and reasoning on another occasion (2 Cor. 11:16-22), taking up "this confidence of boasting" (v.17) to cut off those whose deceptions might make headway among the believing. So now also here, to protect the true people of God, he takes up the argument momentarily on the opponents' ground to cut it out from beneath them. "Since many boast according to the flesh, I will boast also" (2 Cor. 11:18).

Verse 5 – "circumcised the eighth day, of the nation of Israel, of the tribe of Benjamin, a Hebrew of Hebrews; as to the Law, a Pharisee;"

The Apostle to the Gentiles now begins listing the seven reasons he could, should he so choose, rest the weight of his confidence upon his superior Torah-standing. This, however, he will not do, for all that he will

---

52 "it denotes increase, a greater quantity, a larger measure, a higher degree" (Thayer, 387-388).
53 Used "of subjective opinion" and thus often translated "think, presume, suppose" (Friberg, 119).

enumerate here is mere "rubbish" compared to "the surpassing value of knowing Christ" (v.8). These he has gladly "suffered the loss" of (v.7) for that very purpose. For "a righteousness of my own derived from the Law" (v.9) will never stand up to God's holy, perfect standard (Matt. 5:48; 1 Pet. 1:16). But Paul had found in Christ "the righteousness which comes from God" and is given "on the basis of faith" (v.9).

The first of Paul's Jewish credentials is that he was "circumcised the eighth day" (περιτομῇ ὀκταήμερος). The noun (περιτομῇ) is a dative of reference, i.e., "with reference to circumcision."[54] The adjective (ὀκταήμερος) qualifies the noun and might be rendered "an 'eighth-dayer.'"[55] The entire phrase might literally be rendered "a person-of-eight-days relative to circumcision."[56] This takes us back to the moment God gave circumcision to Abraham and his descendants as a sign of His covenant with them. He commanded, "every male among you who is eight days old shall be circumcised throughout your generations" (Gen. 17:12). Thus Abraham circumcised Isaac on the eighth day (Acts 7:8). This then became part of the regulations God handed down to Moses (Lev. 12:3). John the Baptist's parents followed this regulation (Luke 1:59). Jesus' parents also, in observance of the Law, had Him circumcised on the eighth day (Luke 2:21). Thus too Paul's parents had him so circumcised. Paul's Law-righteousness began before he could personally will it to be so, as the first four of the seven items he enumerates reveal. "Converts to Judaism were circumcised in maturity: Ishmaelites in their thirteenth year. He was thus shown to be neither a heathen nor an Ishmaelite."[57]

The second of Paul's potential trusts was the fact that he was born "of the nation of Israel" (ἐκ γένους Ἰσραήλ). For the Jew, to be "of the nation of Israel" was to be within the circle of salvation, to have come under the favor of God, to be the elect of God. Not surprisingly we find Paul not infrequently providing his credentials as such when it served a

---

54 Fee, 306; Robertson, *Grammar,* 523; O'Brien, 369.
55 Harmon, 318; O'Brien, 369.
56 BDAG, 5249.
57 Vincent, *Word Studies,* 3:445.

purpose. When the Jews nearly killed Paul in Jerusalem and the Roman commander who rescued him mistook him for an infamous, marauding Egyptian, Paul said to him, "I am a Jew of Tarsus in Cilicia" (Acts 21:39). When allowed to speak to those Jews who sought his life, he witnessed, "I am a Jew, born in Tarsus of Cilicia, but brought up in this city, educated under Gamaliel, strictly according to the law of our fathers, being zealous for God just as you all are today" (Acts 22:3). When reasoning with the Romans he asked, "God has not rejected His people, has He?" His answer was emphatic, "May it never be!" and as his first line of evidence he said, "I too am an Israelite, a descendant of Abraham, of the tribe of Benjamin" (Rom. 11:1). When false apostles threatened the church in Corinth and downgraded Paul, he asked the believers, "Are they Hebrews? So am I. Are they Israelites? So am I. Are they descendants of Abraham? So am I" (2 Cor. 11:22).

Paul asked the Romans, "Then what advantage has the Jew? Or what is the benefit of circumcision?" He answered, "Great in every respect. First of all, that they were entrusted with the oracles of God" (Rom. 3:1-2). He was correct when he said it is the "Israelites, to whom belongs the adoption as sons, and the glory and the covenants and the giving of the Law and the temple service and the promises, whose are the fathers, and from whom is the Christ according to the flesh, who is over all, God blessed forever. Amen" (Rom. 9:4-5). He reminded Gentile believers of their unbelieving days, saying, "you were at that time separate from Christ, excluded from the commonwealth of Israel, and strangers to the covenants of promise, having no hope and without God in the world" (Eph. 2:12). Yet sadly Paul could also say, "What Israel is seeking, it has not obtained" (Rom. 11:7). The fact is, "they are not all Israel who are descended from Israel" (Rom. 9:6). Paul called it a "mystery ... that a partial hardening has happened to Israel until the fullness of the Gentiles has come in" (Rom. 11:25). But he also promised, "all Israel will be saved; just as it is written, 'THE DELIVERER WILL COME FROM ZION, HE WILL REMOVE UNGODLINESS FROM JACOB'" (v.26).

As a subset of his citizenship within Israel Paul identified himself as "of the tribe of Benjamin" (φυλῆς Βενιαμίν). The tribe of Benjamin was fiercely proud. Benjamin, was the youngest of Jacob's children and thus held an especially dear place in his heart. He was born of Jacob's favored wife, Rachel. He alone of Jacob's sons was born in the land of promise. In the march to the Promised Land the tribe that came from Benjamin took their position with Ephraim and Manasseh, who stood in Jacob's favor in Joseph's place (Numb. 2:18-24). Their allotment in the land fell between that of Judah and Joseph's sons (Josh. 18:11). They were afforded special rank at the head of the military (Judges 5:14; Hosea 5:8). The eventual capital of the nation, Jerusalem, was within their boundaries. Ehud, the left-handed judge, came from Benjamin. The men of Benjamin defended Israel under Deborah and Barak (Judg. 3:14). The nation's first king had arisen from their ranks, and the Apostle's Hebrew name (Saul) probably reflected this point of pride. There were, of course, ignominious moments in the tribe's history as well, such as their resistance of David even after his ascendancy to the throne, Shimei's cursing of David as he fled under Absalom's revolt (2 Sam. 16:5ff), and the revolt against David under the Benjamite Sheba (20:1ff). Yet the greater portion of the tribe stayed loyal to Judah in the revolt against Rehoboam (1 Kings 12:21, 23; 2 Chron. 11:10, 12, 23; 14:8; 15:2, 9). During the time of Exile it was a Benjamite, Mordecai, who helped deliver the Jews from extinction (Esther 2:5), an event memorialized in the Jewish celebration of Purim. Upon return from Exile there were among the intrepid returnees people of the tribe of Benjamin who resettled the land (Neh. 11:7-9, 31-36). F.F. Bruce points out that "From some of these Paul's family may have traced its descent."[58] Early Christian interpreters saw the character of Benjamin, as viewed through Jacob's blessing upon him, as evidenced in Paul's zealous, pre-conversion persecution of Christians: "Benjamin is a ravenous wolf; In the morning he devours the prey, And in the evening he divides the spoil" (Gen. 49:27).

> **Ministry Maxim**
>
> Religious pedigree never gives the rest of faith that comes only through Jesus Christ.

---

58 Bruce, *Philippians*, 108.

Descendants of Benjamin, including Paul, no doubt remembered the bright spots best, as human nature tends to do. The point was that Paul came from faithful stock within God's holy people. His ancestry was not in doubt and he could document his carefully recorded lineage.

Indeed, Paul was "a Hebrew of Hebrews" (Ἑβραῖος ἐξ Ἑβραίων). Does this mean he was a Hebrew *par excellence*?[59] Or does it mean that he was a good Hebrew born from good Hebrew parents?[60] In either case his point is likely that he was not a Hellenized Jew of the Diaspora. Though he was born among the Diaspora, in Tarsus, his parents maintained their strict Judaism, including use of the Hebrew language and all the attending customs which some diaspora Jews let fade away under pressure to accommodate to a contrary culture. Paul was raised in Jerusalem and was schooled there by the great Hebrew teacher, Gamaliel (Acts 22:3).

Paul shifts to a different grammatical form for the final three markers. And in doing so he shifts from those things in which he played no determinative role (items 1-4 of the litany) to those in which he played a direct role (items 5-7). He makes comparative statements using the preposition κατὰ. In each case the NASU translates κατὰ with "as to." A paraphrase might be, "measured according to" or "tested by the standard of."[61] In each case Paul then offers the results of the measurement of himself "according to" each category, a measurement which in every instance puts him at the head of the class.

In the first instance, the comparison is "as to the Law" (κατὰ νόμον). The Law of Moses, of course, was the great pride of the nation of Israel and of the Judaizers in particular. The historical record of the Gospels makes clear that to their mind all things—including Jesus Himself—must answer to the Law. But what they failed to see or fully appreciate is that the Law-giver Himself stood before them in the person of Jesus Christ. In Christ an entirely new order had come. The Father had appointed Jesus "a priest forever according to the order of Melchizedek" (Psalm 110:4; Heb.

---

59 Wallace, 103, 298.

60 Robertson, *Grammar*, 398; Vincent, Word Studies, 3:445.

61 Kennedy, 451.

5:6; 6:20; 7:17, 21). He would "become a priest, not on the basis of a legal requirement ... but by the power of an indestructible life" (Heb. 7:16, ESV). And "when the priesthood is changed, of necessity there takes place a change of law also" (v.12). This the Jews and Judaizers had missed and thus all their calculations and measurements were by necessity in error. But Paul meets them on their own ground. As if to say, "Let me for the sake of argument cede to you the ground of the Law. Let's just for the moment measure according to your standard." In that regard and according to that standard Paul could rightly say he was "a Pharisee" (Φαρισαῖος). Just what this meant to Paul is revealed in his testimony before King Agrippa, "I lived as a Pharisee according to the strictest sect of our religion" (Acts 26:5). He told the ruling council of Israel, "Brethren, I am a Pharisee, a son of Pharisees" (Acts 23:6). No group of people within Judaism took strict adherence to the Law more seriously. By his own testimony Paul had been "educated under Gamaliel, strictly according to the law of our fathers, being zealous for God" (Acts 22:3). Pharisees were unusually aggressive in all things pertaining to the Law and within their circle Paul was markedly more so: "I was advancing in Judaism beyond many of my contemporaries among my countrymen, being more extremely zealous for my ancestral traditions" (Gal. 1:14).

Verse 6 – "as to zeal, a persecutor of the church; as to the righteousness which is in the Law, found blameless."

Paul continues his litany of seven reasons he might have "confidence in the flesh" (v.4). Number six measures "as to zeal" (κατὰ ζῆλος). Zeal can be a good thing, for it marked the life of Jesus (John 2:17). But it must not be blind "zeal." It must accord with a knowledge of reality (Rom. 10:2). But being "zealous for the law" (Acts 21:20) was code for viewing the Law as an end in itself, of seeing in it a means of righteousness. In the followers of Christ, Saul of Tarsus saw a

> **Ministry Maxim**
>
> The currency of religious performance is not legal tender in the economy of heaven.

new end being pursued, the Lord Himself (Phil. 3:7-10). He perceived in them a new kind of righteousness being relied upon (v.9). Having already identified himself as at least a second generation Pharisee, he narrowed the identification even further. Wuest contends that ζῆλος ("zeal") "would almost have a technical meaning at that time for a strict Jew who was a member of the fanatical party among the Pharisees who called themselves Zealots."[62] Whether or not Paul's words can be so strictly interpreted, he certainly here identifies himself with a rich heritage of those who exemplified themselves in Israel for their zeal (e.g., Phinehas [Num. 25:6-13] and Mattathias [1 Macc. 2:19-28]).[63] Being blinded by his misplaced zeal Paul became "a persecutor of the church" (διώκων τὴν ἐκκλησίαν). Thus he "used to persecute the church of God beyond measure, and tried to destroy it" (Gal. 1:13). He could honestly say that he was "more extremely zealous for [his] ancestral traditions" than any of his contemporaries (v.14). In his zeal Paul lived as "a persecutor and a violent aggressor" against all who followed Christ (1 Tim. 1:13). He spent his time "ravaging the church, entering house after house, and dragging off men and women, he would put them in prison" (Acts 8:3). He went about "breathing threats and murder against the disciples of the Lord," even seeking "letters from [the high priest] to the synagogues at Damascus, so that if he found any belonging to the Way, both men and women, he might bring them bound to Jerusalem" (Acts 9:1). Reflecting upon his past, Paul said, "I persecuted this Way to the death, binding and putting both men and women into prisons, as also the high priest and all the Council of the elders can testify. From them I also received letters to the brethren, and started off for Damascus in order to bring even those who were there to Jerusalem as prisoners to be punished" (Acts 22:4-5). Paul was not surpassed in zeal and if it is upon the basis of zeal that the Judaizers wanted to measure one another, they would take second place.

The final standard of measure was "as to the righteousness which is in the Law" (κατὰ δικαιοσύνην τὴν ἐν νόμῳ). As Paul began his litany on

---

62 Wuest, 89.

63 Bockmuehl, 199; Harmon, 324-325.

the matter of most concern to the Judaizers (circumcision, v.5), so he now artfully brings it to an end by raising that which is at the heart of the matter—how is one accounted righteous before God? Momentarily he will take up that matter for explanation (v.9), but for the moment and to make his point Paul is content to yield to his opponents the notion that there is some form of righteousness to be found in the Law. They were "pursuing a law of righteousness" (Rom. 9:31). That is to say, Israel "tried so hard to get right with God by keeping the law" (NLT). This is ever a losing proposition, for the righteousness God accepts is not available on the basis of works, but only by faith (v.32). The righteousness of law-keeping may "clean the outside of the cup and dish," but it leaves the inside "full of robbery and self-indulgence" (Matt. 23:25). What is required by God is a "righteousness [that] surpasses that of the scribes and Pharisees" (Matt. 5:20). But be that as it may, simply meeting the opponents on their own turf, Paul could say that with regard to that external righteousness he had lived a life in which he was "found blameless" (γενόμενος ἄμεμπτος). The word "blameless" (ἄμεμπτος), is used only five times in the NT, two of which are here in Philippians (2:15; 3:6). It meant to be "free from fault or defect" and thus "deserving no censure."[64] It obviously, then, described "pers[ons] of exceptional merit."[65] Luke, under the inspiration of the Holy Spirit, said that Zechariah and Elizabeth were deemed as such (Luke 1:6). Paul prayed that the Thessalonian believers might love one another "so that He may establish your hearts without blame [ἀμέμπτους] in holiness before our God and Father at the coming of our Lord Jesus with all His saints" (1 Thess. 3:13). It points not to sinless perfection, but to living in such a way that there is no legitimate basis for blame by others. The verb (γενόμενος, "found") means more simply "become." The aorist tense pictures "the quality Paul had actually reached."[66] He had worked hard to make good on the strict foundation that had been afforded him. He had become "blameless" as far as the dictates of the Law were concerned. This

---

64 Thayer, 31.

65 BDAG, 394.

66 Lenski, 834.

did not mean he was without sin, but that within the purview of the Law he had obeyed and where he had not, he employed the means outlined by the Law to find provision for his sins.[67] And he knew no one could arise to contradict the verdict over his pre-Christian life: Blameless "as to the righteousness which is in the Law."

Kennedy rightly marks out the example of the young man of great wealth who came to Jesus asking what he must do to obtain eternal life (Matt. 19:16).[68] Jesus, revealing the young man's heart to himself, said, "if you wish to enter into life, keep the commandments" (v.17). The young man replied, "All these things I have kept" (v.20a). He believed himself able to say—with Paul—"as to the righteousness which is in the Law, [I am] found blameless." It was, however, what came next (v.7) that revealed his shortcoming in God's eyes. When Jesus told him, "If you wish to be complete, go and sell your possessions and give to the poor, and you will have treasure in heaven; and come, follow Me" (v.21). But "when the young man heard this statement, he went away grieving; for he was one who owned much property" (v.22). He could not say along with Paul, "those things I have counted as loss for the sake of Christ" (Phil. 3:7b).

> **Digging Deeper:**
> 1. In what way does righteousness by "religious pedigree" show up in your local church?
> 2. What are the key elements of righteousness by "religious performance" where you live and minister?
> 3. How have you tended to rely upon "zeal" for God rather than upon the righteousness of Christ? What effect has it had upon you?

---

[67] Harmon, 326-327.
[68] Kennedy, 451-452.

Verse 7 – "But whatever things were gain to me, those things I have counted as loss for the sake of Christ."

The manuscript evidence is varied regarding the genuineness of the opening conjunction (Ἀλλὰ, "But"). It is omitted in some of the earliest manuscripts, yet clearly Paul is making a marked turn in his thoughts. It is thus possible a copyist may have "corrected" the text by adding the adversative conjunction at a later time. In any case, the reality of the contrast from verses 5 and 6 to what now follows in verses 7 through 14 is not removed.[69]

When Paul refers to "whatever things were gain to me" (ἅτινα ἦν μοι κέρδη) he is speaking of the seven items he has just enumerated in verses 5 and 6 regarding his religious pedigree and performance. The relative neuter pronoun in the plural (ἅτινα, "whatever things") casts the possibilities as widely and all-inclusively as possible, including the items specifically listed in verse 5 and 6, but also including others of like character. Paul is speaking personally, as the personal pronoun reveals (μοι, "to me"). He stands unrivaled with regard[70] to the possibilities of "confidence in the flesh" (v.4). The imperfect tense of ἦν ("were") points to the ongoing nature of how Paul viewed his life before Christ. It looks back to a time when he counted all those things he has listed in verses 5 and 6 as personal "gain" (κέρδη). The plural form pictures each and every one of those items, almost an itemized list of "gains." This is the same word Paul had used earlier to tell the Philippian believers "For to me, to live is Christ and to die is gain [κέρδος]" (1:21). It is used elsewhere in Biblical literature only in Titus 1:11: "who must be silenced because they are upsetting whole families, teaching things they should not teach for the sake of sordid gain [κέρδους]." The cognate verb is used more frequently and is found in the next verse (κερδήσω, "I may gain"). The noun describes whatever might be to one's profit, advantage, or gain. The word was used at times in the first century to describe gains realized through interest. Paul's life had begun with significant inherited advantages (items 1-4, v.5) and he has zealously

---

69 Cf. Fee's discussion of the evidence, 311.
70 A dative of advantage, meaning "in my estimation" (O'Brien, 384).

labored to add to them (items 5-7, vv.5b-6). The net effect was an accrued "gain" which he had at one time gloried in.

Despite all that might provide "confidence in the flesh" (v.4) Paul has "counted as loss" (ἥγημαι ... ζημίαν) all "these things" (ταῦτα). The demonstrative pronoun in the neuter plural form (ταῦτα, "these things") takes up the "whatever things" (ἅτινα) of the previous clause which was also neuter plural. Both pronouns are emphatic by being thrust to the head of their respective clauses.[71] The verb (ἥγημαι, "counted") is used by Paul eleven times, six of those are here in Philippians (2:3, 6, 25; 3:7, 8 [2x]). It means to think, consider or regard.[72] It denotes "a belief resting not on one's inner feeling or sentiment, but on the due consideration of external grounds, the weighing and comparing, of facts."[73] The perfect tense presents the action as having occurred at a point in the past, but with an abiding nature. It points thus to the settled state of determined thinking to which Paul has come. The verb is deponent, thus the middle voice has an active meaning. Significantly, Paul used it earlier to refer to Christ's inward reckoning when he "did not regard [ἡγήσατο] equality with God a thing to be grasped" (2:6). By way of application, then, believers are to similarly "regard [ἡγούμενοι] one another as more important than yourselves" (2:3). Also significantly, he uses it three times in the present context to describe his own inward reckoning regarding his own self-righteousness (3:7-8). Paul has held up the standard as we have it in Christ (2:6), called the Philippian believers to emulate it (2:3) and now sets forth his own example in this regard (3:7-8). It is hard to escape the notion

> **Ministry Maxim**
>
> When once the heart has been awakened to the beauty and value of Christ all else in life loses its luster.

---

71 Alford, 3:179; Fee, 316.

72 BDAG, 3410.2.

73 Thayer, 276.

that Paul is drawing an intentional parallel between Christ's actions on his behalf (2:6) and his own actions on Christ's behalf (3:7-8).[74]

All these various gains (κέρδη, plural) Paul has now come to view as one great "loss" (ζημίαν, singular). Lightfoot represents this transition from the plural to the singular by paraphrasing: "All such things which I used to count up as distinct items with a miserly greed and reckon to my credit—these I have massed together under one general head as loss."[75] The word is used but four times in the NT, here and the next verse from Paul's pen and twice by Luke as he quotes Paul. Luke cites Paul in the cataclysmic loss of all goods and lives through shipwreck (Acts 27:10, 21). It describes "coming into a worsened situation from previous advantage."[76] All that Paul had by his heritage and training been taught to enter in the credit ledger he has now transferred and listed as a debit.[77] This final word (ζημίαν, "loss") "ends the sentence with a dull thud."[78] Indeed, both κέρδη ("gain") and ζημίαν ("loss") receive emphasis by being placed last in their respective clauses.[79]

It is not just that where once Paul was ahead, now he is behind. It isn't just that he has experienced a reversal of fortunes. This is no riches-to-rags story where the positives have been replaced by some negatives. It is that the positives themselves have become the negatives; the assets are now the liabilities. What once were life-preservers are now a millstone around one's neck. What once was evidence for the defense now makes the prosecution's case. What once would have filled a trophy case is now left for the latrine (cf. σκύβαλα, "rubbish," v.8). It is difficult even to imagine

---

74 The verbal parallels continue to mount up, demonstrating the intentionality of Paul's parallel between the present passage and 2:5-11: μορφή ("form," 2:7) and συμμορφίζω ("being conformed," 3:10); εὑρίσκω ("being made," 2:7; "may be found," 3:9); κύριος ("Lord," 2:11; 3:8). (Silva, 155)

75 Lightfoot, 163.

76 Friberg, 186.

77 Robertson, *Word Pictures*, 4:453.

78 Robertson, *Paul's Joy in Christ*, 187.

79 Fee, 316.

the personal, inward drama of that moment when the light of Christ broke through to Paul's pharisaic heart and the new, heavenly accounting of his life was laid bare in the bright light of the gospel of Jesus Christ (Acts 9:3-20).

Yet Paul has embraced this new accounting of his life and he has done so, "for the sake of Christ" (διὰ τὸν Χριστὸν). The preposition (διὰ, "for the sake of") is used "of the reason or cause on account of which anything is or is done, or ought to be done."[80] It can point to the aim one has in mind[81] and thus it may here point to becoming "a partner of Christ" and be "equivalent to ἵνα Χριστόν κερδήσω" in the next verse.[82] Christ is, as Paul has come to see, "the one and only gain."[83] The double use of διὰ in verse 8 appears to confirm this understanding.

Jesus used these words to summarize for His disciples the radical, life-redirecting nature of discipleship: "For whoever wishes to save his life will lose it, but whoever loses his life for My sake and the gospel's will save it. For what does it profit a man to gain [κερδῆσαι] the whole world, and forfeit [ζημιωθῆναι[84]] his soul?" (Mark 8:35-36).[85]

Verse 8 – "More than that, I count all things to be loss in view of the surpassing value of knowing Christ Jesus my Lord, for whom I have suffered the loss of all things, and count them but rubbish so that I may gain Christ,"

The Apostle begins a long sentence (running through verse 11) which grows grammatically complex, but whose point is generally clear and even artfully and memorably made. The conjunction ἀλλὰ is used here "to

---

80   Thayer, 134.
81   Robertson, *Grammar*, 584.
82   Thayer, 134.
83   Lenski, 835.
84   Cognate verb to the noun used by Paul in verse 7 and used by Paul in verse 8 ("I have suffered the loss").
85   Harmon, 333.

indicate that the preceding is to be regarded as a settled matter, thus forming a transition to someth[ing] new."[86] It is here paired with the rare particle μενοῦνγε and καί. The former (a contraction of μέν, οὖν, γέ) is used only three times in the NT, all by Paul (Rom. 9:20; 10:18; Phil. 3:8). It is usually employed in answering a question so as to correct or emphasize what has been posited.[87] Together they emphatically reinforce what Paul has just set forth in verse 7 and prepare both to underscore and escalate the discussion ("More than that"). Robertson says they bring a climactic force to Paul's words.[88] Together they "could be translated 'yes the previous is true but more than that I also... .'"[89]

In saying "I count" (ἡγοῦμαι), Paul returns to the verb he has just used in verse 7 ("I have counted [ἥγημαι] as loss"). It has also been used significantly of what Christ did not do ("did not regard [ἡγήσατο] equality with God a thing to be grasped," 2:6) and of what all believers are to do ("regard [ἡγούμενοι] one another as more important than yourselves," 2:3; cf. also 2:25). Here the present tense underscores Paul's continuing evaluation of things. What Paul had decisively concluded in the past ("I have counted as loss," v.7; perfect tense) he now continuously applies again and again in each and every case ("I count"; present tense). The verb is deponent so while it is in form a middle voice, it has an active meaning. See the discussion under verse 7 for more on the nuances of this verb's meaning.

That which Paul now tallies up are "all things" (πάντα) and he calculates them "to be loss" (ζημίαν εἶναι). The Apostle is still actively engaged in his accounting, as the repetition of ζημίαν ("loss") from the previous verse confirms. But now the expansive "whatever things" (ἅτινα) which became "those things" (ταῦτα, v.7), have been expanded even more graphically to include "all things" (πάντα). It is as if Paul, seeing all the potential advantages of life arrayed before him, with a sweep of his arm across the table rakes all of them into one bin, which he has labeled as "loss"! Into

---

86 BDAG, 336.3.
87 Ibid., 4814.
88 Robertson, *Grammar*, 1148.
89 Rienecker, 557.

the compost pile with, not only his Jewish privileges, but "all things" that might vie for his reliance and trust before God!

It is not as though there is no value in these things at all (vv.5-6), for Paul has demonstrated that he does not downgrade entirely his heritage or his inherited ethnic/religious advantages (Rom. 3:1-2; 9:1-5; 11:1). Rather the "loss" is calculated afresh because of something new and of infinite value that has come upon the scene. The porch light that illumines the way to your front door at night does not cease to shine because the sun rises in the morning. But its practical value diminishes and is eclipsed by the dawn of a greater light.

Thus for Paul the new accounting is "in view of the surpassing value of knowing Christ Jesus my Lord" (διὰ τὸ ὑπερέχον τῆς γνώσεως Χριστοῦ Ἰησοῦ τοῦ κυρίου μου). Here again (cf. v.7b) we meet a clause governed by διά ("in view of"). It is the first of two consecutive διά clauses in the present sentence. The articular neuter participle (τὸ ὑπερέχον, "the surpassing value") is used as an abstract substantive. The present tense points to the abiding nature of the value. It is not and never will be eclipsed by something of higher or greater worth. The word is used but five times in the NT, four of those by Paul and three of those here in Philippians (2:3; 3:8; 4:7).

That upon which such unsurpassed value is placed is "knowing Christ Jesus my Lord" (τῆς γνώσεως Χριστοῦ Ἰησοῦ τοῦ κυρίου μου). Note the unusual four-fold genitive construction. The first, τῆς γνώσεως ("knowing"), is probably best understood as a genitive of apposition, meaning that it is this knowledge which is beyond compare ("surpassing value"). The second, Χριστοῦ Ἰησοῦ, is an objective genitive, making Christ Jesus the one who is known (as opposed to a subjective genitive which would make this the knowledge Christ possesses, though that too is a notion Paul does not shy away from, e.g. 1 Cor. 13:12; Gal. 4:9). The third genitive, τοῦ κυρίου, is in apposition to "Christ Jesus" (Χριστοῦ Ἰησοῦ) and designates Him by another term, which actually escalates and heightens

His identity (see below). And the fourth genitive, μου, is best understood as a possessive genitive.[90]

This full designation (Χριστοῦ Ἰησοῦ τοῦ κυρίου μου, "Christ Jesus my Lord") is used to present Jesus in His fullness and splendor. He is the anointed of God, the Messiah (Χριστοῦ, "Christ"), the long-awaited, promised One, the fulfillment of every OT hope. He is the incarnate God in human flesh (Ἰησοῦ, "Jesus"). His earthly father was instructed to give the child this name because "He will save His people from their sins" (Matt. 1:21). He is "the Lord" (τοῦ κυρίου). It is the Greek term used in the LXX to translate the Hebrew for Yahweh. The God of the OT, the only true God, has come among us in Jesus Christ. In this very letter the Apostle has gone to great lengths to describe just why the title "Lord" rightly belongs to Jesus (Phil. 2:5-11). Jesus is thus the Sovereign of all, and that includes Paul himself (μου, "my"). There is a note of remarkable intimacy in this. The One to whom every knee in history will bow and of whom every tongue will confess that He is truly and uniquely "Lord" is right now in this world the personal "Lord" who has conquered and rules Paul's heart and life. This "knowing" (τῆς γνώσεως) Him in actual relationship is of incalculable worth. Note the definite article accompanies the noun; it more literally "*the* knowing" of Christ Himself. This is a knowledge Paul intended when using "for the sake of Christ" (v.7) and what he will speak of momentarily when saying, "so that I may gain Christ and may be found in Him" (vv.8b-9a).

Jesus told us, "The kingdom of heaven is like a treasure hidden in the field, which a man found and hid again; and from joy over it he goes and sells all that he has and buys that field" (Matt. 13:44). Like that man, Paul had sold everything that he might gain Christ. Similarly, Jesus added, "Again, the kingdom of heaven is like a merchant seeking fine pearls, and upon finding one pearl of great value, he went and sold all that he had and bought it" (vv.44-45). Like the merchant, Paul saw in Christ the pearl of great price and gave everything to know Him. "For what will it profit a

---

90   Harmon, 334; O'Brien, 387.

man if he gains [κερδήσῃ] the whole world and forfeits [ζημιωθῇ] his soul? Or what will a man give in exchange for his soul?" (16:26).

Christ Himself and knowing Him personally and experientially is of such value that Paul could say it is He "for whom I have suffered the loss of all things" (δι' ὃν τὰ πάντα ἐζημιώθην). Again for the third time in verses 7 and 8 we have a διά clause. The antecedent of ὅν ("whom") is clearly "Christ Jesus my Lord" from the previous clause. The "all things" (τὰ πάντα) is an echo of the preceding "whatever things" (ἅτινα)

> **Ministry Maxim**
>
> Idols are most effectively identified and removed not by devaluing them, but by the revelation of Jesus Christ.

and "those things" (ταῦτα) of verse 7 as well as the "all things" (πάντα) earlier in this verse. But, while it is a repetition from earlier in the verse, it now is accompanied by the definite article. Paul continues to expand his frame of reference and at the same time to get increasingly specific with regard to that which cannot compare with the knowledge of Christ. Indeed, Paul can say, for Jesus "I have suffered the loss" (ἐζημιώθην) of everything. The verb is cognate to the noun used in verse 7 and earlier in this same verse (ζημίαν, "loss"). The same commercial imagery present in the noun is also found in the verb. The aorist tense depicts the loss as actual, in time and space. The passive voice pictures Paul being overtaken by the Lord Himself. As the sun rises to overwhelm all other sources of light so when Christ appeared to him all else of value faded into worthlessness in comparison. While on his way to Damascus to persecute the followers of Jesus, "suddenly a light from heaven flashed around him" (Acts 9:3) and Paul would never be able to see anything the same way again: "though his eyes were open, he saw nothing" (v.8). That literal blindness gave way to physical sight by the healing mercy of the Lord (vv.12, 17-18), but the eyes of Paul's heart could never see and calculate the value of anything the same way again.

Another (καί, "and") way of describing the loss is that Paul has come to "count them as rubbish" (ἡγοῦμαι σκύβαλα). The verb is repeated for a third time (see vv.7 and 8a) as Paul continues cycling back over the same ground, but always expanding and deepening with passion and artful skill the point he is making. See the previous discussion regarding the background of the word and its connections thematically with the whole of Philippians. The present tense, as in its previous usage, emphasizes Paul's continuing evaluation of things. "This is no momentary impulse, no spasmodic rhapsody on Paul's part."[91] Robertson says the middle voice may be intensive.[92] Here Paul's calculations set a value on all things outside of knowing Christ. They are "as rubbish" (σκύβαλα). The word appears only here in Biblical literature. It designates "useless or undesirable material that is subject to disposal," thus garbage or refuse and is used in varying senses of "excrement, manure, garbage, kitchen scraps."[93] Its usage is thus broad, covering all that is useless, detestable, disgusting, "but 'dung' is probably what Paul meant" in our present context.[94] Spicq, seeking to convey "the crudity of the Greek," renders it: "It's all crap."[95] Indeed, "The two elements in σκύβαλον, namely, worthlessness and filth, are best expressed by a term like 'dung.'"[96] In Classical Greek it "means rubbish and muck of many kinds: excrement, rotten food, bits left at a meal as not worth eating, a rotting corpse. Nastiness and decay are the constant elements of its meaning; it is a coarse, ugly, violent word implying worthlessness, uselessness, and repulsiveness."[97] These are remarkable words coming from Paul, the former Pharisee, who had been trained to see all of life in terms of "clean" and "unclean." Yet here he is classing all his ethnic and religious righteousness—along with "all [other] things"—as unclean filth compared to personal, saving knowledge of Christ! Isaiah was correct, "all our righteous deeds are like a filthy garment" (Isa. 64:6).

---

91   Robertson, *Paul's Joy in Christ*, 187.
92   Robertson, *Grammar*, 812.
93   BDAG, 6725.
94   Moulton and Milligan, 579.
95   Spicq, 3:265.
96   TDNT, 7:447.
97   NIDNTT, 1:480.

How could Paul view in such terms that which had once been to him more precious than life? It was by way of comparison, or perhaps we should say for the sake of mission, for he states it in a purpose clause: "so that I may gain Christ" (ἵνα Χριστὸν κερδήσω). The verb is cognate to the noun "gain" (κέρδη) in verse 7. It means "to acquire by effort or investment" and thus to "gain" something or someone.[98] The aorist pictures the actual transaction, a gaining of Christ in definite relationship. The subjunctive is used with ἵνα to form the purpose clause. Of course Paul is not saying that by his own effort or works he gained Christ. Quite the opposite! He considers all such effort and works (vv.5-6) as garbage since, as he will tell us in verse 9, the gaining of such relationship with Christ is offered only by a righteousness that "comes from God on the basis of faith." The purpose statement here may have been hinted at in the command "rejoice in the Lord" (v.1) and is akin to "for the sake of Christ" (v.7). Its essence will be touched upon again in the notion of to "be found in Him" (v.9) and in his desire to "know Him" (v.10).

To the one who puzzles as to how Paul can speak both of a present knowledge of Christ ("knowing Christ Jesus my Lord") and still speak of such knowledge as yet future ("that I may gain Christ"), A.W. Tozer simply says, "To have found God and still to pursue Him is the soul's paradox of love."[99]

Verse 9 – "and may be found in Him, not having a righteousness of my own derived from *the* Law, but that which is through faith in Christ, the righteousness which *comes* from God on the basis of faith,"

We find Paul here in mid-sentence (which runs from verse 7 through the end of verse 11), in fact he is mid-clause. He introduced a purpose clause at the end of verse 8 (ἵνα Χριστὸν κερδήσω, "so that I may gain Christ") and he now adds (καὶ, "and") a second part to that purpose: "may be found in Him" (εὑρεθῶ ἐν αὐτῷ). The καὶ is epexegetical; "may

---

98 BDAG, 4209.

99 Tozer, 15.

be found in Him" is simply another, expanded way of saying "may gain Christ."[100] Again, as with its partner verb, the subjunctive mood works with the previous ἵνα (v.8) to form a purpose statement. The aorist tense points to a definitive standing that is actually entered into. The passive voice pictures Paul as being discovered in this standing, out of no doing of his own, the fact of which He will expand upon in the rest of this verse.

It has been said that all Paul's theology can be summed up in the simple phrase "in Christ." He returns now to this matter of union with Christ as he speaks of being "in Him" (ἐν αὐτῷ). The antecedent of "Him" is clearly "Christ" (Χριστὸν) from the first half of this two-part purpose statement (v.8). The preposition is often used by Paul "to designate a close personal relation in which the referent of the ἐν-term is viewed as the controlling influence."[101] Paul began the letter by addressing it to "To all the saints in [ἐν] Christ Jesus who are in [ἐν] Philippi" (1:1), emphasizing the dual nature of their walk of faith.[102]

The rest of the verse expounds upon and explains further what the passive voice of the verb hinted at, how Paul came to be "found in Him."[103] In so doing he emphasizes that it was not by his own doing, but purely by the grace of God. The point is made by way of a "not ... but" (μὴ ... ἀλλὰ) contrast. It is helpful to see Paul's point set out as a chiastic construction, the center point of which gains the prominence.

μὴ ἔχων (not having)
    ἐμὴν (my own)
        δικαιοσύνην (righteousness)
            τὴν ἐκ νόμου (that out of the Law)
                ἀλλὰ τὴν διὰ πίστεως Χριστοῦ, (but that through faith in Christ)

---

100 O'Brien, 392; Silva, 159.

101 BDAG, 2581.4c.

102 cf. also Phil. 1:13, 14, 26; 2:1, 19, 24, 29; 3:1, 3, 14; 4:1, 2, 4, 7, 10, 13, 19, 21.

103 For the verb cf. 2:8: σχήματι εὑρεθεὶς ὡς ἄνθρωπος ("Being found in appearance as a man").

τὴν ἐκ θεοῦ (that out of God)
δικαιοσύνην (righteousness)
ἐπὶ τῇ πίστει (on the basis of faith)[104]

First, Paul develops the negative, how this relationship did not (and can never) come about. It was "not having a righteousness of my own derived from the Law" (μὴ ἔχων ἐμὴν δικαιοσύνην τὴν ἐκ νόμου). The key to relationship to Jesus Christ is possessing (ἔχων, "having"[105]) the "righteousness" (δικαιοσύνην) to stand before Him. The problem is how one can come into the possession of such righteousness. Paul's strict Torah observance ("as to the righteousness which is in the Law, found blameless," v.6) was unable to provide this righteousness. It cannot be self-generated, for our sin ever prohibits us from attaining such a standing before God. Thus Paul says it was a righteousness "not ... of my own" (μὴ ... ἐμὴν). Paul is clear and unequivocal when writing the Roman believers, "THERE IS NONE RIGHTEOUS, NOT EVEN ONE" (Rom. 3:10, quoting Psalm 53:1). Job asked, "How then can a man be just with God? Or how can he be clean who is born of woman?" (Job 25:4). Jesus reminded us that "No one is good except God alone." (Mark 10:18). Obtaining a standing before God on such a basis is impossible for "the unrighteous will not inherit the kingdom of God" (1 Cor. 6:9a). Clearly, the root of our problem before God is a lack of the requisite righteousness necessary to be found in the presence of Him who is perfectly righteous. By adding "derived from the Law" (τὴν ἐκ νόμου) Paul lays his finger upon the heart of the Judaizers' approach to solving this problem. The definite article (τὴν) agrees in gender, case and number with δικαιοσύνην and specifies the kind of "righteousness" that is under consideration, functioning as a relative pronoun.[106] It is that which is,

---

104 Harmon, 339; O'Brien, 394; Silva, 160; contra Fee, 321-322.

105 The participle should be understood as modal, expressing the manner in which one is found in Christ. cf. Harmon, 340; O'Brien, 393; Vincent, 102.

106 Wallace, 215.

literally, "out of Law" (ἐκ νόμου), the genitive being used "to denote derivation" of the righteousness under consideration. [107]

The noun νόμου itself lacks the definite article and thus the NASU has put "the" in italics to indicate that it is not found in the original Greek text. But clearly, given the context of battling Judaizing elements (vv.2-6), Paul has in mind the Mosaic Law as defined and delineated by the Pharisees (and thus the translators render it with a capital "L"). Yet it may be that Paul did not employ the definite article so he could point out that true righteousness cannot be derived from obedience to any principle of law, not only that rendered to the Law of Moses, but by conformity to any humanly-established set of laws. As "a Pharisee" (v.5) Paul knew what it was to expand upon the Law and add to its dictates. The religious have, down through the centuries, done the same—from pagans to some in the name of Christ—setting up standards of conduct by which it is believed one must become acceptable before God. But Paul is clear: no law—whether one written by God or by man—can call forth the righteousness necessary to enter relationship with God. For that "Law" necessarily becomes an instrument for self-produced righteousness.

This, says the Apostle, can never be. So, having dismissed with the matter of how the reality of being "found in Him" was not (and can never be) established, Paul proceeds to explain how he did come to this relationship with Christ. The strong adversative (ἀλλὰ, "but") marks the utter distinction between the negative and the positive. It was "that [righteousness] which is through faith in Christ" (τὴν διὰ πίστεως Χριστοῦ). The preposition διὰ ("through") expresses that "faith" is the instrument or agency through which we are thus "found in Him." Faith is not the generating cause or meritorious ground, but the instrument/agency through which we come to be found in such a state of righteousness before God. Χριστοῦ is an objective genitive (Christ is the object of the faith), rather than a subjective genitive (Christ as the one exercising the faith or demonstrating the

---

107 BDAG, 2317.3c.

faithfulness).[108] The definite article τὴν is repeated in the accusative and is translated "that," functioning again, as in the previous instance, as a relative pronoun.[109] It finds its antecedent in δικαιοσύνην ("righteousness"). It thus sets up a contrast between the two kinds of righteousness envisioned: τὴν ἐκ νόμου (lit., "that out of law") and τὴν διὰ πίστεως Χριστοῦ (lit., "that through faith in Christ").

He further expands upon this statement and expounds upon the precise nature of the righteousness he has in mind

> **Ministry Maxim**
>
> The righteousness which is required of us can never arise out of us or our efforts, but only out of Him who is alone righteous.

by adding, "the righteousness that comes from God on the basis of faith" (τὴν ἐκ θεοῦ δικαιοσύνην ἐπὶ τῇ πίστει). Paul tucks "of God' (ἐκ θεοῦ) between the noun and its definite article, in the attributive position. This emphasizes the nature of the righteousness he has in mind. It is, to be woodenly literal, "the-out of-God-righteousness" that is in view. It should also be noted that the present ἐκ ("from") stands in parallel and contrast to the ἐκ of the previous, contrasting clause. Paul is laying side-by-side a righteousness that arises out of (ἐκ) "the Law" and one that arises out of (ἐκ) "God." The former would of necessity be a self-generated righteousness (ἐμὴν, "of my own"), while the latter would be a divinely provided righteousness. The former would of necessity rest upon the performance

---

108 There has been much debate about how to understand the genitive. Among those viewing it as a subjective genitive are Wallace (114-116), Sumney (80), and O'Brien (398-400). Among those viewing it as an objective genitive are Fee (324-326), Harmon (340-341), Lenski (839), Lightfoot (164), Müller (115), Silva (161), Robertson (*Word Pictures*, 4:453; *Paul's Joy in Christ*, 192), and Vincent (ICC, 102). The objective genitive presents Christ as the ground and object of our faith. The subjective genitive would present Christ's faithfulness (in perfectly keeping and fulfilling the Law) as righteousness which God provides us by means of imputation. The points made by viewing it as a subjective genitive and those made by viewing it as an objective genitive are both confirmed as true elsewhere in Scripture. The question at hand is which point the Apostle seeks to make in this context. In that case it would seem to be that Christ is the object and ground of the faith which comes into possession of the "righteousness which comes from God" and is "on the basis of faith."

109 Wallace, 215.

of the individual (in keeping the Law), the latter is had only "on the basis of faith" (ἐπὶ τῇ πίστει). That is to say, the former must of necessity and with personal effort be extracted "from the Law" (ἐκ νόμου). The latter is divinely initiated and generated and arises thus "from God" (ἐκ θεοῦ). The only part the individual plays is to personally exercise "faith" (τῇ πίστει).

Note again the presence of the definite article. It is not merely "faith" generally considered, but it is (literally) "*the* faith" (τῇ πίστει)—the faith that comes to see that there is no hope of self-generated righteousness extracted from the Law by any amount of human effort and achievement, but rather that the only hope is to reach out in faith and receive the gift of righteousness that arises out of the heart of God and is extended to us in the already accomplished work of Christ. We come to rest, then, in Christ's own righteousness by being brought into union with Him through faith.

This "righteousness" rests "upon" (ἐπὶ) faith. The preposition serves as a "marker of [the] basis for a state of being, action, or result."[110] The righteousness of God is ours, not because of works performed on our part, but because it rests upon the foundation of simple, trusting faith in the provision of God in Christ. This righteousness becomes ours through the instrument/agency (διὰ) of faith and thus our continuing personal standing in this righteousness rests "upon" (ἐπὶ) the foundation of that faith.

Silva points out that this latter part of Paul's extended sentence serves as a succinct summation of his theology, compassing justification (v.9), sanctification (v.10), and glorification (v.11).[111] That is to say, in verse 9 Paul explains how one comes to relationship with God, in verse 10 how one lives in that relationship to God, and in verse 11 how one's relationship with God culminates in the next life.

---

110 BDAG, 2922.6a.

111 Silva, 155, 159.

Verse 10 – "that I may know Him and the power of His resurrection and the fellowship of His sufferings, being conformed to His death;"

While continuing the sentence (which runs through verse 11), Paul shifts his attention from matters of establishing relationship with God (justification, v.9) to matters of living in relationship with Christ (sanctification, v.10). He makes the transition by means of an articular aorist infinitive (τοῦ γνῶναι, "that I may know"). The aorist is ingressive, emphasizing the entrance into such knowledge.[112] The infinitive is used to express purpose ("*that* I may know")[113] and thus makes for an extended third purpose clause modifying "I count all things to be loss" (ἡγοῦμαι πάντα ζημίαν εἶναι, v.8a).[114]

Justification is not an end itself, but is designed to usher in a life of intimate fellowship and union with the Lord who justifies. True justification lands the individual into the midst of a process of sanctification, which witnesses to the reality of the justification. The verb emphasizes the personal, experiential nature of the knowledge and thus transitions us from the forensic world of righteousness (v.9) to the experiential world of relationship (v.10), though the two are never truly separate and distinct. "The word often implies a personal relation between the knower and the known, involving the influence of the object of knowledge upon the knower."[115] He has just used the cognate verb to speak of "the surpassing value of knowing [τῆς γνώσεως] Christ Jesus my Lord" (v.8), a beautiful mystery into which he further delves in this present verse.

---

112 Lenski, 840; Robertson, *Word Pictures*, 4:453. "… he is here speaking … of his *coming into* a knowledge of Christ in the *process* of his experience" (Vincent, ICC, 103-104, emphasis original). Contra O'Brien (402) who sees the aorist as focusing on the final goal.

113 Rienecker, 557; Robertson, *Grammar*, 990, 1002, 1067, 1088. Vincent calls it an "infinitive of design, setting forth the end contemplated in the righteousness of faith" (Vincent, ICC, 103)

114 Harmon, 343; O'Brien, 400-401; contra Silva who says it is a second purpose clause (163). The three are: "so that I may gain Christ" (v.8), "so that I … may be found in Him" (v.9), and "that I may know Him …" (v.10-11).

115 Rienecker, 557.

The object of this knowledge is "Him" (αὐτὸν), the antecedent of which is found in the towering statement of Christ's identity in verse 8 to which all else has answered throughout this current, lengthy sentence: "Christ Jesus my Lord" (Χριστοῦ Ἰησοῦ τοῦ κυρίου μου). The value of such a personal knowledge of Christ is worth the loss of all things. That pearl of great price is a gift given by God to us through the imputed righteousness of Christ (v.9) and explored and enjoyed through a lifetime of fellowship with Christ (v.10) and which culminates in an eternity of fully-realized resurrection life (v.11).

Just how does the twice-repeated καὶ ("and") function? Do both function merely to coordinate the clauses, holding three statements in parallel with one another: "that I know Him and the power of His resurrection and the fellowship of His sufferings"? Or does one or both of them serve epexegetically?[116] If exegetically then the latter two clauses would either more fully develop the first ("that I may know Him") or have each clause further explaining the previous one, so that "that I may know Him" would be enlarged and explained by "the power of His resurrection" which in turn would be expounded by "the fellowship of His sufferings." Vincent says, that here καὶ "is more than a simple connective. It introduces a definition and fuller explanation of αὐτὸν." Indeed, he says the latter two clauses "furnish two specific points further defining the knowledge of Him."[117] The three statements are not strictly parallel, for to know "Him" is more fully rounded and ultimate than "the power of His resurrection" or "the fellowship of His sufferings." Indeed the original accusative form of the pronoun αὐτὸν ("Him") points to Christ Himself and is followed by three instances of the same pronoun in the genitive (αὐτοῦ) which point to matters which derive their reality from Christ. Christ is clearly the center. Thus we view the first instance of καὶ as epexegetical and the second as coordinating.

The Apostle elaborates and enlarges upon this the experience (τοῦ γνῶναι, "that I would know") by speaking of "the power of His

---

116 Lenski, 841.

117 Vincent, *Word Studies*, 3:448; cf. Fee, 328; O'Brien, 402.

resurrection" (τὴν δύναμιν τῆς ἀναστάσεως αὐτοῦ). Just how are we to understand Paul's intent here? It would be tempting to see a development from justification (v.9) to regeneration (v.10). Or should we see a reference to Christ's own resurrection from the dead? Or should we see here a reference to Paul's anticipated resurrection at Christ's return? It seems best to see here a reference, not to Jesus' own resurrection per se (that he dealt with in 2:9ff.) nor to Paul's future resurrection (he will take that up at the end of the sentence, v.11), but to the present experience of His risen, indwelling life actualized in us through the ministry of the Holy Spirit (Acts 16:7; Phil. 1:19). It is not so much faith resting upon a past reality (Christ's resurrection) nor is it anticipation of a future reality (Paul's resurrection at Christ's return), but a present experiential reality (Christ's present and powerful indwelling through the Holy Spirit). As with the previous statement, "it describes a subjective experience. It is the power of the risen Christ as it becomes a subject of practical knowledge and a power in Paul's inner life."[118] The Apostle witnessed to this reality when he said, "if the Spirit of Him who raised Jesus from the dead dwells in you, He who raised Christ Jesus from the dead will also give life to your mortal bodies through His Spirit who dwells in you" (Rom. 8:11). The idea here is of a piece with his extended statements to the Romans earlier in that letter:

> **Ministry Maxim**
>
> Personal, relational knowledge of Christ is the essence of salvation.

> Therefore we have been buried with Him through baptism into death, so that as Christ was raised from the dead through the glory of the Father, so we too might walk in newness of life. For if we have become united with Him in the likeness of His death, certainly we shall also be in the likeness of His resurrection, knowing this, that our old self was crucified with Him, in order that our body of sin might be done away with, so that we would no longer be slaves to sin; for he who has died is freed from sin. Now if we

---

118 Vincent, ICC, 104.

have died with Christ, we believe that we shall also live with Him, knowing that Christ, having been raised from the dead, is never to die again; death no longer is master over Him. For the death that He died, He died to sin once for all; but the life that He lives, He lives to God. Even so consider yourselves to be dead to sin, but alive to God in Christ Jesus." (Rom. 6:4-11)

Paul clearly sees himself, along with all believers, as already raised up with Christ. He told the Ephesian believers that God "made us alive together with Christ ... and raised us up with Him, and seated us with Him in the heavenly places in Christ Jesus" (Eph. 2:5-6). He told the Colossians that "you have been raised up with Christ" and spoke to them of "Christ, who is our life" (Col. 3:1, 4). To the Galatians he said, "I have been crucified with Christ; and it is no longer I who live, but Christ lives in me; and the life which I now live in the flesh I live by faith in the Son of God, who loved me and gave Himself up for me" (Gal. 2:20). Paul prayed that the believers in Ephesus might know "the immeasurable greatness of his power toward us who believe, according to the working of his great might that he worked in Christ when he raised him from the dead and seated him at his right hand in the heavenly places, far above all rule and authority and power and dominion, and above every name that is named, not only in this age but also in the one to come" (Eph. 1:19-21, ESV). To know the living Christ as not just risen, but as the living, indwelling, powerful essence of life itself—this was Paul's great quest, as it is the yearning and desire of every true child of God.

To this he adds (καὶ, "and") a knowledge of "the fellowship of His sufferings" ([τὴν] κοινωνίαν [τῶν] παθημάτων αὐτοῦ). The textual issue of the genuineness of the two definite articles is not insignificant. They were probably added after the fact by scribes seeking to conform it to the previous clause.[119] Their absence means that this clause is united with the previous clause under one definite article, stressing the closeness of the

---

119 "The two definite articles in this phrase are later insertions.... The articles may have been added to create symmetry with the preceding phrase, where as there is little reason for a copyist to drop them out." (Sumney, 81).

realities of knowing the resurrection life of Jesus and sharing in the "fellowship of His sufferings." This was a "fellowship" into which Paul was called personally by Christ at the beginning of His journey of faith: "I will show him how much he must suffer for My name's sake" (Act 9:16). The noun "the fellowship" ([τὴν] κοινωνίαν) is a familiar one to Paul's writings. Here in Philippians he has already spoken of the Philippian believers' "participation [τῇ κοινωνίᾳ] in the gospel" (1:5) and the consequent "fellowship [κοινωνία] of the Spirit" (2:1) which they enjoy. The word has a range of meaning that includes the concepts of *participation* (to share in something), *impartation* (to give a share in something), and *fellowship* (in a more absolute sense).[120] Paul uses the word here in the first sense, of sharing with someone in something.[121]

In this case Paul seeks to share with Christ "His sufferings" ([τῶν] παθημάτων αὐτοῦ). The noun πάθημα ("sufferings") can be used of sinful desire (Rom. 7:5; Gal. 5:24). But Paul uses it most often to describe "sufferings," always in the plural. The consistency of the plural form reminds us that the specifics may vary, but pain is the common core of them all. In Paul's case they included, as Timothy was aware, the "persecutions, and sufferings [τοῖς παθήμασιν], such as happened to me at Antioch, at Iconium and at Lystra; what persecutions I endured, and out of them all the Lord rescued me!" (2 Tim. 3:11). By linking "persecutions and sufferings" Paul makes clear that the suffering was *for* Christ. But it was more than simply *for* Christ; it was in some way a suffering *with* Christ. He could tell the Corinthian believers that "the sufferings of Christ [τὰ παθήματα τοῦ Χριστοῦ] are ours in abundance" (2 Cor. 1:5). He could tell the Colossian believers, "Now I rejoice in my sufferings [τοῖς παθήμασιν] for your sake, and in my flesh I do my share on behalf of His body, which is the church, in filling up what is lacking in Christ's afflictions" (Col. 1:24).

Neither Paul's nor any other believer's sufferings possess atoning power, as Christ's alone did, but amount to a fellowship of a deep and experiential nature. Additionally, that bond is not only vertical (between

---

120 TDNT, 3:798, 804-809.

121 Ibid., 3:804.

the individual believer and his Lord), but horizontal (a fellowship created among Christ's follows in union with their living Head): "But if we are afflicted, it is for your comfort and salvation; or if we are comforted, it is for your comfort, which is effective in the patient enduring of the same sufferings [παθημάτων] which we also suffer" (2 Cor. 1:6). Thus the genitive ([τῶν] παθημάτων αὐτοῦ, lit., "the sufferings of Him") is understood as objective.[122] The sufferings are Christ's, we share them with Him. Or perhaps even better, we become the stage upon which Christ's own sufferings are played out, and thus we come to "know" Him the more deeply. The witness of the saints for millennia confirms that the deepest fellowship with and knowledge of Christ Himself comes in life's lowest moments and deepest pains. The Apostle simply affirms that if this is what is required to know Christ, then he welcomes the pain. Knowing Christ is the very essence of eternal life (John 17:3). Anything that would hinder such knowledge is "counted as loss" (Phil. 3:7-8). Anything that will enhance such knowledge is embraced. If Jesus is my goal, anything and everything can be my friend. To live in Christ's "power" (τὴν δύναμιν) comes through "fellowship" ([τὴν] κοινωνίαν) with Him in His sufferings.

Paul adds a participial qualifier: "being conformed to His death" (συμμορφιζόμενος τῷ θανάτῳ αὐτοῦ). The verb (συμμορφιζόμενος, "being conformed") is found only here in Biblical literature. In fact some believe Paul may have coined the term himself.[123] The cognate adjective, however, is found in verse 21: "who will transform the body of our humble state into conformity [σύμμορφον] with the body of His glory, by the exertion of the power that He has even to subject all things to Himself." The adjective is also found in Rom. 8:29: "For those whom He foreknew, He also predestined to become conformed [συμμόρφους] to the image of His Son, so that He would be the firstborn among many brethren." The verb means to "conform to the same form" and denotes "an inward similarity of attitudes and character."[124] Of note is the common root it shares with signifi-

---

122 Robertson, *Word Pictures*, 4:454.

123 O'Brien, 408; Robertson, *Grammar*, 150.

124 Friberg, 362.

cant statements made previously about Christ, who "existed in the form [μορφῇ] of God" (2:6) and yet took "the form [μορφὴν] of a bond-servant" (2:7). So too here Paul desires to be "conformed" (συμμορφιζόμενος) to His death.

Just what does the participial phrase qualify? It probably is best seen as qualifying "that I may know Him" (τοῦ γνῶναι αὐτὸν).[125] The participle itself should probably be understood as expressing means[126]—it is by means of conformity to Jesus' death that we come to know Him experientially, deeply, and relationally. The present tense views this as an ongoing process rather than a cataclysmic event. It is a journey that continues throughout the disciple's earthly journey with Christ. The passive depicts the work of bringing about our conformity to Christ in His death as coming from outside ourselves. The hands of God—the master potter (Isa. 29:16; 45:9; 64:8; Jer. 18:2-6)—are placed upon our lives and circumstances to press us into the image of Christ (Rom. 8:29; 2 Cor. 3:18; cf. Rom. 12:2).

Paul is not so much thinking here of his own martyrdom (Phil 1:20-23), but of the daily death to sin and self which the journey of discipleship requires of every follower of Christ. Indeed, his Master and ours said, "The Son of Man must suffer many things and be rejected by the elders and chief priests and scribes, and be killed and be raised up on the third day.' And He was saying to them all, 'If anyone wishes to come after Me, he must deny himself, and take up his cross daily and follow Me. For whoever wishes to save his life will lose it, but whoever loses his life for My sake, he is the one who will save it'" (Luke 9:22-24). Thus Paul could say, "I die daily" (1 Cor. 15:31b). And he could refer to "... always carrying about in the body the dying of Jesus, so that the life of Jesus also may be manifested in our body" (2 Cor. 4:10). Indeed, he adds: "For we who live are constantly being delivered over to death for Jesus' sake, so that the life of Jesus also may be manifested in our mortal flesh. So death works in us, but life in you" (vv.11-12). And this was not unusual to Paul as an Apostle; it is the path for all followers of Christ. He told the Roman believers, "Or

---

125 O'Brien, 406.

126 Harmon, 347.

do you not know that all of us who have been baptized into Christ Jesus have been baptized into His death? Therefore we have been buried with Him through baptism into death, so that as Christ was raised from the dead through the glory of the Father, so we too might walk in newness of life. For if we have become united with Him in the likeness of His death, certainly we shall also be in the likeness of His resurrection" (Rom 6:3-5). Vincent well says, "The most radical conformity is thus indicated: not merely undergoing physical death like Christ, but conformity to the spirit and temper, the meekness and submissiveness of Christ; to His unselfish love and devotion, and His anguish over human sin."[127]

Note then the progression of thought that traces backward from the ultimate to what is necessary to experience it: Knowledge of Christ – of His resurrection power—of His sufferings—of His death. To truly know Christ in experiential reality, we must die to sin and self, taking the opportunities of meeting and knowing Him in the midst of the suffering He allows to come our way for His sake, and then, in that place, He exerts the power of His resurrection life within us and through us and we in this way and in these places come into the experience of knowing Christ deeply, personally, immediately.

Robertson was correct; in these present words "We are in Paul's Holy of Holies in his relation with Christ."[128] The sandals should come off and we ought to linger worshipfully before the Lord, considering just what these things say to each one of us.

Verse 11 – "in order that I may attain to the resurrection from the dead."

Paul adds one last clause to the sentence that began in verse 8. Just what does this final clause modify and in what way? The combination of εἴ πως is rendered as a conditional statement by some translations (e.g., "if," KJV, NKJV, NRSV, RSV), but the NASU, along with a number of other

---

127 Vincent, *Word Studies*, 3:448.

128 Robertson, *Paul's Joy in Christ*, 194.

English translations, treats it as expressing purpose ("in order that"; or "that," "so" or "so that," cf. ESV, NET, NIV, NLT). The combination εἴ πως is found three other times in the NT (Acts 27:12; Rom. 1:10; 11:14). It means "if perhaps" or "if somehow."[129] It "introduces a clause expressing a possibility which is the object of hope or desire."[130] The εἴ introduces the element of conditionality, suggesting some level of uncertainty about the attainment of the goal. Some view the uncertainty as related to the means by which the goal will take place.[131] Others reject this notion, leaving the uncertainty more general in nature.[132] We should probably hold in balance the Apostle who is utterly confident about his future resurrection (Rom. 8:30-31; 2 Tim. 1:12) and the one who does not wish to give any hint of presumption about his own faithfulness (1 Cor. 9:27; 10:12; 2 Cor. 13:5; Gal. 4:19-20). Having already cast aside any self-reliance (Phil. 3:3-8) and having put the full weight of his hope upon what only God can do in declaring him righteous (v.9), Paul at present exposes the great hunger this gift of righteousness unleashed within him to see its full work realized in his own life (vv.12-14). He rests ever and always in the gracious hands of God and seeks to wait in humble, obedient, peaceful faith for His good pleasure to be worked out.

> **Ministry Maxim**
>
> Only Christ's return will give us all we truly desire.

The phrase modifies the participle "being conformed" (συμμορφιζόμενος) in verse 10. The great and ultimate goal of knowing Christ in this life—both in His resurrection power and in His sufferings and death (v.10)—is that Paul might in the end be united with Christ at His coming when "the Lord Himself will descend from heaven ... and the dead in Christ will rise first" (1 Thess. 4:16). He desires that "I might attain" (καταντήσω) to this. The verb is used thirteen times in the NT;

---

129 BDAG, 2233.6.n.

130 Rienecker, 557.

131 E.g., O'Brien, 411-413.

132 E.g., Harmon, 348-350; Silva,165-167.

nine of those are in the travelogue of the book of Acts mostly reporting an arrival at a certain destination (Acts 16:1; 18:19, 24; 20:15; 21:7; 25:13; 27:12; 28:13). It can also mean, however, to reach or attain a goal and thus here it means to arrive at something so as to possess that thing (cf. also Acts 26:7; Eph. 4:13).[133] There is some question as to the verbal form; it can be either aorist active subjunctive or future active indicative. Most understand it as the former, which might add an air of confidence to the conditionality of the matter, though the context would have to indicate how much confidence one might read into the condition.[134]

That which is the Apostle's great desire and goal is identified by the preposition εἰς ("to"). That goal is "the resurrection from the dead" (τὴν ἐξανάστασιν τὴν ἐκ νεκρῶν). The word for "resurrection" (ἐξανάστασις) is the compounded form made up of the word for "resurrection" in verse 10 (ἀνάστασις) and the prefix ἐκ- ("out of"). This compounded found is found only here in the NT The prefixed ἐκ- and then the independent ἐκ double up to emphasize the arising *out of* or *out from* the dead. The compounded form of the verb may be used because it "connotes a coming to fullness of life" as depicted and developed in verses that follow (vv.12-21).[135] Or it may be that it is used to distinguish Paul's bodily resurrection from the dead at the return of Christ from the "resurrection" life as a present reality (v.10). Doubling up the definite articles marks the uniqueness and exclusivity of what is being considered, it is "the out-resurrection, the one out from the dead."

Is this not the great longing of the Apostle, of which he spoke so eloquently in Romans 8?

> ... and if children, heirs also, heirs of God and fellow heirs with Christ, if indeed we suffer with Him so that we may also be glorified with Him. For I consider that the sufferings of this present time are not worthy to be compared with the glory that is to

---

133 BDAG, 4023.2.a.

134 Harmon, 349; Sumney, 82; Wallace, 450-451, 469-470.

135 BDAG, 2739.

be revealed to us. For the anxious longing of the creation waits eagerly for the revealing of the sons of God. For the creation was subjected to futility, not willingly, but because of Him who subjected it, in hope that the creation itself also will be set free from its slavery to corruption into the freedom of the glory of the children of God. For we know that the whole creation groans and suffers the pains of childbirth together until now. And not only this, but also we ourselves, having the first fruits of the Spirit, even we ourselves groan within ourselves, waiting eagerly for our adoption as sons, the redemption of our body. (Rom. 8:17-23)

Thus in the present context Paul, having spoken of his justification (v.9) and sanctification (v.10), culminates this extended sentence with a passionate, enraptured view of his glorification (v.11).[136]

> **Digging Deeper:**
> 1. What "things were gain" to you that you must count "as loss for the sake of Christ"? (vv.7-8)
> 2. In what way have you observed people establishing a law by which to seek righteousness before God? (v.9)
> 3. In what way has God allowed you to both taste of Christ's resurrection power and share in His sufferings? (v.10)

Verse 12 – "Not that I have already obtained *it* or have already become perfect, but I press on so that I may lay hold of that for which also I was laid hold of by Christ Jesus."

The Apostle wishes to clarify his position, lest his passion be misread. He makes his clarification by means of a "Not ... but" (Οὐχ ... δὲ) parallelism. There are two things that are clearly not true. The first is "that I have

---

[136] Silva, 165.

already obtained" (ὅτι ἤδη ἔλαβον) this resurrection.[137] The adverb ἤδη ("already") refers to "a point of time prior to another point of time" (i.e., this present life over against the fuller entrance into life that will come at Christ's second coming) with the "implication of completion."[138] It modifies the verb ἔλαβον ("I have ... obtained"), whose aorist tense underscores any sense of final arrival at the point considered. Paul's emphasis upon the indwelling resurrection life of Christ (v.10) is not to be mistaken for a sense of ultimate arrival, which can only take place at Christ's coming (v.11).[139] The object of the verb's action is not made explicit and it has become the cause of a great deal of spilt ink. It seems best to make the knowing of Christ (vv.8, 10) that after which Paul grasps.[140] This, as we have seen above, is explained and expounded in the statements "I may gain Christ" (v.8) and "may be found in Him" (v.9). In this way Paul seems to gather up the whole of verses 8-11 and assume their content here, though he does not explicitly identify the object of the verb.

> **Ministry Maxim**
>
> Passionate, unceasing pursuit of Christ is the texture of true salvation.

The second (ἤ, "or") matter which is not true, is that "I ... have already become perfect" (ἤδη τετελείωμαι). Again the adverb is repeated with the same emphasis. The verb τετελείωμαι ("I ... have ... become perfect") is in the perfect tense, expressing the notion of having arrived at some point in the past into what has become a settled state of being. The term was

---

137 There is no object expressed so the translators have added "*it*" in italics. It seems best to view the implied object as all that has come before in the matter of knowing Christ as expressed in verses 7-11 (Sumney, 84).

138 BDAG, 3413.1.

139 Several important manuscripts contain here the phrase ἤ ἤδη δεδικαίωμαι ("or have already been justified"), including the influential P[46] and D. The debates concerning its authenticity grow complicated and intricate, but in the end most commentators believe the external evidence swings in favor of the shorter reading (e.g., Fee, 337, 343; O'Brien, 417-418; Silva, 187; Sumney, 84; contra Bockmuehl, 220).

140 Fee, 341, 342-343; Kent, 11:142; Hellerman, 199; O'Brien, 421-422; Sumney, 84.

used in the mystery religions to speak of being consecrated or fully initiated into the higher knowledge of the god under consideration.[141] There may be some such flavoring that spills over to Paul's present discussion or he may simply be using the verb in the sense of being made perfect, with the nuance of having arrived at one's intended destination.[142] Note the cognate in verse 15 (τέλειοι, "perfect") and its possibilities in view of the Judaizing influence in Philippi. The verb appears over twenty times in the NT but this is Paul's only usage, though Acts 20:24 has it upon his lips when testifying before the Ephesian elders. There he spoke in an echo of Philippians 3:3-8, saying, "I do not consider my life of any account as dear to myself ..." And this loss was "so that I may finish [τελειῶσαι] my course and the ministry which I received from the Lord Jesus." Comparing the two verbs under consideration, Robertson says, ἔλαβον "denies the sufficiency of Paul's past achievement, τετελείωμαι, denies it as a present reality."[143]

There is no triumphalism in Paul. He was not boasting of having attained a higher state of consciousness. He is not exalting himself above either his opponents or the ordinary believers that live in Philippi. Far from it! To the contrary (δὲ, "but") he is a man taken captive by a passion to "press on" (διώκω) until he can "lay hold" (καταλάβω) of his goal. The former verb is in the present tense, depicting an ongoing, unceasing quest forward toward a prize. The latter verb is in the aorist tense, picturing the victory of actually possessing that which so zealously has been sought. Paul has just used διώκω (v.6) to describe his zealous persecution of the church. When Christ met Saul on the road to Damascus, where he was in route to punish Christ-followers, the event did not rob him of his zeal, it reoriented it and rerouted it and intensified it by setting it upon the Christ who had in fact been the actual object of his persecution. "... and he fell to the ground and heard a voice saying to him, 'Saul, Saul, why are you persecuting [διώκεις] Me?' And he said, 'Who are You, Lord?' And

---

141 BDAG, 7300.3.

142 Ibid., 7300.2.e.

143 Robertson, *Grammar*, 901.

He said, 'I am Jesus whom you are persecuting [διώκεις]'" (Act 9:4-5). The zeal which once had found expression in the form of persecution had since that encounter been poured out in a continual, never-resting press forward toward that same Christ whom He had previously persecuted (Phil. 3:12, 14).

That toward which Paul pressed is the possibility (εἰ καί, "so that … may"; lit., "if indeed") that he might "lay hold" of Christ in fullest fellowship and deepest knowledge. Here again, as in verse 11, we encounter εἰ plus a subjunctive verb. The condition is uncertain as to fulfillment, but it may be considered possible or even probable. The καί is used in an emphatic sense, underscoring the ultimate nature of the prize which Paul pursues. The verb is a compounded form of the second verb above: κατά ("down") and λαμβάνω ("take hold of"), with the prefix giving a sense of movement downward with an element of purpose behind it. The prefix can be viewed as influencing the root verb in a number of ways, from extending an intensifying or perfecting influence upon the root that can carry the idea of "seize," with even a hint of violence and power in the action[144], giving a note of certainty to the action ("attain")[145] or simply underscoring the effort involved.[146] It depicts the divine hand of God powerfully being laid upon Saul for a particular purpose.

The two verbs are found together also in another context where Paul is discussing justifying righteousness: "What shall we say then? That Gentiles, who did not pursue [διώκοντα] righteousness, attained [κατέλαβεν] righteousness, even the righteousness which is by faith, but Israel, pursuing [διώκων] a law of righteousness, did not arrive at that law" (Rom. 9:30-31). Again as here Paul places the emphasis not upon human desire or initiative, but upon God's own initiative in extending the grace that declares one righteous in His sight.

The combination ἐφ' ᾧ ("for which") is found only five times in the NT (Acts 7:33; Rom. 5:12; 2 Cor. 5:4; Phil. 3:12; 4:10). Some take the phrase

---

144 BDAG, 4000; O'Brien, 424.

145 Friberg, 219.

146 Louw-Nida, 57.56.

as expressing cause, others see it as consecutive.¹⁴⁷ It may also express purpose or aim.¹⁴⁸ The combination of ἐφ' ᾧ καὶ ("for which also") is found only here and in 4:10. Paul repeats the second verb: "I was laid hold of" (κατελήμφθην). The aorist tense pictures Christ encountering Saul along the road to Damascus. The passive voice stands over against the previous active form ("I may lay hold of") and puts the initiative and completing power entirely on the divine side (ὑπὸ Χριστοῦ [Ἰησοῦ], "by Christ Jesus") with Paul now the object of the action. In a sudden, cataclysmic encounter Jesus introduced Himself into Saul's life and in so doing took hold of his life forevermore. Now Paul finds himself in passionate pursuit of the very thing for which Christ took hold of him. Previously he stood in front of the Lord, opposing Him and His people. Now he finds himself having stepped alongside the Lord Jesus, in passionate pursuit of the very goal in his life which the Lord is also pursuing. Paul similarly set forth the dynamic interplay between divine initiative and human response in Philippians 2:12-13.

There is a parallelism at work in this section of the letter that might be expressed in the following way:

A   "Not that I have already obtained *it* or have already become perfect" (v.12a)

B   "but I press on so that I may lay hold of that for which also I was laid hold of by Christ Jesus. (v.12b)

A   "Brethren, I do not regard myself as having laid hold of *it* yet;" (v.13a)

B   "but one thing *I do*: forgetting what *lies* behind and reaching forward to what *lies* ahead, I press on toward the goal for the prize of the upward call of God in Christ Jesus." (vv.13b-14)

---

147 Hellerman, 202; Sumney, 85.

148 Robertson, *Grammar*, 605.

Verse 13 – "Brethren, I do not regard myself as having laid hold of *it* yet; but one thing *I do*: forgetting what *lies* behind and reaching forward to what *lies* ahead,"

Paul addresses the believers in Philippi as "Brethren" (ἀδελφοί) something he does six other times in the letter (1:12; 3:1, 17; 4:1, 8, 21; the term is not gender specific, but references both male and female believers). In all the impassioned expression of his great pursuit of Christ he wants to make clear that he is not placing himself in an elite category spiritually, a status which might separate him from other believers in Christ. Their bond in Christ remains and is defining for their relationship. Yet he continues speaking very personally, as the combination of the emphatic personal pronoun (ἐγὼ, "I") and the masculine singular form of the reflexive pronoun (ἐμαυτὸν, "myself") attest. He is referencing his inner self-perceptions, speaking first of how he "does not regard" (οὐ λογίζομαι) himself. The verb was originally primarily a mathematical and accounting term, but then began to be applied to the cognitive process more generally.[149] There is a special emphasis upon the careful and logical nature of such thinking.[150] The present tense points to Paul's settled state of thinking. The verb is deponent, so the middle voice has an active meaning. It is negated by οὐ ("not").[151] That which he does not think of himself as having done is expressed through the infinitive κατειληφέναι ("having laid hold of"). We have here a clear echo of verse 12a. The present verb was twice used in the previous verse. See there for more on the meaning of this compound word. The perfect tense points to a settled state achieved at some point in the past and now made an abiding place. While Paul truly knows Christ already, he does not yet know Him in His unfiltered fullness. Quite a statement for a man who can speak as he does in 2 Corinthians 12:1-10.

---

149 BDAG, 4598.

150 Friberg, 247; Louw-Nida, 30.9.

151 Some manuscripts have οὔπω ("not yet") instead of οὐ ("not"). The weight of evidence probably rests with οὐ (cf. Sumney, 86), but the force is not greatly different between the two. The context supplies the idea of "yet," which may have motivated a scribe to alter it to the more explicit οὔπω (O'Brien, 418; Silva, 187).

It is a reminder that no matter how deeply, personally and profoundly we are privileged to know Christ there are yet more depths to know.

It is these very depths of possibility that beckon Paul forward, more deeply into Christ. In contrast (δέ, "but") to the very notion of "having [already] laid hold" of the fullness of knowing Christ, Paul has "one thing" (ἕν) in mind.[152] The translators have added "I do" in an attempt to make for smoother reading in English, but the Greek is more abrupt, and the more powerful for being so. Paul says simply, "but one thing." In his abruptness the Apostle allows the phrase to dangle before the eyes of our hearts that we might wonder at what "one thing" might be so compelling that it could captivate the entire life of a man such as Paul. No, it is more than that. What could be so beautiful that it might captivate the eternity of not only a man like Paul but every truly regenerate person?

That "one thing" is artfully withheld until verse fourteen where we find it is "I press on" (διώκω). But before Paul takes us there, he sets the table with two participial phrases in the remainder of verse thirteen. The two are held in contrasting parallel by means of a μὲν ... δὲ (i.e., "on the one hand ... on the other hand") arrangement. Together they both qualify the main verb "I press on" (διώκω,v.14), indicating the manner[153] or means[154] by which Paul presses toward the goal before him.

First, Paul's forward press is done "forgetting what lies behind" (τὰ ... ὀπίσω ἐπιλανθανόμενος). The accusative neuter plural τὰ stands in contrast to the accusative neuter singular ἕν ("one thing"). Paul has traded the

---

152 As did David: "One thing I have asked from the LORD, that I shall seek: That I may dwell in the house of the LORD all the days of my life, To behold the beauty of the LORD And to meditate in His temple" (Psa. 27:4). As did Mary: "But the Lord answered and said to her, 'Martha, Martha, you are worried and bothered about so many things; but only one thing is necessary, for Mary has chosen the good part, which shall not be taken away from her'" (Luke 10:41-42). As did the blind man whom Jesus healed: "He then answered, 'Whether He is a sinner, I do not know; one thing I do know, that though I was blind, now I see'" (John 9:25). And is this not what Jesus meant by "Blessed are the pure in heart" (Matt. 5:8) given that καθαρός ("pure") can carry the connotation of singular/unmixed? Kierkegaard put it succinctly: "Purity of heart is to will one thing."

153 Fee, 347; O'Brien, 428.

154 Harmon, 356.

many for the one. The "one" is of such beauty and value that all other things lose their glimmer and sheen. Paul sees but "one thing" and all else is stripped of its power to attract and consume. Paul has found the pearl of great price, and he has sold everything to obtain it (Matt. 13:45-46). He has found the treasure buried in the field and he divests himself of everything in order to buy that field and get that treasure (v.44). Paul has seen that when one has Christ he possesses all things; when one knows not Christ all else is empty chaff. "For from Him and through Him and to Him are all things" (Rom. 11:36). "He put all things in subjection under His feet, and gave Him as head over all things to the church" (Eph. 1:22). Indeed, He possesses "the power ... even to subject all things to Himself" (Phil. 3:21). And thus to bring us to "the summing up of all things in Christ, things in the heavens and things on the earth" (Eph. 1:10). Thus he may ask, "how will He not also with Him freely give us all things?" (Rom 8:32). Possess Christ and you possess all else; aim to possess all else and you will have neither them nor Christ, and die empty-handed.

> **Ministry Maxim**
>
> The Christian life is lived in drive, not in reverse.

To what does "what lies behind" (τὰ ... ὀπίσω) apply precisely? On the one hand, Paul clearly includes all the spiritual privileges already listed in verses 4-6.[155] But could he have also in mind the positive spiritual experiences that have characterized his life in Christ thus far?[156] Or does he perhaps include both, all his positive past experiences from both his pre-Christian and Christian life?[157] At times we hear believers using this to refer to the negative experiences of life with an added exhortation to move on from those things. But Paul is primarily thinking here of what might be counted as positive riches to be pursued and to which one might cling. These are, we might say, idols left behind that one might pursue the one

---

155 Fee, 348; Lenski, 848.

156 O'Brien, 428-429; Robertson, *Paul's Joy in Christ*, 200-201; Vincent, ICC, 100.

157 Harmon, 356; Martin, 153; Silva, 176

true God.[158] These things Paul is "forgetting" (ἐπιλανθανόμενος). The verb is used often in the LXX, but only eight times in the NT and only here by Paul. The present tense expresses this as Paul's normal pattern of thinking. The middle voice pictures Paul's inward decision to no longer regard these things. This "forgetting" is not an accidental lapse of memory, but an settled disposition of mind that refuses to any longer calculate the value of such things or regard them as precious and worthy any longer of pursuit. It is another way of saying what he has already established: "I count all things to be loss in view of the surpassing value of knowing Christ Jesus my Lord, for whom I have suffered the loss of all things, and count them but rubbish so that I may gain Christ" (v.8).

This he has replaced with "reaching forward to what lies ahead" (τοῖς ... ἔμπροσθεν ἐπεκτεινόμενος). We note that "what lies ahead" (τοῖς ... ἔμπροσθεν) is in the plural. Underscoring again that when we pursue the "one thing" (ἓν) of knowing Christ we come into possession of "all things." Such is the lot of all who are "found in Him" (v.9). "For all things belong to you, whether Paul or Apollos or Cephas or the world or life or death or things present or things to come; all things belong to you, and you belong to Christ; and Christ belongs to God" (1 Cor. 3:21b-23). The one who is in Christ has been "blessed ... with every spiritual blessing in the heavenly places in Christ" (Eph. 1:3). Thus Paul is ever "reaching forward" (ἐπεκτεινόμενος). Again, as with the parallel participle, the present tense expresses the ongoing nature of Paul's pursuit and the middle voice pictures Paul's inward resolve to attain that which has captured his heart. Both participles indicate the manner in which or just how it is Paul is able to "press on" (v.14).[159] The present verb is found only here in Biblical literature. It is a double compound:

---

158 "We all know the past was never as clean and bright as we remember it. Nostalgia paints history gold, just as unforgiveness paints it black. Actually, nostalgia ... is ... second cousin to unforgiveness. Both unforgiveness and nostalgia share the trait of an unreconciled past. Nostalgia is a vain attempt to reconcile the past through wistfulness, whereas unforgiveness is a doomed attempt to reconcile it through vengeance" (Buchanan, 119; cf. his entire helpful discussion on pp.118-120).

159 Hawthorne, WBC, 253-254; Hellerman, 204.

ἐπί ("after") plus ἐκ ("out of" or "forth") plus τείνω ("to stretch").[160] The prepositions in compound add both direction to the action as well as underscoring the intensity of the effort. It "is used figuratively to suggest intense effort as well as firm purpose."[161] We may well have here the imagery of a runner in the games—exerting every last ounce of energy as he strains toward the finish line. So too Paul has been captured by the thought of winning Christ.

Throughout the latter part of verse 13 Paul has been echoing verse 12b and continues to do so into the next verse where he will bring the sentence to completion.

Verse 14 – "I press on toward the goal for the prize of the upward call of God in Christ Jesus."

Now the main verb to which the previous discussion (v.13b) has been leading is at long last unveiled: "I press on" (διώκω). This too, like καταλαμβάνω in verse 13b, is a repeat from verse 12, further underscoring the parallelism noted in the discussion under that verse. For the meaning of the verb see the discussion there. Again the present tense pictures the ongoing tenacity and drive of Paul's pursuit.

This he does "toward the goal" (κατὰ σκοπὸν). The expression is thrust forward in the clause for emphasis. The noun (σκοπὸν, "the goal") is used only here in the NT though Paul uses the cognate verb σκοπέω in 2:4 and 3:17. It comes from "a root denoting 'to spy,' 'peer,' 'look into the distance.'"[162] We derive the English words tele*scope* and micro*scope* from this root. A mountain peak just northeast of ancient Jerusalem was named Mount Scopus because it served as a vantage point from which an expansive view of the capital city could be gained. It could thus denote "that toward which movement or activity is directed."[163] As such it could be used

---

160 Vincent, *Word Studies*, 3:450.
161 Louw-Nida, 16.20.
162 Thayer, 579.
163 Louw-Nida, 84.28.

of a target in an archery contest (Job 16:12; Lam. 3:12). And it became a descriptive "metaphor drawn from athletics for what one aims to achieve in the Christian life" and thus can be translated "mark" or "goal."[164] It is "toward" (κατὰ) this goal that Paul is constantly pressing. The preposition with the accusative noun serves as "a marker of spatial aspect" and is descriptive of an "extension toward" something.[165] The nuance of the preposition may be to "Bear *down* upon (κατὰ)" the goal.[166]

He presses forward "toward" (κατὰ) the goal, but it is "for the prize" (εἰς τὸ βραβεῖον) that he truly strives. The preposition indicates "motion into a thing or into its immediate vicinity or relation to something."[167] That into which he wishes to emerge is "the prize" (τὸ βραβεῖον). It is the word used to describe that which was awarded to the victor in the ancient games. The only other NT use of the noun makes the imagery of a race even more explicit: "Do you not know that those who run in a race all run, but only one receives the prize [τὸ βραβεῖον]? Run in such a way that you may win" (1 Cor. 9:24). There is no need to distinguish between the "goal" (σκοπὸν) and "the prize" (τὸ βραβεῖον).[168] The prize is the goal and the goal is attainment of the prize.

The actual identity of the prize is the realization of that to which the "the call" (τῆς ... κλήσεως) beckons the believer. The reference is not to Paul's unique and personal call to apostleship, but to the call that is common to all believers as recipients of God's gracious gift of eternal life. The idea of the believer being under a call is a favorite of Paul, nine of the eleven NT usages of the noun coming from his pen (Rom. 11:29; 1 Cor. 1:26; 7:20; Eph. 1:18; 4:1, 4; Phil. 3:14; 2 Thess. 1:11; 2 Tim. 1:9). This calling is qualified in three ways.

> **Ministry Maxim**
>
> For the believer the call of God always rings louder than any other voice.

---

164 Friberg, 351.

165 BDAG, 3938.B.1.b.

166 Vincent, *Word Studies*, 3:450.

167 BDAG, 2291.

168 Kennedy, 458.

First, it is "upward" (ἄνω). The calling is directional, leading away from present experience into something higher. It is not "behind" (ὀπίσω), but "ahead" (ἔμπροσθεν), indeed not only "ahead," but "upward" (ἄνω). To precisely what is Paul referring when he speaks of "the call"? Is it, as an "upward" call, simply a reference to the resurrection to take place at Christ's return (cf. "in order that I may attain to the resurrection from the dead," v.11; cf. 3:20-21)? Yes, it is that, but is it simply and only that? Paul is sparing in his use of this adverb, but he employs it tellingly in Colossians 3:1-2: "Therefore if you have been raised up with Christ, keep seeking the things above [ἄνω], where Christ is, seated at the right hand of God. Set your mind on the things above [ἄνω], not on the things that are on earth." What he demanded of the Colossian believers he testifies to personally with the Philippians. This "upward calling" is thus ultimately to the resurrection at the coming of Christ (and the fullness of life that event inaugurates), but it includes the continual pressing forward and upward in one's present walk of faith with Christ. All that this life's journey has desired and pursued (and in increasing, but ever-muted measure truly realized) will become our fullest possession at the return of Christ and the resurrection of the dead to eternal life. The present indwelling life of the risen Christ is of a piece with the fullness of life into which He will usher us at His return. The adverb is in the attributive position, tucked between the noun and its definite article. This emphasizes the qualitative nature of "the ... call."

Second, it is the call "of God" (τοῦ θεοῦ). The call is divinely authoritative and therefore cannot be dismissed without consequence. The call is personal, with God Himself issuing the call.

Finally, the call is realized "in Christ Jesus" (ἐν Χριστῷ Ἰησοῦ.). Some want to connect this all the way back to διώκω ("I press on"), but it's position in the sentence moves us to understand it as qualifying "the call" (τῆς ... κλήσεως).[169] The preposition (ἐν, "in") depicts the sphere in which the call is both issued and realized. The call is profoundly relational, issuing from God the Father and culminating in God the Son.

---

169 Lightfoot, 166.

In all of this vivid imagery our minds run quickly to the picture set before us by the author of Hebrews: "… let us also lay aside every encumbrance and the sin which so easily entangles us, and let us run with endurance the race that is set before us, fixing our eyes on Jesus" (Heb. 12:1b-2a).

> **Digging Deeper:**
> 1. Is this pursuit of Christ (v.12) more a set of the will or a state of the emotions? What difference does your answer make?
> 2. What "lies behind" that you need to forget (v.13)? Practically how can this become a reality in your life?
> 3. Define precisely what God's call is upon your life (v.14)? What can you do to make that a more defining a part of your every moment?

Verse 15 – "Let us therefore, as many as are perfect, have this attitude; and if in anything you have a different attitude, God will reveal that also to you;"

In the face of Judaizing influences in the Philippian church (vv.2-3) Paul rejected any notion of personal righteousness (vv.4-7) and clearly cast his hope upon the righteousness that comes from God through Jesus Christ (vv.8-9). He thus described his passionate pursuit of knowing Christ and being found in Him (vv.10-14). Paul now employs οὖν ("therefore") to signal that he is about to set forth a logical conclusion that arises from these realities.

The implications arise primarily in the realm of thinking: "Let us have this attitude" (φρονῶμεν). As we have noted, throughout the letter Paul maintains a steady emphasis upon the world of the mind. The verb appears twenty-six times in the NT, of which twenty-three are by Paul. Of those twenty-three usages ten appear here in Philippians (1:7; 2:2 [2x], 5; 3:15 [2x], 19; 4:2, 10 [2x]), more than in any other NT book. The verb means "to have an opinion with regard to someth[ing]"; to "think, form/hold an opinion" or to "judge."[170] Thus it seems to speak not merely of individual thoughts, but of "a certain way of looking at things, thus 'mindset.'"[171] Paul has revealed how he thinks about them (1:7) and has emphatically set forth the template for Christian thinking as found in Christ Himself (2:2, 5). He will use the verb again to confront erroneous (3:19) and divisive (4:2) thinking as well has to praise the selfless, generous thinking of the Philippian believers (4:10). Paul's frequent use of the word underscores the high place he affords the Christian mind. The subjunctive mood is hortatory in emphasis and presses upon the Philippians with the force of a command the way of thinking Paul has been espousing. The present tense looks for action that is abiding, continual, or habitual. Though Paul has been speaking in highly personal terms, the implications he draws are corporate, for we note the plural form of the verb ("Let *us* ... have this attitude," emphasis added). The specific pattern of thinking is identified by the demonstrative pronoun τοῦτο ("this"). The neuter singular form gathers up what Paul has been exposing about his own thinking throughout vv.2-14 and regards the rejection of personally generated righteousness (vv.4-7), rest upon the divinely provided righteousness of Christ (vv.8-9), and the resulting pursuit of knowing Christ and being found in Him (vv.10-14).

> **Ministry Maxim**
>
> The God who gives the truth can be trusted to make the implications of that truth clear.

He applies this specifically to "as many as are perfect" (Ὅσοι ... τέλειοι). In making the designation "perfect" (τέλειοι) Paul uses an adjective which is cognate to the verb in verse 12: "Not that I ... have already become perfect [τετελείωμαι]." What he denied possessing in verse 12 does he now claim to possess along with some of the Philippian believers? The adjective generally describes something which has attained its appointed purpose or end. It is thus complete or perfect.[172] In the

---

170 BDAG, 7819.

171 Fee, 185.

172 BDAG, 7298.

first century the word was also used in the context of the pagan mystery religions. There it served as a technical term to designate an individual who had passed into the mystic rites as an initiate.[173] In those settings the word distinguished the fully instructed from the novice.[174] It is tempting to see such a nuance in the present context, though there is no hint in the text that Paul used the word in this specialized sense.[175] The word also had a strong history of usage in Jewish contexts where it applied to those who were entire and wholehearted in their efforts to honor God (e.g. the LXX for Gen. 6:9; 1 Kings 8:61; 11:4).[176] Similarly, in the Qumran community the corresponding Hebrew word was used in a technical sense to describe those who lived "faithfully by the Law as it is normatively expounded by the Teacher of Righteousness."[177]

Some see the word being used here with a sense of irony[178] while others deny this.[179] If Paul was employing irony to make his point here, the term could be an intentional polemic against those who believe themselves to have "arrived" by means of observance of the Law (3:2). All Paul's labors are focused on presenting every believer mature and "complete [τέλειον] in Christ" (Col. 1:28). But some may have believed they had "arrived" by means of a different route. The NET Bible seems to support this reading by placing the word in quotation marks: "Therefore let those of us who are 'perfect' embrace this point of view." Again, if irony is to be read here, Paul does not believe them to be so, but may be sarcastically employing their own term to single them out for note by the other believers in Philippi.

---

173 Ibid, 7298.3.

174 Vincent, *Word Studies*, 3:480.

175 Harmon, 365; Kennedy, 459; Lenski, 851-852; O'Brien, 434; Robertson, *Paul's Joy in Christ*, 206; Sumney, 88.

176 Bockmuehl, 225.

177 Ibid.

178 Hanson, 257-258; Hawthorne, WBC, 211; Lightfoot, 167; Robertson, *Paul's Joy in Christ*, 206, Silva, 177.

179 Bockmuehl, 225-226; Fee, 353; Harmon, 365; Kennedy, 459; Lenski, 851-852; Martin, 155; O'Brien, 435-436; Sumney, 88; Vincent, ICC, 112-113.

Could it be that what Paul denied possessing himself (v.12) he, for the sake of argument, labeled the opposition with in order to make his point? If so, this helps avoid the awkwardness of Paul now claiming to possess what he has expressly denied possessing (v.12).

This reading is attractive, but it may make too much of the cognate words (τετελείωμαι, "have already become perfect," v.12; τέλειοι, "perfect," v.15), ignore the separate nuances they may communicate, and demand they support a more nuanced meaning that they may legitimately bear in the present context. It is possible that Paul is holding forth that which is the truly mature ("perfect") Christian view of the matters under discussion. In this case Paul would be saying maturity is found not in having "arrived" in some sense in this life, but in the continuing quest to know Christ and be found in Him. Maturity eschews (vv.7-8) any righteousness arising from the human side of religious pedigree or performance (vv.5-6), rests entirely upon the righteousness that comes from God through Christ (v.9), and makes the passionate pursuit of knowing Christ more deeply their quest in this life (vv.10-14).

Paul uses the plural form of the relative pronoun (Ὅσοι, "As many as") to cast the net broadly enough to gather in whoever might fit under these terms. He is not naming names, but letting the net fall where the facts necessitate.

Paul tacks on an additional line thought (καὶ, "and") which he forms around a conditional statement: "if in anything you have a different attitude" (εἴ τι ἑτέρως φρονεῖτε). He takes up again the verb he has just used in the first half of the verse (φρονεῖτε, "attitude"). There he set forth the prescribed attitude, one that echoes that of Christ Himself (2:5-8) and which has been exemplified in Timothy (2:19-24), Epaphroditus (2:25-30) and himself (3:3-14). But now it is a "different" (ἑτέρως) way of thinking that he addresses. While the verb is the same as earlier in the verse he has shifted from the subjunctive to the indicative and from the first person plural to the second person plural form. Whereas in the first half of the verse he spoke inclusively ("us"), now he directly addresses those who comprise the Philippian church alone ("you"). Whereas he spoke with imperatival force ("Let us ... have this attitude"), he now speaks categorically ("you have a different attitude"). The adverb ἑτέρως ("differently") is found only here in the NT, though the cognate adjective is common.

The variety of ways in which the difference may be manifest is cast as widely as possible (τι, "in anything"). The different way of thinking may be along the specific lines of a perfectionism that could have been showing up in some within the Philippian church (under influence of Judaizing elements or with a seepage of pagan, mystical thought) or it may have taken some other form of divergent thinking. As different as those ways of reasoning may be from one another they are unified in one great whole in the fact that they are "different" from the pattern of thinking God, through His Apostle, calls for from His people. The condition is a simple one, where the matter under consideration is considered true. Paul knew there to be those in the midst of the Philippian church who did not think along these lines. As his letter was read before the gathered congregation those people would come under the white hot glare of God's truth.

To such people Paul is content to say, "God will reveal that also to you" (καὶ τοῦτο ὁ θεὸς ὑμῖν ἀποκαλύψει). By "that" (τοῦτο) Paul means the "different attitude" (ἑτέρως φρονεῖτε) which he has just called out into the light of truth. In saying this Paul might be understood along two lines. He might be saying that if, as this letter is read before the congregation, some in their midst were exposed for their divergent thinking, they should consider it not a matter of Paul's doing, but God's. Or having exposed the divergent nature of their thinking to the larger congregation by way of this letter, Paul may be content to simply leave them to God and allow Him to continue to expose them for what they are. In either case Paul has stated the truth and now he is content to let God defend His truth.

When Paul says "God will reveal" (ὁ θεὸς ... ἀποκαλύψει) he uses a verb that means to bring to light or uncover things that could not be seen in any other way except by the illuminating work of the Holy Spirit.[180] This is a good reminder that we—let alone an apostle!—do not have the power to illuminate a human heart and bring them to understanding. Only God can do this. Our part is to set forth the truth from the

---

180 BDAG, 928.b.

Scriptures; God alone can illumine a heart to see, understand, believe and obey. Like the Apostle, let us as His servants find a passionate, but restful repose in His faithfulness to do His work in His way through His Word.

The plural form of the personal pronoun (ὑμῖν, "you") may indicate that the problem was more than a single person within the congregation, but at least potentially was made up of a movement of folks who had begun to trend in contrary directions, dividing the congregation. Thus Paul's calls for unity throughout the epistle may have been intended in this direction, though there may have been other areas of conflict and division within the church as well.

Just how should we understand the καὶ ("also")? The word order argues against reading καὶ with ὑμῖν, so that he would be saying "to you also (i.e., in addition to us) God will reveal this." Rather it should be taken with τοῦτο which follows immediately. This revelation is apparently in addition to something else God has made or will make clear to them. To just what does the conjunction point? Is there again a touch of sarcasm here, so that this illumination of truth would be in addition to a claimed "revelation" regarding perfection? In which case Paul might be saying in essence, "As the great 'enlightened' ones who have seen what the rest of us cannot, God will surely also bring you into this revelation as well!" Or does he use it more generally, simply leaving this matter, as all others, to the illuminating work of God?

Verse 16 – "however, let us keep living by that same *standard* to which we have attained."

Paul adds a contrasting thought (πλὴν, "however") to what he has just set forth in verse 15. That transition may be made by translating, as the NASU does ("however") or by "only" (ESV, NIV, RSV, NRSV), "nevertheless" (NET, NKJV), or "but" (NLT). The word is used in "breaking off a discussion and emphasizing what is important."[181] Thus Paul is rounding out what he has been saying throughout the chapter.

---

181 BDAG, 5977.1.c.

The present tense infinitive στοιχεῖν carries the force of an imperative or hortatory call ("let us keep living").[182] The verb originally came from the military world and meant to "be drawn up in line," but came to be used figuratively and meant "to be in line with a pers[on] or thing considered as standard for one's conduct."[183] It thus means to "hold to, agree with, follow, conform."[184] If a hint of the military background of the word remains there may be here another subtle call to move forward together in unity, marching as one toward the goal.[185]

The measuring mark for such agreement is "that same *standard*" (τῷ αὐτῷ). The cryptic expression has given rise to what appear to be insertions into the Greek text. Most extant manuscripts include κανόνι (standard) in various places throughout the sentence, though it appears to be an addition to the text intended perhaps to clarify what is otherwise enigmatic. The shorter text has good support from some of the earliest manuscripts. "The translation adds 'standard' because of English requirements, not because of textual basis."[186] Yet the verb στοιχέω, as used elsewhere, seems to imply some measure against which the action is judged (Acts 21:24 = "keeping the Law"; Rom. 4:12 = "the faith of our father Abraham"; Gal. 5:25 = "the Spirit"; 6:16 = "this rule") and so the idea, if not the actual verbiage, for something like "standard" is present.[187]

The expression τῷ αὐτῷ ("that same") is more fully explained by that "to which we have attained" (εἰς ὃ ἐφθάσαμεν). Wallace calls τῷ αὐτῷ a dative of rule in that it "specifies the rule or code a person follows or the standard of conduct to which he or she conforms."[188] The preposition εἰς ("to") signals movement into something. The relative pronoun (ὃ, "which") is that into which the movement is made. The verb (ἐφθάσαμεν, "we have

---

182 It draws upon the hortatory power of φρονῶμεν ("Let us ... have this attitude") in verse 15 (Robertson, *Grammar*, 943-944; cf. Wallace, 608).

183 BDAG, 6837.

184 Ibid.

185 O'Brien, 442.

186 NET Bible, explaining their inclusion of the word "standard."

187 O'Brien, 441-442.

188 Wallace, 157-158; Vincent calls it "the dative of the norm or standard" (ICC, 114).

attained") can mean to come to one thing before another, but here has the simpler meaning of coming up to something or reaching/attaining something.[189] The aorist tense points to an attainment accomplished.

The question is just what is it Paul and the Philippians might together have been considered to have attained? Clearly they had not "attained" a righteousness of their own (v.9a), but rested through faith in the gracious gift of righteousness that comes from God through inclusion in Christ (v.9b). They had not "attained" perfection (v.12a), but were in the process of being sanctified (vv.12b-14). This statement needs to be read in balance with those which Paul has just made: "Not that I have already obtained it or have already become perfect" (v.12), "I do not regard myself as having laid hold of it yet" (v.13), and the fact that his hope was to "attain to the resurrection of the dead" at a point still in the future (v.11). What has thus been "attained" was the pattern and direction of life as one who is in pursuit of knowing Christ ever more deeply (v.8), being "found in him" (v.9), and entering into the fullness of these things through the resurrection from the dead at Christ's return (v.11). Perfection is not yet, but passion has found the path that will take us there by His mercies. Stay this course. Follow this path. Stay in pursuit of Christ. Along this way the Lord will Himself reveal to you the matters that remain in question.

> **Ministry Maxim**
>
> A disciple never surrenders ground gained in the pursuit of Christ.

Digging Deeper:

1. How do verses 15 and 16 inform our understanding of what Christian maturity looks like?
2. In what way does verse 15 give you confidence in the power of God's Word and His commitment to honor it? What implications does this have for you as to preach and teach His Word?
3. What is the standard which the Christian must never surrender? (v.16)

---

189 BDAG, 7716.3.

Verse 17 – "Brethren, join in following my example, and observe those who walk according to the pattern you have in us."

By again (cf. 1:12, 14; 2:25; 3:1, 13; 4:1, 8, 21) using ἀδελφοί ("Brethren") Paul keeps the tone humble, inclusive and conciliatory. Paul sets before the believers in Philippi two commands, each balanced over against the other by the coordinating conjunction (καὶ, "and").

The expression "join in following my example" is more literally "fellow-imitators of me be." The noun Συμμιμηταί is used only here in the Biblical literature. It is a compound comprised of σύν ("with") and μιμητής ("imitator") and designates co-imitators, those who have joined with others in imitating someone or something. Perhaps Lenski is on target: "The idea is that they are to aid and support each other in imitating Paul."[190] The prefix (σύν) is another hint at Paul's efforts to unify the body of believers in Philippi. The present tense imperative (γίνεσθε) calls for repeated and continual action. Paul makes himself the standard for their imitation (μου, "my example" or more simply and literally, "of me"). While God would be the ultimate standard for imitation (Eph. 5:1), Paul issues a similar call to other believers in places like Corinth (1 Cor. 4:16; 11:1) and Thessalonica (1 Thess. 1:6; 2 Thess. 3:7, 9). He called Timothy to live in such a way that others in Ephesus might imitate his life (1 Tim. 4:12). He will repeat himself again later in this letter: "The things you have learned and received and heard and seen in me, practice these things" (Phil. 4:9).

To this Paul adds (καὶ, "and") a second command: "observe" (σκοπεῖτε). The verb means "to pay careful attention to," "look (out) for" or intentionally take "notice" of something or someone.[191] Again it is a present tense imperative, calling for repeated and continual vigilance in this watchful observance. The word is used only six times in the NT, five of which are by Paul and two of which he employs here in Philippians

---

190 Lenski, 856.

191 BDAG, 6715.

(Luke 11:35; Rom. 16:17; 2 Cor. 4:18; Gal. 6:1; Phil. 2:4; 3:17). He used the verb earlier to exhort the believers, saying, "do not merely look out for [σκοποῦντες] your own personal interests" (2:4). The cognate noun (σκοπός) is found in 3:14 where it is "the goal" which Paul pursues with single-minded devotion.[192] As Paul taught the believers to unselfishly look to the cares and concerns of one another he now calls them to look together at him as their example in what it means to follow Christ. Paul was a man of "one thing" (v.13) and he calls the believers to be just as fixed and immovable in their pursuit of Christ.

That which is to be thus observed is identified by the accusative of person or thing, in this case: τοὺς οὕτω περιπατοῦντας ("those who walk according to"). The participle with its definite article is used substantively ("those who walk," emphasis added). The present tense points to the consistent pattern of the lives under consideration. The verb is used often by Paul to refer to the pattern and unfolding nature of one's life (e.g., Eph. 2:2, 10; 4:1, 17; 5:2, 8, 15). The picturesque nature of the metaphor can be lost in the commonness of the verb's appearance—life is lived one step, one choice at a time. As followers of Jesus Christ we are responsible to string together individual steps (choices) that establish a particular pattern of life. The adverb (οὕτω, "according to," lit., "the ones walking *thus*") is in the attributive position, tucked between the participle and its definite article, thus emphasizing the qualitative nature of these people's lives. It is used correlatively with καθὼς and means something like "in this way"

> **Ministry Maxim**
>
> A pattern for living is as important as a pattern for thinking.

or "as follows."[193] It is used to point to a pattern of living that is fleshed out by "the pattern you have in us" (καθὼς ἔχετε τύπον ἡμᾶς). Lit., "as you have a pattern in us." The pronoun is plural (ἡμᾶς, "us") and includes at least Paul (3:4-14), Timothy (1:1; 2:19-24), Epaphroditus (2:25-30), and these others here as well (cf. also "as many as," 3:15). The verb (ἔχετε,

---

192 Harmon, 370; Silva, 179.

193 BDAG, 5445.2.

"you have") is in the present tense, underscoring the consistency and ongoing nature of the life Paul has lived out before the Philippian believers and thus of the gift they possess in that "pattern" (τύπον). The noun can be used technically to describe a "type" (Rom. 5:14; 1 Cor. 10:6 [cf. v.11]), an official "standard" against which something is measured (Rom. 6:17), and, as here, an "example" (1 Thess. 1:17; 2 Thess. 3:9; 1 Tim. 4:12) or "model" (Tit. 2:7) in matters ethical and moral.[194]

Paul was not egotistical in calling for conformity to his own lifestyle, for in similar fashion he called the believers to follow others who walked as he did. And the ultimate standard is Christ Himself: "Be imitators of me, just as I also am of Christ" (1 Cor. 11:1; cf. 1 Thess. 1:6). Note the telescoping pattern of relationships that emerges: Christ – Paul imitates Christ – others also imitate Christ – the Philippians are to imitate Paul and the others who, like him, imitate Christ.

> **Digging Deeper:**
> 1. Paul called the Philippians to follow his example (v.17a), but should a pastor follow his example in telling people similarly to follow him?
> 2. What precisely from Philippians would constitute "the pattern you have in us" (v.17b)?

Verse 18 – "For many walk, of whom I often told you, and now tell you even weeping, *that they are* enemies of the cross of Christ,"

The sentence Paul begins here stretches through verse 19. It is introduced by an explanatory γὰρ ("For"). What follows explains why selecting the right models for conduct is so important (v.17). Paul certainly is not alone as a suitable model (v.17), but the possibilities in the other direction are "many" (πολλοί). Again, as in verse 17, he uses the verb περιπατέω

---

194 Spicq, 3:387.

("walk") as descriptive of the unfolding, step-by-step, pattern and conduct of life. Again the present tense pictures the consistent nature of the life under consideration.

Most of the remainder of the sentence is comprised of three relative clauses all beginning with some form of ὅς in the masculine plural, one of them here in verse 18 and two of them in verse 19. Here it is the genitive masculine plural form (οὕς, "of whom"). A warning about such individuals has "often" (πολλάκις) been the subject of Paul's speech (ἔλεγον, I … told you") in the past[195] and are so "now" (νῦν) again in the present (λέγω, "tell"). The same verb is used in both cases, the first in the imperfect tense to underscore the repeated nature of Paul's past warnings and the latter in the present tense to underscore the present necessity and urgency of his continued warning. The past had been frequently (πολλάκις, "often") punctuated with such warnings (cf. "write the same things," v.1). The present (νῦν, "now") form of the warnings "even" (καὶ) includes "weeping" (κλαίων). In this latter word the participial form is used to express manner.[196] The present tense underscores that this is no passing emotional outburst for the Apostle. We are not told precisely what evokes the emotion in Paul. It could be the eternal danger of the individuals involved, the danger they pose to the Philippian believers or the offense to Christ Himself they represent.

> **Ministry Maxim**
>
> We declare our position by our "walk" as much as by our words.

The frequent warnings of the past and the urgency of their present form all tell the same story: such people are "enemies of the cross of Christ" (τοὺς ἐχθροὺς τοῦ σταυροῦ τοῦ Χριστοῦ). There is no verb present; "that they are" has been

---

195 It had likely been over ten years since Paul founded the church in Philippi. These warnings probably took place during what had possibly been three different visits to the city: at its founding (Acts 16:11-40) and again later as he came and went through Macedonia (Acts 20:1-6; 2 Cor. 1:16). They also could have taken place through trusted associates who had contact with the church in Paul's name and perhaps also in other written communication that we know nothing more about and which God has not preserved.

196 Sumney, 93; Wallace, 628.

added by the translators in an effort at smoother English reading. The Greek text is the more stark and jarring for its brevity. The noun "enemies" (τοὺς ἐχθροὺς) is accompanied by the definite article so that these folk are not just qualitatively "enemies," but, more literally, "*the* enemies." They have, by their pattern of conduct, classed themselves as "enemies" of Christ.[197] Perhaps they had not verbally declared themselves enemies of Christ, but by their lifestyle they had taken a definitive stand against "the cross of Christ" (τοῦ σταυροῦ τοῦ Χριστοῦ) and all it means and sought to secure for Christ's people. We enter this world as enemies of God (Rom. 5:10; Col. 1:21) and these individuals—whatever else they may say about Christ and His sacrifice—by their actions prove they continue in enmity toward Him in the present. That place where Jesus found His ultimate and final expression of humble saving love (Phil. 2:8) has no real meaning to them and they evidence by their lifestyle (περιπατοῦσιν, "walk") that they have no understanding of it nor share in the saving grace it represents. An individual is likely to defect from Christ morally before he departs from Him theologically. The fault lines of a failing faith often reveal themselves first in one's conduct, rather than in one's confession.

Just who are these individuals? That has been a matter of great debate. They might have been non-believing pagans, the Judaizing element that held to Christ as Messiah but held to a righteousness that was at least in part humanly produced by conformity to the Law (3:2, 9)[198], or they could have been professed believers who took the gift of righteousness from God (v.9) as license for a profligate lifestyle (v.19).[199] Final dogmatism is not warranted[200], but the balance of the evidence would appear to support the view that these were professed believers who had taken grace as a license for unholy indulgence and sin under the banner of "Christian

---

197 Alford, 3:185; Vincent, ICC, 117.

198 Lenski, 857-858; Müller, 130; O'Brien, 454-458; Silva, 180-181.

199 Fee, 375; Harmon, 372-373; Hendriksen, 178; Lightfoot, 168; Robertson, *Paul's Joy in Christ*, 214; Wuest, 101.

200 Some like Martin (158-160; which see for a good summary of how various sides find support in the grammar of the sentence) and Vincent (ICC, 116-117) believe agnosticism on the matter is the best route.

freedom." Granted, the previous discussion related to the Judaizing element would lend some contextual support to that view and the context does not seem to have prepared us for a sudden reference to a different group. Yet the actual descriptors here seem to best support this understanding.[201] They were apparently a sizeable group (πολλοί, "many").[202] Paul was dealing with them as a grouping, rather than thinking of individual faces and names within the Philippian church. Thus he may have been considering them as a larger entity, bound together by their similar lifestyle (περιπατοῦσιν, "walk"), rather than as specific individuals. They are identified by the kind of life they lead, rather than the doctrines they promoted, though life choices arise out of the "truth" we profess and propagate. They probably considered themselves followers of Christ, for the verb is typically reserved in Paul for the lives of believers.[203] The way Paul combines both first (ἔλεγον, "I ... told you"), second (ὑμῖν, "you"), and third (οὕς, "of whom") person seems to indicate that he is speaking of a group separate from the Philippian church itself.[204] Perhaps they represent the kind of challenge that God's people face wherever they seek to live out discipleship to Jesus. That they are professed followers of Christ is hinted at by the fact of the Apostle's "weeping" (κλαίων). While Paul was capable of strong emotion over the lost (Rom. 9:2), elsewhere he seems to reserve this term for that which takes place within "Christian" relationships (Rom. 12:15; 1 Cor. 7:30; cf. Acts 21:13).[205]

What a heart wrenching scene it is! Standing among those who laid claim to Christ's saving acts of humble incarnation, living obedience, dying sacrifice and triumphant resurrection (2:5-11) were those who treated these

---

201 For a good summary of how the following clauses might be understood in reference to Judaizers see Martin (158-160) and Müller (130-132).

202 The use of this adjective makes it unlikely Paul is referencing a group confined only to the Philippian church, for it is unlikely that there are "many" (πολλοί) within such a small congregation (Hellerman, 215). It seems more likely that he views these professed followers of Christ as a group, though spread across the landscape of Christ's larger Body at that time.

203 Except in Ephesians 2:2; 4:17; Colossians 3:7 (Fee, 367).

204 Fee, 368.

205 cf. also his use of δάκρυον ("tears") in 2 Corinthians 2:4 and 2 Timothy 1:4 (Fee, 369).

holy realities with such contempt that they might justly be called "enemies of the cross of Christ"! The church gathers in its various locations and diverse settings and the Apostle knows that within their shared circle of confessed faith are included some "enemies of the cross of Christ!" Little wonder he wept. Such blasphemous effrontery in the face of divine grace was more than the Apostle's heart could take. Should there not be a similar response within anyone who has truly found life in that grace?

Verse 19 – "whose end is destruction, whose god is *their* appetite, and *whose* glory is in their shame, who set their minds on earthly things."

The second and third relative clauses which qualify πολλοὶ ... περιπατοῦσιν ("many walk") in verse 18 lead the way here. Both use the genitive masculine plural form ὧν ("whose").

The second clause describes those "whose end is destruction" (ὧν τὸ τέλος ἀπώλεια). The noun (τὸ τέλος, "end") is accompanied by the definite article and points to the final stop on their journey of existence. The noun carries within it the notion of arriving at the goal or outcome toward which effort has been expended. There is a sense of the outworking of logic and purpose here. There may be an intended play on words between "have already become perfect" (τετελείωμαι, v.12), "mature" (τέλειοι, v.15) and "end" (τὸ τέλος) here.[206] Rather than pursuing maturity in Christ, they have chosen a course that can only end in judgment. The inevitable and just outcome of such a lifestyle can only be "destruction" (ἀπώλεια). The word is a strong one. The antichrist is called "the son of destruction" (ὁ υἱὸς τῆς ἀπωλείας, 2 Thess. 2:3). The same phrase is used to call Judas "the son of perdition" (ὁ υἱὸς τῆς ἀπωλείας, John 17:12). The word is used to speak of the

> **Ministry Maxim**
>
> That done in the name of Christian "freedom" may be simply worship of a lesser god.

---

206 Fee, 370; Harmon, 374.

destruction awaiting one who has chosen the broad path (Matt. 7:13). It pictures the lot of those who go to hell (Rev. 17:8, 11). Peter used the word five times in rapid succession in his description of false prophets, speaking of both the current destructiveness of their ways and teaching (2 Peter 2:1) and of the eschatological judgment awaiting them (2 Peter 2:1, 3; 3:7, 16). Thayer says the word describes "the destruction which consists in the loss of eternal life."[207] Indeed, it is held over against "salvation" earlier in this letter (1:28). There Paul had already said that this "destruction" is what awaits the unregenerate "opponents" of the believers in Philippi and now he must apply it to some within the circle of confessed faith in Jesus Christ!

It is easy to allow these words to pass before our eyes and trace through our minds without taking in the gravity of that which the Apostle is depicting. He does not equivocate and hint, "It is possible that there are some within the 'visible,' 'gathered' church who might not genuinely possess eternal life." He did not simply query, "Will everyone here eventually make it to heaven?" He declared, "Some among us are on their way to hell!" One can imagine the shockwaves this would have sent through the congregation. What powerful, Bible-grounded, Spirit-guided self-searching this would have induced!

In this the Apostle Paul is echoing our Master, who said, "Not everyone who says to Me, 'Lord, Lord,' will enter the kingdom of heaven, but he who does the will of My Father who is in heaven will enter. Many will say to Me on that day, 'Lord, Lord, did we not prophesy in Your name, and in Your name cast out demons, and in Your name perform many miracles?' And then I will declare to them, 'I never knew you; DEPART FROM ME, YOU WHO PRACTICE LAWLESSNESS'" (Matt. 7:21-23). Jesus justly asks, "Why do you call Me, 'Lord, Lord,' and do not do what I say?" (Luke 6:46).

Paul's charges do not end here. The third clause describes them as those "whose god is their appetite and whose glory is in their shame" (ὧν ὁ θεὸς ἡ κοιλία καὶ ἡ δόξα ἐν τῇ αἰσχύνῃ αὐτῶν). There are no verbs in

---

[207] Thayer, 71.

these relative clauses and the statements are the more powerful for their abrupt and truncated nature. The first portion of this third clause simply and literally says "the god the stomach" (ὁ θεὸς ἡ κοιλία). Elsewhere Paul used κοιλία to speak of both the "womb" (Gal. 1:15; cf. Acts 3:2; 16:18) and the "stomach" (1 Cor. 6:13). The physical organ is probably here used to represent that sensation most associated with it, "appetite."[208] Paul seems to use it in a similar way when he warns the believers of Rome against charlatan "Christians": "For such men are slaves, not of our Lord Christ but of their own appetites [κοιλίᾳ]; and by their smooth and flattering speech they deceive the hearts of the unsuspecting" (Rom. 16:18). What he depicts there as slavery he pictures here as worship, for the charge here is nothing less than idolatry. By way of application we may see here a condemnation not only of the idolatry of gluttony or a whole host of eating disorders, but of any lifestyle which is dominated and dictated by the senses, drives and appetites of our bodies.[209] What is often dealt with under the label of "addiction" may also need to be explored under the realm of the spiritual and as false, idolatrous worship. There may be not only chemical/physiological and psychological/emotional components to be dealt with, but a spiritual one as well. True, God "richly supplies us with all things to enjoy" (1 Tim. 6:17) and no food is inherently unclean (Mark 7:19). The call here is not to asceticism, but to Spirit-controlled balance for the glory of God. We are able to fall off this line on either side—by being overly restrictive, as the Judaizers probably were[210] or by being overly indulgent. Paul struck the balance needed when he counseled the Corinthian believers: "All things are lawful for me, but not all things are profitable. All things are lawful for me, but I will not be mastered by anything. Food is for the stomach and the stomach is for food, but God will do away with both of them.

---

208 BDAG, 3538.4.b.

209 Kennedy says κοιλία "is probably used as a general term to include all that belongs most essentially to the bodily, fleshly life of man and therefore inevitably perishes" (Kennedy, 462; cf. Robertson, *Paul's Joy in Christ*, 216).

210 That is how those who see Judaizers in verses18 and 19 understand this expression (e.g., Müller, 130-131; O'Brien, 455; TDNT, 3:788).

Yet the body is not for immorality, but for the Lord, and the Lord is for the body" (1 Cor. 6:12-13).

To this is added (καὶ, "and") "whose glory is in their shame" (ἡ δόξα ἐν τῇ αἰσχύνῃ αὐτῶν). Again the absence of the verb makes the expression abrupt and jarring. It is simply, "the glory in the shame of them." Both nouns have definite articles which may be understood as possessive ("whose … their"). The contrast between "glory" (ἡ δόξα) and "shame" (τῇ αἰσχύνῃ) carries a strong sense of irony in it. That which ought to cause them to blush instead prompts them to boasting. That which ought to move them to withdraw in embarrassment instead is the stimulus to a misguided confidence. What they call a "Christian liberty" is in fact an offense to the Christ whose salvation they claim. Their subjective evaluation (ἡ δόξα, "glory") is out of touch with objective reality (τῇ αἰσχύνῃ, "shame").[211] The true believer is promised and rightly anticipates sharing in the Lord's own "glory" at His return, but these folk are headed to a different destination. They have traded the legitimate hope that God "will transform the body of our humble state into conformity with the body of His glory" (v.21) for a libertine lifestyle which they wrongly assess as honoring to Christ. What they see as light is in fact darkness (Isa. 5:20; Mal. 2:17). What they believe is true is in fact false. What they believe to be their "glory" is in fact their "shame." They are morally blind and yet arrogantly demand that it is they who "see"!

The sentence begun in verse 18 now closes with what in English sounds like another relative clause: "who set their minds on earthly things" (οἱ τὰ ἐπίγεια φρονοῦντες). It is, however, a nominative participial clause that has caused translators some angst as they seek to determine precisely its role and to connect it to what precedes. The NIV has simply made it a separate sentence. It defies standard grammatical construction, but is probably best understood as standing in relation to the opening main clause: πολλοὶ … περιπατοῦσιν ("many walk").[212] The adjective "earthly" (τὰ ἐπίγεια) is used as a substantive (thus "things") and is accompanied by the definite

---

211 Alford, 3:185.

212 Kennedy, 462; Sumney, 94.

article. The word is used only seven times in the NT, five of those by Paul and two of those here in Philippians (John 3:12; 1 Cor. 15:40 [2x]; 2 Cor. 5:1; Phil. 2:10; 3:19; James 3:15). He used it in the grand description of the triumphant Christ when he said every knee will bow to Him "of those who are in heaven and on earth [ἐπιγείων] and under the earth" (2:10). It is tucked in the attributive position between the nominative participle (φρονοῦντες, "who set their minds") and its definite article (οἱ)[213], emphasizing the qualitative nature of the thinking under consideration. Both τὰ ἐπίγεια ("earthly things") and ἡ κοιλία ("their belly," ESV, i.e., the lower regions of their body) stand in contrast to the ἐν οὐρανοῖς ("in heaven") in verse 20. The participle is used substantively ("*who* set their minds," emphasis added). The present tense is descriptive of the ongoing nature of their thinking; it has become the "set" of their outlook on and interpretation of life. The verb is by now a familiar one here in Philippians (1:7; 2:2 [2x], 5; 3:15 [2x], 19; 4:2, 10 [2x]). See above under verse 15 for more on this important verb. It is used strategically here in Philippians to depict the attitude which was in Jesus (2:5) and which must likewise be in us (2:2; 3:15). The root of such self-deception and self-destruction is in unenlightened thinking.

Throughout the letter the Apostle stresses the strategic significance of both *what* we think and *how* we think. Here these who believe themselves servants of Christ are in fact too earthly minded to be of any heavenly good. We do well to note the direct connection between the set of our minds (v.19b) and the manner of our "walk" (v.18a). Ideas have consequences. Both what we think and how we reason cannot help but find expression in how we live, the choices we make, the words we speak, the things we value, the goals we pursue, the attitudes with which we act. We need to hear all the more urgently Paul's paradigmatic call: "Have this attitude in yourselves which was also in Christ Jesus" (2:5)! Similarly he used the same verb to exhort the Colossian believers: "Set your minds on things that are above, not on things that are on earth" (Col. 3:2).

---

[213] The definite article may set them apart as a special class of individuals (Alford, 3:185) or it might be possessive ("who set *their* minds").

> **Digging Deeper:**
> 1. What is the appropriate role of weeping in preaching (v.18)? In a pastor's personal ministry to others? In what way can it be abused? How might it be used by God?
> 2. In what ways are you currently struggling against the "god [of your own] appetite" (v.19a)?
> 3. In what way does glorying in shame threaten to enter the church today (v.19b)?

Verse 20 – "For our citizenship is in heaven, from which also we eagerly wait for a Savior, the Lord Jesus Christ;"

Paul now closes out this chapter and the long thread of his thoughts with one more sentence which spans the final two verses of this chapter.[214] The use of γὰρ ("For") signals that Paul is explaining why the Philippian believers should imitate him and others like him (v.17) as opposed to those self-deceived ones over whom he weeps (vv.18-19). Clearly Paul is contrasting "earthly things" (τὰ ἐπίγεια, v.19) and "citizenship ... in heaven" (τὸ πολίτευμα ἐν οὐρανοῖς, v.20), "their" (αὐτῶν, v.19) and "our" (ἡμῶν, v.20), and what one group finds to be "glory" (ἡ δόξα, v.19) over against the hope of conformity with "the body of His glory" (τῷ σώματι τῆς δόξης αὐτοῦ, v.21).

The main assertion of this extended sentence is that "our citizenship is in heaven" (ἡμῶν ... τὸ πολίτευμα ἐν οὐρανοῖς ὑπάρχει). Paul places the plural pronoun (ἡμῶν, "our") emphatically at the beginning of the sentence and in so doing denotes with emphasis the distinction between those described in verses 18 and 19 and those he now addresses.[215] This is the only occur-

---

[214] Because of striking parallels between 2:6-11 and 3:20-21 and because of what some detect as a lyric lilt to these closing lines, some have wondered if these final two verses of chapter 3 with which Paul takes us to a soaring conclusion are not a fragment of some preexisting hymn. The assumption that Paul was incapable of artful expression is uncalled for. O'Brien covers the arguments in favor of the hymn-fragment theory and finds them inadequate (cf. O'Brien, 467-472).

[215] Lightfoot, 169; Sumney, 94-95.

rence of the noun (τὸ πολίτευμα, "citizenship") in the NT. It does echo the note Paul sounded early in the letter when he issued a call concerning how the Philippian believers were to "conduct" (πολιτεύεσθε) themselves (1:27). That verb, cognate to our present noun, is used elsewhere only in Acts 23:1 where it is again in Paul's mouth as he testified to the Jewish ruling Council, "Brethren, I have lived my life [πεπολίτευμαι] with a perfectly good conscience before God up to this day." The verbal form literally means to "live as a citizen."[216] In Hellenistic writings it means "*to conduct oneself as pledged to some law of life*"[217] or to "discharge your obligations as citizens."[218] As for the noun, there is debate as to its precise emphasis. Does it carry a verbal emphasis ("conversation," KJV) or is it more objective, emphasizing the status of those so designated ("citizenship," ESV, NASU, NIV, NRSV)? The "meaning is more likely to be that of 'capital or native city, which keeps the citizens on its registers.'"[219] The noun designates what Spicq calls a "resident community of foreign nationals."[220] That this is the correct understanding of the noun is confirmed by the fact that the "second half of the verse requires a place to be meant here, in order to make sense of the remark 'and from it we await'."[221]

Philippi had been granted the status of "colonia," which raised it to the status of a "mini-Rome,"[222] and thus the citizenry took their privileges and obligations as a matter of pride. As Paul wrote from Rome to Philippi it was a natural word for him to employ. Indeed, while earlier in Philippi he had called upon his Roman citizenship personally and their standing as a Roman "colonia" when the local authorities arrested him (Acts 16:12, 37-38).[223] Perhaps the Apostle played upon this background in his choice

---

216 Friberg, 321.

217 Thayer, 528.

218 BDAG, 6035.3.

219 NIDNTT, 2:804.

220 Spicq, 3:124.

221 NIDNTT, 2:804.

222 Rienecker, 548.

223 Lightfoot, 120.

of the present theme. A sense of obligation and accountability is inherent in the word and thus it perfectly fits the Apostle's need as he exhorts them in the pathway of Christian discipleship. The use of these two cognates serves as an inclusion, framing his discussion of the kind of life discipleship to Jesus requires (Phil. 1:27-3:21). The noun used here in verse 20 was often used in Greek literature generally to denote "a colony of foreigners or relocated veterans."[224] We are a spiritually displaced people—physically residing upon earth, but whose true home and true loyalties are found in heaven from which Christ reigns. We are "fellow citizens with the saints" (Eph. 2:19). But on earth we are "those who reside as aliens" in this world (1 Pet. 1:1). We are "aliens and strangers" (2:11) in a foreign land. The men and women of faith before us "confessed that they were strangers and exiles on the earth" (Heb. 11:13), and so must we.

> **Ministry Maxim**
>
> Our identity and directives arise from realities outside this world, and thus we are forever alien and stranger to that which this world values and demands.

Paul now stands with the Philippians with regard to this citizenship (ἡμῶν, "our"). There were "many" (v.18) in the other group, but the Apostle stands with the band of true disciples of Christ. Again, "in heaven" (ἐν οὐρανοῖς) stands in direct contrast to the focus of the appetites of the others (τὰ ἐπίγεια, "earthly things," v.19). The plural form (as we have here, despite the singular English rendering "heaven") tends to be used when designating "heaven" as a transcendent dwelling place.[225]

Paul's use of the verb ὑπάρχω rather than the far more common ἐστί is worthy of note. The present verb (ὑπάρχει, "is") has the basic connotation of "come into being fr[om] an originating point and so take place."[226] Its only other use in Philippians is strategic in describing the pre-existence of Jesus ("although He existed [ὑπάρχων] in the form of God, did not regard

---

224 BDAG, 6034.

225 Ibid., 5437.2.

226 BDAG, 7525.

equality with God a thing to be grasped," 2:6, see our comments there).[227] What Jesus did in humbling Himself to come and save us arose out of His eternal, preexisting divine nature. What we are called upon to render by way of obedient discipleship here on earth arises from our true identity as citizens of heaven who are in union with Christ the King. The placement of the verb at the end of the clause places emphases upon it and stamps the essence and abiding nature of our identity as arising from and resting in a Kingdom that lies outside of this world. When this world's appetites and allurements call, we remember that we have a preexisting commitment to another realm. The present tense of the verb emphasizes the present reality of such "citizenship." While the fullness of the Kingdom will come only at Christ's return, the reality of our "citizenship" in heaven is a present one. Thus Vincent may say:

> ... those who are in Christ, whose 'life is hid with Christ in God' (Col. iii. 3), for whom 'to live is Christ' (Phil. i. 21), who are 'crucified with Christ' and live their present life by faith in him (Gal. ii. 20), are *now* members of the heavenly commonwealth, and live and act under its laws. Their allegiance is rendered to it. They receive their impulses to action and conduct from it. Their connection with it is the basis of their life ... They are 'fellow-citizens with the saints and of the household of God (Eph. ii. 19). The commonwealth of believers *is* an actual fact on earth ...[228]

---

[227] As will be pointed out in the comments on verses 20 and 21 there are a number of key verbal parallels between 2:6-11 and 3:20-21. Garland (12:249) nicely summarizes them: μορφῇ ("form," 2:6), μορφὴν ("form," 2:7), σύμμορφον ("into conformity with," 3:21); ὑπάρχων ("existed," 2:6), ὑπάρχει ("is," 3:20); σχήματι ("in the likeness," 2:7), μετασχηματίσει ("will transform," 3:21); ἐταπείνωσεν ("humbled," 2:8), ταπεινώσεως ("humble state," 3:21); ἐπουρανίων ("in heaven," 2:10), οὐρανοῖς ("heaven," 3:20); "every knee should bow ... every tongue confess" (2:10-11), "bring everything under his control" (3:21); κύριος Ἰησοῦς Χριστὸς ("Jesus Christ is Lord," 2:11), κύριον Ἰησοῦν Χριστόν ("the Lord Jesus Christ," 3:20); δόξαν ("glory," 2:11), δόξης ("glory," 3:21).

[228] Vincent, ICC, 118-119.

Not only do our ultimate loyalties lie in and our directives arise from citizenship "in heaven" (ἐν οὐρανοῖς), but all our hope is set there as well, for it is heaven "from which also we eagerly await a Savior" (ἐξ οὗ καὶ σωτῆρα ἀπεκδεχόμεθα). The relative pronoun (οὗ, "which") finds its antecedent in (οὐρανοῖς, "heaven").[229] In addition to (καὶ, "also") our citizenship arising out of (ἐξ) heaven, "we eagerly await" (ἀπεκδεχόμεθα) our Savior from that place. In all of Greek literature the verb appears first in the NT and may have been coined by one of the first century believers.[230] It is found eight times in the NT, six of which are from the pen of Paul. In all six the Apostle uses it with regard to the return of Jesus Christ and the fullness of salvation into which He will bring His people at that time (Rom. 8:19, 23, 25; 1 Cor. 1:7; Gal. 5:5; Phil. 3:20). It is here, as always, in the present tense, underscoring the abiding and ongoing nature of the waiting. It is a double compound: ἀπό ("from"), ἐκ ("out of") and δέχομαι ("to receive"). The prepositions in compound "indicate the eager but patient waiting."[231] Burton explains that the first preposition (ἀπό, "from") "intensifies the verb," while the second (ἐκ, "out of") "indicates 'to be receiving from a distance' i.e. 'to be intently awaiting.'"[232] The middle voice views the subject as taking action upon himself—thus again emphasizing the inward nature of the action and the patience involved in the waiting. God's people by faith have always longed and looked for "a better country, that is, a heavenly one" and it is for this very reason that "God is not ashamed to be called their God; for He has prepared a city for them" (Heb. 11:16).

Given our present, earthly realities and the nature of the promises we've been given regarding the future, our hearts wait expectantly for "a

---

229 This despite the fact that οὗ is singular and οὐρανοῖς is plural; and this better than reading οὗ as neuter so as to take it with τὸ πολίτευμα ("citizenship"). See Müller, 133; O'Brien, 461; Robertson, *Grammar*, 714; Silva, 189; Sumney, 95; contra. Martin, 161; Lenski, 862.

230 Hellerman, 223.

231 Rienecker, 559.

232 Cited by Rienecker, 515.

Savior" (σωτῆρα).²³³ It may come as something of a surprise that, outside the Pastoral Epistles (where it is found ten times), Paul uses the noun sparingly—only here and in Ephesians 5:23. The verbal form, however, appears nearly three times as often—though not once here in Philippians. Perhaps Paul used the noun more rarely because of its common use in reference to heathen deities and also of the Roman Caesar. In the latter connotation its use here is perfectly appropriate, for the imagery of "citizenship ... in heaven" necessarily demands an allegiance to "the King of kings" (1 Tim. 6:15). The noun is used extensively in the OT to describe God as our Savior. Thus there may be here another acknowledgement of the deity of Jesus Christ.²³⁴ In the immediate context, Christ as "Savior" of His people most emphatically stands in contrast to the "destruction" (ἀπώλεια, v.19) that will be visited upon those outside His saving rule when He returns.²³⁵ This "Savior" is none other than "the Lord Jesus Christ" (κύριον Ἰησοῦν Χριστόν). This latter phrase stands in apposition to the noun (σωτῆρα, "Savior")—thus further identifying just who is the awaited "Savior." While Paul is not shy about employing the full title, he uses it four times here in Philippians (Phil. 1:2; 2:11; 3:20; 4:23), more than in any other single letter, except 2 Thessalonians. See our comments on 1:2 for the emphasis that stands behind Paul's use of this full title. At the great climax of all history, the return of Christ, "every tongue will confess that Jesus Christ is Lord" (2:11). As subjects of Christ we are to live out the reality of that confession in every aspect of our thinking, speaking, relating, and doing. Being present subjects of Christ's rule we have a jump on that to which every being in heaven and earth will one day subscribe. Thus, while we live now as aliens in a strange world under a foreign ruler, we can live confidently because of the assured end of human history.

---

233 A predicate accusative (Robertson, *Paul's Joy in Christ*, 221). O'Brien says, "The absence of the definite article indicates that σωτήρ is to be understood in a descriptive sense, i.e., pointing to his role or capacity as the Saviour; it is not a title of reference" (462).

234 Fee, 381.

235 Martin, 162.

Verse 21 – "who will transform the body of our humble state into conformity with the body of His glory, by the exertion of the power that He has even to subject all things to Himself."

Paul's "who" (ὅς) modifies "the Lord Jesus Christ" (κύριον Ἰησοῦν Χριστόν) in verse 20. The entirety of verse 21 comprises a relative clause that expounds upon what "the Lord Jesus Christ" (v.20) will do to bring history to its appointed end and His people into the fullness of redemption. In this Paul pictures the return of Christ and the resurrection of believers to the fullness of life and redemption. This is what Paul has yearned for and pursued with single-minded devotion (v.11). It is for him "the goal" and "the prize," "the upward call of God in Christ Jesus" (v.14).

At His return Jesus "will transform" (μετασχηματίσει) us into a state capable of sharing fully in His presence, life and Kingdom. The verb appears five times in the NT, all in Paul's letters (1 Cor. 4:6; 2 Cor. 11:13, 14, 15; Phil. 3:21). The basic connotation of the word is to change the form of something. In the middle voice Paul can use the verb in a negative way to speak of the deceit of false apostles who "disguise" themselves as true apostles (2 Cor. 11:13, 14, 15). That is to say they present themselves as one thing when in fact they are another. He can also use it to make a connection between one thing and another, thus using it to describe his application of the metaphors of servanthood, stewardship and judgment to himself and Apollos (1 Cor. 4:6).[236] But here the basic notion is clearly his intent—Jesus will, at His coming, change the bodies of His followers into a different kind of body.

Though Paul speaks of a reality in which all our bodies share (and thus the plural ἡμῶν, "our") he uses here the singular "body" (τὸ σῶμα), employing the singular as a collective noun which includes all the individuals who together share commonly in "the body of our humble state" (τὸ σῶμα τῆς ταπεινώσεως ἡμῶν). The genitive (τῆς ταπεινώσεως, "of ... humble state") is attributive, functioning as an adjective would, but being

---

236 BDAG, 4859.

"more emphatic"[237] or it "expresses quality ... with more sharpness and distinctness."[238] Identifying the precise intent of the genitive is a matter of some debate. Perhaps, rather than something like "our lowly bodies" (NIV), it is best to see it as asserting that "the body is the means through which our humiliation is experienced"[239] or "the body in which our mortal state of humiliation is clothed."[240] Paul intendeds no slight to the bodies God has created for us in this world. He was neither Stoic nor Gnostic in his views, as if the body is inherently evil and only the spirit is essential and redeemable. The body is God's creation (Psalm 139:13-16). We are made in the image of God (Gen. 1:27). The body is the earthly home of our spirit (1 Cor. 2:11), and, for the redeemed, the dwelling place of God's own Spirit (1 Cor. 6:19). It is the vehicle in which and by which we are to glorify God in this world (1 Cor. 6:20). But it is in this body that we suffer the effects of the fall and the humiliation that sin brings upon us. Paul used the verb form to describe how Christ "humbled" (ἐταπείνωσεν; 2:8) Himself in order to save us. It designates the very glory into which Christ will bring us to share (2:9-11). Paul himself has learned "how to get along with humble means [ταπεινοῦσθαι]" (4:12). Rightly, Paul looks forward, with all God's people, to a time in which all will be "glory."

Those created in the image of God have fallen and it is as embodied souls that we have experienced some measure of the humiliation which sin must bring upon those who embrace it. But this body in which we have experienced the depths of humility will be changed "into conformity with" (σύμμορφον) that of Christ Himself. The grammar is somewhat ambiguous here, leading some early scribe(s) to venture an attempt at smoothing out the intent by adding a clause. But all the manuscripts containing this expansion are late and the shorter reading is clearly the more difficult and therefore the more likely to be original. It may be best to see the adjective

---

237 Wallace, 87.

238 Robertson, *Grammar*, 496.

239 Sumney, 96.

240 Vincent, ICC, 120; cf. Martin, 163; Müller, 134; O'Brien, 464; Robertson, *Paul's Joy in Christ*, 222.

as "in apposition with the previous τὸ σῶμα."[241] The adjective is used only twice in the NT, here and Romans 8:29: "For those whom He foreknew, He also predestined to become conformed [συμμόρφους] to the image of His Son, so that He would be the firstborn among many brethren." That which was determined before time will find its fulfillment finally at the return of Christ. It is a compound word built from σύν ("with") and μορφή ("form"). It is an instance of the associative instrumental case.[242] Paul uses the main root of the word, significantly, to speak of Jesus' fundamental existence ("although He existed in the form [μορφῇ] of God," 2:6) and of His redemptive pursuit ("taking the form [μορφὴν] of a servant," 2:7). The same is found again in compounded form when Paul longs for "being conformed [συμμορφιζόμενος] to His death" (3:10). Paul aimed to be conformed to Christ's death in this life (v.10) so that after death he might be conformed to His eternal, glorious life (v.21; cf. Rom. 6:5). What described Jesus' essential nature, what Jesus voluntarily did, what Paul longed for, God's people will experience at His return. The root of μετασχηματίσει ("transform") is σχῆμα (cf. our English *scheme, schematic*; and cf. "found in appearance [σχήματι] as a man," 2:7), denoting "change of outward fashion."[243] The root of σύμμορφον ("conformity") is μορφή, and denotes "conformity which is inward and thorough, and not merely superficial."[244]

The outcome will be our likeness to "the body of His glory" (τῷ σώματι τῆς δόξης αὐτοῦ). The genitive may be understood to signify "the body in which he is clothed in his glorified state ... the form in which his perfect spiritual being is manifest."[245] The physical body of Jesus was transformed through His resurrection from the dead. It is definite and substantive (Luke 24:39), both recognizable (Luke 24:39; John 21:12) and unrecognizable as the previous body (Luke 24:16; John 20:14; 21:4), capable of being touched (John 20:27) and of consuming food (Luke

---

241 Sumney, 96; Vincent, ICC, 120.

242 Robertson, *Word Pictures*, 4:457.

243 Vincent, ICC, 121; cf. Lenski, 863.

244 Vincent, ICC, 121.

245 Ibid.; cf. Martin, 163; Müller, 134; O'Brien, 464.

24:43), and yet not bound by the limitations of the physical body (John 20:19). "The body of glory will replace the body of humiliation which Christians now bear."[246] Jesus now dwells in glory, the riches of which are the measure by which God meets the present needs of His children (Phil. 4:19). Paul has denounced false believers whose "glory is in their shame" (3:19), but true believers, then and now, are "looking for … the appearing of the glory of our great God and Savior, Christ Jesus" (Tit. 2:13) at which time we will, as Paul tells us in the present passage, come into "conformity with the body of His glory." Indeed, "When Christ, who is our life, is revealed, then you also will be revealed with Him in glory" (Col. 3:4). At the resurrection, what has been "sown a perishable body," will be "raised an imperishable body," what has been "sown in dishonor" will be "raised in glory," what has been "sown in weakness," will be "raised in power," what has been "sown a natural body," will be "raised a spiritual body." Indeed, "If there is a natural body, there is also a spiritual body" (1 Cor. 15:42-44). Paul can confidently say "we will also bear the image of the heavenly" (v.49).

> Now I say this, brethren, that flesh and blood cannot inherit the kingdom of God; nor does the perishable inherit the imperishable. Behold, I tell you a mystery; we will not all sleep, but we will all be changed, in a moment, in the twinkling of an eye, at the last trumpet; for the trumpet will sound, and the dead will be raised imperishable, and we will be changed. For this perishable must put on the imperishable, and this mortal must put on immortality. But when this perishable will have put on the imperishable, and this mortal will have put on immortality, then will come about the saying that is written, 'DEATH IS SWALLOWED UP in victory. (1 Cor. 15:50-54)

All this will come about "by the exertion of the power that He has" (κατὰ τὴν ἐνέργειαν τοῦ δύνασθαι αὐτὸν). The translators understand κατὰ

---

246 TDNT, 7:957.

to indicate the instrument "by" which the transformation takes place. It could perhaps better be rendered "according to," indicating "the norm by which our bodies are transformed"[247] or perhaps by wedding the concepts of norm and reason.[248] The articular infinitive (τοῦ δύνασθαι) is substantive and is thus translated "the power."[249] It may function epexegetically, modifying "the exertion" (τὴν ἐνέργειαν).[250] Vincent suggests a literal translation of: "the energy of His being able."[251] The word for "power" (δύναμαι) expresses what is an innate ability or faculty. The word translated "the exertion" (ἐνέργεια), which is always in the NT used of divine or supernatural working, expresses "power in exercise" or in motion.[252] The former is the power of possibility; the later the power of actuality. At the return of Christ the innate possibilities of God's power will be put in motion to utterly transform the child of God into conformity with the likeness of Jesus' own body.

This is a power which is sufficient "even to subject all things to Himself" (καὶ ὑποτάξαι αὐτῷ τὰ πάντα). Paul's words are a reflection of Psalm 8:6 and perhaps also of Daniel 7:27.[253] The personal pronoun αὐτῷ ("to Himself") is reflexive in meaning.[254] At His return Christ will become the center, the orientation point of "all things." The καί ("even") marks the full extent of the exercise of His power—the transformation will include not only the believer's body, but "all things" (τὰ πάντα), it will bring not only His people into conformity with His body, but will make all things

---

247 Sumney, 96; cf. Vincent, ICC, 122.

248 "… so that 'in accordance with' and 'because of' are merged"(O'Brien, 464).

249 Wallace, 234-235.

250 Ibid., 607.

251 Vincent, *Word Studies*, 3:454.

252 Ibid.

253 See Harmon's extensive treatment of these OT connections (388-389).

254 Wallace, 325.

"subject" to His rule.[255] At Jesus' return "EVERY KNEE WILL BOW, of those who are in heaven and on earth and under the earth, and ... every tongue will confess that Jesus Christ is Lord, to the glory of God the Father" (2:10-11). The word (ὑποτάξαι, "to subject") carries the connotation of authority and the order that results from arranging life under it. Paul uses the word to describe the church in subjection to Christ (Eph. 5:24), believers in subjection to one another (Eph. 5:21), wives to husbands (Eph. 5:24; Col. 3:18; Tit. 2:5), slaves to masters (Tit. 2:9), citizens to civic leaders (Rom. 13:1, 5; Tit. 3:1), women in worship (1 Cor. 14:34), creation to futility (Rom. 8:20), and the spirits of the prophets to the prophets themselves (1 Cor. 14:32). And he uses it, as here, to speak of all things in subjection to Christ (1 Cor. 15:27-28; Eph. 1:22). Paul was willing to lose his whole world (τὰ πάντα, "all things," v.8) so that "all things" might come under the rule of Christ (v.21). We should not miss how important this simple adjective has been throughout this letter where it is used over thirty times. It has frequently been used as a subtle reminder of the unity which the Apostle was seeking throughout the letter (1:1, 4, 7, 8, etc.). The unity of the local church under Christ is a reflection and foretaste of the universal submission of "all things" at the return of Christ. If we, like Paul, direct all our desire and energy toward that day (vv.8, 14) we will dwell together in unity as God's people in the present. Vincent says of this coming subjection, "It is to bring all things within His divine economy; to marshal them under Himself in the new heaven and the new earth in which shall dwell righteousness.

> **Ministry Maxim**
>
> With the same sweep of His mighty arm God will bring His people into their final glory and His enemies into their final horrors.

---

255 "Here is the final word of assurance to the Philippians. In keeping with the same power by which he will transform their present bodies that are suffering at the hand of opposition in Philippi, Christ will likewise subject 'all things' to himself, including the emperor himself and all those who in his name are causing the Philippians to suffer. As Paul has already said in 1:28 and 3:19, their own salvation 'from God' will at the same time result in the 'destruction' of the opposition." (Fee, 384)

Hence the perfected heavenly state as depicted by John is thrown into the figure of a city, an organized commonwealth. The verb is thus in harmony with ver. 20."[256] Paul could "count all things [πάντα] loss" (3:8) in the present in order that he might gain Christ; for in the end, when Christ returns, "all things" [τὰ πάντα] will be arranged under His Lordship and available once again to His children, this time able to enjoy them in a holy and healthy way and in fullest fellowship with their Lord.

> **Digging Deeper:**
> 1. How does one practically and actively bring heavenly citizenship to bear on earthly realities? (v.20a)
> 2. In what way does the promise of a transformed body offer you hope? (v.21a)
> 3. If "conformity with the body of [Jesus'] glory" is your destiny as a child of God, what does it demand of your focus right now? (v.21b)

---

256 Vincent, *Word Studies*, 3:454.

PHILIPPIANS 4

Verse 1 – "Therefore, my beloved brethren whom I long *to see*, my joy and crown, in this way stand firm in the Lord, my beloved."

As the new chapter begins, its exhortations rest upon what has gone before in chapter 3. Ὥστε ("Therefore") marks the continuation of the thought as Paul draws logical implications from what has already been said. But at the same time he turns a corner and begins the move that will eventually bring the epistle to a close. This continuation/transition has led to a great deal of debate about where to make a divide in the text. The exhortation he is about to issue rests upon the realities of spiritual defection (3:17-19) and glorious promise (3:20-21).

For the fifth of seven times in this letter Paul addresses them as "brethren" (ἀδελφοί; 1:12; 3:1, 13, 17; 4:1, 8, 21). Those whom he has just discussed apparently counted themselves within the circle of the church, but Paul marked them as "enemies of the cross, whose end is destruction" (3:18-19). Paul's attention now falls upon them, whose "citizenship is in heaven" (3:20) and who with him await the coming of the Lord Jesus (v.21). With them he is bound together in the family of God (μου, "my"). They are, more than that, marked out in four distinctive ways, set before us in two pairs, held together in each instance by καὶ ("and"). The first two are adjectives qualifying "brethren" (ἀδελφοί).

They are, first of all, "beloved" (ἀγαπητοί). Paul used the same expression in 2:12 where he was making a major transition away from the exalted celebration of Jesus (2:6-11) and into more direct applicational comments. The expression probably functions similarly here, as Paul has in similar fashion been caught up into the glories of Christ (3:20-21) and now transitions to make application of those doxological truths. Here he uses the word twice, also affixing it as the final word of the sentence and thus laying even more emphasis upon it. Paul is laying on the love and laying bare his heart as he calls upon them for a united stand in the Lord.

In addition (καὶ, "and") they are, Paul confesses, those for whom "I long" (ἐπιπόθητοι). The adjective captures a verbal concept and thus the translators have added *to see*. The word occurs only here in the NT, though the verbal cognate has already been used twice in this letter: "For God is my witness, how I long for [ἐπιποθῶ] you all with the affection of Christ Jesus" (1:8) and Epaphroditus "was longing for [ἐπιποθῶν] you all and was distressed because you had heard that he was sick" (2:26). The adjective clearly designates one who is "very dear" and thus "yearned for," "longed for."[1] Paul and his compatriot find their heart-strings entangled with the welfare of their fellow believers in Philippi.

Now Paul turns to the second pair of descriptors, transitioning to the use of nouns. Whereas the adjectives qualified ἀδελφοί ("brethren") this pair of nouns stands in apposition to it. They are the Apostle's "joy" (χαρά). The theme of joy is a rich vein running through the entire letter to the Philippians (χαίρω: 1:18 [2x], 2:17, 18, 28; 3:1; 4:4 [2x], 10; συγχαίρω: 2:17, 18; χαρά: 1:4, 25; 2:2, 29; 4:1). Paul here objectifies all he is after in this regard and makes them the cause for celebration in his life and ministry.

Finally, Paul adds (καὶ, "and") that they are his "crown" (στέφανός). Of the twenty-five times the word is used in the NT, only four are found in Paul's writings (1 Cor. 9:25; Phil. 4:1; 1 Thess. 2:19; 2 Tim. 4:8), though see the related verb in 2 Timothy 2:5 (στεφανόω; "is not crowned," ESV). The noun designated the laurel wreath placed upon the head of the victor

---

1   Friberg, 166.

in the athletic games of Greece. Throughout the NT the noun is coupled with genitive nouns to describe the reward anticipated by faithful believers. We read of the "crown of exultation" (1 Thess. 2:19), the "crown of life" (James 1:12; Rev. 2:10), the "crown of glory" (1 Peter 5:4), a "crown of twelve stars" (Rev. 12:1), and a "crown of righteousness" (2 Tim. 4:8). Here the Philippian "brethren" are viewed as the very crown itself. They stand as the sign of Paul's victorious completion of the ministry handed to him by Christ. If they continue in faith, says Paul, "in the day of Christ I will have reason to glory because I did not run in vain nor toil in vain" (2:16).[2] And again, for the second time, Paul marks this as deeply personal (μου, "my").

Having identified the Philippian believers in such overflowing ways, Paul now issues his command: "stand firm" (στήκετε). The present imperative calls for an ongoing, unceasing action. Paul already used the verb in the indicative to urge them to live "in a manner worthy of the gospel of Christ, so that whether I come and see you or remain absent, I will hear of you that you are standing firm [στήκετε] in one spirit, with one mind striving together for the faith of the gospel" (1:27). Paul issued the same command to the believers in Corinth (1 Cor. 16:13), Galatia (Gal. 5:1) and Thessalonica (2 Thess. 2:15; cf. 1 Thess. 3:8). It is a call "to be firmly committed in conviction or belief."[3]

Paul's metaphors are being stretched a bit, for his commitment to "press on" (3:12a, 14a) and to be ever "reaching forward" (3:13b) have given way to the call to "stand firm" (4:1). While the strict categories of the metaphors may be strained, the truth behind them is not. Part of standing firm is, in a gospel-defined lifestyle, to be ever moving forward in pursuit of Christ. Indeed, this is what it means to "keep living by that same standard to which we have attained" (3:16). What we have "attained" (by continuously pressing on and "reaching forward") is that in which we now "stand firm."

---

2   Müller, 137.

3   BDAG, 6823.

This stand is to be taken "in the Lord" (ἐν κυρίῳ). By "the Lord" (κυρίῳ) Paul uses shorthand for the full title with which he opened the letter (1:2) and which he just employed in his previous sentence: "the Lord Jesus Christ" (κύριον Ἰησοῦν Χριστόν, v.20). And it echoes that cry which will arise from every creature in all creation: "Jesus Christ is Lord" (2:11). The phrase ἐν κυρίῳ ("in the Lord") is found more than forty-five times in Paul (nine of them here in Philippians), and only elsewhere in the NT in Revelation 14:13. The preposition

> **Ministry Maxim**
>
> The gospel frees us not only to love God, but to deeply and personally love His people.

(ἐν, "in") points to the sphere of the activity. They are to stand "in the Lord" in that they steadfastly hold to all the truth and grace which is found in the Lord. Already they have become confident "in the Lord" (1:14; cf. 1:26), Paul hopes "in the Lord" to send Timothy (2:19), he trusts "in the Lord" that he himself will be able to soon visit (2:24), the Philippians are to receive Epaphroditus "in the Lord" (2:29), they are to rejoice "in the Lord" (3:1; 4:4) even as Paul did himself (4:10), and they are to live in harmony "in the Lord" (4:2). And it is here they are to take their stand (4:1). He will tell them "my God will supply all your needs according to His riches in glory in Christ Jesus" (4:19) and thus they should take their stand immovable in Christ. Thus Paul can testify "I can do all things through Him who strengthens me" (4:13). Christ is the object of all the believer's thinking (2:5; 4:2) and choices (2:12-16), the context of all his relationships (2:29), the fount of all his joy (3:1; 44, 10) and hope (2:19; 3:20-21), the source of all his encouragement (2:1) and strength (4:19), the locus of all his desire (3:8), the origin of all his righteousness (3:9), the garrison of all his security (4:7), the goal of all his energies (3:8), and the measure of all his possibilities (4:13). How very different is the essence of their life than that of those just enumerated (3:19)! It is "in Christ Jesus" that they find their standing as "saints" (1:1; 4:21) and it is "in the Lord" which they are now to stand firm and resolute, as one body in Christ.

This "stand" which they are to take and maintain is measured by something (οὕτως, "thus"). The adverb itself can be used either to point to that which came before or to that which will follow.[4] It is repeated from 3:17 and signals that it is 3:17-21 that form the logical basis for the present exhortation to "stand firm." It would apply most directly to the descriptors Paul has used of them: as citizens of the heavenly kingdom (3:20), as those awaiting the transformation of resurrection at Christ's return (3:21), as those loved and longed after, as those who are "my joy and crown," as those who comprise the family of God ("brothers," 4:1). And "thus" (οὕτως) they are to stand firm in the Lord. Without denying this connection, it may also serve to prepare for the exhortation of verses 2 and 3. Thus verse 1 serves as a transitional verse, successfully wrapping up what has been said to this point and also preparing to launch into what is just ahead. As Silva says, "… one should not assume, with regard to 4:1 as a whole, that a backward and a forward reference are mutually exclusive."[5] Indeed, he has pointed out the verbal connections that make this highly probable: πολιτεύομαι ("conduct," 1:27)/πολίτευμα ("citizenship, 3:20), στήκω ("stand," 1:27; 4:1), and συναθλέω ("striving together," 1:27; "have shared my struggle," 4:3).[6] Clearly Paul is revisiting his original concerns and applying them more specifically to the immediate threats to the welfare of the congregation. In this, 4:1 serves as a Janus, looking both backward and forward in the Apostle's presentation of his concerns.

Paul repeats "beloved" (ἀγαπητοί) for the second time in this sentence, emphasizing again the passionate and affectionate nature of his appeal.

> **Digging Deeper:**
> 1. Why do you think Paul piled up the expressions of personal affection as he called the Philippians to "stand firm" in the faith?
> 2. At this moment what specific pressures most challenge you with regard to standing firm in your faith?

---

4   Ibid., 5445.

5   Silva, 186.

6   Ibid.

Verse 2 – "I urge Euodia and I urge Syntyche to live in harmony in the Lord."

For all the nuanced piling up of relational terms in verse 1, the Apostle now becomes blunt and pointed. Dropping all subtlety and finesse Paul with abruptness now simply names names—two women who are presumably a part of the church in Philippi. Paul was not unwilling to name names if need be to warn a believer or church of potential harm (e.g., 1 Tim. 1:20; 2 Tim. 2:17; 4:12), but he did not in his letters frequently call out specific individuals for reproof (cf. Col. 4:17). Both "Euodia" (Εὐοδίαν) and "Syntyche" (Συντύχην) are feminine proper nouns, common female names in the first century as numerous inscriptions bear out. The former means "prosperous journey"[7] while the latter means something like "pleasant acquaintance" or "good luck."[8] Neither is mentioned elsewhere in Scripture and we do not know the precise nature of their role among the Philippian believers, their relationship to one another, nor how their issues may have been affecting the overall health of the church there.[9] Given the frequent efforts Paul has made throughout the letter to make for unity among the Philippian believers and given the exhortation he now makes specifically to these two we may safely surmise that

---

7 Thayer, 260.

8 Robertson, *Word Pictures*, 4:458; cf. Vincent, *Word Studies*, 3:455. There are aural similarities between the proper name Εὐοδίαν (Euodia, v.2) and the noun εὐωδίας ("fragrant," v.18). Did Paul intentionally select the word in verse 18 to make a subtle point to Euodia, discretely urging her to make sure that she resolves the present dispute with her sister in Christ so as to become once again a sweet aroma *to* Christ and *of* Christ to those around her? See the comments below on verse 18.

9 In the absence of further information many speculative suggestions have been made in an attempt to further identify these two women. Some suggest they were not only significant servants in the ministry of the gospel in Philippi, but were office holders (deaconesses?) within the church. Some have made one or the other to be Lydia who played an important role in the founding of the church in Philippi (Acts 16:14-15). Some have thought these two to be the ringleaders in a divide between Philippian Christians of a Hebraic mindset and those of a Hellenistic mindset. Some have found here an opportunity to wax eloquent on the unusual and prominent place women held in Macedonian society in general. All these suggestions go well beyond the evidence available to us in the Biblical text, which is limited to verses 2 and 3 of this chapter of Philippians.

in some way or another these two women had become at odds with one another. Perhaps their personal schism was threatening to spill over into the larger body of believers, thus threatening the oneness of the church. Too often what begins as an interpersonal matter becomes a controversy for the whole church.

Paul appears to be attempting to head off any advance of the conflict with his twice-repeated exhortation (παρακαλῶ, "I urge"). Just why Paul repeats the verb twice when he could have easily used it just once and still made it apply to both women is unclear. It may have been that he did not want either name to stand closer nor further from the verb, thereby implying that one or the other needed the exhortation more than the other. By repeating it in immediate connection with each name he makes them equally responsible for the issues between them and for the actions necessary to see that breech closed and the relationship healed. The verb "I urge" (παρακαλῶ) is a compound, built from the verb καλέω ("to call") and the prepositional prefix παρά ("beside"). The bare combination might mean "to call alongside." It appears in all of the Apostle's letters (except Galatians). It has a range of meaning that can swing from the softer sense of "comfort" to the sharper edge of "exhort." It is translated variously according to context by words such as "appeal" (Philem. 9, 10), "comfort" (2 Cor. 1:4, 6), "encourage" (1 Cor. 16:12), "exhort" (1 Cor. 1:10), "implore" (2 Cor. 12:8), and "urge" (Rom. 12:1). The cognate noun, in the masculine singular form, became a title for the Holy Spirit (John 14:16, 26; 15:26; 16:7) and the Lord Jesus Christ (1 John 2:1).

> **Ministry Maxim**
> Personal conflict has corporate consequences.

Paul urges these two women "to live in harmony" (τὸ αὐτὸ φρονεῖν). The verb is by now familiar as one of Paul's favorite in this letter (1:7; 2:2 [2x], 5; 3:15 [2x], 19; 4:2, 10 [2x]), used here more than in any other NT book. Paul has employed it throughout the letter to demonstrate the significant role of the mind in the outworking of the Christian life. The verb means "to have an opinion with regard to someth[ing]"; to "think, form/hold an opinion" or to "judge."[10] Thus it seems to speak not merely of individual thoughts, but of "a certain way of looking at things, thus 'mindset.'"[11] The translation "to live" lays the emphasis not upon the interior foundation of thinking to which Paul points, but to the active unfolding of a pattern of behavior. While the behavioral is not out of the picture, the emphasis rests upon the role of one's mind in achieving that pattern of life. The present tense looks for a settled, ongoing state of mind and outlook of life.

This is a clear echo of Paul's more general exhortation to the entire church in Philippi to be "of the same mind" (τὸ αὐτὸ φρονῆτε, 2:2). What was intended for all is now made specific to two from among them. The articular personal pronoun (τὸ αὐτὸ) is found in both passages and in each rendered "the same." The singular form emphasizes the singularity and commonality of that which they are thus to think together. Taken at face value it may sound like an impossible proposition: two people who are at odds with one another are now ordered to think the same thing as one another. The nature of human conflict is such that by definition they do not see the issues in the same light or from the same angle; neither wishes to yield to the other. How then are they to suddenly think the same thing? Is one to simply give up what they think and adopt the mindset of the other?

The answer is found in how Paul handled the original, more generally stated exhortation in chapter 2. The same verb was repeated in 2:5 in demanding, "Have this attitude [φρονεῖτε] in yourselves which was also in Christ Jesus." That mindset was unfolded more fully in 2:6-11. The "mind" or "attitude" they each possess is to be set to that which Christ possessed. Christ is the tuning fork and as each mind is set to His thinking, they will together have "the same mind." In this way the pattern of reconciliation is found not in conceding to the other the rightness of their thinking, but in each confessing the distance of their own thinking from that of Christ, then dropping their thoughts to embrace His way of reasoning.

---

10 BDAG, 7819.

11 Fee, 185.

In this way, as each deals personally with Christ, they find themselves meeting in unity in Christ, which is precisely what he demands here. This must take place and can only take place "in the Lord" (ἐν κυρίῳ). It is only by living union with Christ Himself and by the indwelling graces of His life expressed through us by His Spirit that unity can be reclaimed where division has erupted. The repetition from the preceding sentence should not be lost on us. Part of standing firm "in the Lord" (ἐν κυρίῳ, v.1) is found in living in harmony "in the Lord" (ἐν κυρίῳ).

Verse 3 – "Indeed, true companion, I ask you also to help these women who have shared my struggle in *the cause of* the gospel, together with Clement also and the rest of my fellow workers, whose names are in the book of life."

Before moving on (vv.4ff) the Apostle wishes to underscore the exhortation just made (v.2). He signals this by the use of ναὶ ("Indeed") which is used "in emphatic repetition of one's own statement."[12] Having named the two individuals at the heart of the controversy (v.2), Paul now calls upon a third individual to aid them in working out their differences. But just who this individual is remains something of a mystery. The designation σύζυγε ("true companion") has been an enigma that has baffled commentators throughout church history. Some have read it as a proper name, an otherwise unknown "Syzygos," but, since no evidence has been found of its being used as a personal name, it seems best to regard it as a descriptive noun. It is no surprise that attempts at identifying this individual have ranged far and wide.[13] The reality is that whether it is viewed as a proper name or a descriptive appellative the outcome is the same; we know nothing more about this individual than we learn here. The form of the word is masculine, so we can safely assume it refers to a male, but beyond that it is impossible now to identify the person Paul has in mind.

---

12 BDAG, 5038.c.
13 For various options see for example Lenski, 860-870 and Müller, 138.

It would seem that it is his role that is most important for us to note, not his personal identity.

Presumably he was someone Paul considered to be in a position of sufficient influence "to help" (συλλαμβάνου) bring a resolution to the problem between these two women and reconciliation to their relationship, and perhaps also to the larger congregation-wide division that may have attended their issues with one another. The word most literally means "yolk-fellow."[14] Thus tracing out the imagery we can picture this individual as one who similarly serves the gospel-cause, and is thus yoked commonly with the Apostle Paul as a servant of Christ. If it is an actual name Paul probably plays off its meaning much as he does with Onesimus (Philemon 10).[15] If it is simply a descriptive moniker it was chosen for the same reason.

In this venture he is "true" (γνήσιε). The word originally referred to one born in wedlock and thus as being legitimate.[16] It is used only four times in the NT, all by Paul. Twice he uses it, once each in reference to Timothy (1 Tim. 1:2) and Titus (Titus 1:4) as his "true child" in the faith. In 2 Corinthians 8:8 it describes a "genuine" love. One might say this individual was "born for this" role, or, technically, "reborn for this role." The addition of this qualifying adjective makes it doubtful that σύζυγε was intended as a proper noun.[17]

In addition (καὶ, "also") to his direct appeal to the Euodia and Syntyche (v.2), Paul now makes a personal (σέ, "you") and direct appeal (ρωτῶ, "I ask") for help in resolving whatever differences may exist between the two of them. The combination of καὶ σέ ("you also") means that his actions will be in addition to those of Euodia and Syntyche.[18] Sometimes conflict comes to the place that a third party is necessary to help two people reach the resolution they desire. The verb (ρωτῶ, "I ask") is used frequently

---

14 BDAG, 6925.

15 See the author's *Colossians and Philemon for Pastors*, 382-383.

16 BDAG, 1656.1.

17 Friberg, 360.

18 O'Brien, 479-480.

throughout the Gospels, but only four times by the Apostle Paul, and all the others are in his communication with the church in Thessalonica (1 Thess. 4:1; 5:12; 2 Thess. 2:1), meaning he restricted his use to the churches in Macedonia. Given the intimate and personal nature of Paul's relationship to both churches it may signal a special depth of relationship and a concerted expression of respect even while making a request. It "may be a polite term implying that both writer and addressee are equals."[19] Note that in 1 Thessalonians 4:1 it is, as here, found in conjunction with the verb παρακαλέω ("I urge," v.2).

The request is "to help" (συλλαμβάνου). The verb is a compound comprised of σύν ("with") and λαμβάνω ("to take/grasp") and yields a literal sense of "take hold of together."[20] The word can be used both literally (e.g., Luke 1:24, 31, 36) and figuratively (James 1:15) to describe conception. It is tempting to see it in this light here, given the literal sense of the adjective γνήσιε ("true"). But given that the adjective is used metaphorically and clearly the verb is as well, it is best to look elsewhere for the sense of the action called for here. In the middle, as it is here, it means to seize for oneself, either in a hostile way (Acts 26:21), or, as here, in the sense of "assist" or "help."[21]

> **Ministry Maxim**
>
> Sometimes it takes more than four hands to fix a relationship.

It is used thus of Simon's call for help to preserve the great catch of fish the Lord enabled (Luke 5:7, 9). They needed more hands to be laid to the nets to bring in the haul. So too these ladies needed aid from their "yoke-fellow" in resolving their differences and reconciling their relationship. Paul pictures this man joining hands with Euodia and Syntyche as they take up Paul's exhortation and seek to implement it in their relationship with one another. The assistance is to be given to "them" (αὐταῖς; feminine plural), but it may be that Paul pictures this "true companion" joining hands with these two ladies in a picture of solidarity and assistance. Silva says, "The

---

19 Ibid., 479.
20 BDAG, 6936.4.
21 Thayer, 595.

striking emphasis of this letter on corporate responsibility reaches a dramatic high point in the exhortation of verse 3. The discord between Euodia and Syntyche cannot be viewed by the congregant as a personal matter. These courageous women ... needed the assistance of the whole church to resolve their differences."[22]

These are women "who have shared my struggle *in the cause of* the gospel" (αἵτινες ἐν τῷ εὐαγγελίῳ συνήθλησάν μοι). The feminine plural form of the personal pronoun (αἵτινες, "who") makes it clear Paul is still referring to Euodia and Syntyche. It may serve as an expression of cause ("*since* they have contended at my side," NIV, emphasis added; cf. also NLT, NRSV).[23] The translators have added "in the cause of." The simple expression in the Greek is "in the gospel" (ἐν τῷ εὐαγγελίῳ), but it is an example of metonymy which uses the simple to describe the more complex, in this case "the gospel" standing for all the activity that attends and advances it.[24] That activity is a "struggle" (συνήθλησάν). And that struggle is uniquely and especially, though not exclusively, Paul's own (μοι, "my") as an apostle. The verb sets before us another compound made of up of a σύν– prefix. It is constructed from σύν ("with") and ἀθλέω ("to strive/compete" as in an athletic context, used in the NT only twice, both in 2 Tim. 2:5). The imagery here may be military, rather than athletic, in which case there may be an emphasis here on the previous bravery demonstrated by Euodia and Syntyche.[25] The compound verb is used only here and in Philippians 1:27, another signal Paul is wrapping up a point he has been striving to make since the first chapter. There he exhorts the Philippians to so live in harmony with one another that they are "with one mind striving together [συναθλοῦντες] for the faith of the gospel." He is in the present context using the same verb to remind all who hear these words of the sacrificial and significant role these two women have played in the establishment and advancement of the gospel in Philippi.

---

22 Silva, 193.
23 Robertson, *Grammar*, 727-728; cf. O'Brien, 481.
24 NET Bible.
25 BDAG, 7010.

This, Paul can testify, they have previously done "with me" (μοι). Having once locked arms with Paul in the cause of the gospel he now calls upon them—and those with them—to do so once again with one another. We recall that when Paul and his ministry companions first arrived in Philippi over a decade before, they found the Jewish place of prayer beside a river and "we sat down and began speaking to the women who had assembled" (Acts 16:13). Lydia is mentioned as a prominent member of that group (v.14), but whether these two women were also present from the beginning is not known. If not from the first day, certainly at some point in the church's distant past these two came to faith in Christ and put that faith into action by serving the cause of the gospel among their fellow believers and fellow citizens of Philippi.

Their struggle has not only been in fellowship with the great Apostle, but with other servants of Christ as well.[26] It was, firstly, "with Clement also" (μετὰ καὶ Κλήμεντος). This "Clement" is mentioned only here in the NT, but was obviously well known to both Paul and the Philippian believers. Origen identified him as the Clement who became the third bishop of Rome and whose name appears as the author of a later letter to Corinthian believers. This, however, cannot be proven and it is unnecessary for the understanding of the present passage. He was clearly a tested and trusted gospel partner with Paul and the other believers, the mention of whose name here carried impact with the believers in Philippi.

The common struggle was also (καὶ, "and") with "the rest of my fellow workers" (τῶν λοιπῶν συνεργῶν μου). In calling them "fellow workers" (συνεργῶν) Paul uses the fourth σύν- compound in this verse. Paul continues to consistently drive home the theme of unity. The noun is one Paul uses twelve times in his letters (elsewhere only in 3 John 8). He has already used it in this letter to describe Epaphroditus (Phil. 2:25; see the comments there for more on the noun). He uses it elsewhere also of Prisca and Aquila (Rom. 16:3), Urbanus (16:9), Timothy (16:21; 1 Thess. 3:2), Titus (2 Cor. 8:23), Philemon (Philem. v.1), Mark, Aristarchus, Demas,

---

26 Lightfoot connected "with Clement also and the rest of my fellow workers" to "help these women," rather than "who have shared my struggle," but this seems to work against the natural construction of the sentence, as most commentators contend.

and Luke (v.24). He also uses it to describe himself and the Corinthian believers as co-workers with God (1 Cor. 3:9). Here they are seen as joining their labors to those of the Apostle (μου, "my"). They labor side-by-side with Paul. They each are "workers" and together they are "fellow workers" (συνεργῶν). By referring to "the rest" (λοιπῶν), Paul makes the noun applicable not only to these individuals, but also to Clement, Euodia and Syntyche.

All of these are those "whose names are in the book of life" (ὧν τὰ ὀνόματα ἐν βίβλῳ ζωῆς). The relative pronoun (ὧν, "whose") is masculine plural in form and includes Clement and the other "fellow workers" just mentioned, but may well also include Euodia and Syntyche.[27] Not all their names made it into Paul's letter, but they were all recorded "in the book of life" (ἐν βίβλῳ ζωῆς).[28] We may not know their names, but God does. Early in the Scriptural revelation reference is made to a "book" that God keeps (Exod. 32:32). David specifically calls it "the book of life" (Psalm 69:28). The prophets continued the imagery (Isa. 4:3; Ezek. 13:9; Dan. 12:1). Jesus spoke of those whose "names are recorded in heaven" (Luke 10:20; cf. Heb. 12:23). It is Revelation, however, that speaks most frequently of the "book of life" (Rev. 3:5; 13:8; 17:8; 20:12, 15; 21:27). In this way Paul speaks of these individuals as not only sharing his labors in the Lord, but also, and more essentially, the life he has in the Lord. They labor together because they live together! In an earlier connection between this life and his labors, Paul said, "But if I am to live on in the flesh, this will mean fruitful labor for me; and I do not know which to choose" (1:22). Paul has already tasted of that life, for "to live is Christ" (1:21). But he cast his vote for physical death, if it would mean life more immediately in Christ's presence (1:23). Note the order: labor growing out of new life. It is never laboring ones way into life, but by the mercies of God coming into this life and then, from the font of life bubbling up within, laboring in order that others might know this life as well. He speaks thus of all these as the true people of God who, despite their

---

27 O'Brien, 482; Sumney, 101.

28 Vincent, ICC, 132.

differences, are true partakers of life, as opposed to those "whose end is destruction" (3:19).

> **Digging Deeper:**
> 1. How have you seen personal conflict spill over to affect the broader congregation? (v.2)
> 2. What does this letter teach you about how to help, should you be called upon to serve as an intermediary between divided parties? (v.3)

**Verse 4 – "Rejoice in the Lord always;
again I will say, rejoice!"**

Paul moves from intensely personal exhortations (vv.2-3) to ones more generally directed to all believers in the Philippian church (vv.4-9). Seven commands (vv.4-9) come at us in rapid fire, staccato fashion, in short sentences which heighten the rhetorical effect. In so doing Paul picks up the pace of the epistle and whisks the readers forward toward more pleasant topics upon which all believers ought to dwell. These largely positive commands nicely balance the more direct and difficult orders for unity between Euodia and Syntyche.

The Apostle orders the faithful to "Rejoice" (Χαίρετε). As a present imperative it demands action that is repeated, ongoing, and habitual. Joy is to become the fabric of their lives, together and individually. The second plural form is inclusive of all who make up the church in Philippi. But this is not news, he has already issued this command (3:1) and joy has been a vein of gold running throughout the letter (χαίρω: 1:18 [2x]; 2:17, 18, 28; 3:1; 4:4 [2x], 10; συγχαίρω: 2:17, 18; χαρά: 1:4, 25; 2:2, 29; 4:1). Nor should we lose sight of the fact that the one writing does so from prison (1:7, 13). He is a man whose case is still pending and for whom things could turn in the direction of death (1:21-22). The one who commands joy is also one who has suffered deeply (2 Cor. 11:23-29). He who writes is one over whom the Lord spoke these portentous words at his conversion: "I will show him how much he must suffer for My name's sake" (Acts 9:16). These Philippian believers had first-hand knowledge of Paul as a prisoner and some among them had heard him sing his songs of joy in night (Acts 16:25). Given that joy is set before us here as an imperative, we realize that what he commands is more than mere emotion. It surely includes emotion, but only secondarily. It is a willful and deliberate outlook upon oneself, one's circumstances and relationships, and one's purpose. This is joy that can be known and practiced in the midst of "conflict" (1:28; 4:2-3) and suffering (1:29), and while living "in the midst of a crooked and perverse generation" (2:15).

It is only "in the Lord" (ἐν κυρίῳ) that such a command can be fulfilled. The preposition expresses the sphere (ἐν) "in" which the joy is to be found. Indeed, it is only "in the Lord" that such rejoicing can take place. Just as they are to "stand firm" (v.1) and "live in harmony" (v.2) "in the Lord," so now they are to "Rejoice" in union with Him.

This rejoicing is to take place "always" (πάντοτε). Paul has already used the adverb to remind them that he gives thanks for them "always" (1:4), that he will "always" honor Christ in his body (1:20), and they have "always" obeyed in the past (2:12). So there will never be a time that rejoicing is inappropriate, out of place, uncalled for, or unfitting. If in doubt, rejoice! It is ever in style and always in vogue (cf. 1 Thess. 5:16). Matthew Henry was right to say, "It is our duty and privilege to rejoice in God, and to rejoice in him always; at all times, in all conditions; even when we suffer for him, or are afflicted by him. We must not think the worse of him or of his ways for the hardships we meet with in his service. There is enough in God to furnish us with matter of joy in the worst circumstance on earth."[29] The consolations of grace are always sufficient to overwhelm whatever sorrows the world may cast upon us. It is our duty to dwell upon them (v.8) until "the God of peace" (v.9)

> **Ministry Maxim**
>
> Joy is never out of reach for one brought into living union with the Lord of all things.

---

29 Henry, 2328.

restores "the peace of God" (v.7) and joy returns. Invariably, though sometimes more slowly that I wish, when I usher God and His mercies back to the center of my thoughts and settle Him once again upon the throne of my will, soon enough my emotions catch up and join the party.

To underscore and reinforce the imperative, the Apostle repeats himself. Rejoicing is so fundamental to a Christ-follower's existence that Paul will ever and always make this his command to the believers. Note the future tense of the introduction of the repetition: "I will say" (ἐρῶ). There isn't going to be a time or a set of circumstances in which his apostolic orders will ever change. It is "As if he had considered all the possibilities of sorrow."[30] He says it here "again" (πάλιν), and he will ever and always order it again and again. The second occurrence of the command to "rejoice" (χαίρετε) emphatically underscores and emphasizes the urgency of the need and appropriateness for joy. There is in these commands an echo of what we hear so often throughout the Psalms (e.g., Psa. 32:11; 34:1-2; 37:4; 63:5; 94:19; 104:34).

We do well to remind ourselves again that the imperative is laid down in the plural form: "Rejoice" (Χαίρετε). This is a call not only to personal rejoicing, but to personal rejoicing that becomes united, corporate rejoicing. This lays bare the notion that when one is feeling too low because of some sorrow or hardship, that abstaining from corporate worship may be justified. Nay, rather it is all the more necessary and needful. For the obedience of the larger body of Christ—worshiping in the fullness of the His strength—may lift the weakened, weary one to a plane of joy unattainable on their own and unknowable if they sever themselves from the corporate worship of the local assembly of God's people.

Verse 5 – "Let your gentle *spirit* be known to all men. The Lord is near."

The third of the seven commands is again bluntly stated. The imperative is to "Let ... be known" (γνωσθήτω). The aorist imperative form calls

---

30 Vincent, ICC, 133.

for action that is urgent and that must be immediately undertaken. It is the only one of the seven imperatives (vv.4-9) which is not in the present tense. That fact underscores even further the urgency of the present command. The verb is used five other times in the letter (1:12; 2:19, 22; 3:10; 4:8), but this is the first and only time it appears as an imperative. It, and its kindred verb in verse 6, stand alone among the seven being in the third person singular, the others being in the second person plural. Some things must be made known to men (v.5) and some should be made known only to God (v.6). The English translation may sound like it is merely granting permission ("Let ... be known"), but the "Greek is stronger than a mere option, engaging the volition and placing a requirement on the individual."[31]

It is "your gentle *spirit*" (τὸ ἐπιεικὲς ὑμῶν) which is to "be known." By active obedience they will release, as it were, the "gentle *spirit*" which they possess as individuals and as a fellowship in Christ. The adjective appears only five times in the NT (Phil. 4:5; 1 Tim. 3:3; Tit. 3:2; James 3:17; 1 Pet. 2:18). It comes from εἰκός (what is reasonable) and means "equitable, fair, mild, gentle."[32] It denotes one who does not insist "on every right of letter of law or custom" and thus describes that which is "yielding, gentle, kind, courteous, tolerant." [33] Spicq says it combines the ideas of "moderation and measure" as well as "goodness, courtesy, generosity" and suggests a translation here of "friendly equilibrium."[34] "It is," says Robertson, "graciousness with strength and poise of character. It is the opposite of obstinacy. The word is not negative restraint simply, but positive giving up

> **Ministry Maxim**
>
> Demanding our rights may do more damage to the gospel than persecution from our enemies.

---

31 Wallace, 486.

32 Thayer, 238.

33 BDAG, 2950.

34 Spicq, 2:38.

to the reasonable desires of others. It is the mildness of disposition that leads one to be fair and to go beyond the letter of the law."[35] It "was used for a considerate, thoughtful attitude in legal relationships which was prepared to mitigate the rigours of justice, with its laws and claims, in contrast to the attitude which demands that rights, including one's own, should be upheld at all costs."[36] The presence of the definite article substantivizes the abstract quality[37] which the translators have sought to represent by adding "spirit." Other English translations opt for renderings such as "reasonableness" (ESV), "gentleness" (NET, NIV, NKJV, NRSV), "forbearance" (RSV) or the like. Essentially we have a return, then, to what Paul so fundamentally called the Philippians to in 2:3-4: "Do nothing from selfishness or empty conceit, but with humility of mind regard one another as more important than yourselves; do not merely look out for your own personal interests, but also for the interests of others."[38] Indeed, the cognate noun is used elsewhere of Christ Himself: "Now I, Paul, myself urge you by the meekness and gentleness [ἐπιεικείας] of Christ" (2 Cor. 10:1). In the present directive Paul is echoing again the theme set forth in Philippians 2:5 when he commanded them to "Have this attitude in yourselves which was also in Christ Jesus."

This singular quality is to mark the entirety of the congregation, both as individuals and as a whole. This kind of "spirit" ought to characterize their personal lives and therefore also their corporate life. The Philippian believers are to demonstrably give evidence that such an attitude is their very nature. "This favorable reputation and especially this attractiveness are self-evident."[39] And this revelation is to become obvious to "all men" (πᾶσιν ἀνθρώποις), believing and unbelieving, rich and poor, educated and uneducated, male and female, whatever strata of society they come from or whatever religious background they represent.

---

35 Robertson, *Paul's Joy in Christ*, 233.
36 NIDNTT, 2:256.
37 Hellerman, 236.
38 Silva, 194.
39 Spicq, 2:38.

It would include people such as ill-motivated preachers (1:15, 17), those who have imprisoned the Apostle (1:19), the Philippians' "opponents" (1:28) who are bringing suffering upon them (1:29-30), Epaphroditus, who may have returned prematurely in the minds of some (2:25-30), "the dogs ... the evil workers ... the false circumcision" (3:2), those who "have a different attitude" (3:15), the "enemies of the cross of Christ" (3:18-19), and Euodia and Syntyche (4:2). This will become obvious to such folks as they are made the object of attitudes, words and actions that are worthy of being described as yielding, gentle, kind, courteous, tolerant, equitable, and fair. This command serves as reinforcement of the themes of both internal unity and outward witness.

This is an important word for our day in which tolerance has undergone radical redefinition. The new "tolerance" has become the inviolable social virtue. By "tolerance" is not meant the ability to hold with respect and dignity those of differing opinions while disagreeing about truth, but the notion that any and every position is of equal worth and truthfulness. We have become unable to separate ideas from the people who hold and defend them. In the past we were able to debate the truthfulness or untruthfulness of propositions and positions without demeaning the people propagating them. Now to differ in opinion is to denigrate the one of differing position. We have set ourselves on an unsustainable trajectory, one in which all ideas must be able to co-exist as equally truthful and valid. Perhaps, at least in part, this has happened because we as the people of God have failed to demonstrate the quality God demands of us here. In its absence the culture around us has filled in the void with its own secular virtue, what they now call "tolerance."

Added tersely and without a connective is the stubbly, separate sentence: "The Lord is near" (ὁ κύριος ἐγγύς). So abrupt is the sentence that it does not contain a verb; the translators adding "is," though it is absent from the Greek text, as the understood intent of the author. The question regards just what Paul intended by "near" (ἐγγύς). It does not seem to signal physical proximity, for "the Lord," being a Spirit who is omnipresent, is not near or far with regard to physical distance. His is a matter of relational distance. It could be a reference to this mystical, spiritual distance of relationship. It probably points at least to proximity in terms of time and likely refers to the Parousia of Christ.[40] Earlier Paul made powerful reference to what will transpire at Jesus' return (2:9-11) and has just spoken passionately and hopefully again of Christ's return (3:20-21). In this respect it is probably used here much like it appears to be in 1 Corinthians 13:11: "now salvation is nearer [ἐγγύτερον] to us than when we believed." It may be similar as well to the Aramaic expression, "Maranatha" (1 Cor. 16:22; "Our Lord, come!" ESV). It is, then, not unlike James 5:8 in intent: "You too be patient; strengthen your hearts, for the coming of the Lord is near."

The point then seems to be that, since Jesus may appear at any moment, we ought to treat every moment and each person with great care and patience, for Jesus may soon appear. Even if He does not appear in that moment, it can't be long (at least along the eternal continuum) before He does appear, and at that time my patient gentleness will be both relieved and rewarded. While the temporal idea seems primary here, we may be amiss to entirely exclude the notion of relational, spiritual proximity, for the transition to matters of prayer (vv.6-7) may build on this.[41] Indeed, this brief sentence may serve as a transition to the matter of dealing with anxiety (v.6; note the punctuation of the ESV). In fact we may have here an allusion to Psalm 145:18: "The LORD is near to all who call upon Him, To all who call upon Him in truth." The nearness of the Lord Jesus' return and the proximity of His ever-present existence change both our interactions with one another (v.5a) and our dealings with ourselves (v.6).

---

40 BDAG, 2170.2a.
41 Carson, 109-110; Fee, 408; Harmon, 409; Hellerman, 238; O'Brien, 489-490.

> **Digging Deeper:**
> 1. In what ways is the exercise of rejoicing a strictly private matter? In what ways is it attainable only in shared experience with God's people? (v.4)
> 2. In what ways is a "gentle spirit" (v.5a) similar to modern "tolerance"? In what ways is it distinct?
> 3. How does the knowledge that "the Lord is near" (v.5b) affect how we ought to go about conflict resolution (vv.2-3)? How does it affect the matter of one's anxiety (v.6)?

Verse 6 – "Be anxious for nothing, but in everything by prayer and supplication with thanksgiving let your requests be made known to God."

The fourth and fifth commands of the seven that make up verses 4 through 9 are found here. The fourth is a prohibition on anxiety: "Be anxious for nothing" (μηδὲν μεριμνᾶτε). Paul elsewhere used the verb to speak both of positive concern for "the things of the Lord" and of negative anxiety over "the things of the world" (1 Cor. 7:32-33, 34). It can describe legitimate and Spirit-induced care for other believers (1 Cor. 12:25). Indeed, Paul used it earlier in this letter to describe Timothy's legitimate concern for the Philippian believers (Phil. 2:20). But here it clearly has a dark hue and refers to unhealthy anxiety and worry. In this sense Jesus used it of worry about food, drink and clothing (Matt. 6:25-34) and of what to say when persecuted (10:19). It was Martha's problem as she hustled about in efforts to host Jesus in her home (Luke 10:41). Peter used the cognate noun to call for "casting all your anxiety on Him, because He cares for you" (1 Pet. 5:7).

In the present passage the verb is in the form of a present imperative, stressing the ongoing, unending nature of the prohibition. It may indicate that Paul is aware the Philippian believers had given way to anxiety and that he here bids them to stop letting it rule over them. Just as the prohibition extends for all time, it also is absolute, permitting anxiety "for nothing" (μηδὲν). It "can be rendered *not ... at all, in no way*."[42] Here is Paul, a prisoner for the Lord (Phil. 1:7, 13, 14, 17), instructing these freedmen to stop their worrying! They worried about the gospel's advance with the great apostle imprisoned (1:12-18), they worried about his welfare while incarcerated (1:21-26), they had worried over Epaphroditus' physical condition (2:26-28), they may have worried over why he had now returned prematurely from his mission (2:29-30), they may have worried over their opposition (1:27-30; 3:2), and they may have worried about their own differences with one another (4:2). Paul's teaching here is in accord with, and perhaps a purposeful application of, Jesus' own teaching in Matthew 6:25-34.

In strong and emphatic contrast (ἀλλ', "But") to their chronic anxiety, Paul sets forth what ought to occupy the energies and thoughts of Christ's people. Instead of worrying, and as an antidote to such anxiety, you are to "let your requests be made known" (τὰ αἰτήματα ὑμῶν γνωριζέσθω). The verb was used in 1:22 to refer to Paul's having nothing to say concerning God's will in the matter of his living or dying. The verb seems to point either to knowledge possessed or knowledge expressed; something known or something made known. It is used here in the latter sense. The present tense of the verb demands action that is repeated and habitual. For the emphasis of the third person singular imperative see the comments on verse 5 (γνωσθήτω, "Let ... be known"). The passive voice pictures "the requests" (τὰ αἰτήματα) being acted upon by the one praying as "the requests" are articulated to God. The plural neuter form is inclusive of any and all matters that may distress. The plural form coupled with the present tense of the verb is descriptive of repeated approach to God on these matters.[43] The word encourages specificity in our "requests" as contrasted with vague generalities.[44] The noun is used only two other times in the NT, once of the demands of the Jews that Jesus be crucified (Luke 23:24)

---

42 BDAG, 4889.2.b.

43 Hellerman, 240.

44 NIDNTT, 2:858.

and once by the Apostle John in describing prayer (1 John 5:15). How odd that the word describing the request made for Jesus' crucifixion is elsewhere only used of the freedom we have because of His death to bring our requests to God through Him.

This forms the skeletal frame of the sentence, but it is qualified by several clauses. One tells us that this is to happen "in everything" (ἐν παντὶ). As the prohibition on worry is total (μηδὲν, "for nothing") so the inclusiveness of prayer is also total (ἐν παντὶ, "in everything"). The adjective παντὶ ("everything") is to be understood as a substantive. Some have wanted to connect it to τῇ προσευχῇ ("every kind of prayer"), but their differing genders weighs in favor of reading it as an independent substantive.[45]

This is to take place "by"[46] two activities. The first is "by prayer" (τῇ προσευχῇ). Of the two this is the more general word.[47] It is the word used of Paul's first evangelistic contact with citizens of Philippi, as he and his traveling companions (Silas, Timothy, and Luke) went to the Jewish place of prayer by a river and found there women seeking God's presence (Acts 16:13, 16). Now, over a decade later, he reminds them of the primacy and power of making one's requests known unto God. In addition (καὶ, "and") to such praying is "petition" (τῇ δεήσει). Paul has already used this to describe his prayers for the Philippians (1:4) and their prayers for him (1:19). The word

> **Ministry Maxim**
>
> The presence of a sovereign Father and the existence of anxiety are mutually exclusive— to seek the one is to abandon the other.

designates making a specific request. Rienecker reports, "The verb from which the noun is derived had the meaning 'to chance upon,' then 'to have an audience w[ith] a king,' to have the good fortune to be admitted

---

45 Sumney, 103.

46 These two dative forms designate the means or instrument by which the requests are made known to God. (Wallace, 162-163; 434-435).

47 BDAG, 1741.

to an audience, so to present a petition. The word was a regular term for a petition to a superior and in the papyri it was constantly used of any writing addressed to the king."[48] Kennedy says that the former emphasizes "prayer as an act of worship or devotion," while the latter is a "cry of personal need."[49] Thayer makes προσευχή ("prayer) emphasize devotion and δέησις ("petition") the expression of a personal need.[50] It is possible that the two, while possessing some distinct nuance of meaning, are used here in a largely synonymous fashion. Both nouns are accompanied by the definite article, which may point toward the specific prayer/supplication made in each case or they may be possessive (i.e., "*your* prayer and *your* petition").[51] Paul elsewhere uses these two words in combination in Ephesians 6:18 and in reverse order in 1 Timothy 2:1 and 5:5.

Accompanying (μετὰ, "with") all such requests is to be "thanksgiving" (εὐχαριστίας). Part of the defeat of anxiety is appreciation of what one already possesses. Gratitude dispels fear and anxiety, for it recognizes that one is not alone. There is another present and that One is good and is responsible for any good that can be found. That One is present with all the possibilities inherent in infinite power under the direction of immeasurable love and goodness. By nature anxiety causes one thing to dominate a person's outlook. The disciplined practice of "thanksgiving" causes that one fearful thing to find its measured place in proportion to the other good realities of life. It does not eliminate the basis for legitimate concern, but it does make it take its proper place in line for one's attention and emotions. Paul's emphasis on the pervasive power of thanksgiving is consistent (e.g., 1 Cor. 1:4; Eph. 1:16; 5:20; Col. 1:3, 12; 2:7; 3:17; 1 Thess. 1:2; 2:13; 5:18; 2 Thess. 1:3; 2:13; 1 Tim. 2:1). It was upon this very note that he began the present letter (Phil. 1:3) and it is to thanksgiving that he will turn next (4:10-20) as he prepares to close the letter.

---

48 Rienecker, 618-619.
49 Kennedy, 467.
50 Thayer, 126.
51 O'Brien, 493; Lenski, 878; Vincent, ICC, 134.

All this is more than mental games, therapeutic exercises and emotional coping mechanisms, for it is directed "to God" (πρὸς τὸν θεόν). God is; and He rewards those who seek Him (Heb. 11:6). The preposition πρὸς ("to") signals more than would have the mere dative; it is descriptive of motion toward or orientation to God.[52] Kennedy calls it, "A delicate and suggestive way of hinting that God's presence is always there, that it is the atmosphere surrounding them. Anxious foreboding is out of place in a Father's presence."[53] We are reminded that in contrast to Martha's worry was Mary's worship (Luke 10:39, 42) and so here the opposite of and cure for anxiety is to draw near to the Lord in prayer.

> In seasons of distress and grief,
> My soul has often found relief,
> And oft escaped the tempter's snare,
> By thy return, sweet hour of prayer!
>
> And since He bids me seek His face,
> Believe His Word, and trust His grace,
> I'll cast on Him my every care
> And wait for thee, sweet hour of prayer![54]

Digging Deeper:
1. In what way is anxiety a present challenge in your own life? In the lives of the people who make up your local church?
2. What three words would you use to describe the true nature of your personal prayer life? What words would you use to describe the corporate prayer life of your local church?
3. In what needs might you become more specific in your requests to God right now?

---

52 BDAG, 6247.3; Hellerman, 240.
53 Kennedy, 467.
54 William W. Walford (1772-1850), "Sweet Hour of Prayer."

Verse 7 – "And the peace of God, which surpasses all comprehension, will guard your hearts and your minds in Christ Jesus."

The connective καὶ ("And") stands out in a section where conjunctions have been conspicuously absent (v.4ff). It signals that Paul is adding now a promise to the command of verse 6. The two sentences then serve as condition (v.6) and promise (v.7). When we obediently deal with anxiety through a disciplined prayer life (as outlined in v.6) we can expect "the peace of God" (ἡ εἰρήνη τοῦ θεοῦ) as a result.[55] Paul began the letter by extending to them "peace from God" (εἰρήνη ἀπὸ θεοῦ; 1:2), something he does in every NT letter, except 1 Thessalonians. Here "peace" (ἡ εἰρήνη) must be understood over against the prohibition in verse 6 against being "anxious" (μεριμνᾶτε). There are those who seek to make this not the peace that soothes the anxious individual, but the peace that makes as one the contentious parties within the Philippian church.[56] Many others view Paul's concern here the personal, inward peace that meets the demands of anxiety (v.6).[57] There may be wisdom among those who see it as reflecting both personal and corporate peace[58], though the personal would have to come first so that its effect might be found in their relationships. It is sometimes argued that this verse's closest parallel (Col. 3:15) has corporate peace in view. But the present immediate context holds more sway and it is difficult to see how interpersonal peace could be the cure for personal anxiety and worry (v.6).

---

55 This is the only use of this precise expression in the NT, though cf. "the peace of Christ" (ἡ εἰρήνη τοῦ Χριστοῦ) in Colossians 3:15.

56 E.g. Hellerman, 240; Lightfoot, 174.

57 E.g. Alford, 3:189; Carson, 114; Cousar, 85-86; Hendriksen, 196-197; Kent, 11:152; Lenski, 880; Martin, 170-171; Müller, 142-143; Robertson, *Paul's Joy in Christ*, 237; Silva, 199; Vincent, ICC, 135.

58 Harmon, 414; Kennedy, 467; Silva, 196; Fee, 411-412 (though he sees the social peace as primary, not the personal).

Just how are we to understand the genitive (τοῦ θεοῦ, "of God")? It is unlikely to be an objective genitive (the peace which God Himself possesses or experiences) but more likely is a subjective genitive[59] ("the peace that God has and gives"[60]). The definite article sets this peace apart as qualitatively distinct from all else that might go under the generic label. Indeed, this is peace "which surpasses all comprehension" (ἡ ὑπερέχουσα πάντα νοῦν). The participle with its definite article (ἡ ὑπερέχουσα, "which surpasses") is used as an adjective, modifying "peace" (ἡ εἰρήνη).[61] It is a compound comprised of ὑπέρ ("over/above") and ἔχω ("to have/hold"). It occurs but five times in the NT, four of those by Paul. Three of those four appear conspicuously here in Philippians, and always with some connection to one's thought life. Paul exhorted them to "regard one another as more important [ὑπερέχοντας] than yourselves" (2:3). Paul spoke personally of "the surpassing value [ὑπερέχον] of knowing Christ Jesus my Lord" (3:8). And now it is peace "which surpasses [ἡ ὑπερέχουσα] all comprehension." It means here "to surpass in quality or value."[62] The present tense points to the abiding nature of the value. It is not and never will be eclipsed by any "peace" of higher or greater worth. Indeed, it surpasses "all comprehension" (πάντα νοῦν).

The noun "comprehension" (νοῦν) denotes "the faculty of intellectual perception."[63] It is a favorite of the Apostle Paul (of its twenty-four appearances in the NT, it comes from Paul's pen twenty-one times). Born into this world, we have a "fleshly mind" (Col. 2:18), a "depraved mind" (Rom. 1:28; 1 Tim. 6:5; 2 Tim. 3:8), a "defiled" mind (Tit. 1:15). He warns against "the futility of" the unredeemed mind (Eph. 4:17). The mind is the place we reason, weigh evidence, make moral choices and in which we must be

---

59 Wallace prefers to call it a genitive of production, saying the genitive substantive ("of God") produces the noun to which it is related ("peace") 104-106. Others call it a genitive of source (e.g., Harmon, 414; Sumney, 102).

60 Robertson, *Grammar*, 499.

61 Hellerman, 241.

62 BDAG, 7565.3.

63 Ibid., 5144.

convinced of the path we are to take (Rom. 14:5). The mind governs our utterances (1 Cor. 14:14, 15, 19). Paul distinguishes the "mind" from the "spirit" (1 Cor. 14:14, 15) and sets it over against the "flesh" (Rom. 7:25). He speaks of a "law of the mind" that may be over against "the law of sin" (Rom. 7:23). One's mind may be "shaken" (2 Thess. 2:2). And God's people are to "be made complete in the same mind" with one another (1 Cor. 1:10). As we have discovered here in Philippians (2:5), that can only happen as we share "the mind of the Lord" and fortunately we are promised that "we have the mind of Christ" (1 Cor. 2:16). Though surely we will never entirely share His mind ("Who has known the mind of the Lord?" Rom. 11:34) we are commanded to "be renewed in the spirit of your mind" (Eph. 4:23) and to "be transformed by the renewing of your mind" (Rom. 12:2). Yes, ultimately it is the Lord Jesus Himself who must open our minds to understand (Luke 24:45). This important word becomes a significant additional part of the emphasis the Apostle has already laid upon the role of the believer's thinking and mind (e.g. 1:7; 2:2, 5; 3:15, 19; 4:2).

> **Ministry Maxim**
>
> The peace which God gives is both incalculable by the mind and unconquerable by our worries.

Some take this clause to mean that "the peace of God" surpasses what the human mind can produce in its efforts to deal with anxiety.[64] But it seems best to read it as not surpassing what the human mind can produce, but infinitely exceeding what the human mind can understand with regard to the peace God brings.[65] In our present passage Paul adds to the noun the adjective πάντα ("all").[66] This has the effect of pressing the boundaries and possibilities of the fully redeemed and renewed mind to its furthest

---

64 Fee, 410; Lenski, 879; Müller, 142; Vincent, ICC, 135-136.

65 Carson, 114; Harmon, 414; Hendrisken, 196-197; Kent, 11:152; Kennedy, 467; Martin, 170; O'Brien, 497; Robertson, *Paul's Joy in Christ*, 237; Silva, 195-196.

66 Note how Paul continually presses the boundaries by placing emphasis upon "all" in the present context: "Rejoice in the Lord always [πάντοτε]" (v.4), "Let your gentle spirit be known to all [πᾶσιν] men" (v.5), "Be anxious for nothing [παντὶ]" (v.5), "the peace of God, which surpasses all [πάντα] comprehension" (v.7).

limits. Thus a peace that comes from the infinite God Himself is a peace which transcends our highest intellectual capacity to understand, evaluate, comprehend and entirely grasp. Not even a redeemed, renewed, and transformed mind will be able to completely trace out just how this peace works or in what way it so powerfully puts at ease the one who is made its recipient. Having as yet not "obtained … or already become perfect" (3:12) we can never entirely comprehend how an encounter with "the God of peace" (v.9) and the resulting "peace of God" (v.7) can so powerfully displace the anxiety of our hearts.

The promise is that this all-surpassing peace "will guard" (φρουρήσει) the Philippians. The word could be used of the literal guarding of a city (2 Cor. 11:32). Moulton and Milligan explain the imagery as "a garrison keeping ward over a town."[67] It is a military word and would depict a powerful image for the people of Philippi, a Roman Colony populated with many retired military personnel and, even as they read this letter, encompassed by a Roman garrison appointed to guard the Roman *Pax*.[68] Then too, Paul was writing from imprisonment and may have thought of the supervision under which he dwelt. Clearly the term is used here in a metaphorical sense. How interesting that Paul would have used a military word to depict the truth about peace.[69] The future tense looks to a time when the conditions of verse 6 are kept in an individual's life.

That which is thus guarded is two-fold: "your hearts and your minds" (τὰς καρδίας ὑμῶν καὶ τὰ νοήματα ὑμῶν). Though joining the two nouns together by means of καί ("and"), Paul intentionally separates them by repetition of the possessive personal pronoun (ὑμῶν, "your") and by giving each noun its own definite article. It would seem he is thereby separating them conceptually, while uniting them ideologically. The heart (καρδία) is often considered the seat of the whole inner life, encompassing the mind, emotions and will. But given that it is coupled here with νόημα

---

67   Moulton and Milligan, 4595.

68   Fee, 411.

69   "A verbal paradox, for to guard is a warrior's duty" (Lightfoot, 174).

(the individual thoughts produced by the νοῦς[70]) he may be emphasizing the emotional and volitional element of καρδία. Thus together the two terms are all-encompassing, but by being separated conceptually Paul emphatically emphasizes the uniqueness of each. The entire inner life of the believer—the thoughts, the emotions, and the will—shall be garrisoned about by this all-surpassing "peace of God."

This will ever only take place "in Christ Jesus" (ἐν Χριστῷ Ἰησοῦ). The preposition (ἐν, "in") points to the sphere in which such peace can have its powerful effect. Paul similarly comforted the Colossian believers, telling them their "life is hidden with Christ in God" (Col. 3:3). There, no harm can touch us. There, no errant, inward desire can topple us from the safety of God's own hand. It is only in living union with Christ Himself that "the peace of God" can be known. The OT prophets held out peace as the great goal and outcome of the longed for Messianic salvation (e.g., Isa. 48:18; 52:7; 53:5; 54:10, 13; 57:19; 60:17; 66:12)[71] so it is not surprising to find Paul emphasizing that this peace is only available "in Christ Jesus." The order is thus not casual: "Christ" (Χριστῷ, i.e., the anointed one, Messiah), and then "Jesus" (Ἰησοῦ).

The present expression (ἡ εἰρήνη τοῦ θεοῦ, "the peace of God") will be echoed by "the God of peace" (ὁ θεὸς τῆς εἰρήνης) in verse 9. The two phrases serve as an inclusion, framing into a unit the discussion in verses 7 through 9. The "peace of God" will remain elusive until you encounter "the God of peace." It is through "peace with God" (Rom. 5:1), wrought through the shed blood of Christ (Col. 1:20), that one comes into relationship with "the God of peace" (Phil. 4:9). Only thus are we in a position to know and experience "the peace of God" (4:7). Even when in relationship to "the God of peace," "the peace of God" does not come about by accident, but by an intentional, disciplined life devoted to seeking God in the midst of our complex and often painful lives. This can never come about via independence, but only "in Christ Jesus."

---

70 BDAG, 5117.1a; "νόημα is the result of the activity of the νοῦς" (TDNT, 4:960); Kennedy, 467.
71 BDAG, 2285.2.b.

Oh, what peace we often forfeit,
Oh what needless pain we bear,
All because we do not carry
Everything to God in prayer.[72]

> **Digging Deeper:**
> 1. Describe for someone a time when you experienced God's peace in a profound way.
> 2. In what ways did you find yourself struggling for words to adequately express what you experienced?
> 3. In what way is "the peace of God" a deliverance from anxiety (v.6) and in what ways is it a "guard" against anxiety (v.7)?

Verse 8 – "Finally, brethren, whatever is true, whatever is honorable, whatever is right, whatever is pure, whatever is lovely, whatever is of good repute, if there is any excellence and if anything worthy of praise, dwell on these things."

By means of an extended sentence that runs through verse 9 Paul will bring the present series of exhortations to a close before he transitions to matters related to their recent financial gift of support (vv.10-20). Commands number six and seven close out the series of imperatives that have held verses 4 through 9 together.

Τὸ λοιπόν ("Finally") is used by Paul only four times in the NT, two of those here in Philippians (1 Cor. 7:29; Phil. 3:1; 4:8; 2 Thess. 3:1). See our comments on 3:1 where Paul used it to introduce a new subject. But here it seems he uses it not to begin a new subject (for, as we shall see momentarily, in reality he underscores with fresh power a theme he has been building throughout the letter), but to make the first turn toward concluding this letter. He is completing his exhortations and after a final, necessary word of thanks for their financial gift (vv.10-20), he will bring the letter

---

72 Joseph M. Scriven (1819-1886), "What a Friend We Have in Jesus."

to a close. He uses again the familiar ἀδελφοί ("brethren") which he has employed already five times (1:12; 3:1, 13, 17; 4:1) and will use again to close the letter (4:21). This underscores the relational nature of his commands and that what he says, he says in the context of Christian "family."

Paul is known to offer strings of either vices (e.g., Rom. 1:29-31; 1 Cor. 6:9-10; Gal. 5:19-21; Col. 3:5, 8) or virtues (e.g., Gal. 5:22-23; Col. 3:12) to make a point. What we have presently is a superlative example of the latter. He will set forth eight items in all, the first six are held together by the repeated relative pronoun ὅσα ("whatever") and the last two set out as conditional clauses (εἴ, "if"). The six-fold use of the relative pronoun is unprecedented. Nowhere else in either the NT or the LXX do we find such a concentration in one statement. It indicates the inclusive nature of Paul's intent—anything and everything, as many as may fit the description of these six items is to be included.

As for the first six items, they are all set out by neuter adjectives in the nominative case and plural form. The first is joined to the simple verb ἐστίν ("is"); the remaining five assume the verb, but without repeating it. We probably miss the Apostle's point if we seek fine distinctions in definition between each of these items. While each has its own nuance, Paul is setting out to make one great point. It is as if Paul holds out one magnificent diamond before our eyes, turning it to allow the sunlight momentarily to catch different facets of its beauty and to beg for our contemplation. We note also that most of the terms used here were familiar in secular Hellenistic philosophic dialogue and writings. Some have suggested that the Apostle is appealing to their common knowledge of what was valued and venerated in the secular culture and to aim at not offending these in their relationships to the lost around them.[73] But surely this misses the point. Silva is closer to the mark when he says, "The idea that at this point in the letter Paul descends from such heights and asks his brothers merely to act like well-behaved Greek citizens can hardly be

---

73   E.g., Lightfoot, 175.

taken seriously."[74] He is correct, "we must understand Paul's list as representing distinctly Christian virtues."[75]

The first item in the catalogue of virtues is "true" (ἀληθῆ). The word denotes that which conforms to reality, to the facts as they are in actuality.[76] It "often means 'real' as opposed to imaginary or metaphorical."[77] This is of the utmost importance and the logical jumping off point for the Apostle's list because above all God is "true" (John 3:33; 8:26) as is Jesus Christ whom He has sent (John 14:6). Satan is, fundamentally, a deceiver (2 Cor. 11:3; 2 Thess. 2:9) and liar (John 8:44). The devil, as "the god of this world" (2 Cor. 4:4), fundamentally seeks to set everything before our eyes in such a way as to distort what is in fact reality and to guide us into calling what is light, darkness, and what is truth, error (Isa. 5:20). The essence of this first item in the list is echoed in the emphasis of the imperative λογίζεσθε ("dwell upon," see below).

The second item in the list is "honorable" (σεμνά). The word describes that which is august or venerable.[78] "The word denotes moral earnestness, affecting outward demeanor as well as interior intention."[79] The adjective and its cognate noun reveal that this quality should be true of our thoughts (Phil. 4:8) and the result of prayer (1 Tim. 2:2). Such should be true of overseer's children (1 Tim. 3:4), deacons (1 Tim. 3:8), deaconesses (3:11), and Paul's representative (Titus 2:7). The word "has to do not only with bearing and attitude … one's comportment in general … or even collective behavior … but with a religious and moral posture that bears the mark of excellence."[80] If the first term calls for conformity to reality, whatever the prevailing social opinion may be, this second term calls for

---

74 Silva, 197.

75 Ibid.

76 BDAG, 326.2; Friberg, 43; Louw-Nida, 72.1.

77 Spicq, 1:83.

78 Thayer, 573.

79 Rienecker, 619.

80 Spicq, 3:246.

thinking that takes into consideration the opinions and seeks the respect of others.

The third item is "right" (δίκαια). The word has a wide range of meaning, depending upon its context. It "denotes that which is obligatory in view of certain requirements of justice."[81] It was used in the secular world of the standard of model citizenship in the Greco-Roman world.[82] But in the NT the rightness of something is defined by its conformity to the character and truth of God. Often the context makes explicit that the rightness of particular actions and attitudes is defined by who God is and how He acts (e.g. Acts 4:19; Eph. 6:1; Col. 4:1). To set one's mind on that which is "right" is to contemplate the nature of God as the plumb line by which all else is evaluated.

The fourth term is "pure" (ἁγνά). Originally the term served as descriptive of the character and nature of a deity and thus was used ritually. But over time its emphasis shifted to the moral realm and here it denotes "moral purity and sincerity."[83] The term was applied to sexual matters (2 Cor. 11:2; Titus 2:5), but it was used also more widely. It is the first and fundamental quality of "the wisdom from above" (James 3:17). It should be true of a believing wife's conduct (1 Pet. 3:2). It comes from anticipating the return of Christ (1 John 3:3; cf. 2 Cor. 11:2). It applies to appointing church leaders (1 Tim. 5:22) and in matters of church discipline (2 Cor. 7:11).

The fifth quality is "lovely" (προσφιλῆ). The term appears only here in the NT. It is a compound word made up of πρός ("toward") and φιλέω ("to love").[84] The basic sense of the preposition is movement from one place "toward" another, so the idea may be "Whatever calls forth love."[85] It is used in a passive sense of that which is viewed by others as pleasing

---

81 BDAG, 2003.2.
82 Gingrich, 1687.
83 TDNT, 1:122.
84 Robertson, *Word Pictures*, 4:460.
85 Vincent, ICC, 139.

or "lovely." It is "the graciousness that wins and charms."[86] Acceptable renderings include "pleasing," "agreeable," "lovely," or "amiable."[87]

The sixth term is "of good report" (εὔφημα). This term also appears only here in the NT. It originally described careful, circumspect speech used in deference to some transcendent power or to some personage of higher social standing in fear that what is said might prove unlucky or inappropriate in their eyes.[88] Over time it began to be used more widely and came to refer more generally to that which is deserving of approval or praise, of "things spoken in a kindly spirit, with good-will to others."[89] Martin says it "means not 'well spoken of' but 'speaking well of.'"[90]

Paul now switches from the relative pronoun ὅσα ("whatever") to finish off the listing with two conditional clauses (εἴ τις, "if there is any"). The conditional statements may be considered as first class conditions, assuming that the conditions are fulfilled. Such things do indeed exist, so seek them out and "dwell on such things." The indefinite adjective τις ("any") is repeated in both clauses to again cast the net as widely as possible.

The first (or seventh, in terms of the entire list) of these is "excellence" (ἀρετή). The term is used only five times in the NT and only here by Paul. Peter applies the term in the plural to "the excellencies of" God (1 Pet. 2:9) and uses it in the singular to describe His "own glory and excellence" (2 Pet. 1:3). But he also indicates that this should be added the believer's life as one of the basic building blocks of faith (2 Pet. 1:5 [2x]). It is in this latter sense that Paul uses it here, though without losing the defining connection to God's all-surpassing nature. We should let our minds investigate and ponder over wherever and in whatever God's glory is reflected.

Finally, to this is added (καὶ, "and") all that may be "worthy of praise" (ἔπαινος). Paul used the term of what God deserves in view of His glory (Eph. 1:6, 12, 14; Phil. 1:11). But he also used it of praise which comes to

---

86 Robertson, *Paul's Joy in Christ*, 241.
87 BDAG, 6351.
88 Ibid., 3313.
89 Thayer, 263.
90 Martin, 172.

us from God (Rom. 2:29; 1 Cor. 4:5) or others (Rom. 13:3; 2 Cor. 8:18). In the later sense both Paul (Rom. 13:3) and Peter (1 Pet. 2:14) use it of praise that comes to law-abiding citizens from divinely-appointed political leaders. Here it "probably denotes the kind of conduct that wins the praise of fellow humans."[91]

Having built momentum through the listing of these eight superior qualities, Paul then commands the Philippian believers: "dwell on such things" (ταῦτα λογίζεσθε). The demonstrative pronoun ταῦτα ("such things") gathers up all eight items in the preceding list and summarizes them in one term. The verb can mean "to calculate by mathematical processes" and can thus be rendered "calculate" or "reckon."[92] But here it probably has the notion of "to give careful thought to a matter" and might be rendered "think (about), consider, ponder" or, as in the NASB, "let one's mind dwell on."[93]

> **Ministry Maxim**
>
> The discipline of one's mind has direct bearing on the disposition of one's heart.

There is a strong emphasis in the word on the logical nature of the thinking. It is "to think about something in a detailed and logical manner."[94] Just as one reconciles one's checkbook to the monthly bank statement, so one must reconcile one's thinking to the standard of truth and reality. Paul has provided an itemized accounting of what is fundamentally, above all else, "true" (ἀληθῆ, see above under the first word in the list) and thus the standard to which our thinking must be constantly calibrated, reconciled and conformed. The present imperative form calls for the action to be repeated, habitually becoming a pattern of life. "It is not the mere flash of thought like the flitting of a sparrow, but deliberate and prolonged contemplation as if one is weighing a mathematical problem."[95] In some

---

91 O'Brien, 507.
92 BDAG, 4598.1.
93 Ibid., 4598.2.
94 Louw-Nida, 30.9.
95 Robertson, *Paul's Joy in Christ*, 242.

words of mental action the middle voice, though deponent, retains something of its personal emphasis.[96] One is to take action inwardly or upon oneself to think in such terms.

Paul thus once again sounds the theme of the importance of the mind, what one thinks and how one thinks. He has just spoken of "comprehension" (νοῦν) and our "minds" (τὰ νοήματα, v.7) to which he has now added the disciplined application of thought (λογίζεσθε, "dwell upon"). Paul ten times throughout the letter used the verb φρονέω to speak of the significance of one's "attitude" or "mind" (1:7; 2:2 [2x], 5; 3:15 [2x], 19; 4:2, 10 [2x]), most significantly in 2:5 when he called upon the Philippians to "Have this attitude in yourselves which was also in Christ Jesus." Thus in a world of anxiety (v.6) our experience of peace (v.7) has directly to do with the discipline of our minds (v.8) and our application of what we have learned in Christ through godly leaders (v.9).

Verse 9 – "The things you have learned and received and heard and seen in me, practice these things, and the God of peace will be with you."

Though most English translations begin a new sentence with verse nine, the Greek sentence continues from verse eight. The seventh and final command (πράσσετε, "practice") of the string of imperatives that began in verse 4 parallels and is held in balance with[97] "dwell on" (λογίζεσθε) in verse 8. In fact there is a much more extensive and intentional symmetry between the first half of the sentence (v.8) and the latter half (v.9). Both main verbs are present imperatives in the second person plural forms and are held to the end of their respective and extended clauses. Both are accompanied by ταῦτα ("these things"). The relative pronouns (ὅσα, "whatever") of the first half are matched here by ἃ ("The things"). As the repeated ὅσα ("whatever") coordinates the list in verse 8 so the repeated

---

96 Robertson, *Grammar*, 812.

97 Though the balance is not made by use of καὶ or any other connective, continuing the asyndeton that has predominated since verse 4.

καὶ coordinates the list in verse 9. The virtuous qualities listed in the first half are matched here by a listing of four verbs, all of which are aorist active indicatives in the second person plural form. The first seven of the virtues listed in verse 8 end in either -η or -α. Here in verse 9 all four of the subordinate verbs end in either -ετε or -ατε.[98] The rhetorical effect is powerful and effective.

The switch from ὅσα ("whatever," v.8) to ἃ ("The things," v.9), says Fee, indicates the difference between "'indefinite' and 'definite' (i.e., 'whatever things in general' and 'what things in particular.'")[99] Paul is moving from the theoretical to the actual; from the philosophical to the concrete.

The parallel imperatives depict two powerful components in practical sanctification: thinking (λογίζεσθε, "dwell on") and doing (πράσσετε, "practice"). The interface of pondering and practicing is not only essential, but automatic. What our minds dwell upon our hands will carry out. The one follows the other like the day the dawn. This is why Solomon warned, "Watch over your heart with all diligence, For from it flow the springs of life" (Prov. 4:23). This is why Jesus said, "For the mouth speaks out of that which fills the heart. The good man brings out of his good treasure what is good; and the evil man brings out of his evil treasure what is evil" (Matt. 12:34b-35). "And He was saying, 'That which proceeds out of the man, that is what defiles the man. For from within, out of the heart of men, proceed the evil thoughts, fornications, thefts, murders, adulteries, deeds of coveting and wickedness, as well as deceit, sensuality, envy, slander, pride and foolishness. All these evil things proceed from within and defile the man'" (Mark 7:20-23). James added his witness, saying, "But each one is tempted when he is carried away and enticed by his

> **Ministry Maxim**
>
> When personal instruction and personal example are wed together in a single life, ministry is made powerful.

---

98 cf. Fee, 413-414.

99 Ibid., 414.

own lust. Then when lust has conceived, it gives birth to sin; and when sin is accomplished, it brings forth death" (James 1:14-15).

Those things which were abstract, conceptual and theoretical (v.8) are now made concrete, personal and specific (v.9). What were considered as qualities (by use of adjectives and two nouns) are now considered as actions (by means of four verbs). Paul was never merely philosophizing in verse 8; he intended all along that the qualities should be seen through cruciform lenses and in the living example of the Apostle himself. All these actions share alike in being able to be witnessed "in me" (ἐν ἐμοί,). Paul makes much of the power of personal example (e.g., 1 Cor. 11:1; 1 Thess. 1:6; 2:14; 4:1; 2 Thess. 3:6). Here in Philippians he has already held out the example of Jesus (2:5-11), Timothy (2:19-24), Epaphroditus (2:25-30), and himself (3:4-16). He then followed up these examples by the explicit command: "Brethren, join in following my example, and observe those who walk according to the pattern you have in us" (3:17).

The four verbs are held in parallel relationships by the four-fold use of καὶ ("both ... and ... and ... and ..." KJV). The verbs themselves are both familiar and frequently used in the NT. The first is "learned" (ἐμάθετε). It means to gain information or skill through the instruction of another.[100] Paul himself "learned" (ἔμαθον) to live in contentment (4:11). It is a standard verb for describing one's introduction to the gospel of God's grace in Christ (e.g., Rom. 16:17; Eph. 4:20; Col. 1:7; 2 Tim. 3:14) as well as the ongoing life of discipleship (e.g., 1 Cor. 4:6; Tit. 3:14). The verb "received" (παρελάβετε) is used to describe one's embrace of Jesus Christ unto salvation (1 Cor. 15:1; Gal. 1:9, 12; Col. 2:6; 1 Thess. 2:13). It communicates not only giving an audience to the instructor, but personally accepting that of which the instructor speaks. The word served as a semitechnical term for the receiving of tradition. By using it Paul portrays himself as "a link in the chain of tradition" and "implies that the obligation of the Philippians was not only to receive it, believe it, and act upon it but also to pass it carefully on to others."[101] The third verb, "heard"

---

[100] BDAG, 4704.1.

[101] Hawthorne, WBC, 253.

(ἠκούσατε), depicts that the transmission of the gospel and its teachings was oral and audible. But their ears not only picked up the sound waves, they "heard" with understanding and welcomed the instruction concerning Jesus and the life of His apostle, Paul. But the gospel-instruction was not merely oral; it was visually depicted in the actions of the one communicating. Thus it was "seen" (εἴδετε) as well as "heard." Paul told the Philippians that they were "experiencing the same conflict which you saw [εἴδετε] in me, and now hear [ἀκούετε] to be in me" (1:30). Of the four verbs employed here, the first two may refer to Paul's preaching and teaching, the latter two to his lifestyle and conduct.

To the imperative Paul adds (καὶ, "and") a promise: "the God of peace will be with you" (ὁ θεὸς τῆς εἰρήνης ἔσται μεθ' ὑμῶν). As in verse 7, the future tense preceded by an imperative and joined by καὶ ("and") has the effect of a conditional clause which takes on the force of a result.[102] Paul uses the same designation for God in communicating with another much-beloved congregation who was also in Macedonia and was similarly beset with challenges from without and potential division from within (1 Thess. 5:23; cf. Rom. 15:33; 16:20; 1 Cor. 14:33; 2 Cor. 13:11; 2 Thess. 3:16).[103] The title echoes the promise of verse 7 ("the peace of God ... will guard your hearts and minds") and serves to bring the inclusion to a close. In this case the genitive is what Wallace calls a genitive of product.[104] He is the God "who alone creates peace."[105] God is the one who produces the longed for peace. One will never know "the peace of God" (v.7) until he has drawn near "the God of peace" (v.9). Paul is not interested in peace as an abstract concept, but as a personal, relational reality. This involves disciplined prayer (v.6), thinking (v.8) and obedience (v.9). The future tense of the verb (ἔσται, "will be") points to the assured outcome of one who in this way draws near to God. The plural (μεθ' ὑμῶν, "with you") assures

---

102 Rienecker, 561.

103 Fee says "... that in every instance it occurs in contexts where there is strife or unrest close at hand" (420).

104 Wallace, 106-107.

105 Spicq, 1:432.

each individual who makes up the body of Christ in Philippi as well as the congregation as a whole.

> **Digging Deeper:**
> 1. Can you identify something that illustrates each of the eight qualities mentioned in verse 8? What would it look like for you to "dwell upon these things"?
> 2. Who is one from whom you have "learned and received and heard and seen" a gospel-shaped life? (v.9)
> 3. Explain to someone the interplay between having "the peace of God" (v.7) and knowing "the God of peace" (v.9).

Verse 10 – "But I rejoiced in the Lord greatly, that now at last you have revived your concern for me; indeed, you were concerned *before*, but you lacked opportunity."

Paul turns from his final exhortations (vv.1-9) and, before a final, formal farewell (vv.21-23), he turns to the personal matter of expressing thanks for the recent gift of monetary support that had come from the hands of the Philippian believers (vv.10-20). The transition is marked by the use of δὲ ("But").

The first note struck is a positive one (Ἐχάρην, "I rejoiced") and one which echoes the theme of rejoicing so often found in the letter (cf. use of the same verb in 1:18 [2x]; 2:17, 18, 28; 3:1; 4:4 [2x], 10). The aorist tense harkens back to the event of his having received their gift. Epaphroditus had arrived bearing their gift (4:18; cf. 2:25, 30) and the result had been an arousal of fresh joy. The passive voice pictures the moving effect of that gift upon Paul. His rejoicing was not so much in the gift, as it was 'in the Lord" (ἐν κυρίῳ) who moved them to consider him and send their support. Here again in this matter of being in Christ we find another

> **Ministry Maxim**
>
> Unexpressed concern does as much good as total indifference.

strong theme of the letter repeated (cf. the use of this very phrase in 1:14; 2:19, 24, 29; 3:1; 4:1, 2, 4, 10). The call to joy and the expression ἐν κυρίῳ ("in the Lord") have been joined previously in 3:1 and 4:4. This rejoicing was not mild in its effect, but welled up "greatly" (μεγάλως) within him. This is the only NT use of the adverb, though its kindred adjective is found frequently and its root is often compounded with other words. It is used here to intensify the verb Ἐχάρην ("I rejoiced"). The uniqueness of the expression is further emphasized by the emphatic placement of the adverb at the end of the clause.[106] The Philippian believers' gift had achieved its desired effect.

Though some have taken ὅτι ("that") as indicating cause ("I rejoiced greatly because ...")[107] it probably signals that which aroused Paul's joy. The conjunction ὅτι appears frequently with χαίρω to indicate the source of one's "joy."[108] It wasn't even so much their gift of money, but that "you have revived your concern for me" (ἀνεθάλετε τὸ ὑπὲρ ἐμοῦ φρονεῖν). The articular infinitive construction (τὸ ὑπὲρ ἐμοῦ φρονεῖν, "your concern for me") probably depicts the direct object of the verb (ἀνεθάλετε, "you revived").[109] The addition of ὑπὲρ ἐμοῦ ("for me") emphasizes the personal nature of the concern.[110] The verb (φρονεῖν, "concern") takes up again a word employed by the Apostle frequently in this letter (1:7; 2:2 [2x], 5; 3:15 [2x], 19; 4:2, 10 [2x]). The word has underscored the powerful place of the mind in Christian discipleship. Here it points to thinking of another in the sense of being concerned for them.[111] Hellerman notes that "Through their gift the Philippians expressed the mind-set Paul enjoins elsewhere."[112] Paul has used the power of example throughout the letter, supremely that of Christ (2:5-11), and secondarily that of Timothy

---

106 O'Brien, 516; Vincent, ICC, 142.

107 e.g. Fee, 428-429; Hellerman, 255.

108 BDAG, 5414.1.e.

109 Wallace, 601-602; Robertson calls it the accusative of general reference (*Grammar*, 487).

110 O'Brien, 518, 519.

111 BDAG, 7819.1.

112 Hellerman, 255.

(2:19-24), Epaphroditus (2:25-30), and himself (3:4-14). Could he now subtly be highlighting the positive example of the Philippians themselves in this unselfish act of their thoughtful, sacrificial gift of support (4:10-19)? Is this a hint that they have already begun to emulate the example of Christ Himself?[113]

The phrase ἤδη ποτὲ ("now at last") denotes "more the notion of culmination ('now at last') than of time."[114] The phrase is found elsewhere only in Romans 1:10. That their care for Paul had been "revived" (ἀνεθάλετε) means, of course, that this was not the first time they had shown such interest in his needs. Indeed, he will soon enough recount their history of financial support for his ministry (vv.15-16; cf. 2 Cor. 11:8-9). Indeed, their sacrificial generosity is legendary (2 Cor. 8:1-5). This is the only use of the verb in the NT. It is a compound built from ἀνά ("again") and θάλλω ("to sprout/grow"). Interpreters are divided over whether to take the verb as intransitive ("bloom again") or transitive ("to cause to grow/bloom again").[115] The meaning is changed little in either case.

Lest Paul sound as if he held some negative feelings regarding the gap since their last financial gift he adds quickly, "indeed you were concerned" (ἐφ᾽ ᾧ καὶ ἐφρονεῖτε). Robertson makes ἐφ᾽ ᾧ causal[116], but it may be best to read it with the sense of "with regard to which"[117] and connect it with the concern for Paul just expressed. The verb is repeated here from the infinitive form just prior (φρονεῖν, "your concern"). The imperfect form here underscores the ongoing nature of their concern in the past, which is reflected in the addition of "before" by the translators. The καὶ ("indeed") further underscores the repeated verb.

---

113 "... after assuring the Philippians that he had the right frame of mind toward them (1:7), and then rebuking them for not having the right frame of mind toward one another (2:2, 5; 3:15; 4:2), here at the end [he] encourages them by recognizing a very positive trait in their attitude" (Silva, 208-209).

114 Robertson, *Grammar*, 1147; cf. BDAG, 3413.2.

115 BDAG, 474.

116 Robertson, *Grammar*, 963.

117 Fee, 430; Hellerman, 256; O'Brien, 518; cf. Sumney, 110.

There stood, however, something between their ongoing concern and some concrete expression of that care. The δέ is used as an adversative ("but"), setting forth the obstacle. The problem was they had "lacked opportunity" (ἠκαιρεῖσθε) to express their concern. The verb appears only here in Biblical literature. The imperfect tense again underscores the ongoing nature of their past condition. While they had continuously been giving thought to Paul's needs they had also continuously lacked the opportunity to do something about relieving them. At the root of the word is καιρός ("time").[118] But the root word emphasizes not merely time, but the strategic nature of the time in question. Thus the present verb might speak in temporal ("no time") or circumstantial terms ("no opportunity"). Probably it is some combination of the two, "no opportune time."[119] It is not clear just why no such strategic opportunity had presented itself. Was it something on their side (i.e., lack of resources [cf. 2 Cor. 8:1-2], lack of knowledge of the Apostle's needs, lack of someone to carry the gift)? Or was it something on his side (i.e., until imprisonment his needs were not acute, or because of his mobile ministry and lifestyle they would not know where to reach him prior to his imprisonment)? A definitive answer is not provided and is thus ultimately unnecessary. Good intentions meet many obstacles.

The verse is marked both by the use of rare (ἤδη ποτὲ; elsewhere only in Rom. 1:10) or otherwise unknown language (three *hapax legomenon*: μεγάλως, ἀνεθάλετε, ἠκαιρεῖσθε), but also by the use of highly thematic and by now familiar terms or phrases (Ἐχάρην, ἐν κυρίῳ, φρονεῖν, ἐφρονεῖτε). Some have highlighted the unique language and found cause for questioning whether verses 10-19 are original or an addition by a later hand. But the use of familiar themes argues for the authenticity of this section. The uncommon terms may be explained by the uniqueness of the

---

118 Here the α- privative negates the root word. Its opposite is εὐκαιρέω (Mark 6:31; Acts 17:21; 1 Cor. 16:12).

119 BDAG, 238.

material being covered.[120] Fee is correct, "One must dance with unlimited sidesteps to remove this passage from the rest of the letter."[121]

Verse 11 – "Not that I speak from want, for I have learned to be content in whatever circumstances I am."

Paul qualifies his opening comments in v.10.[122] Paul did not want his overflowing gratitude (v.10) to be misconstrued as discontent with God's providential handling of his circumstances while in prison. Thus he says, "Not that I speak from want" (οὐχ ὅτι καθ' ὑστέρησιν λέγω). The phrase οὐχ ὅτι is used by Paul three times in this letter (3:12; 4:11, 17).[123] He employs it "to guard against misapprehension."[124] The use of οὐχ ("Not") makes the denial absolute and categorical.[125] The noun ὑστέρησις ("want") is used elsewhere in the Bible only in Mark 12:44 where it speaks of the widow who gave to God the last of "all she owned, all she had to live on." It is not "from" (καθ') want that Paul speaks. The preposition here combines the ideas of both norm/standard and the reason for his speaking. It joins the notions of "in accordance with" and "because of."[126] It was neither *because of* or *in measure with* a sense of want or lack in his life that Paul has rejoiced so deeply (v.10).

Paul now explains (γὰρ, "for") why this is not the case: "I have learned to be content in whatever circumstances I am" (ἐγὼ ... ἔμαθον ἐν οἷς εἰμι αὐτάρκης εἶναι). Paul speaks personally (ἐγὼ, "I") from hard

---

120 Sumney, 110.

121 Fee, 425.

122 cf. Fee's (424-425) insightful framing of vv.10-20 as a threefold repetition of acknowledgement (vv.10a, 14, 18), initial qualification (vv.10b, 15-16, 19) and final qualification (vv.11-13, 17, 20).

123 He used it three times in 2 Corinthians (1:24; 3:5 [also in the context of sufficiency]; 7:9) as well as 2 Thess. 3:9.

124 Robertson, *Paul's Joy in Christ*, 248.

125 Thayer, 408.

126 BDAG, 3938.5.δ.

won wisdom arising out of difficult experience. Contentment does not come naturally to even a great Apostle. It must be "learned" (ἔμαθον). The verb with the accompanying infinitive (εἰμί) lays the emphasis upon "learned how" rather than "learned that."[127] The aorist tense of the verb looks back over the entire course of Paul's ministry, viewing it as one experience.[128] Vincent well says, "The tuition has extended over his whole experience up to the present."[129] The emphasis is upon the completion of the action, not its beginning.[130] Just as they had "learned" from Paul (4:9), so he had

> **Ministry Maxim**
>
> Complete dependence upon Christ is contented independence from all else.

"learned" from God the secret of contentment. And he matriculated this course when he met Christ, "who, although He existed in the form of God, did not regard equality with God a thing to be grasped, but emptied Himself, taking the form of a bond-servant, and being made in the likeness of men" (2:6-7).[131] Technically the relative pronoun (οἷς) is specific ("in the state in which I am"[132]), but given its plural form and the surrounding context (ἐν παντὶ καὶ ἐν πᾶσιν, "in any and every circumstance," v.12) it probably broadens into a wider, more generalized reference (i.e., "whatever" as per most English versions).[133] In the person of Christ Paul had observed the secret of living (εἰμί, "I am") contentedly

---

127 Robertson, *Grammar*, 1040-1041.

128 Robertson, *Paul's Joy in Christ*, 250. This in contrast to Martin: "The lesson he learnt came to him in a moment of time, as the aorist tense of the verb indicates. It did not come through patient discipline and concentrated endeavor; it broke upon him at his conversion, and his subsequent career and experience are but the outworking of that intimacy with the living Lord which began at that time" (176).

129 Vincent, ICC, 143.

130 Robertson, *Grammar*, 835.

131 Harmon, 441.

132 Vincent, 143; "The neuter phrase … is not indefinite … It refers to his present circumstances in Rome, 'in which circumstances'" (Kent, 11:155).

133 Fee, 431; Hellerman, 258; O'Brien, 521; Sumney, 111.

within (ἐν, "in") whatever realities a sovereign Father permitted him. The transition from the aorist (ἔμαθον, "I learned") to the present (εἰμι, "I am") underscores that a lesson once learned now abides in Paul's ongoing experience.

What had been learned and was presently experienced is "to be content" (αὐτάρκης εἶναι). The verb speaks of one's state of being. The present tense underscores the abiding nature of this condition. The adjective (αὐτάρκης, "content") is used only here in the NT (and in the LXX only in Prov. 30:8; cf. its cognate noun in 2 Cor. 9:8 and 1 Tim. 6:6). It is a compound built from αὐτός ("self") and ἀρκέω ("to be enough/sufficient").[134]

Paul sounds like a Stoic here, but his "self-sufficiency" is ultimately a Christ-sufficiency. As Fee says, "The net result is that Paul and Seneca, while appearing to be close, are a thousand leagues apart. The Stoic's … 'sufficiency/contentment' comes from within oneself; Paul's comes from without, from being 'a man in Christ,' on whom he is totally 'dependent' and thus not 'independent' at all in the Stoic sense."[135] And it is precisely "Because Paul and the Philippians are both 'in Christ,' [that] neither is dependent on the other for life in the world; but also because they are both 'in Christ,' Paul received their gift with joy, because this is how Christ helped him to 'abound' in this case."[136] Findlay says, "The self-sufficiency of the Christian is relative: an independence of the world through dependence upon God. The Stoic self-sufficiency pretends to be absolute. One is the contentment of faith, the other of pride. Cato (a Roman Stoic) and Paul both stand erect and fearless before a persecuting world: one with a look of rigid, defiant scorn, the other with a face now lighted up with unutterable joy in God."[137]

---

134 Thayer, 85.

135 Fee, 427.

136 Ibid.

137 Quoted by Hellerman, 259.

Digging Deeper:
1. Is there someone for whom you have shown support in the past who needs you to "revive your concern for" them? (v.10) In what form should you express that concern presently?
2. Outline how it is God has taught you contentment personally (v.11).
3. In what way do your present circumstances require contentment? (v.11)
4. How can a husband/father help his family learn the contentment that God is seeking to teach him?

Verse 12 – "I know how to get along with humble means, and I also know how to live in prosperity; in any and every circumstance I have learned the secret of being filled and going hungry, both of having abundance and suffering need."

Paul now continues to qualify himself with regard to this matter of contentment. He does so now more expansively and extensively than in verse 11. The present sentence continues through verse 13, though most English versions make verse 13 to stand on its own. The present verse is built around three perfect tense verbs to which are attached a series of six present tense infinitives. These infinitives are arranged in three pairs of two, each pair offering polar extremes of experience. In all three pairs the contrast is effectively set forward by the formula καὶ ... καὶ (i.e., "both ... and" or "not only ... but also"). All six infinitives are in the present tense and in each pair one is in the passive voice, probably emphasizing either the press of Paul's circumstances or the directive hand of God in the circumstances in which he finds himself.

The first two main verbs are identical, "I know" (οἶδα). The verb (in contrast to γινώσκω) originally stressed the completeness of the knowledge, rather than the process of gaining that knowledge through experience or relationship. In the NT, however, the two are often used synonymously.

Here it seems Paul had come to a settled state of conviction through his past experiences.[138] The form is perfect tense, though it normally has a present tense meaning. However, given that the third main verb is also in the perfect tense, it is likely that the two occurrences of οἶδα should also be read as true perfect tenses. The sense would then be that of a past action that continues to be true in the present. In this sense it might read, "I have come to know."

That which has been learned and is now known is set forth in the contrasting infinitives. When οἶδα is followed by an infinitive, as here, the emphasis is not on acquired information, but that one has learned "how" to do something.[139] The first infinitive is ταπεινοῦσθαι ("to get along with humble means"). It is the same verb used in 2:8 to describe Christ's self-humbling in the incarnation (ἐταπείνωσεν ἑαυτόν, "He humbled Himself"). It can mean "to subject to strict discipline" and might be translated "constrain" or "mortify."[140] This is reflective of OT usage (e.g. Lev. 16:29, 31; 23:27; Psalm 34:13; Isa. 58:3) in which one humbled oneself through fasting and other acts of self-denial in order to seek God and His will. But here the form is passive,[141] reflecting either what God Himself worked into Paul or what had been the effect of circumstances upon the Apostle as he sought to fulfill his Lord's commission to take the gospel to the Gentiles. Here the context seems to demand a meaning something like "to live in poor circumstances," "to live in want," or "to be straitened."[142]

To the second occurrence of οἶδα ("I know") is added the contrasting opposite: περισσεύειν ("to live in prosperity"). The verb means "to exceed a fixed number or measure; to be over and above a certain number or

---

138 For a catalogue of some of those experiences see 2 Corinthians 6:4-10; 11:23-33.

139 BDAG, 5205.3; Robertson, *Grammar*, 1045; 1103; O'Brien, 523; Vincent, ICC, 143-144.

140 BDAG, 7258.4.

141 "The voice is likely pass., rather than mid., since the discussion assumes the effect of external circumstances beyond Paul's control" (Hellerman, 260).

142 TDNT, 8:17-18.

measure."[143] Paul repeats the word later in this verse as the first half of the final contrasting pair of infinitives. He has already used the word in 1:9 ("that your love may abound [περισσεύῃ]) and 1:26 ("so that your proud confidence in me may abound [περισσεύῃ]"). He will employ it again in 4:18 ("I have received everything in full and have an abundance [περισσεύω]). Obviously, then, the word can describe an overflowing of both tangible (material or financial) and non-tangible realities ("love" and "confidence"). Paul has known both extremes and has come to know how to gladly love God in the midst of either.

The third main verb is "I have learned the secret" (μεμύημαι). This is its only NT use. It was, however, common in the literature of the day as a technical term for initiation into the Greek mystery religions. There was "secret" knowledge in those cults which was available only to those who had been fully initiated. Presently it is used, of course, more generally and indicates that in the matters under consideration Paul is no neophyte. He has an advanced degree in both ends of the spectrum of experience. The perfect tense emphasizes the abiding result of a process rather than the secret nature of the knowledge gained.[144] The passive voice again either views the knowledge as the imprint of circumstances to which Paul had been subjected or to the direct hand of God in the formative experiences of which Paul speaks.

> **Ministry Maxim**
>
> Contentment is an acquired virtue that includes both pain and pleasure in its curriculum.

Four infinitives, in two contrastive pairs, are attached to this verb. The first is χορτάζεσθαι ("of being filled"). This is Paul's only use of the verb, though it appears extensively in the Synoptic Gospels and is also employed by John (John 6:26; Rev. 19:21) and James (James 2:16). Every other NT usage relates, either literally or figuratively, to food, feeding on it or being by it filled or satisfied. It originally applied to the feeding and

---

143 Thayer, 505.
144 Hellerman, 260.

fattening of animals in a stall, though by the time of Paul it had generalized in meaning.[145] The matching opposite, naturally, is πεινᾶν ("going hungry"). With hunger pangs or a contentedly satisfied belly, Paul knew how to happily give thanks to God and get on with His work.

The last pair of infinitives is περισσεύειν ("having abundance") and ὑστερεῖσθαι ("suffering need"). The former was used in the first contrasting pair in this verse (see above). He had used it to describe the Macedonian believers' (which clearly at least included the Philippians) generosity at the time of the love offering for Judean believers suffering from famine ("their abundance of joy and their deep poverty overflowed [ἐπερίσσευσεν] in the wealth of their liberality," 2 Cor. 8:2; cf. 8:7; 9:8, 12). The latter word means to "be late, arrive late, too late," but also to "let oneself be outrun" or "left behind," and this with a hint of inferiority or even insufficiency and inefficacy.[146] It is used of the prodigal son, who, after squandering all his money, "began to be impoverished [ὑστερεῖσθαι]" (Luke 15:14). The faithful of God were "destitute [ὑστερούμενοι], afflicted, ill-treated" (Heb. 11:37). The present verb comes from ὕστερος ("behind") and the "phrase 'to fall behind' is popularly used of one in straitened circumstances, or in debt."[147] There are "many who know what it is to be behind in one's accounts with nothing in the bank to draw on."[148] The Apostle was one of them; but a contented one. The passive form that is presently before us stresses that the lack was created by Paul's circumstances as directed by the sovereign hand of God.[149]

This is true "in any and every circumstance" (ἐν παντὶ καὶ ἐν πᾶσιν). The repetition of the indefinite pronoun serves to take in all possibilities. The first occurrence is singular (ἐν παντὶ, "in any"), bringing into

---

145 Vincent, *Word Studies*, 1:38.

146 Spicq, 3:428-429.

147 Vincent, ICC, 144; cf. Lenski, 890.

148 Robertson, *Paul's Joy in Christ*, 255.

149 BDAG, 7659.5.b; Thayer, 646; contra Vincent who sees it as a middle voice emphasizing "the *feeling* of the pressure of want" (ICC, 145).

consideration each circumstance individually. The second occurrence is plural (ἐν πᾶσιν, "every"), gathering all the possibilities up and considering them collectively.[150] There won't be any one circumstance that will stand outside Paul's circle of experience and there won't be any found on all the broad plane of possibilities that might do likewise. The neuter form serves also to generalize and make as expansive as possible those things under consideration. The neuter reflects the neuter οἷς ("whatever circumstances") of verse 11 and continues the generalizing Paul began there.[151] Indeed, his "in whatever circumstances I am" (ἐν οἷς εἰμι, v.11) has been rounded out and enlarged here by "in any and every circumstance" (ἐν παντὶ καὶ ἐν πᾶσιν) and will be further enlarged by "all things" (πάντα) in verse 13.

Verse 13 – "I can do all things through Him who strengthens me."

Paul claimed he had learned "to be content" (αὐτάρκης εἶναι, v.11) no matter his circumstances. Now he harkens back to this statement and reveals just how this is possible. Far from Stoic self-reliance which looks inward to one's own reserves, it is possible rather only through a genuine personal relationship with the Lord Himself. Such contentment is not a matter of looking within oneself, but of being in Christ (ἐν τῷ ἐνδυναμοῦντί, lit., "in the one who strengthens").

The indefinite adjective πάντα ("all things") is thrust forward for emphasis. What had been "whatever circumstances" (οἷς, v.11) and then "any and every circumstance" (ἐν παντὶ καὶ ἐν πᾶσιν, v.12) has become "all things" (πάντα). The neuter gender and plural number generalize so as to include all possibilities.

---

150 Lightfoot, 164.

151 Vincent, ICC, 144.

The verb (ἰσχύω, "I can do") speaks of ability, capability, and capacity.[152] It means to "be competent," to "have power" or to "be able."[153] Its present tense form, stresses the readiness and availability of that ability for whatever the moment requires. By means of the prepositional phrase Paul reveals the sole basis upon which such an audacious claim can be made: "through Him who strengthens me" (ἐν τῷ ἐνδυναμοῦντί με). The preposition ἐν is understood by the translators as expressing personal agency ("though"[154]), but perhaps it should be allowed its natural sense of sphere ("in").[155] Thus the telling matter for any believer in Christ is not the conditions in which one finds himself (v.11), but the union with Christ into which he has been placed by the Father. The articular participle (τῷ ἐνδυναμοῦντί) is used as a substantive ("him who strengthens").[156] The word is used six times by Paul (Rom. 4:20; Eph. 6:10; Phil. 4:13), half of them in his correspondence to Timothy (1 Tim. 1:12; 2 Tim. 2:1; 4:17). This is the power that enabled Paul in the earliest days of his ministry (Acts 9:22), throughout the years of his service (1 Tim. 1:12) and in his final, darkest hours (2 Tim. 4:17). It is a compound word, being composed of "in" (ἐν) and "power" (δυναμόω). In the NT it points toward inner, moral or spiritual strength.[157] The present tense underscores the continual empowering of Christ to the one who draws upon Him for enabling. The individual's continual ability (ἰσχύω, "I can do") is possible only because of Christ's continual empowering (τῷ ἐνδυναμοῦντί, "him who strengthens"). That inward, unseen empowering (τῷ ἐνδυναμοῦντί)

---

152 TDNT, 3:397-398.

153 Friberg, 207.

154 Harmon, 444-445; NIDNTT, 3:1210,

155 The NASU marginal reading; cf. Fee, 434; Lenski, 890; O'Brien, 527; Sumney, 113; Vincent, ICC, 145.

156 Most Greek manuscripts include Χριστῷ here, to specify that "Him who strengthens" is Christ Himself. It, however, is not likely to be original, for the shorter reading is the more difficult and therefore more likely to be original. The addition smacks of a scribe's attempt to clarify a more spare statement. The intent is noble, for it is Christ of whom the Apostle speaks, but the addition is unnecessary.

157 Friberg, 149.

is made manifest in our obedience (ἰσχύω, "I can do"). The world only sees the power of Christ when His people draw upon it to perform His will with glad and contented hearts. This clarifies any misconception of Paul's intent in verse 11 when he used the Stoic word αὐτάρκης ("content," i.e., self-sufficient).[158]

Note the doubling up of the preposition ἐν ("in"), stressing the indwelling of the living Christ with all His mighty power and His bringing to each circumstance His enabling might. The preposition in compound graphically depicts the inflow of Christ's life and power as Paul needs it in each circumstance ("infuses strength into me"[159]). Paul's use of the preposition in this simple statement thus beautifully communicates the mystery of the believer's union with Christ. Standing alone the preposition depicts the reality of Paul's being "in Christ" (e.g. 1:1, 13, 26; 2:1, 5; 3:3, 14; 4:7, 19, 21). The preposition in compound depicts the reality of Christ indwelling Paul (e.g. Rom. 8:11; 1 Cor. 3:16; 2 Cor. 12:9; Eph. 3:17; Col. 1:27; 3:4). Me "in Christ" and Christ in me; herein lies every hope of every believer!

Note then the powerful use of the preposition in Paul's current line of reasoning: I may be "in whatever circumstances" (ἐν οἷς, v.11), but "in any and every circumstance" (ἐν παντὶ καὶ ἐν πᾶσιν, v.12) in which I find myself the reality upon which I count is that I am "in" (ἐν) Christ, who has all power and who indwells me with all that saving potential (τῷ ἐνδυναμοῦντί, "him who strengthens," v.13).

Paul personally was the object of this inward strengthening ("me," με). "The source of all Paul's capacity in face of the reality of human life is Christ ... He who is in Christ partakes of a power which makes all things possible. Here, then, is the source of the Christian's power."[160] This, then, is "the secret" which Paul has "learned," which he has come to "know" (v.12) and into which he has been initiated by the grace of God—union with the living Christ! This is what makes Paul's claim ("I can do")

---

158 Vincent, ICC, 145.

159 Ibid.

160 TDNT, 3:398.

something more than self-confidence and positive thinking. There is a dynamic reality indwelling him that makes "I can do" both a humble and truthful statement. This is "the surpassing value of knowing Christ Jesus my Lord" (3:8a). This is why Paul can "suffer the loss of all things, and count them but rubbish" ... all "so that I may gain Christ" (3:8b). This is to "know Him and the power of His resurrection and the fellowship of His sufferings" (3:10). This is the fulfillment of Paul's great desire: "For me, to live is Christ" (1:21a).

The context must be kept as a controlling influence when it comes to making application of this well-known and much-beloved promise. It is often wrenched from its surroundings here and made to apply in ways that Paul probably did not have in mind. The emphasis here is on the Apostle's ability—by Christ's indwelling presence, life and strength—to be content in any and every circumstance. It is not a promise that you or I can do any and every wild-eyed thing of which we may dream. It is not a promise that I may be super-human, but that I can be fully obedient. If the Son of God humbled himself to become incarnate (2:6-7) and then to humbly live among us (v.8a), and to give up His life in our place in the most painful and shameful of deaths (v.8b), then He, dwelling within me by His Spirit, knows how to enable me to walk humbly whatever His will may require of me.

> **Ministry Maxim**
>
> Circumstances do not define me; union with Christ defines both my identity and capabilities.

It is not uncommon to find "Phil. 4:13" written with a magic marker on the athletic tape wrapped around an athlete's wrist or ankle. He dreams of a pro career. She pictures herself in the Olympic Games. Christ is the One who can make that happen! But the promise might be more appropriately applied if he is never drafted or she has a career-ending injury, yet finds through Christ the grace to do so in faith and hope, giving glory to God all the while. Or, if one of them does achieve the dream, to do so humbly, without being ensnared by the powerful trappings that surround such success and fame.

> **Digging Deeper:**
> 1. When were "circumstances" at their worst for you physically and financially? When were they at their best? What was your experience with contentment in each of those times? (v.12)
> 2. How does the knowledge that you are in Christ and that Christ indwells you transform your present pressures into opportunities to know and see Christ? (v.13)
> 3. In what specific way do you need Christ to strengthen you right now?

Verse 14 – "Nevertheless, you have done well to share *with me* in my affliction."

Paul expressed his gratitude for the Philippians' gift (v.10) and then, lest he sound discontent with God's handling of his life, he qualified his statement once (v.11) and again (vv.12-13). But now, lest his extended qualifications sound ungrateful to the Philippians, he again commends their generosity (v.14). Paul uses πλὴν ("Nevertheless") as a means of "breaking off a discussion and emphasizing what is important."[161] Paul may be using it, as in 3:16, "at the end of an argument to single out the main point."[162]

Paul transitions from what he can do (v.13) to what the Philippians "have done" (ἐποιήσατε). The aorist points to the act of their generosity in sending a gift by the hand of Epaphroditus (v.18). They have cared for Paul since the birth of their church, at least ten years prior, and that love found expression again and again in expression of partnership through financial support (vv.10, 15-16; cf. 2 Cor. 11:8-9) and had now done so again in this most recent gift. In so acting, they have done "well" (καλῶς) and God is pleased. Paul stresses this fact by placing the adverb forward, before the verb it qualifies. In combination with this verb it may mean

---

161 BDAG, 5977.1.c.

162 Robertson, *Grammar*, 1187; cf. also its use in 1:18.

"kind enough to do something."¹⁶³ This is more than a tip of the hat for their kindness, but "positive and generous praise."¹⁶⁴

Then, by use of a participle, he specifies the action of which he is speaking: "to share" (συγκοινωνήσαντές). The participle functions adverbially, identifying the way in which they took action ("by sharing").¹⁶⁵ The action of the participle is to be understood as simultaneous with the main verb.¹⁶⁶ The verb is found only two other times in the NT and only here positively. Once when Paul warns: "Do not participate in [συγκοινωνεῖτε] the unfruitful deeds of darkness" (Eph. 5:11). And in a similar warning from an angel: "I heard another voice from heaven, saying, 'Come out of her, my people, so that you will not participate in [συγκοινωνήσητε] her sins and receive of her plagues'" (Rev. 18:4). It is a compound made up of σύν ("with") and κοινωνέω ("to share in"). The main root is another echo of a major theme running through Philippians, struck by the noun κοινωνία (1:5; 2:1; 3:10) and its kindred verb κοινωνέω (4:15). The preposition in compound intensifies "the emphasis on the mutuality and solidarity of the Philippians and Paul."¹⁶⁷ The resulting word means "to become a partaker together with others."¹⁶⁸ It may describe a sympathetic attitude¹⁶⁹ or interest.¹⁷⁰ This interest and attitude, however, was given expression in concrete action (ἐποιήσατε, "you have done"), as love must ever do. Paul opened the letter by using the kindred noun to describe their relationship to him: "both in my imprisonment and in the defense and confirmation of the gospel, you all are partakers [συγκοινωνούς] of grace with me" (1:7). They had shared in the same grace so they shared in his affliction, evidencing this by their recent financial gift.

---

163 BDAG, 3904.4.a.

164 O'Brien, 528.

165 Hellerman, 262.

166 Robertson, *Word Pictures*, 4:462.

167 Hansen, 316.

168 Thayer, 593.

169 Friberg, 360.

170 BDAG, 6902.1.b.

This sharing is "in my affliction" (μου τῇ θλίψει). The noun (τῇ θλίψει) describes pressure or a pressing and thus points to distress brought on by outward circumstances and the pressure they bring.[171] Here the presence of the definite article makes specific and concrete the "affliction" that is under consideration—Paul's imprisonment. It was used earlier to describe the effect sought by those preachers of the gospel who proclaimed the message out of selfish ambition (1:17). Paul's imprisonment in itself was an "affliction," but it was intensified by what took place outside of his confinement. The dative form both identifies that in which the Philippians share with Paul[172] and serves to emphasize "the 'togetherness' inherent in the συν prefix. The result is even greater emphasis on their being sharers in the affliction itself."[173] The personal pronoun (μου, "my") placed before the articular noun stresses the personal nature of the distress.[174]

All of this is a "filling up what is lacking in Christ's afflictions [τῶν θλίψεων τοῦ Χριστοῦ]" (Col. 1:24). Some have connected the present passage with these words of the Apostle to the Colossians and have given the present passage a particularly pointed eschatological significance. At times θλῖψις can draw upon its usage in the LXX and be used in the NT in a technical sense to describe the Messianic sufferings that signal the final stages of God's salvation program before Christ's return (e.g. Matt. 24:21, 29; Mark 13:19; 2 Thess. 1:6). Some have seen in Paul's present words a hint at this, suggesting that Paul hereby enlarges the discussion to let the Philippian believers know that their gift is far more than a personal expression of care for Paul as an individual, but a part of hastening the return of

> **Ministry Maxim**
>
> A gift is not just sharing what you have with another, but joining them in what they are experiencing.

---

171 Ibid., 3588.

172 O'Brien, 528.

173 Fee, 439.

174 Kennedy, 471.

their Lord.[175] The context, however, does not seem to point us explicitly in that direction. Rather, the word seems to be used in its more general sense. What is clear is that Paul shared in Christ's afflictions (cf. Phil. 3:10) and now the Philippians are sharing in his. Shared suffering is one of the truly unifying experiences of the body of Christ—unifying believers with the Lord and with one another.

> **Digging Deeper:**
> 1. Who do you know that is suffering "affliction" of some kind right now?
> 2. In what way can you "share with" them in that affliction by an act of generosity and thoughtfulness that expresses your solidarity with them?

Verse 15 – "You yourselves also know, Philippians, that at the first preaching of the gospel, after I left Macedonia, no church shared with me in the matter of giving and receiving but you alone;"

This new sentence begins with δὲ used as a continuative, but it is left untranslated by the NASU (though note "And" in the NASB, NET, ESV, and RSV; cf. "Now," KJV, NKJV; "Moreover," NIV). Paul appeals now to what the Philippians themselves "know" (οἴδατε). He has just used the same verb twice in verse 12 to speak of what he knows. See there for more on the meaning. The καί ("also") compares the knowledge of the Philippians with that of Paul. They knew as well as he did the truth about these matters. Paul appeals directly to the church as a collective whole (Φιλιππήσιοι, "Philippians"). Such a direct address is not a common occurrence in Paul's letters (cf. 2 Cor. 6:11; Gal. 3:1), but might be read here as expressing "earnestness and affectionate remembrance."[176]

---

175 e.g. Harmon, 447-448; Martin, 178-179.

176 Vincent, 147.

The personal pronoun in the plural form (ὑμεῖς) along with the second person plural form of the verb doubles up the emphasis even further ("You yourselves"). Paul is speaking quite directly and personally.

That which they know is set forth by a ὅτι ("that') clause. He harkens back to an earlier time "at the first preaching of the gospel" (ἐν ἀρχῇ τοῦ εὐαγγελίου). The "gospel" (τοῦ εὐαγγελίου) has been much on Paul's mind throughout this letter, from the Philippians own partnership with Paul in the gospel (1:5, 7), the status of the gospel's advance with the great Apostle incarcerated (1:12, 16), the gospel's demand to shape the entire lives of those who embrace it (1:27a), its power to unify diverse peoples (1:27b), and the service of various others in advancing this gospel (2:22; 4:3). His statement here is more literally "in [the] beginning of the gospel."[177] He means, of course, not the absolute beginning of the gospel's origins, but refers to the gospel's first coming to them some ten years or more prior to the time of this letter, which was, incidentally, the first recorded arrival of the gospel in Europe (Acts 16:11-40). As Paul opened the letter he spoke of their "participation in the gospel from the first day" (Phil. 1:5). He now enlarges upon how, "from the first day," they have uniquely, among all the churches begun by Paul, consistently partnered with him in advancing the gospel.

The account in Acts 16 dramatically describes the efforts of Paul's missionary band to find God's will with regard to the gospel's advance. At multiple points they found their efforts being restricted. They were "forbidden by the Holy Spirit to speak the word in Asia" (v.6b). They "were trying to go into Bithynia, and the Spirit of Jesus would not permit them" (v.7). But when they came to Troas "A vision appeared to Paul in the night: a man of Macedonia was standing and appealing to him, and saying, 'Come over to Macedonia and help us'" (v.9). Knowing they had gained God's direction for their course, "immediately we sought to go to Macedonia, concluding that God had called us to preach the gospel to them" (v.10).

---

177 cf. Ἀρχὴ τοῦ εὐαγγελίου ("The beginning of the gospel," Mark 1:1).

But Paul is focusing his attention not so much on the way the gospel first came to them in Philippi, but what happened with it once he had moved on beyond them, for he further specifies the time to which he refers by adding "after I left Macedonia" (ὅτε ἐξῆλθον ἀπὸ Μακεδονίας). The aorist tense of the verb is used to signify not the precise moment of his departure, but the general period after he left the province.[178] Philippi was a leading city of the Roman province of Macedonia. From Philippi he made his way to Thessalonica, the capital of the province of Macedonia. There the nucleus of a church was formed, though under stiff persecution from the Jews of the city (Acts 17:1-9). Fleeing Thessalonica, he made his way to Berea where he found them to be "more noble-minded than those in Thessalonica" (v.11a), for "they received the word with great eagerness, examining the Scriptures daily to see whether these things were so" (v.11b). Wonderfully, "many of them believed, along with a number of prominent Greek women and men" (v.12). But the Jews came from Thessalonica and created a disturbance which pushed Paul out of Macedonia altogether and on to Athens (Acts 17:16-34) and then to Corinth (18:1-17), both of which resided in the province of Achaia. Paul had traveled ahead of his associates, leaving Silas and Timothy in Berea (17:14). When he arrived in Corinth he supported himself by making tents (18:3) and giving witness to the gospel as he was able in the synagogues (18:4). When Silas and Timothy caught up with Paul in Corinth, they appear to have brought some financial gift with them, for from that point "Paul began devoting himself completely to the word, solemnly testifying to the Jews that Jesus was the Christ" (Acts. 18:5).

From that point, the church in Philippi, uniquely among those which Paul had been blessed to plant, continued to track the Apostle's journey and ministry, participating with him in it by their prayers and giving. He could honestly tell them, "no church shared with me in the matter of giving and receiving but you alone" (οὐδεμία μοι ἐκκλησία ἐκοινώνησεν εἰς λόγον δόσεως καὶ λήμψεως εἰ μὴ ὑμεῖς μόνοι). Paul elsewhere, in the face of accusation and criticism, defended his right to make his living from the

---

178 Lightfoot, 182; cf. Fee, 441; O'Brien, 533.

gospel (1 Cor. 9:3-14), but he also stoutly refused to do so lest the testimony of the gospel be harmed through him (vv.15-18; Acts 20:33-34; 1 Cor. 4:12; 2 Cor. 11:7-9; 1 Thess. 2:9; 2 Thess. 3:7-10). Thus the Philippian church must have been insistent in their efforts to continue supporting Paul. From Athens Paul moved on to Corinth. He would later remind the Corinthian believers that while he was among them "the brethren came from Macedonia"—a probable reference to people from the Philippian church—and "they fully supplied my need" (2 Cor. 11:9; cf. Acts 18:5).

> **Ministry Maxim**
>
> True friendship finds concrete ways to evidence mutuality and reciprocity in a common cause.

This he presently refers to as having "shared" (ἐκοινώνησεν) of their substance with him in his ministry and in his need. This was evidence of their partnership with him in the gospel. The κοινωνία word family has played a key role in the development of this entire letter. The compound verb of verse 14 (συγκοινωνήσαντές, "to share") and the present use of the uncompounded verb (ἐκοινώνησεν, "shared") serve with τῇ κοινωνίᾳ ("participation," 1:5) and συγκοινωνούς ("partakers," 1:7) to round out an inclusion that wraps its arms around the entire letter. The letter is dominated by this theme of shared participation and fellowship (1:5; 2:1; 3:10; 4:14, 15). The theme headlines the letter (1:5, 7) and rounds out its final words (4:14, 15).

Their desire for partnership with the Apostle found expression "in the matter of giving and receiving" (εἰς λόγον δόσεως καὶ λήμψεως). The noun λόγος, while often signifying a "word," has a broad range of meaning and is employed here as a technical term from the commercial world which was used of the settling of one's accounts, as it seems to again in verse 17.[179] The nouns δόσεως ("giving")[180] and λήμψεως ("receiving")[181] were both technical terms from the commercial world of the first century.

---

179 BDAG, 4605.2.b.

180 Elsewhere in the NT only in James 1:17.

181 Used only here in the NT.

The former was "used for a payment or an installment," while the latter "the receiving of a payment."[182] Together they were used "in the sense of 'credit and debit.'"[183] Paul elsewhere made clear that those who received spiritual grace might appropriately share physical goods as a response (Rom. 15:27; 1 Cor. 9:11; Gal. 6:6; cf. Matt. 10:10). It appears that for the Philippians this was a reflex response born of their appreciation for the spiritual life and liberty into which they had been brought through the Apostle's ministry. But this had clearly not been the case in most instances, for the negation was universal and absolute (οὐδεμία ... ἐκκλησία, "no church") with one caveat: "except for you only" (εἰ μὴ ὑμεῖς μόνοι).

A swath of scholars have read tension and ill-ease into Paul's use of financial and commercial terms as he comments here on the gift of the Philippians. But research into the use of these terms in the secular writings of the day reveals that they communicate just the opposite. Marshall summarizes, saying "Rather than pointing to tension or embarrassment on Paul's part over the gift, the language implies the opposite. It reflects a warm and lasting relationship. He not only receives the gift gladly as a sign of their continuing concern, but also recalls the mutual exchange of services and affection which they had shared in the past."[184] Fee adds, "This usage is so well established both in the papyri and in literary works that it is quite impossible for the Philippians to have understood it differently."[185]

Verse 16 – "for even in Thessalonica you sent *a gift* more than once for my needs."

Paul stretches out the thought begun in verse 15 before ending the sentence here. He has established the fact that no other church partnered with him as did these Philippians, for after he left the province of Macedonia they sent their gifts of concern more than once. Now he effectively circles back

---

182 Rienecker, 563.

183 Ibid.

184 O'Brien (534) quoting Marshall, *Enmity in Corinth*, 163-164.

185 Fee, 443.

to an incident that took place even prior to his original departure from the province of Macedonia.

The ὅτι is understood as introducing an explanation ("for"). His words here are an expansion upon and further explanation of the distinctiveness of the Philippian believers' role in supporting the gospel ministry through him. The first καὶ ("even") stresses the uniqueness—and therefore the further confirmatory nature—of the event he is about to recall. He harkens to an experience "in Thessalonica" (ἐν Θεσσαλονίκῃ) as evidence of his point (Acts 17:1-9). Thus he provides evidence of the Philippian believers' eagerness to share with him in the ministry of the gospel.

Even so closely upon the heels of his ministry among them, he can say, "you sent a gift" (ἐπέμψατε). The words "a gift" have been added by the translators; though they are not found in the original text, the context leads us to expect them and they are appropriate here. Placing the verb at the end of the clause serves to add emphasis. The aorist looks to the moment their love found concrete expression in giving. The verb has been used several times in this letter to emphasize the care of Paul and the Philippians for one another. Paul hoped to send Timothy to them (2:19, 23), just as they had sent Epaphroditus to him as their "messenger and minister to my need" (2:25). And Paul was now sending Epaphroditus back to them, knowing his care for them and their concern for him (2:28). Love always finds a way to become concrete in its expression—whether through sending one of your own to meet a need or in sending some of your substance to provide in an hour of crisis or opportunity.

> **Ministry Maxim**
>
> Where there is eagerness and consistency in giving there can be assurance of the gospel's impact.

This they did "more than once" (καὶ ἅπαξ καὶ δίς). The double use of καὶ means "both … and." The adverbs mean "once" (ἅπαξ) and "twice" (δίς). Thus a literal rendering would be "both once and twice," though the phrase was an idiomatic way of indicating a repeated action (cf. 1 Thess.

2:18). Stählin's suggestion of "repeatedly" as a translation[186] may overstate the case here, for that might sound like a long string of gifts were sent. Paul's point seems to be simply that they did this more than once, but not necessarily unendingly (for in this most recent gift Paul can speak of their "revived ... concern" for him, v.10). Thessalonica, like Philippi, was a city within the province of Macedonia. When Paul had left Philippi, his next ministry stop was Thessalonica. There too he faced persecution and was likely only in the city a relatively short time, perhaps a few weeks at most. It is thus surprising that the Philippians found time to send gifts of support more than once in such a relatively short period of time. The primary obstacle would not have been distance, but time. Yet so eager and ready was their love that they made sure his needs were met while he was sharing with their neighbors the gospel which had brought them new life. Paul made a point in Thessalonica not to rely upon the support of the locals, but to work with his own hands (1 Thess. 2:9; 2 Thess. 3:7-10). It might thus be surmised that the gifts sent by the Philippians at that time were not substantial enough to relieve Paul of all need for self-supporting labor. But whatever the size of the gift, it was the giving of it that meant the most.

More than once their love found expression. These acts were expressions of great love and care because they were "for my needs" (εἰς τὴν χρείαν μοι). The preposition εἰς[187] ("for") has been understood variously as denoting reference/respect[188] or purpose.[189] When used in a commercial context it can describe "the object of gifts, collections, etc., or the various items in an account which have to be met."[190] The dative pronoun functions as the indirect object (μοι; i.e., "sent ... to me"). The noun τὴν χρείαν ("needs") "often has the nuance of destitution, indigence, privation,

---

186 TDNT, 1:381.

187 The preposition is missing in some manuscripts, but is probably original. The omission probably occurred because of the identical ending of the previous word, δὶς (Silva, 209).

188 Sumney, 116.

189 εἰς + accusative, Hellerman, 265; O'Brien, 536.

190 Kennedy, 471.

distress."¹⁹¹ His needs were indeed true needs, though Paul should not be understood as indicating he was approaching starvation. The article may designate a specific need of Paul's at the time¹⁹² or it may be possessive ("*my* needs").¹⁹³ Paul will shortly make use of the same noun to assure them that as they have thought of his needs and sacrificed to meet them, so they can rest assured that God knows all their needs and will see that they too are met "according to His riches in glory" (v.19).

> **Digging Deeper:**
> 1. What does the pattern of giving in a local church say about the people's embrace of the gospel? What does the pattern of your personal giving say?
> 2. To what ministry have you most consistently invested your financial gifts? Why?

Verse 17 – "Not that I seek the gift itself, but I seek for the profit which increases to your account."

Paul once again balances what he's just said (cf. 3:12 and 4:11 where he also opened with οὐχ ὅτι). He seems intent on making a carefully nuanced point and not wanting to be misunderstood on either side of the matter. Lightfoot calls it his "nervous anxiety to clear himself,"¹⁹⁴ but Robertson questions the negative bent in his wording and suggests it might better be understood as "delicate courtesy"¹⁹⁵ that drives Paul's clarification here. He makes his present balancing comment by way of a "Not ... but" (οὐχ

---

191 Spicq, 1:97.
192 Fee, 446; Hellerman, 265; O'Brien, 536; contra. Sumney, 116.
193 Vincent, ICC, 148.
194 Lightfoot, 183.
195 Robertson, *Word Pictures*, 4:462; cf. Lenski, 894.

... ἀλλὰ) statement. The negation (οὐχ, "Not") is absolute and categorical.[196] It introduces the point at which he hopes he will not be misunderstood. The adversative (ἀλλὰ, "but") is strong and emphatic and sets forth the point he wishes to make.

The idea to be denied is "that I seek the gift itself" (ὅτι ἐπιζητῶ τὸ δόμα). The verb is used in both clauses of this verse (and only one other time in Paul, Romans 11:7). It is a compound comprised of ἐπί ("on/upon") and ζητέω ("to seek"). The preposition in compound is directive, rather than intensive[197], thus "indicating the concentration of the action upon some object."[198] It is "presumably somewhat more emphatic or goal-directed than in the case of ζητέω" alone.[199] The present tense underscores the present and abiding nature of Paul's pursuit. The noun (τὸ δόμα, "the gift") is elsewhere in the NT used of both tangible gifts between fathers and their sons (Matt. 7:11; Luke 11:13) and spiritual gifts from our heavenly Father to us as His children (Eph. 4:8). The definite article designates the specific contribution recently sent from the Philippians by the hand of Epaphroditus (Phil. 4:18), but it also particularizes the matter of the gift so that "itself" has been added to distinguish "the gift" from "the profit" it might bring to those doing the giving.

In strong contrast (ἀλλὰ, "but") to any possible greedy, money-mongering quest for their financial gifts is that which should be understood. Paul confesses, "I seek for the profit" (ἐπιζητῶ τὸν καρπὸν) which would come to the Philippian believers. The verb is repeated from the previous clause; a repetition Alford calls "solemn and emphatic."[200] The articular noun τὸν καρπὸν ("the profit") is more literally "the fruit." Paul opened the letter telling them he prays they would be "filled with the fruit [καρπὸν] of righteousness that comes through Jesus Christ, to the glory and praise

---

196 Thayer, 408.

197 Ibid., 238.

198 Rienecker, 563.

199 Louw-Nida, 27.42.

200 Alford, 3:194.

of God" (1:11). And Paul could speak from personal experience, for to him physical life equaled fruitful service: "If I am to live in the flesh, that means fruitful [καρπός] labor for me" (1:22). Paul's great concern is not "the gift" *per se*, but what their giving represented regarding their spiritual relationship to God and the reward He would surely heap upon it for their benefit. To borrow from his Corinthian correspondence: "I do not seek what is yours, but you" (2 Cor. 12:14).

God rewards obedience and Paul was confident He would reward the Philippians. As definite as was the gift (τὸ δόμα, "*the* gift") so also—though spiritual—"*the* profit" will be just as definite (τὸν καρπὸν; italics added).[201] The spiritual is as real as the physical. But this is more than that; he is confident that their gift will redound to God in the giving of thanks by those who will in the future come to faith in Christ through him, enabled now by the gift the Philippians have given to sustain him. In his extended instruction to the Corinthians regarding giving (2 Cor. 8-9), where he used the example of these Philippians as motivation (8:1-5; 9:4), he said "the ministry of this service [i.e., giving to relieve the suffering of their brothers and sisters in Christ in Judea] is not only fully supplying the needs of the saints, but is also overflowing through many thanksgivings to God. Because of the proof given by this ministry they will glorify God for your obedience to your confession of the gospel of Christ, and for the liberality of your contribution to them and to all, while they also, by prayer on your behalf, yearn for you because of the surpassing grace of God in you." (9:12-14).

> **Ministry Maxim**
>
> It is a tricky thing to teach the blessedness of giving without misrepresenting your motives.

Paul further qualifies the profit which he is seeking for the benefit of the Philippian believers. It is that "which increases to your account" (τὸν πλεονάζοντα εἰς λόγον ὑμῶν). The present tense participle pictures an ongoing escalation in the yield of "profit" from their obedience to God.

---

201 Lenski, 894.

And this he pictures being recorded in "your account" (λόγον ὑμῶν). He has just used λόγος as a commercial technical term ("the matter," v.15) and he does so now again. Paul is ever conscious of his eschatological reward (e.g., 2 Cor. 1:14; 1 Thess. 2:19-20; 3:9) and is overtly so in the present letter (Phil. 2:16; 4:1).[202] He is now seeking to steer the believers of Philippi into obedience because he knew it to be not merely an individual, personal expenditure between them and himself, but an investment that God would reward with unending and ever-increasing "profit" accrued to their "account" and which would be enjoyed both here (in smaller measure) and in eternity (in fullest measure). As he told the Corinthian believers: "he who sows sparingly will also reap sparingly, and he who sows bountifully will also reap bountifully" (2 Cor. 9:6). Jesus Himself said, "It is more blessed to give than to receive" (Acts 20:35) and "Give, and it will be given to you. They will pour into your lap a good measure—pressed down, shaken together, and running over. For by your standard of measure it will be measured to you in return" (Luke 6:38).

Verse 18 – "But I have received everything in full and have an abundance; I am amply supplied, having received from Epaphroditus what you have sent, a fragrant aroma, an acceptable sacrifice, well-pleasing to God."

As verse 11 qualified and clarified Paul's statement in verse 10, so verse 17 qualifies and clarifies Paul's statement in verse 15 and 16. And as verse 12 expanded further upon the qualification of verse 11, so here verse 18 expands further upon what Paul has set forth in verse 17.

The sentence opens with δὲ used as a mild adversative. Paul is reinforcing the idea that he does not "seek the gift" from the Philippians (v.17a). He is motivated neither by greed nor destitution. Quite the contrary, now that he has "received from Epaphroditus what [they] have sent." Paul, continuing the commercial metaphors, piles up three expressions

---

202 Hellerman, 266.

to emphasize what the gift from the Philippians represented with regard to him. Then, shifting the metaphor to that of worship, he balanced this by using three more expressions to explain what their gift was with regard to God.

With regard to Paul their gift, firstly, represents "everything in full" (πάντα). The adjective is an important one in Paul's discussion of their gift (vv.10-20). He knows how to live "in any [παντὶ] and every [πᾶσιν] circumstance" (v.12). He testified, "I can do all things [πάντα] through Him who strengthens me" (v.13). In the next line he will assure them, "my God will supply all [πᾶσαν] your needs" (v.19). So when he uses it here it has both an expansive, absolute sense and is also restricted to the concerns of the immediate context. It means, most simply, "all." But to say he has received "all" begs the question, "all *of what*?" The translation "everything in full" represents the intent—"everything" they sent by the hand of Epaphroditus, "in full" and without anything missing. It functions thus as a receipt, providing an accounting of the transaction and affirming the faithfulness of Epaphroditus as its courier. All they sent he has "received" (ἀπέχω) safely and faithfully from the hand of their beloved courier. The verb when used intransitively emphasizes putting distance between two things and means "abstain from" (1 Thess. 4:3; 5:22; 1 Tim. 4:3). But used transitively, as it is here, it was a commercial term (added to the list of other commercial technical terms used in this section, cf. vv.15-17) that meant "provide a receipt for a sum paid in full."[203] While this is true, the statement also seems to underscore Paul's contentment with what they have sent. The use of the term αὐτάρκης in verse 11 ("content") means he may also here be stressing that the Philippians' gift has brought him into that place of self-sufficiency and contentment. He is contented, he has "all" that he needs. Their gift has achieved its intent. He is cared for.

To this Paul adds (καὶ, "and") that their gift is to him "an abundance" (περισσεύω). Though the translators represent it as a noun, it is in fact a

---

203 BDAG, 870.1; TDNT, 2:828.

verb in the original text. The present tense underscores the current reality into which their gift has set him. The verb has played a key role in the letter. Paul prays that their "love may abound [περισσεύῃ] still more and more" (1:9). He wants to so live, he says, that their "proud confidence in me may abound [περισσεύῃ] in Christ Jesus" (1:26). Paul could genuinely testify: "I know how to get along with humble means, and I also know how to live in prosperity [περισσεύειν]; in any and every circumstance I have learned the secret of being filled and going hungry, both of having abundance [περισσεύειν] and suffering need" (4:12).[204] So now, the gift from the Philippians has put him in the latter category. All that they sent is more than all he needed.

Thirdly, Paul can say, "I am amply supplied" (πεπλήρωμαι). The verb is a common one, used over eighty times in the NT. It generally conveys the notion of making full or filling up completely.[205] And again here the verb is part of a series of usages throughout the letter. Paul prays for them so that they may stand before Christ at His coming, "having been filled [πεπληρωμένοι] with the fruit of righteousness which comes through Jesus Christ, to the glory and praise of God" (1:11). He calls upon them, in view of their blessings in Christ, to "make my joy complete [πληρώσατέ]" (2:2). And he will promise in the next verse "And my God will supply [πληρώσει] all your needs" (4:19). Presently it is in the perfect tense, underscoring the abiding state into which their gift has brought the Apostle. The passive voice emphasizes that it is their act in sending the gift that has placed Paul in this position of abundance.

Paul can honestly claim such blessedness and abundance, "having received from Epaphroditus what you have sent" (δεξάμενος παρὰ Ἐπαφροδίτου τὰ παρ' ὑμῶν). The aorist tense of the verb pictures the moment of receipt, when Epaphroditus transferred to Paul's hands the gift he had so carefully protected on the long journey to Rome. The participle explains how Paul has come to possess "everything in full," to have "an abundance," and to be "amply supplied." It expresses action

---

204 cf. also the use of the kindred adverb περισσοτέρως in 1:14 ("far more").

205 Friberg, 317.

contemporaneous with (he was amply supplied when he received their gift)²⁰⁶ or antecedent to ("now that I have received")²⁰⁷ the main verb. For more on Epaphroditus and his relationship to both the church in Philippi and the Apostle Paul see 2:25-30. The words "what you have sent" (τὰ παρ' ὑμῶν) are more simply and literally rendered, "the things from you."

> **Ministry Maxim**
>
> I honor Christ's bodily sacrifice when I sacrifice of my substance for His glory and other's good.

Note Paul's emphasis: the gift was "from you" (παρ' ὑμῶν, plural, i.e., the entire church) and it was, in ultimate terms, given "to God" (τῷ θεῷ)²⁰⁸, but it was sent by and thus received "from Epaphroditus" (παρὰ Ἐπαφροδίτου). And all this was to the great benefit of Paul.

Thus we can say there are four parties involved in the practical matter of giving: *We give* as an expression of worship *to God* via some *human agency* for the benefit of *other people*. The fact that the gift is physically (or electronically) put into the hands or care of a person or church or ministry does not negate that it is being given "to God." A divine responsibility lies then upon that human being, church or ministry that serves as the agency of the gift, to see that it is used for the glory of God in the lives of those for whom it is intended.

Paul added a clause in apposition to what he has said about the nature of their gift as it relates to him personally. The clause expresses his judgment as to how God views their act of giving.²⁰⁹ With regard to God, their gift was "a fragrant aroma" (ὀσμὴν εὐωδίας). The noun translated "aroma"

---

206 Rienecker, 563.

207 Hellernman, 267.

208 There are numerous verbal similarities to Leviticus 1:9, 13, 17, which speak of "an offering by fire of a soothing aroma to the LORD" (κάρπωμά ἐστιν θυσία ὀσμὴ εὐωδίας τῷ κυρίῳ). This probably signals the Apostle's intentional dependence upon these texts and his intent to stress that their financial gift to him was ultimately an expression of worship to God (Sumney, 118; Vincent, 150). Note O'Brien's contrary view, 542.

209 Alford, 3:194.

(ὀσμὴν) was used literally of the aroma, fragrance or odor that something emitted, whether pleasant or repulsive. But it was also frequently used in a metaphorical sense where "the Middle Eastern concept that an odor from something is communicating its power."[210] The noun "fragrant" (εὐωδίας) is positive and denotes that which is pleasing to the olfactory instrument. Both words are stock terminology from the OT sacrificial system. To one listening to this letter as it was read aloud, the aural similarities of εὐωδίας ("fragrant") and Εὐοδίαν (Euodia, v.2) would be striking.[211] It is impossible to determine whether Paul intended some subtleties of connection and meaning here, but given his attention to detail it would not be surprising. Was there in this a subtle hint that Euodia see to it that whatever contention has arisen between her and Syntyche must be resolved so as to become a pleasing aroma to the Lord?

Both of the nouns appear together in the NT in Ephesians 5:2 where Christ, in His death, was a "sacrifice to God as a fragrant aroma [ὀσμὴν εὐωδίας]." They appear also in 2 Corinthians 2 where believers are called "the aroma [εὐωδία] of Christ" (v.15) and where God "manifests through us the sweet aroma [τὴν ὀσμὴν] of the knowledge of Him in every place" (v.14). To the perishing we are "a fragrance [ὀσμὴ] from death to death" and to the believing "a fragrance [ὀσμὴ] from life to life" (v.16). Christ in His saving death is "a fragrant aroma" that makes us into a purveyor of that sweet savor to those around us. One means by which that takes place is through our sacrificial, strategic and mission-critical giving. We perpetuate the beauty and power of Jesus' sacrifice to God on our behalf when we, in grateful reflection upon His sacrifice, make sacrifices of service or substance to see that more people know of His sacrificial love.

Indeed, their gift was not one of convenience and made from excess, but was a "sacrifice" (θυσίαν). These people understood sacrificial giving. When Paul described the giving of these Philippians to the famine relief fund he was collecting, he said that it was "in a great ordeal of affliction" that "their abundance of joy and their deep poverty overflowed in the

---

210 Friberg, 286.

211 Sumney, 118,

wealth of their liberality" (2 Cor. 8:2). It was "according to their ability, and beyond their ability" that they gave "of their own accord, begging us with much urging for the favor of participation in the support of the saints" (vv.3-4). In response to Jesus' giving Himself as "a sacrifice to God" (Eph. 5:2) we are called to give ourselves to God as "living sacrifices" (Rom. 12:1). When Paul used the example of these Macedonian believers' giving in order to motivate the Corinthians believers in their giving, he noted "they first gave themselves to the Lord and to us by the will of God" (2 Cor. 8:5). Little wonder Paul earlier in this letter could describe the faith of the Philippian believers as a "sacrifice and service" to God (Phil. 2:17). Their present gift to the Apostle no doubt came from some similar level of sacrifice and thus he wanted them to know it was "acceptable" (δεκτήν) to God. That is to say, they could be assured their gift brought pleasure to God because He approved of their sacrifice.[212]

Their gift was given "to God" (τῷ θεῷ) even though it was put in the hands of Epaphroditus as the agent and ultimately into Paul's as the recipient of the gift. And to God it was "well-pleasing" (εὐάρεστον). Throughout the Greco-Roman world the word was "commonly said of things and esp. of pers. noted for their civic-minded generosity and who endeavor to do things that are pleasing."[213] It is used nine times in the NT, eight of which are by Paul. It describes the will of God (Rom. 12:2) and the sacrifice of oneself made to Christ (v.1). It thus generally describes that which is "well-pleasing" to God (Rom. 14:18; 2 Cor. 5:9; Eph. 5:10; Col. 3:20; cf. Heb. 13:21). Only once does it describe what is acceptable to human beings (Tit. 2:9). It is used only here as a verdict rendered retrospectively.[214]

There are multiple verbal parallels with Paul's opening prayer for the Philippians (1:9-11) which may signal that he is employing an inclusion to round out and bring the letter to a close:[215]

---

212 BDAG, 1767.2.
213 Ibid., 3204.
214 TDNT, 1:457.
215 Hellerman, 267.

1:9-11	4:17-20
πεπληρωμένοι ("having been filled," v.11)	πεπλήρωμαι ("I am amply supplied," v.18; cf. 19)
καρπὸν δικαιοσύνης ("the fruit of righteousness," v.11)	τὸν καρπὸν ("the profit," v.17)
περισσεύῃ ("abound," v.9)	περισσεύω ("have an abundance," v.18; cf. v.12)
εἰς δόξαν ("to the glory," v.11)	δόξῃ ("glory," v.19); δόξα ("glory," v.20)

> **Digging Deeper:**
>
> 1. How can a pastor urge his people to give generously without sounding self-serving? (v.17)
> 2. Does the contentment of the pastor encourage the people to faithfully give or discourage sacrificial giving? (v.18)
> 3. Do the people in your fellowship see themselves as giving to "the church" or to God? (v.18) What practical difference does it make?

Verse 19 – "And my God will supply all your needs according to His riches in glory in Christ Jesus."

Using δὲ ("And") as a transitional particle, Paul moves now to wrap up his comments regarding their gift (vv.10-20). The Apostle has learned "how to get along with humble means" and "how to live in prosperity," how "being filled and going hungry" feels, as well as what "having abundance and suffering need" is like (v.12). So he speaks from experience when he assures them that "my God will supply all your needs" (ὁ ... θεός μου πληρώσει πᾶσαν χρείαν ὑμῶν). Paul can speak of "my God" (ὁ ... θεός μου) not because he has an exclusive claim upon God and His grace, but because Paul has yielded himself exclusively to Him and out of a wealth of personal experience he can testify to God's faithfulness in meeting his needs and making him content (v.11) regardless of his circumstances. He has again and again seen Christ's indwelling strength be sufficient to meet every situation (v.13). The noun with the article makes specific the object of the Apostle's trust—God; not just any god, but, literally, "*the* God." And He is "my" (μου) God—the One who has made me, redeemed me, kept and supplied me, and now rules and owns my life. Paul opened the letter by calling Him "my God" (τῷ θεῷ μου, 1:3) and now he bookends the letter with the same reference (4:19; cf. also Rom. 1:8; 1 Cor. 1:4; 2 Cor. 12:21; Philem. 3).

> **Ministry Maxim**
> The servant of God will never lack what is necessary to express his love in service to God.

This faithful God "will supply" (πληρώσει) when it is needed. This is the same verb Paul just used to assure the Philippians "I have received everything in full [πεπλήρωμαι] and have an abundance" (v.18). The sense is, "As God, through you, has done for me, so He will do also for you in your needs." The verb means "to fill something completely."[216] For more on the verb and its thematic use throughout the letter see our comments above on verse 18. The future tense looks not only to their present needs, but also to the broad expanse of possibilities that may arise in the future and assures the believers that nothing will come upon them that will outstrip God's ability and faithfulness to "supply" fully "all your needs" (πᾶσαν χρείαν ὑμῶν). The indicative is used to make "a non-contingent (or unqualified) statement."[217] God will do what He promises here. The boldness of this promise obviously made some scribes nervous and so some manuscripts have an aorist optative in place of the future indicative,

---

216 TDNT, 6:291.

217 Wallace, 449.

transforming this into a prayerful wish of the Apostle rather than an assured promise. But both the manuscript evidence and the difficulty of the reading support the indicative reading.[218] We should not take the sharp edge off of "this comprehensive, apparently unqualified promise."[219]

Paul has used the noun in this letter to admit to his present needs as a prisoner of Rome (2:25) as well as the needs he had experienced shortly after leaving their city the first time (4:16). Clearly Paul knew the needs experienced in life's low points ("humble ... going hungry," v.12) as well as the unique needs that life's high points present us ("prosperity ... having abundance," v.12). These people also knew what "a great ordeal of affliction" and "deep poverty" is like (2 Cor. 8:2). Not only is Paul calling on his own personal experience with God, but he is reminding the Philippian believers of their experience with God when "according to their ability, and beyond their ability, they gave of their own accord" to aid those they deemed to be in greater need (2 Cor. 8:3).

Their mutual knowledge of one another's experiences and the fact that they had come to have deeper fellowship in Christ through these experiences (1:5, 7; 2:1; 3:10; 4:14, 15) packs even more power behind the Apostle's promise here. He is appealing thus not only to the imagination concerning what might come to pass, but to the memory to recall what had already come to pass.

The indefinite singular adjective πᾶσαν ("all") looks to each and every thing that will become the experience of the Philippians (ὑμῶν, "your") as they continue in the path of discipleship. Under the care of a sovereign God nothing will arise that will outstrip His ability and commitment to provide what is needed to continue in the way of obedience to Him. It is the divine promise here that enables Paul's previous bold claim: "I can do all things through Him who strengthens me" (4:13).

The assurance is not simply that God will meet their needs, but that He will do so generously and lavishly. His provision will be not "from" [NLT] or "out of" [NJB] the wealth of all He has available to Him in

---

218 See O'Brien (516, 545-546) for a thorough accounting of the related issues.
219 Hellerman, 268.

the salvation He has provided in His Son, but "according to [κατὰ] His riches in glory in Christ Jesus."[220] If Paul had said "from" it would indicate source. If he had said "out of" it would have indicated some portion taken from a larger whole. But by using κατὰ ("according to") he indicates both source and lavish proportionality.[221] The preposition here "denotes reference, relation, proportion."[222] It points not merely to origin, but dimension, proportion and ratio. It focuses us not simply on the size of the gift, but on the scope and magnitude of that in accordance with which it is measured. It speaks not primarily to the dimensions of the gift, but the intentions and generosity of the Giver.

That against which the provision is measured is "His riches" (τὸ πλοῦτος αὐτοῦ). The noun is a favorite of Paul's. He uses it just once in a literal way (1 Tim. 6:17), but often in speaking of the wealth and magnitude of God's goodness. It describes the plenteous supply of something.[223] He speaks of "the riches of His kindness and tolerance and patience" (Rom. 2:4), "the riches of His glory" (Rom. 9:23; Eph. 3:16), "the riches both of the wisdom and knowledge of God" exclaiming "How unsearchable are His judgments and unfathomable His ways!" (Rom. 11:33). He speaks of "the riches of His grace" (Eph. 1:7), "the riches of the glory of His inheritance in the saints" (Eph. 1:18), "the surpassing riches of His grace" (2:7), "the unfathomable riches of Christ" (3:8), "the riches of the glory of this mystery among the Gentiles, which is Christ in you, the hope of glory" (Col. 1:27), and "the wealth that comes from the full assurance of understanding, resulting in a true knowledge of God's mystery, that is, Christ Himself" (Col. 2:2). And, interestingly, the Apostle used it also to describe the generosity of these very believers, speaking of how "their deep poverty overflowed in the wealth [πλοῦτος] of their liberality" (2 Cor. 8:2).

---

220 Ibid., 270.

221 Ibid; cf. Hendriksen, 209-210; Kent, 11:157; Lenski, 898; Robertson, *Paul's Joy in Christ*, 262; Vincent, ICC, 151; Wuest, 117.

222 Thayer, 328.

223 BDAG, 5996.2.

To what should the prepositional phrase "in glory" (ἐν δόξῃ) be connected? Some see it modifying the previous prepositional phrase (κατὰ τὸ πλοῦτος αὐτοῦ, "according to the riches of His").²²⁴ Others see it as standing alongside that prepositional phrase in modifying the verb (πληρώσε, "will supply").²²⁵ The latter would view the phrase adverbially and communicate the manner in which the needs will be met: *gloriously*. But given the position of the phrase in the sentence, it is probably better to read it as modifying πλοῦτος ("riches") and signaling where the riches are found—in relationship to God in His glory. That they are "in glory" (ἐν δόξῃ) does not mean that they will only be realized in the eschatological fulfillment of all things when Christ returns.²²⁶ Certainly they will be most fully realized then, but they presently exist in the sphere (ἐν, "in") of God's presence (δόξῃ, "glory") and may become the experience of His people as He pours them out upon them in time and space. The prepositional phrase probably should not be read as adjectival ("his *glorious* riches", NET and NLT, emphasis added). Rather "This glory is God in the splendor of his majesty and the omnipotence of his interventions."²²⁷ God's provision in this world will be in accordance with all that God presently possesses in all its infinite vastness.

These riches will be supplied to them "in Christ Jesus" (ἐν Χριστῷ Ἰησοῦ).²²⁸ This underscores that what God gives is not simply "stuff," but Himself in the person of His Son. Even when the provision is tangible, the promise and its fulfillment are warm, relational, and personal. But this also reminds us that God is not a heavenly vending machine to which we may submit our payment in worship or service and expect our selection from among His "riches." The promise finds fulfillment in the flow of a loving,

---

224 E.g., Hellerman, 270; Kent, 11:157; Martin, 183-184; Sumney, 119.

225 E.g., Alford, 3:194; Müller, 152; O'Brien, 548-549; Vincent, ICC, 151.

226 As per Kennedy (472); cf. Müller (152).

227 Spicq, 1:370.

228 This final prepositional phrase modifies the verb πληρώσει ("will supply") rather than the previous prepositional phrase ἐν δόξῃ ("in glory"). As per Hellerman, 270; O'Brien, 549; Vincent, ICC, 151; contra Sumney, 119.

submissive, obedient relationship to God through His Son. It is "in Christ Jesus" (ἐν Χριστῷ Ἰησοῦ, v.7b) that they live and move and have their being as believers (1:1), that they think in accord with God's grace (2:5), that they worship God and rest in His gifted-righteousness (3:3), that they are called heavenward (3:14), and that "the God of peace" (v.9b) makes "the peace of God" experiential and real in our lives (v.7a). So it is with all the riches of God's grace to us. The preposition again has the locative sense of sphere[229] (or perhaps it is used instrumentally[230])—it is in the sphere of all God has provided in covenant with His Son and in relationship to Him as those "in Christ" that these riches exist, are realized and experienced.

> **Digging Deeper:**
> 1. How have you seen the promise of verse 19 proven true in your personal experience?
> 2. How do you need to see this promise proven true in your experience (or that of your family or church) right now?
> 3. What will claiming this promise by faith need to look like at this precise moment?

Verse 20 – "Now to our God and Father *be* the glory forever and ever. Amen."

The expansive nature of the promise and the mention of God's "glory" (v.19) has set the Apostle's heart soaring and he moves to bring the matter of their gift and his gratitude to a close (vv.10-20). All that will be left are greetings (vv.21-22) and a blessing (v.23) and the letter will be concluded. So by use of the transitional particle δὲ ("Now") the Apostle moves from promise to praise, from heavenly assurance to worshipful ascription. He has transitioned from "my God" (ὁ ... θεός μου, v.19) to "our God and Father" (τῷ ... θεῷ καὶ πατρὶ ἡμῶν). He is both personally and corporately

---

229 Harmon, 462; Hellerman, 270; Martin, 184; Müller, 152; Sumney, 119.
230 i.e., "*through* Christ Jesus" if taken as connected with πληρώσει (O'Brien, 549).

related to us, to us each one and all of us together. By transitioning to the plural pronoun ἡμῶν ('our") Paul makes one more attempt at gathering all the varied individuals of the Philippian church in all their wide-ranging opinions around their one focal point in united praise. The genitive ἡμῶν ("our") should be read with both θεῷ ("God") and πατρὶ ("Father").[231] "God" tells us what He is in His essential being and "Father" who He is with regard to position and role.[232] He is both, "God" and "Father" essentially and eternally. He is both "our God and Father" (cf. Gal. 1:4; 1 Thess. 1:2; 3:11, 13) and "the God and Father of our Lord Jesus Christ" (Rom. 15:6; 2 Cor. 1:3; 11:31; Eph. 1:3; cf. 1 Pet. 1:3; Rev. 1:6). He is also the "God and Father of all" (Eph. 4:6). But as *our* Father "He chose us in Him [Christ] before the foundation of the world" (Eph. 1:4). The brevity of the sentence and the breathlessness of the utterance have left us to assume the verb, which the translators have added as "*be.*"

The word ("glory," ἡ δόξα) probably arose from the verb δοκέω which means "to seem." It meant, then, an opinion or judgment that was made.[233] But Spicq can say, "The semantic evolution of *doxa* is probably the most extraordinary in the Bible. Not once in the LXX (except for Eccl 10:1) or the NT does this noun mean 'opinion.'"[234] It, rather, translated the Hebrew כָּבֵד ("glory") which came from a root meaning "heavy" and then, by extension, pointed to esteem, respect and even power and wealth.[235] When applied to God, "glory" denotes "the splendor of his majesty and the

> **Ministry Maxim**
>
> At the end of every matter is the ultimate goal of God's glory.

---

231 Robertson, *Grammar*, 785.

232 This is an example of the validity of the Granville Sharp rule. In simple terms the rule states that when two nouns of the same case are joined by καὶ and the first is preceded by the definite article, but the second is not, then both nouns refer to the same person (cf. Robertson, *Grammar*, 785; Wallace, 270-274).

233 Spicq, 1:362; Thayer, 155.

234 Spicq, 1:364.

235 Ibid.

omnipotence of his interventions."²³⁶ The definite article underscores this "glory" and the unique, exclusive domain of that which belongs to God alone. It will reach a crescendo at Jesus' return when "every tongue will confess that Jesus Christ is Lord, to the glory of God the Father" (Phil. 2:11). The crescendo, however, will last throughout eternity without slacking, for this "glory" is God's due "forever and ever" (εἰς τοὺς αἰῶνας τῶν αἰώνων), or more literally, "unto the ages of the ages." No greater expression for eternity could be found in the Greek language (Gal. 1:5; Phil. 4:20; 2 Tim. 4:18). He who is "King of the ages" (1 Tim. 1:17) will throughout all the ages deserve all "glory." How sad then for those who have found their glory "in their shame" (Phil. 3:19). But how infinitely wonderful when, at Christ's return, the "body of our humble state" will be brought "into conformity with the body of His glory, by the exertion of the power that He has even to subject all things to Himself" (3:21)! Then, for all eternity, we shall come into the full inheritance of "His riches in glory in Christ Jesus" (4:19).

The Apostle's doxology concludes with a reverberating "Amen" (ἀμήν). The expression was carried over directly from Hebrew where it was long used as a way to acknowledge "a word which is valid, and the validity of which is binding for me."²³⁷ Paul often ended his expressions of praise in this way (cf. Rom. 1:25; 9:5; 11:36; 16:27; Gal. 1:5; Eph. 3:21; Phil. 4:20; 1 Tim. 1:17; 6:16). When so used it means something like "so it is," "so be it" or "may it be fulfilled."²³⁸ All who read (or heard) these words would be moved to reciprocate with an affirming "Amen." Thus the Apostle, as he closes his letter, invites the entire membership of the Philippian church, fractured and fearful as they may presently be, to unite themselves with one voice and one word around the glorious God they serve through the enabling of His Son, Jesus Christ.

---

236 Ibid., 1:370.

237 TDNT, 1:335-337.

238 Thayer, 32.

Verse 21 – "Greet every saint in Christ Jesus. The brethren who are with me greet you."

Paul, as he so often does in his letters, turns to send greetings, both personal and those from others. He begins here by commanding that his own greetings be extended: "Greet every saint in Christ Jesus" (Ἀσπάσασθε πάντα ἅγιον ἐν Χριστῷ Ἰησοῦ). As he does here, Paul often employs the imperative form of the verb to command the recipients of his letters to thus "greet" others in the Body of Christ (e.g. Rom. 16:3, 5-16; 1 Cor. 16:20; 2 Cor. 13:12; Col. 4:15; 1 Thess. 5:26; Titus 3:15). The verb "Greet" (Ἀσπάσασθε) is used by Paul forty times, always in the final chapter of one of his letters. He always uses it in the middle/passive form, but the meaning is that of the active voice. Here the aorist imperative demands that action be taken at once. The second person plural form does not demand that the entire body of the church greet one another (in which case he would have used ἀσπάσασθε ἀλλήλους, "greet one another"; cf. Rom. 16:16; 1 Cor. 16:20; 2 Cor. 13:12; 1 Pet. 5:14), but commands that some group within the church, greet the larger body of the church on the Apostle's behalf. It is not immediately clear just who Paul would have been addressing, but "the overseers and deacons" (1:1) is a good guess.[239] In any case, the reading of the letter before the congregation would have fulfilled the command.

Paul's personal greetings are to go to "every saint" (πάντα ἅγιον). The singular forms indicate that Paul wants each individual saint to receive his greeting as if personally directed to him or her. This is interesting for in the opening of the letter he greeted them with the plural form ("to all the saints," πᾶσιν τοῖς ἁγίοις), embracing them as a whole (1:1). Perhaps this is why Paul takes the rather unusual step of not including any personal greetings as he closes this most intimate of his letters. Where, one may wonder, are

> **Ministry Maxim**
> When unity is the goal inclusiveness is the pathway.

---

239 O'Brien, 552.

greetings to figures so significant in the narrative description of Acts depicting the church's founding in Philippi—people like Lydia (Acts 16:14-15, 40) and the jailer and his household (16:27-34)? Perhaps the absence of such individual greetings is just another one of the Apostle's attempts to underscore the unity and humility to which he has been calling the church throughout the letter (2:1-11; 4:3). "Paul may have omitted all personal salutations so as not to give any suggestion of partiality."[240] They, as we, are "saints" only by virtue of being "in Christ Jesus" (ἐν Χριστῷ Ἰησοῦ).[241] Union with Him who is holy sets a person apart also as holy, and makes him a "saint."

Having extended his own greetings, Paul then passed on the greetings of the other believers with him: "The brethren who are with me greet you" (ἀσπάζονται ὑμᾶς οἱ σὺν ἐμοὶ ἀδελφοί). We have now the same verb, but this time in the indicative form. Paul frequently uses the indicative to convey his own personal greetings or those of others who are with him (e.g., Rom. 16:21-23; 1 Cor. 16:19-20; 2 Cor. 13:12; Phil. 4:21-22; Col. 4:10, 12, 14; Titus 3:15). Just who is with Paul and might be sending their greetings? Certainly it includes Timothy (1:1). Colossians and Philemon, which also were written from this imprisonment (though not necessarily at the same specific time), included greetings from Aristarchus, Mark (Col. 4:10; Philem. 24), "Jesus who is called Justice" (Col. 4:11), Epaphras (v.12; cf. Philem. 23), Luke, and Demas (Col. 4:14; Philem. 24). Perhaps some or all of these were with Paul when he penned the present letter. Some of these may have by this time been absent and others may have been present, given that the party of brothers around Paul at any given time seems to have been somewhat fluid. Minimally they demonstrate the kind of servants of Christ that gathered around Paul even while he was imprisoned. To seek further identity of those "who are with me" would be speculative. "All we know is that just as he does not mention anyone in Philippi by name, neither does he mention any of his companions, even though his greeting makes it clear

---

240 Ibid., 553.

241 Having ἐν Χριστῷ Ἰησοῦ ("in Christ Jesus") modify πάντα ἅγιον ("every saint") rather than Ἀσπάσασθε ("greet") is the better choice in view of 1:1 where the similar connection is required (Hellerman, 275; Müller, 154; O'Brien, 553; Contra Lightfoot, 185).

that some of them are still with him."²⁴² What is clear is that Paul wanted to bring to the fore the connectivity of the larger Body of Christ. The exchange of greetings is more than a social convention, but sets their continuance in obedience in the context of important relationships and the support and accountability they provide. They are a part of a large and eternally significant work; their continuance in faith and obedience is a connected and vital part to the whole.

Verse 22 – "All the saints greet you, especially those of Caesar's household.

Paul broadens the greetings from those of his most immediate ministry associates (v.21) to that of "All the saints" (ἀσπάζονται ὑμᾶς πάντες οἱ ἅγιοι). The extensive greetings in Romans 16 (the longest such section in Paul's letters) bears witness to the impact of the gospel in the city of Rome and its environs and may give some indication of both the identities and the volume of those who "greet" the Philippians from the capital city of the Empire. Others suggest that those mentioned in Philippians 1:15-17 and 2:20-21, though of baser motives in their service for Christ, may be included here.²⁴³

> **Ministry Maxim**
>
> The gospel often overcomes its oppressors by winning from within.

And Paul, with great effect, says the greetings come from "especially those of Caesar's household" (μάλιστα δὲ οἱ ἐκ τῆς Καίσαρος οἰκίας).²⁴⁴ Paul had gone to great lengths early in the letter to assure them that his incarceration had not hindered the gospel (1:12). In fact he had told them that the reason for his imprisonment had "become well known throughout the whole praetorian guard" (v.13). The gospel had cracked

---

242 Fee, 458.

243 e.g., O'Brien, 554.

244 This reference, while not proving the Apostle wrote the epistle from Rome, when taken with the other lines of evidence provides good evidence to that effect.

the elite troops of Caesar himself! In addition, the gospel had extended "to everyone else" (v.13). The imprisonment of the great Apostle had not hindered the gospel's advance, but sped it on its way to many of "those of Caesar's household."[245] The expression here could refer to the members of Caesar's immediate household, but that seems unlikely. It probably indicates those of both slaves and freedmen who made up the staff that kept the Emperor's household running.[246] "Christ is challenging Caesar in his own home."[247] The significance of this would not be lost on the citizens of a Roman colony like Philippi, where patriotism and loyalty to Caesar ran deep. The command center of the Roman Empire had become the nerve center of the gospel's advance! These were "especially" (μάλιστα) anxious that the believers in Philippi, of which they had probably heard so much, know of their sense of common union and cause. The adverb (μάλιστα, "especially") is a superlative of the adverb μάλα which means "very" or "exceedingly."[248] It is used to point to "the highest point in the extent of something" and means something like "most of all," "especially," or "above all."[249] There is urgency and feeling in the ink of these lines, as if to say: "Think of it! You have brothers and sisters in Christ within the inner circle of Nero's household who know of you, pray for you, and want you to know of their kinship in Christ with you!"

Verse 23 – "The grace of the Lord Jesus Christ be with your spirit."

The wording of this entire verse is identical to that of Philemon 25 (and very nearly to Gal. 6:18). The opening portion (Ἡ χάρις τοῦ κυρίου Ἰησοῦ Χριστοῦ, "The grace of our Lord Jesus Christ") is also identical to a portion of 2 Corinthians 13:13.

---

245 See Lightfoot's excursus on Caesar's household and its makeup, 185-192.

246 TDNT, 5:133.

247 Robertson, *Paul's Joy in Christ*, 265.

248 BDAG, 4689.

249 Friberg, 252.

As Paul so often does in his letters, he opens and closes with "grace" (χάρις; cf. 1:2). The inclusion serves to wrap the entire letter, with all its contents and challenges, in "The grace of the Lord Jesus Christ." Note the use of the definite article—this is "*The* grace" that is exclusively "of our Lord Jesus Christ" and can be found nowhere else. The full title is reminiscent of the high point of the letter: "every tongue will confess that Jesus Christ is Lord, to the glory of God the Father" (2:11). Here, as there, the full title is not used casually. "Jesus" is His human name—the name under which He embraced His humble downward movement into humanity and in which He walked that road all the way "to the point of death, even death on a cross" (2:8). "Christ" points to His rightful office as the anointed of God, the One who fulfills all that God promised and prophesied prior to His arrival. And "Lord" unveils His all-encompassing supremacy and marks Him as truly divine (2:9). The humble One ("Jesus") is now the exalted One ("Lord"). The anointed One ("Christ") will at His coming be openly acknowledged as supreme.

The noun "spirit" (τοῦ πνεύματος) is singular while the pronoun (ὑμῶν, "your") is plural. The noun is to be understood as a distributive singular.[250] "Christ's grace is 'to rest and abide upon the spirit of *each one* of his readers."[251] The plural pronoun returns the attention to the wider audience of the opening of the letter (1:3). The phrase "with your spirit" (μετὰ τοῦ πνεύματος ὑμῶν; cf. Gal. 6:18; 2 Tim. 4:22; Philem. 25) is probably not intended to have a more expansive meaning than the simpler "with you" (μεθ' ὑμῶν; as in his other letters, e.g. Col. 4:18).[252] Many manuscripts conclude with "Amen" (ἀμήν; cf. KJV, NKJV, NIV), but the best manuscripts omit it. Most

> **Ministry Maxim**
>
> Wrapped in grace, even the most divided relationships can come to honor God.

---

250 Hellerman, 278; Sumney, 123.

251 O'Brien, 555, emphasis original.

252 Fee, 461; Sumney, 124; Silva, 210.

manuscripts of NT letters contain such a tag to their conclusion, perhaps the addition of reverent scribes.

It is easy to read such words with a casual flair—as if, because of Paul's common use of such language at the close of his letters, he really doesn't give them much thought or that he uses them as mere conventions. Yet Paul never in any of his writings makes light of "grace." It is absurd that he would do so here, in a letter where he has called upon the Philippians to demonstrate interpersonal grace under the stresses of both external pressures and internal strife. No, all Paul's inward strength lies behind his pen as he sends this final grace-wish, for he knows that apart from it the reconciliation and unity he has pursued from the opening words of the letter will not be possible. But, with grace, nothing is beyond the reach of those who take up God's will.

> **Digging Deeper:**
> 1. How do the closing themes of worship (v.20), fellowship (vv.21-22), and enablement (v.23) contribute to the goal of Paul in writing the letter to the Philippians?
> 2. How specifically will you encourage your fellow believers this week to focus on God (v.20), strengthen their ties with one another (vv.21-22), and personally rely upon God's enabling (v.23)?

APPENDIX A

PREACHING AND TEACHING PHILIPPIANS

Preaching is one of the great privileges of a pastor. The NT has much to say about faithfully preaching God's Word. It is my conviction that expository preaching should be the regular practice of every local church pastor.[1] Of course, even among those of similar conviction, there is not always consensus on just what constitutes expository preaching. Similarly, each pastor is comfortable preaching passages of different lengths and series of varying duration. Local circumstances also permit (or require) sermon series of differing lengths.

What follows are suggestive attempts at projecting both preaching series and their individual sermons. First, I offer an exegetical outline of Philippians. Then I offer three possibilities for preaching Philippians—a single message covering the entire book, a shorter series of messages, and a more extended series of messages. These may, of course, be expanded even further. In some cases you may divide the letter differently than I have suggested here. My hope is that these suggestions will provide fodder for your preaching of these portions of sacred Scripture. It is your duty as a

---

1 See the author's *Revival in the Rubble* (chapter 9) for more on the primacy and practice of expository preaching.

servant of God to wrestle with the text of Scripture until God brings you forth with a message for His people which arises from His Word.

"I solemnly charge you in the presence of God and of Christ Jesus, who is to judge the living and the dead, and by His appearing and His kingdom: preach the word; be ready in season and out of season; reprove, rebuke, exhort, with great patience and instruction" (2 Tim. 4:1-2).

EXEGETICAL OUTLINE

I. **Paul's Salutation. (1:1-2)**
 A. The letter's author: Paul. (1:1a)
  1. The author's associate: Timothy. (1:1a)
 B. The letter's recipients. (1:1b-e)
  1. All those "in Christ Jesus." (1:1c)
  2. All the believers "in Philippi." (1:1d)
  3. All the church's leadership. (1:1e)
 C. The author's blessing. (1:2)

II. **Paul's Thanksgiving and Prayer. (1:3-11)**
 A. Paul's Thankfulness for the Philippians. (1:3-8)
  1. The regularity of Paul's gratitude. (1:3-4)
  2. The reasons for Paul's gratitude. (1:5-6)
   a. The faithfulness of the Philippians in gospel-partnership. (1:5)
   b. The faithfulness of God to finish His work in the Philippians. (1:6)
  3. The rationale of Paul's gratitude. (1:7-8)
   a. The sharing of divine grace. (1:7)
   b. The sharing of divine affection. (1:8)
 B. Paul's Prayer for the Philippians. (1:9-11)
  1. Abounding love. (1:9)
  2. Increasing discernment. (1:10)
  3. Growing fruitfulness. (1:11)

III. Explanation of Paul's Circumstances. (1:12-26)
  A. The advance of the gospel despite imprisonment. (1:12-18b)
    1. Two results of Paul's imprisonment. (1:12-13)
      a. A motivation to believers. (1:12)
      b. A witness to unbelievers. (1:13)
    2. Two effects upon the believers. (14-17)
      a. Some are fearful. (1:14a, implied)
      b. Some are emboldened. (1:14)
    3. Two attitudes among the emboldened. (1:15)
      a. Some preach from envy. (1:15a)
      b. Some preach from good will. (1:15b)
    4. Two motivations among the emboldened. (1:16-17)
      a. Love. (1:16)
      b. Selfish ambition. (1:17)
    5. Two kinds of action among the emboldened. (1:18a)
      a. Some acted in accord with truth. (1:18a)
      b. Some acted in accord with pretense. (1:18a)
    6. One cause for joy: Christ is proclaimed! (1:18b)
  B. The adversity of the Apostle during imprisonment. (1:18c-26)
    1. Paul knows he will be delivered. (1:19-22)
      a. With dependence upon others. (1:19)
        i. Dependence upon the Philippians' prayers. (1:19b)
        ii. Dependence upon the help of the Spirit. (1:19c)
      b. With hope to honor Christ in either case. (1:20-22)
        i. For live or die, Paul wins! (1:21-22a)
          aa. Living = Christ. (1:21a)
          bb. Dying = Gain. (1:21b)
          cc. Living = fruitful labor. (1:22a)
        ii. But live or die? Paul can't choose! (1:22b)
    2. Paul doesn't know which to choose. (1:23-24)
      a. To depart and be with Christ is his desire. (1:23)
      b. To remain and serve is his call. (1:24)

3. Paul knows he will live. (1:25-26)
   a. He will live for the Philippians' progress and joy in the faith. (1:25)
   b. He will live with the result that the Philippians may glory in Christ Jesus. (1:26)

IV. Exhortations and Examples of Lives Worthy of the Gospel. (1:27-4:9)
  A. Exhortations: Unity! (1:27-2:4)
   1. Live lives worthy of the gospel. (1:27-30)
      a. Live a strong testimony. (1:27a)
         i. A testimony that can be visually confirmed. (1:27b)
         ii. A testimony that is verbally communicated. (1:27b)
      b. Live a steadfast faith. (1:27c-30)
         i. Steadfast faith existing in community. (1:27c)
         ii. Steadfast faith existing in courage. (1:28a)
            aa. Steadfast faith is a sign concerning the lost. (1:28b)
            bb. Steadfast faith is a sign concerning oneself. (1:28c)
         iii. Steadfast faith existing in grace. (1:29-30)
            aa. Grace to believe in Christ. (1:29b)
            bb. Grace to suffer for Christ. (1:29c-30)
   2. Live lives witnessing unity. (2:1-4)
      a. What you have received in Christ. (2:1)
         i. Encouragement in Christ. (2:1a)
         ii. Consolation of love. (2:1b)
         iii. Fellowship of the Spirit. (2:1c)
         iv. Affection and compassion. (2:1d)
      b. What you reciprocate in Christ. (2:2-4)
         i. Maintaining the same love. (2:2b)
         ii. Being united in spirit. (2:2c)
         iii. Being intent on one purpose. (2:2d)
         iv. Unselfishly exalting one another. (2:3)
         v. Acting in the interest of others. (2:4)

B. Example: Christ. (2:5-11)
  1. Christ reasoned in a particular way. (2:5-8)
     a. Christ thought of Himself in a particular way. (2:6)
        i. Not in a self-protective way.
     b. Christ emptied Himself in a particular way. (2:7)
        i. By taking the form of a bond-servant. (2:7a)
        ii. By being made in the likeness of men. (2:7b)
     c. Christ humbled Himself in a particular way. (2:8)
        i. By being found in appearance as a man. (2:8a)
        ii. By becoming obedient unto death. (2:8b)
  2. Christ was rewarded in a particular way. (2:9-11)
     a. Christ was exalted by God. (2:9a)
     b. Christ was named by God. (2:9b-11)
        i. So that at His name all would bow to Jesus as Lord. (2:10)
        ii. So that at His name all would confess Jesus as Lord. (2:11a)
           aa. That God the Father might get the glory that is His due. (2:11b)
C. Exhortation: Diligence! (2:12-18)
  1. Work out your salvation. (2:12-13)
     a. As in Paul's presence, so in his absence. (2:12a)
     b. With fear and trembling. (2:12b)
     c. Knowing God is the one enabling you. (2:13)
  2. Do all things without grumbling. (2:14-16)
     a. That the Philippians may prove to be God's children in a dark world. (2:15)
        i. Holding fast the word of life. (2:16a)
           aa. So that Paul may have grounds to glory on the day of Christ. (2:16b)
  3. Rejoice! (2:17-18)
     a. I rejoice with you. (2:17b)
        i. Even as my life is poured out like a drink offering upon the sacrifice and service of your faith. (2:17a)
     b. You, rejoice with me. (2:18)

D. Example: Fellow-workers. (2:19-30)
1. The example of Timothy. (2:19-24)
   a. Timothy's example: Genuine concern. (2:20)
      i. Others: Self-interest. (2:21)
      ii. Timothy: Proven worth. (2:22)
   b. Paul's hope. (2:23-24)
      i. To send Timothy to the Philippians soon. (2:23)
      ii. To visit the Philippians himself. (2:24)
2. The example of Epaphroditus. (2:25-30)
   a. Paul explained sending Epaphroditus back. (2:25-28)
      i. The necessity of sending Epaphroditus. (2:25a)
         aa. The character of Epaphroditus. (2:25b)
            (i). Paul's brother.
            (ii). Paul's fellow worker.
            (iii). Paul's fellow soldier.
            (iv). The Philippians' messenger.
            (v). The Philippians' minister to Paul's need.
         bb. The longing of Epaphroditus. (2:26a)
         cc. The distress of Epaphroditus. (2:26b-27)
      ii. The eagerness in sending Epaphroditus. (2:28)
         aa. That you may rejoice in seeing him again. (2:28a)
         bb. That I may be less anxious. (2:28b)
   b. Paul explained the matter of welcoming Epaphroditus. (2:29-30)
      i. Receive him. (2:29a)
         aa. Receive him "in the Lord."
         bb. Receive him with all joy.
      ii. Honor him. (2:29b-30)
         aa. Because he nearly died in service for Christ. (2:30)

E. Exhortation: Vigilance! (3:1-6)
   1. Reminder. (3:1)
      a. Rejoice in the Lord. (3:1a)
      b. Remember Paul's teaching. (3:1b)
   2. Warning. (3:2-6)
      a. Watch out for Judaizers! (3:2-6)
         i. Explanation for Paul's warning. (3:3-6)
            aa. We are the true circumcision. (3:3-4)
               (i). Yet Paul had more reason for confidence in the flesh than anyone. (3:4b-6)
                  (aa). His religious pedigree. (3:5a-d)
                     i. Rites. (3:5a)
                     ii. Religion. (3:5b)
                     iii. Family. (3:5c)
                     iv. Ethnicity. (3:5d)
                  (bb). His religious performance. (3:5e-6)
                     i. Precision. (3:5e)
                     ii. Passion. (3:6a)
                     iii. Performance. (3:6b)
F. Example: Paul. (3:7-14)
   1. Paul counted all things loss. (3:7-11)
      a. That which is counted. (3:7-8)
         i. Every gain. (3:7)
         ii. Everything. (3:8)
      b. How it is counted. (3:7b-8)
         i. Loss. (3:7b, 8a)
         ii. Rubbish. (3:8b)
      c. The reason for the counting. (3:7b-8a)
         i. For the sake of Christ. (3:7b)
         ii. For the sake of knowing Christ Jesus my Lord. (3:8a)
      d. The goal of the counting. (3:8b-9)
         i. That Paul might gain Christ. (3:8b)
         ii. That Paul might be found in Christ. (3:9a)
            aa. Through gifted-righteousness. (3:9b)

- e. The quest of the counting. (3:10)
    - i. That Paul might know Christ personally. (3:10a)
    - ii. That Paul might know Christ's power. (3:10b)
    - iii. That Paul might know Christ's sufferings. (3:10c)
        - aa. By being conformed to Christ's death. (3:10d)
- f. The purpose of the counting. (3:11)
    - i. That Paul might attain to the resurrection from the dead. (3:11)
2. Paul counted one thing essential. (3:12-14)
    - a. Pressing on. (3:12-14)
        - i. The motive: What lies within. (3:12-13a)
            - aa. Because of Paul's imperfections. (3:12a, 13a)
            - bb. Because Christ has made Paul His own. (3:12b)
        - ii. The focus: What lies ahead. (3:13b)
        - iii. The call: What lies above. (3:14)
    - b. Growing up. (3:15)
        - i. Mature in thinking. (3:15a)
        - ii. Restful in trust. (3:15b)
    - c. Holding true. (3:16)
- G. Exhortation: Resolve! (3:17-4:9)
    1. Stand against compromised faith. (3:17-19)
        - a. Moral examples. (3:17)
        - b. Immoral examples. (3:18-19)
            - i. Enemies of the cross of Christ. (3:18)
                - aa. Their destiny. (3:19a)
                - bb. Their idolatry. (3:19b)
                - cc. Their glory. (3:19c)
                - dd. Their ideology. (3:19d)
    2. Stand in hopeful faith. (3:20-21)
        - a. Heavenly citizenship. (3:20a)
        - b. Heavenly hope. (3:20b-21)
    3. Stand in resolute faith. (4:1)
        - a. Deeply loved. (4:1a)

        b. Deeply committed. (4:1b)
    4. Stand in conflicted faith. (4:2-5)
        a. Divided members. (4:2)
        b. United efforts. (4:2-5)
            i. Thinking together. (4:2)
            ii. Working together. (4:3)
            iii. Rejoicing together. (4:4)
            iv. Relating together. (4:5)
    5. Stand in peaceful faith. (4:6-9)
        a. Committed prayer. (4:6)
        b. Contented peace. (4:7)
        c. Concentrated pondering. (4:8)
        d. Consecrated practice. (4:9)

V. Gratitude for the Philippians' Gift of Support. (4:10-19)
    A. A learned contentment. (4:10-13)
        1. By rejoicing in the Lord. (4:10)
        2. By learning from the Lord. (4:11-12)
        3. By relying on the Lord. (4:13)
    B. A lasting collaboration. (4:14-19)
        1. A shared affliction. (4:14)
        2. A shared mission. (4:15-16)
        3. A shared commitment. (4:17)
        4. A shared worship. (4:18)
        5. A shared source. (4:19)

VI. Glory, Greetings and Grace. (4:20-23)
    A. Paul ascribes glory to God. (4:20)
    B. Paul sends greetings to the Philippians. (4:21-22)
        1. Paul sends His own greetings. (4:21a)
        2. Paul sends other's greetings. (4:21b-22)
    C. Paul extends grace to the Philippians. (4:23)

EXPOSITIONAL OUTLINES

Single Message:
Pursuing Joy
The pursuit of joy begins in our minds.

I. **A United Mind. (1)**
   A. United in prayer. (1:1-11)
   B. United in gospel witness. (1:12-17)
   C. United in suffering and serving. (1:18-30)
II. **An Unselfish Mind. (2)**
   A. The unselfish thinking of Christ. (2:1-11)
   B. The unselfish thinking of Christ's servants. (2:12-30)
III. **An Undistracted Mind. (3)**
   A. Undistracted by the past. (3:1-7)
   B. Undistracted from Christ. (3:8-16)
   C. Undistracted from hope. (3:17-21)
IV. **An Undivided Mind. (4)**
   A. Undivided in fellowship. (4:2-3)
   B. Undivided in worry. (4:4-9)
   C. Undivided in contentment. (4:10-23)

Shorter Series (9 Messages)
Title: The Pursuit of Joy

#1 **1:1-11 Pursuing Joy in our Relationships**
God designed joy to find its fullness in the context of relationships.

I. **The Joy of Being Spoken to. (1:1-2)**
   A. Identity: "in Christ." (1:1b)
   B. Locality: "at Philippi." (1:1c)
   C. Capacity: "with the overseers and deacons." (1:1d)
   D. Ability: "Grace and peace to you from God ..." (1:2)

II. The Joy of Being Prayed for. (1:3-11)
   A. The Object of Gratitude. (1:3-8)
      1. Regular Gratitude. (1:3-4)
      2. Reasoned Gratitude. (1:5-6)
         a. Gospel-centered thanksgiving. (1:5)
         b. God-centered thanksgiving. (1:6)
      3. Relational gratitude. (1:7-8)
         a. The sharing of divine grace. (1:7)
         b. The sharing of divine affection. (1:8)
   B. The Object of Intercession. (1:9-11)
      1. Asking for abounding love. (1:9)
      2. Asking for increasing discernment. (1:10)
      3. Asking for growing fruitfulness. (1:11)

#2   1:12-18a Pursuing Joy in our Circumstances
God can give you joy right where you are.
(See the chart "Gospel Work and Gospel Motives" in Appendix C)

I. There are two results of unwanted circumstances. (1:12-13)
   A. A motivation to believers. (1:12)
   B. A witness to unbelievers. (1:13)

II. There are two effects of our choices in unwanted circumstances. (1:14)
   A. Fear. (1:14, implied)
   B. Emboldened. (1:14)

III. There are two attitudes we can hold in unwanted circumstances. (1:15)
   A. Envy. (1:15a)
   B. Good will. (1:15b)

IV. There are two motivations that can move us in unwanted circumstances. (1:16-17)
   A. Selfish ambition. (1:17)
   B. Love. (16)

V. There are two different actions that can come to pass in unwanted circumstances. (18a)
   A. Pretense. (1:18a)
   B. Truth. (1:18a)

#3 **1:18b-30 Pursuing Joy at Life's Decision Points**
God will give us joy at the decision points of life.

I. **Decide to live in joy. (1:21a)**
   A. An exchanged life. (1:21a)
   B. A fruitful life. (1:22a)
   C. An unselfish life. (1:25-26)
      1. Living for the good of others. (1:25)
      2. Living for the glory of God. (1:26)
   D. An honorable life. (1:20b)
      1. Living courageously. (1:20b)
      2. Living shamelessly. (1:20a)
      3. Living joyfully. (1:18b)
      4. Living hopefully. (1:19, 20a, 25)

II. **Decide to die in joy. (1:21b)**
   A. A winning transaction. (1:21b)
   B. An honorable transition. (1:20b)
      1. Dying courageously. (1:20b)
      2. Dying shamelessly. (1:20a)
      3. Dying joyfully. (1:18b)
      4. Dying hopefully. (1:20a)

III. **Decide to stand in joy. (1:27-30)**
   A. Stand in community. (1:27)
      1. Unity that can be seen firsthand. (1:27a)
      2. Unity that can be spoken of second hand. (1:27b)
   B. Stand in courage. (1:28)
      1. Courage that says something about the persecutors. (1:28a)
      2. Courage that says something about the persecuted. (1:28b)

  C. Stand in calling. (1:29-30)
    1. The gift of believing. (1:29a)
    2. The gift of suffering. (1:29b-30)

#4 **2:1-11 Purusing Joy in Christlikeness**
Joy comes as we draw nearer to Jesus.

 I. Joy in what we have received in Christ. (2:1)
  A. Encouragement. (2:1a)
  B. Comfort. (2:1b)
  C. Relationship. (2:1c)
  D. Empathy. (2:1d)
 II. Joy in what we have heard from Christ. (2:2-4)
  A. Oneness in attitude. (2:2)
  B. Selflessness in attitude. (2:3)
  C. Helpfulness in actions. (2:4)
 III. Joy in what we have seen in Christ. (2:5-11)
  A. The mind of Christ. (2:5-8)
    1. Self-surrendering thinking. (2:6)
    2. Self-emptying thinking. (2:7)
    3. Self-humbling thinking. (2:8)
  B. The reward of Christ. (2:9-11)
    1. Exalted by God. (2:9a)
    2. Named by God. (2:9b)
     a. That all might bow to Christ. (2:10)
     b. That all might confess Christ. (2:11)

#5 **2:12-30 Pursuing Joy in Daily Life**
Joy is found in living life moment-by-moment.

 I. The pathway of daily life. (2:12-18)
  A. Work out the gospel. (2:12-13)
    1. Work it out faithfully. (2:12a)
    2. Work it out reverently. (2:12b)
    3. Work it out dependently. (2:13)

B. Hold out the gospel. (2:14-16)
　　　　　1. Hold out the gospel in contrast. (2:15)
　　　　　2. Hold out the gospel in contentment. (2:14)
　　　　　3. Hold out the gospel in anticipation. (2:16)
　　　C. Pour out your life. (2:17-18)
　　　　　1. Pour out your life in worship to God. (2:17a)
　　　　　2. Pour out your life in fellowship with others. (2:17b-18)
　II. **The picture of daily life. (2:19-30)**
　　　A. Timothy was an example of Christlikeness. (2:19-24)
　　　　　1. He exemplified the mind of Christ. (2:20-21)
　　　　　2. He exemplified the character of Christ. (2:22)
　　　B. Epaphroditus was an example of Christlikeness. (2:25-30)
　　　　　1. He exemplified painful love. (2:26)
　　　　　2. He exemplified costly service. (2:27)
　　　C. Paul was an example of Christlikeness. (2:19, 23-25, 28)
　　　　　1. He exemplified purposeful connectedness. (2:19, 23-24, 28)
　　　　　2. He exemplified shared honor. (2:25)
　　　D. The Philippians were to be examples of Christlikeness. (2:29-30)
　　　　　1. We must receive our brothers. (2:29a)
　　　　　2. We must honor our servants. (2:29b-30)

#6　3:1-16 Pursuing Joy by Growing Mature

Joy grows as we mature in Christ.

　I. **Maturity in righteousness. (3:1-6)**
　　　A. False righteousness: gained by what I do. (3:2, 5-6)
　　　B. True righteousness: gained by what Christ has done. (3:1, 3-4, 9)

II. Maturity in pursuit. (3:7-11)
   A. Pursue gaining Christ. (3:7-9)
   B. Pursue knowing Christ. (3:10)
   C. Pursue joining Christ. (3:11)
III. Maturity in thinking. (3:12-16)
   A. I have not arrived. (3:12a, 13a)
   B. I will not quit. (3:12b, 14)
   C. I will be focused. (3:13b)
   D. I will let God be God. (3:15b)
   E. I will not retreat. (3:16)

#7   **3:17-4:1 Pursuing Joy by Standing Firm**
Joy is secure when resting upon three legs.

I. Following godly examples. (3:17)
II. Fleeing ungodly examples. (3:18-19)
   A. Their identity. (3:18c)
   B. Their destiny. (3:19a)
   C. Their idolatry. (3:19b)
   D. Their glory. (3:19c)
   E. Their ideology. (3:19d)
III. Focusing on God's kingdom. (3:20-21)
   A. People with a transcendent allegiance. (3:20a)
   B. People with a transcendent expectation. (3:20b)
   C. People with a transcendent authority. (3:20c)
   D. People with a transcendent hope. (3:21a)
   E. People with a transcendent goal. (3:21b)

#8   **4:1-9 Pursuing Joy in Conflict**
God gives joy to those who seek peace.

I. Seek peace among God's people. (4:1-5)
   A. Stand together. (4:1)
   B. Think together. (4:2)
   C. Work together. (4:3)

D. Worship together. (4:4)
E. Yield together. (4:5a)
F. Remember together. (4:5b)
II. **Seek peace from God's throne. (4:6-9)**
   A. A committed life of prayer. (4:6-7)
   B. A disciplined life of the mind. (4:8)
   C. An active life of obedience. (4:9)

#9   4:10-23 Pursuing Joy in God's Assignment
Joy is found where God plants us for the glory of His name.

I. **Contentment in our circumstances. (4:10-13)**
   A. Contentment through focus. (4:10)
   B. Contentment through learning. (4:11-12)
   C. Contentment through dependence. (4:13)
II. **Partnership in our mission. (4:14-23)**
   A. A shared affliction. (4:14)
   B. A shared mission. (4:15-16)
   C. A shared commitment. (4:17)
   D. A shared worship. (4:18)
   E. A shared source. (4:19)
III. **Fellowship in our calling. (4:20-23)**
   A. The praise of God's glory. (4:20)
   B. The sending of our greetings. (4:21-22)
   C. The giving of God's grace. (4:23)

Longer Series (18 Messages)
Title: Discovering Joy under the Circumstances

#1 **1:1-2 Discovering Joy in our Assignment**
We discover joy when we live within our God-given assignment.

    I. **Living in our spiritual identity. (1:1a-b)**
        A. We are bond-servants. (1:1a)
        B. We are saints. (1:1b)
    II. **Living in our physical locality.** ("at Philippi," 1:1c)
    III. **Living in our ministry capacity.** ("including the overseers and deacons," 1:1d)
    IV. **Living in our divine enabling.** ("Grace to you …," 1:2)

#2 **1:3-11 Discovering Joy in Prayer**
Talking to God about one another maximizes the joy in our relationships.

    I. **The Object of Gratitude. (1:3-8)**
        A. Regular Gratitude. (1:3-4)
        B. Reasoned Gratitude. (1:5-6)
            1. Gospel-centered thanksgiving. (1:5)
            2. God-centered thanksgiving. (1:6)
        C. Relational Gratitude. (1:7-8)
            1. The sharing of divine grace. (1:7)
            2. The sharing of divine affection. (1:8)
    II. **The Object of Intercession. (1:9-11)**
        A. Asking for abounding Love. (1:9)
        B. Asking for increasing discernment. (1:10)
        C. Asking for growing fruitfulness. (1:11)

#3 **1:12-18a Discovering Joy under the Circumstances**
Even unwanted circumstances can become a source of joy.
(see the chart "Gospel Work and Gospel Motives" in Appendix C)

I. There are two results of unwanted circumstances. (1:12-13)
   A. A motivation to believers. (1:12)
   B. A witness to unbelievers. (1:13)
II. There are two effects of our choices in unwanted circumstances. (1:14)
   A. Fear. (1:14, implied)
   B. Emboldened. (1:14)
III. There are two attitudes we can hold in unwanted circumstances. (1:15)
   A. Envy. (1:15a)
   B. Good will. (1:15b)
IV. There are two motivations that can move us in unwanted circumstances. (1:16-17)
   A. Selfish ambition. (1:17)
   B. Love. (16)
V. There are two different actions that can come to pass in unwanted circumstances. (18a)
   A. Pretense. (1:18a)
   B. Truth. (1:18a)

#4 **1:18b-26 Discovering Joy in Life and Death**
Live or die, joy will be ours if we choose …

I. **A life worth living. (1:21a)**
   A. An exchanged life. (1:21a)
   B. A fruitful life. (1:22a)
   C. An unselfish life. (1:25-26)
      1. Living for the good of others. (1:25)
      2. Living for the glory of God. (1:26)
   D. An honorable life. (1:20b)
      1. Living courageously. (1:20b)
      2. Living shamelessly. (1:20a)
      3. Living joyfully. (1:18b)
      4. Living hopefully. (1:19, 20a, 25)

II. A death worth dying. (1:21b)
  A. A winning transaction. (1:21b)
  B. An honorable transition. (1:20b)
    1. Dying courageously. (1:20b)
    2. Dying shamelessly. (1:20a)
    3. Dying joyfully. (1:18b)
    4. Dying hopefully. (1:20a)

#5 1:27-30 Discovering Joy in Steadfastness
Joy is found in a gospel-centered life lived steadfastly.

I. Steadfast in community. (1:27)
  A. Unity that can be seen firsthand. (1:27a)
  B. Unity that can be spoken of second hand. (1:27b)

II. Steadfast in courage. (1:28)
  A. Courage that says something about the persecutors. (1:28a)
  B. Courage that says something about the persecuted. (1:28b)

III. Steadfast in calling. (1:29-30)
  A. The gift of believing. (1:29a)
  B. The gift of suffering. (1:29b-30)

#6 2:1-4 Discovering Joy in Unity
Living in community for Christ is made possible by living in fellowship with Christ.

I. We are called to live in community for Christ. (2:2b-4)
  A. Love. (2:2b)
  B. Commitment. (2:2c)
  C. Thinking. (2:2d)
  D. Actions. (2:3)
  E. Priorities. (2:4)

II. We are called to live in fellowship with Christ. (2:1)
   A. Encouragement. (2:1a)
   B. Comfort. (2:1b)
   C. Relationship. (2:1c)
   D. Empathy. (2:1d)

#7 **2:5-11 Discovering Joy in Humility**
Glorying in Christ requires thinking like Christ.

I. We must think like Christ ... (2:5-8)
   A. Self-surrendering thinking. (2:6)
   B. Self-emptying thinking. (2:7)
   C. Self-humbling thinking. (2:8)
II. That we might glory in Christ. (2:9-11)
   A. Exalted by God. (2:9a)
   B. Named by God. (2:9b-11)
      1. That all might bow to Christ. (2:10)
      2. That all might confess Christ. (2:11)

#8 **2:12-18 Discovering Joy in Discipleship**
Joy in following Christ requires our active participation.

I. Work out your salvation. (2:12-13)
   A. Work it out faithfully. (2:12a)
   B. Work it out reverently. (2:12b)
   C. Work it out dependently. (2:13)
II. Hold out the gospel. (2:14-16)
   A. Hold out the gospel in contrast. (2:15)
   B. Hold out the gospel in contentment. (2:14)
   C. Hold out the gospel in anticipation. (2:16)
III. Pour out your life. (2:17-18)
   A. Pour out your life in worship to God. (2:17a)
   B. Pour out your life in fellowship with others. (2:17b-18)

#9 2:19-30 Discovering Joy in Ordinary Relationships
Christlikeness is found in the most ordinary of relationships.

- I. **Timothy was an example of Christlikeness. (2:19-24)**
  - A. He exemplified the mind of Christ. (2:20-21)
  - B. He exemplified the character of Christ. (2:22)
- II. **Epaphroditus was an example of Christlikeness. (2:25-30)**
  - A. He exemplified painful love. (2:26)
  - B. He exemplified costly service. (2:27)
- III. **Paul was an example of Christlikeness. (2:19, 23-25, 28)**
  - A. He exemplified purposeful connectedness. (2:19, 23-24, 28)
  - B. He exemplified shared honor. (2:25)
- IV. **The Philippians were to be examples of Christlikeness. (2:29-30)**
  - A. We must receive our brothers. (2:29a)
  - B. We must honor our servants. (2:29b-30)

#10 3:1-6 Discovering Joy in Gifted-Righteousness
Joy is found in gifted-righteousness, not religious righteousness.

- I. **The profile of religious righteousness. (3:5-6)**
  - A. Reliance upon religious pedigree. (3:5)
    1. The right "rites." (3:5a)
    2. The right religion. (3:5b)
    3. The right family. (3:5c)
    4. The right ethnicity. (3:5d)
  - B. Reliance upon religious performance. (3:5e-6)
    1. Precision: "Be right!" (3:5e)
    2. Passion: "Be zealous!" (3:6a)
    3. Performance: "Be perfect!" (3:6b)
- II. **The problem with religious righteousness. (3:1-4)**
  - A. It steals our joy. (3:1a)
  - B. It distorts our thinking. (3:1b)
  - C. It misleads our efforts. (3:2)
  - D. It misdirects our confidence. (3:3-4)

#11   **3:7-11 Discovering Joy in Christ**
Joy comes in pursuit of Christ.

      I. **Pursue gaining Christ. (3:7-9)**
      II. **Pursue knowing Christ. (3:10)**
      III. **Pursue joining Christ. (3:11)**

#12   **3:12-16 Discovering Joy in a Maturing Mind**
Joy deepens as we continue to mature in our thinking.

      I. **I have not arrived. (3:12a, 13a)**
      II. **I will not quit. (3:12b, 14)**
      III. **I will be focused. (3:13b)**
      IV. **I will let God be God. (3:15b)**
      V. **I will not retreat. (3:16)**

#13   **3:17-4:1 Discovering Joy in Standing Firm**
Joy abides when it rests upon three legs.

      I. **Following godly examples. (3:17)**
      II. **Fleeing ungodly examples. (3:18-19)**
          A. Their identity. (3:18c)
          B. Their destiny. (3:19a)
          C. Their idolatry. (3:19b)
          D. Their glory. (3:19c)
          E. Their ideology. (3:19d)
      III. **Focusing on God's kingdom. (3:20-21)**
          A. People with a transcendent allegiance. (3:20a)
          B. People with a transcendent expectation. (3:20b)
          C. People with a transcendent authority. (3:20c)
          D. People with a transcendent hope. (3:21a)
          E. People with a transcendent goal. (3:21b)

#14   4:1-5 Discovering Joy in Conflict
Joy can be wrung from conflict when God's people …

    I. Stand together. (4:1)
    II. Think together. (4:2)
    III. Work together. (4:3)
    IV. Worship together. (4:4)
    V. Yield together (4:5a)
    VI. Remember together. (4:5b)

#15   4:6-9 Discovering Joy in Chaos
The God of peace will grant us the peace of God.

    I. A committed life of prayer. (4:6-7)
    II. A disciplined life of the mind. (4:8)
    III. An active life of obedience. (4:9)

#16   4:10-13 Discovering Joy in Contentment
Contentment can be ours no matter our circumstances.

    I. Contentment is a matter of focus. (4:10)
    II. Contentment is a matter of learning. (4:11-12)
    III. Contentment is a matter of dependence. (4:13)

#17   4:14-19 Discovering Joy in Gospel Partnership
The joy of giving is discovered together in …

    I. A shared affliction. (4:14)
    II. A shared mission. (4:15-16)
    III. A shared commitment. (4:17)
    IV. A shared worship. (4:18)
    V. A shared source. (4:19)

#18   4:20-23 Discovering Joy in the Basics of Life
Joy is found in sharing the basics of life in Christ.

    I. **The praise of God's glory. (4:20)**
    II. **The extension of our greetings. (4:21-22)**
    III. **The giving of God's grace. (4:23)**

APPENDIX B

A TOPICAL INDEX TO THE MINISTRY MAXIMS

What follows is a topical index of the Ministry Maxims found in each verse of the commentary. In many cases each verse could have multiple Ministry Maxims formulated for it, so this does not serve as a comprehensive index of all Philippians teaches. Rather this index serves as a quick guide to locating some of its teaching on various subjects, as capsulated in the Ministry Maxims. These topics may provide a starting point in dealing with particular issues in your personal study or training church leaders.

Accountability	1:9, 29; 2:12; 3:20, 21
Anxiety	2:26; 4:6, 7, 8, 11, 12, 19
Apologetics	1:16, 27, 28, 29; 2:16; 3:2; 4:22
Assurance	1:6; 3:5, 6, 9
Blessing	1:2; 4:12, 23
Choices	2:12; 3:4, 12, 13; 4:4, 5; 4:13
Christ	2:2, 10; 3:3, 7, 8
Exaltation of	2:10; 4:20
Humility of	2:8, 9; 4:18
Knowing Him	3:8, 10
Pursuit of	3:12, 13, 14, 16

Return of	1:9; 3:11, 20, 21; 4:20
Union with	1:5, 21, 23; 4:4, 13
Circumstances	1:1, 29, 30; 2:23; 4:11, 12, 13, 19, 20
Comfort	2:1, 27, 28
Commitment	1:20, 24, 25, 29, 30; 4:13, 18
Compassion	2:1, 26, 27; 4:14
Complaint	2:14, 15
Concern	4:10
Confidence	2:24; 3:5; 4:13, 19
Conflict	2:3; 3:18, 19; 4:2, 3, 5, 21
Contentment	2:14, 15; 3:7; 4:11, 12, 13, 19
Death	1:23, 24; 2:8, 17, 30; 3:10
Dependence	4:11, 12, 13, 19
Discernment	1:9; 3:18, 20
Discipline	4:8
Disunity/division	2:14; 3:18, 19; 4:2, 3, 20, 21, 23
Empowerment	1:19, 21; 2:1, 13; 3:3; 4:13, 19
Encouragement	2:1; 4:1, 14, 15
Envy	1:15; 3:7; 4:11, 12, 13
Example	1:14, 15, 16, 26, 27, 28, 29; 2:11, 12, 16, 17, 20, 21, 28; 3:4, 17; 4:2, 9
Faith	1:29; 3:4, 5; 4:11, 12, 13, 19
Faithfulness	1:1, 20, 26, 27, 28, 29; 2:11, 12, 16, 17, 20, 21, 28; 3:15; 4:15, 19
Fellowship	1:5, 7, 27, 28; 2:1, 2, 3, 4, 5, 18, 19, 22, 25, 26, 29; 3:15; 4:1, 2, 3, 10, 14, 15, 20, 21, 23
Fruitfulness	1:22, 24, 25, 26, 29; 4:13, 19
Giving	4:10, 14, 15, 16, 17, 18, 19
God	
Faithfulness of	2:24; 4:19
Sovereignty of	1:6, 12, 13, 19, 24, 29, 30; 2:9, 10, 23; 3:21; 4:6, 7, 19, 20
Gospel	1:16, 27, 28; 3:4, 7, 9; 4:1, 5, 15, 16, 22
Grace	1:2, 7, 22, 29; 2:1; 3:4, 5, 6, 7, 9; 4:19, 23

Gratitude	1:3, 4; 4:6
Great Commission	1:13, 14, 17, 18, 17, 29; 2:15, 16; 4:15, 19
Heaven	1:23, 24; 3:20, 21
Holy Spirit	1:19; 2:1, 13; 3:3
Honor	2:29; 4:18, 20
Hope	1:23; 3:5, 11, 14, 20, 21; 4:19
Humility	2:8, 9, 26; 4:12, 13, 20
Identity	1:1; 2:7, 25, 29; 3:20, 21; 4:13
Idols	3:8
Independence	4:11, 12, 13
Irony	1:12; 3:2
Joy	1:4; 2:18; 4:4
Judgment	1:9; 2:12; 3:21
Knowledge	1:9; 4:7
Love	1:7, 8, 9, 16, 27; 2:1, 4, 26; 4:1, 14, 15
Martyrdom	1:20, 21, 23, 24, 29, 30; 2:17
Maturity	3:1, 13, 16, 19
Mercy	2:27
Mind	2:2, 5, 26; 3:15, 17, 19; 4:7, 8
Ministry	1:8, 15, 18, 21, 22, 23, 24, 25, 26, 29, 30; 2:5, 7, 20, 30; 3:15; 4:3, 9, 10, 13, 14, 15, 19
Motives	1:15, 17, 18, 23, 25; 2:21, 28; 4:17, 18, 20
Obedience	2:8, 12, 13, 19, 30; 3:4, 14; 4:13, 19
Opposition	1:28, 29, 30; 3:18, 19; 4:22, 23
Partnership	1:5, 7; 4:10, 14, 15, 16, 21, 23
Patience	2:10; 4:5
Peace	2:24; 4:6, 7, 8, 11, 12
Prayer	1:4, 18; 4:6
Providence	1:6, 12, 13, 19, 24, 29, 30; 2:9, 10, 23; 4:12, 13, 19
Rebellion	2:8, 14; 3:18
Relationships	1:2, 3, 17, 18, 26, 27, 28, 30; 2:1, 2, 3, 4, 5, 7, 19, 27; 3:4, 15; 4:1, 2, 3, 5, 10, 14, 15, 16, 21, 23
Religion	3:5, 6, 7, 9
Reminder	3:1

Reputation	2:25, 29; 4:17
Responsibility	2:4, 13, 28; 3:15, 20; 4:8, 13
Revelation	3:8
Reward	2:9, 10, 24; 3:20, 21; 4:17, 19
Righteousness	
Imputed	1:11; 3:5, 6, 9
Acted	1:11; 3:9; 4:13, 19
Rights	2:6; 4:5
Sacrifice	2:29, 30; 3:4, 7, 8; 4:12, 13, 15, 16, 17
Salvation	1:6, 21, 28, 29; 2:1; 3:5, 10, 12, 13, 20, 21; 4:1
Sanctification	1:11, 20, 21, 27; 2:1, 4, 5, 6, 7, 13, 14, 15, 25; 3:1, 12, 13, 14, 15, 16, 19; 4:11, 12, 13
Servant/service	2:7, 20, 21, 22, 25, 29, 30; 3:3; 4:3, 10, 13, 14, 15, 19
Sin	1:17
Suffering	1:12, 13, 14, 16, 17, 26, 28, 29, 30; 2:17, 18; 3:10; 4:11, 12, 13, 14
Support	4:10, 15, 16, 18, 19
Teaching	4:17
Thanksgiving	1:3, 4; 4:6
Thinking	2:2, 5, 26; 3:15, 17, 19; 4:5, 8; 4:11, 12, 13
Truth	3:15
Unity	1:7, 27; 2:2, 3, 4, 5, 6, 10, 14, 18, 19, 25, 27, 28; 4:1, 2, 3, 5, 14, 15, 20, 21, 23
Unselfishness	2:4, 5, 21, 25, 26, 29; 4:5, 14, 15, 18
Vindication	2:10, 29; 3:20, 21; 4:19
Waiting	2:10; 3:20, 21
Wisdom	1:2; 2:23
Witness	1:13, 14, 17, 18, 26, 27, 28, 29; 2:15, 16; 4:5, 22
Worry	2:26; 4:6, 7, 8, 11, 12, 13
Worship	2:17, 18; 3:3, 19; 4:18, 20
Worth	2:7

APPENDIX C

ASSORTED CHARTS

The charts found here are referred to at several points in the commentary and are intended as aids in instruction and application.

Does Paul's Use of σύν in Philippians Contribute to the Theme of Unity?

Comparison of Paul's use of σύν in all his NT letters

Book	Total # of Words	Use of σύν	Use of σύν in compound	%
Romans	7111	4	47	0.717
1 Corinthians	6830	7	47	0.791
2 Corinthians	4477	7	32	0.871
Galatians	2230	4	10	0.628
Ephesians	2422	2	16	0.743
Philippians	1629	4	16	1.228
Colossians	1582	7	15	1.391
1 Thesss.	1481	4	2	0.405
2 Thess.	823	0	1	0.121
1 Timothy	1591	0	4	0.251
2 Timothy	1238	0	7	0.565
Titus	659	0	1	0.152
Philemon	335	0	4	1.194

It is of note that three of the four Prison Epistles have the highest percentage use of σύν and σύν– prefixed words: Philippians, Colossians and Philemon. Ephesians alone of the Prison Epistles ranks on a par with others of Paul's longer letters. This may be explained, perhaps, by the fact that many believe it was prepared as a cyclical letter designed to be circulated among the churches of Asia Minor and thus is lacking some of the personal touches of the other Prison Epistles. Colossians and Philemon together deal with two highly personal issues: a virulent heresy brewing in the area and the return of the runaway slave Onesimus.[1] This may explain the higher percentages of σύν– related words in these two letters. The high percentage in Philippians may be attributed to the strong emphasis on unity throughout the letter.[2] The frequent use of σύν and σύν– prefixed words is one major contributor to this emphasis.

Uses of σύν in Philippians

σύν in Philippians
- 1:1 – "Paul and Timothy, bond-servants of Christ Jesus, To all the saints in Christ Jesus who are in Philippi, including [σύν] the overseers and deacons:"
- 1:23 – But I am hard-pressed from both directions, having the desire to depart and be with [σύν] Christ, for that is very much better"
- 2:22 – "But you know of his proven worth, that he served with [σύν] me in the furtherance of the gospel like a child serving his father."
- 4:21 – "Greet every saint in Christ Jesus. The brethren who are with [σύν] me greet you."

---

1 See the author's *Colossians and Philemon for Pastors*.
2 See the Introduction: "Theology: What does Philippians Teach us?"

σύν as a prefix in Philippians
- συγκοινωνός – "partakers" (1:7)
- συνέχω – "I am hard-pressed" (1:23)
- συναθλέω – "striving together" (1:27)
- σύμψυχος – "united in spirit" (2:2)
- συγχαίρω – "share … joy with" (2:17, 18)
- συνεργός – "fellow worker" (2:25)
  - συνεργός – **"fellow workers" (4:3)**
- συστρατιώτης – "fellow soldier" (2:25)
- συμμορφίζω – "being conformed to" (3:10)
- συμμιμητής – "join in following" (3:17)
- σύμμορφος – "into conformity with" (3:21)
- Συντύχη – "Syntyche" (4:2)
- σύζυγος – "true companion" (4:3)
- συλλαμβάνω – "help" (4:3)
- συναθλέω – "share … struggle" (4:3)
- συγκοινωνέω – "share with" (4:14)

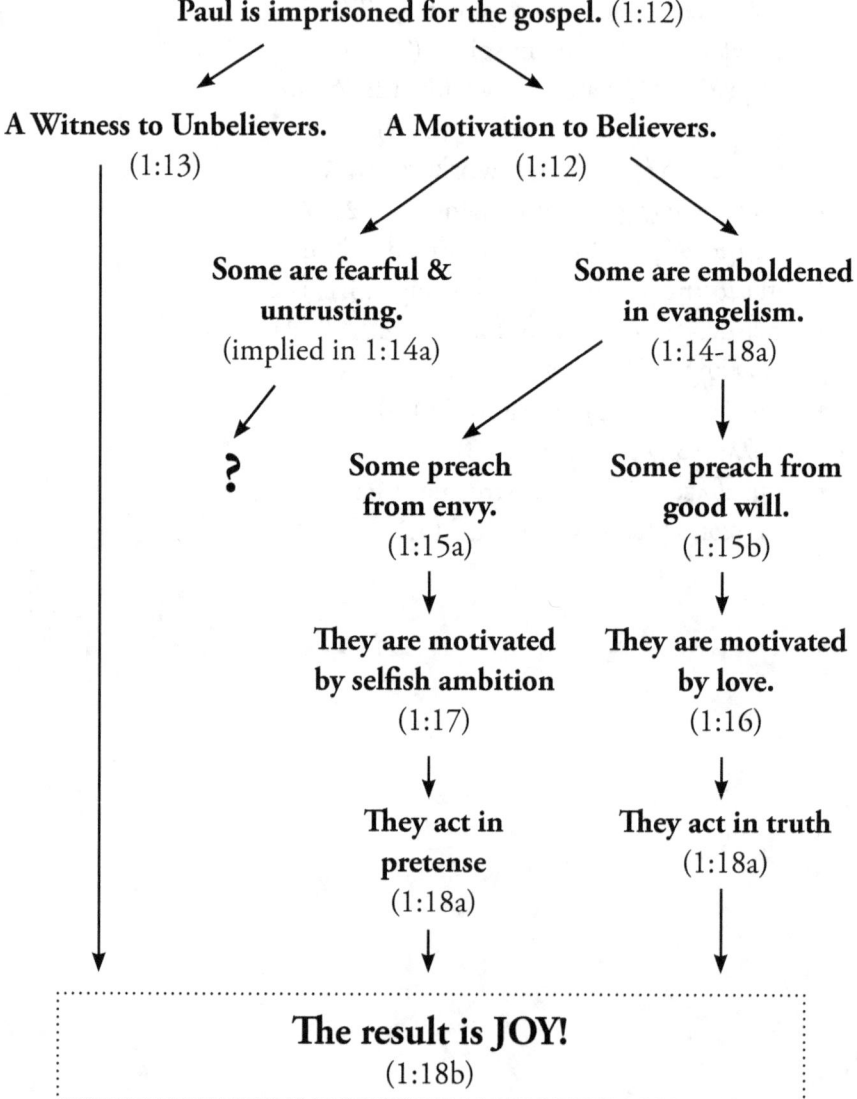

The only scenario in which joy is not the outcome of Paul's difficult circumstances is when people allow those circumstances to inhibit their witness for Christ.

APPENDIX D
ANNOTATED BIBLIOGRAPHY

This annotated bibliography is provided to help pastors determine how to invest their money in commentaries before preaching Philippians. I believe a pastor should interact with the Greek text at the greatest depth his training and available tools afford him. My comments will come from this perspective.

As I prepare to preach a book of the NT I seek several commentaries that work closely and carefully with the Greek text, engage in technical discussions and provide in-depth insights into the original text. I then look for two or three commentaries that are more exegetical or theological in nature. Finally, I want one or two that are more expositional or homiletical in character. After my own exegetical work, I work through the commentaries in that order. Those in the first category help me with analysis (taking the pieces apart). Those in the second category assist in the transition from analysis to synthesis (putting the pieces back together). Those in the last category help me move from text to message. To that end, then, I would want to have (in addition to this current volume!):

Technical Commentaries: O'Brien, Hellerman, Hawthorne/Martin (WBC). Theological/exegetical Commentaries: Harmon, Fee (NIC), Hansen. Expositional Commentaries: Merida/Chan, Robertson (*Paul's Joy in Christ*), Hughes.

In the annotations that follow, my observations are personal reflections and each reader may come to different conclusions about a given commentary.

Alford, Henry. *Alford's Greek Testament: An Exegetical and Critical Commentary.* 5 vols. Grand Rapids, Michigan: Baker Book House, reprint 1980 from the 1871 version.

Based on the Greek text. Its age limits its usefulness, but there are occasional gems to be found here.

Anders, Max E. *Galatians, Ephesians, Philippians, Colossians.* Holman New Testament Commentary. Nashville: Broadman and Holman, 1999.

Anders serves both as the editor for the entire series as well as the author of this volume, which covers four of Paul's letters. Given that the author aims to cover so much material in one volume (of 358 pages) the comments tend to be light in terms of exegetical detail. A two page introduction suffices for the letter to the Philippians (in which Anders asserts Paul writes from his first Roman imprisonment). The commentary moves chapter by chapter through each letter, first providing an introduction for that chapter which sounds very much like a sermon introduction. The actual commentary on the given portion of Scripture is more sermonic in content. In fact the commentary has a homiletic outline imbedded in it (and then presented again at the end of the chapter under a section titled: "Teaching Outline"). The work is primarily devotional and homiletic in nature and the pastor seeking help at that level may find assistance here.

Ash, Anthony L. *Philippians, Colossians & Philemon.* The College Press NIV Commentary. Joplin: College Press Publishing Company, 1994.

Moves through the text systematically, at times offering insight into the Greek text. The publishing house is primarily associated with the Christian Churches/Churches of Christ, so the reader should be aware of their particular theological emphases.

Barclay, William. *The Letters to the Philippians, Colossians, and Thessalonians*. The Daily Study Bible. Philadelphia: The Westminster Press, 1959.

Barclay is not always where we would like him to be on some matters, but he occasionally provides excellent background material.

Beare, F.W. *The Epistle to the Philippians*. Black's New Testament Commentary. London: Adam and Charles Black, 1959.

Beare believes that our Philippians is a composite work knit together from three other Pauline letters. One of these (3:2-4:1), he believes, may not even have been written to Philippi.

Bentley, Michael. *Shining in the Darkness: Philippians Simply Explained*. Welwyn Commmentary Series. Darlington: Evangelical Press, 1998.

It appears this volume has been replaced in the series by the volume by Hywel R. Jones (see below).

Blair, Edward P. *Philippians, Colossians and First and Second Thessalonians*. Basic Bible Commentary. Nashville: Abingdon, 1988.

Brief (158 pages) and, true to the series' name, basic. Cannot decide between Ephesus, Rome and Caesarea as the place of origin for the letter (11). He is equally agnostic as to the unity of the letter (12). Pastor/exegetes will look elsewhere for help.

Bockmuehl, Markus. *The Epistle to the Philippians*. Black's New Testament Commentary. Grand Rapids: Baker Publishing Group, 1998.

The author is Dean Ireland's Professor of the Exegesis of Holy Scripture at Keble College in Oxford. He believes that seeing Paul as writing the letter from his first Roman imprisonment "remains the least problematic" of the possible views, and therefore "most likely" (32). This volume is often cited by other more recent works, giving evidence both of the author's respected stature in the academic community and the enduring value of his insights on Philippians. He touches insightfully upon nearly every point of the text and while it may not be among the few "must have" resources for the pastor-exegete, it is a valuable resource that will prove worth your investment.

Boice, James Montgomery. *Philippians: An Expositional Commentary*. Grand Rapids: Baker Books, 2006.

A helpful contribution from a beloved and renowned exegete of the Scriptures. Boice offers real help by modeling how to make the transition from exegesis to preaching and in how to offer appropriate application of the text.

Bruce, F.F. *Philippians*. New Interational Biblical Commentary of the New Testament. Peabody: Hendrickson Publishers, 1989.

Yet another helpful volume from the hand of the renowned British NT scholar. He leans toward seeing Paul writing from a Roman imprisonment (11-16) and assumes the letter's unity (19). While he interacts with the Greek text (mostly in the "Additional Notes" and always transliterated), he offers a thoughtful theological commentary. The commentary is valuable and worth having.

Carson, D.A. *Basics for Believers: An Exposition of Philippians*. Grand Rapids: Baker Academic, 1996.

A brief exposition of the letter by a celebrated scholar. The expositions were originally given as messages at a conference, but have been reworked for the printed page. He believes Paul probably wrote from his first Roman imprisonment (15). Carson offers a helpful example of how to bridge from study to sermon, making insightful and sound application of the text.

Chapman, David. *Philippians: Rejoicing and Thanksgiving*. Focus on the Bible Commentary. Fern: Christian Focus Publications, 2012.

A solid, basic commentary of 290 pages that provides a good examination of the letter.

Cohick, Lynn H. *Philippians*. The Story of God Bible Commentary. Grand Rapids: Zondervan, 2013.

> As the series title conveys, the authors seek to set the particular book of the Bible within the larger narrative of the entire Bible. The series seeks to help readers not only understand what the text says, but what it means for today. Each volume comes to the text to explain it from three angles: Listen to the Story (includes the text of Scripture under consideration as well as suggestive cross references for reflection), Explain the Story (explanatory and exegetical insights to understand the text as given to us), Live the Story (helps with application and sometimes helpful illustrations). Cohick believes Paul wrote from his first Roman imprisonment and affirms the letter's unity. There is sparse interaction with the Greek text, but where there is the Greek is transliterated. The value in this volume (and series) may be found in placing it within the development of the larger narrative of redemption conveyed through the whole of the Bible.

Comfort, Philip W., "Philippians." *Cornerstone Biblical Commentary – Volume 16: Ephesians-2 Thessalonians, Philemon*. Carol Stream, IL: Tyndale House, 2008. WORD*search* CROSS e-book.

> The commentary on Philippians is a part of one volume (covering six NT books) in a series covering the entire Bible. Comfort believes Paul wrote these letters from a Roman imprisonment. The volume offers brief exegetical insights on each verse then provides a more expansive section of commentary from a theological angle. Its greatest usefulness will likely come in bridging from one's exegesis to sermon crafting and as one seeks to identify appropriate application of the text to a contemporary audience.

Cousar, Charles B. *Philippians and Philemon: A Commentary*. The New Testament Library. Louisville: Westminster John Knox Press, 2009.

> Cousar's commentary is quite brief—only five pages of actual commentary on Philemon! Nevertheless, he packs in more than one

might expect from such a slim volume. He believes Paul wrote from an Ephesian imprisonment (11). Due to the length of the work, he devotes little space to interaction with the views of others. He believes 2:6-11 is a "pre-Pauline" adaptation of the Apostle; seems astonished that many other recent commentators don't join him in this view (52-53).

Craddock, Fred B. *Philippians*. Interpretation. Louisville: Westminister John Knox Press, 1984.

This volume was written by a renowned professor of preaching from a more mainline tradition. The series aims to hold out "the integrated result of historical and theological work with the biblical text" and is aimed for "those who teach, preach, and study the Bible in the community of faith" (v). The work is light on exegetical depth and interaction with the text of Scripture. It majors on theological reflection and moves quickly to matters of application and integration within the life of the church. It is a brief work (only 84 pages long). He seems at pains to avoid stating his position on the unity of the letter (e.g., 54).

Eadie, John A. *A Commentary on the Greek Text of the Epistle of Paul to the Philippians*. New York: Robert Carter and Brothers, 1859.

Though the volume is dated, if offers good help in dealing with the Greek text. Eadie affirms the unity of the epistle (xxxi) and that Paul wrote it from his first Roman imprisonment (xxxiv-xxxvi). The work is scholarly in tone, but there is warmth in the insights and applications drawn. This would be a valuable addition to the expositor's library. The entire volume is available online at Google Books.

Fee, Gordon D. *Paul's Letter to the Philippians*. New International Commentary on the New Testament. Grand Rapids: William B. Eerdmans Publishing Company, 1995.

Fee's volume replaced the older contribution of Müller (1955, see below) in this series. The present volume is a much more expansive

(497 pages compared to 162 pages of commentary on Philippians) contribution. Fee believes Paul writes from his first Roman imprisonment (34) and also argues against those who see fragments of letters later pieced together and thus for the unity of the present letter (21-23). Fee is clearly well-read on the literature (cf. his massive 26 page bibliography) and reflects carefully on the various views of scholars in the body of the commentary. Fee views the letter as a Christian hortatory letter of friendship. His theological reflections are astute and helpful. This commentary should be among the pastor's select tools as he preaches/teaches through the letter.

Fee, Gordon D. *Philippians.* InterVarsity Press New Testament Commentary. InterVarsity Press, 1999.

A briefer commentary than Fee's NICNT offering (see just above), which may appeal to those looking for less technical detail and with less time to invest. Given its relative size it naturally lacks the detailed argumentation of the larger volume, but for this reason it is more accessible to a wider audience. Fee's NIC volume is more theologically robust, this volume more accessible (as per this series' intent). The pastor/exegete should choose Fee's NICNT volume. The entire text of this shorter volume is available for free online: (https://www.biblegateway.com/resources/commentaries/index.php?action=getBookSections&cid=8&source=).

Ferguson, Sinclair B. *Let's Study Philippians.* Edinburgh: Banner of Truth, 1998.

A popular introduction to the letter from a well-respected Reformed theologian/pastor (153 pages). The publisher's stated aim for the series is "to combine explanation and application. The aim is the exposition of Scripture written in the language of a friend, seated alongside you with an open Bible."

Fleming, Dean. *Philippians: A Commentary in the Wesleyan Tradition*. New Beacon Bible Commentary. Kansas City: Beacon Hill Press, 2009.

As per the subtitle, the volume along with the entire series seeks to offer pastors and students "the best scholarship in the Wesleyan tradition" (7). Fleming holds that Paul wrote from his first Roman imprisonment. He affirms the unity of the letter.

Foulks, Francis "Philippians." *The New Bible Commentary: Revised*. Donald Guthrie and J.A. Motyer, editors. Grand Rapids: William B. Eerdmans Publishing Company, 1970.

Foulks sees Paul writing the letter from his first Roman imprisonment. As part of a one-volume commentary his comments are helpful, but are generally too brief to be of significant help to the serious expositor.

Fowl, Stephen E. *Philippians*. The Two Horizon New Testament Commentary. Grand Rapids: Eerdmans Publishing House, 2005.

The series avoids matters of "philology, grammar, syntax, and concerns of a historical nature" and focuses instead upon "theological readings of the text" (i). If pressed, he would say Paul probably wrote from his first Roman imprisonment though "it is not clear that one's decisions on these matters makes much interpretive difference" (9). He affirms the unity of the letter (8).

Garland, David E. "Philippians," *Revised Expositor's Bible Commentary: Revised Edition*, vol. 12. Grand Rapids: Zondervan, 2006.

A solid, contribution from a well-regarded scholar. The volume is briefer than one might wish, given that it is just one part of a volume containing commentaries on all the Prison Epistles. Garland's contribution replaces that of Kent (see below) in the original edition of the series. Garland believes Paul wrote from his first Roman imprisonment.

Gavin, James C. and Ronald A. Beers, contributing eds. *Philippians, Colossians, Philemon*. Life Application Bible Commentary. Carol Stream: Tyndale House Publishers, Inc., 1995.

> The series aims to provide "verse-by-verse explanation, background and application for every verse in the New Testament" (iv). A brief introduction is provided (the authors believe Paul wrote from Rome). The running commentary is primarily focused on making application of the text. Call-out boxes are sprinkled generously throughout the text, offering material that further focuses on application, and which offer quotes from famous Christian leaders and illustrations. There is little help here for the expositor; the work will best serve leaders of Bible discussion groups.

Greenlee, J. Harold. *An Exegetical Summary of Philippians*. 2nd ed. Dallas: Summer Institute of Linguistics, 1992, 2008.

> Not a commentary in the usual sense, this volume was prepared with Bible translators in mind. It gathers insights from twenty-seven commentaries and reference works and presents the findings in a verse-by-verse format under two headings: "Lexicon" and "Question" (in which various answers to key questions related to the text are provided). This volume "makes more sources of exegetical help available than most translators have access to" (6). It can be helpful in quickly surveying the exegetical options on key questions concerning the text of Scripture. May prove helpful to the busy pastor with limited resources and time.

Gromacki, Robert G. *Stand United in Joy: An Exposition of Philippians*. The Woodlands: Kress Biblical Resources, 2003.

> A brief, but insightful collection of expositions. A good outline frames the comments. Best suited for adult Sunday School teachers and lay readers.

Hamm, Dennis. *Philippians, Colossians, Philemon*. Catholic Commentary on Sacred Scripture. Grand Rapids: Baker Academic, 2013.

> Catholic. Believes any decision about where Paul was when he wrote the letters is "a matter of educated guesswork" (18).

Hansen, G. Walter. *The Letter to the Philippians*. The Pillar New Testament Commentary. Grand Rapids: William B. Eerdmans Publishing Company, 2009.

> The entire series is designed "for serious pastors and teachers of the Bible" (ix), seeking to interact with contemporary scholarship while avoiding getting bogged down in technical detail. Hansen seems to achieve these goals with "a blend of rigorous exegesis and exposition, with an eye alert to both biblical theology and contemporary relevance" of the letter (ix). While Hansen interacts carefully and thoroughly with the text, he does not offer a lot in terms of grammar or other matters of the original language. While not ignoring these matters he spends his time searching out the theological implications of the text. He consistently offers a good survey of possible interpretations, along with the strengths and weaknesses of each. Hansen leans toward the letter arising from an Ephesian imprisonment (24-25). He believes 2:6-11 is of non-Pauline origin (131), perhaps having been written by Stephen (132). He sees 3:20-21 as also having poetic/hymnic qualities and sees it as completing what was begun in 2:6-11 (276-277). The volume will serve the careful student of the Scripture well in theological reflection on the text, but you'll want to also seek insights into the Greek text from the likes of O'Brien or Hellerman.

Harmon, Matthew. *Philippians: A Mentor Commentary*. Fern: Christian Focus Publications, 2015.

> A newer commentary that interacts significantly with the Greek text, but does so in a way that is accessible to non-Greek students. Harmon provides careful notes on the text, thoughtful exploration of the theological themes of the letter, and insightful application of the truth

uncovered in the text. He consistently provides thorough exploration of linguistic connections between Paul's letter and the OT. A commentary well worth the price and which will prove valuable to the busy pastor. You'll want to own this one.

Harrell, Pat Edwin. *The Letter of Paul to the Philippians*. The Living Word Commentary. Austin: R.B. Sweet Co., Inc. 1969.

Finds no good reason to deny the origin of the letter as arising from Paul's first Roman imprisonment (22). He seems to lean toward the unity of the letter, except for the possibility of 2:6-11 being a non-Pauline hymn inserted by the apostle (18). Makes some reference the Greek text (using transliteration).

Hawthorne, Gerald F. and Ralph P. Martin. *Philippians*. Word Biblical Commentaries 43. Nashville: Thomas Nelson, 2004.

The volume was originally written by Hawthorne and was then later revised by Martin after Hawthorne's passing. I am not alone in finding the format of the series a bit frustrating. The volume is a bit briefer than most contributions in this series, yet it offers a substantive treatment of the letter and of the scholarship that has arisen around it that will prove helpful to the serious student of the letter. The authors find "no compelling reason to doubt the integrity" (xx) of the letter as we have it. The original volume by Hawthorne believed the letter was written from Caesarea, while Martin's revision holds to an Ephesian imprisonment as the place of origin (l). As a technical commentary it will find its place behind O'Brien in usefulness to the pastor/expositor, but will prove helpful to those who use it.

Hellerman, Joseph H. *Philippians*. Exegetical Guide to the Greek New Testament. Nashville: Broadman and Holman Publishing Group, 2015.

Not a commentary in the usual sense, but each volume in the series "aims to close the gap between the Greek text and the available tools" and "aims to provide all the necessary information for understanding the Greek text" (xvi). The book proceeds on a paragraph-by-paragraph basis offering at each stop the Greek text, structural ananlysis, discussion of each phrase, various translations of key words, suggested topics for further study with a bibliography, and homiletical suggestions. Hellerman dedicates this volume "To all God's shepherds who learned Greek in seminary, who made it a priority over the years to retain the language, and who continue to draw upon the riches of the Greek New Testament for ministry in the church today" (vii). The works by Hellerman, Greenlee and Sumney are not identical, but cover some of the same ground. All are helpful, and each of us will want to make our choice based upon individual needs and familiarity and facility with Greek, but if I was pressed to own just one it would be Hellerman.

Hendriksen, William. *Philippians, Colossians and Philemon*. New Testament Commentary. Grand Rapids: Baker Book House, 1962.

Trusted, evangelical, conservative, and from a Reformed perspective. He views Paul as writing from his first imprisonment in Rome. A fine commentary filled with rich insights. Worth the investment.

Henry, Matthew. *Matthew Henry's Commentary on the Whole Bible: Complete and Unabridged in One Volume*. Peabody, Massachusetts: Hendrickson Publishers, Inc., 1991.

Dated, but devotionally warm and thus sometimes helpful in homiletical development.

Houlden, J.L. *Paul's Letters from Prison*. Pelican New Testament Commentaries. Philadelphia: The Westminster Press, 1977.

As part of a volume covering multiple letters from Paul the contribution for Philippians is brief (16 pages of introduction and 69 pages of commentary). Houlden tentatively sides with Paul's first Roman imprisonment as the most likely point of origin for the letter (43) and appears tentative about its unity (41).

Hughes, R. Kent. *Philippians: The Fellowship of the Gospel.* Preaching the Word. Wheaton: Crossway Books, 2007.

A trusted expositor who is also the editor of the entire *Preaching the Word* series. He offers excellent expositions of the letter that model well what expository preaching might look like. This volume offers the pastor aid as he moves from his exegetical work to the crafting of his sermon.

Hybels, Bill. *Philippians: Run the Race.* Grand Rapids: Zondervan, 1999.

A brief (96 page) six-part Bible study guide with a few comments sprinkled in. Little here to help the serious student of the Scripture. More attune to an informal Bible discussion group.

Ironside, Henry A. *Philippians and Colossians.* Ironside Expository Commentary. Grand Rapids: Kregel, 2007.

Devotional expositions from a much-loved Bible teacher from a previous generation.

Joersz, Jerald. *Galatians, Ephesians, Philippians.* Reformation Heritage Bible Commentary. St. Louis: Concordia Publishing House, 2013.

This series draws upon the heritage of such Reformers as Hus, Luther, Melanchthon, Knox, Calvin, and Wesley. While it is written from a Lutheran perspective it does include works from reformers outside that tradition. The text of the commentary provides both the ESV and KJV in parallel columns at the beginning of each section. The introductions are brief, but helpful.

Johnson, Dennis E. *Philippians.* Reformed Expository Commentary. Phillipsburg, New Jersey: Puritan and Reformed Publishers, 2013.

This series of commentaries seeks to encourage the reader's confidence in the clarity and power of the Scriptures and to uphold the doctrinal heritage of the Reformed faith (xiii). This particular volume sets forth a series of eighteen sermons preached by a professor of practical theology at Westminster Seminary California as an associate pastor of a local church. The goal is to model how to preach this particular letter. Affirms Pauline authorship from his first Roman imprisonment as well as the unity of the letter (xvi).

Jones, Hywel R. *Philippians*. Focus on the Bible. Fern: Christian Focus Publications, 1993.

It appears this volume has been replaced in the series by the volume by David Chapman (see above).

Jones, Hywel R. *Philippians: For the Sake of the Gospel*. Welwyn Commentary Series. Darlington: EP Books, 2010.

A solid, basic, thorough unfolding of the book from a Reformed perspective.

Kent, Homer A., Jr. *Philippians*. The Expositor's Bible Commentary, vol.11. Grand Rapids: Zondervan Publishing House, 1978.

A fine commentary by a respected exegete and conservative scholar who has written a number of helpful commentaries on NT books. He believes Paul wrote from his first Roman imprisonment. Though Kent's comments are necessarily brief as part of a multivolume series, he consistently offers helpful insights that may prove valuable to the preaching pastor. The series has been updated and the newer volume is by Garland (see above).

Knight, John A. *Philippians*. Beacon Bible Commentary. Vol. 9. Kansas City: Beacon Hill Press of Kansas City, 1965.

A simple commentary which states its positions in a straightforward manner. Knight provides just eight pages of introduction, but there he sees Paul writing from his first Roman imprisonment (13) and upholds the unity of the letter (11-12).

Kuschel, Harlyn J. *Philippians, Colossians, Philemon*. The People's Bible. Milwaukee: Northwestern Publishing House, 1986.

The series aims to be above all Christ-centered it its orientation, also practical and directed to a lay audience in its focus (vii). The book provides popular level studies from a Lutheran perspective, having been commissioned by the Wisconsin Evangelical Lutheran Synod.

Lenski, R.C.H. *The Interpretation of St. Paul's Epistles to the Galatians, Ephesians and Philippians*. Minneapolis: Augsburg Publishing House. Copyright 1937, Lutheran Book Concern, 1946, The Wartburg Press. Copyright assigned to Augsburg Publishing House, 1961.

The classic Lutheran commentator. Because of its age some newer developments are not touched upon, yet often helpful and intriguing on the Greek text. Helpful in giving a Lutheran perspective on difficult passages. Often the source of a valuable nugget of insight.

Lighfoot, J.B. *Philippians*. The Crossway Classic Commentaries, Alistar McGrath and J.I. Packer, editors. Wheaton: Crossway Books, 1994.

Though an older volume, Lightfoot provides excellent help with the Greek text. There is help here for the expositor, though you'll want to be sure to have one of the more recent technical commentaries as well.

Lightner, Robert P. "Philippians." *The Bible Knowledge Commentary: New Testament*, John F. Walvrood and Roy B. Zuck, Editors. Victor Books, 1983.

Solid, conservative, evangelical. Good as far as it goes, but too brief to be of substantive help to the serious expositor.

Lloyd-Jones, D. Martyn. *The Life of Joy: An Exposition of Philippians 1 and 2*. Grand Rapids: Baker, 1989.

Classic expositions by the master preacher from the United Kingdom. These are expositions characteristic of Lloyd-Jones's other works. See the companion volume just below.

Lloyd-Jones, D. Martyn. *The Life of Peace: An Exposition of Philippians 3 and 4*. Grand Rapids: Baker, 1990.

See the comments on the companion volume just above.

MacArthur, John. *MacArthur New Testament Commentary – Philippians*. Chicago: Moody Press, 2001. WORDsearch CROSS e-book.

The introduction is characteristically brief (he argues for Paul writing from his first Roman imprisonment), but this is classic MacArthur, providing strong work in the text. MacArthur is conservative and consistent. One will want to have a good technical commentary on hand (O'Brien or Hellerman), but this is a valuable resource for the preaching pastor.

Marshall, I. Howard. *The Epistle to the Philippians*. Epworth Commentary Series. London: Epworth Press, 1993.

A brief offering (127 pages) by a renowned Scottish NT scholar. Marshall was an evangelical Methodist by persuasion. He leans toward the letter being written by Paul from his first Roman imprisonment (xviii-xx). He argues for the unity of the letter (xxxi-xxxii). The comments are generally insightful and helpful in a way disproportionate to the volume's size.

Martin, Ralph P. *A Hymn of Christ: Philippians 2:5-11 in Recent Interpretation and in the Setting of Early Christian Worship*. Downers Grove: Inter-Varsity Press, 1997.

Martin seems to have been the go-to scholar for publishers seeking commentary on Philippians in the sixties, seventies, and eighties. This is a massive study (372 pages) devoted to just seven verses—albeit, highly significant verses. It is a republication of his original *Carmen Christi* (originally published by Oxford Press in 1967) with a new preface. Though this has stood as a definitive technical study of this pivotal pericope of Scripture, the preaching pastor will probably pass on this volume and gravitate toward one of Martin's commentaries covering the whole of the letter.

Martin, Ralph P. *The Epistle of Paul to the Philippians: An Introduction and Commentary.* Tyndale New Testament Commentaries. Revised edition. Grand Rapids: William B.Eerdmans Publishing Company, 1959, 1987.

This is a revised edition of his original 1959 offering to this much relied upon series of commentaries. Characteristic of all the volumes in the series, this is a brief commentary (187 pages). Martin updates the commentary based on more recent scholarly works and discussion on Philippians. It is clear, concise and often helpful. One will find Martin's more recent (2004) update of Hawthorne's original contribution on Philippians in the Word Biblical Commentaries to be more thorough (as well, obviously, as more conversant with even more recent scholarship) and will find him there interacting more extensively with the academic matters related to the letter. The pastor/exegete will probably wish to own one of Martin's volumes, but will want to decide based upon the other works he possesses and just what he wished for from the commentary.

Martin, Ralph P. *Philippians.* New Century Bible Commentary. Grand Rapids: Eerdmans Publishing House, 1976.

Similar in length (176 pages) to Martin's TNTC contribution, but newer than the original 1959 contribution to that series and not as new as the updated version of that series (1987). Martin leans a bit more into technical matters in the present volume that he does in his Tyndale volume. He does not find sufficient reason to doubt the unity of the letter (21). He cautions about accepting the traditional view of Rome as the place of the letter's origin (56).

Melick, Richard R. *New American Commentary – Volume 32: Philippians, Colossians, Philemon.* Nashville, TN: Broadman Press, 1991. WORD*search* CROSS e-book.

> This was the first volume to be published in this series, for which Melick serves as a consulting editor. Melick is conservative and helpful. He believes the evidence supports Paul writing the letter from his first Roman imprisonment. The commentary is likely to provide some good help to the pastor/expositor.

Merida, Tony and Francis Chan. *Exalting God in Philippians.* Christ-Centered Exposition Commentary. Nashville: Holman Reference, 2016.

> The series fully and unashamedly affirms the full inspiration, inerrancy and authority of the Scriptures. The series aims to be exegetically accurate, helpful to pastors in particular, provide helpful illustrations and theologically driven applications of the text, and to highlight the centrality of Jesus in understanding each text. The focus on a pastoral audience is evident as each section of the commentary begins with a helpful and suggestive homiletical outline of the pericope under consideration. The comments are an interesting blend of comment on the text (often citing others' insights) and reflective questions that move toward application. The pastor will find this a helpful and insightful addition to his tools on Philippians.

Meyer, F.B. *The Epistle to the Philippians: A Devotional Commentary.* London: The Religious Tract Society, 1905.

> A series of twenty-seven devotional expositions taking one through the letter under the guidance of a much-loved Bible teacher of a bygone era.

Michael, J. Hugh. *The Epistle of Paul to the Philippians.* The Moffatt New Testament Commentary. London: Hodder and Stoughton Limited, 1928.

> A dated work. Michael wavers on the unity of the letter (xi-xii) and believes it was composed while Paul was a prisoner in Ephesus (xxi).

Motyer, J. Alec. *The Message of Philippians.* The Bible Speaks Today. Downers Grove: Inter-Varsity Academic, 1997.

A helpful volume from the hand of a trusted scholar and exegete. Gobble up just about anything Motyer writes. The strength of this series is not insight into individual texts within the given Bible book, but its flow and its theological development. That is true of the present volume, but one is often surprised by just how much insight Motyer can pack into a brevity of words. He brings many complex things within the grasp of simpler minds.

Müller, Jac. J. *The Epistle of Paul to the Philippians.* New International Commentary on the New Testament. Grand Rapids: William B. Eerdmans, 1984.

A fine commentary, but unusually brief for the series in which it is found. The insights are helpful, but one wishes at times that Müller had been willing to offer us more. He believes Paul wrote from an imprisonment in Rome. This volume has been replaced in the series by Fee's 1995 volume (see above).

O'Brien, Peter T. *The Epistle to the Philippians.* The New International Greek Testament Commetnary. Grand Rapids: William B. Eerdmans Publishing Company, 1991.

O'Brien is a well-respected scholar and the author of numerous well-received commentaries. This present contribution does not disappoint. He believes the evidence favors Paul's authoring the letter from his first Roman imprisonment. His work is comprehensive and thorough (597 pages), touching upon every point in the text that the careful student of Scripture is likely be concerned about. He is, of course, thorough in dealing with the Greek text. Even one unskilled in the Greek language can benefit from the commentary if he has a Greek interlinear side-by-side with the commentary. O'Brien thoroughly surveys the options where interpretive challenges are met, in the end providing reasoned justification for where he lands. This is the best current volume available on the Greek text and should be among the first technical commentaries to which you turn in your study of Philippians.

Osiek, Carolyn. *Philippians and Philiemon*. Abingdon New Testament Commentaries. Nashville: Abingdon Press, 2000.

The series aims to offer "compact, critical commentaries" on the books of the NT. They are aimed at theological students, but may have secondary value to pastors and other church leaders (9). Argues for the unity of the letter (17-19). Believes it most likely that Paul wrote from an Ephesian imprisonment (30).

Pentecost, J. Dwight. *The Joy of Living: A Study of Philippians*. Grand Rapids: Zondervan Publishing House, 1973.

A series of popular expositions by a stalwart scholar of the dispensational persuasion. Useful for devotional insights.

Phillips, John. *Exploring Philippians*. John Phillips Commentary Series. Grand Rapids: Kregel, 2002.

The forte of Phillips' commentaries lies in the strong outlines he provides and the present volume is no exception. His alliterative approach may or may not appeal to you, but in either case you may find helpful insights into how to expound the letter in classical fashion.

Plummer, Alfred. *A Commentary on St. Paul's Epistle to the Philippians*. London: Robert Scott Roxburghe House Paternoster Row, E.C. 1919.

A dated work from a previous era. Does comment on the Greek text in places. Purchase O'Brien and bypass this dated work.

Reumann, John. *Philippians*. The Anchor Yale Bible Commentaries. Yale University Press, 2008.

A massive (808 pages) technical commentary that displays a grand intellect and over thirty years work on the letter to the Philippians by one who was emeritus Professor of New Testament and Greek at Lutheran Theological Seminary, Philadelphia. Reumann was an active participant in the Lutheran-Catholic dialogue on justification which resulted in the Joint Declaration of 1999. Not only does the sheer size of the volume turn most away, the formatting makes the book difficult to use. Reumann's adherence to various partition theories for the letter also obscures and misdirects. There is surely some help here, but the effort to mine it out will prove more than the average pastor is able to pull off in his week-by-week sermon preparation.

Robbins, Ray Frank. *Philippians: Rejoice in the Lord.* Nashville: Convention Press, 1980.

A brief (144 page) series of comments on the letter that are mostly devotional in nature.

Robertson, Archibald Thomas. *Paul's Joy in Christ: Studies in Philippians.* Grand Rapids: Baker Book House, 1917 by Fleming H. Revell Company, Baker reprint, 1979.

Expositions by a trusted New Testament scholar of a previous generation. Though dated, Robertson models wonderfully how to interact carefully with the text while communicating it helpfully to lay people. Despite its brevity, it consistently offers significant help in understanding the text. You'll need to hunt for a used copy, but it is well worth having in your select few resources.

Silva, Moisés. *Phlippians.* Baker Exegetical Commentary on the New Testament. Grand Rapids: Baker Academic. Second edition, 2005.

This volume was originally published in 1988 as part of the Wycliffe Exegetical Commentary series. It was subsequently picked up by Baker and, with only minor changes, made the inaugural volume in the Baker Exegetical Commentaries on the NT (1995). It has proven so popular that this is now the second edition of the work in the BECNT. Little has changed in Silva's views from the previous volumes. Silva believes Paul wrote from his first Roman imprisonment. He sees the primary theme of Philippians to be that of perseverance, resting upon the twin pillars of human responsibility and divine sovereignty. This is a fine commentary by a good thinker who carefully reflects upon the text and who gives helpful insight into the Greek. The commentary is not as expansive as O'Brien, Fee or Hansen's contributions (248 pages, compared to 597, 497, 355 respectively) and notwithstanding all of his insightful comments, at times it seems Silva does not comment at all on a particular or two with which the student may be concerned. All in all, it is a helpful and insightful commentary that will prove a genuine help to the busy pastor who is serious about his study and preparation.

Smiles, Vincent M. *First Thessalonians, Philippians, Second Thessalonians, Colossians, Ephesians*. The New Collegeville Bible Commentary. Collegeville, Minnesota: Liturgical Press, 2005.

A contemporary Catholic treatment of these letters of Paul. It is no surprise then that the comments are based upon the New American Bible. The comments are, given the breadth of the one volume, general and there is little interaction with the text itself. Believes Paul wrote the letter to the Philippians from an Ephesian imprisonment.

Still, Todd D. *Philippians and Philemon*. Smyth and Helwyns Bible Commentary. Macon: Smyth and Helwyns Publishing, 2011.

The series aims at being "visually stimulating" and "user friendly" and "as close to multimedia in print as possible" (xv). The volume is thus filled with many photographs, charts, maps, and call-out boxes with additional information. Still argues for the unity of the letter (12-13) says he is "presently inclined to think that Paul wrote Philippians from Rome" (15). He references the Greek with some regularity, always in transliterated form.

Sumney, Jerry L. *Philippians: A Greek Student's Intermediate Reader*. Peabody, Massachusetts: Hendrickson Publishers, Inc., 2007.

> Not a commentary per se, but written "to help students who have finished their initial year of Greek grammar" (ix) read Philippians with better understanding. Section by section the book provides "the Greek text, an interpretive translation, and comments on the constructions of each phrase" (ix). It offers helpful interpretive options at difficult points and why some options are better than others in the given context. The volume is helpful to the pastor who wants to incorporate his basic knowledge of Greek into his exegesis, but is pressed for time.

Taylor, Preston A. *Philippians: Joy in Jesus*. Chicago: Moody Press, 1976.

> A brief (160 pages) book of simple comments based on a sermon series preached at the author's church (10). Perhaps best for devotional reading or as a Sunday School class guide.

Tenney, Merrill C. *Philippians: The Gospel at Work*. Grand Rapids: William B. Eerdmans Publishing Company, 1956.

> A brief (102 pages) series of expositions of the letter by a highly respected NT scholar.

Thielman, Frank S. *Philippians*. NIV Application Commentary. Grand Rapids: Zondervan, 1995.

> The series aims to help the reader bridge the gap between the present century and the first century. Thielman believes Paul wrote from an Ephesian imprisonment and places its date of composition just after that of Galatians and just before 1 Corinthians. He affirms the unity of the letter. The commentary, as with each volume in this series, proceeds through the letter by sections, at each turn considering that portion under the lenses of "Original Meaning," "Bridging Contexts," and "Contemporary Significance." The commentary will serve best in making the transition from exegesis to application and homiletics, though

I personally have seldom found the "Contemporary Significance" sections in this series to be of great help in this regard.

Thurston, Bonnie B. and Judith M. Ryan. *Philippians and Philemon*. Sacra Pagina Series. Vol. 10. Collegeville, Minnesota: Liturgical Press.

A series that says it is Catholic in that it is "inclusive in its methods and perspectives, and shaped by the context of the Catholic tradition." Thurston tentatively holds to an Ephesian imprisonment as the likely origin of the letter (30). She holds to the unity of Philippians as a single letter (33).

Tomlin, Graham, ed. *Philippians, Colossians*. Reformation Commentary on Scripture. Vol. XI. Downers Grove: IVP Academic, 2003.

The series seeks to expose modern students to the rich writings of the reformers. The commentary proceeds section by section through each of the letters, offering a number of extended quotations from the writings of the reformers as they may relate to the text or themes of that particular passage.

Vincent, Marvin R. *A Critical and Exegetical Commentary on the Epistles to the Philippians and to Philemon*. The International Critical Commentary. Edinburgh: T. & T. Clark, 1897.

Vincent's contribution is dated, but is still an genuine help to the pastor as he wrestles with the Greek text. If you can find a used copy at a good price, grab it.

Walvrood, John F. *Philippians: Triumph in Christ*. Everyman's Bible Commentary. Chicago: Moody Press, 1971.

A brief, simple commentary that is written, as the title of the series indicates, to be accessible for everyone. Walvrood holds to Rome as the place of composition (13). The volume is brief and most helpful to laymen and those teaching simple Sunday School classes or Bible studies.

Weidmann, Frederick W. *Philippians, First and Second Thessalonians, and Philemon.* Westminster Bible Companion. Louisville: Westminster/John Knox Press, 2012.

The series is designed primarily for the laity of the church. The scope of this one volume is such that the comments on any one section of any one letter are more brief than the serious student of the text seeks. Weidmann believes Paul wrote from an Ephesian imprisonment. The pastor/exegete will want to invest his resources in another direction.

Wiersbe, Warren W. *The Bible Exposition Commentary: New Testament*, vol. 2. Colorado Springs: Victor Books, 2001.

Wiersbe's reputation as an outstanding Bible teacher who faithfully opens the Scriptures for hungry hearts is well deserved. The size and nature of the volume necessitates that much technical material is left untouched, yet he seldom fails to provide some insightful and helpful homiletical tidbit.

Witherington, Ben III. *Friendship and Finances in Philippi: The Letter of Paul to the Philippians.* Valley Forge: Trinity Press International, 1994.

This is Witherington's earlier effort on the letter to the Philippians. He believes Paul wrote from his first Roman imprisonment (26) and upholds the unity of the letter (28). His dependence upon socio-rhetorical interpretation is in evidence here. See below.

Witherington, Ben III. *Paul's Letter to the Philippians: A Socio-Rhetorical Commentary.* Grand Rapids: Eerdmans Publishing House, 2011.

As in his earlier volume, Witherington believes Paul writes from his Roman incarceration and affirms the unity of the letter as one original document from the Apostle himself. Argues extensively against Paul following the format of a "friendship letter" (17-20). The work focuses its attention upon understanding the first century cultural setting of the author, the letter, and its recipients and how this influenced Paul's manner of writing.

Wuest, Kenneth S. *Philippians in the Greek New Testament for the English Reader.* Grand Rapids: William B. Eerdmans Publishing Company, 1942.

A brief volume that may be one of the best contributions among Wuest's studies on the books of the NT. He is simple and straightforward. He aims to make the gems of the Greek NT accessible to those who lack facility with the original language. Probably most helpful to laymen and lay Bible study leaders.

www.ingramcontent.com/pod-product-compliance
Lightning Source LLC
Chambersburg PA
CBHW051406230426
43669CB00011B/1779